UNIVERSITY
of
GLASGOW

Law Class
Library

WALKER

on

THE SCOTTISH LEGAL SYSTEM

THE SCOTTISH LEGAL SYSTEM

AN INTRODUCTION TO THE STUDY OF SCOTS LAW

BY

DAVID M. WALKER

M.A., LL.B.(Glas.), LL.D.(Lond.), Ph.D., LL.D., Hon. LL.D.(Edin.), F.S.A.Scot.,
One of Her Majesty's Counsel in Scotland,
Of the Middle Temple, Barrister,
Regius Professor of Law in the University of Glasgow

FOURTH EDITION, REVISED

EDINBURGH
W. GREEN & SON LTD.
LAW PUBLISHERS
1976

First Edition	.	.	.	1959	By D. M. Walker
Second Edition	.	.	.	1963	,, ,,
Third Edition	.	.	.	1969	,, ,,
Fourth Edition	.	.	.	1976	,, ,,

ISBN 0 414 00591 0

©

D. M. Walker, 1976

GLASGOW UNIVERSITY
LAW LIBRARY

Printed in Great Britain by The Eastern Press, Ltd., London and Reading

PREFACE

THIS book was written primarily to provide a textbook for the introductory course in the legal curriculum of Glasgow University, which is designated Scottish Legal System. Nevertheless I hope that it may prove of interest and utility to other persons concerned to obtain a general conspectus of the subject.

That course, and consequently this book, is intended not as a first or general introductory course on Scots Law itself, but as an attempt to tackle the problem of teaching the novice law student how to go about the study of law and an attempt to equip him to do so. It is an introduction to the *study*, not to the law itself. The traditional method of plunging the law student at once into the subject-matter of various branches of the law was quite unsatisfactory, because he did not at that stage have the knowledge or skill necessary to study the law with understanding and effect. This book is therefore not an elementary book on the principles of Scots Law but an attempt to acquaint the student at the very outset of his studies with the background and the basic knowledge requisite to enable him intelligently and profitably to pursue legal studies, and with the materials of legal study and the methods of working.

The study of this book is not intended to supersede the necessity for later, closer and more detailed study of each of the topics it covers, as well as of the doctrinal principles of the substantive law. Every topic discussed herein has been deliberately treated in a preliminary and elementary way, and many details, qualifications, subtleties and difficulties have been glossed over. Considerations of space and expense have further severely limited or even prevented altogether the discussion of many points.

I have deliberately avoided the detailed treatment and the full citation of authority which might be expected in a more advanced book, and much bibliographical material has been mentioned in footnotes not so much to vouch the statements in the text as to indicate the sources of further information.

This fourth edition has been completely revised to take account

v

of developments in the law since the last edition and in the hope of clarifying some of the difficulties.

I am greatly indebted to my colleagues, who have brought to my notice many points requiring revision, to my wife, who has assisted me at every stage of the book, to the publishers who undertook the preparation of the Tables of Statutes and of Cases, and to the printers who have taken such pains and trouble over this book. I have tried to take account of all developments down to the date of this Preface.

D. M. W.

THE UNIVERSITY,
 GLASGOW, G12 8QQ.
1st January, 1976.

CONTENTS

LIST OF ILLUSTRATIONS
from drawings by the author

ix

TABLE OF CASES

TABLE OF STATUTES

ABBREVIATIONS

A.J.C.L.	American Journal of Comparative Law
A.J.I.L.	American Journal of International Law
A.P.S.	Acts of the Parliaments of Scotland (Record Edition, 12 vols.)
B.J.A.L.	British Journal of Administrative Law
B.Y.I.L.	British Year Book of International Law
Can.B.R.	Canadian Bar Review
C.L.J.	Cambridge Law Journal
C.L.P.	Current Legal Problems
C.L.Y.	Current Law Year Book
Col.L.R.	Columbia Law Review
H.L.R.	Harvard Law Review
I.C.L.Q.	International and Comparative Law Quarterly
J.Crim.L.	Journal of Criminal Law
J.R.	Juridical Review
J.S.P.T.L.	Journal of the Society of Public Teachers of Law
L.Q.R.	Law Quarterly Review
M.L.R.	Modern Law Review
N.I.L.Q.	Northern Ireland Law Quarterly
N.Y.U.L.Q.R.	New York University Law Quarterly Review
Pub.L.	Public Law
S.H.R.	Scottish Historical Review
S.L.R.	Scottish Law Review
S.L.T.	Scots Law Times
Yale L.J.	Yale Law Journal

INTRODUCTION

THE Scottish legal system is the general name for a complex of institutions (*e.g.* legislative bodies, executive agencies, courts, companies, prisons),[1] of persons (*e.g.* legislators, administrators, judges, lawyers, business men, police, social workers, prison officers and ordinary citizens),[2] of ideas and theories (*e.g.* justice, peace, freedom, order, implementing undertakings, compensation for wrong) expressed in principles and rules for regulating conduct, which are formulated in words (*e.g.* you should perform your undertakings, take care for the safety of your neighbour, not steal), grouped in logically related sets,[3] and systematically stated in books,[4] of methods and techniques of law-making,[5] law-finding,[6] fact-finding,[7] law-applying,[8] and law-reforming,[9] and of means of adjudicating, of procedures and practices.[10] This complex exists in relation to the people living in Scotland. It co-exists with social, political, economic, religious and other systems in the community and interacts with them. It must be seen in the light of its development,[11] and in its place among other legal systems in the world, *e.g.* the French legal system, and other branches of the study of legal science, *e.g.* legal theory,[12] while the study of legal science or law in all its branches must in turn be seen as a subject of study and in its place among the bodies of human knowledge which men seek to understand, particularly those other bodies also concerned with Man in Society.[13]

---

[1] Chaps. 5–7.
[2] Chap. 8.
[3] Chap. 9.
[4] Chaps. 10–11. These sets of principles and rules comprise what is usually called " the law ".
[5] Chap. 10.
[6] Chaps. 11–12.
[7] Chaps. 13–14.
[8] Chaps. 13–14.
[9] Chap. 15.
[10] Chaps. 13–14.
[11] Chap. 4.
[12] Chap. 3.
[13] Chaps. 1–2.

Chapter 1

LAW AND OTHER STUDIES

THE field of human knowledge and inquiry is roughly divisible into three major areas, known as the humanities, the social sciences, and the natural sciences (or the physical and biological sciences, or simply " science ").[1] These areas of knowledge and inquiry comprise respectively the studies which consider, discuss, criticise and evaluate the products of human reasoning, speculation and imagination,[2] which examine, analyse and seek to explain particular facets of the conduct, attitudes, interaction and interrelations of human beings living and working together in organised and civilised society,[3] and those which investigate the universe and the phenomena, creatures and things which are found in it.[4] It is only since the Renaissance that these different areas of thought and study have come to be thus divided, and further subdivided into branches and subjects of study; in ancient and medieval times the polymath could know something of all.[5] To Plato philosophy embraced almost the whole field of knowledge. Aristotle wrote on a wide variety of subjects. But division and subdivision, with their necessarily concomitant specialisation and compartmentation of knowledge, are inevitable consequences of the enormous and continuing growth in the extent, complexity and detail of knowledge in every field and of thinking, investigation and writing thereon,[6] though this increasingly tends to give rise to the division between the Two Cultures, of Arts (and Social Sciences) and of Science,[7] in which persons knowledgeable in one field are frequently largely ignorant in the other.

---

[1] Universities frequently recognise this general division in the form of the distribution of subject-matter of study between Faculties of Arts (or Letters), of Social Sciences, and of Science, though in some the social sciences are included in the Faculty of Arts. Other Faculties are specialised offshoots of these main groups, concerned more particularly with the studies relevant to certain major professions.

[2] e.g., philosophy in its various branches, languages, literature, fine art, music.

[3] e.g., politics, economics, history, sociology, anthropology. The humanities and the social sciences are together sometimes spoken of as dealing with super-organic phenomena.

[4] e.g., physics, chemistry, geology, astronomy (physical sciences dealing with inanimate nature and inorganic phenomena); botany, zoology, physiology, biochemistry (biological sciences dealing with living creatures, plants and organic phenomena).

[5] Encyclopaedia of the Social Sciences, Introd. II—The Social Sciences as Disciplines (Vol. I, 231 et seq.).

[6] See Encyclopaedia of the Social Sciences, Introd. I—The Development of Social Thought and Institutions (Vol. 1, 8–228).

[7] See C. P. Snow, The Two Cultures: And, A Second Look (1964). See also Aldous Huxley, Literature and Science (1963).

A more refined analysis [8] distinguishes ten major divisions of knowledge, nine of which are concerned with *what is known* by means of the particular sciences such as physics, economics and the like about the universe and the things in it, including Man and all his doings, and the tenth with the branches of learning or departments of scholarship themselves, with *how*

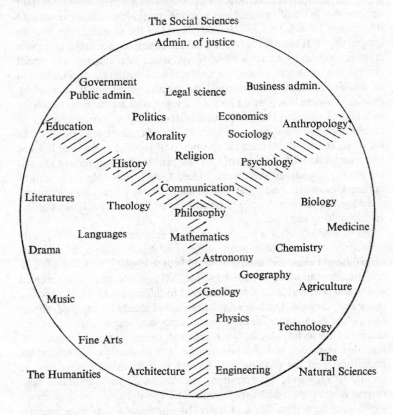

Within the circle which represents the sphere of human knowledge the most general and fundamental studies are at the centre and the others so placed as to show related studies close to one another. These belong to the three major areas of the Humanities, the Social Sciences and the Natural Sciences. The divisions between the three areas and between one study and another are not sharp or clearly defined, and there are no barriers to the linking of any one study with any other as in History of Fine Art, Philosophy of Science, Psychological Medicine and Engineering Economics. No significance attaches to which studies are shown at the top, as the circle can be looked at from any angle and any point can be at the top.

---

[8] *Encyclopaedia Britannica* (15th ed., 1974) Propaedia volume.

we know that which we know, with the nature, history and methods of inquiry, argument and demonstration of the various branches of knowledge or scholarly disciplines themselves, and also with three particular branches of knowledge, namely logic and scientific method, mathematics and philosophy, all of which are both studies in themselves and also have important applications in thinking about and working out problems in the other nine divisions of knowledge.[9] In this analysis one of the nine divisions has the general title of Human Society and is held to comprise the studies of human culture, studied by social anthropology, social organisation and social change, studied by sociology, the production, distribution and utilisation of wealth, studied by economics, politics and government, studied by political science, law, studied by legal science, and education, studied by educational science. The assignment of law to the group of studies or divisions of learning concerned with Human Society does not elide the fact that, at both the theoretical and practical levels, the study of law has important links with branches of knowledge in the fields of human life and behaviour, technology and others. Indeed there is probably no branch of human knowledge which may not in some circumstances be relevant to some legal problem and have to be considered for the light it casts on an issue requiring legal decision.

No scheme of division is, however, rigid and the areas are not strictly defined or self-contained; many subjects of study partake of elements from different areas and are therefore difficult to classify,[10] and many more run into one another, but the tripartite division is a generally accepted and useful one, and does also correspond to differences in the methods of study and research. The humanities are studied chiefly by study of written texts, close examination of arguments, reasoning, verbal disputation and criticism; the social sciences by observation, examination and analysis of recorded instances of human behaviour, and deduction of conclusions therefrom; and the physical and biological sciences by observation of natural phenomena, classification, measurement, the tabulation and comparison of the results of experiments, the induction of hypotheses which explain the results and observed phenomena, and experimental verification, correction and amplification of these hypotheses.

[9] To these might have been added Communication and Language, as the major means of written and oral argument, of thinking and communication. In the human or social sciences communication of ideas by words is very important. Moreover in some branches of legal study much of the literature is in French, German, Italian or Spanish, while knowledge of Greek and Latin is frequently also necessary.

[10] Thus psychology is partly derived from introspection and reasoning, partly from observation of human and animal conduct, partly from planned experiments; geography is partly social science, dealing with human activities, partly physical science, dealing with the characteristics of the world inhabited by man; architecture is partly a fine art, partly an applied science; history may be regarded as among the humanities, or as a social science; and so on. Many studies, such as psychology, moral philosophy, geography, medicine, biology, linguistics and others have important social implications quite apart from their own substance and technicalities.

Each one of these branches of study, moreover, has its own body of theory and philosophy, its own course of historical development, and its own body of recognised principles, constantly being modified in the light of changing conditions and progressive research and criticism; each one also has its more theoretical and abstract side, in which it is regarded primarily as a more or less coherent body of knowledge and studied with little or no regard to its utility, and its more practical and applied side, in which it is considered mainly as a system of useful principles capable of application to practical needs and ends, to solving actual problems and surmounting real difficulties.

In this general pattern legal science, or the study of law in its most general sense, falls to be grouped with the social sciences [11]: it deals, that is, with one aspect of the relations and interactions of individuals living in society, namely, with the institutions, machinery and principles which particular societies have developed for the purposes of defining the claims and liabilities of persons against one another in various circumstances, and of providing means for vindicating just claims and peaceably resolving their disputes and controversies in accordance with the principles accepted as fair and right in the particular community at a given time.[12] Moreover, the content of law is influenced and even determined by the views of society and it has important consequences for society and individuals. The existence of a legal order in society is furthermore presupposed by most other social sciences, so that law and the other social sciences are interdependent and, as studies, overlap.

Law is, indeed, a part of human culture, of " that complex whole which includes knowledge, belief, art, morals, law, custom and any other capabilities acquired by man as a member of society." [13] It is both a product of civilisation, in that wherever groups of individuals have attained that

[11] *Cf. Encyc.Soc.Sc.*, I, 3, defining social sciences as " those mental or cultural sciences which deal with the activities of the individual as a member of a group." The *Encyclopaedia of the Social Sciences* (1930) distinguished the social sciences (politics, economics, law, anthropology, sociology, penology and social work), the semi-social sciences (ethics, education, philosophy and psychology) and the sciences with social implications (biology, geography, medicine, linguistics and art). The *International Encyclopaedia of the Social Sciences* (1968), though disclaiming finality in its decision of what are social sciences, deals with anthropology, economics, geography, history, law, political science, psychiatry, psychology, sociology and statistics. Cairns (*Law and the Social Sciences*) considers the relations of law and anthropology, economics, sociology, political science and psychology. Similarly the Dewey Decimal Classification of books (18th ed., 1971) developed for the particular purpose of classifying books in libraries and rather artificially dividing and subdividing by tens, recognises as one of the ten major divisions the social sciences, and includes within that division the ten subjects of sociology, statistics, political science, economics, law, public administration, social pathology and crime, education, commerce, transport and communications, and custom and folklore.
[12] Patterson, *Jurisprudence*, 50, points out that so far as jurists deal with precepts for conduct which *ought to be* followed, law is not a social science but a philosophic discipline, akin to moral philosophy.
[13] Tylor, *Primitive Culture*, 1.

stage of organisation and of control over their environment which we call civilisation, some kind of legal ordering of society is found,[14] and it is also an essential of the continuance and development of civilisation, in that without a legal order to regulate conflicting claims and to resolve differences, civilisation would slip back into anarchy. The intimate connection between the legal system and the general culture of our society is well illustrated by the extent to which legal institutions are pictured in English literature [15] and legal phraseology has penetrated into common speech.[16]

The origins of all the social sciences go back to the ancient Greeks and their rationalist inquiries into the nature of man, the state, and morality but they began to develop more rapidly, and to become increasingly differentiated after the Renaissance and particularly from the eighteenth century. All were affected by the English, American and French Revolutions, the Industrial Revolution, urbanisation, the development of democracy and other similar factors.

Law a True Science

Law, moreover, is truly a science,[17] that is, a systematic body of coherent and ordered knowledge about the institutions, principles and rules regulating human conduct in society.[18] It is " an organised and critically controlled body of knowledge both of legal institutions and legal precepts

---

[14] Thus, highly developed legal systems existed in ancient Mesopotamia (see Driver and Miles, *The Babylonian Laws*, 2 vols.; *The Assyrian Laws*), Asia Minor (see Neufeld, *The Hittite Laws*), Palestine (see Kent, *Israel's Laws and Legal Precedents*) and elsewhere.

[15] See, *e.g.*, Underhill, *Shakespeare's England*, Chap. 13; Keeton, *Shakespeare and His Legal Problems*; Holdsworth, *Charles Dickens as a Legal Historian*; McNair, *Dr. Johnson and the Law*; Marshall, *Sir Walter Scott and Scots Law*; Cardozo, " Law and Literature " in *Selected Writings*, 339; Holdsworth, " Literature in Law Books " in *Essays in Law and History*, 219; Lord Macmillan, " Law and Letters " and " Law and Language " in *Law and Other Things*; Windolph, *Reflections on the Law in Literature*; Collins, *Dickens and Crime*.

[16] See, *e.g.*, Simon, " English Idioms from the Law " (1960) 76 L.Q.R. 283, 429; (1962) 78 L.Q.R. 245; (1965) 81 L.Q.R. 52.

[17] The word " science " is not confined, or appropriate only, to natural science; it is applicable to the systematised knowledge of any subject of intellectual inquiry.

[18] Lord Atkin once said: " That law is a scientific subject, I suggest, cannot be disputed. I think it was Burke who said that law is one of the finest and noblest of human sciences: a science which does more to quicken and invigorate the understanding than all the other kinds of learning put together." (" Law as an Educational Subject " (1932) J.S.P.T.L. 27.) Stair (*Institutions*, I, 1, 17) affirmed that law could, and should, be handled as a rational discipline, having principles from whence its conclusions may be deduced. Alexander Bayne (Professor of Scots Law at Edinburgh, 1722–37, on whom see Menzies, " Alex. Bayne of Rires " (1924) 36 J.R. 60) in *A Discourse on the Rise and Progress of the Law of Scotland*, annexed to his edition of Hope's *Minor Practicks* (1726), wrote that the Science of the Law was of the highest character among the humane sciences, the most useful to mankind, and best entitled to first place among them. Similarly Blackstone (*Commentaries on the Laws of England*, I, 34) wrote: " Law is to be considered not only as a matter of practice, but also as a rational science." (On Blackstone see further: Boorstin, *The Mysterious Science of the Law*, and Hanbury, *The Vinerian Chair and Legal Education*.) *Cf.* also Pollock, *First Book of Jurisprudence*, 46; Langdell, Introduction to *Cases on the Law of Contract* (1886).

and of the legal order, that is, the legal ordering of society . . . a science of
achieving social control by means of or with the aid of laws . . . a science
of the adjustment of human relations through the public administration of
justice, or, more specifically, a science of the securing of interests in civilised
society by means of an ordered judicial and administrative adjustment of
relations." [19] Legal science, or jurisprudence (in the wider sense of that
word), includes all thinking and writing about and systematic study and
knowledge of the making, exposition and analysis, development and
transmission of law, and also legal dogmatics, or the study of the actual
content of the legal system, of the body of propositions, precepts, doctrines,
principles and rules accepted in a particular community and of their
applications.[20]   Law in a modern community does not consist of a great
mass of particular, specific, unrelated rules which have to be looked up, as
in a telephone directory, and the study of law does not consist in memoris-
ing, or even in learning how to look up, such a directory. The scientific
element in law consists in that a system of law comprises a body of reasonably consistent principles and rules, susceptible of arrangement under
heads and sub-heads and of systematic study, defining rules for and
standards of conduct and the consequences of their non-observance in
particular kinds of circumstances. These can be applied to an infinite
number and variety of problem-situations, whether known or foreseeable
or not, and can solve them in accordance with overriding principles of
justice, in the same way as propositions and formulae about the triangle
can be applied to any actual triangle.[21] Furthermore, law can be studied by
scientific methods just as can any other science.   Experiment, or the
observation of phenomena under conditions controlled by the investigator,
is possible only to a very limited extent,[22] but observation, classification,
analysis and synthesis, inductive and deductive inference, and comparison
and analogy are all applicable to legal problems as much as to those of
other sciences.   Observation and classification in particular are clearly
illustrated by the common and centuries-old legal practice of having
interesting cases noted or reported under legal headings, so that jurists can
subsequently read what the courts have done and said in solving particular

---

[19] Pound, *Jurisprudence*, I, 16–17.

[20] *Cf.* Kantorowicz, *The Definition of Law*, 11–13; Schulz, *History of Roman Legal
Science*, 1.

[21] *Cf.* Fraser Tytler's *Memoirs of Lord Kames*, I, 114: " The examination of various
cases which turn upon one common *ratio decidendi*, familiarises the mind, in all
points of doubt to recur immediately to a principle; and this habit of reference will
not only be found of the utmost benefit when any abstruse or intricate question is
the subject of discussion; but it tends from the agreeable and vigorous exercise it
affords to the intellectual powers, to give to jurisprudence that dignity as a science
which it merits, and to render the study of the laws, instead of a servile drudgery, the
manly employment of a philosophic mind."

[22] It is possible to some extent in such contexts as trying different methods of
treatment of criminals, or different methods of control of anti-social activities, such
as gambling.

problems,[23] and can classify and study together cases relating to similar problems. Analysis involves the breaking down of a legal problem or reported decision into its elements, into the particular factors which constitute it, so as to discern what is unknown or different from other comparable cases, while synthesis is the building up of the legal elements involved in a factual situation which go to impose liability or provide a valid defence or justify a legal remedy in the particular circumstances. Inductive inference consists in drawing a general principle from a number of similar observed instances; deductive inference is the process of applying general principles to suitable particular instances. Both are illustrated repeatedly in the way the courts handle previous reported decisions to help them solve a new problem before them.[24] Comparison and analogy involve the recognition of greater or lesser degrees of similarity between one case and another or others, and again these are techniques regularly resorted to in legal reasoning.[25]

Law must not be thought of solely or even primarily as a body of professional knowledge, the stock-in-trade of the practitioners of certain professions, or as purely a practical or applied science. It is primarily a social science, a pure science, an area in the field of studies of men's relations with one another. The knowledge gained from that study can of course be used to understand and to solve actual everyday problems, as a basis for advice, decision or action; to that extent it forms part of the background knowledge employed by several professions, but the same is true of economics, physiology and many other subjects. The evident utility and manifold applications of the knowledge should not be allowed to obscure the status of the subject as a major department of the social sciences, indeed one of the most ancient of them, and one which has in every age and country attracted the attention and devotion of some of the ablest minds of the time.

Relations of Law with other Studies

Legal science deals with only one facet of human conduct and of the relations of people in society, and cannot ignore those other sciences which study other facets of the same relations.[26] One particular piece of conduct

---

[23] " Case law has a scientific aim, namely, the prediction of events by means of past experience ": Pollock, " The Science of Case Law " in *Essays in Jurisprudence and Ethics*, 237, and in *Jurisprudence and Legal Essays*, 169.

[24] *Cf.* the inductive inference in *Donoghue* v. *Stevenson*, 1932 S.C.(H.L.) 31, of the general principle implicit in various particular earlier decisions, and the deduction from that general principle of the particular decision in *Lockhart* v. *Barr*, 1943 S.C.(H.L.) 1.

[25] See further Levi, *Introduction to Legal Reasoning.*

[26] *Cf.* Lord Kames's Preface to his *Elucidations respecting the Law of Scotland*: " Were law taught as a rational science, its principles unfolded, and its connection with manners and politics, it would prove an enticing study to every person who has an appetite for knowledge."

may be of interest to the students of many disciplines; an assault by one man on another is to the sociologist a deviation from normal conduct, to the psychologist a problem of motivation, to the philosopher a problem of right and wrong, to the psychiatrist a possible manifestation of a diseased mind, and to the lawyer a breach of a legal duty which is punishable. The relations between law and the principal other social sciences are so close and important as to justify more detailed individual examination.[27]

Law and Anthropology

Anthropology is the study of man as a physical and social being as he is found in different environments in the world, and of this one aspect is social anthropology which deals with the life of primitive peoples living in primitive conditions at the present day, and studies their conduct, habits, institutions and attitudes, their beliefs, taboos, marriage customs, kinship relations, trading relations, reactions to wrongdoing and so on. Such studies seek to discover the origins of civilisation and culture, and provide important indications of the origins and bases of modern social institutions and the patterns of conduct of civilised peoples. They serve to stimulate, illustrate and modify thinking about law and its origins and nature rather than to influence it today or to provide material to which it is applicable. From such studies it is apparent that means of social control, some approximating in substance to law, can exist without writing or lawyers, without force or formal procedure, in such communities.[28]

Law and Sociology

Sociology is the study of society, social groups, social phenomena, the forms of social institutions, social relationships, social structure, social change and development,[29] and it therefore deals with much that is the background to, and the justification for and explanation of, the legal system. Not least sociology examines criminal classes and their attitude to society and such problem groups as drug-addicts, the poor, and minority groups. In its study of the interaction and relationships of individuals and groups it deals with the same subject-matter as does the law, but from a

---

[27] See generally Cairns, *Law and the Social Sciences*; Stone, *Law and the Social Sciences in the Second Half Century*.

[28] See further, generally, Boas, " Anthropology " in *Encyc.Soc.Sc.*, II, 73; Greenberg and others, " Anthropology " in *Int.Encyc.Soc.Sc.*; Chappel and Coon, *Principles of Anthropology*; Piddington, *Introduction to Social Anthropology* (2 vols.); Lowie *Primitive Society*; and, on points of legal interest, Hartland, *Primitive Law*; Diamond *Primitive Law*; Malinowski, *Crime and Custom in Savage Society*; Hogbin, *Law and Order in Polynesia*; Gluckman, *The Judicial Process among the Barotse of Northern Rhodesia*; *Politics, Law and Ritual in Tribal Society*; Llewellyn and Hoebel, *The Cheyenne Way*; Hoebel, *The Law of Primitive Man*; see also Robson, *Civilisation and the Growth of Law*; Cairns, " Law and Anthropology " (1931) 31 Col.L.R. 32.

[29] See generally MacIver, " Sociology " in *Encyc.Soc.Sc.*, XIV, 232; Reiss and others, " Sociology " in *Int.Encyc.Soc.Sc.*

different standpoint. Social institutions, such as the family, marriage and inheritance are in fact regulated in large part by legal rules and are legal institutions as well as sociological.[30] Sociology is also concerned with society's reactions to social problems, such as welfare services and prisons.

To the sociologist law is necessarily a matter of interest because law is, like custom, habit, morals, taboos and fashion, one of the forces of social control which tend to regulate conduct and impose uniformities of behaviour, and is moreover the most widespread and powerful of these forces.[31] Law is also largely a product of social requirements and changes, and of custom and accepted social practices, and develops to take account of such social changes; if it does not, it becomes out of date, out of touch with the requirements and the feelings of the community and to that extent fails to serve its purpose.[32] In the present century there has indeed developed a branch of study called sociology of law, studying law as a specialised phase of the study of society.[33]

To the student of law, sociology explains much of the society in which his legal system works and for which it exists.[34] It enables him to take account of social facts in the framing of new legislation or the enforcement of existing rules, and requires him to reconsider time-honoured rules or institutions in the light of changed conditions. What is social disorganisation to the sociologist includes what are to the lawyer also problems, such as of crime, divorce, illegitimacy, racial discrimination, street and industrial accidents, and town planning. Sociology both helps to explain the institutions of the legal order, and itself assumes them in its own studies.

Law and Politics

The relationship in this case is obviously close. Politics is the study of the organisation adopted by the members of a society living in a defined area for their own government in the general interest of peace and order.[35]

---

[30] See generally MacIver and Page: *Society, an Introductory Analysis*; Johnson, *Sociology, a Systematic Introduction*; Ogburn and Nimkoff, *Handbook of Sociology*; Ginsberg, *Essays in Sociology and Social Philosophy*, 3 vols.; Michael and Adler, *Crime, Law and Social Science*; Glueck and Hall, *Crime, Theft and Society*.

[31] See Pound, *Social Control Through Law*; " Sociology and Law " in Ogburn and Goldenweiser, *The Social Sciences* (1921) 319.

[32] See further Friedmann, *Law in a Changing Society*; Ginsburg (ed.), *Law and Opinion in England in the 20th Century*; Sawer, *Law in Society*.

[33] See Timasheff, *The Sociology of Law*; Ehrlich, *Fundamental Principles of the Sociology of Law*; Gurvitch, *Sociology of Law*; Aubert (ed.) *Sociology of Law*; sociology of law is closely related to sociological jurisprudence, which is rather the " applied " aspect of the relations of law and society, examining the legal system functionally, as it works and operates in society. On the latter, see Pound, *Jurisprudence*, I, 291 *et seq.*

[34] John Millar, Professor of Law in Glasgow University 1761–1801, wrote on *The Origin of the Distinction of Ranks*, which is important as an early sociological study. It is reprinted with a valuable introduction in Lehmann, *John Millar of Glasgow* (1961). See also Lehmann, " John Millar " (1961) 6 J.R.(N.S.) 218.

[35] See further Heller, " Political Science " in *Encyc.Soc.Sc.*, XII, 207; Brecht and Wolin, " Political Theory " in *Int.Encyc.Soc.Sc.*

Politics may be distinguished into political theory, thought or philosophy, the more theoretical study, concerned with the ways in which thinkers have considered that power in a state should be distributed and exercised,[36] and political science, the systematic study of political institutions, behaviour and the operation of political systems.[37] The framework of the political organisation of a community, its constitution, is set out in legal terms and legal forms and secured by legal means, and the subordinate standards, such as the structure and powers of the legislative assembly, the rights and liberties of citizens, the powers and duties of officials, the position of the police and their powers, the system of taxation and so on, are all defined by law. Even in a dictatorial regime, the dictator commonly secures his powers by law; in a democracy every power, control and regulation is a matter of law and effected by legal forms.

Conversely, the political structure of a society has as one of its primary purposes and duties the maintenance of a legal system, of law and order in the community, and in most modern organised societies the modification and reformation of the law in the interests of the community, or possibly of the politically dominant group thereof, is the prerogative of the legislative assembly, which is a part of the political framework, while the application to particular cases and enforcement of the legal principles is the function of other branches of the political organisation. It is clear, therefore, that the nature and content of a legal system may be largely determined by the views of those politically dominant at any given time.

As studies jurisprudence and politics are interdependent and almost indistinguishable in origin, and the most profound thinking on the theoretical side, such as Aristotle's *Politics*, is common to both. In practice the studies of law and politics are inextricably enmeshed and inseparable.[38]

Law and Economics

Law and economics similarly overlap at many points. Economics is the study of human action in relation to the production, exchange and distribution of wealth, or of " social phenomena centring about the provision for the material needs of the individual and of organised groups." [39]

As a study economics emerged from ethical, legal and political thinking. Adam Smith lectured and wrote on ethics and legal theory as well as on economics, and only in the nineteenth century did economics become

---

[36] *e.g.* Plato, *Republic*; Aristotle, *Politics*; Hobbes, *Leviathan*; Bentham, *Fragment on Government*; and see generally Sabine, *History of Political Theory.*

[37] See *e.g.* Finer, *Major Governments of Modern Europe*; Wheare, *Federal Government*; Jennings, *Parliament* and *Cabinet Government.*

[38] See further Pound, *Jurisprudence*, II, 283; Bryce, *Studies in History and Jurisprudence*, Essay X.

[39] Seligman, " Economics " in *Encyc.Soc.Sc.*, V, 344; and see Robinson, " Law and Economics " (1938) 2 M.L.R. 257; de Roover and others, " Economic Thought " in *Int.Encyc.Soc.Sc.*

distinct.[40] Like other studies economics is distinguishable into economic theory or economic thought and applied economics.

Much law springs from the necessity of regulating economic relations and exists for that purpose, while economic activities, such as buying and selling, transport, manufacture and financial transactions can flourish only within a regime of law and order and are shaped materially by the legal forms recognised in the community. Associations, such as companies and trade unions, are formed in legal ways and subject to legal regulation for economic ends. The salient economic relations such as sale, hiring, transport and employment are effected within a legal framework. The ancillaries which facilitate such relations, such as credit, bills, cheques, money and other modes of payment, securities for payment and insurance against loss, are all regulated by law. Monopolies,[41] restrictive trading agreements, hire-purchase transactions and the protection of consumers from defective quality are spheres in which law and economics are increasingly interacting. General concepts, such as contract, property and succession on death, taxation and many more, need to be and can profitably be studied from both standpoints. Not merely those engaged in industry or commerce but every individual every day enters into numerous transactions which have both legal and economic significance, the law determining whether it is permissible and in what form it may or must be effected, what its legal effect and consequences are and what can be done to enforce performance, and considerations of economics determining whether that transaction should be entered into or deferred or abandoned, on what terms, and whether completion will give satisfaction or not.

Law and Psychology

Psychology is concerned with investigating the mental processes of the individual, his instincts, beliefs, emotions, means of perception, feeling, remembering and thinking.[42] In legal contexts it is frequently material to determine such facts as the intention of a party, whether he could have or should have known something, the motive for his conduct, and so on. While the courts normally are content to ignore the underlying mental processes and draw inferences from facts external to the individual, the

---

[40] Adam Smith's work includes *The Theory of Morai Sentiments* and *Lectures on Justice, Police, Revenue and Arms* as well as the *Wealth of Nations*. See further Scott, *Adam Smith as Student and Professor*; Fay, *Adam Smith and the Scotland of His Day*; Cooke, " Adam Smith and Jurisprudence " (1935) 51 L.Q.R. 326; and, more generally, Gide and Rist, *History of Economic Doctrines*; Roll, *History of Economic Thought*. See also Jones, *Historical Introduction to the Theory of Law*, Chap. 10—" Law and Economic Theory."

[41] See, *e.g.*, Lewis, " Monopoly and the Law " (1943) 6 M.L.R. 97; Hunter, *Competition and the Law*.

[42] See Jastrow, " Psychology " in *Encyc.Soc.Sc.*, XII, 588; Bernard, " Social Psychology " in the same, XIV, 151; Waters and others, " Psychology " in *Int.Encyc. Soc.Sc.*

individual's mental state may be acutely important, as where issues of insanity or diminished responsibility arise in criminal cases, and psychology may be valuable as giving insight into the springs of the conduct under investigation. In another context, psychology can cast light on the value or fallibility of human evidence and on the ways by which judges think.[43]

Social psychology is the study of persons' conduct in their interactions with one another with reference to the effects of this on their thoughts, feelings, emotions and habits. It stems from both psychology and sociology. Social conduct, and the person and the group's prejudices, convictions, attitudes, frames of reference and values may all be highly relevant to law and help to explain facts giving rise to legal issues.[44]

In investigating delinquency and criminal behaviour psychology can sometimes assist by explaining the reasons for criminal conduct, by helping to devise suitable treatment and in persuading the offender to refrain from such conduct in future.

Law and History

History involves not only the tracing of the order of past happenings but elucidating the causal factors which helped to determine these happenings, and their effects and influence on every facet of the life of the society or institution whose history is being studied.[45] The connection of law with history is very close. In the first place every branch of law, international, supra-national and national, has its own history and course of development which can be traced, and which alone can in many cases provide the explanation for the existence today of apparently peculiar or irrational rules. In the second place that history itself is only one facet of the general development of international and supra-national institutions and relations, of the growth of the structure and organisation of the particular nation-state, and of the communities therein, and has to be related to the other facets, social, political, economic, religious and so on, of that history. Legal history is, moreover, not merely a facet but largely a product of the more general history of the particular society and may repeatedly have been powerfully influenced by important events in other sectors of the general history of the community.[46] A country's legal history is inextricably entangled with its social, political, constitutional, economic and ecclesiastical history, and events primarily within any one of these facets of history may affect legal development. Thus in Scottish legal history important

---

[43] See Frank, *Law and the Modern Mind* and *Courts on Trial.*

[44] See further Thouless, *General and Social Psychology*; McDougall, *Introduction to Social Psychology*; Newcomb, *Social Psychology*; Kimball Young, *Handbook of Social Psychology*; Jones, *Historical Introduction to the Theory of Law*, Chap. 7— " The Psychological Theories."

[45] See generally Berr and others, " History and Historiography " in *Encyc.Soc.Sc.*, VII, 357 *et seq.*; Gardiner and others, " History " in *Int.Encyc.Soc.Sc.*

[46] See further Pound, *Interpretations of Legal History.*

legal changes have been brought about by such events as the struggle for independence, the religious Reformation, the political unions with England under the Commonwealth and Protectorate and, since 1707, the Jacobite rebellions, the industrial revolution, the two world wars and so on.[47]

Historical study of law is of particular importance not only because it can frequently explain what is rationally inexplicable, but because it makes clear that particular rules cannot always be considered as immutable, or as embodying eternal or universal principles; they may proceed only from the prejudices or the exigencies of a particular time; their history explains them but does not justify them, leaving them open to criticism on other grounds.

Law and Religion

Religion is not always regarded as a social science, but it is inseparable from the social sciences. Many of the most critical problems in the social sciences involve a religious factor. The attitudes, beliefs, faiths and practices which constitute religion have important connections with law. In its early forms law is completely entangled with religion. Like law, religion is a vast subject of study with its own history, philosophy, theology, institutions, variant bodies of dogma and forms [48] but in practice it provides ways of life and codes of conduct which are major forces regulating men's actings in many contexts, which impel men to act in certain ways and deter them from acting in others.

Christianity has powerfully influenced all the legal systems of Western Europe both in general, and in particular ways at particular times. Thus the supremacy of Puritanism or of Calvinism have at different times affected the law. It has always had a particular concern with marriage and the family structure, and church law has greatly influenced state law in this sphere. The Christian Church itself developed an extensive and refined system of law, the canon law,[49] which had wide influence on many spheres of activity, particularly before the Reformation, and had permanent influence on secular legal systems. The underlying ideas of religion,

---

[47] On these points, see further Chap. 4, *infra. Cf.* Kames, *Historical Law Tracts,* preface, where he says: " Law in particular becomes then only a rational study, when it is traced historically, from its first rudiments among savages, through successive changes, to its highest improvements in a civilised society." See also Fraser Tytler's *Memoirs of Lord Kames,* I, 208: " There cannot indeed be a more pleasing exercise for the understanding, nor any that affords a greater scope for ingenuity, than the reciprocal elucidation of Law and of History, by the aids which they borrow from each other. Every law is a key to the history of the times in which it was framed, and may, in most instances, be traced up to the political emergency which required its enactment."

[48] There are many parallels between law and religion, the books of authority, the ritual of courts, the part played by priests and judges, the complicated bodies of dogma, the distinction between crime and sin, and others.

[49] On the canon law see further Chap. 3.

belief in the value of the human personality, in justice, sympathy, charity, forgiveness, honour and truth have similarly penetrated legal practices and influenced legal rules.

The religious and social and political and economic orderings of society are everywhere interactive and since the early middle ages the conflict between Church and State has been a constant theme in some countries.[50]

The connections of law with two other branches of knowledge also require examination.

Law and Language

Law consists of precepts and norms for regulating conduct, of statements of doctrines, principles, rules and standards, all formulated in words. It is set out in statutes, decisions and books, all conveying meaning verbally. It operates through deeds and writs, pleadings and letters, sentences and judgments, all expressed in words. Legal argument takes place in words; witnesses give evidence in words. The study of language, word-meaning, word-usage, word-order, grammar, sentence-structure, modes of verbal expression, composition and interpretation are all of the greatest importance and the highest practical use in legal study and legal practice, while in some circumstances one is faced also with the difficulties of translation and of the understanding of texts written initially in a foreign language. A branch of linguistic study important for legal study is semantics.

Semantics is the study of the theories as to the meanings and mental influences of words and other symbols used in communication. The results of semantic study are particularly important in legal thinking, writing and argument, since so many of the terms and concepts used in law and legal books are inherently vague and capable of conveying different ideas in different circumstances; such words as " right," " wrong," " negligence," " malice " are susceptible of different meanings in different contexts. It is fatal to legal study to think that any such words have a fixed meaning; they all have many shades of meaning in different contexts and when used for different purposes, and even have uses other than pure communication;

---

[50] See generally Yinger, *The Scientific Study of Religion*; Weber, *The Protestant Ethic and the Spirit of Capitalism*; Tawney, *Religion and the Rise of Capitalism*; Lenski, *The Religious Factor: A Sociological Study of Religion's Impact on Politics, Economics and Family Life;* Hill, *Society and Puritanism in Pre-Revolutionary England*; St. John-Stevas, *Life, Death and the Law.*

thus such words as " worker ", " democratic " and even " consumer " have a strong emotional flavour.[51]

Lastly, it is necessary to look at some of the major points of contact between law and philosophy.

Law and Philosophy

On its theoretical side the study of law, as of other social sciences, inevitably impinges on various aspects of philosophy.[52] Philosophy is thinking about the most general and most ultimate problems of every branch of knowledge and human activity, and about how we think and acquire knowledge itself. It is not so much a body of knowledge as a questioning attitude of mind, a seeking for understanding. It consists of man's efforts to reflect deeply in a rational, methodical and systematic way on the problems of greatest concern to man. For centuries law and politics had a common philosophic foundation,[53] while economics and sociology emerged later from this same body of thought. Only in the nineteenth century did law tend to be divorced from politics and economics, but a counter-movement, starting in the latter half of the nineteenth century, urged the unification of the social sciences, stressing the interrelation and interaction of all and their common background of philosophical thinking. The study of law, as of all the other social sciences, inevitably leads to questions of the rightness or wrongness of conduct, the ends sought to be attained, the justifiability of means and ends, the problem of justice, the validity of reasoning, the meanings of the terms used and the proper use of terminology, and so on, all of which are essentially philosophic problems. The philosophy of law, or the critical examination of the propositions, presuppositions and underlying ideas of legal systems in the light of philosophical ideas and methods is an important part of jurisprudence (in the narrower sense of that word).

Of the recognised branches of philosophy two, logic and scientific method, and moral philosophy, are vitally important, for the light they cast on problems of law and the study of law in relation to and in the light of these branches forms legal philosophy or philosophy of law. Other

---

[51] The standard books on semantics are Ogden and Richards, *The Meaning of Meaning*, 8th ed., and Carnap, *Philosophy and Logical Syntax*. See also Cohen and Nagel, *Introduction to Logic and Scientific Method*; Philbrick, *Language and the Law*; Chase, *The Tyranny of Words*; Hexner, *Studies in Legal Terminology*; Jensen, *The Nature of Legal Argument*; Wasserstrom, *The Judicial Decision*; Mellinkoff, *The Language of the Law*; Hart, " Definition and Theory in Jurisprudence " (1954) 70 L.Q.R. 37; Williams, " Language and the Law " (1945) 61 L.Q.R. 71, 179, 293, 384; (1946) 62 L.Q.R. 387.

[52] See Dewey, " Philosophy " in *Encyc.Soc.Sc.*, XII, 118; Emmet and Hobbs, " Ethics " in *Int.Encyc.Soc.Sc.*

[53] See Cairns, *Legal Philosophy from Plato to Hegel*; Cohen, " Philosophy and Legal Science " (1932) 32 Col.L.R. 1103.

branches such as epistemology, philosophy of man, philosophy of mind, aesthetics and metaphysics have lesser connection with legal studies.

Logic and scientific method serves an important purpose by clarifying ideas as to thinking and reasoning, and as to the validity of inferences drawn from initial propositions.[54] Law has many logical characteristics; it is a body of propositions, some general, some particular, forming a more or less systematic structure, and legal principles and problems can be classified, defined and distinguished. While logic does assist in legal thinking, it does not by itself ensure legally correct or just answers. At most it tests the correctness of thinking, but the basis for the reasoning may still be legally inaccurate,[55] and the final determination of a legal issue may be a matter of policy or discretion [56] not determined by logic at all. Logic does not provide, or guarantee the correctness of, the bases for reasoning. Thus a judge's finding that one spouse had committed adultery is a basis for logical reasoning to a legal conclusion, but cannot itself be checked or controverted by logic.[57]

Ethics or moral philosophy is the normative science of the conduct of human beings living in societies; it studies human conduct and seeks to determine standards for judging its goodness or badness, rightness or wrongness, and accordingly evaluates conduct by reference to some such criterion as whether it promotes the general happiness or could without absurdity be generalised into a universal rule of conduct.[58] It examines the validity of such standards and the meaning of such concepts as " right," " duty," " good " and " ought." Distinct from but related to moral philosophy is practical morality, the examination of what people in practice regard as right or wrong, which also has great relevance to legal issues. Its overlap with law is obvious; both study and approve or censure human conduct, but using different standards. Acutely difficult but interesting problems arise as to whether, and how far, law should seek to promote and secure ethical values; should it, for example, punish conduct which is morally objectionable but may be harmless to the general community?

---

[54] " No science affords more opportunity for exerting the reasoning faculty than that of law ": Kames, *Elucidations*, preface.

[55] Thus logically valid conclusions in a particular case could be drawn from an initial general premiss such as: In Scotland a wife can divorce her husband for incompatibility of temperament, though that premiss is legally unsound, and any conclusion therefrom consequently legally unsound also.

[56] *e.g.*, the appropriate sum to award as damages, the appropriate penalty, whether to give custody of a child to one parent or the other.

[57] On the place of logic in law, see further Cohen, " The Place of Logic in the Law " (1915) 29 H.L.R. 622; Dewey, " Logical Method and Law " (1924) 10 Cornell L.Q. 17; Lloyd, " Reason and Logic in the Common Law " (1948) 64 L.Q.R. 468; Guest, " Logic in the Law " in *Oxford Essays in Jurisprudence*, 176; Castberg, *Problems of Legal Philosophy*, Chap. 3.

[58] The literature is enormous; good modern introductions are Lillie, *An Introduction to Ethics*; Hospers, *Human Conduct: An Introduction to the Problems of Ethics*. See also Sidgwick, *History of Ethics*.

How far can a child of five be held " responsible " for wrongdoing? How far, again, are a person's motives and intentions relevant to his moral guilt, and to his legal guilt? Legal phenomena are also moral phenomena.[59] In some respects the law treats of matters ethically neutral, as when it lays down the rule of the road and the rules as to authentication of deeds, where there has to be a rule, though the rule currently adopted in Scotland can hardly be said to be good or bad in comparison with the alternative, but many matters raising legal issues also raise moral issues.[60] The concept of justice and the relations between human law and ideal justice are other topics of common interest to law and ethics.

The examination of moral problems inherent in legal issues leads on in some cases to metaphysical problems such as, for example, the status and existence of universal propositions, such as that all persons should obey the law, or what a rule of law, in the most general sense, is, or to the examination of the most abstract general ideas, such as Right, Freedom or Liability. One point at which everyday law touches metaphysics is when we speak of an accident " causing " injuries and are driven to inquire what is really meant by " cause " and " causation." [61] So too, deep study of legal issues leads on into theology, to such questions as human and divine justice, crime and sin, the dissolubility of Christian marriage, and the legal attitude to life and death.[62] All these and similar problems go to make up that part of jurisprudence known as philosophy of law.

The Theoretical and Practical Sides of Legal Science

Like the other main social sciences, legal science has two sides to its study; there is the theoretical and philosophical study, seeking to classify, rationalise, explain, restate, criticise and evaluate the existing principles of law, to trace their origins, examine their consistency one with another,

---

[59] Miller, *Lectures on the Philosophy of Law*, 9.

[60] See among many books, Pound, *Law and Morals; Introduction to the Philosophy of Law*; *Jurisprudence*, II, 215; Stone, *Province and Function of Law*, Chap. 16; Friedmann, *Legal Theory*; Cahn, *The Moral Decision*; Goodhart, *English Law and the Moral Law*; Lloyd, *Public Policy*; Hart, *Punishment and Responsibility*; *Law, Liberty and Morality*; see also Ames, " Law and Morals " (1909) 22 H.L.R. 97; Winfield, " Ethics in English Case Law " (1931) 45 H.L.R. 112, and *Select Legal Essays*, 266; Cohen, " Philosophy and Legal Science " (1932) 32 Col.L.R. 1103, and in *Law and the Social Order* (1933), 219; Cohen, " Law and Scientific Method " in the same, 184; Cohen, " Moral Aspects of the Criminal Law " (1940) 49 Yale L.J. 987; Hart, " Positivism and the Separation of Law and Morals " (1958) 71 H.L.R. 593; Fuller, " Positivism and Fidelity to Law," ibid. 630.

[61] See Hart and Honore, *Causation in the Law*; Castberg, *Problems of Legal Philosophy*, Chap. 4.

[62] Books casting interesting light on such problems are Williams, *The Sanctity of Life and the Criminal Law*, and Stevas, *Life, Death and the Law*. See also Daube, *Studies in Biblical Law*; Bryce, " The Relations of Law and Religion " in *Studies in History and Jurisprudence*, II, 638; Lord Devlin, " The Enforcement of Morals " (British Academy Maccabaean Lecture, 1959), also in *The Enforcement of Morals* (1968); Hart, *Law, Liberty and Morality*

compare them with those accepted at earlier periods or in other contemporary societies, to relate them to their philosophical bases and evaluate them by ideal standards, and to give consideration to their amendment and reform. This side is concerned with such questions as why the law is what it is, what it has been, what it is elsewhere, how its terms are used, and its rules classified and arranged, whether it is fair or not and whether it should be otherwise. Secondly there is the study of law as a reasonably coherent and systematic body of principles and rules capable of practical application to the affairs of men in everyday life, to the defining of their claims and liabilities in particular circumstances and to the resolution of their controversies and the decision of disputes. This side is concerned with what the existing law prescribes, permits or forbids, and with its application to specific people in particular circumstances. Sir Frederick Pollock once distinguished between the practice of law as an art, and the study of law as a science. So, too, law has been called " social engineering " by analogy with the way in which principles of physical science can be used by engineers for useful ends. In the university the emphasis is naturally on the study of law as a science, with pure law; in everyday life the emphasis is on law as a practical art, with applied law.

This distinction is sometimes drawn in some other studies by a distinction in names, such as that between theology and religion, economic theory or economic science and applied economics, political theory or philosophy and political science or politics, social theory or philosophy and sociology or social science, moral philosophy and moral science or morality, pure (natural) science or natural philosophy and applied science, and so on, though the terminology is not always consistent and there is no clear or sharp line of division between any two. In legal studies this same distinction is sometimes drawn between jurisprudence [63] or legal theory and philosophy, and law or legal principles or legal dogmatics or even legal science (in a narrower sense of that phrase), though the term Law is more

---

[63] The term jurisprudence may accordingly be used, firstly, as earlier in this chapter, in its widest and most general sense, as *juris prudentia* or *juris scientia*, for legal science, or the science of law; secondly, for that branch of legal science which deals with general problems of the theory of law, particularly with the examination of the concepts and terminology of law, " the comparative anatomy of developed systems of law," and sometimes including also problems of the philosophy of law (on this sense, see further p. 65, *infra*); and occasionally, thirdly, as a grandiloquent synonym for the dogmatic principles of one legal system or a branch thereof, *e.g.*, Scottish jurisprudence, medical jurisprudence. In France *la jurisprudence* means what we call case-law (on which see Chap. 10). Jurisprudence in its second sense is an important element in legal studies, just as is law, *i.e.*, the dogmatic exposition of accepted principles. The terminology is further complicated by the fact that some writers speak of " the science of jurisprudence " (in the second sense), or call jurisprudence (in the second sense) the " science of law," as distinct from dogmatic exposition of law, which itself is sometimes called " legal science " (in the narrower sense of that phrase). These words and phrases do not have completely fixed or settled usages or meanings. See further Campbell, " A Note on the Word ' Jurisprudence ' " (1942) 58 L.Q.R. 334.

commonly used for both sides of legal science. In every case the pure or more theoretical and philosophical study and the applied or more practical overlap and their problems constantly run into one another. A problem of practical application may require for its answer a thorough examination of the theoretical basis of the principle to be applied. But it is important to note that law is not only, or even primarily, a body of rules or formulae for practical application to the solution of concrete problems. This is the obvious, the common, aspect of law but not by any means the whole of law as a science or as a study, since the theory and the abstract principles underlie every particular rule and application.

Conclusion

Legal science, or jurisprudence (in its broad sense), or law in its most general sense, is a body of knowledge akin to and related to politics, economics, history and other studies of human behaviour, activities and relations; like them it has an historical aspect, a theoretical and philosophic aspect (jurisprudence in the narrow sense [64]), a comparative aspect and a dogmatic aspect, dealing with the actual content of specific legal systems, international, supra-national and national, which sets out the currently accepted principles and rules. The present book seeks to deal with some of the main elements in the historical, comparative and theoretical aspects of the law of Scotland and of its most general doctrines and structure as an introduction to the detailed study of its dogmatic content and of the applications thereof to particular problems, and ultimately to the study of the philosophy of law.

FURTHER READING

Law as a University Study
Brown: " Purpose and Method of a Law School " (1902) 18 L.Q.R. 78, 192.
Brownlie: " Legal Education in the Scottish Universities " (1955) 67 J.R. 26.
Cardozo: " Law and the University " (1931) 47 L.Q.R. 19.
Denning: " The Universities and Law Reform " (1949) 1 J.S.P.T.L.(N.S.) 258.
Gavit: *Introduction to the Study of Law.*
Gower: " English Legal Training " (1950) 15 M.L.R. 137.
Hamson: " The Teaching of Law " (1952) 2 J.S.P.T.L.(N.S.) 19.
Hanbury, *The Vinerian Chair and Legal Education.*
Hughes Parry: " Some Reflections on Legal Education " (1949) 1 J.S.P.T.L. (N.S.) 249.
Jones: " Modern Discussions of the Aims and Methods of Legal Science " (1932) 47 L.Q.R. 62.
Kennedy: " A Project of Legal Education " 1937 S.L.T.(News) 1, 17, 21.
Llewellyn: *The Bramble Bush.*
Montrose: " Law, Science and the Humanities " (1957) 4 J.S.P.T.L.(N.S.) 61.

---

[64] Some books on jurisprudence are mainly concerned with legal theory (classification, terminology, etc.), others with legal philosophy (ideals, justice, etc.), but the two branches are not separable and the titles of books on jurisprudence frequently use the terms " theory " and " philosophy " indifferently.

Smalley Baker: " The Teaching of Law as one of the Social Sciences " (1947) 1 J.S.P.T.L.(N.S.) 69.
Stallybrass: " Law in the Universities " (1948) 1 J.S.P.T.L.(N.S.) 157.
Vanderbilt (ed.): *Studying Law.*
Walker: " Law as a Liberal Education " 1956 S.L.T.(News) 57.
 " Legal Studies in the Scottish Universities " 1957 J.R. 21.
Williams: *Learning the Law.*
Wright: " The Study of Law " (1939) 54 L.Q.R. 185.

Law and the Social Sciences
Arnold: *The Folklore of Capitalism.*
Barnes and Becker: *Social Thought from Lore to Science.*
Cairns: *Law and the Social Sciences.*
Carlston: *Law and the Structures of Social Action.*
Cohen: *Law and the Social Order.*
Cohen and Cohen: *Readings in Jurisprudence and Legal Philosophy*, Part 4.
Commons: *Legal Foundations of Capitalism.*
Dicey: *Law and Public Opinion in England in the Nineteenth Century.*
Friedmann: *Law in a Changing Society.*
Ginsberg (ed.): *Law and Opinion in England in the Twentieth Century.*
Gregg: *Social and Economic History of Modern Britain.*
Gurvitch: *Sociology of Law.*
Hall: *Readings in Jurisprudence*, Part 3.
Hartley and Griffith: *Government and Law.*
Ogburn and Goldenweiser (eds.): *The Social Sciences and their Interrelations.*
Patterson *Jurisprudence.*
Pound: *Social Control through Law.*
Renner: *The Institutions of Private Law and their Social Functions.*
Robson: *Civilisation and the Growth of Law.*
Sawer: *Law in Society.*
Stone: *The Province and Function of Law*, Part 3.
 Social Dimensions of Law and Justice.
Welford: *Society: Problems and Methods of Study.*
Wootton: *Social Science and Social Pathology.*

Law and History
Assoc. of American Law Schools: *Essays in Anglo-American Legal History*, 3 vols.
 General Survey of Continental Legal History.
Bryce: *Studies in History and Jurisprudence.*
Diamond: *Evolution of Law and Order.*
 Primitive Law, Past and Present.
Holdsworth: *Sources and Literature of English Law.*
 History of English Law, 17 vols.
Keir: *Constitutional History of Modern Britain.*
Macdonnell and Manson (ed.): *Great Jurists of the World.*
McKechnie (ed.): *Sources and Literature of Scots Law.*
Maine: *Ancient Law.*
 Early History of Institutions.
 Early Law and Custom.
Paton (ed.): *Introduction to Scottish Legal History.*
Pollock and Maitland: *History of English Law before Edward I.*

Ullman: *Mediaeval Idea of Law.*
  Principles of Government and Politics in the Middle Ages.
Vinogradoff: *Historical Jurisprudence*, 2 vols.
Wigmore: *Evolution of Law Series*, 3 vols.
Winfield: *Chief Sources of English Legal History.*

Law and Philosophy
Barker: *Principles of Social and Political Theory.*
Berolzheimer: *The World's Legal Philosophies.*
Cahn: *The Moral Decision.*
Cairns: *Legal Philosophy from Plato to Hegel.*
  Theory of Legal Science.
Cohen: *Ethical Systems and Legal Ideals.*
Cohen and Cohen: *Readings in Jurisprudence and Legal Philosophy*, Part 3.
D'Entreves: *Natural Law.*
Friedmann: *Legal Theory.*
Friedrich: *Philosophy of Law in Historical Perspective.*
Goodhart: *English Law and the Moral Law.*
Hall: *Readings in Jurisprudence*, Part 1.
  Studies in Jurisprudence and Criminal Theory.
Hamburger: *Morals and Law—Aristotle's Legal Theory.*
Hart: *Punishment and Responsibility.*
Jones: *Historical Introduction to the Theory of Law.*
Lamont: *Principles of Moral Judgement.*
Micklem: *Law and the Laws.*
Morris: *The Great Legal Philosophers.*
Patterson: *Jurisprudence.*
Pound: *Law and Morals.*
  Introduction to the Philosophy of Law.
Radin: *Law as Logic and Experience.*
Stone: *The Province and Function of Law*, Parts 1 and 2.
  Legal System and Lawyer's Reasonings.
  Human Law and Human Justice.

CHAPTER 2

THE STUDY OF LEGAL SCIENCE

LEGAL science is the systematised body of knowledge concerned with law in the most general sense of that word. What then is law? A full study of the nature of law is an important branch of jurisprudence and legal philosophy and it is a topic of much complexity. But it is desirable at an early stage in legal studies to formulate a provisional idea of the general nature of law which can be corrected and refined in the light of later study. It is necessary at once to put aside such uses of the term " law " as in " law of gravitation " or the other " laws " of the natural sciences, since these physical or scientific " laws " are generalisations explaining various uniformities in the phenomena of nature, *descriptive of what happens* in certain defined circumstances,[1] and also such uses as " natural " or " moral " law, which expresses an ideal standard of conduct to which rules of positive law, *i.e.*, the law laid down in particular communities, *ought to* conform so as to make human conduct be in accordance with moral beliefs as to right and wrong. This latter use of the term " law " is, however, nearer to the jural significance in that it has the connotation of a rule for human conduct which is absent from the former, purely descriptive use.

In the sense which is of jural significance the law consists of a body of rules or precepts or norms for the regulation of social conduct, recognised as obligatory, and enforceable. Rules of law are *prescriptive* of conduct, not merely descriptive of what happens. Different jurists emphasise different aspects of this body of rules. Thus some [2] stress the fact that those rules which are termed " law " are based on the will and force of the organised political community, the state, and define law as the commands of superior authority. This serves to distinguish rules of law from customary practices and rules voluntarily agreed upon and observed by particular groups, from conduct merely habitual or accepted by reason of moral or religious belief.

Others emphasise the end to be attained by those rules of social conduct, defining it, for example, as " the body of principles recognised and applied by the state in the administration of justice " [3] or " the expression of the idea of right involved in the relation of two or more human beings," [4] or " the sum of the rules of justice administered in a

---

[1] Salmond, *Jurisprudence*, 11th ed., 24; Holland, *Jurisprudence*, 13th ed., 17.

[2] *e.g.*, Hobbes, Bentham, Austin, Amos, Markby, Holland.

[3] Salmond, *Jurisprudence*, 41.

[4] Miller, *Philosophy of Law*, 9.

state and by its authority " [5]; and these views reflect the very prevalent belief that law is and should be related to right and justice, that it does not exist merely to regulate life or resolve controversies but to do so in a manner consistent with justice.

In recent times law has been regarded and defined largely by reference to its function in society, sometimes with an emphasis on the way in which it is applied by the courts. For example: " The prophecies of what courts will do in fact and nothing more pretentious, are what I mean by the law " [6]; "What these officials [judges or sheriffs or clerks or jailers or lawyers] do about disputes is, to my mind, the law itself " [7]; " A body of social rules prescribing external conduct and considered justiciable." [8] Other definitions emphasise that its function is to resolve conflicts of claims and interests of individuals and groups and to harmonise their differing desires with the minimum of disagreement. Thus: " The legal order is a régime of adjusting relations and ordering conduct through the systematic and orderly application of the force of a politically organised society, in order to prevent friction in human use and enjoyment of the goods of existence and eliminate waste of them." [9] Stress is also sometimes laid on the fact that the legal order of society is more than the abstract rules. The law is " the body of precepts and received ideals and the technique of using them, established or recognised by organised human society for the delimitation and securing of interests " (an interest being a demand or want or desire which human beings either individually or in groups seek to satisfy and of which the ordering of human relations in civilised society must take account).[10]

Law as Social Control

The legal system of a country is in substance a form of social control, that is, a body of principles and rules regulative of human conduct in society, persuading persons to do some things and constraining them from doing others.[11] It is thus intimately related to the social functions that are the subject-matter of the other social sciences and to the regulative influence of religious and moral beliefs. The main bodies of rules which exist and operate as social controls in this way are law, religion, morals,

[5] Pollock, *First Book of Jurisprudence*, 17.
[6] Holmes, " The Path of the Law " (1897) 10 H.L.R. 457, 461.
[7] Llewellyn, *The Bramble Bush*, 3.
[8] Kantorowicz, *The Definition of Law*, 79.
[9] Pound, " Introduction to American Law," in Vanderbilt, *Studying Law*, 379.
[10] Pound, " Theory of Social Interests," in Hall, *Readings in Jurisprudence*, 238; see also Pound, " A Survey of Social Interests " (1943) 57 H.L.R. 1, reprinted in Vanderbilt, *Studying Law*, 439, and *Jurisprudence*, III, Chaps. 14 and 15.
[11] On social controls generally, see MacIver and Page, *Society*, 137 *et seq.*; 175–181. The concept is a sociological one and an example of the influence this science has had on the study of law. See further Everett, " Social Control," *Encyc.Soc.Sc.*, IV, 344; Pound, *Social Control through Law*; Bodenheimer, *Jurisprudence*, Chap. 13.

custom, fashion, convention, etiquette, and professional, club, trade or union rules. Each has its distinctive forms of sanction brought to bear on one who transgresses the rules. In many particular sets of circumstances conduct such as stealing may contravene several sets of rules and several of these social controls may all be operating simultaneously on an individual and influencing his conduct. Thus conscience pricks him for doing wrong, religious feeling causes remorse for sin, custom and habit of society frown on his conduct and may result in his being shunned, despised or ostracised, while the legal order may cause him to be fined or imprisoned or forced to pay compensation for what he has done.

State law, however, differs from the other social controls in that it is more widespread, extending to and covering far more activities than does any other form of control, its rules are more fixed and definite, being frequently prescribed in a strict verbal form, its operation extends in general to all persons subject to the state's authority, its authority is greater in that it may override and cancel the prescriptions of other social controls, and, lastly, it alone may be enforced by the whole authority of the state by means of fines, imprisonment or pecuniary compensation. Law is accordingly a very important form of social control, of regulative influence, over practically every form of human conduct.

The concept of law as social control is one which provides a readily comprehensible idea of the notion of law in general, and the other definitions quoted may be treated as simply more particularised statements, emphasising respectively the fact of enforcement by the state, the aim of securing justice, and the mode of functioning of the law.

Law and the Legal System

The application of the controlling factor in society which is called " law " to various sets of circumstances requires the existence in each independent society of a legal system, which comprises a complex of legislative organs,[12] executive agencies,[13] an establishment of courts and tribunals,[14] of individuals who act as judges, clerks, prosecutors, gaolers, legal representatives and advisers, and in other capacities,[15] a coherent body of particular principles, doctrines and rules of law,[16] with techniques of handling them [16] and means for amending, restating and adding to them,[17] and an apparatus of procedure whereby individuals may bring controversies and conflicts of claims before the courts for resolution.[18]

[12] Chap. 5, *infra.*
[13] Chap. 6, *infra.*
[14] Chap. 7, *infra.*
[15] Chap. 8, *infra.*
[16] Chaps. 9–12, *infra.*
[17] Chap. 15, *infra.*
[18] Chaps. 13–14, *infra.*

It is this legal system in any particular country which individualises the general conception of law into specific rules and applies them to the determination of specific controversies.

Law and the State

The precise organisation of the legal system and the content of the rules of law vary from one country to another. These elements are closely connected with the form of human association known as the state, which is the organisation or association of all the persons living within a demarcated extent of territory and organised into a distinct political community.[19] It is possibly the most important form of human association and an essential basis for peace, order, civilisation and good government. One of the main functions of the state as a political and legal organisation is to establish and maintain for its subjects a legal order, and to enforce a system of law and order. The identification of a legal system with a particular state is not, however, invariable in that within the territory of one political state there may exist simultaneously several distinct legal systems, each in a distinct portion,[20] or even for different classes of individuals in the same area,[21] while one system of law might in theory be applied throughout several political states.

A second main function of the state is the maintenance of its own existence and integrity, its freedom and that of its inhabitants from external aggression and domination; and this is a prerequisite of the maintenance of its own system of law and order.

The adequate performance of these main functions has required each state to set up a taxing apparatus to obtain the revenue required and a legislative, judicial and administrative system, so that the principles on which justice is to be administered and the territory governed may be decided, and those principles applied and worked out in detail in specific cases. There is further implied in the performance of these functions that this association of persons should have a definite organisation, a determinate and systematic form, structure and organisation, and not be merely a temporary or casual union. The organisation of a modern state is of great complexity and embodies a great mass of legal rules and principles.

In modern times an important group of functions has been annexed to the responsibilities of the state. It provides a postal system, highways and bridges, engages in scientific research, controls building and

---

[19] See further Sidgwick, *Elements of Politics*, 217; MacIver, *The Modern State*, 22; Salmond, *Jurisprudence*, 10th ed., 129; Field, *Political Theory*, 54–56; Barker, *Principles of Social and Political Theory*, 3; Vinogradoff, *Historical Jurisprudence*, I, 85; and see generally, Pound, *Jurisprudence*, II, 283.
[20] As in the United Kingdom and U.S.A.
[21] *e.g.* Hindu and Mohammedan law in certain relationships in India.

the use of land; it has assumed the duties of providing for the health, welfare, education and well-being of its citizens,[22] and to a considerable extent the conservation of national natural resources,[23] as well as the management and regulation of enterprises,[24] public utility services,[25] and industries,[26] which are of paramount importance for the national economy. This tendency towards an extension of state organisation and control leads to a great increase in the volume of legal rules regulating the conduct of individuals and groups of individuals and restricting their freedom of action in various respects in the interest of what is conceived to be the general welfare.[27]

The Methods of Legal Science

The full understanding of a legal system or any branch of it requires study from four standpoints; these are the analytical, breaking down the problem-situation and ascertaining what elements compose it and what rules are applicable to each part of the subject and its problems; the historical, ascertaining how and why these rules have come to be accepted and to take their modern form; the philosophical, considering whether those rules are consistent with the needs of society, and with accepted ideas of right and justice; and the comparative, seeing how other societies at a similar stage of civilisation face up to the same or corresponding problems. For proper appreciation, that is, one must find out what the rules are here and now, what they once were and how and why they have come to be what they are, whether they are satisfactory judged by an ideal standard, and how they appear compared with the rules which are accepted elsewhere.[28]

The Scottish Legal System

Within the territorial limits designated as Scotland the state has developed an organisation of courts and legal practitioners, a body of principles, rules and precepts, and a body of knowledge and thinking about law which amounts to the Scottish legal system It is largely indigenous having grown and developed naturally within the country rather than having been imposed from without, yet it is not narrowly parochial, having shared in drawing something from the legal systems of antiquity, nor yet insular, having strong historical connections and logical affinities

---

[22] Thus in Britain the Education Acts, National Health Service Acts, National Insurance Acts, Factories Acts, Children Acts, etc.

[23] *e.g.,* Petroleum Acts, work of the Forestry Commission.

[24] *e.g.,* B.B.C., Independent Broadcasting Authority.

[25] *e.g.,* the railways, electricity and gas authorities.

[26] *e.g.,* coal-mining, steel-making.

[27] The legal monopolies of coal-mining, broadcasting, generation of electricity, etc., prevent individuals commencing business enterprises in these fields.

[28] Bryce, " The Methods of Legal Science " in *Studies in History and Jurisprudence,* II, 607.

with legal systems of and derived from continental Europe. It is unitary
in that it has grown as a body rather than been formed by aggregation or
merging of substantially different elements; it is reasonably simple in being
remarkably free from anomalies, absurdities and historical survivals which
have outlived their usefulness and their justification; and it is firmly rooted
in general principles, so that much can be explained as deduction from, or
detailed working out of, great overriding principles based on reason and
justice. Accordingly, the main elements in the Scottish legal system which
will require detailed examination are the history and systematic structure
of the law, the organisation of courts, and the personnel of the law, and
the principles and rules applicable to various sets of circumstances. But
several further preliminary matters remain to be discussed.

LAW AND FACT

Elements in a Legal Situation

The situations which the judge or lawyer has to deal with are seldom
exclusively matters of pure law and may indeed involve law only incidentally. In every such situation there are four elements; there are principles and rules of law, which are abstract and general, facts, which are
concrete and specific, persons, who are complex, possibly irrational
and unpredictable, and the physical, social, intellectual, economic,
political and other environments which form the background to the
acts and events spotlighted for investigation and inquiry in the particular
situation which has arisen. Of these elements two require special attention, though the others remain factors which cannot be ignored: those
two are fact and law.

Fact and Law

In all legal discussion the distinction between fact and law has to
be kept in mind, for it is a distinction of fundamental importance in
many connections.[29] A question of fact concerns the existence in past
or present time of some act or event or state of things, cognisable or
ascertainable by the senses; a question of law concerns the existence, or
content, or applicability, of some doctrine, rule or principle of the legal
system. Thus, for example, what A said, what B heard, whether
C's car was going fast at the moment of impact, whether D intended
to kill E, whether F warned G of his danger, whether lamps were lit,
questions of time, place, speed, direction, colour, temperature, visibility,
mental state, identity, and generally anything cognisable by the senses,

---

[29] See further Corbin, " Legal Analysis and Terminology " (1919) 29 Yale L.J.
163 and in Hall, *Readings in Jurisprudence*, 471; Wilson, " A Note on Fact and
Law " (1963) 26 M.L.R. 609.

or by inference from sense-data, are questions of fact. On the other hand whether J's conduct was legally reckless, whether K's departure from his wife amounted in law to desertion, whether L's killing amounted legally to murder or not, whether M's vehicle was a " trailer " within the meaning of the Act, and so on, are questions of law, which cannot be decided by the senses but only by determination of whether or not the fact in issue falls within the verbally defined limits of some doctrine, principle, rule, category or standard of law, from which certain legal consequences will follow, such as entitlement to some remedy or liability to some remedy or liability to some penalty. A question of law, that is, concerns the existence, or content, or applicability of a precept of law to certain circumstances. Thus whether S is liable in damages for defamation depends on (a) what he said, and the circumstances in which he said it (fact), and (b) whether these words in these circumstances are legally defamatory (law). So too other legal controversies and problems can be resolved into factual and legal elements, though it should be remembered that either the factual or legal element may be admitted on all sides, or be so clear as to be beyond argument. Thus it may be admitted that X struck the blow, but be argued that in the circumstances it was not murder but culpable homicide, or it may be admitted that the killing of Y was murder but be disputed whether X was the person who did it. The proper meaning or interpretation of statutes and documents, or statements made, are always questions of law.

Certain consequences of this distinction must also be borne in mind. A question of fact has to be determined, if disputed, by proof, by adducing evidence of what happened, what was said, or seen, or heard, or done, and so on. Questions of law on the other hand are determined not by evidence [30] but by legal argument, by adducing to the judges or other persons concerned with making the decision, statements in cases, statutes and books of authority which persuade them to the view that the appropriate rule of the legal system is one to a particular effect *e.g.* that a mistake by a man as to his wife's previous chastity does not give him ground for having the marriage annulled.[31] A court or other tribunal is presumed to know the law of its own country; accordingly one need not, and must not, seek to prove the law to it, but must simply seek to persuade it by legal argument as to which particular rule or exception should be applied in the circumstances. But one must enlighten

---

[30] An exception to this principle arises in the cases where the law of *another* country is in issue, *e.g.*, a matter of English law in a Scottish court, and vice versa. In such cases the foreign law is treated as a question of fact (since the court does not have judicial knowledge of a foreign system) and its rules must be proved by evidence, as by producing as witnesses practitioners of the other systems involved, *e.g.*, English barristers, as in *Rosses* v. *Bhagvat Sinhjee* (1891) 19 R. 31, or by remitting to the courts of the other system for a statement on their law.

[31] *Lang* v. *Lang*, 1921 S.C. 44, overruling *Stein* v. *Stein*, 1914 S.C. 903.

a court as to the facts in issue by leading evidence of them, unless those facts are admitted or not in dispute.

While these are the fundamental distinctions between questions of fact and questions of law, subsidiary meanings of the terms are also found. Thus in the determination of certain litigated controversies a jury has a part to play and matters which are for the decision of the jury are rather arbitrarily called questions of fact and matters reserved for the decision of the presiding judge are called questions of law, and this nomenclature persists notwithstanding that certain of the matters which are committed to the judge may be in their nature questions of fact.[32] This difficulty is not so apparent in cases decided by a judge sitting alone since he has to decide issues both of fact and law.

Again, any question which is determined by some rule of law, such as the punishment for treason, may be called a question of law, as distinct from a question of fact, which depends on the facts and circumstances of the case,[33] or which is determined by the exercise of the judge's discretion.[34]

Lastly, a question of law may be a question as to what the true rule of law is, applicable to a particular matter. Thus in special cases and stated cases [35] certain admitted or proved facts are set before the court and a question of law formulated, raising a problem of the applicability or otherwise of some rule or principle of law, whether a statutory provision applies, or whether a particular doctrine deduced from case-law governs the case thus presented, or what effect a particular rule has in the circumstances.

Transformation of Fact into Law

As the law develops and grows in complexity there is in some circumstances a tendency for matters which in their nature are truly matters of fact to be treated as matters of law and determined by rules of law accordingly. Thus in some cases legal presumptions arise by virtue of which the law deems some state of fact to exist, whether in truth it exists or not. For example, there is a legal presumption that children under eight are incapable of committing crime, which applies despite any indications of capacity or intention in fact; no contrary proof can counter-

---

[32] Thus in a case of damages for malicious prosecution, the pursuer must prove that the defender initiated the prosecution maliciously and without probable cause. It is a question for the judge whether facts have been proved which suffice to imply malice and lack of probable cause, even though this is factual in nature.

[33] Thus under the Sale of Goods Act 1893, unsatisfactory goods must be returned "within a reasonable time," and what is a reasonable time is a question of fact, *i.e.,* it has to be decided in the circumstances of each case. There is no rule laid down as to what is a reasonable time, no rule that a week or a month is reasonable.

[34] Thus in a divorce case the judge has a discretion to which parent to give custody of the children and he is not bound by law to give to one rather than the other.

[35] As to these, see Chap. 13, *infra.*

vail. Again, certain conduct may by a legal fiction be " deemed to be " fraudulent or criminal with the result that it will be so in law whatever it may have been in fact. A further class of presumptions exists whereby certain factual circumstances have certain legal validity and consequences, unless the presumption is rebutted, that is, unless it can be shown that in fact and in truth the circumstances were otherwise: thus every man is presumed sane, every man is presumed innocent, and so on. Again, once it has been decided in one case that certain facts amount to cruelty or adultery or culpable homicide or such other legal category, similar facts arising subsequently will have the same effect as a matter of law, by the operation of the doctrine of judicial precedent.[36]

In all these cases the circumstances of fact have ceased to be purely factual in that certain legal force and effect necessarily attaches to them by operation of law from the mere fact of their existence.

Questions of Discretion

Matters of judicial discretion are matters which are not of pure fact in that they are not wholly determinable or ascertainable by evidence or proof, nor yet are they determinable by the application of a rule of law, but they are questions of moral judgment in which the court must try to determine what is good or reasonable or fair or equitable or right or just in the circumstances. Thus the punishment for murder is fixed by law, but the punishment for other crimes is a matter for the discretion of the judge, within certain limits; he may imprison, or fine or discharge, as he thinks right in the circumstances. The tendency is as the legal system progresses and develops, to convert questions of discretion into questions of law since a body of decisions on prior similar sets of facts grows up, tending to limit and define the ways in which and the extent to which the judicial discretion should be exercised.[37] " In respect of questions as to what is just, right, and reasonable, the purpose and effect of a system of law is to exclude and supersede to a very large extent the individual moral judgment of the courts, and to compel them to determine these questions in accordance with fixed and authoritative principles which express the established and permanent moral judgment of the community at large." [38] While this tendency is constantly at work, statute or judicial decision may sometimes overrule the growth of such a body of limiting rules and restore freedom of judicial discretion.

---

[36] On judicial precedent, see further Chap. 10, *infra.*

[37] Consider the body of decisions which has grown up as to the exercise of judicial discretion on such questions as: to which parent is custody of a child to be given? In what circumstances can one apply for a winding-up order under the " just and equitable " clause—Companies Act 1948, s. 222 (*f*)? In these and other cases the judge's discretion is not free but limited by earlier decisions, which tend to harden into rules that in cases like X something must be done, and in cases like Y the reverse must be done.

[38] Salmond, *Jurisprudence*, 11th ed., 71.

Mixed Questions of Fact and Law

Questions frequently arise in which elements of fact and of law are both present and intermixed. These arise in two forms: the problem may be really a composite one depending both on the existence of a state of fact and also on the sufficiency of these facts for some legal purpose. Thus the question whether partnership exists between two persons depends on the terms of the agreement entered into by them (fact) and also on the sufficiency of an agreement in those terms to constitute what the law will recognise as a partnership (law). Very many questions which arise are of this type, such as whether A had murdered B, whether C had slandered D, whether E had married F, whether G had wrongfully imprisoned H, and so on, and a very common fault in pleading before a court is to make statements of this composite kind which beg the question whether the facts are truly legally sufficient to justify the use of the term having a legal connotation. Thus to state that " by letters of 1st and 2nd May the pursuer and the defender *contracted* to . . ." begs the question whether the letters (the existence and terms of which are facts) did, as interpreted by the court, truly constitute a contract, which is a matter of law.

Secondly, mixed questions of fact and law may arise where a judicial discretion may be exercised only within legally determined limits. Many powers of imposing fines and imprisonment are of this kind and in such cases the question for the court is one of fact so far as concerns the appropriate measure of punishment to be imposed in any particular case in the exercise of its discretion, and one of law so far as concerns the limits within which the discretion may operate.[39]

Again, the questions set to juries and answered by their general verdicts are frequently problems of mixed fact and law. When a jury returns a verdict that the prisoner is guilty of culpable homicide they are truly reporting two things: that in their view the prisoner had done certain things (fact), *and* that these happenings amounted in the circumstances to culpable homicide, as that legal category has been explained to the jury by the presiding judge in his charge to the jury (law).

Difficulties as to Facts or Law

The preceding discussion must not obscure the difficulty that in many cases matters of fact or of law or of both remain doubtful or disputed till in the end the final decision in a litigation reaches a conclusion which binds the parties. Facts in a textbook problem or a reported case are set down as matters fixed and established but in practice matters of fact may remain in doubt. The judge or jury in hearing evidence is trying

[39] In such a case there is, of course, frequently a prior mixed question of fact and law on the matter of liability, *e.g.*, was the accused guilty of reckless driving? before the question as to punishment arises. The latter question alone would arise if the accused pleaded guilty or were convicted.

to reconstruct what really happened, as in a detective novel, from fragmentary, misleading and inaccurate clues. What emerges may be not a
finding of what happened, but of what the judge or jury *think* must have
happened, as being the sequence of happenings most consistent, in their
view, with the bulk of the testimony.[40] The facts finally held to have been
" proved " are at the mercy of witnesses who could not be found, who
did not notice, who cannot remember, of parties who have failed to keep
letters, who cannot recall where or when, who did not think something
was worth mentioning to the lawyer, or who have died, of cars which
did not stop, workmen who have left no address, bystanders who did not
give their names, and so on. Accordingly the facts disclosed by a client
to his legal adviser frequently contain gaps and uncertainties, and
they almost certainly and invariably conflict with some of the evidence
adduced by the opposing party. Frequently much of this arises from the
fact that something happens quickly and suddenly and is all over before
anyone has had a chance to observe what was happening. The human
senses are in any event fallible recorders of events, and honest testimony
may be very inaccurate. Difficulties as to facts and discrepancies in evidence arise far more from faulty observation, or inattention, or forgetfulness, or the unavailability of witnesses or of corroborative evidence than
from dishonesty by witnesses, though there is a great deal of lying, in
criminal cases particularly.

Similarly, even if and when some state of facts is " found " by the court
to have " happened, " it may still be uncertain precisely which principle
or rule of law, or what precise verbal formulation of it, falls to be applied.
It may not be at all clear what rule applies, or whether any existing rule
can be applied, or whether resort must be had to analogy, to formulating
a new rule or modifying an old one to cover the case, because principles
and rules of law are frequently much vaguer and less precise than the
exact and categorical prescriptions which laymen think of as rules of law.

Even thereafter much may depend on the temperament of the judge.
Where he has to apply a flexible standard of law, such as " reasonable
care," the answer to the problem whether reasonable care was in fact
taken in the circumstances held to have happened depends not on any
fixed touchstone but on whether that judge *thinks* that reasonable care
was taken. Another judge might think differently.

THE EXPRESSION OF LEGAL PRECEPTS

The precepts of the law which have to be applied to different sets of
facts are not all of the same form, and the form they take in particular

---

[40] On the uncertainty of judicial fact-finding, see Frank, *Courts on Trial* (1949),
and " What Courts do in Fact " in Hall, *Readings in Jurisprudence*, 1103.

cases does not depend on their source, that is, whether the precepts in question are laid down by statute or have been developed in cases. There are four distinguishable kinds of legal precepts, namely, principles, rules, concepts and standards, and it is through these forms that legal ideas are expressed.

Principles

Principles are the broad formulations of reason or generalisations which underlie and comprehend particular rules. They are broader than rules and justify and explain various particular rules. Principles may be so broad as to be indefinite and uncertain, yet they can frequently be expressed concisely and accurately, embracing within them numerous particular rules and yet harmonising these rules. They are the authoritative starting-point or basis for legal reasoning wherever legal provision must be made for a situation not governed by a strict or precise rule of law. Principles are not commonly laid down by statute or case, but more commonly arrived at inductively by jurists from consideration of the particular decisions of various cases and then set out in textbooks; they are sometimes hinted at or even tentatively formulated by judges in particular cases,[41] though such formulations may subsequently be found in the light of criticism and other cases to be too wide or too narrow, or otherwise to require correction or reformulation.

Thus it is a principle that a person should not be allowed to profit from another's loss when there was no intention to gift or otherwise to confer benefit. This principle explains, connects into a coherent body, and justifies such specific rules as that a payment made when it was not due may be recovered, that payment made on the faith of an agreement which later fails is recoverable, and that work done voluntarily in emergency on behalf of an absent person should be recompensed. Again, it is a principle that no valid right in security can be created over corporeal things without transferring them to the security-holder, and there are many more similarly general principles. Again it is a principle that an employer must take reasonable care for the safety of his employees. This principle justifies numerous particular rules worked out in particular cases, such as that in this case the employer should have given a warning, in that case put up protective fencing, in another case should have ensured that a ladder was safe, and so on. Moreover, from a principle it is possible to deduce other particular rules applicable to circumstances hitherto unrecognised so that one great merit of a legal principle is that it has not been exhausted by the deduction of the

---

[41] *e.g., Hadley* v. *Baxendale* (1854) 9 Ex. 341, restated in *Victoria Laundry* v. *Newman* [1949] 2 K.B. 528; *Rylands* v. *Fletcher* (1868) L.R. 3 H.L. 330, restated in *Read* v. *Lyons* [1947] A.C. 156; *Donoghue* v. *Stevenson*, 1932 S.C.(H.L.) 31.

recognised specific rules from it but remains a reservoir of future rules. It is largely through principles that the law grows and develops and keeps in touch with the feelings and beliefs of the community; principles need to be elastic and flexible yet not wholly formless.

Rules

Rules are categorical precepts attaching a distinct, definite and detailed legal effect or consequence to follow on definite prescribed facts. They are more specific and detailed than principles. Thus it is a legal rule that a person convicted of treason is punishable by death, that a formal deed must be signed by the granter and attested by two witnesses, that a loan of money must be proved by the borrower's writ or admission on oath, that a person cannot marry till sixteen, and so on. Rules may be laid down by statute, by the decision of a court, or set out in an authoritative book. Such rules may be rigid, or may be flexible, as where they confer a measure of discretion; thus the rule is that if a person has been injured by the negligence of another, the other must pay such damages in compensation as the court may think reasonable to award. A common advantage of a rule is that it is definite and certain, but it may on that account be unadaptable to new conditions or changing circumstances [42]; it may become out of date and obsolete, though these dangers are less likely if the rule contains within it a standard rather than a fixed measure or confers a discretion rather than prescribes consequences.

Concepts

Both legal principles and legal rules are built up of and stated in terms of legal concepts; a legal concept is a general word which serves as a category of legal thought or classification, the title given to a set of facts and circumstances which satisfies certain legal requirements and has certain legal consequences. It is a generally understood category into which facts may be put in order that definite principles or rules may be applicable thereto. Thus marriage, contract, negligence, culpable homicide, partnership, duty, tenure and many more terms are legal concepts. These and other similar concepts are the terms of legal thought and expression, in that rules and principles are built up of them and legal consequences attach to them. Thus if a court holds that the relationship between two persons was a " marriage," there immediately attach to them all the legal consequences which many statutes, cases and authoritative books have prescribed as the legal consequences of marriage, such as the duty to adhere and to aliment, the inability of either to marry another, and so on. If the court holds that the relationship in the circumstances was merely concubin-

---

[42] Thus, *e.g.*, a rule formulated in the days of horse-drawn traffic may be unsuitable for mechanised traffic.

age different legal consequences attach. The connotations of concepts frequently convey complex and abstract legal ideas, and one task of jurisprudence is to analyse the constituents and requisites of particular legal concepts, to see how the words are used and what they mean in different contexts and different branches of the law. Endless controversy for example, has raged over the concept of " possession." British law is in some ways deficient in legal concepts in that some ideas are not clearly formulated in a legal concept and statutes frequently establish their own definitions of words for the purpose of that statute only, rather than generally. Some legal concepts, such as those of corporate personality, property and future interests in land, are highly abstract and not always easy to explain or to comprehend. The definition of a " crime," for example, has given rise to much thought, discussion and writing and probably no concise yet comprehensive description of the indicia and characteristics of a crime has yet been made.

Two of the commonest and most important concepts deserve particular mention, rights and duties. Principles and rules sometimes confer legal rights, that is, state what one party is legally entitled to claim as against another, or impose legal duties, that is, state what the party affected is legally obliged to do. Both concepts are frequently misused and there is a considerable literature on the uses of these terms.[43]

It has to be noticed particularly that legal concepts do not always coincide in connotation with the everyday uses of the same verbal form. Thus not everything which in common speech is called " negligence " truly amounts to negligence in law, nor is every " contract " or " crime " truly such in law. In each department of the law considerable attention must be paid to discovering the constituent elements of the concepts used so that legally accurate uses of the word may be distinguished from instances which have apparent similarities. Statutes frequently contain long interpretation sections defining particular terms in special, frequently very extended, ways, so that such everyday words as " factory," " development " and " family " may become legal concepts with meanings materially different from their everyday meaning in the context of these statutes and cases thereon and with important legal consequences. So, too, in decided cases concepts may be explained and in the course of time refined and modified.[44]

Standards

Sometimes principles and rules do not prescribe specific or definite

---

[43] See, *e.g.*, Salmond, *Jurisprudence*, 11th ed., Chaps. 10–11; Kocourek, *Jural Relations*; Hohfield, *Fundamental Legal Conceptions*; Pound, *Jurisprudence*, IV, 39; Hall, *Readings in Jurisprudence*, Chap. 11.

[44] For discussions of various concepts and legal words see the list of *Words and Phrases* in the Current Law Yearbooks referring to cases in which the concepts and words have been discussed.

legal consequences but prescribe standards of conduct or evaluation. A legal standard is a measure for conduct, to be applied according to the circumstances of each individual case. The standard is the main means whereby both legal principles and rules maintain flexibility. Where the standard is employed principles and rules are usually expressed not in absolute but in relative terms and this enables the court in a particular case to consider the precise circumstances of that case and to determine whether the conduct falls short of or comes up to the desired level. The law is full of expressions of such standards as " the reasonable man," " the prudent trustee," " the *bonus paterfamilias*," " fair rent," " reasonable precautions," " the normally skilful practitioner." The use of such standards enables account to be taken of individual circumstances; consider how much more flexible is the rule " unsatisfactory goods must be returned within a reasonable time " than such a rigid rule as " . . . within seven days." The former gives room for discretion and allows account to be taken of difficulties; the latter might be very unfair in particular cases. Sometimes the law does impose fixed rather than relative standards, as where it prescribes a speed limit of thirty miles per hour in built-up areas.

In practice the formulation of the law on any topic may utilise all four forms of expression. Thus it is a *principle* that a person injured by the fault of another is entitled to recover compensation from him, and one *rule* derived from this is that a person who by driving *without reasonable care* (*standard*) causes injury to another is legally *negligent* (*concept*) and therefore liable in damages to the injured person. But it is not always easy to say whether a decision of a particular case lays down a rule or merely applies a wider principle to particular facts or merely holds that the facts fall within or without the standard set up by a principle or rule. Every case must be interpreted on its own, regard being had to the language used, to the definiteness or vagueness, to the presence or absence of detail, and to the reference to a standard or otherwise, in the formulation of the decision. In legal study, important though specific rules are, the main task of the jurist and the student of law must be to ascertain the general principle involved, relate the rules and specific cases thereto, and to examine, evaluate and criticise the principles as elements in a systematic body of principles of social regulation.

Doctrines

The term " doctrine " is sometimes used for the most general systematic fitting together of principles, rules, concepts and standards relating to particular situations or fields of the legal order. Thus one may speak of the doctrine of public policy, or the doctrine of fault-liability.[45] These are almost entirely the work of the jurists and found in their textbooks, through which they influence legal reasoning and decisions.[46]

THE VOCABULARY OF LAW

Language and Words

Since the legal order consists of the regulation of conduct by the application of various kinds of principles and rules to various sets of factual circumstances the enormous importance in legal connections of language and words must not be overlooked. For the principles and rules and other precepts of law are formulated verbally in statutes and orders, in judicial and administrative decisions, and in books of authority, and the circumstances of fact to which rules of law are to be applied are frequently expressed in verbal form in contracts, agreements, wills, deeds, dispositions and other writings, are brought before courts by way of written pleadings, indictments or complaints, while oral evidence of facts is given in verbal form. It is apparent then that an important part of both the study and the application of law consists of the correct appreciation and understanding of the uses and meanings of words, the accurate formulation of thought in words so as to convey precisely the meaning intended, and the nice analysis of language used so as to extract from it the precise connotations and implications inherent in it.[47] Attention to word-meaning and usage is of practical importance in legal study and accordingly good textbooks devote considerable attention to the analysis of the legal terms and words relevant to their subject-matter, while this analysis is also pursued in jurisprudence.[48]

Law unfortunately does not have a large, highly technical vocabulary as do medicine and engineering. Legal thinking and writing would be much clearer if it did, but in fact law for the most part utilises everyday words of the English language.

It has to be admitted that many terms used in legal connections, and many more in social, ethical and political studies, are vague and do not necessarily cause the hearer immediately to have in mind the same thing

---

[45] *i.e.*, the body of principles and rules all embodying the idea that liability in damages arises from harm caused by fault, by commission or omission, and not merely from the occurrence of harm.

[46] See further Pound, " Hierarchy of Sources and Forms " in Hall, *Readings in Jurisprudence*, 661; Pound, *Jurisprudence*, II, 124 *et seq.*

[47] See Sapir, " Language," in *Encyc.Soc.Sc.*, IX, 158.

[48] A valuable discussion of this topic in legal connections is Williams, " Language and the Law " (1945) 61 L.Q.R. 71, 179, 293 and 384; (1946) 62 L.Q.R. 387. See also Corbin, " Legal Analysis and Terminology " (1919) 29 Yale L.J. 163; Chafee, " The Disorderly Conduct of Words " (1941) 41 Col.L.R. 381.

The student interested in pursuing this topic should make the acquaintance of such works as Fowler's *Modern English Usage* and *The King's English* and make frequent reference to both legal and standard English dictionaries. The study of literature and other languages does much to develop the sensitive weighing and handling of words.

as the speaker had in mind. Thus such phrases as " reasonable care," " unreasonable restraint of trade," " satisfied beyond reasonable doubt," leave room for differences of opinion and do not refer to a concrete measurable criterion. It is this vagueness which can easily permit judges to differ in opinion as to the decision of a case even though the facts may be established and the law well settled. Thus if the law is that rejected goods must be returned to the seller " within a reasonable time " and they have in fact been returned in ten days, one judge may consider that ten days was reasonable in the circumstances of the case and another that it was not reasonable but unduly delayed. This is even more so in the case of such words as " just, " " wrong," " unconstitutional " which are sometimes used emotionally and with no clear significance at all.

Again many words have several senses or meanings which require to be carefully distinguished since the word is not always used with the same connotation in all legal discourse. Thus " malice " may mean simply the deliberate doing of a legally wrongful act, or it may mean malevolence, spite or ill-will; " property " may mean the legal rights of proprietorship [49] or may mean the actual object to which these legal rights relate.[50]

There are again numerous words which have two or more distinct senses, one or more in ordinary everyday speech and one with a particular and rather different meaning in legal discourse. Thus " negligence " in ordinary speech means carelessness, whereas in law it means a failure to fulfil the duty of care imposed in the circumstances by the law, whether or not that be carelessness in the common sense. " Charity " in everyday speech means helping the needy but it has a wider meaning in law and the interpretation of the word " charity " in legal contexts has given rise to immense controversy. Particular statutes sometimes define particular words for the purposes of that statute, sometimes more narrowly, sometimes more broadly than the everyday meaning of the word.

This category of words is again distinct from the category of words which have definite legal meanings only and which are seldom, if ever, used in everyday discourse at all, words such as " vitious intromitter," " bailee." English law was formerly rich in words peculiarly legal but many have now disappeared. Scots law has not so many peculiarly legal terms, but all British law is weak in accurate technical terminology as compared with medicine or engineering.

This close attention to words and the verbal form of statutes, deeds and other legal expressions must extend to the commonest and most

---

[49] Thus in the Sale of Goods Act 1893, there are rules for the passing or trans- ference of the " property," which is quite a distinct matter from the transfer of the goods sold.

[50] As in the estate agent's phrase " a desirable property."

ordinary parts of speech since it may be of crucial importance whether " or " or " and " be used, " may " or " shall, " " among " or " between," and every indication of meaning which can be gathered from a grammatical shift may be important. Again, the precise position of the word " only " in a sentence may be crucial.

Closely connected with this topic is the body of guiding principles and presumptions which have been developed by the courts to assist them in the difficult task of statutory interpretation,[51] a problem which perplexes courts and legal advisers precisely because the communication of ideas by words can never be achieved with complete accuracy and perfect freedom from ambiguity.

FURTHER READING

The Nature of Law
Cohen and Cohen: *Readings in Jurisprudence and Legal Philosophy*.
D'Entreves: *Natural Law*.
Hall: *Readings in Jurisprudence*.
Hart: *The Concept of Law*.
Kantorowicz: *The Definition of Law*.
Lloyd: *Introduction to Jurisprudence*.
Morris: *The Great Legal Philosophers*.
Pound: *Jurisprudence*, Vol. 2.
Stone: *The Province and Function of Law*.

Law and Fact
Cardozo: *Nature of the Judicial Process*; (also in *Selected Writings of Benjamin N. Cardozo*, 107).
Dowling, Patterson & Powell: *Legal Method*.
Salmond: *Jurisprudence*, Chap. 3.
Wigmore: *Principles of Judicial Proof*.

The Expression of Legal Precepts
Hohfeld: *Fundamental Legal Conceptions*.
Kocourek: *Jural Relations*.

The Vocabulary of Law
Bell: *Dictionary and Digest of the Law of Scotland*.
Broom: *Legal Maxims*.
Chase: *The Tyranny of Words*.
Hexner: *Studies in Legal Terminology*.
Jowitt: *Dictionary of English Law*.
Lloyd: *Introduction to Jurisprudence*.
Philbrick: *Language and the Law*.
Pollock and Wright: *Possession in the Common Law*.
Trayner: *Latin Maxims and Phrases*.
Wharton: *Law Lexicon*.
Williams: " Language and the Law " (1945) 61 L.Q.R. 71, 179, 293, 384; (1946) 62 L.Q.R. 387.
" International Law and the Controversy concerning the word Law " (1945) 22 B.Y.I.L. 146, and in Laslett (ed.) *Philosophy, Politics and Society*, 134.

---

[51] These principles are discussed in Chap. 10, *infra*.

CHAPTER 3

THE BRANCHES OF LEGAL SCIENCE

IT conduces to completeness of understanding and effective study of legal science to divide up the whole subject-matter of legal science into a number of distinguishable and fairly distinct branches or subjects.[1] No division of the subject-matter of legal studies is wholly satisfactory [2] and, however it be done, some topics are difficult to classify while others again fall logically into more than one class. There is necessarily overlapping at the edges in any such classification, but this is no bad thing since it emphasises that the whole of legal knowledge is ultimately a unity which in turn has very indefinite frontiers with other fields of knowledge.[3] Knowledge gained from the study of one branch may cast light on a problem within another branch. Moreover, legal controversies not infrequently involve issues pertaining to several of the branches so that the convenience of such a division should not be allowed to lead to mental compartmentation. Proper classification of legal problems may also be of practical importance with regard both to finding the law, and correct application of the rules.

A generally satisfactory fundamental division of legal science is into (1) legal history, or the study of the development of legal institutions, ideas and doctrines in civilised communities, and particularly in our own community; (2) legal theory and philosophy, or jurisprudence, dealing with the most general ideas about law; (3) comparative legal studies, comparing and contrasting the attitudes adopted by different legal systems to particular problems, their different organisations of justice and courts, their different modes of thinking, and so on; (4) international law, or the body of law governing international institutions such as the United Nations and existing as between independent sovereign states and political communities; (5) supranational law, or the law of regional organisations of political communities; and (6) the various bodies of state, national or municipal law operating within these various states and communities and within the provinces thereof which have distinct legal systems, differing from each other in greater or less extent. Each of these branches may be further subdivided into distinct heads and subheads for study.

---

[1] The student should observe that the division into branches does not necessarily correspond in number, name or scope with the subjects of a university degree curriculum.

[2] Stair, I, 1, 3–12, distinguishes the law of nature, or equity, or the moral law, the positive law of God, and human law, which is distinguished into the law of nations (i.e., international law) and the law of each society of people, or their civil law. Erskine, I, 1, 7, divides law into the law of nature (i.e., roughly jurisprudence), the law of nations, and civil or municipal law. So too Mackenzie, *Inst.*, I, 1, 3.

[3] *Cf.* Chap. 1, *supra.*

I.—LEGAL HISTORY

Legal history is of importance as showing how legal institutions, such as courts, legal concepts, such as contract or landownership, and legal principles, such as liability for harm done without justification, have originated and developed, or been imposed by one legal system on another, or been copied or borrowed by one from another. It is also of importance as revealing in many cases the original scope of and justification for a particular institution, rule or concept, and in many cases a modern rule can be understood only in the light of its origins and development.

There are two main aspects of legal history, first the development of law in human societies generally and more particularly in those civilisations which have contributed to the general Western tradition in law, as in general spiritual and intellectual matters, and secondly, the development of legal institutions and law within particular countries, that is the histories of distinct legal systems. These two aspects are interrelated and cannot be divorced.[4]

The more general aspects of legal history are sometimes known as Historical Jurisprudence. Historical jurisprudence studies the origins and development of legal institutions and ideas generally, of law as a factor in human society. In default of evidence from written records as to the administration of justice and law in ancient and primitive societies jurists draw inferences from the legal practices of primitive peoples living at the present day, whose customs and ways of life are recorded by social anthropologists. Legal history proper differs from historical jurisprudence in that it seeks simply to follow out, record, explain and understand the changes and developments which have taken place in the evolution of each particular system of law, to discover the causes of the specific changes which have taken place and to disclose the historical origins, bases and justifications of modern rules. It follows that there is a body of historical knowledge relative to every distinct system of law, though in the earlier periods one system tends to resemble and overlap other related systems,[5] and the influence of, and deliberate borrowing from, other systems are factors always to be kept in mind.

Legal history necessarily overlaps with constitutional history, though the latter subject is more particularly concerned with tracing the origins and development of governmental institutions, such as the legislative body, the superior executive body, the Council of Ministers or Cabinet and so on, which are matters of public law, while legal history is alone concerned with the development of rules of private law such as contract and succession.

---

[4] The history of law in Scotland is dealt with in Chap. 4.

[5] Thus in the period prior to the War of Independence, Scottish legal development very much resembles that of England. So too all the European systems deriving from Roman law have marked affinities in the medieval period.

Both legal and constitutional history are concerned with such topics as the development of the courts and the rights of the subject, though even there a difference of emphasis is usually discernible, the one study being more concerned with the legal aspects and the other with the political aspects. So too both legal and constitutional history necessarily overlap with social, political, religious and economic history since these studies relate to and cast light on the background in which the legal system developed and frequently provide the explanation for purely legal changes. Law does not develop in a vacuum, sealed off from other facets of the development of the society it relates to; it is an integral part of society and changes with it.

The study of legal history necessarily depends on the discovery, examination and interpretation of records and archives and in most countries legal societies exist for the purpose of bringing to light, editing and publishing material from public and private collections of historical material,[6] but diligent search and a discerning eye can find information of legal importance in every kind of historical material, charters, rent-rolls, taxation lists, memoirs, letters, parish registers and similar records. In Scotland the study of legal history has hitherto been inadequately pursued and a great deal of research still remains to be done.

LAW IN EARLY CIVILISATIONS

Extensive remains exist of various bodies of written laws from some of the early civilisations of the Middle East, which evidence not only a high degree of general civilisation but also a degree of legal maturity and sophistication. The earliest fragments date from about 2900 B.C. It is known that in the time of the Third Dynasty in Egypt (2815–2690 B.C.) formal documents were required for important legal transactions, but detailed knowledge of the legal institutions and rules is scanty.[7]

The most substantial body of law is the Laws of King Hammurabi of Babylon,[8] dating from about 1800 B.C., which take the form, not so much of a code or statement of the law but a series of amendments to the common law of Babylon, classified under major headings. Though ancient they are not primitive, but evidence considerable legal maturity. Thousands of legal documents containing contracts, conveyances and reported cases have also been recovered from Babylonia, dating down to about 300 B.C. Then there are fragmentary records of Old Assyrian laws and legal documents of about 2300 B.C. and more extensive records of Middle

---

[6] In Scotland the Stair Society exists for this purpose, but much legal material has been published by the Scottish History Society, the Scottish Text Society and the Scottish Burgh Records Society and by such older clubs as the Maitland and Bannatyne Clubs and the Spalding Club. In England the great legal-historical society is the Selden Society.

[7] Seidl, " Law " in Glanville (ed.) *The Legacy of Egypt*, 198.

[8] See Driver and Miles, *The Babylonian Laws*, 2 vols.

Assyrian enactments dating from between 1450 and 1250 B.C., also modifications of pre-existing customary law.[9]

From Asia Minor have come Hittite treaties and laws from the period 1600–1300 B.C.,[10] and from Palestine some primitive codes of about 750 B.C. and, more importantly, the bodies of rules found in various books of the Old Testament, dating from about 600 B.C.,[11] which through the spread of Christianity have entered into the basic beliefs of much of Western civilisation, though more through religious and moral prescription than by direct legal influence.

In Greece there are fragmentary records of lawgivers and laws, such as Lycurgus at Sparta, *c.* 875 B.C., Draco at Athens, *c.* 625 B.C., and Solon at Athens, *c.* 595 B.C., covering roughly from the ninth to the sixth centuries B.C. The Code of Gortyn in Crete probably belongs to the fifth century B.C.[12] Classical Athens had an extensive and developed system of law [13] but more significant for the ideas of law and justice in later Western civilisation was the contribution of the Greek thinkers, much of whose work, particularly some of the writings of Plato and Aristotle, has had permanent influence on Western thinking about law and justice as much as about morals or politics.

But historically interesting as these early bodies of law are they have had little direct or permanent influence on any modern Western European legal system. It is, however, otherwise with the law of Rome.

CIVIL OR ROMAN LAW

The Civil or Roman law is in the first place the law of the ancient city of Rome and the Roman empire from the foundation of the city (traditionally 753 B.C.) to the fall of the Western empire in the fifth century A.D. and even thereafter till the fall of the Eastern empire with the capture of Constantinople by the Turks in 1453. The system really begins [14] with the adoption of the Laws of the Twelve Tables about 450 B.C. which established a system of law for Roman citizens only (*jus civile*), characterised by rigidity and formality.

In 242 B.C. the increase of foreigners at Rome made it necessary to appoint a special judge, the peregrine praetor, to deal with causes in which

---

[9] See Driver and Miles, *The Assyrian Laws.*

[10] See Neufeld, *The Hittite Laws.*

[11] These include particularly Exodus, xx–xxiii; Leviticus, xvii–xxvi; Deuteronomy, v–xxvi; and Ezekiel, xl–xlviii. See further Kent, *Israel's Laws and Legal Precedents*; Daube, *Studies in Biblical Law.*

[12] Vinogradoff, *Historical Jurisprudence*, Vol. II; Wyse, in *Companion to Greek Studies* (ed. Whibley), 429–490.

[13] Jones, *Law and Legal Theory of the Greeks*; Harrison, *Law of Athens.*

[14] For the history, see Muirhead, *Historical Introduction to the Private Law of Rome*, 3rd ed.; Jolowicz, *Historical Introduction to the Study of Roman Law*, 3rd ed. For the law, see Buckland, *Text-book of Roman Law from Augustus to Justinian*; Girard, *Manuel Élémentaire de droit romain*, 8th ed.

a foreigner was involved, and he and the urban praetor, who dealt with cases involving only citizens, both issued edicts defining the circumstances in which they would give particular remedies, and these edicts became important sources of new and revised law which came to be known as *jus praetorium* or *jus honorarium*. In the late republican period, from about 150 B.C. to 27 B.C., this was the chief reforming factor in Roman law.[15] Also in this period the *jus gentium* came to be of importance; this was the body of law applicable equally to Roman citizens and to foreigners, a system based on common principles of the Mediterranean peoples with a strong Roman flavouring but free from formalistic elements, and it was later applied to Roman provincials also. It came to be connected with the theoretical idea of a law common to all peoples and dictated by nature, a notion taken over by the Romans from Greek philosophy.

In the early empire (27 B.C. to A.D. 100) legal literature developed [16] and the praetors' edicts tended to become fixed and carried on from year to year, as is evidenced by the growing practice of writing commentaries on the edict. In or about A.D. 131 the emperor Hadrian had the jurist Salvius Julianus revise and settle the edicts, which thereafter became fixed and alterable only by the emperor. The classical age of the law was reached in the second century and the first half of the third, considerably later than the classical age of Latin literature, and it is marked by extensive juristic writing and the detailed working out of principles. The great age was short and soon over; Papinian was killed in 212, Ulpian in 228, and Ulpian's pupil Modestinus was the last of the great jurists. By A.D. 300 jurisprudence was stricken with sterility. The most important work surviving in its original form from this period is the *Institutes* of Gaius, a student's textbook written about A.D. 161, which subsequently formed the basis of Justinian's *Institutes* and is of unique importance as evidence of the state of the law in the classical period.

While the law did not stand still there was a falling off in legal literature after 235; new ideas were introduced, especially from the East, while the law was also influenced by the growing importance of the eastern half of the empire with its capital at Constantinople. More and more, law-making had become the function of the emperor, and in the third and later centuries attempts were made to collect the mass of imperial constitutions. Two unofficial collections are known, the *Codex Gregorianus* containing constitutions from Hadrian to Diocletian, and the *Codex Hermogenianus* containing mainly those of Diocletian's time. They may have been made in the East, for the tendency was for the imperial centre to shift eastwards and Constantine in 326–328 removed the imperial court to Byzantium, now

---

[15] Watson, *Law Making in the Later Roman Republic*, Chaps. 3–6.
[16] On this, see Schulz, *History of Roman Legal Science*.

renamed Constantinople, while in the fourth century the seat of the Western government was removed first to Milan and then to Ravenna. In 438 the *Codex Theodosianus* was promulgated: it was an official collection of imperial statutes beginning with Constantine I, a collection rather than a code, but by the time it was issued the barbarians were already striking at the empire.[17]

Fall of the Western Empire

In the fourth and fifth centuries the encroachments of barbarian tribes on the empire increased and twice the empire was divided into East and West portions for ease of administration and defence. The weakness of successive Western emperors culminated in the capture and sack of Rome by the Visigoths under Alaric in 410. The Franks and Burgundians founded kingdoms in northern Gaul, the Visigoths in southern Gaul, while the Vandals passed through Spain and conquered North Africa. Rome was again sacked in 454, by the Vandals, and the empire in the West came to an end in 476 when the last puppet emperor was deposed. The Eastern half was, however, to stand for another thousand years until the Turks captured Constantinople in 1453. The two halves had never become completely unified or integrated and remained Greek and Latin though united politically. By the end of the fifth century Germanic kingdoms, superficially romanised, had been established all over Western Europe, Visigoths in south-west Gaul and Spain, Burgundians in south-east Gaul, Ostrogoths in Italy, Vandals in Africa. Rather later the Franks established themselves between the Rhine and the Somme, the Alemanni on the upper Rhine and Danube, the Bavarians on the Danube and in the Alps, the Angles, Jutes and Saxons in South Britain.

Roman Law in the West

The Western provinces of the former Roman Empire adhered to the former law summed up in the *Codex Theodosianus* of A.D. 438. There was legislation by the emperors down to that date, fragments of older legislation contained in the private collections known as the *Codex Gregorianus* and the *Codex Hermogenianus*, numerous *Novellae* of early fifth-century emperors and a great volume of older jurisprudence laid down in opinions and treatises going back to the classical age. The temporary reconquering of part of Italy by Justinian's troops in the sixth century had no legal or permanent consequences and his legislation was ineffective there. But other law was beginning; the barbarians had been writing down their

---

[17] A valuable summary of the later days of the Roman empire is in *The European Inheritance*, I, 222–249. For a fuller account, see *Cambridge Medieval History*, Vol. IV, esp. Chap. 21. See also Gibbon, *Decline and Fall of the Roman Empire*, Chap. 44; Bryce's *Holy Roman Empire*, Chaps. II and III; Bury's *Invasion of Europe by the Barbarians*, *passim*.

customs and barbarian kings had begun to issue law-books for their Roman subjects, while books of ecclesiastical law were also being compiled.

Roman law in the provinces had become a debased body of rules by the fifth century when many races of foreigners were within the Empire, and occupying posts of authority and importance in the civil and military administration. For such peoples in the provinces various statements of barbarised Roman law were prepared in the late fifth and early sixth centuries. The principal were the *Edictum Theodorici* for the Ostrogothic kingdom (*c*. A.D. 500), the *Lex Romana Burgundionum* (*c*. A.D. 500) and the *Lex Romana Visigothorum*, also known as the *Breviarium Alaricianum* (A.D. 506) of which the last became the standard source of Roman law in Western Europe during the first half of the Middle Ages. It was a more or less complete code for the use of the Roman populace in France and Spain, comprising the enactments of the later Empire with interpretations of the text designed to make the sense of the laws as clear as possible, and consisted of three main portions, an introductory survey for beginners, legal and jurisprudential doctrines laid down by authorities and a body of enactments by recent emperors.[18] But the most important event for the subsequent history and influence of Roman law happened in the East after the fall of the Western Empire.

Justinian

When Justinian became emperor at Constantinople in 527 he set out to collect, codify and reform the mass of law which had grown up over the centuries. His efforts resulted in the promulgation of (a) *The Old Codex*: a new collection of imperial constitutions superseding the older ones and including later legislation; (b) *The Fifty Decisions*: a collection of fifty constitutions settling matters of dispute and abolishing some institutions and distinctions no longer of practical importance; (c) *The Digest or Pandects*: a collection of excerpts from the works of jurists, amended and omitting obsolete or superfluous matter, arranged in fifty books according to subject-matter: the *Digest* preserved the writings of the classical jurists who were really responsible for the greatness of the Roman law; (d) *The Institutes*: this was a systematic new book for the elementary instruction of students based on Gaius' *Institutes*, and on other elementary works; (e) *The New Codex*: this was a revision of the Old Codex in the light of the Fifty Decisions and other later constitutions; (f) *The Novels* (*Novellae*

---

[18] For a valuable comparison of the Breviary with Justinian's *Corpus Juris*, see Vinogradoff, *Roman Law in Medieval Europe*, 2nd ed., 18–21, where he shows how much the Breviary evidences intellectual decay. See also Roby, " Roman Law," 2 *Camb.Med.Hist.*, Chap. 3.

Constitutiones) or later legislation. The Institutes, Digest, (new) Code and Novels together form the *Corpus Juris Civilis.*[19]

After Justinian's time Greek versions of parts of the *Corpus Juris* were made in the East and selections published modifying some of the enactments particularly to make the law more consonant with Christian principles. Under Leo the Wise (886–911) was prepared the *Basilica*[20] in which are fused, in sixty books, all the parts of Justinian's compilations, in Greek versions of the sixth and seventh centuries, with some changes. This remained the law of the Eastern Empire until the fall of Constantinople in 1453. There was some revival of legal studies in the eleventh century and later, and about 1345 the *Hexabiblos* was compiled at Thessalonica. This still had a measure of authority in Greece until the promulgation of the modern Civil Code in 1946.

The West after Justinian

Justinian's *Corpus Juris* was long accepted and even known only in the East and in parts of Italy. The *Breviarium Alaricianum* still comprised the Roman law for the West, and legal knowledge decayed seriously in the Dark Ages. The *Lex Romana Curiensis* of the late eighth century, a statement of legal custom for the population of Eastern Switzerland, and used also in the Tyrol and Northern Italy, testifies to even greater decadence and is little more than custom flavoured by Roman law.

In the Dark Ages and early Middle Ages law was essentially personal and local rather than territorial, since no state was strong enough to enforce a legal order or system of its own. Moreover, the entry of Goths, Franks and Lombards into the former Roman provinces had not involved the disappearance of Roman inhabitants and their special legal status was allowed to continue and relations between them were governed by their own racial law. So, too, men of each nation, such as Burgundians or Bavarians or Salian Franks, lived under their own law, which raised difficulties when members of different nationalities wished to enter into legal transactions. This system of national laws gave rise to problems of conflict of laws.[21]

Moreover, in most districts local customs arose to regulate the ordinary dealings of the people and these tended to take their colouring from the

---

[19] The standard edition is the Berlin one edited by Krueger, Mommsen and Schoell in three volumes: The parts are cited by book, title, and paragraph or fragment: thus Inst. I, iii, 3; D. (or Dig.) IX, 2, 7, 1; C.I., xviii, 12; the *Novels* are cited by number, *e.g.*, Nov. 118. The compendious title *Corpus Juris Civilis* was not given till much later, being copied from the title *Corpus Juris Canonici.*

[20] See further Lawson, " The Basilica " (1931–32) 46 L.Q.R. 486; 47 L.Q.R. 536; Collinet, " Byzantine Legislation," *Camb.Med.Hist.*, IV, Chap. 20.

[21] In a famous letter from Bishop Agobard of Lyons to Ludwig the Pious about 850 it is narrated that " It often occurs that five men walking or sitting together are each of them living under a different law," and it became customary for the parties to a deed or action to make an express declaration of which system they lived by.

prevailing national majority and to modify any surviving traces of Roman law. Thus legal customs were built on a basis of Roman law in Southern Italy till the advent of the Saracens and Normans, where the Byzantine Empire still held sway, in the Romagna, and in Southern France and Northern Spain where the *Breviarium Alaricianum* was applied.[22]

In other districts, Northern France, Germany and England, the barbarian laws applied but Roman institutions and legal customs still had influence, particularly since the clergy still followed Roman law. Roman influence was strongest in the case of the Ostrogoths of Northern Italy and Austria and of the Visigoths of Spain and France who adopted Roman enactments wholesale quite apart from Imperial Roman law codified for Roman fellow-citizens.[23]

Legal learning did not, however, entirely disappear in these times and still survived in part and can be found in medieval salvage of the wreckage of antiquity such as in Bishop Isidore of Seville's *Etymologiae* and in clerical abstracts and glosses or explanations of older texts.[24]

The Corpus Juris in the West

In the West, Justinian's law was rediscovered in Italy in the eleventh century.[25] The study centred on Bologna [26] where Irnerius [27] began the succession of Glossators,[28] or scholars who wrote glosses on the text, settling its form, explaining it, resolving contradictions, deducing maxims and discussing concrete cases, becoming in the end a commentary. The men who administered local laws and customs were trained in the *Corpus Juris* and its more civilised rules influenced the natural growth of the law of developing communities. The *Summa* of Azo (*fl. c.* 1190) was an indispensable text while the Gloss of Accursius (*ob. c.* 1260) was a standard commentary on the text.

About 1300 there arose the school of Commentators [29] of whom the greatest were Bartolus of Sassoferrato (1314–57) and his pupil Baldus (1327–1400). They sought to make the Civil Law applicable to the practice of their time, adapting it to living conditions, and to harmonise it with the

---

[22] Vinogradoff, *op. cit.* 28.

[23] *Op. cit.* 30.

[24] *Op. cit.* 37–41; see also Jenks, *Law and Politics in the Middle Ages*, Chaps. 1, 2.

[25] The great authority on the later Roman law is Savigny's *Geschichte des Römischen Rechts im Mittelalter* (1822); see also *Continental Legal History Series*, Vol. I, for a general survey.

[26] Provence, Pavia and Ravenna were also early centres of the revival.

[27] See Dove Wilson, " Irnerius " (1894) 6 J.R. 304.

[28] See Vinogradoff, *Roman Law in Medieval Europe*, 2nd ed., Chap. 2; Hazeltine, " Roman and Canon Law in the Middle Ages," *Camb.Med.Hist.*, V, 697; Hazeltine, " Glossators," in *Encyc.Soc.Sciences*, VI, 679; Hazeltine, Introd. to Ullman, *Medieval Idea of Law*; Kantorowicz and Buckland, *Studies in the Glossators of the Roman Law*.

[29] See Hazeltine, " Commentators," in *Encyc.Soc. Sciences*, III, 679; Woolf, *Bartolus of Sassoferrato*; Ullman, " Bartolus on Customary Law " (1941) 52 J.R. 263.

feudal, Germanic or canon laws then in force. They transformed it and made it living law but at the cost of casuistry, pedantry and voluminous confusion. " The great achievement of the Commentators, the Post-Glossators, was in fact the transformation of the Roman law into a medieval Italian law. They created a literature in Romano-Italian law which not only possessed authority in Italy itself, but played a role of great importance in the legal and political life of Europe as a whole. Thus it was the living Romano-Italian law of the Commentators, and not the pure Roman law of Justinian, which crossed the Alps into Germany in the age of the Reception." [30]

During this period from 1100 to 1500 the Roman law became the basis for legal science throughout Western Europe and its importance and influence spread rapidly. Moreover in this period great political and economic changes were taking place, towns were developing, commerce, trade, agriculture, fairs, and the older customary law, gradually elaborated to regulate the relations of men living by agriculture, became inadequate for a populace depending on industry and commerce. Roman law was looked to for its embodiment of the old Roman cultural ideal and as carrying an aura of the old Roman glory and unity, but particularly since it contained principles capable of solving many of the problems of the more cultivated society which was arising and of the developing trade and commerce. It made important contributions to the solution of specific problems and became the basis for much development.

The study spread [31] to France where in the south, the *pays du droit écrit*, it gradually superseded the older Roman law books as the law of the land, modified only by local custom. In northern France, the *pays du droit coûtumier*, it was mingled with the traditional customs in the thirteenth century, and it was freely used in Philippe de Beaumanoir's *Coûtumes de Beauvaisis* (*c.* 1280).

The third great school of Roman law studies is that of the Humanists, which rose following the decline of the Commentators about the beginning of the fifteenth century. They had a historical sense and began to try to reconstruct the classical law from the amended passages found in the *Digest* by detecting the interpolations made in the texts included in the *Corpus Juris* by the compilers. This movement was very strong in France and is represented by such jurists as Cujacius (Jacques Cujas, 1520–90), Donellus (Hugues Doneau, 1527–91) and Faber (Antoine Favre, 1557–

---

[30] Hazeltine, Introd. to Ullman, *Medieval Idea of Law*, xix; see also Hazeltine, *Camb.Med.Hist.*, V, 697, and on the legal and political theories of the Glossators and Commentators, see Carlyle, *History of Medieval Political Theory in the West*, Vols. II and VI.

[31] On the extension, see Munroe Smith, *Development of European Law*; *Continental Legal History Series*, Vol. 1, General Survey; " Law," by Vinogradoff, le Bras and Meynial in *The Legacy of the Middle Ages*; Taylor-Cameron, " Roman Law in the Early Middle Ages " (1895–8) 7 J.R. 241; 8 J.R. 118; 10 J.R. 438.

1624), while Jacobus Gothefredus (Jacques Godefroy, 1587–1652) published a great edition of the Theodosian Code, with commentary. Rather later Pothier [32] in France published in 1748 his *Pandectae Justinianae in novum ordinem digestae*, recreating the correct order of the text, and on that foundation wrote a series of treatises on aspects of French law, such as the *Traité des Obligations* (1761).

In Germany it began to oust the native tribal law in the later Middle Ages, facilitated by the theory of continuity of the Holy Roman Empire with the older Empire of the West,[33] and by the lack of political unity among the Germanic states. About the fourteenth century there took place the " Reception " in Germany of civil and canon law, which were widely studied in the universities. While in theory the *Corpus Juris* was accepted only as subsidiary and its rules to be applied if Germanic law were silent, in practice Germanic law was to a large extent superseded. The central Imperial court adopted Roman law for its guidance as the common law of the Empire in 1495 and it exercised considerable influence on the legal institutions of all the states of the Empire so that the " Reception " spread. Roman law remained a main source of Germanic law until the German Civil Code of 1900, and in the nineteenth century Savigny and his successors created an elaborate, highly systematised body of law (*Pandektenrecht*) on the basis of the *Corpus Juris*. So, too, until the promulgation of the Code Napoleon in 1804 the customs, particularly of Paris, influenced and supplemented by Roman law, constituted the law of France.[34] These codes in turn have been copied repeatedly in codes all over the world.

In Holland resort was had to the Roman law to supplement the inadequacies of general and local customs and Roman law was " received " in all the provinces in varying degrees from the fifteenth to the seventeenth centuries; in Holland also there flourished many great jurists whose writings on law, particularly on Roman law, have been very important and influential.[35] The law of Holland was carried to South Africa by the early Dutch settlers there, though in Holland itself it was superseded by the French civil code during the Napoleonic wars. But in South Africa it took root, developed and survived as the Roman-Dutch law.

Roman law probably entered Scotland [36] initially through the church

---

[32] On Pothier, see Macdonell (ed.), *Great Jurists of the World,* 447.

[33] For an account of this, see Bryce, *The Holy Roman Empire.*

[34] On France, see Brissaud, *Manuel d'Histoire du Droit Français*; Esmein, *Histoire du Droit Français*; Olivier-Martin, *Histoire du Droit Français*.

On Germany, see Hubner, *Institutionen des deutschen Privatrechts* (trans. in *Continental Legal History Series*); Fehr, *Deutsche Rechtsgeschichte.*

[35] In this connection the long-standing practice of Scottish advocates studying in Holland must be remembered since Holland is the channel through which much Roman law came to Scotland.

[36] See further Baird Smith, " Roman Law," in Stair Society, *Sources and Literature of Scots Law,* and references there; Dove Wilson, " Reception of the Roman Law in Scotland " (1898) 9 J.R. 361; Miller, " Reception of Roman Law in Scotland " (1923) 35 J.R. 362.

and the canon law but by the sixteenth century it had come frequently to be referred to in supplement of native customary or common law. Knowledge of Roman law was increased by the long association of Scotland with France and the works of the French jurists of the fifteenth and sixteenth centuries were well known to Scottish students who flooded to such universities as Bourges. Some doctrines of Roman law were introduced by legislation. In the seventeenth century the writings of French and Dutch civilians were well known and when Stair wrote his *Institutions* he naturally turned to Roman law, as developed by these civilians, to fill gaps and harmonise differences. In the seventeenth and eighteenth centuries Scottish students frequented the Dutch universities and the citation of the Dutch and German commentators can be traced in the earlier Scottish collected decisions. The Roman law which was adopted and introduced was generally a simplified form, ignoring elaborate refinements, accepted on its merits and for its reason and equity, not as of binding force. After the Union of 1707 English influence tended to grow and this has been more pronounced with the passage of time. Simultaneously reliance on Roman law has tended to decline and in the twentieth century it is seldom referred to except in matters previously adopted from the Roman law, while reference to the older French, Dutch and German commentators is rare.

The Roman law never became a constituent element of English law but it was influential when legal doctrines were being formulated in the twelfth and thirteenth centuries and was continuously studied in the universities [37] and in particular topics it has been a direct source of English rules. Hence also Roman law has been less influential in the parts of the world settled from England. Thus, apart from Quebec and Louisiana, North America has taken its law initially and fundamentally from England. But, largely through the French and German codes, principles stemming originally from Roman law have spread all over the world.

Permanent Importance of Roman Law

The Roman law is still a material subject of legal study for several reasons; in the first place, the development and working out of their great system of law by the Roman jurists over a thousand years is an excellent example of the modes of growth and development of a legal system; furthermore this development was one of the great intellectual achievements of antiquity and Roman law is entitled to be placed with Greek philosophy and Jewish religious thought as one of the most important and powerful intellectual forces in European civilisation inherited by the

---

[37] Vinogradoff, *op. cit.* 97 *et seq.*; Winfield, *Chief Sources of English Legal History*, Chap. 4; Scrutton, *Influence of Roman Law on the Law of England* in *Essays in Anglo-American Legal History*, I, 208; Potter, *Historical Introduction to English Law*, 4th ed., 631; Plucknett, *Concise History of the Common Law*, 5th ed., 294; Powell, " Roman Law in Common Law Courts," 1958 *Curr.Leg.Prob.* 19.

modern from the ancient world.[38] " Roman law, next to Christianity, was the greatest factor in the creation of modern civilisation, and it is the greatest intellectual legacy of Rome." [39]

Secondly, the rules, doctrines, conceptions and terminology of the Roman law were closely studied everywhere in Europe from the end of the Dark Ages till modern times and have powerfully influenced legal thinking and terminology and the actual content of many modern systems of law. Roman law has unique significance as a common source of legal conceptions. " Roman law is still the foundation for the liberal education of a lawyer, the training and the sharpening of his logical equipment. The methods of reasoning of the Roman jurists their way of approaching a legal problem we still follow today." [40] " It may be said that the Romans have fixed for all time the categories of juristic thought." [41]

Thirdly, the rules of Roman law have been a material source of rules accepted and applied in modern systems, and to the Roman law modern systems have frequently turned for rules to apply to new sets of circumstances. By acquaintance with Roman law the English-speaking legal student gains a key to the understanding of the many modern systems of law which derive ultimately from Rome, of French law, German law and the many systems based on these systems, of the Roman-Dutch law of South Africa,[42] international law and of much of jurisprudence. Roman law is thus fundamental to jurisprudence and comparative legal study. Roman law and English law between them cover a large part of the civilised and most of the uncivilised world.[43] The reception of Roman law created a great body of continental law which served along with the feudal law, canon law, and the law merchant to unify the diverse legal systems of much of Western Europe.[44]

Fourthly, Roman law was taken as the basis of international law by Grotius and his successors. The founders of international law turned unhesitatingly to Roman law for the rules of their system whenever the relations between ruling princes seemed to them to be analogous to those of private persons. The international rules as to territory are still in essentials the Roman rules of property.

---

[38] This point is well brought out in de Burgh, *Legacy of the Ancient World*, esp. Chaps. 7, 8 and 11. See also Vinogradoff, " The Work of Rome," in *Collected Papers*, Vol. I, 222; Meynial, *Roman Law* in *The Legacy of the Middle Ages*; Bryce, Inaugural Lecture, in *Studies in History and Jurisprudence*, II, 860; Lobingier, " The Value and Place of Roman Law in the Technical Curriculum " (1918) 30 J.R. 136.

[39] Buckland (1931) J.S.P.T.L. 25.

[40] Meynial, in *The Legacy of the Middle Ages*, 399.

[41] Cuq, *Institutions juridiques des Romains*, 2nd ed. I, xxiv.

[42] See generally Hahlo and Kahn, *The South African Legal System and its Background*, Part II; see also Smith, " Scots Law and Roman-Dutch Law: A Shared Tradition," 1961 J.R. 32.

[43] Bryce, *Studies in History and Jurisprudence*, I, 74.

[44] Munroe Smith, *General View of European Legal History*, 3, 28. See also Coing, " The Roman Law as Jus Commune on the Continent " (1973) 89 L.Q.R. 505.

" From the purely academic point of view we cannot afford to neglect a branch of legal learning which has had so large an historical effect, a branch of learning which is still so necessary to a scientific study of law. From the purely practical point of view we cannot afford to neglect a branch of learning which is necessary to the proper understanding of international law, and of foreign Codes de Commerce." [45]

The debt of Scots law to Roman law is very great and Roman law still needs to be studied in Scotland as a material source of the living law of Scotland.[46] Scotland, unlike England, " received " the Roman law and it had great influence from the mid-sixteenth to the mid-eighteenth centuries. Mackenzie, Stair, Bankton and Erskine all consider that in default of native statute or custom great weight attaches to the Roman law, and the courts constantly referred to continental treatises on the Roman and canon law. Since about 1800 this influence has been less but it remains a fact that Roman law was a factor of major importance in the formative period of modern Scots law, with particular influence on the law of moveable property and obligations, and its influence is not yet wholly spent.[47]

OTHER INDIGENOUS EUROPEAN SYSTEMS

Early Celtic Law

Of the law of the Celtic peoples who early inhabited much of the British Isles we have only limited knowledge. Later, when the Celtic peoples were pushed north and west, into Scotland, Wales and Ireland there are records of law, but at least in Scotland none of this seems to have had any material influence on later law.[48]

Early Teutonic Law

Among the Teutonic tribes described in Tacitus' *Germania* there was little organised law. Early Teutonic law was primarily the unwritten custom of the tribe, but there is evidence of tribal assemblies and allegiance to kings, and traces of courts of the tribe and the hundred. The law was mostly concerned with wrongs and there was a recognised system of compensation for injuries or death (wergeld) originally paid in cattle.

---

[45] Holdsworth, *Sources and Literature of English Law*, 235. *Cf.* Lobingier " The Value and Place of Roman Law in the Technical Curriculum " (1918) 30 J.R. 136.

[46] Baird Smith in Stair Society, *Sources and Literature*, p. 177; Smith, *Short Commentary on the Law of Scotland*, 19–24; Mackintosh, " Our Debt to Roman Law " (1926) 38 J.R. 327. *Cf. Stewart* v. *L.M.S. Ry.*, 1943 S.C.(H.L.) 19, 38.

[47] " The Roman law, though interesting, is only of service as showing the foundation on which the Scots law rests. The real question must always be what is the law of Scotland." *Cantiere San Rocco* v. *Clyde Shipbuilding Co.*, 1923 S.C.(H.L.) 105, 123, *per* Lord Dunedin.

[48] See Dillon and Chadwick, *The Celtic Realms*, Chap. 5; Cameron, *Celtic Law*; for Wales, Ellis, *Welsh Tribal Law and Custom in the Middle Ages*; Melville, *The Laws of Hywel Dda*; Owen, *Ancient Laws and Institutes of Wales*; and for Ireland, Thurneysen, *Studies in Early Irish Law*; Macneill, *Early Irish Laws and Institutions*; Hennessey and others (ed.), *Ancient Laws of Ireland*.

Much of Gaul and Germany up to the Rhine-Danube frontier was occupied by the Roman legions for the first four centuries of the Christian era, but in the fifth century most of the Roman provinces in the West fell into the hands of the barbarians, and Germanic kingdoms were founded in the former Roman provinces. Thus Franks and Burgundians came to hold Gaul, Visigoths south Gaul and Spain, and Ostrogoths Italy and most of central Europe. Later the Lombards took Italy from the Ostrogoths.

The Leges Barbarorum

From some of these Germanic kingdoms there have survived bodies of law, mainly codifications of criminal law and procedure, partly containing existing customary law and partly new statutory rules. The earliest is the code of the Visigoths, the *Leges Visigothorum*, of the time of King Euric (*c*. 475) which remained in force among the Visigoths of Spain till replaced by that of Leovigild (*c*. 580), when it was made applicable to all the subjects in the kingdom. A new code, applicable to Visigoths and Romans alike, was made by Recesswinth (*c*. 670) and is known as the *Liber judiciorum*, and a recension made in 681 by King Erwig is known as the *Lex Visigothorum renovata*.

Not much later is the *Lex Salica* of the Salian Franks, a compilation of different dates, originally issued by King Chlodwig in North France about 500, and later amended, added to and corrected. It is pre-eminently a penal code, stating the amounts of fines for various crimes, but containing some civil enactments, notably a chapter on succession to land declaring that daughters cannot inherit land. The *Lex Ripuaria* of the Ripuarian Franks is influenced by, and in part adopts, the Salic law.

Among the Burgundians a code, known as the *Lex Burgundionum*, the *Liber Constitutionum*, or *Lex Gundobada*, was compiled by King Gundobad about 500, and shows strong traces of Roman influence. It applied between Burgundians and also to cases between Romans and Burgundians, and was appealed to as late as the eleventh century. Of the laws of the Alamanni there have survived two texts, the *Pactus Alamannorum* of the seventh century, and the *Lex Alamannorum* of the eighth.

The laws of the Lombards, the *Leges Langobardorum*, are more substantial. The first part, the *Edictus Langobardorum* was promulgated by King Rothari at Pavia in 643. This edict is systematically arranged, clearly compiled by jurists who knew Roman law, but presents Germanic law. It was augmented by later rulers, and after the union of the Lombards to the Frankish Kingdom, the capitularies made for the kingdom were applied to Italy, though there were also special capitularies, *Capitula Italica*, for Italy. Compilations were early made in Italy for the use of lawyers. Thus the contents of the edict with its accretions were arranged into a *Concordia de Singulis Causis* (830). In the tenth century was made the *Capitulare*

Langobardorum, a collection of the capitularies in use in Italy, and in the following century, under the influence of the school of law at Pavia appeared the *Liber legis Langobardorum* (also called *Liber Papiensis* and the *Lombarda*) of which there are two versions known as the *Lombarda Casinensis* and the *Lombarda Vulgata*.

The law of the Bavarians, the *Lex Baiuvariorum*, was taken in part from the law of Euric and partly from the *Lex Alamannorum* and the *Lex Salica* and dates from about 745. The *Lex Saxonum*, containing ancient customary enactments of Saxony, dates from about 802, the *Lex Thuringorum*, containing local customs and partly based on the *Capitulare legi Ribuariae additum*, is of about the same date, and there is also a mixed collection of enactments known as the *Lex Frisionum* of about the same date.[49]

Germanic law in England

As part of the great migrations westwards, Angles, Saxons and Jutes moved into south Britain and about 600 Aethelbert of Kent began to write the dooms (or judgments) of the people of Kent. Before 700 there appeared the dooms of Ine in Wessex and later Offa of Mercia is known to have published laws. There are many such bodies of law, partly statements of customary law, partly new law, in the centuries before the Norman Conquest, all in the vernacular, uninfluenced by Roman law and little influenced by canon law.[50] After the Conquest it was one of the achievements of the Angevin kings of England to build up a system and convert the laws of the Mercians, the West Saxons, the Danes and the Normans into the law of England, a task achieved chiefly by the early development of a strong central court from which itinerant justices went out to hear cases in local courts by the law common to all England, the common law of England. By the twelfth century, the king's court had become the most powerful organisation in the kingdom, a highly organised body of officials, with financial, administrative and judicial functions, and Assizes and Ordinances were being promulgated.[51]

CANON LAW

Canon law is the body of laws framed by an ecclesiastical body for its own

---

[49] See generally Canciani, *Barbarorum leges antiquae*; Walter, *Corpus juris germanici antiqui*; *Monumenta Germaniae Historica, Leges*; Brunner, *Deutsche Rechtsgeschichte*.

[50] Brunner, " The Sources of English Law," in *Essays in Anglo-American Legal History*, II, 7; Pollock, " English Law before the Norman Conquest " (1898) 14 L.Q.R. 291; Richardson and Sayles, *Law and Legislation from Aethelberht to Magna Carta*. See also Thorpe, *Ancient Laws and Institutes of England*.

[51] Mrs. Green, " The Centralisation of Norman Justice under Henry II," in *Essays in Anglo-American Legal History*, I, 111. See also Pollock and Maitland, *History of English Law*, Chap. 1; Jenks, *Law and Politics in the Middle Ages*, Chaps. 1 and 2. For development after the Conquest, see Plucknett, *Concise History of the Common Law*, Chap. 2.

regulation, and particularly the law of the Roman Church.[52] In the early centuries of the Christian Church there was no general legislation but the various communities framed rules themselves and in time collections were made in the East of decisions by councils and bishops and rather later in the West. The Churches of Britain tended to remain outside the centralising movement. In the Middle Ages the canon law was a common law for Europe sharing in the authority conceded to the Roman law on which, along with Holy Scripture, it was based. The Roman law was the temporal law of the clergy and the councils and popes drew inspiration therefrom. The canon law, like the Roman, was a principal branch of university study down to the Reformation.

The principal sources of medieval canon law were the New Testament, canons or decrees of councils, oecumenical, national or provincial, and the custom of the Church. Collections of these were made, into which forged documents sometimes found their way.

About 1148 Gratian, a monk of Bologna, published the treatise at first called the *Concordia discordantium canonum* and later the *Decretum* in which he brought together and tried to make into a coherent juridical system the vast body of texts of different periods furnished by earlier collections. Gratian drew on the existing collections, the works of the fathers and the ecclesiastical councils, and the Roman law, as well as later councils, and recent decretals down to the Lateran council of 1139, and fitted the texts into a treatise. The *Decretum* was a work of only private authority but it has subsequently been the basis of instruction in canon law in all universities, been commented on by the most illustrious canonists, and having been cited, corrected and edited by the popes has obtained an authority recognised and accepted by the Roman Church.

The disciples of Gratian collected later papal decretals into five large compilations of which the most important is the *Breviarium extravagantium* compiled about 1190 by Bernard of Pavia, and which were condensed into a single collection by Raymond of Pennaforte in 1234 under the orders of Gregory IX (*Decretales Extravagantes, i.e., extra Decretum vagantes*). Two official collections followed, one prepared by a committee of canonists under Boniface VIII and published in 1298. Since it followed the five books of Gregory IX it was called the *Liber Sextus*. The other collection was called the *Clementinae*, from Pope Clement V, and promulgated in 1314. There are also two later collections of private authority, the *Extravagantes* (*i.e., extra collectiones publicas*) of John XXII and the *Extravagantes communes* of several popes down to Sixtus IV in 1484. These various collections complete the body of law known as the *Corpus Juris*

---

[52] For the history, see *Continental Legal History Series,* Vol. I, 705–724; Munroe Smith, *Development of European Law*, 191–212.

Canonici.[53] All existed separately until gathered together by order of Pope Gregory XIII and published with official authority in 1580. The documents contained in the *Corpus Juris Canonici* were frequently published with glosses or commentaries in the margins; the common gloss on the *Decretum* is that of Joannes Teutonicus (d. 1245), but there were many other commentators on parts of the *Corpus* including Raymond of Pennaforte, Hostiensis (Henricus de Segusio, Bishop of Ostia) (d. 1271), and Panormitanus (Niccolo de' Tudeschis, Archbishop of Palermo) (d. 1445). After the Council of Trent pontifical constitutions continued to appear and a revised Codex of Canon Law was promulgated by Benedict XV in 1917.[54]

In addition the canon law included bodies of local canons, bodies of state law on ecclesiastical matters and the decisions of the Tribunal of the Rota and of the Congregations of Cardinals, while an enormous and valuable literature of commentaries grew up round the texts and decisions.

The canon law in Scotland [55] prior to the Reformation was generally that of the Continent of Europe and the usages of the Church were similar to those in France rather than in England. In the twelfth century Robert, Bishop of St. Andrews, with the consent of David I, promulgated to his clergy the *Exceptiones Ecclesiasticarum Regularum*, the lineage of which has been traced to the *Decretum* of Ivo of Chartres. Canon law was not automatically authoritative in Scotland since in the canons of her national provincial councils she possessed a canon law of her own which was recognised by parliament and the popes, and enforced in the courts. Much of it was doubtless borrowed from the *Corpus Juris Canonici* and English provincial canons, but these portions derived their authority from the Scottish Church, by adoption and not by original promulgation, and the general canon law was received only according to equity and expediency except where it had been acknowledged by parliament or decision of the courts.

In the Middle Ages the Church courts exercised wide civil jurisdiction, including all matters of marriage, legitimacy and succession, with a possible ultimate appeal to Rome. At the Reformation the canon law of marriage, legitimacy and succession was taken over by the Scottish secular

---

[53] This title is met from the twelfth century, but was not officially adopted till 1671. The best edition is by Friedberg (2 vols., Leipzig, 1879–81).

[54] On the modern canon law, see Willock, " A Civil Lawyer looks at The Canon Law " (1962) 11 I.C.L.Q. 89.

[55] For Scotland, see Baird Smith, " Canon Law," in *Sources and Literature of Scots Law*, Stair Society; Mylne, *Canon Law*; *Statuta Ecclesiae Scoticanae* (ed. Robertson); *Statutes of the Scottish Church* (ed. Patrick); Stair, I, 1, 14; Fraser on *Husband and Wife*, Introduction: *Hay's Lectures on Marriage* (Stair Society).

See also Mortimer, *Western Canon Law*; Maitland, *Roman Canon Law in the Church of England*; Moore, *Introduction to English Canon Law*; Galante, " The Modern Study of Canon Law," in *Essays in Legal History* (ed. Vinogradoff).

courts and survived almost unimpaired as part of the common law on these subjects.[56]

In Catholic countries the canon law of the Roman Church has had a continuous influence on the legal and social system, and in practically every system of law stemming from Western Europe it has been influential to some extent. " Decretals and canons of a date earlier than the fifteenth century still govern the administration of the best disciplined and, from the point of view of numbers, the greatest of all monarchies—that of the Sovereign Pontiff—and regulate the religious and social life of the three hundred millions of the faithful of whom it is composed. . . The principles developed by the Church and applied by her during the period when no one disputed her control over all civil matters in which the salvation of souls was concerned, still underlie a considerable portion of the common law of the West, and are predominant in large provinces such as those of marriage or of obligations." [57]

From the renaissance of legal studies in the eleventh century the civil law and canon law were principal subjects of study in the universities of Europe,[58] and the pre-Reformation Scottish universities were founded to study and teach, *inter alia*, civil and canon law.[59] Though since the Reformation the study of canon law has been largely abandoned in Britain, its historical importance was considerable and reference to the canonists as ultimate sources of some of the principles of modern law may still on occasion be required.[60] Public law and the law of nations, criminal law and procedure, civil law and procedure of Western Europe all owe something to canonist principles.

FEUDAL LAW

Feudalism originated in the anarchic kingdom of the Merovingian Franks in the sixth century, where bodies of retainers came to attach themselves to more powerful neighbours for protection, giving some service in return.[61] This protective relationship was constituted by commendation, and gradually each party came to have recognised obligations, the one to serve and respect his superior, the other to aid and support his vassal. It was

---

[56] *Cf.* the list of authorities cited in Fraser on *Husband and Wife*, Vol. II, p. xxxiv; see also *Collins* v. *Collins* (1884) 11 R.(H.L.) 19, 31, *per* Lord Watson.

[57] Le Bras, " Canon Law " in *Legacy of the Middle Ages.*

[58] Rashdall, *The Universities of Europe in the Middle Ages, passim.* See further Mackie, *The University of Glasgow*, 7, 27, 232–234; Grant, *Story of the University of Edinburgh*, I, 35, 63, 123, 167.

[59] Hence the degree in law (LL.B.) is still *baccalaureus utriusque juris* (*i.e.*, both civil and canon laws).

[60] See, *e.g., Kerr* v. *Martin* (1840) 2 D. 752; *Annan* v. *Annan*, 1948 S.C. 532. Notice, too, the reliance on canonists in Lord Fraser's treatise on *Husband and Wife.*

[61] See generally Vinogradoff, *Camb.Med.Hist.*, Vol. II, Chap. 20; Vol. III, Chap. 18; Ganshof, *Feudalism* (trans. Grierson); Bloch, *Feudal Society* (trans. Manyon), and " Feudalism " in *Encyc.Soc.Sc.*

often convenient to bestow on a person sufficient land to maintain him, which was done by a grant of a tenement or benefice, normally for life.

Later the institutions of vassalage and the benefice coalesced and by the time of Charlemagne persons of higher social classes had become prepared to become vassals of the king. The tracts of land granted to them enabled them to create vassals for themselves. Throughout the eighth and ninth centuries the practice spread, coupled with a steady rise in the social status of vassals, and they now included the most important persons in the land. The mutual relationship was created by a promise of fealty by the vassal to his lord. In time the services due from vassal to lord came to be better defined and more specialised and they might include duties in the lord's household or in the management of his estates, but by the ninth century military services were taking precedence over all others. It was also by then recognised that both parties had interests in the benefice, the lord as owner and the vassal as holder in benefice, and by the ninth century benefices were becoming not personal, but inheritable, if the lord confirmed the benefice to the son of the former vassal.

Charlemagne and his advisers also found vassalage a remedy for the lack of administrators, judges and trained soldiers by attaching duties to the position of vassal of a lord, of serving by advice, by administering and by doing justice among sub-vassals, and of giving military service as a mounted knight. By the classical age of feudalism, the tenth to thirteenth centuries, the relationship was worked out in detail and the vassal's tenement came to be known as his fief or fee.

Feudalism in its French form spread into England in the wake of the Norman Conquest, and into other countries.[62] In Northern Italy feudalism attained a character rather different from elsewhere and is illustrated by the *Libri Feudorum* or *Consuetudines Feudorum*,[63] a private compilation made in Lombardy about 1100 by, it is thought, a feudal judge of Milan, but this found general acceptance throughout Western Europe. Feudal relationships became more universal in England than ever in France or Germany, but in each country the rules of the feudal relationship were largely a matter of local or regional custom.

THE LAW MERCHANT

The conduct of commerce by itinerant merchants originated far back in history, particularly in Mediterranean lands and in Europe, and much business was done in medieval times at the great fairs and markets of Europe. Peripatetic merchants needed speedy resolution of their disputes,

---

[62] As to England, see Pollock and Maitland, *History of English Law before Edward I*; Round, *Feudal England*; Stenton, *The First Century of English Feudalism*; *Anglo-Saxon England*; Barrow, *Feudal Britain*.

[63] Ed. Lehmann, 1896; translated by Lord Clyde as Appendix to his translation of Craig's *Jus Feudale*.

and the gathering of merchants from many countries tended to give an international character to the principles applied. During the Middle Ages the custom of merchants seems to have been developed principally in the Mediterranean cities and in Italy. Bills of exchange were probably invented by a Florentine and were well known in the Middle Ages. Insurance was recognised early in the Middle Ages, chambers of insurance to record contracts of insurance in case of dispute being found in Barcelona in the thirteenth century, in Bruges in 1310 and in London in 1574.[64]

By the thirteenth century it was accepted in England that pleas of merchants were wont to be decided by the law merchant at boroughs and fairs and that this law was different from the common law of England. Markets and fairs had their own machinery for resolving disputes, the most famous being the courts of piepowder, specially concerned with merchants who travelled from market to market, but these were later largely superseded by courts of the staple.

Later the law merchant was administered in the English common law courts as a body of customs, to be proved as a fact in each individual case of doubt, but during the Chief Justiceship of Lord Mansfield it was incorporated into the common law, and to a substantial extent it is through following the English decisions that it has come to be incorporated in Scots law also.

Important contributions to the development of this branch of law were made by the writings of commercial men in England in the seventeenth and eighteenth centuries. Malynes' *Lex Mercatoria* (1622) treated of commercial and maritime law, money, bills and the courts in which the law merchant was administered, and set down in permanent form many of the mercantile usages and practices now becoming settled. Marius wrote a tract on bills of exchange in 1651 and in 1676 Molloy dealt with similar topics in his *De Jure Maritimo et Navali*. Later works included Beawes' *Lex Mercatoria Rediviva* (1751) which deals with the matters of trade and all the principal topics of commercial and maritime law, and Magens' essay on insurance (1755).

In England and Scotland, from the eighteenth century onwards, commercial litigation fell into the hands of the ordinary courts and the relevant principles became part of the ordinary law,[65] whereas in European countries generally, commercial law remained separate from the ordinary law and, when legal systems came to be codified, separate codes were normally enacted for civil and for commercial law.

---

[64] See generally Bewes, *Romance of the Law Merchant*; Lord Murray, " The Law Merchant " in (Stair Society) *Sources and Literature of Scots Law*, 241.

[65] In this process of incorporating the principles of the law merchant into the fabric of English law the work of Chief Justices Coke, Holt and Mansfield was of outstanding importance. For England, see generally Holdsworth, *History of English Law*, V, 60; VIII, 99; XII, 524; *Select Cases concerning the Law Merchant* (Selden Society, 3 vols.).

MARITIME LAW

The earliest traces of legal rules on maritime matters come from the Mediterranean.[66] Seaborne commerce there developed early and we know of a body of law, the *Lex Rhodia*, which grew up in the maritime centre of Rhodes two or three centuries before Christ. The *Basilica* of the late ninth century contained a collection of maritime rules and there was another, possibly earlier, collection known as the Rhodian Sea Law.[67]

Later maritime law developed as the custom of various ports and can be found in the custumals of commercial towns, later more widely adopted. Of these particularly important are the Laws or Judgments of Oleron, based on decisions of the merchant court of Oleron, probably dating from the twelfth century, which were adopted by the seaports of Normandy and Brittany, transplanted into England and copied in English compilations, such as the Black Book of the Admiralty,[68] the *Consolato del Mare* of about 1340, compiled from the customs of Barcelona and accepted in the Mediterranean, and the codes of Lubeck and Wisby, current in the Baltic and influenced by the Laws of Oleron. The Wisby sea laws are cited in Scotland in Balfour's *Practicks*. There were others too such as the sea laws of Amalfi and Trani. Welwod, Professor of Law at St. Andrews, published *The Sea Laws of Scotland*[69] in 1590 and in 1613 an *Abridgment of All the Sea Laws*.

In Scotland and England the maritime law was administered by the local Admiralty courts from early times, and also in Scotland by the Dean of Guild and the Water Bailie. It continued to partake of an international character and the main forms of maritime legal documents, such as the charterparty, were settled in outline at an early date.

In Scotland the Court of Admiralty was merged in the Court of Session in 1830, since when at least the maritime law has been administered as part of Scots law. In England the High Court of Admiralty was in 1875 made part of the Probate, Divorce and Admiralty Division of the High Court. Since 1971 it has been part of the Queen's Bench Division.

ENGLISH LAW

The development of the law of England has been as significant for the law of the modern British Commonwealth and of English-speaking parts of the world generally as the Roman law has been for most European countries

[66] See Sanborn, *Origins of the Early English Maritime and Commercial Law*; and " Maritime Law " in *Encyc.Soc.Sc.*; Holdsworth, " The Law Merchant " in *Essays in Anglo-American Legal History*, I, 289.

[67] See Ashburner, *The Rhodian Sea Law*.

[68] Ed. Sir Travers Twiss (Rolls Series). This was a collection of documents for the use of the English court of Admiralty, not earlier than the mid-fifteenth century.

[69] Reprinted in Scottish Text Society Miscellany, 1933.

and the civilisations derived therefrom.[70] The Norman Conquest and the greater power and unifying tendencies of the Norman kings were a decisive influence in creating a common law in place of the pre-existing bodies of local customary law. The kings assumed control of the administration of justice and gradually a system of courts developed out of the Curia Regis. The courts of Exchequer, Common Pleas and King's Bench successively emerged and the Norman and Angevin kings adopted the system of sending out royal justices throughout the kingdom to hold assizes, at first only for criminal but later (1285) also for civil cases, and this was a powerful factor in creating a law common to all England. The characteristic of common law procedure was that there was a separate form of initial writ for each cause of action, and the slow development of various forms of action, which went on for some six centuries, had a profound influence on the development and content of the rules of substantive law. The mode of trial depended on the form of action.

The victory of royal justice over local courts and regional customary law was completed by the rise of the Justices of the Peace in the thirteenth and fourteenth centuries. From 1363 they held sessions quarterly and Parliament regularly added duties both judicial and administrative to their original police function.

Equity

The common law thus early became hidebound by formalism, and hence became rigid and inflexible, and unable to do justice in cases not covered by an existing form of action. The practice developed of petitioning the king for a remedy. He delegated the disposal of these petitions to the Chancellor, always in medieval times an ecclesiastic, as keeper of the King's conscience. In time the Chancellor came to sit regularly to dispose of such petitions and he thereby created the Court of Chancery,[71] which tended to develop the rules for dealing consistently with particular petitions. Thus there developed a body of rules of equity and these were developed particularly by such notable Chancellors as Bacon, Nottingham, Hardwicke and Eldon, though particularly under Eldon Chancery proceedings became intolerably slow and expensive.[72] The principles administered by the Chancellors thus became over the centuries a body of rules mainly concerned to right the injustices and supply the defects of the common law, and its most significant contributions to English law were the rules relating

---

[70] On the development of English law generally, see Plucknett, *Concise History of the Common Law*; Potter, *Historical Introduction to English Law*; Pollock and Maitland, *History of English Law before the time of Edward I* (2 vols.); Holdsworth, *History of English Law* (17 vols.). See also Winfield, *Chief Sources of English Legal History*; Holdsworth, *Sources and Literature of English Law*.

[71] On the development of equity, see Plucknett, *Concise History*, Part 5; Holdsworth, *H.E.L.*, I, 395; Kerly, *Historical Sketch of the Court of Chancery*.

[72] The case of *Jarndyce v. Jarndyce* in Dickens' *Bleak House* is a not unfair picture of the slow working of the Court of Chancery in its last years.

to trusts, many of the rules as to mortgages, the remedies of injunction, specific performance and rescission. Latterly the rules of equity were as well settled and nearly as rigid as the rules of common law, though not quite so trammelled by procedural formalism but more bedevilled by prolixity and delay.

Blackstone

Important in the development was the publication of Blackstone's *Commentaries on The Laws of England* (1765–69), the most complete work hitherto written on English law, accurate in statement, lucid and elegant in exposition. " The *Commentaries* summed up, in accurate and readable form, the logical system which, with some help from the Legislature, had been built up by the legal profession throughout many centuries." [73] It summed up the law as it had developed down to the mid-eighteenth century. Though not blind to the defects of the law Blackstone tended to be satisfied with the law as it was. The book had immense influence in England and in America and remains a legal classic.

Reform in the Nineteenth Century

Extensive reform of the court system was effected in the nineteenth century, culminating in 1875 in the abolition of all the older superior courts and the creation of the modern High Court and Court of Appeal. The High Court was at first divided into five divisions (Exchequer, Common Pleas, Queen's Bench, Chancery, and Probate, Divorce and Admiralty) with jurisdictions corresponding to the separate courts which they replaced, but in 1880 the first three were amalgamated into the Queen's Bench Division. In 1971 the last was renamed the Family Division.

At that time common law and equity were nominally merged and all courts were empowered to give both legal and equitable remedies, but many traces of the former division still survive. Barristers still tend to practise in common law matters or chancery matters, which are dealt with in the divisions of the court corresponding to the old separate courts.

Local courts of limited jurisdiction had largely disappeared in England in medieval times and the modern system of county courts was created in 1846.

Expansion of the Common Law

The law of England went abroad with the Pilgrim Fathers, with later colonists in America and Canada, and later to South Africa, Australia and New Zealand. Though in time these countries, and other former British colonies, developed their own legal systems, it has generally been on the basis of English common law and equity, and in some cases there have

---

[73] Holdsworth, *Sources and Literature of English Law*, 158. On Blackstone, see also Hanbury, *The Vinerian Chair and Legal Education.*

survived abroad elements which have disappeared from the law now known in England. In Quebec the common law did not displace law based on French, ultimately on Roman, law, and in South Africa it influenced but did not supersede the Roman-Dutch law imported by the original Dutch settlers, which is the main basis of South African law.[74]

SCOTS LAW

The development of Scots law is considered in Chapter 4.

II.—LEGAL THEORY AND PHILOSOPHY OR JURISPRUDENCE

The topic of jurisprudence [75] is variously defined as the "examination of the precepts, ideals and techniques of the law in the light derived from present knowledge in disciplines other than the law " [76] or " the body of theories of and about law," [77] " the study and systematic arrangement of the general principles of law in its widest sense," [78] " the science of the first principles of the civil law . . . those more fundamental conceptions and principles which serve as the basis of the concrete details of the law." [79]

It is essentially thinking about law in general, as distinct from seeking to know what the law of any system on a particular matter is. It is concerned with such problems as the nature of law, the historical origins and development from primitive times of legal institutions and ideas generally, their relationship with other social phenomena, the relationship of law with theories of morality and of the state, the relation between law and justice and the manner in which law maintains justice, the sources of the law and their interpretation, the examination of the judicial process and the elucidation of the meaning, significance and use of such fundamental legal conceptions as the terms right, duty, obligation, ownership, possession, malice, intention, motive, liability and so on, but different jurists at

---

[74] On the expansion of the common law, see Bryce, " The Extension of Roman and English Law Throughout the World " in *Studies in History and Jurisprudence*, I, 72; volumes in the series The British Commonwealth; The Development of Its Laws and Constitutions, and since 1965 the *Annual Survey of Commonwealth Law*. On development in America, see Pound, *The Formative Era of American Law*; Wigmore (ed.), *Essays in Anglo-American Legal History* (3 vols.). Kent's *Commentaries on American Law*, founded on Blackstone, were published in 1826–30.

[75] On the meaning of the word itself, see Brown, " Ulpian's Definition of Jurisprudence " (1921) 33 J.R. 128; Campbell, " A Note on The Word Jurisprudence " (1943) 58 L.Q.R. 334. Numerous phrases are used as synonyms of jurisprudence in this sense; they include legal theory or theory of law, legal philosophy or philosophy of law, legal thought, legal science or science of law.

[76] Stone, *Province and Function of Law*, 25; *Legal Systems and Lawyer's Reasonings*, 16.

[77] Patterson, *Jurisprudence: Men and Ideas of the Law*, 1.

[78] Keeton, *Elementary Principles of Jurisprudence*, 4.

[79] Salmond, *Jurisprudence*, 2. See further Allen, " Jurisprudence—What and Why," in *Legal Duties*, 1; Pound, *Jurisprudence*, I, Chap. 1.

different times have approached these and kindred problems from very different angles and have evolved very different and contradictory theories. The one general element in all jurisprudence is the attempt to question presuppositions, to examine critically and analyse and discover the general ideas, principles and theory underlying various sets of actual rules of law.[80]

The literature of jurisprudence is enormous, frequently voluminous and obscure, and in every language, while its pursuit frequently draws heavily on disciplines, such as logic, philosophy and psychology, sociology and political theory, relatively unfamiliar to the legal student but which help to cast light on central problems of legal studies.

Furthermore, the approach of different jurists and different books is very diverse,[81] some dealing in a most abstract way with the most general notions and problems, and having little apparent connection with the legal system actually applied in any country, while others deal almost exclusively with specific systems of law to such an extent as to be in many respects little more than generalised accounts of that legal system, examining general notions entirely in the light of one particular system of law.

Broadly speaking there are three main schools of jurists, or approaches to jurisprudence [82]; the first, the oldest and most voluminous, is philosophical jurisprudence.[83] It deals with such topics as the concept of justice, and its relations with law; the distinction, if any, between the spheres of law, morality and other factors of social control; the ethical significance and validity of fundamental legal conceptions and principles; the criticism of legal institutions and problems of legal reform. This approach has been favoured more on the Continent than in Britain and frequently by scholars who were philosophers primarily rather than jurists, and whose theories of law reflect their philosophical positions. This approach comprises within itself many different and even conflicting theories, arrived at from different philosophic standpoints.

The second is analytical jurisprudence, which has found greatest favour in the English-speaking countries.[84] It has been profoundly influenced by its founder John Austin,[85] and since his time analytical jurisprudence has

---

[80] It is sometimes denied that any principles can be discovered at all: see, *e.g.*, Harvey, " A Job for Jurisprudence " (1944) 7 M.L.R. 42, and the reply, Kennedy, " Another Job for Jurisprudence " (1945) 8 M.L.R. 21.

[81] See Vinogradoff, " The Study of Jurisprudence," in *Collected Papers*, II, 205, and " Aims and Methods of Jurisprudence," *ibid.* 319; Allen, " Jurisprudence—What and Why," in *Legal Duties*, 1.

[82] Stone, *Province and Function of Law*, Chap. 1, pp. 182–187.

[83] Some leading figures of this school are St. Thomas Aquinas, Grotius, Bentham, Kant, Hegel, Jhering, Lorimer, Stammler, del Vecchio, Geny, Duguit.

[84] In fact Austin owed a great deal to Jeremy Bentham. Leading figures include Austin, Markby, Holland, Salmond.

[85] 1790–1859: Professor of Jurisprudence at University College, London, 1826–32; *The Province of Jurisprudence Determined* was first published in 1832. On Austin, see further the article in D.N.B., Vol. II, by Sir John Macdonell; Sarah Austin's Memoir in fifth edition of his *Lectures on Jurisprudence*, and the Introduction to the 1954 edition of the *Province* (ed. Hart) in the Library of Ideas.

usually been regarded in English-speaking countries as the main topic of juristic speculation. It proceeds mainly by seeking to resolve a legal system into its fundamental conceptions, such as rights, obligation, possession, and subjecting these to close examination. Accordingly it relies largely on logic and semantics. But disregard of the moral and social implications of law tends to reduce purely analytical jurisprudence to arid formalism so that it cannot usefully be pursued alone and the later followers of Austin have not avoided all questions of the rightness of law and its relation to justice. A modern development which is the highest development of analytical positivism is the Pure Theory of Hans Kelsen.

The third is sociological jurisprudence, which has been developed very largely in America in the present century.[86] It studies particularly the interaction between social forces and the law, and the ways in which law works and gives effect to the different claims, interests, rights and duties of men interacting in society. This school of jurisprudence has to a large extent superseded and taken over from the nineteenth-century school of historical jurisprudence [87] which was primarily concerned with the manner of growth of legal systems, their evolution and organic development and the evaluation of the various sources and influences which had contributed to their forms and characteristics.[88] One branch of this approach examines law and legal institutions from the Marxist standpoint. Another, the realist movement, concentrates on the way people behave in relation to law.

The importance of jurisprudence cannot be overestimated. It is a fundamental branch of legal study, though too frequently it receives inadequate attention, and legal study generally pays too much attention to dogmatic rules of law. " Philosophy of law lies at the base of all divisions of legal science." [89] " This neglect of legal theory and philosophy, added to a concentration on the substantive rules of law, must inevitably lead to a failure by the general body of lawyers, to appreciate not only the nature and purpose of law but also the place of law among the other social sciences.

---

[86] Leading figures are Pound, Frank, Llewellyn and Stone. Sociological jurisprudence is connected with but distinct from sociology of law which is the sociological analysis of the phenomena of law, such as courts and judges, legislators and lawyers, law-abiding and law-breaking, of the relations between law and society, conflict resolution, and the functioning of law. See Ehrlich, *Fundamental Principles of the Sociology of Law*; Timasheff, *Introduction to the Sociology of Law*; Sawer, *Law in Society*; Selznik " Sociology of Law " in *Int.Encyc.Soc.Sc.*

[87] Some writers treat the historical school as a distinct, fourth, school of jurisprudence.

[88] See further Kantorowicz, " Savigny and the Historical School of Law " (1938) 53 L.Q.R. 326. Leading figures are Savigny, Puchta, Maine, Bryce and Vinogradoff.

[89] Kocourek, *An introduction to the Science of Law* 3.

" We have entered upon a period of profound social and legal adjustments—particularly in the department of social legislation. Yet the general body of English lawyers is wholly untrained in legal science." [90]

It is true that law is a practical matter, but " the law is not identical with the science of the law. Every science is essentially theory; at the very basis of every action, however practical, is always theory, and no science is possible without philosophy." [91]

Jurisprudence, moreover, is not without practical utility and the most fundamentally important cases frequently turn on an essentially jurisprudential point, such as the scope and purpose of the criminal law,[92] or the morality of penalising an attempt at rescue,[93] or the liability to punishment of a person of " diminished responsibility." [94] Similarly the reform of the law of divorce, or abortion, or sexual offences raises jurisprudential and moral problems.

III.—COMPARATIVE LEGAL STUDIES

Despite its name comparative law is neither a body of law nor a branch or department of the law of any country and it would be better named comparative legal studies.[95] It is rather a technique of study and research originating from the facts that different countries have different systems and rules of law, applying different legal solutions to very similar problems, and that it is enlightening and stimulating to see what these other solutions are, so as not to fall into the easy error of thinking that the solution propounded by one's own legal system is the best or the natural or the only one.[96] This involves obtaining at least a general acquaintance with the judicial structure and the sources, literature and main principles of some foreign systems of law. Not only complete legal systems but any major branches of several legal systems can usefully be compared; thus study

---

[90] Parry, " Economic Theories in English Case Law," 47 L.Q.R. 183, 186. Note that the terms legal science and science of law are sometimes used, as here, in the narrow sense of legal theory or jurisprudence.

[91] Kunz, " The American Science of International Law," in *Law: A Century of Progress*, II, 166 at 182.

[92] *Shaw* v. *D.P.P.* [1962] A.C. 220.

[93] *Steel* v. *Glasgow Iron and Steel Co.*, 1944 S.C. 237.

[94] *Kirkwood* v. *H.M. Advocate*, 1939 J.C. 36.

[95] The best general introduction to the subject is Gutteridge, *Comparative Law*, 2nd ed., 1949. See also Derrett (ed.), *An Introduction to Legal Systems*; David and Brierley, *Major Legal Systems in the World Today*; Buckland and McNair, *Roman Law and Common Law*, 2nd ed. by Lawson; Lawson, *A Common Lawyer looks at the Civil Law*; Schmitthoff, " The Science of Comparative Law " (1939) 7 C.L.J. 95; Lord Cooper, " The Importance of Comparative Law in Scotland," in *Selected Papers*, 142; Lord Macmillan, " Scots Law as a subject of Comparative Study " (1933) 48 L.Q.R. 477.

[96] *Cf.* Lepaulle, " The Function of Comparative Law " (1922) 35 H.L.R. 838, 858; Gutteridge, " The Value of Comparative Law " (1931) J.S.P.T.L. 26.

may be directed to comparative constitutions, comparative law of contract, of delict, of matrimonial property or of criminal procedure.[97]

The function of comparative legal study is variously said to be the ascertainment of principles common to all civilised systems of law, or the discovery of the causes which underlie the development and extinction of legal institutions, or the promotion of unification of legal rules followed in civilised communities, but in fact the comparative method is sufficiently elastic to embrace all activities concerned with the study of foreign law, the resemblances and differences between different legal systems and the results achieved by different legal methods, techniques and principles applied to fundamentally similar problems.[98] This study may have practical as well as cultural value as the increase in international intercourse today more frequently requires some appreciation of foreign legal doctrines and conceptions or at least awareness of the salient characteristics of the other systems involved. So too comparative study may suggest ways of law reform or a solution for problems not hitherto determined in the student's own system. Traditionally Scots law has been developed and studied comparatively, and the institutional writers, particularly Stair and Bankton, have a strongly developed comparative approach.[99]

Most of the world's developed legal systems fall conveniently into two families, those which are derived ultimately from the Civil or Roman law, or have absorbed it as a principal ingredient in their modern developed system, and those based on the common law, which, Germanic in origin, was developed from the eleventh century by the English courts and spread over the world with the English people and language.[1] The former is the foundation or a principal element in the law of modern continental Europe, Central and South America, Quebec, Louisiana, South Africa, Ceylon and Scotland,[2] and French, Dutch, Spanish and Portuguese colonies and settlements; the latter is the basis of the law of England and Wales, Ireland, the United States (except Louisiana and Porto Rico), Canada (except Quebec), Australia and New Zealand, of the former British India (except over Hindus and Mohammedans as to inheritance and family law) and generally in British colonies. While there is this familial distinction, some systems, basically of the Roman law family, have been and are being much

---

[97] *Cf.* Hazeltine, " The Study of Comparative Legal History " (1927) J.S.P.T.L. 27.

[98] *Cf.* Walton, " The Study of Foreign Laws " (1934) 46 J.R. 1; Gutteridge, " Comparative Law and the Law of Nations " (1944) 21 B.Y.I.L. 1.

[99] *Cf.* Lord Cooper, " The Importance of Comparative Law in Scotland," in *Selected Papers,* 142.

[1] See Schlesinger, *Comparative Law; Cases and Materials, passim*; von Mehren, *The Civil Law System,* Chap. 1; Symposium on " The Migration of the Common Law " (1960) 76 L.Q.R. 41. See also Wigmore, *Panorama of the World's Legal Systems,* 3 vols.

[2] Rene David, *Introduction à l'Etude du Droit privé de l'Angleterre,* 164, characterises Scots law as " très different du droit anglais," and Levy Ullman, " The Law of Scotland " (1925) 37 Jur.Rev. 370, described it as " absolutely Roman in character."

influenced by common law conceptions and methods, as in the cases of Scotland, Louisiana and South Africa.[3] Since 1945 the system of law developed since 1917 in Russia has been extended as a concomitant of military occupation to all the countries of Eastern Europe and has transformed their legal systems into systems on the Russian model [4] while Communist China has also radically changed its legal system in the same general direction and made it an agency for changing its society.[5] The Scandinavian countries have distinct legal systems which embody features characteristic of both civil law and common law countries.[6] Islamic law, based on the Koran, is a powerful influence in North Africa and the Middle East,[7] and former colonial territories in Africa, on gaining independence, commonly develop legal systems incorporating elements of Islamic or tribal law and of civil or common law from the legal system of the former governing European power.

IV.—PUBLIC INTERNATIONAL LAW

Legal rules regulating international relations and the practices of states *inter se* have existed from a very early period,[8] but modern international law is a product of the turbulent sixteenth and seventeenth centuries which witnessed the break-up of the medieval community of mankind under the Pope and the Emperor and the emergence of independent nation-states, each administered by a separate government with its own particular law, as part of the turmoil produced by the Renaissance and the Reformation.[9] Thus there grew up a body of " rules which determine the conduct of the general body of civilised states in their mutual dealings." [10] The name International Law was invented by Jeremy Bentham in 1780.[11] It may now be described as " the body of customary and conventional rules which are considered legally binding by civilised states in their intercourse with each

---

[3] Amos, " The Common Law and the Civil Law in the British Commonwealth of Nations " (1937) 50 H.L.R. 1249. *Cf.* Lawson, *Rational Strength of English Law*, 5; Jolowicz, " The Civil Law in Louisiana " [1954] *Curr.Leg. Problems*, 1; Hahlo and Kahn, *South Africa: the Development of Its Laws*.
[4] See further Gsovski and Grzybowski, *Government, Law and Courts in the Soviet Union and Eastern Europe*, 2 vols.
[5] Buxbaum, " Preliminary Trends in the Development of the Legal Institutions of Communist China " (1962) 11 I.C.L.Q. 1.
[6] Orfield, *The Growth of Scandinavian Law*; Gomard, " Civil Law, Common Law and Scandinavian Law " (1961) 5 *Scand. Studies in Law*, 27.
[7] Anderson, *Islamic Law in Africa*.
[8] See, *e.g.*, I Samuel xv, 18; II Samuel xii, 31; Greek and Roman instances cited in Holland, *Lectures on International Law*, 10–15; Vinogradoff, " Historical Types in International Law," in *Collected Papers*, II, 248; and generally Walker, *History of the Law of Nations*; Nussbaum, *Short History of the Law of Nations*; Butler and Maccoby, *Development of International Law*.
[9] Lawrence, *Principles of International Law*, Chap. 2; Pollock in 12 Camb.Mod. Hist., Chap. 22.
[10] Lawrence, *Principles of International Law* (7th ed.), 1.
[11] *Principles of Morals and Legislation*, Chap. xvii, s. xxv.

other," [12] or " the body of rules and usages which among civilised independent states are recognised as binding upon their several governments in their dealings with one another and with each other's subjects," [13] or " the principles and rules of conduct declaratory thereof which states feel themselves bound to observe, and, therefore, do commonly observe in their relations with each other." [14]

The modern system dates from the publication in 1625 of Hugo Grotius' *De Jure Belli ac Pacis* [15] though the system had been taking shape in the works of such jurists as Vitoria, Suarez, Ayala and Gentilis in the previous century. The immediate source of his work was to be found in the barbarities of the European Wars of Religion and particularly of the Thirty Years War (1618–48). The first result of the Peace of Westphalia which ended that war was the formal recognition of a society of independent nations occupying defined territory, equal before the law, and transacting with one another as principal parties without reference to Pope or Emperor. Since that time general congresses of states, the practice of establishing embassies and legations at the courts of other states, and diplomatic, commercial and legal relations between states have become formalised. International law accordingly has come to be the body of rules which regulates the actions of civilised states in their dealings with one another, defining the essentials of state personality, the conditions under which states are recognised as coming into existence or disappearing, their rights, duties and privileges *inter se* in time of peace and war, as amicable partners, as belligerents and as neutrals.

This body of law was built up largely from the writings of jurists, such as the followers of Grotius, men such as Pufendorf,[16] Thomasius,[17] Burlamaqui,[18] Wolff,[19] Vattel,[20] Bynkershoek [21] and von Martens.[22] They based their work originally largely on Roman law, theology, canon law and the concept of a " law of nature," and, later, on developing usages.

[12] Oppenheim, *International Law*, I, 4.

[13] Pollock in 12 Camb.Mod.Hist., 703.

[14] Hyde, *International Law*, I, 1; see further Lauterpacht, *The Function of Law in the International Community*.

[15] Hugo de Groot or Grotius: 1585–1645: scholar and jurist; Grand Pensionary of West Friesland and Holland: Swedish ambassador to France, 1634–44. See Lauterpacht, " The Grotian Tradition in International Law " (1946) 23 B.Y.I.L. 1; and Oppenheim, *International Law*, I, 79 *et seq.*

[16] 1632–94; Professor of the Law of Nature and Nations at Heidelberg, 1661; Professor of Jurisprudence at Lund, 1670; *De jure naturae et gentium*, 1672; historiographer at Stockholm, 1677, and at Berlin, 1688.

[17] 1655–1728; Professor at Leipzig and later at Halle; *Fundamenta juris naturae et gentium*, 1705.

[18] 1694–1748; *Principes de droit naturel*, 1747.

[19] 1679–1754; *Institutiones juris naturae et gentium*, Halle, 1750.

[20] 1714–67; *Le droit des gens*, 1758.

[21] 1673–1743; *De dominio maris*, 1702; *De foro legatorum*, 1721; *Questionum juris publici libri duo*, 1737.

[22] 1756–1821; *Précis du droit des gens modernes de l'Europe*, 1788.

It must be remembered that it is disputable how far international law is properly called law in the strict sense of that word in respect that it lacks some of the usually accepted criteria of law.[23]   Thus there is no legislative body which promulgates rules of law, authoritatively declaring the true rule and altering previous rules; there is only a rudimentary and frequently ineffective system of sanction or compulsion in case of disobedience; and the jurisdiction of international tribunals is limited and their decisions are frequently flouted or ignored, and are not enforceable to anything like the same extent as those of domestic tribunals. To a large extent international law is still the custom and practice of nations, a body of rules binding so far as accepted, and for that reason it is still commonly defined in terms of rules and standards of conduct rather than of law.

Thus Hall[24] defines international law as consisting in " certain rules of conduct which modern civilised states regard as being binding on them in their relations with one another with a force comparable in nature and degree to that binding the conscientious person to obey the laws of his country, and which they also regard as being enforceable by appropriate means in case of infringement." In fact, however, this controversy is academic and international law is increasingly and now usually regarded as law, though still underdeveloped in comparison with state law in respect of definiteness and enforcement, and it is being increasingly accepted expressly as binding on states. " The best evidence for the existence of international law is that every actual state recognises that it does exist and that it is itself under an obligation to observe it. States may often violate international law just as individuals often violate municipal law; but no more than individuals do states defend their violations by claiming that they are above the law." [25]

In modern times the practice and custom of states, treaties, alliances and conventions, ordinances of particular states, opinions of jurists to their governments and decisions of international tribunals and courts have added substantially to the volume of law recognised, while more recently the growth and development of international institutions and agencies has also contributed a large volume of new law.[26] The Hague Conferences of 1899 and 1907 reduced to written form many of the rules hitherto unwritten, such as the rights and duties of neutral states. The League of Nations and the United Nations Organisation and their respective subsidiary organs, including the Permanent Court of International Justice

---

[23] See also Ago, " Positive Law and International Law " (1957) 51 A.J.I.L. 691.
[24] *Treatise on International Law*, 8th ed., I.
[25] Brierley, *Outlook for International Law*, 5; see also Fitzmaurice, " Foundations of the Authority of International Law and the Problem of Enforcement " (1956) 19 M.L.R. 1; McNair, " General Principles of Law Recognised by Civilised Nations " (1957) 33 B.Y.I.L. 1.
[26] See Lauterpacht, *The Development of International Law by the International Court.*

(1921) and the International Court of Justice (1946), have made much new law,[27] while increasing international intercourse has continually raised fresh problems.

International administrative, social and economic organisations have developed enormously in the past century and such bodies as the Universal Postal Union (1878) and the International Labour Organisation (1919) have added great volumes to the body of international agreement, while the growth of population, science, industry, commerce, foreign trade and investment in recent times have made international relations even more complex and more in need of legal regulation.[28] The body of law relating to international organisations and peaceful relations now greatly outweighs the subjects of war and neutrality which bulk so largely in the older books. But international law is still a long way short of the developed state attained by the municipal law of the more advanced countries.

Moreover in modern times international law is ceasing to be primarily a body of law between states but " increasingly includes cross-frontier-relationships of individual organisations and corporate bodies which call for appropriate legal regulation on an international basis,[29] problems of economic and technological interdependence requiring the regulation on the basis of common rules of matters which do not *per se* involve inter-state relations in any real sense, and rights designed to protect the individual, and in some cases organisations, with a measure of protection against the individual member states of the international community." [30]   Most modern international law is treaty law, indeed international legislation, and increasingly it deals with trade, commerce, finance and trans-frontier aspects of topics of private law,[31] while the influence of juristic writing in developing international law is diminishing.

V.—SUPRANATIONAL LAW

Supranational law arises where a group of states, without entering into any kind of federation or union, have created new institutions and transferred part of their national sovereign powers thereto; these institutions are not properly international, but only regional and limited in membership, yet

---

[27] See also Lauterpacht, *Private Law Sources and Analogies of International Law*; " Decisions of Municipal Courts as a Source of International Law " (1939) 16 B.Y.I.L. 65; *Development of International Law by the International Court, passim*.

[28] See generally Ball and Killough, *International Relations*.

[29] *e.g.*, the International Civil Aviation Organisation.

[30] Jenks, " The Scope of International Law " (1954) 31 B.Y.I.L. 1.

[31] Jennings, " The State of International Law Today " (1957) 4 J.S.P.T.L.(N.S.) 95; see also Jennings, " The Progressive Development of International Law " (1947) 24 B.Y.I.L. 301; McNair, " International Law in Great Britain, 1920–70 " (1971) 87 L.Q.R. 173.

their organisations and its law are above and wider than national law; it is intermediate in generality between international and national law.[32]

Since 1945, particularly in the face of the Russian threat to the independence of Western European countries, there has been a developing movement for the integration of these countries, towards a goal described by Sir Winston Churchill in 1946 as a " United States of Europe." The first European organisation was created by the Brussels Treaty of 1948 between Britain, France and the Benelux countries, followed closely by the Organisation for European Economic Cooperation in response to the American Marshall Plan to aid the recovery of Europe. In 1949 the Council of Europe was set up by these five countries along with Italy, Ireland and the three Scandinavian countries, with a Committee of Ministers and a Consultative Assembly which can, however, only recommend to member governments.[33] In 1954 the Brussels Treaty Organisation was enlarged and converted into Western European Union, a defence organisation, itself largely superseded since 1955 by NATO.[34] In 1960 a convention for the formation of the Organisation for Economic Cooperation and Development was signed; this included the U.S.A. and Canada and converted OEEC into an Atlantic Organisation (OECD).

The Assembly of the Council of Europe promoted a European Convention for the Protection of Human Rights and Fundamental Freedoms in 1950[35] to be guaranteed by a European Court of Human Rights,[36] and a European Commission of Human Rights, while a separate European Social Charter, dealing with social and economic rights, was signed in 1961, and in 1952 the Assembly adopted a recommendation for the establishment of a European Court of Justice and a European Act for the peaceful settlement of disputes, but later the International Court was put in place of the proposed European Court. The Assembly has also worked on a number of other Conventions of legal importance.

The European Communities

In 1951 France, Germany, Italy, Belgium, Holland and Luxembourg by a Treaty of Paris successfully formed the European Coal and Steel Com-

---

[32] For the meaning of the term " supranational " see Robertson, *European Institutions*, pp. 105–108. See also Efron and Nanes, " The Common Market and Euratom Treaties: Supranationality and the Integration of Europe " (1957) 6 I.C.L.Q. 670.

[33] See generally Robertson, *The Council of Europe*.

[34] France left NATO in 1967 and in consequence NATO headquarters were moved to Brussels.

[35] This is distinct from the United Nations Universal Declaration of Human Rights (1948) on which see Lauterpacht, *International Law and Human Rights*, Chap. 17. See further Robertson, " The Legal Work of the Council of Europe " (1961) 10 I.C.L.Q. 143.

[36] See Waldock, " The European Convention for the Protection of Human Rights and Fundamental Freedoms " (1958) 34 B.Y.I.L. 356; Robertson, " The European Court of Human Rights " (1959) 9 A.J.Comp.L. 1.

munity (ECSC) to pool their resources of iron, steel and coal in a single market without frontier barriers, and in 1957 they signed two treaties of Rome [37] and thereby established the European Economic Community (EEC), (the Common Market), planning an area in which goods, persons, services and capital could move freely without hindrance at national frontiers by tariffs or import restrictions, and the European Atomic Energy Community (Euratom).

These three communities had each a High Authority (ECSC) or Executive Commission (EEC and Euratom) as executive, and a Council. In 1967 the executives were merged into a single European Commission, and they have a single Council of Ministers, one European Parliamentary Assembly and one Court of Justice for all three. All, like some other international organisations, report to the Assembly of the Council of Europe. So too does such a body as the International Institute for the Unification of Private Law. Outside the Common Market the United Kingdom took the lead in forming the European Free Trade Association (EFTA), to establish a free market between its members.[38] Greece and Turkey subsequently sought to be associated with EEC and in 1961 the United Kingdom announced its intention to seek to join EEC and, in 1962, also to join ECSC and Euratom. These approaches were rejected by the European Community at the instance of France, and a further application to join in 1967 was similarly rejected but in 1973 the United Kingdom, Ireland and Denmark joined the three communities.[39] Other countries, such as Malta, have sought association with the European Communities.

The communities thus set up are supranational and have personality under international law. The Council of Ministers, which acts as executive, takes the policy decisions and seeks to co-ordinate the policies of the national governments and those of the Communities as a whole; the Commission has functions of initiative, preparation, decision and execution; the European Parliament meets at Strasbourg, to which the European Commission reports; and the Court of Justice of the Community, sitting at Luxembourg, has to decide whether decisions of the executives and of the Council of Ministers must be annulled and other problems of the legal interpretation of the various treaties. The judgments of the court have the force of law in the community and are directly enforceable on individuals, firms, governments and the European Commission.[40] There are also various consultative committees, *e.g.* on transport or monetary problems.

---

[37] The text of the Paris and Rome Treaties is printed in Sweet & Maxwell's *European Community Treaties*.

[38] See European Free Trade Association Convention (Cmnd. 906, 1960) and European Free Trade Association Act 1960.

[39] European Communities Act 1972.

[40] They are reported in Britain in the *Common Market Law Reports* (1962–), and in the *Recueil de la Jurisprudence de la Cour* (1954–).

The Communities each have legal personality in the law of each member state, but their institutions do not.

As a body which is a distinct legal entity the communities (taken together) have from their foundation been creating a body of law regulating their own organisation and those aspects of the life and work of the member states controlled by the Communities.

A declared object as well as a practical necessity, of the developing European Communities is the approximation of national systems of law, starting with the protection of industrial property and the development of a European law of patents, trade-marks, designs and models, and the development of a common law on bankruptcy, companies, the enforcement of judgments, and so on. British membership also has constitutional significance in involving constitutional limitations on the sovereign powers of Parliament. The political implications of these developments indicate that the developing economic unification of Europe is only a stage towards greater political unification or federation. Thus there is clearly developing a body of law within the European Community distinct both from International Law and also from the national systems of the constituent states. It will come increasingly to affect the legal relations of individuals and the legal systems of the countries. The increasing intercourse between the countries will also give rise to a sharply increased number of problems of international private law, while domestic courts will also have to apply Community Law in certain circumstances since the Treaty of Rome makes Community Law a part of the municipal law of each member state. An understanding of the salient principles and general structure of the domestic legal systems of other Community countries will similarly become of increasing importance.

VI.—STATE OR MUNICIPAL LAW

The bodies of state, national, domestic, civil or municipal law [41] comprise the whole body of doctrines, principles and rules accepted, applied and enforced in a particular state or political community. They are what are commonly called the law of the particular country.[42] Every state and territory recognised as a political entity possesses a whole apparatus of state law which may differ very substantially from that in an adjacent state; indeed many states, such as the United Kingdom and the United States, have several distinct bodies of municipal law in force in different parts of the one state. There are therefore several hundred bodies of municipal law in the world. The similarities and differences were in practice

---

[41] State law is sometimes called civil, as being enacted by a *civitas* or state, or municipal, which originally connoted laws binding *municipia*, or dependent states, but was later extended also to laws enacted by sovereign states: Ersk. I, 1, 18.

[42] *Cf.* Mackenzie, *Inst.* I, 1, 6; " Civil or Municipal Laws are the particular Laws and Customs of every Nation, or People, who are under one Sovereign Power."

formerly dictated by the origins, sources and historical borrowings of the legal system in the state in question and by the existence in many cases of federal or common legislative bodies and final courts of appeal. In modern times differences are dictated more by different social and economic conditions and the different policies pursued by the political superiors in the state in question.

Since there are numerous distinct and independent political communities in the world each having and enforcing its own legal system or systems it is unfortunately true that legal science is not a unified body of knowledge like medical or engineering science which, learned in one country, is valid everywhere. While there are affinities between certain legal systems there is a greater or lesser measure of distinctness so that one state's legal system differs from every other at least in details and sometimes in fundamentals too. For practical purposes accordingly students of law must confine themselves to an intimate knowledge of one or two systems of law with, at most, a general knowledge of some others, and an understanding of those elements of legal thought common to many, if not all, actual systems of law, and of the international and supranational law which holds as between the distinct political communities themselves.

The Subject-Matter of Municipal Law

The subject-matter of these doctrines, principles and rules is rights and duties, that is, those claims, powers, privileges, immunities and other advantages conferred on persons over and against other persons, and those burdens, liabilities and disabilities which are imposed and incumbent on persons in relation to other persons. Those rules of law are binding on all persons in the country under the common authority of the state and are administered by the courts, being invoked as need arises sometimes by a public official, sometimes by an aggrieved individual seeking redress. Thus if A enters a shop and buys a book, the law confers on him a right to obtain delivery of the book, which right it will enforce at his instance, if need be, and imposes on him a duty to pay the agreed price, which duty it will enforce, if need be, at the instance of the bookseller, and it imposes on the bookseller a duty to hand over the book and a right to recover the price.[43] In the majority of cases, of course, people implement their legal rights and duties without compulsion or resort to the courts. The classification, analysis and examination of these concepts of rights and duties is an important element of jurisprudence, but cannot be pursued further here.[44]

It is important to discover the scientific analytical arrangement of the legal principles in force in one community. It reveals that the body of law

[43] Pollock, *First Book of Jurisprudence*, Chap. 4.
[44] See further Holland, *Jurisprudence*, 13th ed., Chap. 7; Salmond, *Jurisprudence*, 12th ed., Chaps. 10–11; Dias, *Jurisprudence*, Chap. 8.

is an ordered system with a coherent logical structure. The mass of legal principles may be classified in various ways.[45] Classification is important as facilitating study, as showing the logical structure of the legal system and permitting scientific examination of its doctrines and principles, and is specially important where legal problems involving a foreign element are present.[46] The method and accuracy of classification of the principles and the cases to which they apply may be of great practical importance. The choice of remedy, or of which court should be approached to grant it may depend on whether a claim is classified as of one kind or another. The same classification is not applicable to all systems of municipal law, because the way a given system groups and classifies its doctrines and rules is usually affected by its history. But certain broad divisions are so commonly found as to deserve mention.

Public Law and Private Law

State law may be divided first into Public Law and Private Law.[47] While the distinction has been current since the time of the Greeks and of the Roman law at least, and is commonly accepted and generally understood, its basis is difficult to define and different jurists distinguish the two bodies of law in different ways, while there is not complete agreement as to whether certain topics should be placed under the one head or the other. One explanation is that public law regulates relations between superior and inferior, private law relations between equal persons. Again it is said that the division corresponds to the twofold activity of the state, in providing an organisation of government and means for the maintenance of order and the repression of disorder, and on the other hand providing machinery for the settlement of disputes and the resolution of conflicts of interest between private persons.[48] Questions between the state and the individual, however, give rise to some difficulty of classification.

Again it is generally true that a mark of public law is that the state or a state department is a party to the legal relationship or controversy, while private law applies as between private individuals.[49] But this test is not by any means invariable since in many legal relationships the state and its agencies are subjected to the ordinary principles of private law, as in owning property and making commercial contracts. Hence " public law

---

[45] See Markby, *Elements of Law*, Chap. 7; Holland, *Jurisprudence*, Chap. 9; Salmond, *Jurisprudence*, Appx. III; Jolowicz, *Lectures on Jurisprudence*, Part III; Paton, *Textbook of Jurisprudence*, 4th ed., Chap. 11; Pound, " Classification of Law " (1934) 11 N.Y.U.L.Q.R. 319.

[46] Hence in international private law (conflict of laws) careful classification of the problem-situation is essential.

[47] On this see further Jones, *Historical Introduction to the Theory of Law*, 139–163; Jolowicz, *Roman Foundations of Modern Law*, Chap. 7; and *Lectures on Jurisprudence*, Chap. 21; Mitchell, " Public law and private law " (1905) 17 J.R. 30.

[48] Keeton, *Elementary Principles of Jurisprudence*, 2nd ed., 227–228.

[49] This was the view of Holland, *Jurisprudence*, 13th ed., 128–129.

comprises the rules which specially relate to the structure, powers, rights and activities of the state. Private law includes all the residue of legal principles. It comprises all those rules which specially concern the subjects of the state in their relations to each other together with those rules which are common to the state and its subjects." [50] Markby [51] in explanation of the distinction drawn in Justinian's *Institutes*,[52] wrote: " Public law is that portion of law in which our attention is directed mainly to the state; private law is that in which it is mainly directed to the individual. I do not think that it means that these topics are capable of exact separation; but that our attitude changes in regard to them. And, according as we assume one attitude or the other, we call law public or private." Pollock [53] expressed the view: " No rule of law can be said, in the last resort, to exist merely for the benefit of the state or merely for the benefit of the individual. But some departments of legal rules have regard in the first instance to the protection and interests of the commonwealth, others to those of its individual members . . . The topics of public and private law are by no means mutually exclusive."

This division is not accordingly wholly clear-cut and there is no essential or inherent difference in nature between the two kinds of law; both may be relevant in particular cases and both come before the same courts; accordingly some would deny the existence of the division, though its general convenience causes it usually to be retained.

Law and Equity

English private law down to 1875 drew a fairly clear distinction between rules of law, or of common law, which were those developed by the King's courts, and equity, which were the rules developed by the Chancellors in the Courts of Chancery or of equity. Thus there came to be legal rights and equitable rights, legal remedies and equitable remedies, and so on, which sometimes overlapped and sometimes conflicted.[54] In 1875 the Judicature Acts abolished the dualism of courts and merged the administration of common law and equity, but did not merge the substantive rules or the rights and remedies, though providing that in cases of conflict the rules of equity should prevail.

This distinction between law and equity was carried over into most of the systems of law founded on English law and still survives in some of them to a greater extent than it does in England. The distinction has, however, never been known in Scots law nor in any system based on Roman law.

---

[50] Salmond, *Jurisprudence*, 506.

[51] *Elements of Law*, 151.

[52] Inst. I, 1, 4. *Jus publicum est quod ad statum rei Romanae spectat, jus privatum quod ad singulorum utilitatem pertinet.*

[53] *First Book of Jurisprudence*, Chap. 4, reprinted in *Jurisprudence and Legal Essays*.

[54] On its origins and development, see p. 63, *supra*.

Civil and Commercial Law

Systems of law, such as the French and the German, which have been strongly influenced by the Roman civil law, commonly divide private law into separate bodies of civil and commercial laws representing fundamentally rules derived from the (Roman) civil law, applicable to ordinary persons, and rules derived from the laws merchant and maritime, applicable to persons engaged in business. Thus French and German laws both have separate Civil and Commercial Codes. This distinction has no significance in Scots or English law.

Civil and Criminal Law

Another fundamental division is that into civil [55] and criminal law,[56] or into civil, administrative and criminal law. This is a cross-division which sub-divides each of public and private law. This distinction is fundamentally one of procedure since the classification of any subject depends mainly on whether infringements and infractions of the rules are pursued in civil courts by civil procedure for the purpose of obtaining a remedy, such as payment of a debt, an award of damages, a divorce, the stopping of a wrong, or the like, or in criminal courts by criminal procedure for the purpose of punishing the wrongdoer, deterring him and others from offending similarly, and maintaining peace, order and the safety of person and property. In fact most legal relationships give rise to remedies in the civil courts only. In the sphere of wrongs there is no universal touchstone by which one can classify some wrongs and injuries as essentially offences against the state or the community at large, or merely against private persons, dealt with respectively in criminal courts by criminal procedure and by civil courts under civil procedure. Some wrongful acts may be either, and pursued in either or even in both ways; many others are one or other only, but the only guidance which can be given as to whether or not a particular course of conduct is a crime, and therefore of concern to the criminal law, is to discover whether or not it is conduct which the state power on behalf of the community has determined to repress and punish

---

[55] The uses of the term " civil law " are numerous and confusing. The main ones are (i) the civil law of Rome, as opposed to the canon law—*Corpus Juris Civilis* and *Corpus Juris Canonici*, the twin subjects of legal study in the Middle Ages; (ii) the civil law of Rome as opposed to the praetorian law—*jus civile* and *jus praetorium*; (iii) civil law as opposed to common law, with reference to the main families of legal systems; (iv) civil (or municipal or state) law as opposed to international law; (v) civil law as opposed to martial or military law (on this see *Green* v. *Lord Advocate*, 1918 S.C. 667); (vi) civil law as opposed to criminal law; (vii) civil law as opposed to ecclesiastical law.

[56] See further on this distinction Salmond, *Jurisprudence*, 507.

by fine and imprisonment.[57] If not, if it is left to the individual to work out a remedy himself by action in the civil courts, the conduct is not criminal nor of concern to the criminal law.

In most developed states today this procedural division is incomplete in that many rights such as to social security benefits are conferred by administrative law and disputes relative thereto determined neither by civil nor by criminal courts but by administrative tribunals.[58] Administrative law is like civil rather than criminal law in nature and content, but is distinct in respect of administration and adjudication. This division might accordingly be regarded as tripartite rather than bipartite.

The volume of civil law is enormously greater and more heterogeneous than the criminal law and for this reason this division is not very helpful since it merely segregates the criminal law from the whole mass. Of greater interest is the issue whether the body of criminal law should be grouped with the public or private spheres of law. It may be classified with private law[59] on the basis that most criminal wrongs are done to individuals, albeit pursued and punished by the state, or with public law[60] on the basis that criminal wrongs, even though done directly to individuals, are indirectly detrimental to the peace and order of the community; moreover they are dealt with by state agencies on behalf of the community and today an increasing number of crimes and petty offences are not done against any individual at all but are declared criminal and repressed simply because of their injurious tendency to the communal interest, to the national economy, or to people generally. Moreover many fundamental public rights are frequently in issue in criminal cases.

Substantive and Adjective Law

Another distinction of great materiality which subdivides each of the major divisions of state law, civil, administrative and criminal, is that between substantive law and adjective law, although at many points the dividing line is difficult to draw. Adjective law is sometimes equated with procedure or procedural law,[61] but properly it covers more than procedure. Broadly speaking substantive law defines the rights and claims, liberties and privileges, duties and liabilities of persons, while adjective law defines

---

[57] Kenny, " The Nature of a Crime," in his *Outlines of Criminal Law*, 16th ed., Appendix I; Allen, " The Nature of Crime " in *Legal Duties*, 220; Hall, *General Principles of Criminal Law*, Chaps. 5–7; Winfield, *Province of the Law of Tort*, Chap. 8; Williams, " The Definition of Crime " [1955] *Curr. Leg. Problems*, 107; Smith and Hogan, *Criminal Law*, Chap. 2. *Cf. Pty. Articles Trade Assocn.* v. *Att.-Gen. for Canada* [1931] A.C. at p. 324.

[58] Thus France has a highly developed system of administrative courts. See Hamson, *Executive Discretion and Judicial Control*; Brown and Garner, *French Administrative Law*.

[59] This view is taken by Salmond, *Jurisprudence*, 507.

[60] As by Holland, Markby and Pollock.

[61] *e.g.*, Holland, *Jurisprudence*, 358.

the means whereby, the circumstances in which, the qualifications under which, and the legal procedure whereby, these rights can be vindicated or these duties enforced.[62]   Adjective law covers evidence, procedure and pleading, matters of practice, the enforcement of decrees and related topics.   There is accordingly a body of adjective law attaching to each of civil and criminal law and their respective sets of courts, while a rather less definite body of adjective law also attaches to administrative law and its tribunals.   The distinction is sometimes put briefly as being that between " right " and " remedy " but this is inaccurate in that substantive rights and duties and remedial rights and duties all equally exist by rules of law, and are distinct from the means whereby remedies are sought and enforced when a substantive right is infringed.   The method by which a right can be enforced sometimes determines to some extent the nature or content of the right.   On the other hand the distinction is at some points quite clear, and accurate delimitation of the two areas may be of crucial importance, as in some problems of conflict of laws.[63]   And it is a distinction not without practical importance,[64] for unless adjective and procedural law works quickly, cheaply and efficiently, substantive law is deprived of much of its value.[65]

FURTHER READING

Arrangement and Classification
Hall: *Readings in Jurisprudence*, Chap. 14.
Holland: *Jurisprudence*, Chap. 9.
Paton: *Jurisprudence*, Chap. 11.
Pound: *Jurisprudence*, Vol. V.

Legal History
Continental Legal History Series: Vol. I—*General Survey.*
Vol. II—*Great Jurists of the World.*
Vol. X—*Progress in the Nineteenth Century.*
Diamond: *Evolution of Law and Order.*
Monier, Cardascia et Imbert: *Histoire des Institutions et des Faits Sociaux.*

Early Law
Jones: *Law and Legal Theory of the Greeks.*
Maine: *Ancient Law.*
Munroe Smith: *Development of European Law.*
Vinogradoff: *Historical Jurisprudence*, 2 vols.

[62] Procedure has been described as " The mode of proceeding by which a legal right is enforced, as distinguished from the law which gives or defines the right, and which by means of the proceeding the court is to administer—the machinery as distinguished from it product ": *Poyser* v. *Minors* (1881) 7 Q.B.D. 329, 333.
[63] See, *e.g., McElroy* v. *McAllister*, 1949 S.C. 110.
[64] Thus, *e.g.,* in Scots law it is a rule that loan of money may be proved by writ or oath only. If I lend money and seek to recover it, but have lost the debtor's written acknowledgment, is my right gone, or only my remedy barred (ignoring, for the sake of argument, the question of the debtor's oath)? What happens, on either of these views, if I later find the debtor's writ?
[65] *Cf.* Harvey, " A Job for Jurisprudence " (1944) 7 M.L.R. 42, 49; Lord Cooper, " Defects in the British Judicial Machinery " in (1953) 2 J.S.P.T.L.(N.S.) 91 and *Selected Papers*, 244.

Roman Law
Bryce: " Extension of Roman and English Law throughout the World," in
    Studies in History and Jurisprudence, I, 72.
Buckland: *Textbook of Roman Law.*
Buckland and McNair: *Roman Law and Common Law.*
Jolowicz: *Historical Introduction to the study of Roman Law.*
    Roman Foundations of Modern Law.
Lawson: *A Common Lawyer looks at the Civil Law.*
Lee: " Modernus Usus Juris Civilis " (1947) 22 Tulane L.R. 135.
Mackintosh: *Roman Law in Modern Practice.*
Schulz: *Classical Roman Law.*
    Roman Legal Science.
Ullman: *The Medieval Idea of Law.*
Vinogradoff: *Roman Law in Mediaeval Europe.*

Canon Law
Maitland: *Roman Canon Law in the Church of England.*
Mortimer: *Western Canon Law.*
Mylne: *Canon Law.*

Feudal Law
Bloch: *Feudal Society.*
Ganshof: *Feudalism.*

Law Merchant
Carter: " Early History of the Law Merchant in England " (1901) 17 L.Q.R.
    232.
Holdsworth: *History of English Law*, Vol. 5.
Mitchell: *The Law Merchant.*
Sanborn: *Origins of the Early English Maritime and Commercial Law.*

Maritime Law
Ashburner: *The Rhodian Sea Law.*
Holdsworth: *History of English Law*, Vol. 5.
Senior: " Early Writers on Maritime Law " (1921) 37 L.Q.R. 323.

English Law
Holdsworth: *Sources and Literature of English Law.*
James: *Introduction to English Law.*
Plucknett: *Concise History of the Common Law.*

Jurisprudence
Allen: *Law in the Making.*
Cairns: *Legal Philosophy from Plato to Hegel.*
Cohen and Cohen: *Readings in Jurisprudence and Legal Philosophy.*
Friedmann: *Legal Theory.*
Friedrich: *Philosophy of Law in Historical Perspective.*
Hall: *Readings in Jurisprudence.*
Hart: *The Concept of Law.*
Jones: *Historical Introduction to the Theory of Law.*
Lloyd: *Introduction to Jurisprudence.*
Morris: *The Great Legal Philosophers.*
Paton: *Jurisprudence.*

Pound: *Jurisprudence*, 5 vols.
    Introduction to the Philosophy of Law.
Simpson and Stone: *Cases and Readings on Law and Society*, 3 vols.
Stone: *Legal System and Lawyers' Reasonings.*
    Human Law and Human Justice.
    Social Dimension of Law and Justice.

Comparative Legal Studies
Amos and Walton: *Introduction to French Law.*
Arminjon, Nolde and Wolff: *Traité de Droit Comparé.*
David: *Traité Elémentaire de Droit Civil Comparé.*
David and De Vries: *The French Legal System.*
Foreign Office: *Manual of German Law*, 2 vols.
Gsovski: *Soviet Civil Law.*
Gutteridge: *Comparative Law.*
International Association of Legal Science: *International Encyclopaedia of Comparative Law*, 16 vols.
James: *Introduction to English Law.*
Lee: *Introduction to Roman-Dutch Law.*
Pound: " Comparative Law in Space and Time " (1955) 4 A.J.C.L. 70.
Roberts-Wray: *Commonwealth Law.*
Schlesinger: *Comparative Law.*
Van Mehren: *The Civil Law System.*
Vyshinsky: *Law of the Soviet State.*
Yntema: " Roman Law as the Basis of Comparative Law " in *Law: A Century of Progress*, II, 346.

Public International Law
Bowett: *Law of International Institutions.*
Butler and Maccoby: *The Development of International Law.*
Lauterpacht: *Function of Law in the International Community.*
    International Law and Human Rights.
    Development of International Law by the International Court.
Schwarzenberger: *Manual of International Law.*
Starke: *Introduction to International Law.*
United Nations Yearbook.
Wright: *The Role of International Law in the Elimination of War.*

Supranational Law
Bebr: *Judicial Control of the European Communities.*
Campbell: *Common Market Law.*
European Yearbook, 1953–
Parry and Hardy: *EEC Law.*
Robertson: *European Institutions.*
    The Council of Europe.
    Law of International Institutions in Europe.
Valentine: *The Court of Justice of the European Communities.*
Wall: *The Court of Justice of the European Communities.*

State or Municipal Law
Dunedin: *Divergencies and Convergencies of English and Scots Law*, Glasgow Univ. Publications, 1935.

Fisher: " Scotland and the Roman Law " (1947) 22 Tulane L.R. 13.

Gibb: " Interrelation of the Legal Systems of Scotland and England " (1937) 53 L.Q.R. 61.

Goudy: *Fate of Roman Law North and South of the Tweed*, 1894.

Keith: *The Spirit of the Law of Scotland* (Holdsworth Club, Birmingham, 1957).

Levy-Ullman: " The Law of Scotland " (1925) 37 J.R. 370.
        The English Legal Tradition.

Lovat-Fraser: " Some Points of Difference between English and Scottish Law " (1895) 10 L.Q.R. 340; 11 L.Q.R. 1.

Macmillan: " Two Ways of Thinking " in *Law and Other Things.*

Normand: *Scottish Judicature and Legal Procedure* (Holdsworth Club, 1941).

Radbruch: " Anglo-American Jurisprudence through Continental Eyes " (1937) 52 L.Q.R. 530.

Smith: *British Justice: The Scottish Contribution.*
        " English Influence on the Law of Scotland " (1954) 3 Am.Jo.Compar. L. 522.
        " The Common Law Cuckoo," 1956 *Butterworth's South African Law Review,* 147.
        " Strange Gods: The Crisis of Scots Law as a Civilian System," 1959 J.R. 119.
        " Scots Law and Roman-Dutch Law," 1961 J.R. 32.

Stein: " Influence of Roman Law on the Law of Scotland " (1957) 23 *Studia et Documenta Historiae et Juris,* 149.

Walker: " Some Characteristics of Scots Law " (1955) 18 M.L.R. 321.

Fisher: " Scotland and the Roman Law " (1947) 22 Tulane L.R. 13.

CHAPTER 4

THE DEVELOPMENT OF SCOTS LAW

THE modern Scottish legal system and the complex body of doctrines, principles and rules which it utilises has not been the creation of a single edict, but represents the present state of a long and slow process of development and evolution, in which numerous factors have played a part, social and economic developments, political and governmental changes, the effects of war, religious upheaval, constitutional moves and so on. At different times different influences have been predominant. Not only does an outline of the historical development of the Scottish legal system show how that system has come to take its present shape, but it helps to explain numerous practices and rules which survived long after the conditions which gave rise to them had passed away, and some of which still survive to upset the simplicity and symmetry of the law and sometimes to cause confusion and even injustice.

Early Times

Very little is known of legal institutions in Scotland prior to the year A.D. 1000 and nothing from any earlier period can be shown to have exercised any material or permanent influence on the development of the modern law.[1] For present purposes accordingly the story starts after that date. In particular it should be noted that the introduction of Roman law into Scotland was not effected by the Roman occupation of the South of Scotland.

I.—THE FEUDAL PERIOD

Introduction of Feudalism

After the victory of Carham over the Northumbrians in 1018 the Scottish kingdom reached its present boundaries by the incorporation of the northern part of Northumbria.[2] Northumbrian influence had penetrated into Lothian prior to then though it was long before the more outlying parts of the kingdom were assimilated and lost their previous characteristics.   Civilisation was confined to the Lothians

---

[1] Rait and Pryde, *Scotland*, 13; Ritchie, *Normans in Scotland*, xiii. Traces of Celtic law are discussed in Cameron, *Celtic Law*. See also Levie, " Celtic Tribal Law and Custom in Scotland " (1927) 39 J.R. 191; Cameron, " Gaelic Notitiae in the Book of Deer " (1939) 51 J.R. 150; Chadwick, *Celtic Britain*, 80; Dillon and Chadwick, *The Celtic Realms*, Chap. 5.

[2] On the formation of the Kingdom, see also Dickinson, *Scotland to 1603*, Chap. 4; Duncan, *Scotland: The Making of the Kingdom*.

and the coastal plain round to the Moray Firth, and particularly the districts near the burghs and baronial and ecclesiastical centres.

In the Gaelic Highlands the populace probably lived under the influence of Celtic customs, traces of which are found in the Senchus Mor and the Book of Aicill. In the Britons of Strathclyde there was a point of contact with the traditions of early Welsh law while in Galloway traces of customary law persisted as late as 1384. Orkney, Shetland, the Western Isles and large tracts of land north of Dingwall had been occupied by Scandinavians and long remained independent, while Orkney and Shetland were governed by Norse law down to 1468.

The Norman Conquest of England in and after 1066 influenced Scotland less immediately and directly than it did England, but gradually it permeated and influenced Lowland Scottish society and institutions and southern influences were potent in Scotland for many years. Normans began to come to Scotland from about 1050 and by 1150 " Scotland was Normanised beyond recall. Normans held the chief offices in Church and State. Land and power had largely passed into Norman hands. The old feudal system had been changed to Norman-feudal. A French aristocracy had been established, a French civilisation implanted." [3]

An important factor in the assimilation of Anglo-Saxon influences was the marriage of Malcolm III (Canmore) (1057–93) to the Saxon princess Margaret about 1070. The queen had great influence on her husband and used it to strengthen the Anglo-Saxon influences on church and state. In the course of the next two centuries the population of the Lowlands became converted into an English-speaking community with life organised on the model of the Anglo-Saxon-Norman Kingdom of England, and spiritually more akin to England than to Gaelic Scotland. [4]

Prior to 1124 Norman feudalism [5] had probably made some headway in the south of Scotland but was not generally accepted. [6] The process of Anglicisation or Anglo-Normanisation was definitely accepted in the reign of David I (1124–53) [7] and the law as much as the court and the Church was subjected to English influence. David, trained as a knight under Henry I of England, did much to reproduce in his own realm the

---

[3] Ritchie, *Normans in Scotland*, xv. For Celtic opposition to Anglo-Norman feudalism, see Dickinson, *op. cit.* 57. See further, Gardner, " Historical Survey of the Law of Scotland prior to the reign of David I " (1945) 57 J.R. 34, 65; Levie, " Anglian Influence on Early Scottish Law " (1940) 52 J.R. 95.

[4] Rait and Pryde, *Scotland*, 13; Ritchie, *op. cit.*, xiii.

[5] On feudalism in general, see Ganshof, *Feudalism* (trs. Grierson); Barrow, *Feudal Britain*, 1066–1314, *passim*; Vinogradoff, " Origins of Feudalism," 2 Camb.Med.Hist., Chap. 20; *idem.*, " Feudalism," 3 Camb.Med.Hist., Chap. 18.

[6] Hume Brown, *History of Scotland*, I, 73; Ritchie, *op. cit.* 67–83, 160–175; Barrow, " Beginnings of Feudalism in Scotland ", *The Kingdom of the Scots*, Chap. 10.

[7] On his reign, see generally, Innes, *Scotland in the Middle Ages*, Chap. 4; Dickinson, Chap. 9; and generally, Cooper in *Introduction to Scottish Legal History* (Stair Society), Chap. 1.

pattern of feudal government and institutions prevailing in Norman England, at least in the southern third of the kingdom.[8] The features of this system, at once a social, military and legal one, were castle-building, the use of professional cavalry, church-building and monastic development, the grant of land in knights' fees to be held in knight-service for the provision of one or more knights,[9] and the requirement of homage and fealty from tenants. Under Malcolm (1153–65) and William the Lion (1165–1214) military feudalism became more intensive.

The feudal system of land tenure whereby land was held by a " vassal " from a lord in return for certain services, the grant being confirmed by written charter, was introduced into Scotland in the twelfth century. The system was by this time well developed in England and on the Continent. After 1153 the practice seems to have been to grant tracts of land in return for the service of a knight or even of a part of a knight, for the Scottish barons were men of lesser substance than their English counterparts.[10] There were, however, large estates held by military service and within them a fairly systematic process of subinfeudation, that is, of giving smaller areas of land to a sub-vassal to be held by him of his lord by the performance of feudal duties.

The characteristics of the system were that it was at once a decentralised method of government and administration, a social and economic system and a system of land tenure. In all these aspects its introduction had lasting importance and influence in Scotland, and the land law is still fundamentally feudal. Moreover a grant of land to be held in feudal tenure naturally conveyed with it the right to hold a court for the feudal tenants and civil and criminal jurisdiction over them, the extent of jurisdiction varying with the rank of the grantee.[11]

This system seems to have fitted quite well into the previously existing Celtic method of land tenure under which land was held by the chief and his near kindred and there seems to have been little racial displacement or dispossession of existing holders of land.[12] Land and the accompanying jurisdiction over the population were conferred by royal charter both upon the king's Anglo-Norman friends and on native Scottish chiefs who had their customary rights confirmed and enlarged by the grant of feudal jurisdiction.[13] By the end of the thirteenth century old Celtic institutions had been feudalised as far as the Moray Firth and in some

---

[8] Ritchie, *op. cit.* 179–190.

[9] Neilson, " Tenure by Knight-Service in Scotland " (1899) 11 J.R. 71, 173; see also Neilson, " Scottish Serjeanties " (1899) 15 L.Q.R. 405.

[10] Barrow, *op. cit.* 293.

[11] Dickinson, *op. cit.* 84–93; Milne, in *Introduction* (Stair Society), Chap. 13; see specimen charter in Dickinson and others, *Source Book of Scottish History*, I, 90–94.

[12] Rait and Pryde, *op. cit.* 19.

[13] *Ibid.* 20; Ritchie, *op. cit.* 237–242.

more remote areas where, however, Celtic custom in the main lasted for several more centuries.[14]

The institution of this land system was the basis of the family in Anglicised Lowland Scotland as much as was the clan system in the Celtic Highlands and extensive grants of land were made in David's lifetime to men of Saxon, Norman or Danish extraction and, particularly in Strathclyde, Lothian and Fife, castles were planted and feudal communities developed, with land held by vassals and sub-vassals of the king, which greatly strengthened the royal authority.[15] The majority of those who farmed the land were tenants, usually from year to year and only gradually did it become common to hold lands for a lifetime, or perpetually, for a fixed money rent. Tenure in feu-farm developed gradually from the twelfth century. Below the free tenants were a great number, the majority of the whole people who had neither secure tenure nor complete personal freedom; they varied from husbandmen to people tied to the soil (*adscripti glebae*) and even to outright slaves. Servile status was, however, tending to disappear.

The trading burghs developed and from the deliberations of the Four Burghs,[16] originally Berwick, Roxburgh, Edinburgh and Stirling, sprang the *Leges Quatuor Burgorum*, a code of municipal regulations, partly copied and adapted from English models.

Feudal Administration

Feudalism introduced the idea that the king was lord of the whole land and the fountain of all justice. The king's court could hear appeals from lower courts and cases relating to important persons or matters. The king sat with the officers of his household and such great men as were with him at the time. Later he began to summon other tenants-in-chief and those regularly called to give the king counsel became his council. In time this council began to sit in various capacities, for finance, for justice, for affairs of state. By the end of the thirteenth century a sitting for discussion, a *parliamentum*, had become primarily a sitting of the council as supreme court which laid down the law or changed it. Parliament was primarily a court of law, while a council, strengthened by summoning additional persons, called a general council, was primarily a deliberative body.[17]

David I also introduced the political officers and institutions of the feudal monarchy, such as the chancellor, chamberlain, justiciar, constable

---

[14] Skene, *Celtic Scotland*, III, 287 *et seq.*
[15] Hume Brown, I, 89–90.
[16] The association of these burghs was the genesis of the Convention of Royal Burghs which survived to 1975.
[17] Dickinson, *op. cit.* 106–107.

and steward.[18] A royal officer, the *iudex*, was important from the eleventh to the thirteenth century. *Iudices* were attached to a province and their commonest function seeems to have been perambulating marches, to determine the lawful boundaries of estates.[19] A network of sheriffdoms began to spread over the whole country, under sheriffs who were the king's representatives and charged with the maintenance of order and the collection of the revenue in the king's name.[20] Periodically the chamberlain held an ayre or court in each royal burgh, at which all the burgesses had to be present, to ensure that the king had his dues from trade and also that there were no breaches of trading or commercial relations. A court was held in the burghs fortnightly, presided over by the king's bailie.

The performance of important services to the king passed into office by invisible steps. A man of importance [21] had rights and privileges and land to support him: he tended to acquire powers, military, administrative, or judicial in a definite area so that his service came to be in effect an office under the crown, and both office and district came to be called a barony and both passed to his heir after confirmation by the king.[22]

A great council of the realm or *Curia Regis* was established on the English model. In theory it consisted of all tenants-in-chief and the chief ecclesiastical dignitaries.[23] The burgesses did not appear till later.

The Justice-Ayres

Under David the justiciars appear as important officials.[24] This office is also of Norman origin. The justiciar or justice-general was originally the king's delegate for administration and the administration of justice. He had originally supreme jurisdiction both in civil and criminal matters and the general administration of justice seems to have been entrusted at an early date to two justiciars, one for the north and one for the south of the kingdom, under whom various inferior judges exercised subordinate and delegated jurisdiction. A third justiciar is also known

---

[18] Dickinson, *op. cit.* 103–104; Ritchie, *op. cit.* 184; Innes, *Scotch Legal Antiquities*, 74–85; Duncan, in *Introduction to Scottish Legal History* (Stair Society), Chap. 23; Bateson, " The Scottish King's Household " (1901) 13 J.R. 405; (1902) 14 J.R. 35; and S.H.S. *Miscellany*, II, 3.

[19] Barrow, *The Kingdom of the Scots*, Chap. 2.

[20] Rait and Pryde, *op. cit.* 21; Hume Brown, I, 88, Dickinson, *op. cit.* 101; see also Vary Campbell, " The Sheriff in Scotland " (1900) 12 J.R. 15; Ferguson, " The Sheriff in Scotland " (1910) 22 J.R. 105. See also *Sheriff Court Book of Fife*, ed. Dickinson (S.H.S.), Appx. D.

[21] In Norman-French " baron " was simply a man, later a man of importance in battle or council.

[22] Ritchie, 222–223. In this way primogeniture became accepted as the rule of succession in heritage.

[23] Dickinson, *op. cit.* 105; Rait and Pryde, 21; Ritchie, 208–209; Rait, *Parliaments of Scotland*, 1.

[24] See generally, Dickinson, in *Introduction to Scottish Legal History* (Stair Society), Chap. 31, and on procedure, *ibid.*, Chap. 33; Barrow, *The Kingdom of the Scots*, Chap. 3.

of later.[25] Their office was to dispense justice in civil and criminal cases not dealt with by the king's court and they had to hold justice-ayres or circuit-courts in spring and autumn for that purpose, though in times of trouble the ayres were irregular. They also had a prominent role in the processes of perambulation and measurement of lands, and in the related act of giving sasine which often followed perambulation. They had further to supervise the sheriffs. At this time the office was not hereditary.[26]

While Edward I had Scotland temporarily subjugated he appointed eight justiciars, and Robert Bruce seems to have maintained five.[27] The justiciars were commonly high nobles and had wide competence, political and governmental as well as legal. The justiciar's court seems to have evolved considerably in the thirteenth century. The office of justice-general, however, later became hereditary and remained so till 1836 when on the death of the Duke of Montrose, the then holder of the office, it was united with that of Lord President of the Court of Session. After the institution of the College of Justice in 1532 the justiciar never judged in civil matters. In 1672 [28] the supreme criminal court was reformed and constituted the High Court of Justiciary.

The limited power of the crown at this time and the inadequate central machinery of government combined with feudal theory to effect a wide dispersion of judicial functions and powers among men and families of importance all over the country, which powers were linked to landholding and readily became not merely territorial but hereditary.[29]

Rise of the Burghs

About the time of David I there began to develop the burghs, which were inhabited places, usually adjacent to a royal castle, latterly, if not originally, possessing charters which granted the burgesses privileges, such as of holding a fair, or freedom from tolls.[30] Burghs were fundamentally economic organisations acting as market-centres for the sheriff-doms, and they tended to attract foreigners and merchants to settle there but they also served as colonies, outposts of political control.[31]

---

[25] See list in Cooper, *Select Scots Cases of the Thirteenth Century.*
[26] Mackinnon, *Constitutional History of Scotland,* 128.
[27] Tytler, I, 248; Dickinson, 161.
[28] Courts Act 1672, c. 16.
[29] Hill Burton, II, 54 *et seq.*
[30] The model was Norman, as with most of David's introductions: Dickinson, 111; Ritchie, *Normans in Scotland,* 323. See also Pryde, " Origin of the Burgh in Scotland " (1935) 47 J.R. 271; " Burghal Administration," in *Source Book of Administrative Law,* 1–11; " The Scottish Burghs " (1949) 28 S.H.R. 155, and *The Burghs of Scotland*; Neilson, " On Some Scottish Burghal Origins " (1902) 14 J.R. 129; Innes, *Scotland in the Middle Ages,* Chap. 5; and specimen burgh charters in *Source Book of Scottish History,* I, 102–105.
[31] Mackenzie, *The Scottish Burghs,* 1–50.

The weekly market in the burgh was the regular occasion for local trade and burghs were frequently granted the monopoly of trade in a particular area, which was known as its "liberty."[32] So too, burghs were the exclusive centres of foreign trade and the trades of the burgh had an exclusive right in craft work. The burgesses soon acquired the right to elect their own provost, bailies and other officers.

These privileges were granted in consideration of liability to provide a share in any grant of money to the king, at first one-fifth and, later one-sixth of the total. The apportionment of this among the individual burghs was the work of the Convention of Royal Burghs, a body which comes into the limelight in the sixteenth century.[33]

Apart from these royal burghs with royal charters there were established from early times burghs dependent on ecclesiastical magnates, burghs of barony, and burghs of regality which were erected by lords of baronies or of regalities. Burghs of barony were founded as early as royal burghs, with similar commercial privileges, and were frequently ecclesiastical foundations. They were always erected by a subject-superior under licence from the king.[34] Many such burghs were erected in the fifteenth, sixteenth and seventeenth centuries. The administration of burghs of barony depended on the superior or on agreement with him and consequently varied from one town to another.

A lord of regality had within his lands a jurisdiction as wide as that of the king, including jurisdiction in the crimes normally reserved to the royal courts, the pleas of the Crown, and such a lord might create a burgh, though his exceptional jurisdiction did not make a corresponding extension of the burgh's commercial powers. That might, however, be done by special arrangement.[35] Burghs of barony or of regality might be raised to royal rank.

Guild Merchants and Burgh Courts

In many burghs a merchant guild was formed and craftsmen were generally admitted to it, and this was probably the first official recognition of self-control as against control by the superior of the burgh. An Act of Parliament in 1593 approved the power and jurisdiction of the Dean of Guild and his council in burghs to deal with actions between merchants or between merchant and mariner.[36] This gradually fell into desuetude but from about the sixteenth century the Dean of Guild

---

[32] *Ibid.* 66.

[33] *Ibid.* 76; Ritchie, *op. cit.* 327–330. See also, Pagan, *The Convention of the Royal Burghs of Scotland*, 53.

[34] *Ibid.* 79–80; Dickinson, 112; see also Ferguson, "The Barony in Scotland" (1912) 24 J.R. 99.

[35] *Ibid.* 78.

[36] Mackenzie, 100–105; McKechnie, in *Source Book of Administrative Law*, 95–104; Pryde in *Introduction to Scottish Legal History* (Stair Society), Chap. 29.

was recognised as having a common law jurisdiction over buildings, nuisances and questions of neighbourhood, and this long survived in the form of jurisdiction to regulate streets and buildings.[37]

Apart from the guild every burgh tended to develop a court to enforce its regulations and settle disputes, which tended in turn to assume powers of administration. All burgesses, unless excused, had to attend the three head courts of the year (Yule, Easter and Michaelmas). The burgh bailies may have had power to try all crimes except the four pleas of the Crown but this was early attenuated to dealing with boundary disputes, failure to use proper weights and measures or observe the market rules and various offences such as encroaching on another's land or allowing animals to trespass on another's fields.[38] The competence of the burgh courts was cut down by the rise of the Court of Session and the justices of the peace, so that the bailies came to be limited to trivial cases and petty disputes.[39]

The Chamberlain had some supervisory functions over burghs. In his annual ayre or circuit he dealt with appeals from the burgh court, decided disputes between burghs, and investigated the mode in which the bailies had been discharging their functions. From 1292 the *Curia Quatuor Burgorum* met under the presidency of the Chamberlain to hear appeals from the burgh courts and from the ayre [40] and to lay down the law of the burghs which may have been influenced by the *Leges Quatuor Burgorum* [41] borrowed from Newcastle. The Chamberlain's power disappeared in the fifteenth century and the *Curia* vanished about 1500.

Only in the fourteenth century, under the necessity of financial stringency, did the great burghs obtain representation in Parliament and from the informal discussions of the burgh commissioners to Parliament there arose the Convention of Royal Burghs (1552) with legislative, executive and financial jurisdiction.[42]

Barony and Regality Courts

The term baron in early feudal law included any considerable tenant but later came to be restricted for the most part to those who held lands direct of the king, which had been erected by the grant *in liberam baron-*

---

[37] McKechnie, *loc. cit.* 100–101; Pryde, in *Introduction* (Stair Society), Chap. 29.

[38] Pryde, in *Source Book of Administrative Law*, 4; Dickinson, 114–115.

[39] Pryde, in *Source Book*, 8.

[40] Pryde, in *Source Book*, 5; Dickinson, 118–119; *Source Book of Scottish History*, I, 228–230.

[41] Printed in A.P.S. I. 329. The four burghs were at first Berwick, Edinburgh, Roxburgh, and Stirling, and later Edinburgh, Stirling, Lanark and Linlithgow.

[42] Dickinson, *op. cit.* 186–187.

iam.[43] Barony tenure was characterised by being a unity, a unit for administration and law, and possessing its own officers and baron-bailie, and when lands were granted *in liberam baroniam* the charters included a clause granting certain rights of public justice. The barony always had a legal *caput* which was inseparable from it and wherein was centred the jurisdiction. The baron by accepting the barony accepted responsibility to the king for ordinary public justice within the lands included in the barony; he had power of pit and gallows, *fossa et furca.*[44] Hence a grant of barony excluded to that extent the king's officers, and in time this exclusion grew greater so that certain barons received all rights of public justice including even the four pleas of the Crown[45] and other royal rights so that they became holders *in regalitatem.* A regality was a barony with fuller jurisdictional and administrative rights, the precise rights depending on the charter of erection.[46] The only right excluded was the right to try treason. Regalities were in fact so much petty kingdoms that the realm was divided into royalty and regality.[47]

Barony jurisdiction appears to have been granted from the twelfth century and such grants were common in the later Middle Ages.[48] The baron usually held court at the *caput baroniae* at various intervals as need arose.[49] For most of the people the baron court of their lord was the one which affected them. It might be presided over by the baron or by his bailie, or by both, or by two bailies, and the judges of the court were the suitors, that is, those tenants who held land by suit of court, for whom attendance at court was a feudal burden attached to the holding of their land,[50] and the sentence or doom was pronounced by the dempster or doomsman.[51] The court had civil jurisdiction in matters of debt, possession, lawburrows,[52] breach of arrestment, bloodwite[53] and deforcement,[54] and criminal jurisdiction in theft and slaughter.[55]

In time these jurisdictions tended to fall into disuse with the development of centralised institutions and courts. By the seventeenth century only regalities or earldoms might still punish capitally and baron courts

---

[43] Dickinson, *op. cit.* 91–92; *Barony Court Book of Carnwath* (ed. Dickinson), xiv. See also Ferguson, " The Barony in Scotland " (1912) 24 J.R. 99.

[44] *Ibid.* xx–xxvi.

[45] Murder, arson, rape and robbery.

[46] *Ibid.* xxxix–xl.

[47] Prior to the Reformation there were over fifty regalities in Scotland: Pryde, *Kirkintilloch Burgh Court Book*, xlii.

[48] On the details of barony jurisdiction, see Innes, *Scotch Legal Antiquities*, 54–60; McIntyre, in *Introduction to Scottish Legal History* (Stair Society), Chap. 28.

[49] *Cf.* Ritchie, *Normans in Scotland*, 311.

[50] On the suitors of the court, see also Hamilton-Grierson in (1917) 14 S.H.R. 1 and Dickinson in *Sheriff Court Book of Fife*, Introd., lxxii.

[51] *Barony Court Book of Carnwath*, lxxx.

[52] Surety for keeping the peace.

[53] Fines for bloodshed.

[54] *Ibid.* civ.

[55] *Ibid.* cvii.

had given up this jurisdiction. They disappeared with the abolition of the heritable jurisdictions in 1747.

The Sheriff Courts

The establishment of the office of sheriff in Scotland is probably to be attributed to David I [56] and many areas were erected into sheriff-doms in the twelfth and thirteenth centuries.[57] England supplied the model, where the Norman kings had introduced their own officer, the *vicecomes* or shire-reeve. The Scottish sheriffdom seems to have been an artificial unit which did not coincide with previous divisions of the land or natural boundaries, and was frequently dependent on a castle.[58] The sheriffs were appointed from among the Scoto-Norman barons and gradually royal sheriffs were established over the whole kingdom, showing the power of the central government. The sheriff was the king's judicial, financial, administrative and military officer and gradually the office became almost uniformly heritable.[59] The office had to be fitted into the existing system and it is uncertain how the office compared with that of the mair, who continued to sit as an assessor in the sheriff's court.[60]

The sheriff court was originally held at the castle and was the king's court of the sheriffdom, which consisted of the lands which owed court duty and military service to the castle.[61] Head courts were held thrice a year and lesser courts at intermediate times at irregular intervals, which probably averaged six weeks. Head courts were courts held at the seat of the sheriffdom, attended by the full complement of those who owed the duty of suit of court [62] and presided over by the sheriff in person; at them all the more important business was transacted. The lesser courts might be held at different places in the sheriffdom. As burghs tended to grow up beneath the walls of the castle, the burgh became the *caput* of the sheriffdom, and by the sixteenth century all courts were held in the tolbooth of the head burgh of the sheriffdom.[63]

The sheriff court was the king's baron court and within the sheriffdom the sheriff administered both civil and criminal justice. He might

---

[56] Dickinson, *op. cit.* 101; *Sheriff Court Book of Fife* (ed. Dickinson, S.H.S.), 347. See also Philip in *Source Book of Administrative Law*, 74–80; Malcolm, " The Office of Sheriff in Scotland " (1923) 20 S.H.R. 129, 222, 290; Milne, *Introduction to Scottish Legal History* (Stair Society), Chap. 25.

[57] *Ibid.* 347–368. On sheriffs in the twelfth century see Barrow, *Regesta Regum Scottorum*, I, 35; II, 28.

[58] *Ibid.* 384; Ritchie, 319.

[59] *Ibid.* xxxi–xxxiii. See specimen sheriff's account in *Source Book of Scottish History*, I, 96–99.

[60] Ritchie, *op. cit.* 321.

[61] *Ibid.* 372. *Cf. ibid.* 311.

[62] See *Source Book of Scottish History*, I, 101.

[63] *Sheriff Court Book of Fife*, xi–xx.

not deal with cases involving the four pleas of the Crown nor exercise jurisdiction over any ecclesiastical person. Nor, of course, had he jurisdiction within stewartries, where the king's steward was the sole competent judge, nor within regalities, nor within burghs, since burgesses claimed to be heard only before their own courts or the Chamberlain's ayre. Personal exemptions were also sometimes granted.[64] In civil matters the sheriff could deal with actions of molestation, removing, ejection, spuilzie, and all kinds of personal actions.[65] Many civil actions could begin only when a complainer presented a brieve bought from the king's chancery, addressed to the sheriff stating a grievance and ordering investigation by a sworn inquest. The sheriff was the presiding officer in the court, controlling procedure, and instructing the suitors in the law, but the judgment was that of the suitors.[66]

The sheriff had also an oversight of the proper administration of justice in inferior courts within the sheriffdom and his court was the court of appeal against decisions of baron courts within the sheriffdom.[67] He had to uphold the Church courts, search for and pursue rebels put to the horn, to guard prisoners, arrest idle men, issue tokens to beg, keep the castles in repair, supervise the efficiency of the arms and the holding of the wappinschaw, execute royal writs and letters and carry out many more administrative duties.[68]

Ecclesiastical Courts

In the medieval kingdom the clergy and the religious houses were of great importance.[69] They were favoured by David I and grew rich and powerful under him. Not least they imported into the kingdom an element of scholarship and of the canon law of the Roman Church and it was probably through this infusion of canon law that Roman law came first to influence Scottish procedure.

A great volume of the litigation in the thirteenth century, even involving laymen, took place before ecclesiastical tribunals, particularly before judges-delegate, usually three in number, who were constituted an *ad hoc* tribunal by mandate from the Pope or papal legate with instructions to carry out specified procedure. These mandates were obtained by the prospective pursuer in the action.[70] The judges-delegate might carry the case to conclusion without further reference to Rome, or refer

---

[64] *Ibid.* xxvii.
[65] *Ibid.* xxxviii and Appx. B.
[66] Appeal lay to the court of the justiciar, when he visited the *caput* of the sheriffdom.
[67] *Ibid.* xxxix.
[68] *Ibid.* xl–xlv.
[69] See generally, Dickinson, *op. cit.* 120–124; Easson, *Scottish Religious Houses*; Dowden, *Medieval Church in Scotland*; Innes, *Scotch Legal Antiquities*, 161–208; and on the Church courts, Donaldson in *Introduction* (Stair Society), Chap. 27.
[70] Cooper, *Select Scottish Cases*, xxvii; see also Stein " Roman Law in Scotland," *Ius Romanum Medii Aevi*, v, 13b, 23.

back for instructions and guidance in case of difficulty, or even report the facts to Rome for final hearing and decision there. Appeals might be made to Rome at any stage. The judges-delegate dealt with a great variety of cases, claims to money, lands, for damages or specific implement, for reduction of a decree arbitral or even for an award of sequestration.[71]

As the thirteenth century proceeded there was increasing resort to lay tribunals [72] and cases were heard before the King in Council or in Parliament, the justiciar, and the sheriff. The justiciars numbered usually two and never more than four, and the sheriffs numbered from twenty to thirty so that the judicial establishment of the country was inadequate. The system of papal judges-delegate lost most of its importance by the time of the War of Independence but the Courts Christian remained.[73]

Procedure

In the period before the foundation of the College of Justice the primary procedural writ was the brieve, a short writ issued from the Chancery, in the form of a command in the king's name, requiring an official, a commissioner or a party to take some action which justice was thought to require.[74] Sometimes the brieve had to be " retoured," in which case the verdict was returned to the Chancery. The system contributed greatly to the development of a uniform system of law, common to the whole country. This system was in operation in the thirteenth century, though not fully developed, and was extended by James I after his return from captivity in 1424.[75]

Scottish brieves were undoubtedly founded on English models though papal practice probably also had some influence. English forms were, however, often discarded or modified and Scotland had fewer and more adaptable basic writs than the great multiplication of writs in the English register.[76] After 1532 brieves tended to give way to other forms of initial writs in litigation; the brieve passed into the summons under the signet and fell into desuetude as a means of initiating litigation.

The brieve had also other uses. In its widest sense a brieve covered any kind of formal writ issued by the king, administrative or judicial.

---

[71] *Ibid.* xxxi–xxxii.

[72] *Ibid.* xxxvii.

[73] Donaldson " Church Courts " in *Introduction to Scottish Legal History* (Stair Society), Chap. 27.

[74] Dickinson, *op. cit.* 107. See generally, McKechnie, *Judicial Process upon Brieves 1219–1532*; Lord Cooper, Introd. to *Register of Brieves* (Stair Society); Innes, *Scotch Legal Antiquities*, 222–240; Hamilton-Grierson (ed.), Bisset's *Rolment of Courtis*, III, 41; Maxwell, in *Introduction to Scottish Legal History*, Chap. 32.

[75] For specimens and the procedure thereunder, see Innes, *op. cit.* 233–237, and *Source Book of Scottish History*, I, 95–98.

[76] On the English register, see Pollock and Maitland's *History of English Law*, I, 150, 195; Plucknett, *Concise History*, 276–277.

Other brieves were used as a means of obtaining the factual answer to problems. Such were the brieves of succession, terce and tutory. Very important was the brieve *de recto* by which the title to heritage could be determined.

Modes of Trial—the Jury

The common modes of trial in early times were battle, compurgation, whereby a man could clear himself by the oath of a prescribed number of oath-helpers or compurgators that they believed his oath to be true, or the ordeal by water or by hot iron.[77] The fourth Lateran Council of 1215 prohibited clerical assistance at ordeals and the withdrawal of religious sanction contributed to its disappearance; it seems to have vanished by 1230. Proof by writ or by witnesses is little heard of in the twelfth and thirteenth centuries and seems to have developed first in the burgh courts.

The jury system came to Scotland in the wake of feudalism and by 1230 it is possible that the jury had definitely superseded the ordeal but at first it was difficult to distinguish the jury from sworn witnesses or from compurgators. The jury was frequently chosen by the pursuer in conjunction with the officers of court. For long there was no settled number for a jury and the rule that the number should be odd was arrived at only gradually and later.[78]

The jury disappeared in nearly all civil cases after 1532 though retained for some special kinds of cases, but remained in criminal cases, though latterly a greatly increased number of criminal cases have been allowed to be heard summarily. In 1815 the jury was imported afresh for civil cases.

Private Law in the Feudal Period

It is difficult to obtain or to present in brief compass a general picture of private law at this early period. Much early law was local and customary.[79] Predominantly it was concerned with complaints against violence and wrongdoing and included much which in later times would have been classed as criminal. The oldest laws describe a system of combined fines and compensation for murder and personal injuries, which represents the beginnings of the commutation of the blood-feud into judicial remedy. There were elaborate tariffs of fines and compensation varying with the status of the injured man and the gravity of his injuries. Wrongs pre-

---

[77] Innes, *Scotch Legal Antiquities*, 209–222; *idem, Scotland in the Middle Ages,* 182–189; Neilson, *Trial by Combat.* As late as 1567 Bothwell, when suspected of Darnley's death, offered to prove his innocence by battle. Compurgation is last mentioned in 1622.

[78] Dickinson, *op. cit.* 108; Dickinson, *Sheriff Court Book of Fife,* Introd. lxxxvi. See also, Willock, *The Jury in Scotland,* 20–37.

[79] See *Source Book of Scottish History,* I, 114–118.

dominate and there is little of contract while testamentary law was within the jurisdiction of the Church. In the earlier thirteenth century there was extensive use of canon law.

Accordingly, in the period immediately before the War of Independence, Scots law appears to have closely resembled Anglo-Norman law but even then to have had distinct differences. There had been borrowing, not wholesale, nor indiscriminate, but critical, with adaptations and simplifications. Scots law and English law were recognisably different, though bearing many marks of close relationship.[80] Canon law had also established itself in many spheres. "Development as compared with England proceeded not on parallel, but on gradually diverging, lines—the divergence being due in part to the inability of Scotland to keep abreast with the rapid progress made in England from Glanvill, through Bracton, to the Edwardian law, and in part to Scotland's deliberate refusal, under the influence of the Romano-canonical tradition, to absorb the more technical and artificial features of the Bractonian law. By the end of the [thirteenth] century the divergence was already marked, not only in the rejection of much that England had introduced, and in the adoption of ideas and expedients which Scotland did not owe to England but in a general effort towards greater simplicity, flexibility and directness." [81] Law and custom, moreover, varied from one area to another depending on the extent of Celtic or Norman tradition. There were still places for Brehon law, the laws of Galloway, the laws of the forest, the laws of the four burghs and even the law of clan MacDuff.

This early period of Scottish legal development was abruptly terminated by the deep division of the War of Independence, though some of the customary and Roman and canon law survived to a later period.

II.—FOURTEENTH TO SIXTEENTH CENTURIES

The War of Independence and After

During the English occupation of Scotland Edward I appointed eight justiciars in 1305 and he took action with a view to establishing an Exchequer on the English model, and possibly also a Chancery, at Berwick.[82] He increased the number of sheriffs while twenty commissioners drew up an Ordinance for the Government of Scotland,[83] but in a few months this existed on paper only.

The period from 1329 to about 1600 is the Dark Age of Scottish legal

---

[80] Cooper, " Scottish Legal Tradition," in *Selected Papers*, 175. See also Cooper, " A Scottish Law Student at Oxford in 1250 " (1944) 56 J.R. 57.

[81] Cooper, Introd. to *Register of Brieves*, 25.

[82] Cooper, *Select Scottish Cases of the Thirteenth Century*, xlv. See also 25 S.H.R. 27.

[83] A.P.S. I, 119: It was sometimes thought that *Regiam Majestatem* was a product of this commission. See also, Barrow, *Robert Bruce*, 191.

history,[84] a period of political strife and economic troubles which was an unkindly background for the development of law. Yet even in this period there were enacted a few statutes which are even yet of fundamental importance. If satisfactory judicial machinery had been established the Scoto-Norman law which had already been developed might have continued to evolve steadily as did English law. But by reason of the absence of a powerful central court and settled government no such development could take place and despite many attempts it was not till 1532 that the requisite court was created.[85] This was the period when Scots law as a science and a philosophy reached its nadir, yet even so the evidence is that there was plenty of law and plenty of lawyers.

Law Books—

Regiam Majestatem and Quoniam Attachiamenta

The principal source of knowledge of Scoto-Norman law in later times is the book called, from its opening words, *Regiam Majestatem*.[86] It probably describes law and practice as they were under Alexander III or even later rather than under David I and was probably privately and unofficially compiled, possibly about 1320; possibly as late as about 1350. It is not original or distinctively Scottish but is based on Glanvill's [87] *De Legibus et Consuetudinibus Angliae* (1187) but with amendments, adaptations to Scottish conditions and variations on the original, since by its time Scots law had progressed beyond the stage described by Glanvill. But Glanvill was the basis as providing an account of the main features of the system which Scotland was developing. There is also heavy drawing on the early Scots statutes and the primitive laws of the Brets and Scots, which probably survived in Galloway into the fourteenth century, and on Roman and canon law,[88] particularly the *Corpus Juris*, the *Decretum* and *Decretals*, the *Summa* of Azo, Tancred's *Ordo Judiciarius*, Raymond of Penaforte's *Summa de Casibus* and other canonists. It attempts to cover the whole field of civil and criminal law and procedure from the standpoint of the royal courts. The arrangement, following Justinian's *Institutes*, is in four books.

---

[84] On this see generally, Cooper, " The Dark Age of Scottish Legal History," in *Selected Papers*, 219; Paton, in *Introduction to Scottish Legal History*, Chap. 2; Levie, " Place of the War of Independence in Scottish Legal History " (1943) 55 J.R. 121; and Nicholson, *Scotland: The Later Middle Ages*.

[85] *Ibid.* 226–227.

[86] Edited with a valuable introduction by Lord Cooper for the Stair Society. See also Buchanan, " The MSS of Regiam Maiestatem " (1937) 49 J.R. 217; Duncan, " Regiam Majestatem: A Reconsideration," 1961 J.R. 199.

[87] While this book is called Glanvill, it was probably written not by Glanvill (Henry II of England's Justiciar) but by his nephew, Hubert Walter: see further, Plucknett, *Concise History of the Common Law*, 5th ed., 256–257.

[88] Richardson, " Roman Law in *Regiam Majestatem* " (1955) 67 J.R. 155; Stein " Source of the Romano-canonical part of *Regiam Majestatem* " (1969) 48 S.H.R. 107; Stein, " Roman Law in Scotland " in *Ius Romanum Medii Aevi*, V, part 13b, 23.

The subsequent history of the *Regiam* has been chequered. It was repeatedly chosen as part of the basis for intended revisions of the laws,[89] was condemned by Stair as "no part of our law," accepted by others and yet was still being cited in court in the twentieth century. The modern view is that it is quite authentic, an attempt, founded on Glanvill, probably made by an unknown cleric in the fourteenth century, to set out the existing law of Scotland.

The *Quoniam Attachiamenta*, usually printed along with the *Regiam*, belongs to the fourteenth century and is exclusively Scottish. It is essentially a systematic manual of procedure in feudal courts based on experience gained in practice. It includes styles and forms and even practical hints and utilises a new technical vocabulary. Nothing is known of its author. It may fairly be described as the earliest purely Scottish legal work.[90]

Developments after 1329 generally

After Bannockburn there followed a period of reconstruction; a great reform and consolidation of the system of land tenure was carried through, probably devised by Bernard de Linton, abbot of Arbroath and Chancellor of the kingdom. Under it the basic unit of land held from the Crown was the barony, usually held by knight service or archer service but sometimes for payment of money or in frankalmoign. The reorganisation was designed to strengthen both defence and the administration of justice.[91]

Many of the provisions of the reforming measures passed at this time assume the existence and use of Anglo-Norman forms of procedure and amend them to an extent which shows that Scotland had progressed considerably towards the construction of an independent legal system.[92]

The feudal pattern of society steadily tended to dissolve and effective power tended to become concentrated in fewer and larger units, though the judicial power continued dispersed, and consequently inefficient, for too long. Yet the period does not lack legal interest. In 1326 there was convoked at Cambuskenneth the first Parliament, so far as known, at which burghal representatives were present. The fifteenth and sixteenth centuries witnessed the passing of much statute law of great immediate and permanent importance. Among the most notable of these statutes are the Leases Act 1449, which gave a tenant a real right against a purchaser of the land from the landlord; the Prescription Act 1469 and later Acts establishing the long negative prescription; and the Act 1573, c. 55,

---

[89] In 1425, 1469, 1566 and 1649. See, Mackay, *Memoir of Stair*, 42–43. Projects of 1574 and 1628 did not expressly refer to *Regiam Majestatem*.
[90] Cooper, Introd. to *Regiam Majestatem*, 47–50.
[91] Rait and Pryde, 33–34; Dickinson, 173–174; Barrow, *Robert Bruce*, 416–421.
[92] Cooper, *Select Cases*, xlii.

which long regulated divorce for desertion. A number of the statutes of this period are still in force.[93] " Had it not been for these statutes, modern Scots law would have been an entirely different thing in many respects, and their enactment is proof positive of the existence of legal statesmanship of a high order at the time when they were passed." [94]

After Bruce's death in 1329 Edward III of England revived the attempt to subjugate Scotland and warfare ensued. Edward Balliol was crowned as vassal of Edward III in 1332 and in 1334 ceded much of the Lowlands to Edward, but most of the ceded territory was recovered by 1341; about this time common enmity towards England gave France and Scotland a common interest and in 1346 David II was captured while invading England and remained a prisoner till 1357; part of the exorbitant ransom was never paid but the extraordinary efforts required of an impoverished kingdom to meet the ransom resulted in important constitutional developments.[95] Meetings of Parliament and of the general council became frequent and burgesses came to attend the former certainly from 1366 and the latter from 1357, since their concurrence in the levying of taxation and the quadrupling of the great custom was thought essential. But the economic drain also militated against the enforcement of law and order.[96]

About this time too there was adopted the practice of delegating parliamentary powers to committees, one which became in time a salient, but regrettable, feature of the Scottish Parliament.[97] One was the Committee of Articles. Out of another, the Committee for Causes, and similar judicial committees, there eventually evolved the Court of Session.[98] Parliament alone was competent to deal with some matters, in particular " falsed dooms " which were brought up from court to court, possibly originating in a baron court and advancing through the court of a sheriff or lord of regality and coming up to Parliament via the justice-ayre. Resort to the king's council could not be had unless due order had been infringed at some stage or the form of law not observed. But questions of unusual character or importance might be remitted to Parliament by the royal ministers.[99]

The Beginnings of Parliament

Parliament is first referred to in Scotland in the latter years of the

---

[93] See Statute Law Revision (Scotland) Act 1964, Sched. 2.
[94] Cooper, *Selected Papers*, 227.
[95] Nicholson, *Scotland: The Later Middle Ages*, Chap. 7.
[96] Dickinson, *op. cit.* 185; see also, *Source Book*, I, 184–188; 194–203.
[97] Hume Brown, I, 181; *Source Book*, I. 204.
[98] On the judicial committees, see *Acta Dominorum Concilii*, *II* (ed. Neilson and Paton) Introd.; Rait, *Parliaments of Scotland*, 458 *et seq.*; Hamilton-Grierson, " Judicial Committees of the Scottish Parliament, 1369–70 to 1544 " (1924) 22 S.H.R. 1.
[99] Hannay, *College of Justice*, 2–3.

thirteenth century[1] and seems to have originated earlier in that century, springing from a reinforced meeting of the King's Council. Two forms of this larger body are distinguishable, namely, Parliament and General Council. The distinction lay in that Parliament was the supreme court of law and, unlike General Council, it was summoned publicly and in accordance with judicial procedure.[2] Both bodies were competent in legislation and finance, but Parliament alone had jurisdiction in cases of treason and appeals from subordinate courts, the latter by the process of " falsing of dooms." About 1530 the term " Convention of Estates " seems to have superseded that of General Council though Conventions do not seem at first to have claimed parliamentary powers.[3]

From the mid-fourteenth century the presence of burgesses was normal and, following French practice, Parliament came to be referred to as the assembly of the three Estates, or the Estates.[4] The three Estates were clergy, tenants-in-chief, and burgesses, though at a late date tenants-in-chief were superseded by Lords of Parliament and commissioners of shires (who were representatives of tenants-in-chief of lower rank than Lords of Parliament) while in its last years, apart from some Officers of State, it was composed of two groups which represented the original estate of tenants-in-chief and of one group which represented the original estate of burgesses.[5] The three Estates met separately for deliberation and discussion as well as in a single chamber for the disposal of business.

An important characteristic of the Scottish Parliament was its practice of delegating functions to committees. A committee of auditors was regularly appointed to hear judicial business and after 1424 the practice developed of appointing a committee known as the Lords of the Articles to discuss the " articles " or proposals of the Crown, probably prepared beforehand by the Council, which reported back to the final meeting of Parliament which passed the proposed legislation. In consequence in the sixteenth and seventeenth centuries sessions of Parliament were brief.[6]

Parliament as Supreme Court

It is quite apparent that from the first Parliament was a meeting of the Estates exercising judicial functions. In 1370 the Estates elected a committee to deal with matters of justice and delegation of judicial functions can be traced from at least 1341. In 1398 the regular holding of

---

[1] On earlier assemblies, see Innes, *Scotch Legal Antiquities*, 99–103.
[2] Rait, *Parliaments of Scotland*, 128.
[3] *Ibid.* 130–164.
[4] Dickinson, *op. cit.* 189–190.
[5] *Ibid.* 165–166. The franchise Act of 1587, largely re-enacting an Act of 1428, regulated the county franchise till 1832: Dickinson, *op. cit.* 214, 363.
[6] *Ibid.* 357–374; Dickinson, *op. cit.* 216–217. See also, *Source Book*, II, 37–44; III, 234–246.

Parliaments was ordained so that the king's subjects might be " servit of the law." [7] It was both a court of first instance and a court of appeal and had jurisdiction in both civil and criminal causes.

As a court of first instance it was specially concerned with cases of treason, most other criminal matters falling to the justiciars and later the High Court of Justiciary. In civil matters there were constant efforts made to limit the judicial functions of the Estates, but even after the establishment of the Court of Session, special circumstances or private influence might bring cases directly to Parliament. [8]

As a court of appeal the most important jurisdiction was the " falsing of dooms " in civil cases. [9] Appeals were allowed from baronial courts to the sheriff, from burgh courts to the court of the Four Burghs and from the sheriff court to the justiciar.

Judicial authority in Parliament belonged to the whole Parliament and to every Estate thereof, but very early came to be exercised by committees. Committees of the Great Council had been appointed to discharge judicial functions even before the War of Independence. In 1341 two auditors were appointed *ad audiendum et terminandum supplicationes et querelas* after the end of the Parliamentary session and judicial commissions were again appointed in 1369 and 1370. These auditors had to hear the cases and probably suggest suitable disposal for them, the final decision being pronounced in Parliament. Thereafter the practice of appointing Lords Auditors was regular. [10]

Ecclesiastical Courts

Before the Reformation the bishop of each diocese had his own consistorial court, presided over by a judge known as the official, who was skilled in the canon and frequently also in the civil law. From his decisions there was normally no appeal to the bishop. [11]

The ecclesiastical courts were chiefly occupied with matrimonial cases, questions of legitimacy and illegitimacy and of dowry, with causes relating to testacy and intestacy, and the interpretation of wills, and with cases of slander. The canon lawyers also tried to extend the jurisdiction of the Church courts to all cases of contract which had been fortified by the oaths of the parties. They also had to deal with disputes as to patronage, or tithes, or concerning Church property, and petty cases

---

[7] A.P.S. I, 573.

[8] Rait, *Parliaments of Scotland*, 456.

[9] A.P.S. II, 246, 254.

[10] Rait, *op. cit.* 459–460.

[11] Dowden, *Medieval Church in Scotland*, 288; Donaldson, in *Introduction to Scottish Legal History*, Chap. 27.

of assaults on ecclesiastics or brawling in sacred places. In addition much business came before the bishop's court by consent of parties.[12]

The majority of the matrimonial causes were instituted with a view to obtaining a declaration of the nullity of a pretended marriage. Marriage was considered indissoluble so long as the spouses lived and the only divorce granted was a separation *a mensa et thoro*, which did not permit remarriage of the parties.[13]

Apart from the body of ecclesiastical legislation which formed the canon law and was the general law of the Church throughout Western Christendom, there was a substantial amount of legislation by provincial synods peculiar to Scotland.[14] Much of this was drawn from the statutes of English councils. Some dealt with clerical duties and conduct but a great deal concerned the laity also.

The Auld Alliance

The period from 1329 to the death of James II in 1460 was also the really significant period of the alliance with France. By 1460 the English had been finally expelled from both Scotland and France and France was now on the threshold of developing into a great European power. Neither any longer needed the alliance but its tradition persisted long after 1460 and led Scotland into disastrous adventures.[15]

The influence of France on Scottish civilisation in these and later years was considerable and it replaced that of England in the legal and administrative as in most other spheres.[16] A number of Scottish practices appear to owe their origin to French influence, such as the sitting of the king *pro tribunali*, analogous to the *Lit de Justice* of the French kings, the institution of the Scottish parliamentary auditors, analogous to the *maitres de requetes*, about 1341, shortly after David II returned from France, the provision of counsel for the poor, found in France in 1400 and 1414 and instituted in Scotland in 1424, the development of a body of practitioners inferior to counsel, *les solliciteurs*.[17] Apart from direct influence, both countries were influenced by feudalism and Scottish

---

[12] *Ibid.* 287. For specimens of the work of the courts, see *Liber Officialis Sancti Andree* (ed. Innes, 1844), and Dowden, 295–298. See also Hannay, " Scotland and the Canon Law " (1937) 49 J.R. 25; Anton, " Medieval Scottish Executors and The Courts Spiritual " (1955) 67 J.R. 129.

[13] *Ibid.* 290.

[14] *Ibid.* 224–239. They may be found in *Statutes of the Scottish Church* (ed. Patrick, S.H.S.).

[15] Rait and Pryde, 40.

[16] *Ibid.* See also Smith, " Influence of the Auld Alliance on the Law of Scotland," 1961 S.L.T. (News) 125.

[17] Neilson and Paton, Introduction to *Acta Dominorum Concilii*, II. See also Gardner, " French and Dutch Influence," in *Sources and Literature* (Stair Society), 226; Walton, " Relationship of the Law of France to the Law of Scotland " (1902) 14 J.R. 19; " Influence of France on Scots Law " (1895) 3 S.L.T. 189; Ross, *Lectures on Conveyancing and Diligence*, I, 180, 235, 414, 420.

students resorted regularly to Orleans, Bourges and Louvain prior to the Reformation and the French connection was the channel through which, particularly in the medieval period, the Roman and feudal laws were received into Scotland.[18]

The Origins of the Session

Warfare, invasion and rebellion continued to be the rule till about 1424 when James I (1406–37), who had been captured at sea in 1405 on his way to refuge in France, was ransomed and released. He returned to Scotland determined to introduce law and order, " to make the key keep the castle and the bracken bush the cow " and set about repressing disorder. He tried to apply to Scotland many ideas learned during his captivity in England. Parliament was summoned frequently and many measures taken to improve the machinery of government.[19]

James early tried to reform the ordinary courts which were always giving cause for complaint by an Act ordaining that there be made officers and ministers of law through all the realm to give law to the king's commons. The attempt failed and the king tried another method. An Act of 1426[20] accordingly decreed that the chancellor and certain discreet persons chosen from each Estate should sit three times a year and determine complaints and causes.[21] Nine members were usually chosen, three from each Estate, with the Clerk Register in attendance. This was modelled on the auditorial committee of Parliament but distinct therefrom and was intended to relieve the council of business and administer justice more regularly than could be done in connection with Parliament. There is little information on the working of the new institution but it flourished sufficiently to acquire the name of " the session " and survived to about 1468 or 1470 when this model of session seems to have been abandoned.[22]

Another Act of 1426 directed all freeholders of the Crown, both great and small, to attend Parliament and General Council in person but in 1428 it was laid down that only the greater tenants-in-chief would be summoned by writ, but the other freeholders need not attend but might be represented by two commissioners from each shire and these were

---

[18] Cameron, " Scottish Students at Paris University, 1466–92 " (1936) 48 J.R. 228; see also Mitchell, " Scottish Law Students in Italy in the Later Middle Ages " (1937) 49 J.R. 19.

[19] *Source Book*, II, 10, 13. See also Hannay, " Observations on the Officers of the Scottish Parliament " (1932) 44 J.R. 125.

[20] A.P.S. II, 11.

[21] Rait and Pryde, 37; Hannay, *College of Justice*, 5–7; and generally, Balfour-Melville, *James I*. See also Duncan, in *Introduction to Scottish Legal History*, Chap. 23; *Source Book*, II, 45–46.

[22] Hannay, 8; Dickinson, 213.

to elect a speaker on the English model. Neither Act seems to have been operative.[23]

Yet another facet of the urge to establish settled government and to enforce law and order was the appointment of a commission in 1425 to examine the books of law, that is, *Regiam Majestatem* and *Quoniam Attachiamenta*, and amend the laws that needed amending. But nothing seems to have come of this.[24] An Act of 1426 provided that all the king's subjects were to be governed by the king's laws, not by particular laws or privileges. Thus there was to be a common law of the realm.[25]

There was also a considerable volume of well-intentioned social and economic regulation, such as the regulation of dress and prices, the prohibition of football and poaching, and the exhortation to hunt wolves and sow peas and beans.[26] It is clear that the executive was inadequate to enforce these Acts.

In 1450 the king was to choose certain discreet persons of the three Estates who were to hold three sessions a year along with the chancellor. In 1456 the Estates themselves chose nine judges, three from each Estate, to sit in three sections after the General Council which appointed them had dispersed, to hear and decide cases. In 1458 the Estates provided that the Session was to be continued till the next Parliament and the Lords of Session were to hold three sittings of forty days each at Edinburgh, Perth and Aberdeen. Three of each Estate were appointed for each sitting. This was supplementary both to the local courts and the parliamentary auditors. Further Sessions seem to have been appointed in 1460, 1464–65 and 1468 but the Parliament of 1467 appointed auditors in two divisions, *ad querelas* and *ad judicia contradicta*, with the provision that causes undecided during the parliamentary session should be decided by the Lords of Council.[27] This " continuing " of cases from Parliament to council became regular after this time.

While Parliament continued to meet regularly during the reign of James III (1460–88) the Lords of the Articles were the virtual masters of the country and their existence was detrimental to the development of a strong and effective Parliament.[28] A committee for causes and complaints, usually of three members from each Estate, was appointed at least fourteen times during the reign. The committee for falsed dooms was appointed less frequently.

In 1471 it was made possible to make direct complaint to the council

---

[23] Rait and Pryde, 38; Hume Brown, I, 218–219; Dickinson, 214–215.

[24] Cooper, *Regiam Majestatem* (Stair Society), 1.

[25] Dickinson, *op. cit.* 212; Nicholson, *op. cit.* 309.

[26] Rait and Pryde, 38; Nicholson, 309; Menzies, " The Social Legislation of James I, 1424–37 " (1927) 39 J.R. 262.

[27] A.P.S. II, 88. For a collection of materials showing the evolution of the central court, see Neilson and Paton (ed.). *Acta Dominorum Concilii*, 1496–1501, pp. x–xxviii.

[28] Hume Brown, I, 289; Nicholson, Chap. 15.

in respect of an error at the trial and in 1487 a summons of reduction was recognised as an alternative to falsing a doom as a mode of appeal. Falsing survived for the better part of another century but the tendency was to facilitate access to the council.[29] In the late fifteenth century it was apparent that the council could not avoid responsibility for civil justice, though it was frequently interrupted by affairs of state.

In 1469 or 1487 there was a revival of the project of revising the law, the king's laws, *Regiam Majestatem*, Acts, statutes and other books, but again nothing came of it and the administration of justice languished during the reign.[30] Sessions of the council for civil causes, as distinct from sessions of the Lords Auditors, began at least as early as 1478,[31] and the council found itself increasingly committed to dealing with civil causes.

In 1488 the king was slain in the course of a rebellion and it is significant of the increased prestige of the monarchy that the rebels deemed it necessary to obtain parliamentary approval of their conduct and sought to explain to the people and to foreign countries that they had not been guilty of rebellion.[32]

Under James IV (1488–1513) there was material improvement in the administration of justice and the king personally took an active part in holding the justice-ayres all over the kingdom.[33]

In 1491 the Chancellor was ordained to sit with certain lords of council or else the lords of session for the disposal of civil causes, three times a year, during the terms which James I had fixed for the auditorial sessions.[34] At first there was no clear distinction between judicial business and General Council business and the personnel were always mixed, partly officers of state, partly members of the privy council and partly others brought in to be lords of session.

In 1495 an attempt was made to settle a " table " or distribution of summonses, in fact, a court roll, and the experiment was tried of disposing of session business in conjunction with that of the justice-ayres. This was unsuccessful as was an attempt in 1503 to group the shires so that cases might come up in order and litigants be aware of approximate dates.[35]

In 1504 the privy council proposed the institution of a council to sit continually in Edinburgh and decide all civil matters, apparently to fill the gaps between sessions but not to supersede the customary sittings

[29] Hannay, 10–11.
[30] Dickinson, *op. cit.* 226–227.
[31] Hannay, *College of Justice*, 22.
[32] Rait and Pryde, 41.
[33] Hume Brown, I, 340–341; Hannay, 15–16; Mackie, *King James IV of Scotland*, 57–58, 192–193.
[34] A.P.S. II, 226.
[35] Hannay, 16–18.

of council. This body was set up, but was to be itinerant and to have the same power as the lords of session, and it came to be known as the " daily council " and in 1505 the lords of session and the king's council sat concurrently on civil business. The term " session " was applied indiscriminately to both, but the association of the lords of session with the Chancellor and the fact that they sat in Edinburgh warrants the conclusion that the Court of Session had now evolved.[36] The whole of the fifteenth century is accordingly a period of experiment, false starts and struggle against arrears of judicial business and the detail of the story is not clear. The burgh courts continued to exercise both civil and criminal jurisdiction in their own spheres and to deal with much legal work of everyday concern.[37]

The College of Justice

The foundation of the College of Justice is legally the most important event in the reign of James V (1513–42).[38] In the early years of the reign there was a growing tendency for the session to become a specialised branch of the council's work. Thus in 1526 eight persons were added to the lords of secret council to sit on the next session and nearly all seem to have been experienced in law.[39] By 1527 eleven of those subsequently appointed senators of the College of Justice in 1532 were already acting.[40] But some settled remuneration was needed if judges were to be permanent and this was still lacking. The king badly needed money and approached the Pope who in July 1531 imposed a tithe on the Scottish Church for three years as a subsidy for the defence of the realm. It probably owed something to pressure on the Pope by the Emperor arising from enmity towards Henry VII of England. In September a further bull was issued, narrating the king's desire to establish a college of judges,[41] and requiring the prelates to contribute a large sum annually for this purpose. The project of the College of Justice seems to have been extemporised as a pretext for obtaining the subsidy.[42] The prelates sought to offer a composition for the perpetual tax and, pending settlement of this issue, a President and fourteen others were named to sit in the interval

---

[36] *Ibid.* 19–21.

[37] Dickinson, *op. cit.* 250–251.

[38] See generally, Irvine Smith, " The Transition to the Modern Law, " in *Introduction to Scottish Legal History* (Stair Society), Chap. 3.

[39] Hannay, 29–30.

[40] *Ibid.* 35.

[41] The view that the College was founded on the model of the Parlement of Paris is a mistake. If it had any model it was the Collegio dei Giudici of Pavia: Hannay, *op. cit.* 49; Stein, " The College of Judges of Pavia " (1952) 64 J.R. 204; McKechnie in *Common Errors in Scottish History* (Historical Assocn., 1956). See also Thomson, " The Old Fifteen " (1921) 33 J.R. 225; J. S. H(enderson), " The Scottish College of Justice in the 16th century " (1934) 50 L.Q.R. 120; " Connection between the Parlement of Paris and the Court of Session " (1897) 5 S.L.T. 72, 74.

[42] Hannay, 50–54; Dickinson, 308.

until the college might be established. No scheme had really been thought out and it was difficult to fit the contemplated college of judges into the pattern of lords of council and session.

It was provided also that the Chancellor, if present, might occupy the presidential chair, and that the king might nominate three or four lords of his great council to take part in the judicial business as extra-ordinary lords. The president and half of the fourteen judges were to be clerics. Negotiations over the ecclesiastical subsidy and preoccupation with defence caused delay and it was not until 1535 that the Pope granted the bull creating the College of Justice.[43] In 1541 Parliament confirmed the first institution of the college in 1532, ratified the papal bull, and or-dained that the college should remain perpetually for the administration of justice to the lieges of the realm.[44] It also gave the senators power to make Acts for the ordering of process and the expedition of justice. The importance for the development of the law and the proper administra-tion of justice of having a permanent supreme court was immense.

At first the court sat as a collegiate body but by about 1554 there is evidence of lords proceeding to the outer tolbooth to hear witnesses and before 1600 it seems to have become settled practice to have two or three ordinary lords sitting in the outer house dealing with bills and witnesses.[45]

Legal Consequences of the Reformation

Anti-Catholic religious doctrines had been making headway in Scot-land for some time before 1546 when the Reformation flared into life with the murder of Cardinal Beaton in St. Andrews castle. The new religious opinions made steady progress despite attempts at repression. In 1559 direct action was resorted to and much ecclesiastical property was damaged.[46]

When the Estates met in 1560 Knox's Confession of Faith[47] was ratified and the national Church abolished, along with the papal authority, the mass, and all practices contrary to the new creed. An Act of that year also abolished all papal jurisdictions and brought to an end the courts of the Officials in the dioceses and appeals therefrom to Rome.

Consistorial cases and all matters formerly competent in the ecclesi-astical tribunals were determined by the Court of Session from 1560 to 1563 though the kirk sessions in various parts of the country consti-tuted themselves consistorial courts. In 1563, however, there was estab-

---

[43] Hannay, 56–61.

[44] A.P.S. II, 371; *Source Book*, II, 48–52.

[45] Hannay, 91–98. See also Cooper, " The King versus the Court of Session " (1946) 58 J.R. 83, and *Selected Papers*, 116; and Cooper, " The Central Courts after 1532," in *Introduction* (Stair Society), Chap. 24.

[46] Hume Brown, II, 20–70; Dickinson, 323–331.

[47] Printed in his *History of the Reformation in Scotland* (ed. Dickinson) II, 257.

lished the commissary court of Edinburgh, with four judges authorised to determine all causes formerly competent in the courts of the Roman Officials, and jurisdiction over all Scotland in matters of marriage, divorce and bastardy.[48]   The office of Commissary was held by some learned lawyers but the slowness of the court's proceedings gave rise to general dissatisfaction.   Appeal lay to the Court of Session.   Despite the change the consistorial law of the old courts, based on the canon law of the pre-Reformation provincial councils of the Scottish Church, continued to be observed, except in so far as expressly altered by the reformers.[49]

The previous marriage law was defective in having excessively extended the forbidden degrees of relationship for marriage [50] which resulted in much uncertainty whether persons were married or not and much ingenuity in finding grounds on which marriages might be declared null.

In 1567 Parliament annulled all laws, acts and constitutions, canon, civil or municipal, contrary to the reformed religion, and later provided that marriage should be open to all related in the second degree or more remotely.[51]

The most material change was, however, in the introduction of judicial divorce.   Prior to the Reformation separation only was recognised in accordance with the general canon law of the West.[52]   Immediately after the Reformation, however, the courts held that divorce for adultery was competent at common law.[53]   In 1573 divorce for malicious desertion, persisted in for four years,[54] was introduced by statute, although the statute narrates that since 1560 it had been the law that divorce was allowed for desertion, and divorces on both grounds were regularly granted from that time onward.[55]

Medieval Legal Literature—Practicks

The establishment of the Court of Session gave rise to a new kind of legal literature, notes of judgments made privately by judges for their own use, passed from hand to hand and frequently copied.   The collections came to be known by the names of their compilers.   Two

---

[48] This court was created by royal charter and ratified by Parliament in 1592.

[49] See further, *Introduction to Scottish Legal History* (Stair Society), Chaps. 6, 7 and 8.

[50] Hay Fleming, *Reformation in Scotland*, 477–502; Dowden, *Medieval Church in Scotland*, 251. See also Fraser, on *Husband and Wife*, 2nd ed., 104–134: Hay's *Lectures on Marriage*, 185 *et seq.*

[51] Hay Fleming, 503; Fraser, 112.

[52] *Cf.* Hay's *Lectures on Marriage*, 59.

[53] Fraser, 1141.

[54] Reduced to three years in 1938; the other grounds of divorce are also modern.

[55] Judicial divorce, as distinct from divorce by Act of Parliament, was not permitted in England till 1857.

kinds of practicks [56] developed, those which contained only notes of decisions, usually in chronological order, and those others which included abstracts of statutes and other sources, such as passages from *Regiam Majestatem*, as well as notes of cases and practical observations, and were usually digested under alphabetical subject-headings. The best-known examples of the latter kind are the *Practicks* of Balfour,[57] Spotiswoode [58] and Hope,[59] and this kind of *Practicks* is the forerunner of the modern textbook or encyclopaedia, while the former kind is the forerunner of the modern law reports. Balfour's *Practicks* in particular is regarded as authoritative and is of the greatest importance for the law of Scotland down to 1579 since it preserves matter from earlier collections now lost and covers the whole field of Scots law. Collections of *Practicks* continued to be made well into the seventeenth century until the decision-Practicks were superseded by the early published reports and the digest-Practicks by the treatises of Craig and Stair.

Private Law, 1328–1600

If informality and lack of precision characterised procedure at this time the substantive law was in no better state. The records contain specimens of many kinds of actions, usually exhibiting the common tendency of undeveloped law " to conceive of any legal question as one of wrongdoing and its suppression." [60] " With insignificant exceptions one and all of them are envisaged simply as the infliction of a wrong by the defender upon the pursuer, as if the only chapter in the law of Scotland were one devoted to delicts or torts. Irrespective of whether the action is one for breach of contract, or for payment of a debt or the price of goods sold, or for damages, or for specific implement, or for delivery, or for warrandice of title, or for reduction of a challenged transaction, or for half a hundred other things, the pursuer simply takes objection to the ' wrangous ' detention and withholding of something, or the ' wrangous ' occupation and labouring of certain lands, and so on; and the common form of judgment is one which simply finds that the defender did ' wrang ' or did ' na wrang,' as the case may be. It is hardly an exaggeration to say that each pursuer eventually presented himself before the tribunal in the guise of ' an infant crying in the night,

---

[56] See McKechnie, " Practicks " in *Sources and Literature* (Stair Society), 25. " Practick " means a decision or precedent, and hence in the plural a collection of decisions.

[57] Published in 1754; reprinted by the Stair Society, 1962–63; see McKechnie, " Balfour's Practicks " (1931) 43 J.R. 179; McNeill, " Sir James Balfour of Pittendreich " (1960) 5 J.R.(N.S.) 1.

[58] Published 1706.

[59] Published by the Stair Society in 1937–38 in two volumes as Hope's *Major Practicks*. A slighter collection by the same Hope was published in 1726 as Hope's *Minor Practicks*.

[60] Daube, " The Scales of Justice " (1951) 63 J.R. 124.

and with no language but a cry' and that the whole of Scots law had been compressed into a single commandment: 'Thou shalt do na wrang'."[61]

While this was the case with litigation, in this same period land law was being developed to a high degree and charters evidence a considerable measure of skill in conveyancing.[62]

III.—THE UNION OF THE CROWNS AND AFTER

The Union of the Crowns brought many changes; it greatly increased the prestige of the monarchy and also removed the king from personal participation in the government of Scotland. James utilised the Tudor device of government by council and the Privy Council became the main executive and, to some extent, the legislative body. He also managed Parliament by utilising the committee of the Lords of the Articles, whose composition was not unlike that of the Privy Council. Even the General Assemblies were convened by him and their work prearranged. The business of government was mainly effected by the great officers of state who were the leading members of the Privy Council and their supervision extended to every branch of the national administration.

James had ordained (1587) that justice-ayres should be held twice a year in every shire, with eight persons specially commissioned to conduct them.[63] In 1609 he enlarged the duties of the office of justice of the peace so as to comprise the functions of a local magistracy. A sufficient number was to be appointed for every shire, those of lesser rank to be paid for their services, and they were endowed with all the duties of magistracy, save that capital offenders and those of high rank were to be referred to the Council, and the powers of provosts and bailies of burghs were also saved.[64] In 1611 Norse law and customs were abolished in Orkney and Shetland and the isles were annexed to the Crown in 1612.[65]

In 1604 a project for the complete union of Scotland and England, a matter urged by the king in his first speech to the English Parliament, resulted in the appointment of commissioners to discuss the issue. The project broke down on account of the English refusal to concede parity to the Scots on account of their greater wealth and resources.[66] The

---

[61] Cooper, " Dark Age," in *Selected Papers*, 219.

[62] Conacher, " Feudal Tenures in Scotland in the 15th and 16th Centuries " (1936) 48 J.R. 189.

[63] A.P.S. III, 458; *Source Book*, III, 283–285.

[64] Hume Brown, II, 277–278; Pryde, *Scotland from 1603*, 5; *Source Book*, III, 278–282.

[65] Pryde, *op. cit.* 5.

[66] Hume Brown, II, 246; Hill Burton, V, 401–408; Rait and Pryde, 60–61. Sir Thomas Craig was one of the Scottish Commissioners and his arguments are printed in *De Unione Regnorum Britanniae Tractatus* (ed. Sanford Terry, S.H.S.). See also *Source Book*, III, 456–461.

furthest James was able to go was to obtain from the English Parliament the repeal of the Acts which treated Scotland as a hostile country, and the decision [67] that Scots born after his accession to the English throne were not aliens in England. A similar concession was made by the Scottish Parliament for the king's English subjects.[68] Beyond that his scheme for an incorporating union failed. James also assumed by proclamation the title of King of Great Britain,[69] while he also gave Scottish trade a measure of commercial freedom in England.

James meanwhile steadily pursued his ecclesiastical policy, directed towards the full restoration of episcopacy in Scotland. Bishops had been restored and their powers extended while in 1610 the king imposed on the country two Courts of High Commission (united in 1615) for the punishment of ecclesiastical offences.[70] Each was under an Archbishop and had authority over the whole populace in life or religion and they came to be a byword for arbitrary action, wide and indefinite powers, unreasonable severity and tyranny.[71]

Mounting Opposition under Charles I

The reign of Charles I opened with trouble. He secured the passage in October 1625 of a very comprehensive Act of Revocation which threatened the resumption by the Crown of all grants of land made by it since 1542, including most of the gifts of old Church lands.[72] This attempt to take back the bulk of the property of the pre-Reformation Church alienated most of the nobles, since most of them had acquired some of the former Church lands, and they tended to ally with the Presbyterians against the king. Charles, however, pushed through his policy in the face of opposition.

In the following year the king initiated legal proceedings for annulling many titles to ecclesiastical lands and teinds or tithes, which had come to be largely in the hands of lay owners, other than the heritors or owners of the lands, and known as titulars, since he planned the provision of a reasonable maintenance for the clergy from the teinds.[73] Only in 1629 was he able to pronounce a final deliverance settling the composition for which the heritors were entitled to purchase their teinds from the titulars. While the plan was sensible and put ministerial stipends on a sure basis, the king's actions antagonised many of the nobles and lords.

Charles even sought to revive one of his father's institutions known

---

[67] *Calvin's Case*, or the case of the *post-nati*: (1608) 2 St.Tr. 459; 7 Co.Rep. 6a.
[68] Hill Burton, V, 409–410; Pryde, *op. cit.* 3.
[69] Rymer, XVI, 603.
[70] Hume Brown, II, 249; *Source Book*, III, 58–60.
[71] *Ibid.* 250.
[72] Rait and Pryde, 63; Hume Brown, II, 286–289. See also Macmillan, " The Court of Session in 1629 " (1900) 12 J.R. 137.
[73] Rait and Pryde, 63; Hume Brown, II, 286–289; *Source Book*, III, 66–67.

as the Commission for Grievances, with enlarged powers which would have virtually made it a Scottish Star Chamber, but strenuous opposition made him desist.[74]

Through control of the Lords of the Articles Charles secured much legislation of the kind he desired, including Acts relative to religion which made clear his intention to make the Church of Scotland conform to the Laudian pattern of the Church of England. This body of legislation excited both attention and hostility and in 1635 a new Book of Canons was imposed, while a new Court of High Commission with more extensive powers was established to secure the operation of the new canons.[75] In 1637 the attempt to impose Laud's Liturgy led to riots, the National Covenant and the Glasgow Assembly of 1638 which swept away all the traces of episcopacy and abolished the Court of High Commission.[76] Then followed the Bishops' Wars and the quarrels between king and Parliament in England which resulted in the Civil War. The struggle between king and Parliament took place mainly in England but not without intervention by the Scottish army. The last stages of Charles's reign and his execution were, however, wholly the acts of his English subjects. During the years 1638–49 the Parliament and the General Assembly had played a larger part than ever before in the affairs of the country, and had made real advances in the government of the country. At the same time the parishes and burghs advanced in importance and the system of shires was extended and completed.[77]

Commonwealth and Protectorate

Scotland espoused the cause of Charles II and came to blows with the English in consequence. Cromwell defeated the Scottish royalist forces at Dunbar (1650) and Worcester (1651) and proceeded to the subjugation of the country. The Estates were captured at Alyth, the royal robes and public records sent from Stirling to London and arrangements made for the government of the country. Eight commissioners were entrusted with the task. The first idea had been to convert Scotland into a province of England, but more generous conditions were proposed later. Scotland and England were to be made into one Commonwealth with all convenient speed, liberty of worship secured, and compensation paid for damage caused to England by the resistance on Charles's behalf.[78] The representatives of the shires and burghs had no option but to acquiesce. Deputies had further to be chosen to go to London not so much to discuss

[74] Hume Brown, II, 285.
[75] *Ibid.* 298–299.
[76] See *Source Book*, III, 90–115.
[77] Pryde, *op. cit.* 10–12.
[78] Hume Brown, II, 365–366. The detailed story is traced in *The Cromwellian Union* (ed. Terry, S.H.S.). See also *Source Book*, III, 146–151.

the proposed union as to supply information for the Bill to effect it. Scotland sent thirty members to the Commonwealth and Protectorate Parliaments, twenty representing the thirty-three shires and ten representing fifty-seven of the burghs; some of the features of this system of representation such as double-county seats and districts of burghs appeared in much later schemes of parliamentary representation.[79] The representation allotted in 1651 was in fact ridiculously inadequate and many of the members were English officers, mere ciphers of the government.[80]

The Privy Council and Court of Session ceased to function on Cromwell's invasion in 1650 and the Commonwealth appointed seven Commissioners, of whom four were English, to administer justice.[81] Their efficiency and impartiality contrasted favourably with their dilatory predecessors. The court sat as a body, each judge acting as president for a week in rotation. The heritable jurisdictions were abolished and the judges went on circuit. The Outer House was abolished but restored in 1655.[82] Scotland benefited on the whole from the firm rule of the Protectorate in matters of administration and justice.

Consideration of union was still proceeding when Cromwell dissolved Parliament and was appointed Protector by the Instrument of Government (1654). Later in that year the Council produced the Ordinance of Union which provided that Scotland was henceforth to make one Commonwealth with England and to send thirty members to the Union Parliament. The Protectorate Parliament was however dissolved before it could confirm the Ordinance of Union.

In 1656 the Commissioners for the government of Scotland were replaced by a Council of State of eight while seven were appointed to supervise the administration of justice, and in the following year the Ordinance of Union was approved by the second Protectorate Parliament but within a year the Long Parliament was restored and the whole question of union reopened.[83] The restoration of the Stuarts put an end to hopes of union and to the English domination yet it has to be conceded that peace and order had been better maintained under the Protectorate than ever before.

The Restoration

The Scottish Parliament met again in 1661, but it was a carefully

---

[79] Pryde, *op. cit.* 14–15.

[80] Rait and Pryde, 67–68; *Source Book*, III, 248–251; 462–468.

[81] Mackay, *Memoir of Stair*, 58–59. The Scots were Sir John Hope of Craighall, Colonel William Lockhart and John Swinton of Swinton. See also McMillan, " Judicial System of the Commonwealth in Scotland " (1937) 49 J.R. 232; Cooper, " Cromwell's Judges and their Influence on Scots Law " (1946) 58 J.R. 20 and in *Selected Papers*, 111.

[82] Mackay, 60–62. Stair was raised to the bench in 1657, but the courts were closed from Cromwell's death in 1658 till the Restoration.

[83] Hume Brown, II, 374–375.

selected body of members and passed a large volume of subservient legislation, restoring the nearly absolute monarchy of the days of James VI.[84] A general Rescissory Act declared null and void the proceedings of every Parliament since 1633. The Privy Council now proceeded to restore episcopacy and from 1662 onwards the Privy Council was the effective government of the country. The Court of High Commission was even revived in 1664 to enforce royal ecclesiastical policy, but was so detested that it fell into abeyance within a couple of years.[85]

The Court of Session was restored, Stair being one of the judges and from 1661 he was named Vice-President [86] but in 1664 he resigned, having refused to take the Declaration that it was unlawful for subjects to enter into Leagues and Covenants, but was then readmitted by the king's personal intervention.[87]

Free trade with England came to an end at the Restoration and Scottish trade began again to suffer from the English Navigation Acts. Charles II was unable to secure for Scotland the privileges obtained by James VI and I. Negotiations in 1667 for a commercial treaty came to naught, but consequent on that failure Commissioners were again appointed by both Parliaments to treat of union.[88] The Commissioners met at Westminster for two months in 1670 and adjourned but did not reassemble. The conference failed on the refusal of the English to accept the Scottish demand that the existing number of members of the Scottish Parliament should sit in a Parliament of Great Britain, and over the difficulty of appeals to Parliament, the Scottish Commissioners being insistent that no appeals could lie from Council and Session to the proposed Parliament of Great Britain.[89] Four years later this problem gave rise to the secession of the Bar.

In a litigation between Lords Dunfermline and Callendar in the Court of Session the defeated party sought to appeal to the Estates of Parliament, and the counsel for the appellants were suspended from their profession. This was taken as an insult to the whole Bar and some fifty members of the Faculty of Advocates seceded and remained out for two years until the matter was compromised in 1676.[90]

The Privy Council continued to govern Scotland in a bitter atmosphere of religious antagonism and repression of Presbyterianism until 1679 when the Duke of York (later James VII) became Royal Com-

---

[84] Gray, " Judicial Proceedings of the Parliaments of Scotland, 1660–88 " (1924) 36 J.R. 135.

[85] Hume Brown, II, 385–393; *Source Book*, III, 152–160.

[86] Mackay, *Memoir of Stair*, 70–71.

[87] *Ibid.* 74–79.

[88] Lord Stair was one of the Commissioners. For the negotiations, see *The Cromwellian Union* (ed. Terry, S.H.S.), Appx.

[89] Rait and Pryde, 75–76; Mackay, *Memoir of Stair*, 90.

[90] See further Mackay, *Memoir of Stair*, 113–116; Hill Burton, VII, 194–195; Sir George Mackenzie's *Memoirs*, 267 *et seq.*

missioner. In 1681 he convened a Parliament which passed a Test Act, prescribing a test to be taken henceforth by all holding offices of trust in Church and State.[91] Stair, Lord President of the Court of Session, and others resigned rather than take the Test. The Privy Council governed for the rest of the reign and persisted in seeking the repression of Covenanters, a task in which Sir George Mackenzie, the Lord Advocate, distinguished himself as a fanatic for the prerogative.[92]

In 1685 James VII succeeded his brother; tyranny and persecution continued. His attempts to grant indulgence to Catholics further roused opposition and by 1688 Scotland as much as England was looking to William of Orange for deliverance. He duly landed at Torbay and James fled to France. A Convention Parliament assembled and in April 1689 made a declaration that James had forfeited the Crown and that the throne was now vacant, and they offered the Crown to William and Mary, bringing to an end the period from 1603 during most of which Scotland had been governed autocratically and repressively.

The High Court of Justiciary [93]

From the feudal period there had existed the institution of justiciars for Scotland and by the middle of James V's reign the office of justice-general was apparently exercised by one individual with various deputes. Down to the sixteenth century the office was not hereditary but it then became hereditary in the family of Argyll. Argyll in 1628 resigned the office into the hands of Charles I but reserved his rights as justice-general for Argyll, Tarbet and the Isles. In 1587 Parliament had again to enact that justice-ayres should be held by the justice-general and his deputes commissioned for the purpose.

In 1672 the office of justice-depute was abolished and the High Court of Justiciary created, consisting of the Justice-General, Justice-Clerk [94] and five [95] judges of the Court of Session as Commissioners of Justiciary, for the trial of criminal causes in Edinburgh.[96] The office of Lord Justice-General became a sinecure post and not till 1808 was it provided that on the death of the existing holder (the Duke of Montrose), which happened in 1837, the office should be held by the Lord President.   The same Act divided the kingdom into three districts and appointed circuit

---

[91] *Source Book*, III, 185–189.

[92] Hume Brown, II, 141–221.

[93] See further Dickinson in *Introduction* (Stair Society), Chap. 31; Scott, " Archives of the High Court of Justiciary " (1891) 3 J.R. 197; 4 J.R. 32, 105, 293.

[94] He was originally clerk of the justiciar's court, later acted as assessor, and did not become a judge till the seventeenth century: see Ersk, I, 3, 26; Hannay, " Office of Justice Clerk " (1935) 47 J.R. 311.

[95] Only in 1887 by the Criminal Procedure Act did all judges of the Court of Session become Lords Commissioners of Justiciary also.

[96] Mackinnon, *Constitutional History of Scotland*, 260–261; Ersk, I, 3, 26; *Source Book*, III, 283–287.

courts to be held each spring, a system which with modifications still survives.

The Public Registers of Deeds

The Scottish registers are in some cases of great antiquity, that of the Great Seal being extant since 1306, but of greatest importance for the land law was the institution in 1617 of the General Register of Sasines, which maintains from henceforth a continuous record of all transactions relating to or affecting landed property, the existence and accuracy of which has been of the greatest value in ensuring the validity and security of such transactions, since search of the Sasine register for the appropriate county will reveal previous transactions with the land and many of the burdens affecting it.[97] In 1672 the system was developed by the requirement of keeping a minute-book recording those in whose favour charters and writs were granted, while permission was given for writs and charters to be written book-wise.

Development of Private Law in the Seventeenth Century

Despite civil war and religious persecution, private law was greatly developed and improved in the seventeenth century.[98] Much legislation of fundamental and permanent importance was passed such as the statutes of prescription,[99] the foundation of the law of entail,[1] new regulations for the conduct of business in the Court of Session,[2] an Act nullifying alienations in defraud of creditors,[3] regulating the execution of deeds,[4] settlement of the law of tithes, rules for the division of commonties and runrig lands, which were complementary to the statutes for the encouragement of agriculture, the statutory recognition of the fundamental principles of bankruptcy, and many other important pieces of legislation. Trading enterprise flourished and many joint-stock companies were established.[5]

It is remarkable that at this time, despite, apart from the disturbances, the extent of royal and other authority and the weakness of Parliament,

---

[97] Registration Act 1617, c. 16; *Source Book*, III, 565. There had been earlier attempts in 1425, 1469, 1555 and 1587. Registration is now governed by the Land Registers (Scotland) Act 1868. Other registers include the Register of Deeds (since 1554) in which, *inter alia*, wills are now registered, the Registers of Inhibitions and Adjudications, of Hornings, of Service of Heirs and others. There are now 15 registers in all, mostly of considerable antiquity and all of great legal and historical value. See further, Milne, *The Scottish Office*, 190–192; *Edinburgh* (Third Statistical Account) 226–229.

[98] See further, Irvine Smith, " The Rise of Modern Scots Law, 1660–1707," in *Introduction to Scottish Legal History*, Chap. 4.

[99] Prescription Acts 1617, c. 12; 1669, c. 9.

[1] Entail Act 1685, c. 22.

[2] Courts Act 1672, c. 16.

[3] Bankruptcy Act 1621, c. 18.

[4] Subscription of Deeds Act 1681, c. 5.

[5] Pryde, *op. cit.* 31. See also Conacher, " Land Tenure in the Seventeenth Century " (1938) 50 J.R. 18.

such importance and beneficial character were
hat the leading lawyers and statesmen must have
had profound knowledge of the law and also a strong desire to develop
and improve the legal system and the judicial institutions.[6]

The Seventeenth-Century Jurists

In the seventeenth century flourished a considerable number of jurists
of great importance for the development of the law whose works are still
of importance and authority.[7]

Sir Thomas Craig of Riccarton (1540–1607), justice-depute in 1564,
was the first systematic writer on law, as distinct from a collector of
decisions and statutes.[8] His *Jus Feudale* (1603, pub. 1654) deals with
the origin of law and traces the progress of the civil, canon and feudal
laws. His exposition of the feudal law makes the work the first Scottish
institutional text. He also wrote on the succession to the English throne,
a treatise on the Union of the Kingdoms of Scotland and England [9]
and much Latin verse.

Sir John Skene (?1549–1611), Lord Advocate and later Lord Clerk
Register, was the first great legal antiquary, somewhat erratic and inaccurate, but deserving of great credit for his work. He first edited the
Regiam Majestatem and *Quoniam Attachiamenta* in 1609 and produced
in *De Verborum Significatione* an invaluable glossary of ancient legal
terms.

Sir Thomas Hope of Craighall (?1580–1646), Lord Advocate and
father of three judges, is said to have been the most eminent advocate
of his time. He compiled the *Major Practicks* [10] and the *Minor Practicks*.[11] He acted for Charles I in the famous revocation of grants of
Church lands in 1625, which led to the law of teinds being put on a
satisfactory footing. He was a partisan of the Solemn League and Covenant and responsible for the legal side of much of the Covenanters'
activities.

Other notables of the Bar about this time were Sir Robert Spotiswoode,
author of the *Practicks*,[12] Sir Thomas Nicolson, Sir John Gilmour, who
defended Montrose in 1641 and held office as Lord President from 1660
to 1670, and Sir John Nisbet who was the last to combine the offices
of Lord Advocate and Lord of Session, which he did in 1664. He wrote

---

[6] See also Gibb, " International Private Law in Scotland in the 16th and 17th
Centuries " (1927) 39 J.R. 369.

[7] See generally, Cooper, " The Scottish Lawyer's Library in the Seventeenth
Century," in *Selected Papers*, 276, and *Introduction* (Stair Society), Chap. 3.

[8] See Fraser Tytler's *Life of Sir Thomas Craig of Riccarton*, *passim*, and Law,
" Cragii Jus Feudale " (1898) 10 J.R. 177.

[9] Published by the Scottish History Society, 1909.

[10] Edited by Lord Clyde, Stair Society, Vols. 3 and 4, 1937–38.

[11] Published 1726 and 1734.

[12] Published in 1706.

Doubts and Questions in the Law[13] which were answered many years later by Sir John Steuart, Lord Advocate under Queen Anne.[14]

Sir John Lauder of Fountainhall (1646–1722) was concerned in most of the great causes of the time. He left voluminous manuscripts and two volumes of printed decisions, too infrequently referred to, since they contain much interesting and entertaining matter about the law, the courts and the personalities of the times, and cast much light on the history and state of Scotland in the middle of the century.

Stair

Born in Ayrshire in 1619, James Dalrymple, later (1664) baronet and (1690) first Viscount Stair, graduated at Glasgow, served with Glencairn's Horse in the Bishops' War and was a regent in philosophy in Glasgow University (1641–47) before passing advocate in 1648. In 1649 he was secretary of the commission sent to The Hague to treat with Charles II and was one of those who met Charles when he landed in Scotland in 1650. In 1657 he became a judge under the Protectorate, being continued in office at the Restoration, but retired from office in 1663 to avoid taking the " declaration " abjuring the right to take up arms against the king. In the following year he resumed office, having made a modified declaration. In 1670 he was one of the Scottish commissioners to London to treat of a Union with England.

In 1671 he was appointed Lord President of the Court of Session and was sworn of the Privy Council and in 1672 was largely responsible for a series of revised regulations governing jurisdiction and procedure,[15] while in the following year he advocated a more clement policy towards the Covenanters.

In 1681 he was ejected from his post for failure to take the Test and retired to his wife's estate in Galloway, where he occupied himself with completing his *Institutions*, and later withdrew to Leyden, whence he published his *Decisions* (two volumes, 1684 and 1687), the first series of reports published in Scotland.[16] In 1688 he returned with William of Orange and in the following year was readmitted as President, which office he held until his death in 1695.

The publication of Stair's *Institutions* in 1681 (second edition, revised and enlarged, 1693) marked the creation of modern Scots law. It is " an original amalgam of Roman law, feudal law and native customary

---

[13] Known as Dirleton's *Doubts*. (His judicial title was Lord Dirleton.) See Young, " Sir John Nisbet of Dirleton " (1909) 21 J.R. 170.

[14] Published as *Dirleton's Doubts and Questions in The Law of Scotland Resolved and Answered* in 1715 and 1762.

[15] Mackay, *Memoir of Stair*, 94–100. See also Thomson, " The First Viscount Stair " (1924) 36 J.R. 33; Duncan, " Viscount Stair " (1934) 46 J.R. 103; Graham, *Annals of the Viscount and First and Second Earls of Stair*.

[16] Durie's *Decisions* relate to an earlier period but were not published till 1690.

law, systematised by resort to the law of nature and the Bible, and illuminated by many flashes of ideal metaphysic." [17] It is not a compendium of municipal law but an essay in historical and comparative jurisprudence. Rules are classed analytically and deduced from principles with frequent reference to the philosophic bases of the positive law.[18] " Its outstanding feature is the emphasis consistently laid upon first principles, and the systematic development of these principles in harmony with the most enlarged and comprehensive views of comparative jurisprudence. The *Institutions* are no mere compendium of Scots Law; for Stair made the whole science of jurisprudence his province." [19]

Mackenzie

Sir George Mackenzie of Rosehaugh,[20] born in 1636, came to the Bar in 1659 and early distinguished himself. In 1677 he became King's Advocate and won his sobriquet of " Bloody " Mackenzie by relentless persecution of the Covenanters. In 1686 he was removed from office for refusal to concur in the exercise of the dispensing power in favour of Catholics, was restored briefly in 1688 and retired to Oxford in 1689 where he pursued literary work till his death in 1691.

His writings include *Aretina*, an early specimen of prose fiction, moral essays, political writings in support of the prerogative,[21] and many legal works, a treatise on criminal law,[22] one on actions, observations on the statutes, commentaries on the bankruptcy Act and the entail Act, and a *Science of Heraldry* (1680) and an *Institutions of the Law of Scotland* (1684). This is, however, a slight work and quite overshadowed by Stair's *Institutions*. As much as anything he will be remembered for the foundation of the Advocates' Library, now the National Library of Scotland, which he inaugurated with a notable oration.[23]

The Movement Towards Union

In 1689 yet another attempt was made to effect a union of the Parlia-

---

[17] Cooper, " Scottish Legal Tradition," in *Selected Papers*, 177.

[18] See further, Campbell, *The Structure of Stair's Institutions*.

[19] Cooper, " Some Classics of Scottish Legal Literature," in *Selected Papers*, 39, 43.

[20] See Lang, *Sir George Mackenzie of Rosehaugh*; article in D.N.B.; Brown, " Sir George Mackenzie " (1901) 13 J.R. 261; Brown, " Sir George Mackenzie of Rosehaugh " (1902) 9 S.L.T. 1, and " Mackenzie's Institutions " (1901) 8 S.L.T. 105, 113, 130, 138, 145, 154, 157; 9 S.L.T. 9. Young, " Sir George Mackenzie of Rosehaugh " (1907) 19 J.R. 266; Most of Mackenzie's writings are collected in his *Works* (2 vols., 1716–22).

[21] *Jus Regium, or the Just and Solid Foundations of Monarchy in General* (1684).

[22] *The Laws and Customs of Scotland in Matters Criminal* (1674).

[23] Dickson, " The Advocates' Library " (1902) 14 J.R. 1, 113, 214; " The National Library of Scotland " (1928) 40 J.R. 172; " David Hume and the Advocates' Library " (1932) 44 J.R. 1. Mackenzie's oration, translated by J. H. Loudon, is in the *Transactions of the Edinburgh Bibliographical Society*, (1946) II, p. 275.

ments.[24] The Scottish Convention appointed commissioners to treat of complete union, except in Church government, and offered to accept King William as arbiter in any dispute about the terms of union. The English Parliament refused, however, to appoint commissioners though William was himself favourable. No further progress could be made during William's reign since he had become personally unpopular and anti-English feelings had been aroused by the massacre of Glencoe and the failure of the Darien Scheme.[25]

In 1700 at the height of the Darien controversy William again recommended to the English Parliament the appointment of commissioners to discuss union, but while the Lords agreed, the Commons declined the royal recommendation. The Lords discussed the matter again in 1701, and in 1702 William renewed his request and it was endorsed by Anne on her accession later in the year. Accordingly a commission sat from October 1702 till February 1703 but again proved fruitless, the insuperable objection being that of the English to free trade between the two countries.[26]

Further consideration of union between the two countries was provoked by the question of the succession to the throne which arose sharply after the death of all Queen Anne's children. The English Parliament in 1701 by the Act of Settlement limited the succession to the English crown on the House of Hanover, but the Scottish Parliament had taken no action and English statesmen feared the possibility of a restoration of the Stuarts, which might endanger the Protestant succession in England and the system of limited constitutional monarchy established in 1688. Hence union became politically desirable for England though there was still great unwillingness to concede the equal privileges of trade with England and the English colonies.[27] The Scottish Parliament sought to take advantage of the Queen's difficult situation and her entanglement in the war of the Spanish Succession against Louis XIV. In 1703 an Act was passed to the effect that no future sovereign should have power to make war or peace without the consent of the Scottish Parliament.[28] Anne consented to this but refused assent to the Bill entitled the Act of Security under which, on the death of Anne without issue, the Scottish Estates were to name a successor from the Protestant descendants of the old royal line of Scotland, but this was not to be the same person as the designated successor to the throne of England unless there were such conditions of government settled and enacted as might secure the honour

---

[24] Stewart, " The Scottish Parliament, 1690–1702 " (1927) 39 J.R. 10, 169, 291, 408.
[25] Rait and Pryde, 76–77; Pryde, *op cit.* 48. See also, *Source Book*, III, 337–344; Pratt Insh, *The Company of Scotland trading to Africa and the Indies*; Prebble, *The Darien Disaster*.
[26] Rait and Pryde, 79; Hume Brown, III, 83–84.
[27] Rait and Pryde, 79–80.
[28] *Source Book*, III, 472.

and sovereignty of the kingdom, the freedom and power of Parliament, the religion, freedom and trade of the nation from English or foreign influence.[29] The Act was passed the following year by dint of Parliament refusing supply for the first time in its history.[30] This and other measures were not designed to force a union since the Country Party had in mind complete separation from England and in this had the support of the Jacobites who wished to avoid the recognition of the Electress of Hanover and her line as heirs to the Scottish crown.[31]

The English Parliament recognised the danger of allowing a settlement to wait till Anne's death. By the Aliens Act of 1705 [32] they again authorised the Queen to negotiate with any commissioners who might be appointed by the Scots and provided further, as a counterweight to the Act of Security, that from Christmas 1705 until the Scottish Parliament should have passed an Act settling the Crown of Scotland upon the designated successor to the Crown of England, every native of Scotland, with a few exceptions, should be an alien in England and that, apart from a few exceptions, trade between England and Scotland should be prohibited.[33]

The debates of the Scottish Parliament that summer were heated and of crucial importance for the future; they took place in an atmosphere of confused excitement and amid popular agitation against union. In September, however, Parliament resolved that commissioners should be nominated not by itself but by the Queen to treat of union, a resolution with the practical consequence that the Scottish commissioners would be selected from advocates of union. In November the English Parliament repealed the threatening clauses of the Aliens Act.[34]

The joint commission met in London in April 1706 and early agreed on three main points, an incorporating union, guarantees by the English of complete freedom of trade, and an undertaking by the Scots to recognise the Electress of Hanover and the heirs of her body being Protestants, as successors to Anne as Queen of Scotland. Agreement was also reached on taxation and the jurisdiction of the Scottish courts but the sharpest difference arose over the number of Scottish representatives in the new Parliament of Great Britain. The Scots asked for fifty members in the House of Commons but the English suggested thirty-eight and later proposed forty-five with sixteen representative peers in the House of Lords,[35] and agreement was reached on this basis. These numbers were

---

[29] *Source Book*, III, 473–477.
[30] Clark, *Later Stuarts*, 275–276; Hume Brown, III, 88–94.
[31] Rait and Pryde, 81.
[32] *Source Book*, III, 477–478.
[33] Clark, 276; Hume Brown, III, 94.
[34] *Source Book*, III, 480.
[35] On these, see Fergusson, *The Sixteen Peers of Scotland*. By the Peerage Act 1963, all Scottish peers became entitled to sit and vote in the House of Lords.

unsatisfactory and inadequate on the basis of population though they were liable to produce great unsettlement of the balance of political forces in the new chambers and they did result during Anne's later years in policy being influenced by the Scottish members. Each country ceased to have exclusive control of its own political affairs, a state which has, however, resulted in the long run in far more English influence on Scotland than the other way.

The English gave up their exclusive commercial privileges, a great sacrifice according to the economic notions of the times which did not foresee the ultimate advantages of an extension of the free-trade area, and paid a sum of £398,085 to the Scottish exchequer as an " Equivalent " for the share of the national debt which Scotland was to assume. The Scots accepted the principle that taxation and trade regulation should be uniform in the two countries in future, though this was made acceptable by substantial tax concessions.[36]

The commissioners completed their work in three months and the articles of union were ratified by the Scottish Estates in January 1707 [37] in the face of many protests and indications of popular disapproval, rioting in Edinburgh and accusations of bribery. They were ratified by the English Parliament in March [38] and came into force on May 1, 1707; in October of that year the first Parliament of Great Britain met at Westminster.[39] The Estates at the same time passed an Act for the Security of the Church of Scotland as an essential part of the union settlement.[40]

The Preservation of Scots Law by the Union

The continuance of Scots law and the Scottish courts was provided for by the Treaty of Union by provisions (Art. XIX) that the Court of Session and Court of Justiciary should continue in all time coming, that the Court of Admiralty should always be continued in Scotland, and that no causes in Scotland should be " cognoscible by the Courts of Chancery, Queen's Bench, Common Pleas or any other court in Westminster Hall " and that there should be a Court of Exchequer in Scotland after the union for deciding questions concerning the revenues of customs and excises. Heritable offices, superiorities and jurisdictions were preserved (Art. XX) and also the rights and privileges of the royal burghs (Art. XXI). Laws concerning regulation of trade, customs and excises were to be the same in both countries after the union but all

[36] Hume Brown, III, 100–110; Pryde, *The Treaty of Union*, 20–24; *Source Book*, III, 480–489.

[37] A.P.S. XI, 406, c. 7.

[38] 6 Anne, c. 11.

[39] Rait and Pryde, 82–83; Clark, 276–278; Hume Brown, III, 110. See also Smith, "The Union of 1707 as Fundamental Law " [1957] Pub.L. 99.

[40] *Source Book*, III, 489–492.

other laws in use in Scotland were after the union and notwithstanding
it to remain in force as before " but alterable by the Parliament of Great
Britain, with this difference betwixt the laws concerning publick right
policy and civil government and those which concern private right, that
the laws which concern publick right policy and civil government may be
made the same throughout the whole United Kingdom; But that no alteration be made in laws which concern private right except for evident utility
of the subjects within Scotland " (Art. XVIII). The right of the House
of Lords to continue to hear appeals from England and to hear appeals
from Scotland was simply evaded by the Treaty since the House of Lords
was not another " court in Westminster Hall."

Nevertheless among the first measures of the new Parliament of Great
Britain were the abolition of the Scottish Privy Council,[41] the regulation
of the system of Justices of the Peace, and the establishment of a Court
of Exchequer in Scotland. A year later in defiance of the Treaty the
Government put through an Act applying one law of treason, the ancient
English one, to both countries,[42] and a commission of Oyer and Terminer
superseded the High Court of Justiciary in this field of law.[43]

IV.—THE EIGHTEENTH CENTURY

In the early years of the eighteenth century there was much dissatisfaction with the union, particularly over questions of taxation and in
particular the malt tax of 1713, which was inequitable and technically contrary to the treaty.[44] In that year a motion for the repeal of the
union was lost in the House of Lords by only four votes.[45] The growing practice of taking appeals from the Court of Session to the
House of Lords seems to have excited little popular discontent or
excitement though ecclesiastical feeling was offended by the decision
in *Greenshields'* case which tolerated the Episcopal Church of Scotland,
and more so by the Act of Toleration in 1712 which sanctioned episcopacy
and prescribed unacceptable oaths for the clergy, both Presbyterian and
Episcopalian.[46] It appears that initially union was in one way or another
distasteful to a majority of both peoples and only made acceptable by
the pressure of events.[47]

Serious grievances appeared during 1707–08 during the passage
of the Act for abolishing the Scottish Privy Council and increasing the

---

[41] *Source Book*, III, 495; McNeill, " The Passing of the Scottish Privy Council,"
1965 J.R. 263.
[42] Dickson, " The Scots Law of Treason " (1899) 10 J.R. 243.
[43] Hume Brown, III, 143–144; Hill Burton, VIII, 210–216.
[44] Clark, 280–281.
[45] Hume Brown, III, 152–153.
[46] Stephen, *History of the Scottish Church*, II, 468; Grub, *Ecclesiastical History
of Scotland*, III, 361–367; Pryde, *op cit.* 94–95.
[47] Rait and Pryde, 86.

powers of the justices of the peace though the objections must be discounted at least in part as those of parties interested in maintaining the instrument for controlling elections.[48]

Again in 1708 Parliament, following a threatened Jacobite landing in the Forth, substituted the English law of treason for that of Scotland and united all the Scottish parties into an unsuccessful opposition, though the motives of some of the peers for the opposition were rather mixed. In 1711 the House of Lords ruled in the case of the Duke of Hamilton and Brandon that no British title could confer on a Scottish noble the right to a seat in the House of Lords and this was deeply resented as a national insult and proof of England's twisting of the Union to its own advantage.[49] In the following year the restoration of lay patronage to ecclesiastical livings aroused fear and anti-union feeling among the Presbyterians. The Act in question [50] was a clear breach of the Treaty both in letter and in spirit.[51]

In 1715 the first Jacobite rebellion broke out. The government sought to preserve the loyalty of Scotland by an Act commonly known as the Clan Act, by which every Crown vassal was to forfeit his lands if found guilty of treasonable correspondence with the Pretender, while entails and settlements in favour of children or other heirs were made void from August 1, 1715, in all time coming. This threat hung over the heads of all lords who might think of departing from allegiance to the Hanoverian dynasty.[52]

The rebellion was a military failure and two Acts followed, one appointing a Commission to deal with estates forfeited during the rebellion and the other for disarming the Highlands as a means of securing the peace of the country.[53] In breach of the Treaty of Union many prisoners were removed from Scotland to Carlisle for trial under the treason law. This caused much bad feeling among all classes in Scotland. Though attempts were made to enforce the new treason law, it is questionable if any instances occurred of punishment by the courts of criminal justice for concern in the insurrection. The penal retributions were inflicted through English tribunals, and were thus treasured in the Scots mind as a national aggression and injury.[54] The proceedings of the Forfeited Estates Commissioners [55] were equally loathed; their actings were hindered by the Scottish Court of Exchequer and the Court of Session and few

---

[48] Rait and Pryde, 86. See further, Riley, *The English Ministers and Scotland,* 1707–1727; McNeill, " The Passing of the Scottish Privy Council," 1965 J.R. 263.
[49] *Ibid.* 87. See also Yeaman, " Edinburgh before the Fifteen " (1937) 49 J.R. 152.
[50] 10 Anne, c. 12.
[51] Rait and Pryde, 87; Hume Brown, III, 143–144.
[52] Hume Brown, III, 162–163.
[53] *Ibid.* 189.
[54] Hill Burton, VIII, 331–338.
[55] Hill Burton, VIII, 348–350.

would buy the forfeited estates until the York Buildings Company, which had been founded to supply London with water from the Thames, came forward as chief purchaser.[56] Further resentment attended the proceedings of a commission of Oyer and Terminer sent to Scotland to take proceedings in absence against Jacobites who had fled. Its failure was proof not of Jacobite sympathies but of Scottish resentment and bitterness at English interference.

Dissatisfaction with the government was also shown in the resistance of the Faculty of Advocates in 1722 to the Crown's appointment of Patrick Haldane, one of the commissioners on the forfeited estates, as a Lord of Session. The court held that Haldane had not made out his qualification to be received as a judge, but this decision was, it need hardly be said, reversed by the House of Lords. The government, however, withdrew the nomination but by statute abolished the court's veto on nominees, leaving the privilege of subjecting the presentee to an examination, and also the extraordinary Lords of Session.[57]

In 1725 an Act for Disarming the Highlands was passed and a serious attempt made to bring the country within civilisation. General Wade began to erect barracks and forts and make roads throughout the Highlands to check cattle-lifting and the gathering of troops,[58] while a little later the Highland regiments began to be raised.

House of Lords Appeals

There was no express provision in the Treaty as to whether any appeal was to be permitted to the House of Lords of the Parliament of Great Britain. In England appeal to the House of Lords by writ of error had become established by the seventeenth century. In Scotland it was an obscure and still uncertain question how far any appeal lay from the Scottish courts to the Scottish Parliament. The Treaty avoided the difficulty but its silence on the matter left open the possibility of appeal.

In 1707–08 the Earl of Rosebery tried an appeal to the House of Lords and the jurisdiction was accepted by the House. In 1711 an Episcopalian clergyman, James Greenshields, was imprisoned in Edinburgh for openly using the Anglican form of service and the Court of Session upheld the action of the presbytery and the magistrates. Appeal was taken to the House of Lords and the Lords reversed the Court of Session and ordered Greenshields' release.[59] The decision caused great alarm in Scotland but

---

[56] Hume Brown, III, 190–193.

[57] Hill Burton, VIII, 352. See also Parker, " A Rejected Judge " (1929) 41 J.R. 193.

[58] Hill Burton, VIII, 368–378; Hume Brown, III, 211–212. On the roads see further, Salmond, *Wade in Scotland.*

[59] There were earlier appeals in 1708, but *Greenshields*' case attracted more attention. See also Malcolm, " The House of Lords and Appeals from Scotland " (1910) 22 J.R. 295.

since then the House of Lords has continued to entertain appeals from Scotland and the practice, however erroneous, is now settled.

Central Government

After the abolition of the Scottish Privy Council in 1708 the government of Scotland was, till 1746, sometimes in the hands of a third Secretary of State but was frequently entrusted to one or other of the joint Secretaries of State.[60] In the intervals Scottish affairs were managed by a Scottish noble or by the Lord Advocate. Responsibility fell to the northern Secretary of State till 1782 and thereafter to the Home Secretary assisted by the Lord Advocate. The management consisted largely of control of elections and the dispensing of patronage. The most successful manager was Henry Dundas, later Viscount Melville, during the years 1783 to 1806.[61]

Local Government

At the time of the Union the functions of local government were distributed among six agencies which had developed with little reference to each other and at different periods. The sheriffs and the burghs had arisen in the twelfth century, baronies and regalities in the fourteenth, kirk sessions in the sixteenth and justices of the peace and commissioners of supply in the seventeenth.

The administrative functions of the sheriff had formerly been the collection of Crown dues, execution of Royal writs, publishing of statutes and latterly making the return of the shire members. These functions were, however, restricted as the sheriffships became heritable in the hands of the great families and administrative power was curtailed while legal jurisdiction increased.[62]

The Royal burghs had each a constitution or " sett " which entrusted power to a provost, bailies and self-elective town councils and they remained into the nineteenth century self-contained agencies of local government frequently enjoying substantial revenues. The merchant guilds and crafts in the burghs had numerous exclusive privileges which legally survived till 1846 though they had been largely abandoned by then. Measures for the control of the burghs were enacted from time to time, notably in 1822, but this was too late and the courts refused to enforce them.[63]

The baronies and regalities had formerly enjoyed substantial jurisdictional rights but by 1707 these had very largely fallen into abeyance. Their executive duties, however, continued; these were to preserve

[60] Lovat Fraser, " Scottish Administration in the Eighteenth Century " (1912) 24 J.R. 122.
[61] Lovat Fraser, " A Famous Lord Advocate " (1902) 14 J.R. 350; " The Impeachment of Lord Melville " (1912) 24 J.R. 235.
[62] Rait and Pryde, 177–178.
[63] Rait and Pryde, 178.

common lands, pastures, woods and mosses, dykes and ditches and to keep the assizes of bread and ale. After the abolition of heritable jurisdictions in 1747 even their administrative functions fell into desuetude though particular instances survived till much later.[64]

The kirk sessions established at the Reformation acted under the general guidance of the commissioners of supply and, in burghs, in co-operation with the town council. Expenditure required the sanction of the heritors of the parish, *i.e.*, the heritable proprietors appearing on the valuation roll of the parish.[65] The kirk session managed the parish schools, paid small allowances to the poor, aged and indigent and distributed charitable relief in case of need. It was permissible to lay assessments on the parish after 1663, half on owners, half on occupiers, but these were unpopular and infrequently resorted to and most funds came from church collections and mortifications for the poor. The poor law system was, however, disintegrating and badly needed reform by the nineteenth century.[66]

In Scotland the justices of the peace never enjoyed either the powers or the prestige of their English counterparts. After 1708, however, they did enjoy considerable administrative powers, having jurisdiction over the settlement of disputes as to work and wages, weights and measures; they had to suppress riots, support customs officers and supervise prisons and almshouses and, from 1718, in conjunction with the commissioners of supply, to see to the maintenance of country roads and bridges.[67]

The commissioners of supply were recognised by statute in 1667 but had existed on a customary basis before then. They were a country committee of wealthy landowners appointed to allocate the monthly cess or land tax, and their organisation made it convenient to entrust them with other duties such as the enforcement of the Education Act of 1696 and, with the justices, the control of vagabonds and the upkeep of roads.[68]

Break-up of the Clan System and the Heritable Jurisdictions

The measures adopted to restore and ensure internal peace after the defeat of the second Jacobite rebellion at Culloden provoked considerable dissatisfaction. The chief constitutional change was the abolitition, in breach of the Treaty of Union, of heritable jurisdictions in 1748.[69] Compensation amounting to £152,000 was paid, of which £21,000 went

---

[64] Hill Burton, VIII, 517–518; Rait and Pryde, 178.
[65] The meaning of the term is discussed at length in Black's *Parochial Ecclesiastical Law of Scotland*, 4th ed., p. 44.
[66] Rait and Pryde, 179; Ferguson, *Dawn of Scottish Social Welfare*, Chap. 7.
[67] Hill Burton, VIII, 210; Rait and Pryde, 179.
[68] Rait and Pryde, 180.
[69] Pryde, *op cit.* 65; Omond, *Lord Advocates of Scotland*, II, 32–38, 41–42. Dickson, " Heritable Jurisdictions " (1897) 9 J.R. 428.

to the Duke of Argyll in compensation for his right of justiciary over Argyll and the Western Isles. Thereafter the power and prestige of the sheriff courts advanced steadily and in 1787 the office of sheriff-substitute was recognised and made a salaried office. So too the holding of land in return for military service was abolished and lands thus held converted to ordinary feudal tenure.[70]

After Culloden the Highlands were treated with unforgiveable savagery and the measures for disarming the Highlands and breaking up the clan system were unnecessarily severe.[71] The tartan and the pipes were proscribed as military and badges of sedition and not legalised again till 1782 while suppression and persecution contributed materially to the great emigration to North America about the middle of the century.[72]

An Act of 1752 disposed of the estates which had been forfeited after the rebellion and devoted their revenues to the improvement of Highland farms, the establishment of schools and the planting of forests.[73] The Act had beneficial results and many areas were greatly improved. A few years later followed another beneficial measure in the Act for the better preservation of turnpike roads under which dues were levied from vehicles and spent on the maintenance of the public roads, while in 1770 Montgomery's Entail Act empowered heirs of entail in possession to grant leases for substantial periods on certain conditions, a provision which greatly tended towards the agricultural improvement of the country.[74]

In 1782–84 the Act prohibiting the wearing of the Highland dress was repealed, and the forfeited estates restored to the legal heirs but on condition that debts charged on them were to go to the public benefit and particularly towards the expense of completing the Forth and Clyde canal and of making roads in the Highlands.[75]

Heritable Jurisdictions and the Inferior Courts

The abolition of the heritable jurisdictions affected not only rights of jurisdiction held by virtue of grants of barony or regality but the office of sheriff all over the country.

The office of sheriff had early tended to become hereditary in the line of a powerful Crown vassal and by 1747 twenty-three out of thirty-three sheriffs held thus. But since about 1357 there had been a growing practice for the sheriff to appoint a qualified depute to perform the judicial

---

[70] Hill Burton, VIII, 503–504; Hume Brown, III, 330.

[71] See Prebble, *Culloden*; Watt, " The Treason Trials at Carlisle after the '45 " (1911) 23 J.R. 124; Bartholomew, " The Highland Clans in the Law of Scotland " (1901) 13 J.R. 205, 307.

[72] Hume Brown, III, 328–329.

[73] Rait and Pryde, 97; Hume Brown, III, 337–338; Pryde, *op cit.* 153.

[74] Hume Brown, III, 345.

[75] *Ibid.* 352–353; Pryde, 155.

work. In 1747 the qualified depute everywhere replaced the hereditary officer and became the sheriff of the county.[76] In 1828 the name Depute was dropped and he became the modern Sheriff, since 1971 called Sheriff-Principal. The Sheriff-Depute in turn appointed sheriffs-substitute who held office during his pleasure and were paid by him. In 1787 it was provided that the substitute should be paid by the Crown, and from 1825 it was provided that the sheriff-substitute should be a trained lawyer while in 1877 that office became a distinct Crown appointment.

Private Law in the Eighteenth Century

The later eighteenth century was the classical age of the Scottish common law, developed and brought to maturity by Erskine and not yet debased or defiled by inconsidered statutes, uncritical following of English principles or ignorant interference by an English House of Lords.[77] It largely coincided with the great days, the golden age, of Edinburgh and the efflorescence of the arts and letters and of the Scottish School of philosophy. Material prosperity advanced and the law had to take account of more settled conditions, developing agriculture, industry and commerce, and a more complicated social and economic order.

Legal Literature—Bankton, Erskine, Millar and Kames

The eighteenth century saw some very distinguished lawyers and judges.[78] On the bench the work of Forbes, Dundas and Ilay Campbell was outstanding.[79] But now among the jurists the academic is becoming for the first time prominent. William Forbes, Professor of Law at Glasgow (1714–46) wrote books on *Bills of Exchange*, *Tithes* and *Justices of the Peace* as well as a small *Institutes of the Law of Scotland*.[80]

In 1751 there appeared the *Institutes* of Andrew McDouall, Lord Bankton, a work still of considerable authority and value and notable

---

[76] For list of the first sheriffs, see Omond, *Lord Advocates*, II, 43–44. See also Malcolm, in *Introduction* (Stair Society), Chap. 26.

[77] See further, Paton, " The Eighteenth Century and Later," in *Introduction to Scottish Legal History*, Chap. 5; Inglis, " Eighteenth Century Pleading " (1907) 19 J.R. 42; Waugh, " Gleanings from the 18th Century Law Reports " (1903) 15 J.R. 164.

[78] See also Ramsay, " Eighteenth Century Advocates and Their Study of Literature " (1939) 51 J.R. 23; Stein, " Legal Thought in Eighteenth Century Scotland " 1957 J.R. 3.

[79] Some impression of practice at the Bar in the 1770s can be gained from Wimsatt and Pottle (ed.), *Boswell for the Defence*; see also Henderson, " James Boswell and his Practice at the Bar " (1905) 17 J.R. 105; Simpson, " Boswell as an Advocate " (1922) 34 J.R. 201; Duke, " Boswell Among the Lawyers " (1926) 38 J.R. 341; Roughead, " The Wandering Jurist " (1931) 43 J.R. 30, 138; Ramsay, " Boswell's First Criminal Case " (1938) 50 J.R. 315; Murray, " Some Civil Cases of James Boswell " (1940) 52 J.R. 222.

[80] Forbes' major work, *The Great Body of the Law of Scotland*, has never been published but remains in manuscript in Glasgow University Library.

for its extensive comparisons with the law of England, but overshadowed by the work of Erskine.

John Erskine of Carnock [81] was born in 1695 and passed advocate in 1719. In 1737 he became professor of Scots Law at Edinburgh, which chair he held till he retired in 1765. In 1754 he published his *Principles of the Law of Scotland* for use as the textbook of the class, a function which in repeated editions it performed until well into the twentieth century. He died in 1768. His larger work, the *Institute of the Law of Scotland*, was not published in his lifetime but appeared posthumously in 1773, and soon achieved a place second only to Stair's *Institutions* in juristic regard. Erskine displays classical Scots law, deduced from principle and considered in leisurely prose, not yet overwhelmed by the citation of difficult or even contradictory decisions or by masses of barely comprehensible statutory amendment. It is as the final and authoritative exponent of the older law of Scotland, resting on the Roman law and the feudal customs, that Erskine stands supreme. His work lacks the philosophic breadth of Stair and the bold insight of Bell, and he probably failed to appreciate that, even when he wrote, the centre of interest in legal studies was shifting from the law of property to commercial law. His treatment is academic, cautious, exact and workmanlike rather than inspired, but yet worthy of the highest admiration and respect. John Millar, professor of law at Glasgow from 1761 to 1801,[82] was the most celebrated and successful law teacher of his time; his writings included *The Origin of the Distinction of Ranks*, an interesting early sociological study, and *An Historical View of the English Government*, the first constitutional history of Britain. He was a notable supporter of the liberties of the subject and an outspoken advocate of parliamentary reform. Also in the eighteenth century appeared some of the collections of styles of deeds, which are the beginning of modern conveyancing practice.[83]

Of the judiciary Henry Home, Lord Kames (1696–1782), was among the most notable. He passed advocate in 1723 and was raised to the Bench in 1752. His literary output was considerable and diverse, collections of decisions,[84] essays on legal subjects, antiquities, on morality and natural religion, literary criticism, farming and education. The works still of most interest and value are the *Historical Law Tracts* (1757) and the *Principles of Equity* (1760), the latter of which examined, with much comparative reference to English law, the principles on which rules of law might be modified in application by an overriding equitable

---

[81] See Grant, *Story of the University of Edinburgh*, II, 372, and D.N.B.

[82] See further, Lehmann, *John Millar of Glasgow*; and " John Millar " (1961) 6 J.R.(N.S.) 218.

[83] See Macmillan, " The Old Scots Conveyancers " (1898–99) 10 J.R. 425; 11 J.R. 41.

[84] *Remarkable Decisions*, 1716–28, continued later, 1730–52; *Select Decisions*, 1752–68 (pub. 1780); *Dictionary of the Decisions of the Court of Session* (completed by Woodhouselee, 4 vols., 1741).

discretion. In this connection he conducted extensive correspondence with Lord Hardwicke and Lord Mansfield in England. "We moderns are hardly enough aware of how much the Scotch lawyer is indebted to Henry Home, Lord Kames. His versatile and truly philosophical mind neglected nothing. He enriched the law of Scotland by his collections of remarkable decisions, by his abridgment of the Statutes, and by a large body of ingenious speculations and criticisms upon law and legal decisions." [85]

The eighteenth century practically saw the end of the old intimacy between Scotland and the Continent and of the practice of young men resorting, formerly to France and later to Holland, for study of the Roman law as expounded by the commentators and the great civilians. Craig, Mackenzie, Spotiswoode and Fountainhall had studied at Orleans, Poitiers, Bourges or Paris. In the seventeenth and eighteenth centuries it is known that about 1,600 Scottish lawyers studied at Leyden alone. Stair was there in exile from 1682 to 1688 [86]; Lord President Forbes studied there and Lord President Dundas at Utrecht. Most cogent evidence of the link can be seen in the older books of the Advocates' Library, founded in 1681, of which the great majority are Continental treatises, mostly from France, Holland and Northern Germany, but some drawn from further away. "From their sojourn in Holland the aspirants to practice in the Parliament House brought back with them not only the principles which they had imbibed from the masters of the Roman-Dutch law but also the treatises with which the law schools of the Dutch Universities were so prolific. No Scots lawyer's library was complete in those days which did not contain the works of Grotius, Vinnius, the Voets, Heineccius and other learned civilians. Collections of decisions of the Scottish judges were few and inaccessible, and the Court of Session, with its predilection for principle rather than precedent, heard many arguments, adorned with citations of the Roman law and its Dutch commentators." [87] Scots law has still, for this reason, an affinity with the Roman-Dutch law of South Africa.

---

[85] Innes, *Scotch Legal Antiquities*, 10. On Kames, see also Fraser Tytler's *Memoirs of the Life and Writings of Henry Home of Kames*; Ross, *Lord Kames and the Scotland of his Day*; Lehmann, *Henry Home, Lord Kames and the Scottish Enlightenment*; Brown, " Kames's Principles of Equity " (1903) 10 S.L.T. 94, 111, 127, 159, 173, 181; Brown, " A Master of Equity " (1904) 20 L.Q.R. 308; Brown, " Lord Kames: A Judicial Historian " (1911) 23 J.R. 180; Brown, " Equity " (1914) 26 J.R. 338; Lehmann, " The Historical Approach in the Juridical Writings of Lord Kames," 1964 J.R. 17. On other judges see Cloyd, *Lord Monboddo*; Walton, " Lord Monboddo" (1896) 8 J.R. 360; Brown, " Lord Monboddo: A Judicial Metaphysician " (1905) 17 J.R. 267; Lyell, " The Real Weir of Hermiston " (1904) 16 J.R. 115.

[86] On Stair's familiarity with Continental jurists, see Campbell, *The Structure of Stair's Institutions.*

[87] *Stewart* v. *L.M.S. Ry.*, 1943 S.C.(H.L.) 19, 38, *per* Lord Macmillan.

V.—THE MODERN PERIOD

The keynotes of the period since the Napoleonic wars have been reform, the increasing volume and importance of public and especially administrative law, the growing bulk and complexity of statutory law, and the increase of English influence and the tendency to assimilate Scots law to English. Constitutionally it has been a period of constant reform and movement towards democracy.

The Movement for Reform

In 1792 the Society of Friends of the People was formed and branches spread over Scotland and England. The doctrines of liberty found ready acceptance. The government became alarmed and prosecutions were initiated. The first in Scotland was of Thomas Muir of Huntershill, a young advocate and champion of reform, who was unfairly tried and sentenced to transportation.[88] Further trials, public excitement and government fears continued but calm was restored by 1795. But the movement for reform continued and grew in strength.

After Waterloo there was a severe economic depression which gave rise to a spirit of unrest and the founding of revolutionary societies. Sedition was feared, especially in Glasgow, and a number of weavers were tried in 1818 but general opinion had changed since Muir's trial and the prosecutions mostly failed.[89]

Discontent and agitation for reform continued throughout the 1820s; fruits of the movement were found in the reforms of the Court of Session in 1808 and 1825 and a measure of 1822 giving jurisdiction over burgh accounts to the Court of Exchequer.

The Scottish Reform Bill was passed in 1832 raising Scottish representation from 45 to 53, redistributing seats and extending the franchise, and the following year saw the reform of the burghs, putting an end to the self-election of the magistrates.[90]

Conflict between Church and State and the Disruption

The courts and the General Assembly of the Church came into sharp conflict in the 1830s. In 1834 the Assembly passed the Veto Act whereby the dissent of a majority of male heads of families was to prevent the presentation of a minister to a charge by the patron of the living. In 1835 the Presbytery rejected a presentee to the church of Auchterarder under the Veto Act. The Court of Session held [91] that the Veto Act

---

[88] Hume Brown, III, 381–382; Craik, *Century of Scottish History*, iI, 149–154; Meikle, *Scotland and the French Revolution*, *passim*; Roughead " An Advocate of Reform " (1938) 50 J.R. 231.

[89] Craik, II, 284–291.

[90] *Ibid.* II, 365–371; Pryde, 192–196.

[91] *Earl of Kinnoull* v. *Fergusson* (1841) 3 D. 778; (1842) 1 Bell 662; (1843) 5 D. 1010.

(of Assembly) was contrary to the Patronage Act (of Parliament) of 1711 and this view was upheld by the House of Lords. The difficulties were also apparent in the Lethendy case,[92] and the Strathbogie [93] and other cases, which resulted in the Assembly defying the court and the court interdicting the Assembly. The controversy continued; appeals to Parliament failed of effect and in 1843 a large body of ministers and laity seceded from the Church and formed the Free Church of Scotland.[94] Patronage was abolished in 1874 but the breach between the Church and the Free Church was healed only in 1929 and then not completely.

Central Government

In the second half of the nineteenth century criticism began to be directed against the system whereby the Lord Advocate under the loose control of the Home Secretary administered Scotland. This administration consisted very largely in the management of elections and the dispensing of patronage. It was brought to its peak of perfection by Henry Dundas, later Viscount Melville, between 1783 and 1806.[95] From 1827 till the creation of the Secretaryship for Scotland in 1885 the Home Secretary was the Minister nominally responsible though *ad hoc* bodies tended to be set up to exercise some administrative functions. Such were the Board of Supervision (for Poor Law) in 1845 and the Prison Commissioners in 1877.[96]

Under the third Reform Act (1884–85) Scotland for the first time was given her proper share of representatives according to population, with 72 members, while the grievance over the maladministration of Scottish affairs was to a small extent remedied by the creation of an under-secretaryship of Home Affairs, with Scotland as his special charge and only a year later was the office of Secretary for Scotland created.[97] About this time too the troubles in Ireland caused many of the Scottish Liberal members [98] to speculate on the need to review the terms of the Union and speak of devolution within the United Kingdom.[99] In 1894

---

[92] *Clark* v. *Stirling* (1839) 1 D. 955.

[93] *Presbytery of Strathbogie* (1839) 2 D. 258, 585, 1047, 1380; *Edwards* v. *Cruickshank* (1840) 3 D. 283; *Presbytery of Strathbogie* (1842) 4 D. 1298; *Edwards* v. *Leith* (1843) 15 Sc.Jur. 375.

[94] Hume Brown, III, 423–431; Pryde, 184–186; Taylor, " Church and State in Scotland " (1957) 2 J.R.(N.S.) 121, 125 *et seq.* See also Crabb Watt, *John Inglis,* 60–73; Craik, *Century of Scottish History,* Chap. 22; Grub, *Ecclesiastical History of Scotland,* IV, 203–235; Cunningham, *Church History of Scotland,* II, 450 *et seq.*: Burleigh, *Church History of Scotland,* 334.

[95] See Matheson, *Life of Henry Dundas, Viscount Melville.*

[96] See the tracing of the development of the office of Secretary of State for Scotland in Milne, *The Scottish Office,* Chap. 2.

[97] On this, see further, Mure Mackenzie, *Scotland in Modern Times,* 267–269; Hanham: " The Creation of the Scottish Office, 1881–87, " 1965 J.R. 205. A list of the holders of the office can be found in Milne, *The Scottish Office,* 216.

[98] The Liberals consistently held most of the Scottish seats from 1833 to 1900.

[99] Rait and Pryde, 121; Mure Mackenzie, 270.

a concession was made to the demand for devolution which from 1889 to 1895 underlay a perennial motion in favour of a separate parliament for Scotland by the establishment of the procedure whereby all Scottish members were included in a Scottish Grand Committee for the consideration of a Bill.[1] It was revived in 1907 as a concession to nationalist sentiment and became a standing committee, while in 1912 the House of Commons approved a resolution to grant equal treatment in the matter of devolution to Scotland and Ireland. Irish affairs, however, were more pressing.[2]

The tendency of the twentieth century has been to increase the direct responsibility of the Secretary of State for Scottish administration and to bring under his control matters formerly entrusted to distinct Boards and Commissions. There has also been an increasing and salutary tendency to assign to the Scottish Secretary matters on which there is a distinctive tradition or body of law or pattern of administration, or where Scottish conditions are notably different from those in England and Wales.

The Reorganisation of Offices (Scotland) Act 1939 brought together the several Scottish Departments which had formerly existed under the control of the Secretary of State for Scotland and these now became branches of the Scottish Office, having their principal home in Edinburgh and a liaison office in London. They are the Scottish Home and Health Department dealing with prison and Borstal services, police, fire and civil defence, public order and safety, national health and welfare services; the Department of Agriculture for Scotland which deals with agriculture, forestry and drainage, and fisheries; the Scottish Education Department responsible for colleges of education and schools and guiding the local education authorities; the Scottish Development Department whose responsibility extends to local government, rating, electricity, roads, housing, town and country planning and prevention of pollution; and the Scottish Economic Planning Department, created in 1973.

In 1951 the group of Ministers responsible for Scottish affairs was increased by the appointment of a Minister of State, Scottish Office, and a third Under-Secretary of State, which, with the Lord Advocate and Solicitor-General, brought up to seven the group in the government available for the direction of Scottish affairs. The salient defect which remains is that all these are primarily politicians, members of a United Kingdom party, and Scottish requirements and interests have to conform to national ones, while legislation is made when London wishes it, too frequently to a pattern settled in London, and discussed

---

[1] *Ibid.* 124; Mure Mackenzie, 273–275.
[2] *Ibid.* 127, and see p. 128 as to the Government of Scotland Bill sought to be introduced in 1913 and 1914, and p. 133 as to Home Rule Bills between 1919 and 1927. See also Mure Mackenzie, 392–398.

in an assembly dominated by party political considerations in which seven-eighths of the members have little knowledge of or interest in Scotland.

Local Government

The reform of local government [3] began with the Acts of 1833 whereby the magistrates and town councils of the sixty-six royal and thirteen parliamentary burghs were to be elected by the £10 householders.

A whole series of statutes authorised royal burghs and burghs of barony (1833), parliamentary burghs (1847) and other populous places (1850, 1862) to adopt a uniform code of " police," covering watching, lighting, paving, cleansing and water supply, and thereby to become " police burghs." In the police burgh authority was entrusted to police magistrates and police commissioners who might or might not be the same as the bailies and councillors and this dual administration lasted to the end of the nineteenth century. Minor reforms included the abrogation of the exclusive rights of guildry and craft and burgess-ship, the abolition of petty customs, transfer to the county council of the duty of maintaining a police force, and authority to appoint a stipendiary magistrate.

This trend culminated in the Burgh Police (Scotland) Acts 1892 and 1903 and the Town Councils (Scotland) Act 1900, under which over two hundred towns administered their own machinery for preserving order, health and good government.

In the counties [4] a regular, paid police force made its appearance under Acts of 1839 and 1857, its administration being entrusted to the commissioners of supply. [5] The justices of the peace also had administrative functions, particularly in connection with roads and bridges.

In 1845 parochial boards were established to take over administration of the poor law; they were composed of elected members, kirk session delegates, heritors and burgh magistrates. The whole of Scotland was supervised by a Board of Supervision of nine members. These parochial boards were given further duties later, in connection with registration (1854) and public health and water supply (1867). [6]

In 1853 the Forbes Mackenzie Act commenced the system of licensing of public-houses, while 1854 saw the introduction of compulsory registration of births, deaths and marriages, and in 1872 popularly elected school boards were set up in each burgh and parish with power to levy a local rate for education and to compel attendance up to the age of thirteen. [7]

---

[3] See generally Pryde, *op cit.* 188–190, and " Burghal Administration," in McLarty (ed.), *Source Book of Administrative Law*, Chap. 1.

[4] On the counties, see Slevin, " Rural Administration," in McLarty (ed.), *Source Book of Administrative Law*, Chap. 2.

[5] Rait and Pryde, 180.

[6] Slevin, " Rural Administration," in McLarty (ed.), *Source Book of Administrative Law*, Chap. 2; Ferguson, *Dawn of Scottish Social Welfare*, Chap. 8.

[7] Rait and Pryde, 181.

In 1878 county road trustees assumed responsibility for all roads and bridges, superseding the older statute-labour roads and turnpike trusts.[8]

In 1889 a substantial reform of local government was effected by the establishment of comprehensive authorities in the shape of popularly elected county councils.[9] They took over the functions of commissioners of supply, justices of the peace and county road trustees, administered the police in smaller burghs and public health services. They were authorised to levy a consolidated rate in place of the former separate assessments. In the larger shires district committees were to act as their agents in matters of roads and public health. As regards police and capital works the final say was given to the standing joint committee composed of seven county councillors and seven commissioners of supply with the sheriff as chairman.[10]

In 1894 popularly elected parish councils were set up in lieu of the old parochial boards and charged with the administration of poor relief and all local matters, with a Local Government Board to co-ordinate their activities.[11] District committees composed of county councillors for the district, and one parish councillor from each parish and from any burgh within the district, formed a link between county and parish.[12]

The Local Government (Scotland) Act 1929 recast the whole system, sweeping away the older and *ad hoc* authorities, and substituting county, town and district councils to which all powers and functions were entrusted. This pattern was amended only in detail in 1947. Burghs were divided into three categories, counties of cities, a small number of large burghs and a larger number of small burghs. The Act provided an admirable scheme but it has been found in practice to remove most power to the larger authorities and to increase reliance on the central government, a tendency visible in other fields of administration also. Various functions have since 1945 been transferred from local to national organisations and dependence on the Exchequer for money is heavy, which tends to effect also a transfer of control. There has also since 1945 been widespread dissatisfaction with the way in which everything of consequence is managed from, or its decisions reached in, London and with remote control which frequently reveals ignorance of local conditions and disregard of local sentiment.

A fresh structure came into force in 1975.[13] Burghs ceased to have functions in local government and all powers were assigned to nine regional, three islands, and fifty-three district councils.

---

[8] Rait and Pryde, 181; Pryde, *op cit*. 207.
[9] Rait and Pryde, 123–124.
[10] *Ibid*. 181; Slevin, *loc cit*. 17–19.
[11] Rait and Pryde, 124.
[12] *Ibid*. 181; Slevin, *loc cit*. 17–19.
[13] Local Government (Scotland) Act, 1973.

Special Authorities

In the Highlands high rents and ejections among the crofters produced much bad feeling and hardship and some outbursts of violence when in 1886 the Crofters' Holdings Act sought to fix fair rents, guarantee security of tenure, enlarge existing holdings and allow compensation for improvements. The Crofters Commission was appointed with executive and judicial functions and toured the northern counties seeking to settle disputes and alleviate difficulties.[14] In 1897 a Congested Districts Board was set up for the settlement of land scheduled as suitable for new holdings and small farms. In 1911 its work was passed to the Board of Agriculture and in 1912 the Crofters Commission gave place to the Scottish Land Court.[15] In 1955, however, a new Crofters Commission was appointed charged with the reorganisation, development and regulation of crofting in the crofting counties.[16]

The House of Lords and Scots Appeals

In the first half of the nineteenth century the reputation of the House of Lords as an appeal court from Scotland, never high, touched its nadir.[17] Appeals were regularly taken to the Lords, frequently merely to waste time. Many appeals were heard by the Lord Chancellor or a single Law Lord sitting with two lay peers to make up a quorum. Some Lord Chancellors frankly confessed their ignorance of Scots law on the matter under appeal, others merely showed it in their judgments, which frequently reversed the Court of Session, while judgments were regularly and normally thought and sometimes spoken in terms of English law and not even translated into the terms of art of Scots law. It is not surprising that decisions of the Lords continued to be worthless as statements of Scots law and, so far as influential, to be seriously detrimental to the principles of Scots law. Repeatedly Lords, in complete ignorance of the principles, asserted that the law of Scotland *must* be the same as the law of England.[18] An infamous example, which fastened on Scots law the wickedly unjust rule of common employment,[19] is *Bartonshill Coal Co.* v. *Reid*[20] where Lord Cranworth, having discussed the English cases, said: " But if such be the law of England, on what ground can it be argued not to be the law of Scotland? " In cases of doubt, moreover, the Lords sometimes consulted

---

[14] Rait and Pryde, 124; Mure Mackenzie, 294.
[15] Mure Mackenzie, 294–295.
[16] Laird, in *Source Book of Administrative Law*, 90–91.
[17] See Gibb, *Law from Over the Border*, Chap. 3.
[18] Gibb, *op. cit.* 57.
[19] Abolished by statute in 1948; the rule was *not* part of Scots law prior to 1858.
[20] (1858) 3 Macq. 266, 285.

the judges, but the *English* judges,[21] and this practice persisted in isolated cases as late as 1904.[22]

By 1866 the position had become intolerable. " For at least a century there had been intense dissatisfaction in Scotland with the constitution of the House of Lords as Court of Appeal. Scottish lawyers in particular felt aggrieved because they had to plead before a foreign tribunal which had to be instructed in the elements of their system . . . the House of Lords, as a bench of competent judges, had thus to a great degree lost the confidence of the profession in Scotland. Lawyers naturally thought the administration of Scots law in the court of last resort could not be entrusted to men who were conversant only with a foreign system, and who showed little or no consideration for the opinions of Scotch judges— at least not that deference accorded to them in the days of Mansfield and Erskine. There were other reasons for the discontent. In many cases —for example, the *Douglas*, the *Roxburghe* and the *Queensberry* cases— property to the value of half a million had been involved. These were great causes and attracted wide notice. But hundreds of others had stood in the same position as far as the feebleness of the House of Lords as the ultimate judicature, constituted without a Scotch judge, was concerned. It was esteemed a radical defect, as indefensible as absurd, that the judges knew little or nothing about the law they had to administer. Even the English members of the bench from time to time kicked against the pricks. Some of them, like Lord Redesdale, who officiated in the *Queensberry* cases (1819) openly confessed that they had to divest themselves of English prejudice before studying a Scotch case. . . . Scotch lawyers have resented the interposition of an English mixture into the solid body of their Roman system." [23] " The general sentiment of the Scottish people was that the House of Lords was not a tribunal which could be trusted, and for a long time it had been felt in the Parliament House, and also among English lawyers, that the court of final appeal would be strengthened by the presence of a judge who was thoroughly acquainted, from practical experience, with the law of Scotland." [24]

Accordingly, so as to have someone in the House who knew something about Scots law, and to be a counterpart in the Upper House as expositor of Scottish measures to the Lord Advocate in the Commons, Lord President McNeill was raised to the peerage as Lord Colonsay in 1866. He did not make any great mark there and died in 1874.

In 1873 the Judicature Act abolished the jurisdiction of the House of Lords but this provision never came into force and in 1876 the Appel-

---

[21] *e.g. Baillie* v. *Grant* (1832) 6 W. & S. 40.

[22] In *Free Church of Scotland* v. *Overtoun* (1904) 7 F.(H.L.) 1: this appears from the *Memoirs of Lord Salvesen* (ed. Andersen, 1949), pp. 66–67. Salvesen was one of the counsel in the case.

[23] Crabb Watt, *John Inglis*, 256–257.

[24] Omond, *Lord Advocates of Scotland, 1834–80*, 146.

late Jurisdiction Act provided for salaried Lords of Appeal in Ordinary with life peerages.[25] While this jurisdiction is still doubtfully satisfactory it is at least less objectionable than before 1867.[26] At least since 1876 the House has never lacked at least one Scottish Law Lord[27] though it is still the case that Scottish appeals are decided by a tribunal all of whom may be, and the majority of whom almost invariably are, English lawyers.

The consequence of this strange jurisdiction has been the introduction of much English law into Scotland, much of it then or subsequently misunderstood, and the assimilation of much Scots law to English, usually to the detriment of the native rule. Opinions still differ as to the merits of the practice of an appeal to Westminster and it is significant that the Scottish criminal law, where no such appeal has ever been permitted, has developed on quite satisfactory lines without the influence of appeal to the Lords. Since 1876, however, Scots law has at least been represented by distinguished jurists in the House and contributed something to its judgments. Lords Watson and Reid in particular have been highly esteemed as much in English as in Scottish appeals.[28]

The Superior Courts

The pattern of the Court of Session remained substantially unchanged from its foundation till after 1800.[29] It remained a unitary court, sitting and deliberating as a whole, though two or three judges might at any time be on duty in rotation in the Outer House acting as Lord Ordinary, dealing with witnesses, oaths and the preliminary stages of actions, or in the Bill Chamber authorising the initiation of exceptional forms of actions, but such judges were delegates of the whole court rather than independent judges. The system had, however, ceased to be satisfactory by the early nineteenth century and the first third of the century saw a flood of reports of commissions and committees, pamphlets and memoranda urging change.

In 1808 the Inner House was divided into the First and Second Divisions, consisting respectively of the Lord President and seven Lords Ordinary, and the Lord Justice-Clerk and six Lords Ordinary. In 1810 the three junior judges of the First Division and the two junior judges of the Second Division became permanent Lords Ordinary sitting only in the Outer House. Further adjustment seemed necessary and in 1825

---

[25] See Stevens, " Final Appeal: Reform of the House of Lords and Privy Council, 1867–76 " (1964) 80 L.Q.R. 343.

[26] See modern cases discussed by Gibb, *op. cit.*, Chap. 4.

[27] The succession has been Lords Gordon, Watson, Robertson, Shaw of Dunfermline, Dunedin, Macmillan, Thankerton, Normand, Reid, Keith of Avonholm, Guest, Kilbrandon and Fraser, while other Scottish judges who were peers, such as Lords Kinnear and Shand have also sat occasionally.

[28] See Blom-Cooper and Drewry, *Final Appeal*, 156–157.

[29] See generally, Cooper, " The Central Courts after 1532," in *Introduction to Scottish Legal History*, Chap. 24.

the court was settled on the basis of an Inner House of two Divisions, each of four judges (including the Lord President and Lord Justice-Clerk in the First and Second Divisions respectively) and an Outer House of seven Lords Ordinary.[30] In 1830 the Outer House was allowed to diminish to five and the total to thirteen but in 1948 the traditional number of fifteen was again authorised [31] and later statutes [32] raised the authorised number to twenty.

An important change in procedure was made in 1850 by the Court of Session Act of that year.[33] Hitherto litigation had been conducted largely by written pleadings, learned and voluminous,[34] but thereafter it was incompetent to order " cases or minutes of debate or other written argument to be prepared by the parties." " These minutes of debate gave employment to scores of men who could not address a judge without blushing or stammering—honest, able worms that burrowed away their lives amid the parchment, the print, and the moths of Voet and Heineccius, of Stair and Erskine, of the Jus Feudale and the Pandects . . . from 1850 forward Vinnius and the Corpus Juris vanished into obscurity." [35] Written pleadings became much briefer and oral argument thereon became normal.

Even after the Act of 1850 reform of procedure was sadly required, for the mills of justice ground slowly. The Distribution of Business Act of 1856 gave some relief and the Court of Session Act of 1868, though attacked as anglicising, instituted an improved and expeditious procedure.

A factor which made for expedition was the change in the method of taking proofs. Down to the beginning of the century the depositions of witnesses were taken by the Lord Ordinary in his week of duty in the Outer House. They then resorted to the device of appointing commissioners to hear witnesses, write down the gist of their testimony and report, but neither commissioner nor judge reported on the import of the evidence or the credibility of the witnesses. This continued till 1866 when it was provided that in all ordinary cases proof should be led before the Lord Ordinary but the success of the change was due largely to the adoption of the practice of having shorthand notes taken, which was first sanctioned by the Conjugal Rights Act of 1861. At first the judges dictated the evidence to the shorthand writer but this was later given over and shorthand notes became competent in all civil

---

[30] See *Purves* v. *Carswell* (1905) 8 F. 351, 354.

[31] Administration of Justice (Scotland) Act 1948, s. 1.

[32] Restrictive Trade Practices Act 1956, s. 32; Criminal Justice (Scotland) Act 1963, s. 49; Resale Prices Act 1964, s. 9; Administration of Justice Act 1968, s. 1.

[33] See further, Maxwell, in *Introduction* (Stair Society), Chap. 32.

[34] A specimen of this style at its best is Thomas Thomson's Memorial on Old Extent, written for the case of *Cranstoun* v. *Gibson*, May 16, 1818, F.C., and printed by the Stair Society in 1946.

[35] Crabb Watt, *John Inglis*, 54–55.

cases in 1866. Some judges, however, such as Inglis, always took the notes themselves.

In 1913 much of the mass of Acts of Sederunt regulating practice was consolidated into the Consolidating Act of Sederunt and this in turn was superseded in 1936 by Rules of Court made under the authority of the Administration of Justice (Scotland) Act 1933. The principal excrescence on a reasonably simple and direct system of procedure was and is the persistence of civil jury trial, an expensive time-wasting alien imposition and an unsuitable mode of trial to boot, which was nevertheless recommended for retention in a restricted sphere by a departmental committee in 1959.[36]

The Admiralty Court

In the sixteenth century [37] the Court of Admiralty sat to exercise the judicial functions of the Admiral of Scotland and but for the opposition of the other courts would probably have captured most of the commercial litigation by reason of the suitability of its jurisdiction and procedure. It had jurisdiction in maritime causes, civil and criminal, over the whole of Scotland. It administered the customary law of the sea, particularly the Laws of Oleron. But the Court of Session and the Court of Justiciary were jealous of this rival and stole business from it despite attempts at parliamentary protection.[38] In 1825 the jurisdiction in prize was transferred to the English Court of Admiralty [39] and in 1828 a jurisdiction in criminal causes, cumulative with that of the Admiralty Court, was conferred on the Court of Justiciary. Finally in 1830 the civil jurisdiction of the Admiralty Court was transferred to the Court of Session and to the sheriffs and thereafter the criminal jurisdiction was merged in that of the Justiciary Court and of the sheriffs.

The Jury Court

The jury as a tribunal for determining disputed issues of fact in civil matters had vanished by the sixteenth century. In 1810, however, a Royal Commission suggested the introduction of civil juries on the English model and in 1815 this was put into effect by the creation of a separate tribunal, first of three and later of five judges, entitled the " Lords Commissioners of the Jury Court in Civil Causes." [40] The Chief Commissioner was William Adam who, though a Scot, had practised

---

[36] *Report of the Committee on Civil Jury Trial in Scotland* (Cmnd. 851, 1959).
[37] See further, *Acta Curiae Admirallatus Scotiae*, ed. Wade, Stair Society, Vol. 2; Baty, " The Judge Admiral of Scotland " (1916) 28 J.R. 144; McMillan, " The Scottish Court of Admiralty " (1922) 34 J.R. 38, 164.
[38] Acts 1609, c. 22, and 1681, c. 82.
[39] A violation of Art. XIX of the Treaty of Union.
[40] For the reasons underlying the introduction of jury trial, see Gibb, *Law from Over the Border*, 45 *et seq.*

only in England. This court had no original jurisdiction but acted only on remit from the Court of Session or Admiralty Court. The experiment never seems to have been much of a success and subsequent statutes limited the causes in which jury trial was requisite.

In 1830 the powers and duties of the Jury Court were transferred to the Court of Session and the court abolished. The Royal Commission of 1868 reported that the institution of civil jury trial had not given general satisfaction but it has nevertheless survived, despite constant criticism and the withering away of civil jury trial in England on the model of which it was established.[41]

The Court of Exchequer

This court was created in 1708 pursuant to the Treaty of Union and consisted of the High Treasurer of Great Britain,[42] a Chief Baron,[43] and four ordinary Barons[43] of Exchequer. The court sat in Edinburgh and was concerned mainly with questions of customs, excise, revenue and Crown debts. During the nineteenth century the functions of the court were curtailed by various statutes and in 1856 it was merged in the Court of Session. Revenue cases coming before the Court of Session continue, however, to be designated Exchequer causes.

The Commissary Courts

The Reformation left undischarged the functions formerly attaching to the courts of the Officials in each diocese by abolishing all jurisdiction depending on papal authority. In 1563 a new Commissary Court was created for Edinburgh and commissaries named for each diocese.[44] The chief court consisted of four with a jurisdiction over the bishopric of Edinburgh and a general jurisdiction over the whole of Scotland in matters of marriage, divorce, legitimacy, status and the moveable succession of Scottish subjects dying abroad or not subject to another jurisdiction. Down to the nineteenth century the commissaries nearly monopolised jurisdiction in actions affecting status and succession, both at first instance and on intermediate appeal, and despite the

---

[41] See *Report of the Committee on Civil Jury Trial* (Cmnd. 851, 1959). For criticisms, see Sidgwick, *Elements of Politics*, 491 *et seq.*; Lord Cooper, " Trial by Jury in Scotland," in *Selected Papers*, pp. 58–70, and " The Scottish Legal Tradition," *ibid.*, pp. 172–200. As to England, see Jackson, " Incidence of Jury Trial during the past Century " (1937) 1 M.L.R. 132, and " Jury Trial Today " (1938) 6 Camb.L.J. 367; Glanville Williams, *The Proof of Guilt*, Chap. 10.

[42] The office of Treasurer has been entrusted since 1714 to a commission consisting of the First Lord of the Treasury, the Chancellor of the Exchequer and the junior Lords of the Treasury. See also, Clerk and Scrope, *Historical View of the Court of Exchequer in Scotland* (1820); *Inland Revenue* v. *Barrs*, 1959 S.C. 273; affd. 1961 S.C.(H.L.) 22.

[43] From Norman-French *baron*, a man; they were not in any sense peers.

[44] Donaldson, " The Church Courts," in *Introduction to Scottish Legal History*, Chap. 27

Reformation continued to develop the law largely in reliance on Continental jurists, canonists and civilians.

In 1823 the inferior commissaries became merged in the sheriff courts, though they were not formally abolished till 1876 and the name still survives in the designation of executry business as " commissary business," just as matrimonial causes are still designated " consistorial causes." The Commissary Court of Edinburgh was abolished in 1836, since when its functions have been performed by the common law courts.

The Teind Court

An Act of 1708 transferred to the Court of Session in the capacity of Commission for the Plantation of Kirks and Valuation of Teinds work relating to parish churches and manses, stipends and teinds previously entrusted to various *ad hoc* commissions. The court in this capacity continued to perform numerous administrative and judicial functions, both those of the older commissions and further duties imposed by later legislation. From 1839 the Lords Commissioners of Teinds comprised the judges of the Inner House together with the second junior Lord Ordinary, any five of whom, it was provided in 1868, should form a quorum. Most of the now much diminished work is today done by the second junior Lord Ordinary as Lord Ordinary on Teinds.

The Bill Chamber

The Bill Chamber originated in an Act of Sederunt of 1532 as a Vacation Court, but in addition acquired a special jurisdiction, granting leave to issue certain kinds of privileged summonses and to use certain kinds of diligence. Down to 1933 it retained control of the processes of suspension or suspension and interdict, and in the nineteenth century statute conferred on the Bill Chamber miscellaneous special jurisdictions, particularly in relation to bankruptcy, entails and judicial factories. The Bill Chamber was, during session, under the junior Lord Ordinary and had its own office and staff and a great deal of peculiar and detailed procedure. In 1933 it was merged with the Court of Session and its jurisdiction became ordinary Outer House jurisdiction.

The Legal Profession

The Faculty of Advocates maintained its position as a learned and influential society as well as one of the most honourable professional bodies; its ranks included not only the most distinguished lawyers but wits, scholars, politicians and men of letters.

The Faculty for long differed from the English Bar in having no formal differentiation between senior and junior [45]; a man " gave up writing "

---

[45] King's Counsel are known in English law from the sixteenth century; Bacon did much to define their position and secure their privileges.

(pleadings) when of sufficient age and experience, but the absence of a distinct status placed the senior advocate in an invidious position when appearing before the House of Lords or meeting English counsel. In 1857–58 the problem of precedence was much discussed and was settled by according ex-law officers precedence postponed only to the Lord Advocate, the Dean of Faculty [46] and the Solicitor-General. In 1892 a petition craving Her Majesty to create a roll of Queen's Counsel in Scotland was granted, since when a formal distinction between senior and junior counsel has subsisted.

The status of the solicitor's profession was immensely promoted by the Law Agents Act of 1873 which for the first time demanded the passing of examinations as a requirement for admission to practice. The former requirement of apprenticeship continued and continues, but since 1873 a significant feature has been the steadily increasing number of apprentices who have graduated in one of the universities. Equally significant has been the increasing number of solicitors employed in local government and in industry.

In 1949 the Law Society of Scotland was established by statute, so that the profession had for the first time a national body including all solicitors. The former societies and the local bodies however continued. It acquired further statutory powers in 1958 and exercises a wide authority over the qualification and professional conduct of solicitors. It was set up partly to administer the legal aid scheme introduced in 1949, which is done through a central and a number of local committees.

Legal Literature—Hume and Bell

Since the early nineteenth century the greatest contributions to the literature of the law have come from the academic lawyers. David Hume (1756–1838), a nephew of the philosopher of the same name, was Professor of Scots Law at Edinburgh from 1786 to 1822, and published the *Commentaries on the Law of Scotland respecting Crimes* in 1797, a book which has always been accepted as of the highest authority on the subject. He also published a valuable volume of *Decisions* and his academic lectures were highly regarded and frequently cited.[47] They have subsequently been published by the Stair Society.[48] Hume had also been a Principal Clerk of Session contemporaneously with Sir Walter Scott and was promoted a Baron of Exchequer in 1822.[49]

George Joseph Bell (1770–1843), his successor as Professor of Scots

---

[46] A list of the Deans of Faculty in the nineteenth century will be found in Crabb Watt, *John Inglis*, 111, and lists of Deans since 1698 and Vice-Deans since 1754 in 1972 S.L.T.(News) 217.

[47] See e.g. *Biggart* v. *City of Glasgow Bank* (1879) 6 R. 470, 475–6, per Lord Deas.

[48] ed. Paton, 6 vols., 1939–57.

[49] See further Paton's *Life of Hume*, in Vol. 6 of the Stair Society edition of the *Lectures*.

Law (1822–43), took an active part in promoting improvements in Court of Session procedure but made his name as a jurist with his *Commentaries on the Law of Scotland and on the Principles of Mercantile Jurisprudence* (1810, based on an earlier book of 1800), which set out to systematise the principles of the law merchant and to reconcile them with the fundamental principles of Scots law, and the *Principles of the Law of Scotland*, published originally as a textbook for students (1829) and later revised and enlarged. He published also *Illustrations from Adjudged Cases of the Law of Scotland* (3 vols., 1836–38) as a companion work for students and an early specimen of the students' case-book, and other legal textbooks. He contributed immensely not only to the exposition but to the creation of mercantile law and to the harmonisation of Scots law on the topic with the decisions of English and other courts. Bell became a Principal Clerk of Session in 1832 and Lord Advocate Jeffrey would have made him a judge had there been a vacancy. Bell's successor, John Schank More (1784–1861), Professor 1843–61, published the standard, modern, annotated edition of Stair in 1832. His *Lectures* were posthumously published.[50]

Walter Ross, W.S., published in 1792 his *Lectures on the History and Practice of the Law of Scotland relative to Conveyancing and Legal Diligence* which are still valuable and which influenced the Society of Writers to the Signet to institute a lectureship in conveyancing in Edinburgh University, which was erected into a chair in 1825. The Juridical Society of Edinburgh first published its *Collection of Styles or Complete System of Conveyancing in* 1787–94, a work of great utility to practitioners. In the sphere of jurisprudence some mark was made by James Lorimer of Edinburgh [51] and Galbraith Miller of Glasgow.[52]

The Bench and Bar in the early nineteenth century continued the tradition of scholarship not confined to the law.[53] Francis Jeffrey was among the brilliant group who founded the *Edinburgh Review*, Henry Cockburn wrote those *Memorials* which are still the finest evocation of the Edinburgh of his young days, while Walter Scott wrote the *Waverley Novels* in the intervals of duty as Principal Clerk of Session and Sheriff-Depute of Selkirk.[54] Thomas Thomson, as depute Clerk Register, laboured

---

[50] Edited by McLaren, two volumes, 1864.

[51] *Institutes of Law* (1872); *Institutes of the Law of Nations* (1883). On him see Flint, " Professor Lorimer " (1890) 2 J.R. 113; Thomson, " Lorimer's Juristic Theory " (1896) 8 J.R. 242.

[52] *Lectures on the Philosophy of Law* (1884); *Law of Nature and Nations in Scotland* (1896); *The Data of Jurisprudence* (1903).

[53] It is noteworthy that the two greatest biographies in the English language, Boswell's *Life of Johnson* and Lockhart's *Life of Scott*, were written by advocates. At the end of the century R. L. Stevenson was an advocate but did not practise. On him see Guthrie " R. L. Stevenson " (1919) 31 J.R. 89, 161; (1920) 32 J.R. 71, 129.

[54] McDonald " Sir Walter Scott's Fee Book " (1950) 62 J.R. 288; Dobie " Law and Lawyers in the Waverley Novels " (1920) 32 J.R. 244, 317; Marshall, *Sir Walter Scott and Scots Law*.

to organise and publish many of the invaluable public records, and through the Bannatyne Club published many more volumes of immense historical interest and value.

Later in the century many judges made important contributions to the development of the law. Over the years 1858–91 Lord President Inglis [55] set out in classic judgments many principles of the steadily developing law while Lord McLaren [56] wrote the standard book on *Wills and Succession* and Lord Fraser [57] authoritative books on *Husband and Wife, Parent and Child* and *Master and Servant*. In the House of Lords Lord Watson [58] and, later, Lord Reid [59] were outstanding judges both in Scottish and English cases.

In the twentieth century Lord Dunedin [60] and Lord Cooper [61] were outstanding on the Bench while Professor Sir John Rankine wrote books still valuable on *Land ownership* and *Leases* and Professor Gloag's book on *Contract* won a high reputation for its breadth and grasp of principle. The foundation of the Stair Society in 1934 showed a quickening interest in Scottish legal history, while the Law Faculties of the universities began to concern themselves as much with the theory, history, philosophy, analysis and criticism of law, and with its wider implications as with its dogmatic exposition and practical applications, and the foundation of the Scottish Universities Law Institute in 1960 marked the beginning of a major undertaking in restating Scots law in modern form.[62]

Developments in Private Law

The two factors which most influenced the development of Scots law since 1800 have been increasing statutory modification of common law doctrines and increasing reliance on English rather than Roman law as a source for borrowing.[63] Hardly any branch of common law has escaped statutory modification, while many topics of entirely statutory creation have developed. Most of these changes reflect changes in public opinion, in prevailing social, political and economic philosophy, and in conceptions of the functions and responsibilities of the state, or the changes wrought by two world wars, which necessitated an unparalleled

---

[55] Crabb Watt, *John Inglis*, McLaren, " Lord President Inglis " (1893) 4 J.R. 14.
[56] Kennedy, " Lord McLaren " (1910) 22 J.R. 181.
[57] Goudy, " Lord Fraser " (1889) 1 J.R. 178.
[58] McNaghten " Lord Watson " (1899) 11 J.R. 269; Stormonth-Darling, *ibid.*, 272; Haldane, *ibid.*, 278.
[59] Blom-Cooper and Drewry, *Final Appeal*, 156.
[60] " Dunedin, the greatest master of the principles of Scots Law in our time ": *per* Lord Macmillan, *Stewart* v. *L.M.S. Ry.*, 1943 S.C.(H.L.) 19 at 38.
[61] See Smith, " The Contribution of Lord Cooper of Culross to the Law of Scotland " (1955) 67 J.R. 249 and in Lord Cooper's *Selected Papers*, xxix.
[62] See 1961 S.L.T.(News) 97.
[63] See also *Introduction to Scottish Legal History*, 53–63.

amount of state control and interference with matters of private concern.[64] Industrial law and social welfare legislation [65] are both almost entirely modern statutory creations.

The nineteenth century was a great period for the formulation and working out of legal principles in cases and judicial decisions, and in many branches of the law the basic modern formulation of the principles is still to be found in nineteenth-century cases. In contrast the twentieth century since 1914 has been concerned increasingly with the interpretation of statutory provisions, and comparatively few common law decisions of really outstanding significance have been pronounced. *Donoghue* v. *Stevenson* [66] is undoubtedly the principal decision of the century to date with the most profound influence on the development of the law.

In nearly all branches of law references to the *Digest* and the civilians have come to be replaced by reference, usually uncritical and too frequently mistaken, to English law and English books.[67] Much unsuitable or misunderstood law has thereby infiltrated into Scotland and warnings have been uttered from the Bench as to the dangers of ignorant use of nonnative sources of law. Students, practitioners, judges and the House of Lords have all on various occasions been decoyed by the similarity of result attained by the two systems into saying that the principle is the same in both countries or into relying on English authorities or more up-to-date English textbooks.

Statute has effected numerous and far-reaching reforms, especially in property law. The fetters which bound entailed property and rendered it unsaleable and unburdenable with debt had subsisted since Sir George Mackenzie's Act of 1685, relieved only by the Act of 1746, which authorised the sale of entailed lands to the Crown for public purposes, and the Montgomery Act of 1770, which further authorised leasing, powers extended by the Rosebery Act of 1836. The Aberdeen Act of 1824 and the Rutherford Act of 1840 conferred wider powers on the heir of entail, the latter legalising under certain conditions the alienation of the estate. Acts of 1875 and 1882 led up to the Act of 1914 which prohibited the creation of future entails.

The feudal system of landholding was simplified and shortened by

---

[64] See generally Dicey, *Lectures on the Relation between Law and Public Opinion in England in the Nineteenth Century*; Ginsberg (ed.), *Law and Opinion in England in the Twentieth Century*; Friedmann, *Law in a Changing Society*; Smith, " Scots Law in the Victorian Era " (1901) 13 J.R. 152; Walker, " Law and Opinion in Britain since 1900," 1956 J.R. 117, 213.

[65] See generally Ferguson, *Dawn of Scottish Social Welfare*; *Scottish Social Welfare, 1864–1914*; Marwick, *Economic Developments in Victorian Scotland*; Mackinnon, *Social and Industrial History of Scotland*; Hutchins and Harrison, *History of the Factory Acts*.

[66] 1932 S.C.(H.L.) 31.

[67] See Henderson, " English Cases as Scots Authorities " (1900) 12 J.R. 304; Burn-Murdoch, " English Law in Scots Practice " (1908–9) 20 J.R. 346; 21 J.R. 59, 148.

a series of Acts leading up to the Consolidation Act of 1868 while Gordon's Act of 1874 made further sweeping changes in the direction of simplifying land transfer, a process continued in the present century in 1924 and 1938.[68]

In the Highlands the proprietors in the late eighteenth and early nineteenth centuries transformed much of the interior of the West and North Highland counties into large sheep-farms, clearing out the crofters and settling them in crofting townships on patches of ground near the coast. When sheep-farming became less profitable owing to wool and mutton coming from Australia and New Zealand, large sheep-farms were turned into deer forests. Population had increased despite emigration but migration and depopulation followed the clearances and the ruin of the kelp industry.[69] The middle years of the nineteenth century were years of great hardship and destitution. The government remedy was emigration, suggested by a commission in 1841: friction and unrest resulted, evictions for non-payment of rent were common and there were instances in the 1880s of violence, resistance to ejection measures and clashes with the police and the military. A Commission of Enquiry was set up in 1883 which resulted in the Crofters' Holdings Act of 1886, which conferred security of tenure on certain conditions, fixed fair rent, compensation for improvements and gave facilities for the enlargement of holdings. It set up the Crofters' Commission which performed executive and judicial functions until superseded by the Land Court under the Small Landholders Act of 1911.[70] A new Crofters' Commission was set up in 1955 to reorganise and develop crofting in the crofting counties.

In the law of persons two of the common law forms of irregular marriage were abolished in 1939 and civil marriage introduced, while the grounds of divorce were widened in 1938 and this, combined with the disturbance to family life effected by the War and a changed social attitude to divorce, made divorce a common form of litigation. Many statutory changes ameliorated the position of the illegitimate child, while changes in guardianship made the welfare of the child the paramount consideration.[71]

During the nineteenth century contract increased in importance as commerce flourished. Towards the end of the century there were passed the Mercantile Law Amendment Act of 1856, designed to assimilate in large measure the laws of Scotland and of England in business matters and the forerunner of the Sale of Goods Act 1893, and other pieces of

---

[68] See further Monteath, in *Introduction* (Stair Society), Chap. 14.
[69] See Campbell, *Scotland since 1707*; Mackenzie, *The Highland Clearances*; Prebble, *The Highland Clearances*.
[70] Mackinnon, *Social and Industrial History of Scotland from the Union*, 74.
[71] See further *Introduction* (Stair Society), Chaps. 8–11.

partial codification, and the Bankruptcy Act of 1856, later superseded by the Act of 1913, and the Merchant Shipping Act 1894.[72]

Conditions contributed very much to the development of the law of reparation. More settled conditions and greater willingness to abide by the law reduced the number of cases of spuilzie and deliberate wrong-doing. At the same time increasing use of machinery and the coming of railways and later of road traffic brought more into prominence wrongs of negligence, particularly personal injuries, arising out of travel and industrial accidents. The increasing congestion of the roads similarly gave rise to the large number of traffic offences dealt with in the summary criminal courts.[73]

From early in the nineteenth century legislation strove to improve the position of factory workers and increasingly to make provision for their safety, health and welfare. The common law claim of an injured employee for damages for injury was reinforced by recognition of his claim for breach of statutory duty, and by his claims, independently of proof of fault on the employer's part, under the Employers' Liability Act 1880, and subsequently to workmen's compensation (1897) and then to industrial injuries benefit (1946). Trade unions were recognised as lawful institutions and collective bargaining, conditions of work fixed by statute, arbitration or independent bodies largely replaced individual contracts of employment.[74]

The great extension, enlargement and development of industrial enterprises in the nineteenth century made for conditions with which the private individual and the partnership could not cope. " After 1720, the foundation of joint-stock companies was controlled by the so-called ' Bubble Act ' of that year, a panic measure passed by Parliament as a direct consequence of the public scandal caused by the collapse of the South Sea Company. This law prohibited the formation of new joint-stock companies unless sanctioned by private Act of Parliament or Crown charter. The law stood unrepealed till 1825. It never affected the continuance of those aristocrats among the older public companies, the East India Company (founded in 1600) or the Hudson's Bay Company (founded in 1670), or the Bank of England. Long before it was repealed as the need for collective capital increased, the ingenuity of lawyers and business men got round the Act by promoting the formation of unincorporate joint-stock associations." [75] This expedient allowed a considerable

---

[72] *Ibid.*, Chap. 19.   [73] *Ibid.*, Chap. 20.
[74] See further, Smith, in *Introduction* (Stair Society), Chap. 12, and " Master and Servant: Further Historical Outlines " (1958) 3 J.R.(N.S.) 215.
[75] Court, *Concise Economic History of Britain from 1750*, 84; see also Brown " The Genesis of Company Law in England and Scotland " (1901) 13 J.R. 185; Roberton Christie, " Company Law: Joint Stock Enterprise in Scotland before the Companies Acts " (1909) 21 J.R. 128; Holdsworth " The Early History of Commercial Societies " (1916) 28 J.R. 305; Campbell, " The Law and the Joint Stock Company in Scotland," in Payne (ed.), *Studies in Scottish Business History*, 136.

growth of company enterprise in certain fields such as insurance. But the old law of partnerships in an age of business instability and enterprise on larger scales frequently brought ruin owing to the absence of limitation on liability.[76] Partnership or unincorporated enterprise was manifestly unsuitable for the great investment in railways after 1840 [77]; it had the economic advantages of combined capital but the members' liability for the debts of the concern was unlimited as in partnership, and legal proceedings by or against the concern were apt to be intricate and laborious. In 1837 it was provided that the privilege of incorporation might be obtained not only by private Act or Crown charter but by letters patent and by the Registration Act of 1844 any company might register by a simple process and thereby become incorporated as a single entity in law. In 1856 limited liability was extended to all registered companies. A consolidating Act in 1862 extended the new facilities to insurance companies, and codified the law. Banks were for long excluded from limited liability and for long were also reluctant to take advantage of the privilege, and in consequence the failure of the joint-stock but unlimited City of Glasgow Bank in 1878 caused widespread ruin.[78] In 1879 the legal difficulties in the way of adoption by the banks of limited liability were removed. The law of companies has several times subsequently been consolidated afresh, each time incorporating new provisions designed to protect the investor from fraud, duplicity or misrepresentation.

Criminal law continued to develop with only small statutory interference, but methods of treatment and reformation of criminals were very largely altered in the twentieth century and the rules affecting punishment and treatment have become much more complicated as attempts have been made to humanise and individualise penalties. Procedure was greatly rationalised by the Criminal Procedure Act of 1887 which greatly simplified indictments, a development extended to the summary criminal courts by the Summary Jurisdiction Act 1907.

In the civil courts procedure was simplified by the Consolidating Act of Sederunt of 1913, itself superseded by the Rules of Court of 1936 (now 1965) while the Sheriff Courts Act of 1907 continued the same process for the sheriff court.

A tendency of great importance has been to remove controversies,

---

[76] *Cf.* the ruin of Sir Walter Scott in the failure of Ballantyne's in 1825, and the cases arising out of the failure of the City of Glasgow Bank in 1878.

[77] On the development of Scottish railways, see Mackinnon, *Social and Industrial History of Scotland from the Union*, 131–143; Pryde, 239–240.

[78] The directors were tried for fraud in the High Court and received various terms of imprisonment. See Wallace, *Trial of the City of Glasgow Bank Directors* (Notable Scottish Trials Series). The call on the shareholders of the bank was very heavy and this gave rise to much litigation in the next few years, mainly by shareholders seeking to have their names removed from the list of shareholders, and thereby to escape contribution. See also Kerr, *History of Banking in Scotland*; Mackinnon, *Social and Industrial History*, 154.

particularly under social welfare legislation, from the courts altogether and to commit them to a great variety of *ad hoc* tribunals.

Overall the tendency of the years since 1914 has been to interfere more and more with the liberty of the subject, to regulate his actings in more and more ways, and to produce a patchwork of *ad hoc* amendments and alterations of the common law to meet particular difficulties. The tendency towards legal chaos has been strong. Parliament has steadily been working, partly by ignorance, partly by the lack of interest of the majority of members, partly by the desire to unify conditions throughout the United Kingdom, and partly by declining to legislate separately for Scotland, for the destruction of Scots law. Occasionally a feature of Scots law has been adopted for England, but more usually the assumption has been that what will do for England is good for Scotland and Sottish members have too often aided and abetted this process, or at least acquiesced in it.

The Resurgence of National Spirit

Over the years since 1707, despite government or misgovernment from remote London, despite harshness, ignorance, apathy and neglect which treated Scotland sometimes as a rather laughable backwood, sometimes as a conquered, sometimes merely as a forgotten, province, there have never been lacking Scots who preserved the idea of Scotland as a nation, though others sought to ape the English in all things, English speech, English-type education, and English-type law.[79] The struggle for home rule rule for Ireland in the latter part of the nineteenth century evoked sympathy from the Scottish Liberals many of whom favoured devolution to local Parliaments, and the Scottish Home Rule Association was instituted, with Liberal support in 1886, and some propaganda for Scottish self-government thereafter continued. But in 1913 and 1914 the Liberal Government refused to consider a Government of Scotland Bill which would have set up a Scottish Parliament similar to what should, but for the war, have come into being in Ireland.

The issue of home rule reasserted itself in the inter-war years. Bills were put before Parliament between 1918 and 1927 and were shelved, though the Scottish Liberals adopted from 1924 a plan for federal government. Governmental indifference and the troubles of the inter-war years secured that nothing happened. In 1928 the Scottish National Party was founded and from the first attracted some public sympathy. Compton Mackenzie in 1931 and John MacCormick in 1950 stood as Scottish Nationalists and were elected Rectors of Glasgow University. In 1934 the moderate home-rulers of a new Scottish party joined the earlier

---

[79] See generally, Coupland, *Welsh and Scottish Nationalism*; Paton, *The Claim of Scotland*; Hanham, *Scottish Nationalism*.

Nationalists to form a broader Scottish National Party and in 1945 Dr. McIntyre won their first parliamentary seat at Motherwell.

The wider powers granted to the Scottish Standing Committee in 1948 were a concession to nationalist sentiment, which was further evidenced by local plebiscites and strong approval from the General Assembly of the Church of Scotland for a separate Scottish Parliament. In 1949 nationalist sympathisers organised the Scottish Covenant movement which obtained some two million signatures from persons supporting the principle of a Scottish Parliament. In 1950 a small group removed the Stone of Destiny from Westminster Abbey and transported it to Scotland. It was returned, draped in a saltire flag, to Arbroath Abbey [80] in April 1951, and the incident was dismissed by some as an idiotic prank, an outrage and sacrilege, and viewed by others as a possibly mistaken but sincere expression of indignation at the perpetuation of an ancient wrong, dissatisfaction with alien rule and a blow for their country. In 1952 on the accession of Queen Elizabeth there were protests against the ill-warranted assumption of the title Queen Elizabeth the Second.[81]

Scottish Affairs in Parliament

In Parliament itself some concessions have been made; since 1948 a public Bill certified by the Speaker as relating only to Scotland is referred for consideration in principle to the Scottish Grand Committee, which comprises all the seventy-one members for Scottish constituencies plus ten to fifteen others so as to maintain the balance of parties in the committee the same as in the House of Commons as a whole. After this the Bill is formally read a second time on the floor of the House and referred for detailed clause-by-clause examination to the Scottish Standing Committee which, set up in 1894 and 1895 and regularly since 1907, comprises thirty members for Scottish constituencies, plus up to twenty more to maintain the balance of parties. Scottish provisions in a United Kingdom Bill may also be referred to the Scottish Standing Committee. The Scottish Grand Committee also since 1948 spends up to six days in any parliamentary session considering the Scottish estimates, as well as two days given to Scottish estimates debates in the full House, and not more than two days in considering specified matters relating exclusively to Scotland which may have been referred for discussion. Since 1899 also

---

[80] An action doubtless intended to, and certainly evoking, memories of the Declaration of Arbroath of 1320, in which the barons of Scotland asserted the liberty of Scotland and declined ever to consent to subject themselves to the dominion of the English. See the text in *Source Book*, I, 151.

[81] See *MacCormick* v. *Lord Advocate*, 1953 S.C. 396. It seems that the question of the Queen's title was just assumed, the Scottish part in forming the United Kingdom and possible Scottish feeling being forgotten. The form of proclamation used in all Commonwealth countries also, equally wrongly, used the number.

there has been the distinctive system of considering private legislation, now regulated by the Private Legislation Procedure (Scotland) Act 1936, whereby a body desiring parliamentary powers applies to the Secretary of State for Scotland for a provisional order granting the desired powers. If the request is opposed, or if an inquiry seems necessary, an inquiry is held in Scotland before four commissioners drawn from panels of members of both Houses of Parliament. If the Secretary of State is satisfied he makes the order as requested and submits it to Parliament for ratification scheduled to a provisional order confirmation Act, which is dealt with under an expedited procedure. This has almost completely superseded private Bill procedure in Scotland.

Scottish Administration

Prior to 1885 Scottish administration was handled nominally by the Home Secretary and in practice by the Lord Advocate. In that year was created the office of Secretary for Scotland and there were transferred to him the functions of the Home Secretary relative to Scotland and certain others discharged by the Privy Council, the Treasury and the Local Government Board. He also became responsible to Parliament for the independent Scottish boards by that time established in Edinburgh, namely, the Board of Supervision, later the Local Government Board for Scotland, the Fishery Board, the Prison Commission, and the General Board of Commissioners in Lunacy, later the General Board of Control for Scotland. Further boards were created later, notably the Congested Districts (Scotland) Commissioners (1897), the Scottish Insurance Commissioners (1911), the Board of Agriculture for Scotland (1912) and the Highlands and Islands (Medical Services) Board (1913). The Scottish Board of Health on its creation in 1919 took over the functions of the Local Government Board for Scotland, the Scottish Insurance Commissioners and the Highlands and Islands (Medical Services) Board.

In 1926 the office of Secretary of Scotland was promoted to that of one of His Majesty's Principal Secretaries of State, and the holder then became Secretary of State for Scotland. In 1928 the Scottish Board of Agriculture, the Scottish Board of Health and the Scottish Prison Commissioners were replaced by the Department of Agriculture for Scotland, the Department of Health for Scotland and the Prisons Department for Scotland, each a statutory body independent of the Secretary of State, but under his control and direction. In the 1930s there was a substantial movement of offices and staff from London to Edinburgh; in 1939 St. Andrew's House, Edinburgh, was opened as the Secretary of State's headquarters, the London office remaining mainly for liaison purposes with Parliament and with departments based in London. Also in 1939 the Reorganisation of Offices (Scotland) Act abolished the independent departments and vested their functions in the Secretary of State, which he accordingly exercised through four departments, the Scottish Home Department, the Department of Health for Scotland, the Scottish Education Department, and the Department of Agriculture for Scotland. In 1962 the first two were rearranged and there came into being the Scottish Home and Health Department and the Scottish Development Department. In addition many Great Britain Departments of State, such as the Ministry of Social Security, have regional offices in Scotland.

The ministerial staff responsible for Scottish affairs has also increased; a Parliamentary Under-Secretary of State was appointed in 1919, a second in 1940 and a third in 1951; in that year also a Minister of State, Scottish Office, was appointed as the Secretary of State's principal deputy; the Lord Advocate and Solicitor-General for Scotland are also available for assistance, though they may not be Members of Parliament.

Since 1945 the Secretary of State's responsibilities have several times been extended. Thus in 1954 he became responsible for Scottish roads, and for the appointment of J.P.s in Scotland. In addition numerous independent bodies, such as the Crofters' Commission (1955), the Red Deer Commission (1959), the Highlands and Islands Development Board (1965), the Scottish Special Housing Association and the like, have close contact with the Secretary of State's Department.[82]

There have accordingly been material moves towards transferring authority from London to Edinburgh. But Parliament, eager to thrust self-government on many underdeveloped and politically immature parts of the Commonwealth, some trivial in size, importance and capacity, and many with no native tradition of law and government, stubbornly refused to consider any real devolution of power, despite growing evidence of pressure of business on Parliament and constant pleas of lack of time to legislate for Scotland.

Inadequacies of the Present System

These steps have not satisfied many people. The Scottish Standing and Scottish Grand Committees have no powers of legislative initiative, nor of veto. They can consider a Bill affecting Scotland at certain stages, but only if and when the Cabinet has decided to legislate for Scotland, and in the terms thus decided. Even the unanimous wish of all the Scottish M.P.s for a Bill on, say, criminal law or divorce or leases could not cause such a Bill to be introduced, and a power of amendment in committee (subject to being wiped out at a later stage) is no equivalent for a power to decide when and whether and in what terms to legislate. Conversely, if the Cabinet resolved to bring in a Bill, say, to abolish Scots law or the Presbyterian Church, the unanimous opposition of the Scottish

---

[82] Report of the Royal Commission on Scottish Affairs, 1953–54, (Cmd. 9219, 1954), Appx. 2.—Summary of the History of Scottish Administration; Milne, *The Scottish Office*; *Handbook on Scottish Administration* (1967 ed.).

M.P.s would not necessarily be able to secure its rejection. Also many fundamental matters of principle are decided for the United Kingdom and it is then a matter of enacting the principle in the terms of the two legal systems. Many fundamental issues are contained in United Kingdom Acts which could not be considered by the Scottish Committee in either of its forms. Scots law is made and unmade, and commonly mangled and ruined, in a legislative assembly in which the Scottish members are outnumbered by eight to one, a body the great majority of whose members have no interest or need to know or to care about the law or government of Scotland. The people of Scotland are not masters of their own fate in law or government. Their strong desire may be ignored, or outvoted in a House of Commons two-thirds empty, and they cannot lawfully resist the most outrageous destruction of their institutions.

These matters have become important only over the past eighty years or so because of, on the one hand, the extensions of the franchise and, on the other, the enormous growth in governmental control and interference with the life of the individual, with liberty of action, with freedom of contract, and with law generally. A basic trouble has been that power and patronage have always lain in London and a Member of Parliament must be an obedient and diligent servant of the London-based and London-centred parties. There is no room in modern British politics for the non-conformist or for independence of mind or thought. It is alleged that Scotland has full control of its affairs by having their administration in Scotland, but the administration merely executes the policy and gives effect to the ideas of others elsewhere. St. Andrew's House has freedom of action only within limits and only to execute what has been enacted in London.

The Tide Runs Strongly

In the late 1960s the feeling grew stronger. In 1967 the Scottish Nationalist candidate won a parliamentary seat at Hamilton and candidates of that party made extensive gains all over the country in local authority elections. The Liberal Party in 1966 and 1968 introduced Bills to give Scotland and Wales separate Parliaments on lines generally similar to that created for Northern Ireland in 1920.

In May 1968 the Leader of the Opposition, Mr. Heath, proposed the creation of an elected Scottish Assembly to take part in legislation in conjunction with Parliament, the details to be worked out by a constitutional committee. The precise constitution, powers and functions of this body were left very vague. Later in the same month the General Assembly of the Church of Scotland overwhelmingly approved a recommendation whereby it " convinced of the need for an effective form of self-government in Scotland within the framework of the United Kingdom, ask Her Majesty's Government for the early appointment of a royal commission, consisting of Scots widely representative of Scottish interests, to meet in Scotland with powers to call for evidence, to make recommendations which may enable the people of Scotland to choose the form and extent of self-government best suited to the nation's well-being, and to treat the matter with the utmost urgency." It did not take the Prime Minister long to refuse this request. A month later a serious B.B.C. programme [83] disclosed the majority opinion of Scots questioned by researchers in favour of greater self-government within the United Kingdom, while a survey commissioned in Glasgow by the *Glasgow Herald* found only small support for the status quo and overwhelming support for greater independence.[84] A few months later the government announced the setting up of a Royal Commission on the constitutional structure of the United Kingdom and the question of devolution.

A report on Scotland's government [85] by a committee appointed by the Conservative party proposed the creation of a Scottish Assembly with power to co-ordinate regional views, meet and question Scottish ministers, discuss government proposals and debate matters of concern to Scotland, and power to participate in the framing and passage of Scottish legislation.

The Royal Commission on the Constitution [86] rejected both the separation of Scotland from the United Kingdom and the creation of a federal structure, but recommended a measure of devolution, in the form of the creation of an elected regional assembly.

In 1974 the number of Scottish Nationalist M.P.s rose to eleven and the Labour government then elected had included in its manifesto a pledge to create a directly-elected Scottish Assembly.

Continuance of the Union of 1707 in its present form is not, and is not now ever again likely to be, generally regarded as satisfactory. Change is necessary, but it remains to be seen when and how and in what form change will be made. The implications of greater independence for the survival of Scots law are clear.

VI.—SOME FACTORS IN SCOTTISH LEGAL HISTORY

It is desirable finally to abstract some elements which have been powerful factors at different times in shaping Scottish legal history.

Feudal Law
The medieval feudal law which came from Normandy through England

---

[83] " The Disunited Kingdom," B.B.C. 1 T.V., June 12, 1968.
[84] *Glasgow Herald*, June 17, 1968. The figures were: No change: 14 per cent.; Complete independence: 21 per cent.: Some Home Rule within the U.K.: 38 per cent.; Greater local and regional freedom: 27 per cent.
[85] *Scotland's Government* (Scottish Constitutional Committee, 1970).
[86] Report, Cmnd. 5460, 1973.

has been the source and is still the ba~   and of heritable
property and succession.[87]   In Scotlan.   ~he War
of Independence, it has developed on its ow.   ~nce
preserved a feudal system simpler and closer   ~n did
England, and also avoided the complications n~   ~ngland
by the premature rigidity of the common law, the consequent rise of
equity and the growth of a dual system of legal and equitable interests
in property.[88]

Canon Law

The pre-Reformation canon law of the Roman Church, in Scotland
as elsewhere, has had a lasting influence on the law of the personal and
domestic relations, marriage, separation and divorce, wills and succession. But the canon law has also had its influence on contract and
on the form of deeds and writs.[89] In most branches, however, its influence
is largely spent and the canonical principles have been overlaid by legislation and a native tradition of decisions. Nevertheless even in the twentieth
century its force cannot be ignored and resort may still have to be had
to the texts and commentaries thereon.

Roman Law

Roman law was profoundly influential in the times of the institutional writers and its force is not yet exhausted.[90] It has been a quarry
of principles, terminology and examples, was accepted as decisive in
countless cases, the traditional fundamental training in legal science,
and a constant subject of study and source for principles to supplement
indigenous doctrines. It was never " received " or adopted entire in

---

[87] *Cf.* Farran, *Principles of Scots and English Land Law.*

[88] See further, Girvan, " Feudal Law " in *Sources and Literature of Scots Law*
(Stair Society), 193.

[89] In 1775 Lord Hailes said (*Maxwell* v. *Gordon*, Hailes' Decisions, 624): " The
Canon Law is not the Law of Scotland, but the Law of Scotland contains much of
the Canon Law. This is so certain that, in many cases, we determine according to
the Canon Law, without knowing it." On canon law influence, see further, Baird
Smith, " Canon Law," in *Sources and Literature of Scots Law* (Stair Society), 183;
Hermand's *Consistorial Decisions*, ed. Walton (Stair Society), *passim.*

[90] See Goudy, *The Fate of Roman Law North and South of the Tweed*, 1894; Dove
Wilson, " Historical Development of Scots Law " (1896) 8 Jur.Rev. 217; *idem*,
" The Reception of Roman Law in Scotland " (1897) 9 Jur.Rev. 361; Miller, " Recep-
tion of Roman Law in Scotland " (1923) 35 J.R. 362; Baird Smith in *Sources and
Literature of Scots Law* (Stair Society) 171; Mackintosh, *Roman Law in Modern
Practice*; Campbell, " The Romanisation of Scottish Law " (1942) 22 Boston Univ.L.R.
581; Fisher, " Scotland and the Roman Law " (1947) 22 Tulane L.R. 13; Stein, " In-
fluence of Roman Law on the Law of Scotland " (1957) 23 *Studia et Documenta
Historiae et Juris*, 149, and 1963 J.R. 205; Smith, " Strange gods: The Crisis of Scots
Law as a Civilian System " (1959) 4 J.R.(N.S.) 119; Campbell, " Diritto scozzese e
diritto romano," in *Bartolo Sassoferrato, Studi e Documenti per il VI centenario,*
I, 75 (1962); Stein, " Roman Law in Scotland " in *Jus Romanum Medii Aevi*, V,
part. 13b.

Scotland as it was in Germany, but woven into the texture of the native law, and no statement of the law of Scotland can avoid reference to it. It is the basis of Scots law on pupils and minors, tutors and curators, moveable property, securities, servitudes, succession to moveables, contract, quasi-contract and delict. Since 1800, however, it has declined in importance and is not now a major force in the development of the law. " Roman law then, is probably spent as a source of new law in Scotland; it is rare for the *Corpus Juris* to be cited in the Court of Session. But the Roman notions which were introduced into Scots law during its formative period were embedded so firmly in its structure that many parts still bear an unmistakably Roman stamp; they cannot be fully comprehended without a knowledge of the Roman institutions from which they derive." [91] It would, however, be advantageous if there were more tendency today, in default of immediate authority, to look to the Roman law and systems founded thereon than to the English common law for guidance.

The Law Merchant

The law merchant was the embodiment of customs and usages established by general convenience and a common sense of justice for the carrying on of trade, gradually and continuously recognised, first locally and eventually internationally. The principles of mercantile law have always been to some extent international, having been developed by the trading intercourse of mercantile communities largely independently of their national systems of law. The trading relations of Scotland with the Continent necessitated and stimulated the adoption of customary rules widely accepted abroad, and strengthened the legal connections with these principles common to Western Europe, to the countries of which, in consequence, Scots law in these branches shows close affinities.

The writings of Bell [92] and adoption of principles already accepted by English courts were material factors in introducing principles from the law merchant.

The development of commercial law in the last two centuries has been greatly stimulated by the industrial revolution and the development of Britain as a great commercial and trading community with commercial interests and connections all over the world. The courts steadily developed mercantile customs and incorporated them into the general body of law, but there was and is no distinct and self-contained body of commercial rules, as in some foreign codes and legal systems.

The Maritime Law

The general maritime law of Europe was also of a largely international

---

[91] Stein, " The Influence of Roman Law on the Law of Scotland," 1963 J.R. 205, 245.

[92] See Bell, *Comm.*, preface.

character in the Middle Ages and was administered in local courts like the law merchant. Gradually the great maritime codes were recognised as authoritative and much Roman principle came to be incorporated. Later the Court of Admiralty developed the principles as does its successor, the Court of Session. From the seventeenth century maritime law in Scotland and England developed on similar lines and in both it was absorbed into the general body of the common law and it is now common to the United Kingdom.

English Law

Since 1800 English law has been a most powerful factor, not so often imported on its merits as taken over and applied by mistake, in ignorance, through reliance on English books or cases, frequently without appreciation of the subtle differences between the two systems of law, and by subordination to a single Parliament often ignorant and careless of Scottish conditions, traditions and sentiment, composed of men sometimes more concerned with party than with country, and by the existence of an ultimate appeal in civil causes to a court composed as to a majority of English lawyers with no necessary knowledge of, qualification in, or sympathy with, the principles of Scots law. In most branches of public law, mercantile and industrial law, and delict, English influence has been powerful; its influence has been least in land law. No branch of law has escaped the influence of legislation, frequently imbued with an English spirit and cast in English models of terminology and procedure, albeit sometimes "translated" for Scotland, while too often Scottish appeals to the House of Lords have been judged from the standpoint of what English law would sanction. The warnings of Bell and some of the greatest Scottish judges against the promiscuous citation, acceptance and following of English authorities have constantly to be borne in mind, of the danger of spoiling Scots law by misunderstanding and misapplying English law.[93]

The Threat to the Scottish Legal Tradition

The greatest threat today to the Scottish legal tradition lies in Scotland, in the apathy and ignorance of Scotsmen, in their failure to study, cherish, conserve, restate and develop their traditional principles. Facile acceptance of English books and judgments, acceptance of English legal training as of value in Scotland, ignorance of everything but narrow practicalities, unwillingness and inability to search far back for a true principle consistent with the traditional development of the native law, have all militated against the vigorous survivance of Scots law. So too

---

[93] See Brodie-Innes, " Some Outstanding Differences between English and Scots Law " (1914–16) 26 J.R. 396; 27 J.R. 28, 175, 312; 28 J.R. 62; Smith, " English Influences on the Law of Scotland," in *Studies Critical and Comparative*, 116.

the growth in parliamentary powers and the ubiquity of legislation have accompanied a decline in the quality of Parliament and an interest in power, and in party and class advantage rather than in good legislation and government.

Scots law is in danger not least because it lacks an independent legislature to effect the necessary amendments; its amendment and restatement are left to be fitted into, and more often left out of, the programme of a national legislature heavily overburdened with national, Commonwealth and international affairs and in any event little interested in Scotland and Scots law, and in which Scots law has little or no voice.

Beyond that the Scottish legal tradition is in danger, like so many other national and traditional institutions, from the modern tendency to amalgamate the smaller into and identify it with the larger, to prescribe from the centre a dead uniformity and to obliterate individual characteristics, to abolish the solid old for the flashy new, and from modern ignorance of the value of the native law. Such tendencies spell the end of what is left of Scotland's independent life and culture, her law included. " The Scottish legal tradition is a thing to be prized both in Scotland and beyond its borders, and the public of Scotland should be more conscious of the fact. It is in a very real sense a typical product of the Scottish ethos, and has attracted to its enthusiastic service some of the greatest figures in our country's history. . . . The truth is that law is the reflection of the spirit of a people, and so long as the Scots are conscious that they are a people, they must preserve their law." [94]

FURTHER READING

The general histories of Tytler, Hill Burton, Hume Brown, Andrew Lang, Agnes Mure Mackenzie, Dickinson and Pryde and the Edinburgh History of Scotland (4 vols.) give the background. More specifically legal are:

Atlay: *The Victorian Chancellors*, 2 vols.
Barrow: *Regesta Regum Scottorum* I: Malcolm IV, 1153–65
                            II: William I, 1165–1215
Brunton and Haig: *Historical Account of the Senators of the College of Justice.*
Campbell: *Lives of the Lord Chancellors*, 10 vols.
Campion (Lord) (ed.): *British Government since* 1918.
Cockburn: *Life of Lord Jeffrey.*
           Memorials of his Time.
           Journal.
           Circuit Journeys.
Cooper (Lord): *Selected Papers.*
Cowan: *The Lord Chancellors of Scotland*, 2 vols.
Crabb Watt: *John Inglis.*
De Foe: *History of the Union between England and Scotland.*
Dicey and Rait: *Thoughts on the Union between England and Scotland.*
Farran: *Principles of Scots and English Land Law.*

---

[94] Cooper, " Scottish Legal Tradition," in *Selected Papers*, 197–198, 199.

Ferguson: *Dawn of Scottish Social Welfare.*
   Scottish Social Welfare, 1864–1914.
Fergusson: *The Sixteen Peers of Scotland.*
Forbes Gray: *Some Old Scots Judges.*
Fraser Tytler: *Memoirs of the Life and Writings of Henry Home of Kames,* 2 vols.
Goudy: *Fate of Roman Law North and South of the Tweed,* 1894.
Grant: *The Faculty of Advocates in Scotland,* 1532–1943 (Sc. Record Society).
Hannay: *The College of Justice.*
   Early History of the Scottish Signet, in revised *History of the Society of Writers to H.M. Signet.*
Heuston: *Lives of the Lord Chancellors, 1885–1940.*
Howden: " History of the Scottish Constitution " (1898–99) 10 J.R. 64; 11 J.R. 209.
Hume Brown: *Union of England and Scotland.*
Innes: *Scotch Legal Antiquities.*
   Scotland in the Middle Ages.
   Sketches of Early Scotch History.
Kames: *Historical Law Tracts.*
Keir: *Constitutional History of Modern Britain since* 1485.
Lang: *Sir George Mackenzie of Rosehaugh.*
Lehmann: *Henry Home, Lord Kames, and the Scottish Enlightenment.*
Mackay: *Memoir of Sir James Dalrymple, First Viscount Stair.*
Mackinnon: *Union of England and Scotland.*
   Constitutional History of Scotland.
   Social and Industrial History of Scotland from the Union.
McLarty (ed.): *Source-book and History of Administrative Law in Scotland.*
Maidment: *Court of Session Garland.*
Marshall: *Sir Walter Scott and Scots Law.*
Menary: *Life and Letters of Duncan Forbes of Culloden.*
Milne: *The Scottish Office.*
Murray: *Early Burgh Organisation in Scotland,* 2 vols.
   Legal Practice in Ayr and the West of Scotland.
Neilson: *Trial by Combat.*
Omond: *The Lord Advocates of Scotland,* 3 vols.
Paton: *The Claim of Scotland.*
Pitcairn: *Scottish Criminal Trials, 1488–1625,* 3 vols.
Pryde: *The Treaty of Union.*
Rait: *The Parliaments of Scotland.*
Rait and Pryde: *Scotland.*
Riddell: *Inquiry into the Law and Practice in Scottish Peerages,* 2 vols.
Ross: *Lord Kames and the Scotland of his Day.*
Scott-Moncrieff: *Record of the Proceedings of the Justiciary Court, 1661–78,* 2 vols.
Seton: *Memoir of Chancellor Seton.*
Speirs: " Catalogue of Senators of the College of Justice, 1834–1972," in 1972 S.L.T. (News) 233.
Stair Society: *Sources and Literature of Scots Law.*
   Introduction to Scottish Legal History.
Stones: *Anglo-Scottish Relations, 1174–1328.*
Terry: *The Scottish Parliament, 1603–1707.*

W.S. Society: *History of the Society of Writers to Her Majesty's Signet.*
Wight: *Inquiry into the Rise and Progress of Parliament, chiefly in Scotland.*

See also publications of the Stair Society, Scottish History Society, Scottish Burgh Records Society, Scottish Text Society, Maitland, Bannatyne and Spalding Clubs, Proceedings of the Society of Antiquaries in Scotland, and of local antiquarian and historical societies, and articles in periodicals, particularly the *Juridical Review* and *Scottish Historical Review.*

TABLE OF SIGNIFICANT EVENTS IN LEGAL HISTORY

Scotland	England	Europe and America
		1000 School of Lombard law at Pavia
		1003 Voyage of Leif Ericsson to America
		1012 Burchard of Worms, *Decretum libri xx*
	1015–6 Canute invades England and becomes King of England	
1016 Battle of Carham secures Scottish possession of Lothian		
1040–57 Macbeth		
		1045 University of Constantinople re-founded
		1047 *Etablissements de Saint Quentin* (earliest code of customs of French town)
		1054 Final breach between Roman and Greek Churches
		1064 *Usatges* of Catalonia (earliest feudal code)
	1066 Normans invade England; William the Conqueror becomes William I Development of feudal state in England	
		1072 *Pravda* (compilation of Russian laws)
		1073 Pope Gregory VII Investiture contest
		1077 Henry II submits to Gregory VII at Canossa
	1085 Domesday Book	
		1095 Ivo of Chartres, *Decretum*

1098 Magnus of Norway conquers Shetland, Orkney and Man	1100 Henry I's Charter of Liberties	1099 Crusaders take Jerusalem and found Latin kingdom of Jerusalem
	1118 *Leges Henrici Primi*	1100 Irnerius and the glossators at Bologna
		1122 Concordat of Worms concludes Investiture contest
1124–53 David I Development of feudal state in Scotland Development of sheriffdoms	1131 Commencement of Pipe Rolls	1139 Gratian's *Decretum*
	1149 Vacarius teaches civil law at Oxford	1154 *Constitutiones Feudales*
	1154–89 Henry II	
	1159 John of Salisbury, *Policraticus*	
	1164 Constitutions of Clarendon (relations of Church and State)	
1165–1214 William the Lion	1166 Assize of Clarendon (criminal procedure)	
	1170 Henry II orders Inquest of Sheriffs	
	1176 Assize of Northampton (criminal justice)	
	1179 Fitz Nigel, *Dialogus de Scaccario*	1180 *Libri Feudorum*
	1181 Assize of Arms	
	1189 Glanville, *De Legibus et Consuetudinibus Angliae*	

Scotland		England		Europe and America	
1192	Scottish Church made "special daughter" of Rome				
		1194	First Plea Roll		
			Articles of the Eyre		
				1195	Bernard of Pavia, *Summa*
				1200	*Très Ancien Coutumier de Normandie*
		1215	John grants Magna Carta	1215	Fourth Lateran Council abolishes
			Court of Common Pleas established		trial by ordeal
			at Westminster	1215	Tancred, *Ordo Judiciarius*
				1219	Honorius III bans teaching Roman
					law in Paris
				1225	Eike von Repkow, *Sachsenspiegel*
		1225	Magna Carta reissued		
		1227	First Register of Writs		
				1230	Azo of Bologna, *Summa Codicis et*
					Institutionum
				1233	Hugolinus, *Summa Digestorum*
		1235	Statute of Merton	1234	Decretals of Gregory IX
		1237	Magna Carta confirmed		
				1250	*Grand Coutumier de Normandie*
				1250	Alfonso of Castile publishes *Fuero*
					Real
				1256–63	Compilation of *Las Siete Partidas*
		1258	Provisions of Oxford		
		1259	Provisions of Westminster		
				1260	Accursius, *Glossa Ordinaria*
1265	Battle of Largs				
1266	Hebrides and Man ceded to Scotland	1267	Statute of Marlborough		
		1268	Bracton, *De Legibus et Consuetudinibus Angliae*		

1270 Etablissements de Saint Louis
1271 Hostiensis, *Summa Aurea*
1274 Thomas Aquinas, *Summa Theologiae*
1274 Magnus Lagaboter establishes common law in Norway
1280 Beaumanoir, *Coutumes de Clermont en Beauvaisis*
1283 Creation of the Court of the Consulate of the Sea for commercial affairs at Valencia.

1272–1307 Edward I
1275 Edward I holds Parliament attended by knights and burgesses
1275 Statute of Westminster I
1278 Edward I initiates Quo Warranto inquiries
1284 Edward I's Statute of Rhuddlan (Statutum Walliae) provides English government for Wales
1285 Statute of Westminster II, De Donis Conditionalibus; System of Nisi Prius justices instituted
1286 Circumspecte Agatis (issues triable in church courts)
1290 Statutes of Quia Emptores and Quo Warranto
1292 The first Year Book
1295 Edward holds " Model Parliament "

1286 Death of Alexander III
1290 Maid of Norway dies
1291 Edward I called on to determine succession to Scottish throne:- " The Great Cause "
1292 Edward awards crown to John Balliol
1296 Edward subdues Scotland; Balliol abdicates

Scotland	England	Europe and America
1297 Wallace defeats English at Stirling Bridge		
	1298	Boniface VIII publishes *Liber Sextus*
	1303 Carta Mercatoria in favour of alien merchants	
1305 Edward's Ordinance for the government of Scotland		
1306 Robert Bruce crowned	1307–27 Edward II	
		1309 Papacy moves to Avignon
		1313 Clement V publishes *Clementinae*
1314 Bruce defeats English at Bannockburn		
? *Regiam Maiestatem*		1317 John XXII publishes *Extravagantes*
1320 Declaration of Arbroath		
1326 Cambuskenneth Parliament attended by burgesses		1324 Marsilius of Padua, *Defensor Pacis*
1328 Treaty of Northampton recognises independence of Scotland	1327–77 Edward III	
1329–71 David II		
		1331 John XXII defines functions of Court of Audience, later known as Rota
	1337–1453 Hundred Years War	1336 Cino da Pistoia, *Lectura in Codicem*
		1340 Johannes Andreae, *Glossa Ordinaria* on *Sext*
		1345 Harmenopulos, *Hexabiblos*
		1348 Johannes Andreae, *Novella* (on canon law)

Scotland	England	Europe
1350 Black Death in Scotland	1351 Statute of Provisors	
	1352 Statute of Treasons	
	1353 Statute of Praemunire	
	1354 Statute of the Staple	
? Regiam Maiestatem	1357 Ordinance for Ireland	1357 Bartolus, *Commentaria in Codicem*
1371–90 Robert II, first Stewart king	1362 Act establishing Quarter Sessions	
1373 Barbour, *The Brus*	1376 First election of a Speaker by Parliament	1378 The Great Schism, Papal courts at Rome and Avignon
?1385 Quoniam Attachiamenta; Iter Camerarii	1380 Wycliffe's English Bible	1390 d'Ableiges, *Le Grand Coutumier de France*
	1381 Peasants' Revolt	
	1393 Great Statute of Praemunire	1400 Baldo degli Ubaldi, commentaries on Roman and canon law
1405 Curia Quatuor Burgorum	1417 Equity jurisdiction of Chancery becomes increasingly important henceforth	1417 End of the Great Schism
1406–24 James I prisoner in England		
1424 James I assumes personal government		
1424 Origin of the Lords of the Articles		
1426 Lords Auditors appointed	1430 Lyndwood, *Provinciale*	Period of the Renaissance

Scotland	England	Europe and America
1437 James II		
1440 Ordo Justiciaria		1440 Lorenzo Valla demonstrates the falsity of the Donation of Constantine
		1453 Turks capture Constantinople; end of Eastern Roman Empire
		1453 End of Hundred Years War
1460 James III		
	1463 Fortescue, De Natura Legis Naturae	1466 Panormitanus, Summa (of canon law)
1468 Orkney and Shetland pledged to Scotland and later annexed	1468 Fortescue, De Laudibus Legum Angliae	
1476 Lord of the Isles surrenders and renounces independence	1476 Fortescue, Governance of England	
	1481 Littleton, Of Tenures	
	1485 Battle of Bosworth; end of the Wars of the Roses; accession of Henry VII	1485 Extravagantes Communes
	1487 Henry VII's Star Chamber Act establishes judicial sub-committee of Council	
1488 James IV		
1491 Sessions to be held thrice a year		1492 Spanish extinguish Moorish kingdom in Spain
		1492 Columbus discovers America
		1493 Pope Alexander VI divides New World between Spain and Portugal
	1494 Poynings Law makes Irish Parliament subordinate to English	
		1495 Reichskammergericht established

Scotland	England	General
1496 Education Act		
		1497 Cabot explores Newfoundland
		1497 Vasco de Gama rounds Cape of Good Hope
		1508 Budé, *Annotationes in Pandectas*
1513 Flodden; James IV killed	1509 Henry VIII	
	1516 Fitzherbert, *Graunde Abridgment*	1516 Luther's 95 Theses begin Reformation in Germany
		1519 Charles V Emperor
		Period of the Reformation
	1523 Saint Germain, *Doctor and Student*	
Reformation ideas begin to develop in Scotland		
	1529 Sir Thomas More, Lord Chancellor	
	1531 Henry VIII becomes Supreme Head of the Church of England	
1532 College of Justice founded		1532 Machiavelli, *The Prince*
		1532 *Carolina*, German criminal code
	1534 Act of Supremacy confers on Henry VIII all powers formerly exercised by Pope in England	
	1534 Fitzherbert, *Natura Brevium*	
	1536 Statute of Uses	1536 Calvin, *Institutes of the Christian Religion*
	1536 Sir Thomas More executed	
	1537 Dyer's Reports, the earliest law reports	
	1539 Statute of Proclamations	
1542–67 Mary Queen of Scots		
		1545–64 Council of Trent; The Counter-Reformation
	1547 Edward VI	
	1553 Queen Mary Tudor	

Scotland	England	Europe and America
1557 National Covenant	1558–1603 Queen Elizabeth	1567 *Nueva Recopilacion*
1559–60 Scottish Reformation		1573 Hotoman, *Franco-Gallia*
1560 Parliament abolishes papal jurisdiction; Confession of Faith approved		1576 Bodin, *Six Livres de la Republique*
1561 Mary Queen of Scots returns to Scotland	1568 Lambarde, *Archaionomia*	1578 Cujas, *Commentaries on Roman Law*
1564 Commissary Courts established	1572–1616 Coke's *Reports*	
1567–1625 King James VI		
	1577–80 Drake's voyage around the world	
1581 Second Confession of Faith	1586 Camden, *Britannia*	
1582 Buchanan, *Rerum Scoticarum Historia*		
1587 Execution of Mary, Queen of Scots	1588 Defeat of the Armada	
1587 Franchise Act		
1592 Presbyterian order of church ratified	1597 Hooker, *Laws of Ecclesiastical Polity*	
1597 Skene, *De Verborum Significatione*	1597 Bacon's *Essays*	
1599 James VI, *Basilikon Doron*		1603 Althusius, *Politica methodice digesta*
1603–25 James VI becomes also James I of England on death of Elizabeth	1605 Gunpowder Plot	
	1606 Bates' case	
	1606 Coke becomes Chief Justice, Common Pleas	

Scotland	England	Europe/America
1609 Skene's *Regiam Maiestatem*	1607 English settlement at Jamestown, Virginia	
1609 J.P.'s appointed	1608 Calvin's case	
1610 Court of High Commission established	1609 Bonham's case	
1611 Abolition of Norse law in Orkney and Shetland	1611 Authorised Version of the Bible	
	1611 First English settlement in India	
	1616 Coke removed from office of Chief Justice	1617 Suarez, *De Legibus ac Deo Legislatore*
1617 Register of Sasines instituted	1617 Bacon, Lord Chancellor	1618–48 Thirty Years War
1618 Five Articles of Perth introducing Anglicanism		1620 Pilgrim Fathers settle in Massachusetts
	1622 Malynes, *Consuetudo vel Lex Mercatoria*	
	Charles I	1625 Grotius, *De Jure Belli ac Pacis*
1625–49	1628 Petition of Right	
	1628 Coke on *Littleton* (Institutes, Part I)	
	1628 Spelman, *Glossary of Law Terms*	
	1629–40 Personal government of Charles I	1630–42 Great migrations from England to America
	1632 Selden's *Mare Clausum*	
1635 New Book of Canons authorised for Scottish church	1637 Case of Ship Money (Hampden's case)	1637 Descartes' *Discours de la Methode*
1638 National Covenant	1639 Selden, *De Jure naturali et gentium*	
1639 General Assembly abolishes Episcopacy		

Scotland	England	Europe and America
	1640 The Long Parliament meets	
	1641 Star Chamber and High Commission abolished	
	1642–44 Coke's *Institutes*, Parts II—IV	
1643 Solemn League and Covenant	1642 Beginning of Civil War	1643 Conring, *De Origine Juris Germanici*
	1648 Pride's Purge of Parliament	1648 Peace of Westphalia ends Thirty Years War
		1648 *General Lawes and Libertyes of Massachusetts*
1649–85 Charles II	1649 Execution of Charles I; England declared a Commonwealth	
	1650 Hale's *Analysis of the Civil Law* proposes codification	
	1651 Hobbes' *Leviathan*	
	1651 First Navigation Act	
	1653 Instrument of Government: Cromwell, Lord Protector	
1654 Scotland and Ireland united with England in Cromwellian Union		1654 Conring, *De Finibus Imperii Germanici*
1655 Craig's *Jus Feudale*	1655 Dugdale, *Monasticon Anglicanum*	
1655 Spottiswoode, *History of the Church and State in Scotland*	1657 Humble Petition and Advice: Cromwell declines Kingship	
	1658 Death of Cromwell	
	1659 Long Parliament meets again	
	1660 Restoration of Charles II	
	1660 Navigation Act	1661 Louis XIV begins personal rule
	1665 London Gazette first issued	1665 Godefroy's *Codex Theodosianus*

Scotland	England and General	Europe
	1666 Great Plague and Great Fire of London	1667 Lamoignon's Code Louis
1671 High Court of Justiciary established	1672 Stop of the Exchequer	1672 Pufendorf, *De Jure Naturae et Gentium*
	1673 Test Act	
	1677 Statute of Frauds	
1678 Mackenzie's *Laws and Customs of Scotland in Matters Criminal*	1678 Hale's *Pleas of the Crown*	
1679 Covenanters—The Killing Time	1678 The Popish Plot	
1681 Stair's *Institutions*	1679 Habeas Corpus Act	
1682 Advocates' Library founded		
1684 Mackenzie's *Institutions*		
1685 King James VII and II		
1687 James VII founds Order of the Thistle	1687 Newton's *Principia Mathematica*	
	1688 William of Orange lands	
1689–1702 William III and Mary II		
1689 The Claim of Right	1689 Bill of Rights	
	1689 Locke, *Two Treatises of Civil Government*	
	1689–1709 L. C. J. Holt	
1690 Confession of Faith Ratification Act		1693 Leibniz, *Codex Juris Gentium Diplomaticus*
1692 Massacre of Glencoe		
1693 Stair's *Institutions*, revised edition	1694 Bank of England founded	
1695 Bank of Scotland founded	1696 Board of Trade and Plantations established	
1698–1700 Darien Expedition	1701 Act of Settlement	

Scotland	England	Europe and America
	Queen Anne	
1702–14 Act of Security	1704–35 Rymer, Foedera	1705 Thomasius, Fundamenta Juris Naturae et Gentium
1704	1704 Alien Act	
1707 Parliaments of Scotland and England unite in Parliament of Great Britain	1709 Copyright Act	
1712 Toleration and Lay Patronage Acts		
	1713 Hale, History of the Common Law of England	1713 Peace of Utrecht
		1713 Gravina, Origines Juris Civilis
1714–27	George I	1714 Boehmer, Jus Ecclesiasticum Protestantium
1715 Jacobite rising	1716 Hawkins' Pleas of the Crown	
	1716 Septennial Act	
	1720 The South Sea Bubble	1720 Vico, De Uno Universi Juris Principio
1722–30 Forbes's Institutes		
1725 Malt riots in Glasgow	1726 Edward Lloyd Issues Lloyd's List	
1726 Wade begins building military roads in Highlands		
1726 Hope's Minor Practicks	George II	
1727–60		
1727 Royal Bank established		
	1733 Proceedings in English courts no longer to be written in Latin	1732 Moser, Foundations of International Law
1736 Porteous riots in Edinburgh	1736 Matthew Bacon, Abridgment of English Law	
	1737–56 Lord Chancellor Hardwicke	
1739–40 Hume, Treatise of Human Nature		
1741 Kames, Dictionary of Decisions		

1745–46 Jacobite rising: Culloden		
1747 Heritable jurisdictions abolished		
1751–53 Bankton's *Institute*	1751 Calendar Act introduces Gregorian Calendar	1748 Montesquieu, *L'Esprit des Lois*
	1751 Beawes' *Lex Mercatoria Rediviva*	1751 Cocceji's Code Frederic replaces Roman law in Prussia
		1751 Diderot's *Encyclopedie*
1752 Appin murder		
1752 Faculty Collection of reports begun		
1752 Forfeited Estates Act	1753 Hardwicke's Marriage Act	
1754 Balfour's *Practicks*		
1754 Erskine's *Principles*	1755 Johnson's *Dictionary*	
1755 Hutcheson, *System of Moral Philosophy*		
	1756–88 Lord Chief Justice Mansfield	1756–63 Seven Years War
1758 Kames's *Historical Law Tracts*	1758 Blackstone appointed Vinerian Professor	1758 Vattel, *Le Droit des Gens*
1759 Robertson's *History of Scotland*		
1760–1820	George III	
1760 Kames's *Equity*		
1762 Kames's *Elements of Criticism*		1762 Rousseau, *Social Contract*
		1764 Beccaria, *On Crimes and Punishments*
	1765 Beginnings of Industrial Revolution	
	1765–69 Blackstone's *Commentaries on the Laws of England*	
1766 Ferguson, *Essay on the History of Civil Society*		
1766–69 The Douglas Cause		
1770–90 Forth and Clyde canal constructed		
1771 *Encyclopaedia Britannica* published		
1773 Erskine's *Institute*		

Scotland	England	Europe and America
1773 Monboddo, Origin and Progress of Language	1775 James Watt perfects his steam engine	1776 American Declaration of Independence
1776 Adam Smith, Wealth of Nations	1776 Bentham's Fragment on Government	
1776 Hailes, Annals of Scotland	1776 Gibbon's Decline and Fall of the Roman Empire	
	1777 Howard, The State of the Prisons	1780 Filangieri, Science of Legislation
1786 Burns' Poems		1788 Constitution of U.S.A. comes into force
1788 Millar, Historical View of the English Government		
1788 Reid, Essay on the Active Powers of the Human Mind	1789 Bentham, Introduction to the Principles of Morals and Legislation	1789 French Revolution begins; Declaration of Rights of Man
1791 Boswell, Life of Johnson		1791 U.S. Bill of Rights ratified
1791 Sinclair, Statistical Account of Scotland		
1791 Dugald Stewart, Elements of the Philosophy of the Human Mind	1792 Fox's Libel Act	
1793 Muir and Palmer transported		1797 Kant, Metaphysical Foundations of the Theory of Right
1797 Hume's Commentaries on Crimes	1799 Mackintosh, Introduction to the Law of Nature and Nations	
1800 Bell's Bankruptcy (later Commentaries)	1800 Act of Union with Ireland	1800 Feuerbach, Encyclopaedia of Penal Jurisprudence
1801–05 Morison's Dictionary of Decisions	1801–06, 1807–27 Lord Chancellor Eldon	
	1802 Health and Morals of Apprentices Act	

	Scotland		Britain / General		Europe / America
1803	Caledonian Canal begun			1804	Code Napoleon (Code Civil) promulgated
				1806	End of the Holy Roman Empire
1808	Divisions of Court of Session established			1808	Eichhorn, *History of German Law*
1811	Burnett's *Criminal Law*			1811	Austrian Civil Code
1814	Scott, *Waverley*			1814	Savigny, *On the Vocation of Our Age for Legislation and Jurisprudence*
1815	Jury Court established	1815	Corn Law; distress causes emigration	1815	Savigny, *History of Roman Law in the Middle Ages*
				1815	Waterloo
1820-30			George IV	1821	Hegel, *Philosophy of Right*
				1823	Monroe doctrine enunciated
		1824	Repeal of Combination Acts	1826	Kent's *Commentaries on American Law*
		1827	Hallam, *Constitutional History of England*		
		1829	Peel founds Metropolitan Police		
		1829	Roman Catholic Relief Act		
1829	Bell's *Principles*		William IV		
1830-37					
1830	Jury Court merged with Court of Session				
1832-33	Alison's *Criminal Law*	1832	Austin, *Province of Jurisprudence Determined*	1832-45	Story's *Commentaries* on branches of American law
1832	Scottish Reform Act	1832	Great Reform Act		
		1833	Civil Procedure Act; Factory Act		
		1834	Poor Law Amendment Act; Abolition of slavery in British Empire		
1834-45	*New Statistical Account*				

Scotland	England	Europe and America
1837–1901 Queen Victoria	1837–50 Great development of railways	
	1838 Foundation of Public Record Office	
1843 Disruption in Church of Scotland		
	1848 Mill, *Principles of Political Economy*	1848 Marx and Engels, *Communist Manifesto*
		1848 Year of revolutions in Europe
	1849 Navigation Acts repealed	
	1852 Common Law Procedure Act	
	1854 Civil Service Commission	1854–56 Crimean War
1856 Mercantile Law Amendment Act		
	1857 Divorce Court established	1857–58 Indian Mutiny
	Rolls Series of texts begun	
1858 County police made mandatory		
	1860 Mill, *Representative Government*	
	1861 Maine, *Ancient Law*	1861–65 American Civil War
	1862 Mill, *Utilitarianism*	
	1864 Bryce, *Holy Roman Empire*	
1867–68 Second Reform Act	1867 Bagehot, *The English Constitution*	1867 Marx, *Capital*, Vol. I
		1870–71 Franco-Prussian War
		1871 Mommsen, *Roman Constitutional Law*
1872 Lorimer's *Institutes of Law*		1872 German Criminal Code
1872 Education to 13 compulsory		
	1874 Stubbs, *Constitutional History*	
	1875 Judicature Act	
	1876 Appellate Jurisdiction Act establishes House of Lords as final appellate court	1876 Lombroso, *L'Uomo delinquente*
	1876 Pollock on *Contract*	
		1878 Congress of Berlin

1884–85 Third Reform Act
1885 Secretary for Scotland appointed
1886 Crofters Holdings Act
1887 Criminal Procedure Act

1889 Elected County Councils
1889 Juridical Review founded

1892 Burgh Police Act

1900–01 Union of Free Church and U.P. Church; the Free Church case

Edward VII
1901–10

1910–36

1914–18

George V

1911 Parliament Act

World War I

1879 Anson, *Law of Contract*
1880 Employers' Liability Act
1882 Married Women's Property Act
1884 Law Quarterly Review founded

1886 Dicey, *Law of the Constitution*
1887 Pollock on Torts
1887 Maitland, *Bracton's Notebook*
1888 Bryce, *American Commonwealth*
1889–94 Anson, *Law and Custom of the Constitution*

1894 Pollock and Maitland, *History of English Law*
1897 Workmen's Compensation Act

1901 Bryce, *Studies in History and Jurisprudence*
1903 Holdsworth; *History of English Law*
1907 Court of Criminal Appeal

1885 Marx, *Capital*, Vol. 2

1890 Bertillon develops identification of criminals
1891 Papal encyclical Rerum Novarum

1899 First Hague Peace Conference

1901 German Civil Code introduced

1907 Second Hague Peace Conference

1917 Russian Revolution
1919 League of Nations
1919 International Labour Organisation founded

Scotland	England	Europe and America
	1921 B.B.C. established	
	1922 Irish Free State proclaimed	1922 Fascist government in Italy
1926 Court of Criminal Appeal	1926 General Strike	
	1926 Adoption Act	
	1928 Parliament rejects revised Prayer Book	
1929 Union of Church of Scotland and United Free Church		
1929 Local Government Act	1930–39 Economic depression	
1929 Gloag on *Contract*	1931 National government	
		1933 Nazi government in Germany
		1933 Roosevelt inaugurates New deal
1936 Stair Society founded	1936 Accession and Abdication of Edward VIII; George VI	1936–39 Spanish civil war
	1937 Matrimonial Causes Act facilitates divorce	
1939 Reorganisation of Offices Act	World War II	
1939–45	1946 Development of Welfare State	1946 United Nations Organisation
1947 Local Government Act		1947 General Agreement on Tariffs and Trade
	1948 Institute of Advanced Legal Studies founded	
1949 Legal Aid Scheme introduced		1949 N.A.T.O. established
		1949 Council of Europe established
1952	Queen Elizabeth II	1952 E.C.S.C. established
	1953 Royal Commission on Capital Punishment	
1954 Summary Jurisdiction Act		1954 European Convention on Human Rights

Year	Event
1955	Crofters' Commission re-established
1955	Commonwealth Law Conference
1956	Restrictive Practices Court established
1958	E.E.C. and Euratom established
1959	E.F.T.A. established
1960	Scottish Universities Law Institute founded
1965	Highlands and Islands Development Board established
1965	Scottish Law Commission established
1965	Death penalty for murder abolished
1965	Law Commission established
1967	Parliamentary Commissioner for Administration established
1968	Children's hearings established
1968	Race Relations Act
1969	Divorce Reform Act; Family Law Reform Act
1971	English courts reorganised
1971	Sheriff Courts Act
1973	Local Government Act
1973	U.K., Ireland and Denmark join European Communities
1973	Collapse of British economy
1974	Consumer Credit Act
1974	Royal Commission on Constitution

Chapter 5

THE LEGISLATIVE ORGANS OF SCOTS LAW

AMONG the important institutions of the Scottish legal system are the bodies and persons having legislative power, that is power to make authoritative declarations of what the law on some matter is, or is to be, power to lay down general rules, or new rules, and to abrogate or alter old rules. They are distinguishable into (a) the treaties establishing the European Communities and the Council of Ministers and the Commission of the Communities which make general rules for the furtherance of their responsibilities under the Treaties; (b) the United Kingdom Parliament having supreme legislative power in all other respects throughout the United Kingdom; and (c) numerous persons and bodies having legislative powers delegated by the United Kingdom Parliament to legislate within limited spheres.

EUROPEAN COMMUNITIES LEGISLATION

The treaties establishing the three European Communities (Coal and Steel Community, Economic Community and Atomic Energy Community) operate by their own force in all member states and accordingly have force equivalent to legislation therein, and also have created law-making organs, namely the Council of Ministers and the Commission of the European Communities, and empowered them to make secondary or more detailed legislation.

The Council of Ministers and the Commission may both make *regulations*, which bind the member states and have the force of law in their territories without need for confirmation or other action by their national legislatures. They may each also issue *directives* addressed to member states and having to be implemented by the states in whatever manner they deem appropriate and *decisions* addressed either to member states or to corporations or individuals therein, binding on the addressee only, but binding completely and leaving no discretion in the manner in which they are carried out. Whether an act of the organs of the Communities is a regulation, directive or decision is determined by its content and object not by its form. Recommendations made under the ECSC Treaty can, but other recommendations, and opinions, issued by Community organs have no binding force and cannot be regarded as legislative. The legality of acts, including binding regulations, directives and decisions, of the Council and the Commission, is controlled by the Court of the European Communities, which can invalidate any act contravening the Treaties.

Publication of European Community Legislation

Regulations must be and in practice directives and decisions of the Council and the Commission are published in the *Official Journal of the European Communities*. Regulations come into force on the date specified in them, or if no date be specified, on the twentieth day following publication. Directives and decisions have to be notified to those to whom they are addressed and take effect on such notification.

Application in the United Kingdom

In their application to the United Kingdom Community legislation is distinguishable into those instruments which are "self-executing," including regulations and many directives and decisions, those, including some directives and decisions, which do not require legislative action by the United Kingdom, those which may be embodied in Orders in Council or other statutory instruments made under the European Communities Act 1972, s. 2, and those for which, under United Kingdom law, a special Act of Parliament or statutory instrument under an Act of Parliament is required.

UNITED KINGDOM LEGISLATION

Supreme legislative power is vested in the United Kingdom Parliament sitting at Westminster and is exercised by considering bills, and if thought fit, of passing them into law as statutes or Acts of Parliament.[1]

Legislative Drafting

The first appearance of official draftsmen of Bills was about 1800 but till 1869 each department of state made its own arrangements for drafting with consequent inconsistency of language, style and arrangement. In 1869 there was established the office of Parliamentary Counsel to the Treasury (consisting of two barristers, with a small office staff), to draft legislation for all government Bills, except Scottish and Irish ones.[2] Scottish Bills were drafted in the Lord Advocate's office. A private member had to, and has to, get his Bill drafted himself, though if the government supports his proposals, it may give him the assistance of a parliamentary

---

[1] The structure, composition and legislative procedures of Parliament belong to constitutional law and are dealt with in books on that subject and in Erskine May's *Parliamentary Practice*. Parliament also has other functions than legislation but legislation occupies much of its time.

[2] Mr. (later Lord) Thring, then Parliamentary Counsel to the Home Office, was the first holder of the office, and was responsible for considerable improvements in the style and arrangement of statutes. The Interpretation Act 1889 assisted the process by generalising the definitions of common terms in statutes. On the history, see Ilbert, *Legislative Methods and Forms*, 77–85, and for practical guidance on drafting, pp. 237–334 thereof. See also Ilbert, *Mechanics of Law Making*, 56 *et seq.* On drafting and the early stages of a Bill, see Ram, "Improvement of the Statute Book," 1951 J.S.P.T.L. 442. On the modern position, see Mackenzie and Grove, *Central Administration in Britain*.

draftsman. Since it was established the office of Parliamentary Counsel has greatly expanded. The Lord Advocate's department is still responsible for drafting legislation affecting Scotland, the work being done by the Lord Advocate's small staff of Legal Secretaries and Parliamentary Draftsmen, on the instructions of the office of the Solicitor to the Secretary of State for Scotland. This latter office is also responsible for the drafting and presentation to Parliament of subordinate legislation affecting Scotland.

Bills

At the present time a projected piece of legislation during its passage through Parliament is called a Bill,[3] and these may be of three kinds, each being subject to different procedure in Parliament. These are (*a*) public Bills which relate to matters of public policy generally, alter the general law, and apply generally to the members of the public who fall within their scope; most of these are Government Bills introduced by Ministers on behalf of the Government in pursuance of the Government's policy and thereby assured of the general support in Parliament of the supporters of the Government.[3] Some public Bills are, however, introduced by private members in the limited time made available to them. These private members' Bills are not sponsored or supported by the Government and may even be contrary to its policy, though they may on the other hand be adopted later by the Government and their passage facilitated.[4]

(*b*) Private Bills, which are for the particular interest or benefit of any person or body and are solicited by the parties concerned, and deal with local or personal matters such as giving special power to a local authority, or dealing with private estates, names, peerage or status. Private Bills are brought in on petition and are usually referred to private Bill committees, before whom the promoters have to establish their case for obtaining the parliamentary powers they seek.[5]

(*c*) Hybrid Bills, which are introduced as public Bills but affect private interests in much the same way as private Bills, and have a special procedure.[6]

There should also be noted Provisional Order Confirmation Bills which are Bills introduced to have confirmed by Parliament orders and schemes made by Ministers. Local authorities and private bodies frequently obtain statutory powers in this way. Their proposals are made to the Secretary of State for Scotland who, if satisfied as to their desirability, and if necessary after a public inquiry, issues a provisional order confirming the schem

---

[3] For procedure see Erskine May, *Parliamentary Practice*, Chap. 21.

[4] Notice that private members' Bills and private Bills are completely different things; the one is introduced by a private member, rather than a Minister, but is a public Bill; the other is sponsored to affect private interests, not general to the whole country.

[5] See Erskine May, *Parliamentary Practice*, Chap. 34.

[6] Erskine May, Chap. 21.

and later introduces (as a public Bill) a Bill confirming the provisional order and giving it statutory effect.[7] This avoids the expense of private Bills.

Acts

When Bills have passed through all their stages and received the Royal Assent they become Acts of Parliament or Statutes. Acts are now [8] classified as public or private [9] and as general or local or personal. A public Act is one which is judicially noticed by the courts and the terms of which accordingly need not be proved, whereas a private Act is one the existence and terms of which have to be proved by the party founding on it in any court in which it is founded on. Every Act passed since 1850 is now deemed public in this sense, and to be judicially taken notice of as such, unless the contrary is expressly provided and declared by the Act.[10] An Act is general or local or personal according to the extent of its operation, applying to the whole community, or to a locality, or to a particular individual. A public Bill may be general, local or personal in nature, but always emerges as a public Act; a private Bill may be local or personal in nature, but emerges as a public Act in the former case and a private Act in the latter because all personal Acts contain a provision that " this Act shall not be deemed to be a public Act."[11] The main distinction is accordingly between public and general Acts on the one hand and public and local and personal on the other. This distinction has been described [12] as follows: " A general Act prima facie is that which applies to the whole community. In the natural meaning of the term it means an Act of Parliament which is unlimited both in its area and as regards the individual in its effects. And as opposed to that you get statutes which may well be public because of the importance of the subjects with which they deal and their general interest to the community, but which are limited in respect of area—a limitation which makes them local—or limited in respect of individuals or persons—a limitation which makes them personal."

---

[7] The procedure is regulated by the Private Legislation Procedure (Scotland) Act 1936. See also Constable, Beveridge and Macmillan: *Provisional Orders*. For examples, see Dunoon Burgh Order Confirmation Act 1954 (2 & 3 Eliz. 2, c. xxiii); Writers to the Signet Widows' Fund Order Confirmation Act 1965 (1965, c. xii); Glasgow Corporation (Carnoustie Street) Bridge Order Confirmation Act 1966 (1966, c. ii). In England procedure by provisional order has been largely superseded by procedure under the Statutory Orders (Special Procedure) Acts 1945 and 1965 (also applicable to Scotland), on which see Molson in (1950) 3 *Parliamentary Affairs*, 458 and Erskine May, *Parliamentary Practice*, Chap. 40.

[8] There were formerly other classifications at different times, for which see Ilbert, *Legislative Methods and Forms*, 26, 49; Craies' *Statute Law* (7th ed.), 56–57; Erskine May, Chaps. 21, 38.

[9] This classification, it should be noted, is entirely different from the classification of Bills before Parliament into public and private.

[10] Interpretation Act 1889, s. 9.

[11] See *e.g.* Arundel Estate Act 1957 (5 & 6 Eliz. 2, c. *I*), s. 8.

[12] *R.* v. *London County Council* [1893] 2 Q.B. 454, 462, *per* Bowen L.J.

Publication of Legislation

When a Bill has been presented to Parliament by a Minister or private member it is printed on blue paper and can be purchased by the public from H.M.S.O. A Bill amended in committee is usually reprinted as amended before report to the House and again when transmitted to the other House.

Once a Bill has received Royal Assent and become an Act it is assigned a chapter number and copies are printed by the Queen's Printer on white paper and may be purchased by the public from H.M.S.O. All the statutes so printed for one year are bound up in one or more volumes and published by H.M.S.O. as the *Public General Statutes* for the calendar year. They are also reprinted in various editions by various publishers.[13]

Nearly all private Acts are printed by the Queen's Printer but are not published as bound volumes. An annual list of titles is issued by H.M.S.O.[14] in which private Acts are classified as (1) (a) ordinary private Acts; (b) public Acts of a local character including Provisional Order Confirmation Acts [15]; and (2) personal Acts. A few personal Acts are not printed; this category is now almost obsolete.

The classification adopted in Queen's Printer's editions of the statutes is now:

(1) Public General Statutes, *i.e.* judicially noticed and also of general application or importance. These have numbers in arabic characters.

(2) Local (formerly local and personal), either

    (*a*) public, *i.e.* judicially noticed, but of a local character,[16] or

    (*b*) not public, *i.e.* declared " not to be deemed a public Act." These have chapter numbers in small Roman numerals.

(3) Personal, *i.e.* relating to individuals' personal affairs, either

    (*a*) printed by the Queen's Printer, or

    (*b*) not so printed (now almost obsolete). These in group (*a*) are numbered in italicised arabic figures.[17]

Other Descriptions of Statutes

Some other terms applied to Acts are merely descriptive and not strictly classificatory. Thus an Act may be called *declaratory* if passed to explain

---

[13] Table of the Local and Personal Acts (including the Public Acts of a local character).

[14] These are numbered indiscriminately in the order of passing and assigned chapter number in small Roman type.

[15] These are numbered and assigned chapter numbers in italic arabic type.

[16] Including Provisional Order Confirmation Acts.

[17] Examples, taken from the 1893 statutes, are: The Rules Publication Act 1893 (56 & 57 Vict. c. 66) (Public general); East Fife Central Railway Act 1893 (56 & 57 Vict. c. cxcvi) (Local); Ryland's Estate Act 1893 (56 & 57 Vict. c. *1*) (Private—printed by the Queen's Printer); and Fleming's Divorce Act 1893 (Private—not printed). Unprinted personal Acts are not numbered and are now almost obsolete. The last private Act dealing with divorce is said to have been passed in 1923.

and declare the pre-existing law on some particular subject to remove doubts thereon, and frequently to set aside what Parliament believes to have been an erroneous interpretation or judicial mistake.[18] A *codifying Act* is passed to reduce to the form of a code the whole of the existing statute law and case-law on a given subject,[19] and thus to state the whole law on that topic in codified form, and a *consolidating Act* to bring together into one Act provisions previously contained in a number of statutes,[20] usually with corrections and minor improvements, but not effecting major changes of substance. Consolidating Acts may, exceptionally, profess to consolidate with amendments, but these are comparatively rare. Consolidating Acts are presumed not to change the law but simply to re-enact it in convenient consolidated form.[21] *Statute Law Revision Acts* are passed periodically to remove from the Statute Book spent, obsolete and unnecessary enactments.[22] *Clauses Acts*, common in the mid-nineteenth century, contained " common form " clauses and provisions intended to be incorporated by reference in common kinds of private Bills, so as to promote uniformity and reduce the length of such Bills.[23]

Long Title and Short Title

Most statutes have a formal long title which appears at the commencement and indicates the scope and purpose of the Act. Thus, *e.g.*," An Act for codifying the Law relating to the Sale of Goods." Old Acts have in many cases a very full and cumbrous long title setting out the purpose of the Act at some length.

It has also long been the practice to provide in a section of each Act, now usually near the end, for a short title, by which name the Act is usually known and cited. Thus section 64 of the above-mentioned Act provides: " This Act may be cited as ' The Sale of Goods Act 1893 '." In 1896 the Short Titles Act was passed, which thus christened a large number of older Acts to facilitate their citation, and the Statute Law Revision Act 1948 continued the process. The 1896 Act also gives collective titles to many groups of statutes relating to the same subject-matter.[24] The Statute Law

---

[18] *e.g.* Territorial Waters Jurisdiction Act 1878, passed to overrule the decision in *R.* v. *Keyn* (1876) 2 Ex.D. 63.

[19] *e.g.* Bills of Exchange Act 1882; Partnership Act 1890; Sale of Goods Act 1893; Marine Insurance Act 1906.

[20] *e.g.* Titles to Land Consolidation Act 1868; Companies Act 1948. Consolidating Acts do *not* seek to incorporate the substance of case-law as do codifying Acts. But it must be noted that the terms " codifying " and " consolidating " are sometimes used carelessly and incorrectly, rather than with their strict connotation.

[21] Much consolidation of statute law has been done since 1945, mostly under the authority of the Consolidation of Enactments (Procedure) Act 1949.

[22] *e.g.* Statute Law Revision (Scotland) Act 1964.

[23] *e.g.* Railways Clauses Consolidation Act 1845; Lands Clauses Consolidation (Scotland) Act 1845.

[24] The current *Index to the Statutes in Force* tells what Acts are comprehended under collective titles.

Revision (Scotland) Act 1964 by Schedule 2 confers short titles on all the surviving Acts of the pre-1707 Parliament of Scotland, which were previously cited by year and chapter number only.

In the case of amending Acts or further Acts on a topic already dealt with by legislation, it is commonly provided that the Act and the prior Acts may be cited together by a collective title, *e.g.* the Merchant Shipping Acts 1894 to 1967. Parts of an amending Act may be cited with certain earlier legislation by one collective title and other parts with other earlier legislation by a different collective title.[25]

Apart from these official titles many Acts have acquired popular titles by which, though entirely unofficially, they are commonly known in the profession and often cited in books, such as the Montgomery and Rutherford Entail Acts, so called from the Lord Advocates who sponsored them.[26]

Date of Royal Assent

Immediately after the title is stated the day, month and year on which the royal assent was given to the Act.[27] This is the date of the "passing of the Act."[28]

Preamble

Statutes sometimes have a preamble setting out the facts or state of the law for which Parliament is proposing to legislate.[29] Most modern statutes have a brief preamble or none at all. Private Bills must have preambles. In modern times the preamble is often superseded in the case of public Bills by a memorandum or White Paper explaining the object of the Bill.

Words of Enactment

After the title or after the preamble, if any, there appears the enacting formula, namely: " Be it enacted by the Queen's Most Excellent Majesty, by and with the advice and consent of the Lords Spiritual and Temporal, and Commons, in this present Parliament assembled, and by the authority of the same, as follows." [30]

Citation of Statutes

The Acts of the Scottish Parliament were formerly cited by the year and chapter number or by the volume, page, and chapter number of the

---

[25] Thus parts of the Companies Act 1967 may be cited with earlier Acts as the Companies Acts 1948 to 1967; other parts may be cited with the Insurance Companies Act 1958 as the Insurance Companies Acts 1958 to 1967.

[26] A list of such popular titles is printed in Craies on *Statute Law*, 6th ed., Appx. A.

[27] Acts of Parliament (Commencement) Act 1793.

[28] *Tomlinson* v. *Bullock* (1879) 4 Q.B.D. 230.

[29] A famous modern preamble is that to the [English] Matrimonial Causes Act 1937.

[30] A modified formula is used in the case of statutes enacted in accordance with the provisions of the Parliament Acts 1911 and 1949.

Record edition, *e.g.* Act 1449, c. 17; A.P.S. II, 127, c. 3. The latter is more common in historical than in legal texts, and the same Act does not always bear the same number in both the Record and the Glendook duodecimo editions.[31] This mode of citation is found in older books and still applies to Scots Acts which have been repealed. The Statute Law Revision (Scotland) Act 1964, Sched. 2, gives short titles to all surviving Acts of the Parliaments of Scotland, and the proper mode of citing such Acts thereafter is by the short title, *e.g.* The Royal Mines Act 1424, or by the calendar year and chapter number, or by the volume, page and chapter number of the Record edition.

By the Interpretation Act 1889, s. 35, an Act may be cited in any Act, instrument or document either by its short title with or without a reference to the chapter, or by reference to the regnal year, and session if more than one, and chapter. By the Acts of Parliament Numbering and Citation Act 1962, s. 1, Acts passed in 1963 and later years may be cited by short title or by the calendar year and chapter number, and this latter mode has now been adopted for the marginal references in post-1962 Acts to pre-1963 legislation.[32]

Statutes of the British and United Kingdom Parliaments prior to 1963 are cited by an antiquated and clumsy method which must, however, be understood. Each Act when it received the Royal Assent was given a number whereby it became a chapter of the session's legislation; the numbers ran consecutively within each session of Parliament; each session of Parliament was numbered according to the regnal year or years of the sovereign during which it sat. Confusion arose from the fact that the sovereign's regnal years did not coincide with calendar years, and sessions of Parliament did not coincide with either.[33]

It may be explained as follows: George VI came to the throne on December 11, 1936, so that the year till December 10, 1937, was I Geo. 6, and so on. The period from December 11, 1951, till his death on February 6, 1952, was therefore 16 Geo. 6. On his death Elizabeth II succeeded and the year to February 5, 1953, was accordingly 1 Eliz. 2, and so on.[34] Each of these regnal years, it will be noted, covers parts of two calendar years.[35]

---

[31] See McN[eill], " Citation of Scots Statutes," 1959 S.L.T.(News) 112. The Acts of the Parliament of Scotland (revised edition, H.M.S.O., 1966) which reprints all the Acts then surviving and as amended gives both the Record edition and the Glendook edition chapter number. Both are also given in the Statute Law Revision (Scotland) Act 1964, Scheds. 1 and 2.

[32] See, *e.g.* marginal references in Queen's Printer's editions of the Law Reform (Miscellaneous Provisions) (Scotland) Act 1966, especially s. 8.

[33] See further, Plucknett, " Legal Chronology," in *Handbook of Dates for Students of English History* (ed. Cheney: Royal Hist. Socy. 1945).

[34] A table of regnal years is printed in the *Parliament House Book* and in Sweet & Maxwell's *Where to Look for Your Law.*

[35] Hence a statute of a particular calendar year, *e.g.* 1950, might belong to either the session 12, 13 & 14 Geo. 6 or the session 14 Geo. 6 or the session 14 & 15 Geo. 6.

Now the session of Parliament [36] normally commences with the state opening by the sovereign about November each year, and continues with occasional adjournments till prorogation the following autumn, but sessions may be longer or shorter than this and so may fall into one, or be spread over two, or even run into a third, regnal year.[37] A new session also starts when Parliament assembles after a General Election.

When any session started it bore the number of the sovereign's regnal year in which the opening took place, say, 3 Eliz. 2, and this continued till the anniversary of her accession when the session became 3 & 4 Eliz. 2; if the same session should have run past the next anniversary of the accession, it would have become 3, 4 & 5 Eliz. 2. The statutes numbered within that session accordingly started as, *e.g.* 3 Eliz. 2, c. 15, and after the anniversary of the accession became renumbered retrospectively as 3 & 4 Eliz. 2, c. 15. It was, however, possible, if a parliamentary session was held wholly within one regnal year (as in 1950) and another session started in the same regnal year and carried on into the next, to have two *different* statutes of the same calendar year (1950), which are cited, *e.g.* 14 Geo. 6, c. 3, and 14 & 15 Geo. 6, c. 3.[38] It also follows from this system that the attribution to a statute of a short title, *e.g.* the —— Act 1938, does not give a certain indication of which volume of statutes the particular Act may be found in; it might be in the 1937–38 volume or the 1938–39 volume.[39] Till 1940 volumes contained the Acts of the parliamentary session, but since 1939 they contain those of the calendar year.

Commencing in 1963 United Kingdom statutes are cited by the calendar year and chapter serial number of that year, *e.g.* 1963, c. 15.[40]

The numbering of statutes as chapters arose, at least in England, from the fact that at one time all the Acts passed in one session were called a

---

[36] A session is the period between the opening of Parliament by the Queen and its prorogation (which ends the session, but not the Parliament) or dissolution (which ends the life of that Parliament and requires a General Election). During a session Parliament may adjourn, and normally does so over Christmas, Easter and the summer: adjournment does not end the session. On prorogation and dissolution (but not on adjournment) all Bills in progress lapse and must be reintroduced in the next session and debated afresh.

[37] Thus the parliamentary session 1948–49 extended into three regnal years and the citation is 12, 13 & 14 Geo. 6, though prints of Acts issued at the start, when it was not certain that the session would extend into the second regnal year, would originally be numbered 12 Geo. 6, and later, but before it was known that the session would extend into the third regnal year, would be renumbered 12 & 13 Geo. 6, and only finally get their definitive numbering. This was followed by a shorter session in 1950 which all fell within one regnal year and is consequently cited as 14 Geo. 6. The next session (1950–51) was 14 & 15 Geo. 6.

[38] See further, Carr, " Citation of Statutes," in *Cambridge Legal Essays*, 72, and (1940) 56 L.Q.R. 460.

[39] Take the case of the Finance Act 1955 (3 & 4 Eliz. 2, c. 15); the Finance (No. 2) Act 1955 (4 Eliz. 2, c. 17); and the Finance Act 1956 (4 & 5 Eliz. 2, c. 54). Despite the dates the latter two belong to the same parliamentary session and the former of them was later renumbered as 4 & 5 Eliz. 2, c. 17.

[40] Acts of Parliament Numbering and Citation Act 1962.

" statute," and the chapters were on distinct topics, but the word " statute " has now for long been used to denote a separate Act and not a collection of Acts, but it is still technically called a chapter.[41]

It should also be noted that public general statutes are numbered in arabic numbers, *e.g.* c. 19, local Acts in small Roman numbers, *e.g.* c. xxvi, and personal Acts by italicised arabic numbers, *e.g.* c. *53*.[42]

Divisions of statutes

Statutes are divided into sections, subsections and paragraphs; thus the Companies Act 1948, s. 10 (2) (*a*) (ii), means sub-paragraph (ii) of paragraph (*a*) of subsection (2) of section 10 of the Act. Lengthy Acts or Acts dealing with distinct topics are frequently divided into numbered parts, and occasionally the parts are divided into numbered chapters.[41] The numbering of the sections runs consecutively through the whole Act. The subject-matter of groups of sections is indicated by brief headings, and the subject-matter of each section is indicated by a brief marginal note. The correct mode of citing the various divisions and subdivisions of legislative instruments should also be noticed. It is as follows:

Bill (before Parliament); clause; subsection; paragraph.

Act of Parliament; section; subsection; paragraph; sub-paragraph.

Schedule to Act; paragraph; sub-paragraph.

Order in Council; article; paragraph; sub-paragraph.

Regulations; regulation; paragraph; sub-paragraph.

Rules; rule; paragraph; sub-paragraph.

Schedules

Schedules are sometimes appended to Acts, containing matter which cannot conveniently be put into the body of the text, such as forms, lists of previous Acts repealed or affected, and matters of detail. The Schedule is part of the enactment and effect may have to be given to something in a Schedule as against an earlier provision in the body of the Act, but the enactment cannot be restrained or limited by the terms of a mere form inserted for convenience in a Schedule. Schedules are numbered and divided into paragraphs and sub-paragraphs, not sections. They may also be divided into parts consisting of groups of paragraphs.

Promulgation of Legislation

No form of public announcement, in the Press or on radio or TV or otherwise, need be made to acquaint the public with the fact that any Act

---

[41] The lengthy Income and Corporation Taxes Act 1970 is divided into 20 parts, each containing several chapters. This is analogous to the division of a textbook into parts and chapters and is a different and modern use of the term in the statutory connection.

[42] For examples, see p. 189, *supra*, note 7.

has been passed. The serious newspapers and professional journals normally report that certain Bills have been passed and the journals also frequently report and comment on the substance of the changes made by new Acts. But the public, lay and professional, are themselves responsible for keeping up with new legislation.

Commencement

The " commencement " of an Act means the time at which the Act comes into operation.[43] Since 1793 it has been the rule that an Act prima facie comes into force on the date on which it receives the Royal Assent and this date is on printed copies set on the first page, immediately below the long title. Hence the phrase " the passing of this Act " means the date of the Royal Assent and not any date fixed by the Act at which it or parts of it are to come into operation.[44] But modern Acts commonly provide for the Act or parts of it coming into force on a specified date,[45] or provide that a particular Minister of the Crown or other person may, by statutory instrument, bring the Act into force on a date selected by him, usually called " the appointed day," and may provide for his bringing different parts of the Act into force on different dates. Hence a statute may have been passed and yet not be, or be only in part, in force, and further research is frequently necessary to discover whether, and what parts of, an Act have been brought into force. A statute, or part thereof, brought into effect is effective from the first moment of the day on which it is brought into effect.[46] Once passed, however, it stands on the Statute Book, whether or not it has been brought into operation in whole or in part, until repealed.

Application

A statute passed by the United Kingdom Parliament prima facie applies to the whole of the United Kingdom.[47] If it is intended not to apply to Scotland this is frequently expressly stated, usually at the end of the Act. If it is intended to apply to Scotland only, this is stated in the Act and the word " (Scotland) " is included in the title.[48] If parts only of an Act are intended to apply to Scotland this may be stated expressly, by making a part of the Act apply expressly to Scotland,[49] by stating in certain sections that

---

[43] Interpretation Act 1889, s. 36.

[44] *Tomlinson* v. *Bullock* (1878) 4 Q.B.D. 230; *R.* v. *Weston* [1910] 1 K.B. 17.

[45] *e.g.* the Succession (Scotland) Act 1964, s. 38 (3), provides that it is to come into operation on the expiry of three months beginning with the date on which it was passed.

[46] *R.* v. *Logan* [1957] 2 Q.B. 589.

[47] *Att.-Gen. for Alberta* v. *Haggard Assets* [1953] A.C. 420.   See further Anton, *Private International Law*, 78–82.

[48] *Cf.* the National Health Service Act 1946 [England and Wales] and the National Health Service (Scotland) Act 1947.

[49] *e.g.* Limitation Act 1963: Part I applies to England and Wales, Part II to Scotland; see also s. 16 (2).

they do not apply to Scotland,[50] or by stating what provisions apply to Scotland in an " application to Scotland " section. But too frequently the application is left in doubt and an Act may be held not to be applicable to Scotland if it is expressed as an amendment of a statute from which Scotland was expressly excluded,[51] or if expressed in technical terms of English law without any mention of their Scottish counterparts.[52] An inference that an Act applies to Scotland may be drawn from the fact that Northern Ireland is clearly included [53] or from the fact that Northern Ireland is expressly excluded.[54] Statutes applicable to the United Kingdom as a whole are usually drafted with English conditions in view and in the terminology of English law, but with an " application to Scotland " section which provides that, in the application of the Act of Scotland, particular Scottish terms are to be read for the English terms used in the body of the Act. This is a clumsy expedient since one legal system can never be translated to suit other conditions in this way and the technical terms of one system are never the exact equivalents of those of the other. The only justification is that it saves parliamentary time, but it is productive of much inconvenience when seeking to read and understand the Act under Scottish conditions.

Similarly the presumption is that a statute applies to all persons and all conduct within the country or area for which Parliament has legislated, but it may appear from the wording of a provision that only certain persons or certain conduct is affected.

Amendment

Any statute, once passed by Parliament, may be amended or altered in any respect and to any extent by any later statute, and the amendments may in turn be amended or repealed. Hence some Acts have accumulated a great accretion of subsequent changes, the tracing of which may be a matter of difficulty. Amendment may be express, as where a later statute provides that some word or passage or section of a prior Act is to be extended or limited or modified in a stated respect, or that some new words or sections are to be added, or to be substituted for something in the original Act; or amendment may be implied from the occurrence in later legislation of a provision which is in some respect inconsistent with an existing statutory provision and which must take effect instead, as it has to be presumed to represent the later view of the legislature on the matter in

---

[50] *e.g.* Sale of Goods Act 1893, ss. 22 (3), 24 (3), 26 (3).

[51] *Westminster Fire Office* v. *Glasgow Provident Investment Socy.* (1888) 15 R.(H.L.) 89, 94; *Levy* v. *Jackson* (1903) 5 F. 1170; *Bell* v. *Mitchell* (1905) 8 F.(J.) 15. But see *Bridges* v. *Fordyce* (1847) 6 Bell 1.

[52] *Scottish Drug Depot* v. *Fraser* (1905) 7 F. 646. But see *Perth Water Commrs.* v. *McDonald* (1879) 6 R. 1050; *Dunlop* v. *Goudie* (1895) 22 R.(J.) 34.

[53] *e.g.* Parliamentary Commissioner Act 1967.

[54] *Scottish Drug Depot* v. *Fraser* (1905) 7 F. 646, 648.

issue.[55] All statutory provisions on one topic must be considered together and read as one so that in case of inconsistency the later must have effect and the earlier must give way: *Leges posteriores priores contrarias abrogant.*

Repeal

A statute, or any part thereof, may be repealed by any subsequent statute. The effect of repeal is complete obliteration of the statute or part affected and it must be considered as if it had never been, except so far as concerns proceedings begun and carried through whilst it was the existing law.[56] A statute may be repealed as regards England and Wales, and remain in force as regards Scotland, or conversely.[57]

Express repeal is effected by a definite statement in a statute that particular prior statutory provisions, frequently listed in a schedule, are repealed. To ascertain whether any statute or section has been expressly repealed reference must be made to the *Chronological Table to the Statutes*, the *Index to the Statutes in Force*, to the Table showing the Effect of the Year's Legislation appended to each annual volume of statutes, and to the Statute Citator in *Current Law*. The *Statutes Revised* print statutes with the omission of sections repealed by later legislation down to the end of 1948 and the *Statutes in Force* (in progress) prints statutes as amended and with repealed portions omitted. A great deal of obsolete law is also periodically expunged by Statute Law Revision Acts which effect wholesale repeal of spent and obsolete legislation which has hitherto escaped express repeal.

Implied repeal is effected when a later Act is so plainly repugnant to and contradictory of an earlier one that the two cannot stand together, in which case the earlier gives way and the later rules.[58] It may be difficult in particular cases to say whether a later provision is consistent with an earlier, or so inconsistent as to take precedence over the earlier. The court is, however, loth to imply a repeal in this way.[59] So, too, a special Act is not repealed by a general Act unless there is some express reference to the previous legislation or unless there is a necessary inconsistency in the two Acts standing together.[60]

A statute or part of a statute may be repealed, expressly or impliedly, by subordinate legislation, but only if power to effect such a repeal is conferred by the enabling statute.

The repeal of an enactment wholly obliterates what has been repealed,

[55] *Mount* v. *Taylor* (1868) L.R. 3 C.P. 645.
[56] *Kay* v. *Goodwin* (1830) 6 Bing. 576, 582; Interpretation Act 1889, s. 38 (2).
[57] Thus the Sexual Offences Act 1956 (applicable to England only) repealed the Criminal Law Amendment Act 1885, but left it in force in Scotland.
[58] *Kutner* v. *Phillips* [1891] 2 Q.B. 267, 272; *Lang* v. *Munro* (1892) 19 R.(J.) 53; *Ross* v. *Ross* (1894) 22 R. 174; *Ellen Street Estates Ltd.* v. *Minister of Health* [1934] 1 K.B. 590.
[59] *Bain* v. *Mackay* (1875) 2 R.(J.) 32; *Dobbs* v. *Grand Junction Waterworks Co.* (1882) 9 Q.B.D. 151.
[60] *Aberdeen Suburban Tramways Co.* v. *Aberdeen Magistrates*, 1927 S.C. 683, 689.

as if it had never been, but, unless the contrary intention appears, does not revive anything not in force or existing at the time when the repeal takes effect.[61] Repeal does not, however, affect the validity of anything done under the repealed Act while it was in force.[62] If a repealing Act or section is itself later repealed the previously repealed statute or section is not thereby revived unless there are express words reviving it.[63] Unrepealed statute-law and case-law is, of course, not affected by the subsequent repeal of a statute which had itself repealed only other parts of the statute-law. Where an Act altering a rule of common law is repealed, the repeal may not revive the common law rule unless a contrary intention appears.[64] In some cases the effect of a repeal is consequently to produce some doubt as to what the surviving law really is.

Desuetude

In Scotland prior to 1707 the doctrine of desuetude was accepted, whereby non-use or contrary usage for a substantial time was held to cancel an Act and imply repeal thereof. It applies now only to pre-1707 Scots Acts. The doctrine required not merely antiquity of the Act, but that there should be no recent instance known in which the Act had been given effect to, that it should have been long disregarded in practice, or that its provisions were out of line with modern conditions.[65] A large number of obsolete Scots Acts were repealed in 1906 and 1964[66] and there is a presumption, which is, however, rebuttable, that any Scots Act left in force thereby is still in observance and not in desuetude.[67]

The modern rule is that post-1707 legislation cannot be abrogated by non-use or even practice to the contrary and there is probably no authority for the application of desuetude to English or United Kingdom statutes of any period.[68]

Duration

Apart from the few cases to which desuetude applies the rule is accordingly that a statute endures, even though it be not brought into force, or

---

[61] Interpretation Act 1889, s. 38 (2) (*a*).

[62] *Ibid.* s. 38 (2) (*b*).

[63] *Ibid.* s. 11 (1). For an example of revival, see Trade Disputes and Trade Unions Act 1946, s. 1, repealing Trade Disputes and Trade Unions Act 1927, reviving " every enactment and rule of law amended or otherwise affected by that Act . . . as if the Act of 1927 had not been passed." For a more complicated example, see Iron and Steel Act 1967.

[64] *Ibid.* s. 38 (2) (*a*).

[65] *McAra* v. *Magistrates of Edinburgh*, 1913 S.C. 1059; *Brown* v. *Magistrates of Edinburgh*, 1931 S.L.T. 456.

[66] Statute Law Revision (Scotland) Acts 1906 and 1964.

[67] See generally, Smith, " Desuetude " (1895) 7 J.R. 173; Philip, " Some Reflections on Desuetude " (1931) 43 J.R. 260. For the text of Scots Acts still unrepealed, and probably not in desuetude, see *Acts of the Parliaments of Scotland* (revised edition, H.M.S.O., 1966).

[68] See Winfield, *Chief Sources of English Legal History*, 78–81.

applied or enforced, until it is repealed. Some statutes, however, are passed for a limited period only and lapse automatically at the end of that period, though each year some such Acts are continued in life for a further period by an Expiring Laws Continuance Act. Some Acts again may be expressed to lapse on a specified future date unless previously renewed, while others may be expressed to continue in force until the occasion which has given rise to them is declared to be at an end by Order in Council. Even of the permanent Acts a few, such as those conferring some privilege or immunity, can be repealed subsequently by a Statute Law Revision Act as having served their purpose and being " spent."

The validity of statutes

If an Act has been agreed to by both Houses of Parliament and received the royal assent, it cannot be challenged in or be disregarded by any court on the ground of irregularity in its introduction or passage through Parliament [69] nor even on the ground that it was procured by fraud.[70] The courts might have to consider whether a document had received the approval necessary to make it an Act of Parliament. In all genuine statutes this is recited in the enacting formula and the sufficiency of consent could only arise in the absence of such a recital.

The authority of statutes

The legislative authority of the Queen in Parliament is supreme, so that, whatever a statute may enact, is absolutely binding on and must be accepted by all courts and citizens. It follows that Parliament cannot bind its successors, nor protect any provision from subsequent repeal.[71] Any statement of law in an Act of Parliament is authoritative above and notwithstanding any inconsistent rule of common law, custom, understanding or statement in legal literature. But in doubtful cases the courts presume that Parliament did not intend to interfere with established principles of common law.

Prerogative Legislation

Apart from legislation passed by Parliament with the Royal Assent, the Crown still retains a residual power of legislating in a limited class of cases by issuing Orders in Council, Letters Patent or Proclamations in the

---

[69] *Edinburgh and Dalkeith Ry.* v. *Wauchope* (1842) 1 Bell 252.

[70] *Lee* v. *Bude and Torrington Junction Ry. Co.* (1871) L.R. 6 C.P. 576.

[71] *Godden* v. *Hales* (1686) 11 St.Tr. 1165, 1197. This principle has developed since the eighteenth century. See *City of London* v. *Wood* (1711) 12 Mod. 687; *Lee, supra.* Previously there were some expressions of view that Parliament could not enact what was contrary to reason or morality. See *Bonham's Case* (1610) 8 Co. Rep. 114, 118; *Day* v. *Savadge* (1615) Hob. 85, 97; Blackstone, *Commentaries*, I, 41. It is open to argument whether in the Act of Union of 1707 the two Parliaments did not seek to bind their successors in perpetuity.

exercise of the royal prerogative.[72] At least in peacetime these powers are not of great importance, since they relate chiefly to the constitutions of overseas territories of the British Commonwealth, appeals to the Judicial Committee of the Privy Council, and matters of colonial currency. The power is also used in wartime to regulate trade, commerce, reprisals and contraband. Such orders are not numerous, nor are they an important source of law within the United Kingdom, but their existence remains possible.

SUBORDINATE OR DELEGATED LEGISLATION

Subordinate legislation [73] consists of the body of legislation, usually entitled rules, orders, regulations or by-laws proceeding from any person or body other than, and usually lower than, Parliament, such as a Minister of the Crown or a Government Department, to whom or which Parliament has delegated power to make such subordinate legislation, and which in the exercise of this power remains subject to the control of Parliament. Difficult questions may arise whether certain instructions issued by a Minister or Department of State are truly legislative, *i.e.* laying down general rules, or executive, *i.e.* dealing with a particular case, applying law rather than making it. The purpose of subordinate legislation is to amplify parliamentary legislation, to provide for matters of detail, and to give effect in particular matters to the general purpose and policy of the Act. The majority of the items of delegated legislation are required to be registered, numbered and published, formerly under the Rules Publication Act 1893 and now under the Statutory Instruments Act 1946. Power conferred on a Department is deemed to have been conferred on the Minister of the Crown in charge of the Department. Delegated legislation, if validly made and within the powers of the delegating Act, has the same force and effect as if it were contained in the Act itself. The chief forms of subordinate legislation are:

(1) *Orders in Council.* Some Orders in Council, as has been mentioned, are issued by the Queen in Council in the exercise of the prerogative power, but Parliament also frequently by statute authorises Her Majesty in Council to make Orders in Council and Orders of this class are properly subordinate legislation. Orders of this latter class are usually drafted in one or other of the Government Departments and while the Order in Council is usually reserved for the most

---

[72] For procedure, see Morrison, " The Privy Council Today " (1948) 2 *Parliamentary Affairs*, 10. Such prerogative Orders in Council must be distinguished from Orders in Council which are used under the delegated legislative power contained in a statute, as a means of delegated legislation. These latter are discussed in the next paragraph.

[73] On the development of the practice of delegating a rule-making power, see Report of the Committee on Ministers' Powers (Cmd. 4060), 13–15; Allen, *Law and Orders*, Chap. 2; Sieghart, *Government by Decree*, Part I; Craies, *Statute Law*, 7th ed., 268.

important and national purposes, there is no strict rule as to whether the subordinate rule-making function is to be exercised by Order in Council or by other means.[74] It depends on how the empowering provision in the parent Act directs that the delegated legislative power is to be exercised.

(2) *Ministerial or Departmental Rules, Orders and Instruments.* This is the most numerous and common kind of delegated legislation, and power to make rules, orders and instruments is regularly conferred by statute on Ministers or Departments of the Crown. Prior to 1948 instances of such legislation were variously called rules, regulations and orders, but by virtue of the Statutory Instruments Act 1946 power conferred on a Minister or Department is now exercisable by statutory instrument and such departmental legislation after 1947 is accordingly called Statutory Instruments.[75] Statutory instruments may relate to any topic at all, as may be authorised by the Act which delegates the legislative power, but subjects commonly covered by statutory instruments are matters of detail, specific requirements for certain purposes of the Act, and lists of items, goods or commodities affected for the time being by statutory provisions.[76] Thus a Minister may be empowered to prescribe by statutory instrument which places or categories of items are affected by some requirement or prohibition in the Act, and he may by further statutory instrument add to or reduce the list of places or categories, or substitute a new list, without the need for further legislation by Parliament.

(3) *Local Authority By-laws.* Power to make by-laws for their own particular area is conferred on local authorities, regional, islands and district councils, by general legislation, such as the Local Government (Scotland) Act 1973 [77] and the Public Health Acts, and also by special private Acts obtained by particular local authorities. A municipal by-law has been defined judicially [78] as " an ordinance affecting the public or some portion of the public imposed by some authority clothed with statutory powers ordering something to be done or not to be done and accompanied by some sanction or penalty for its non-observance. Further, it involves

---

[74] Thus the power of making Defence Regulations under the Emergency Powers (Defence) Acts of 1939 and 1940 was to be exercised by Order in Council.

[75] Statutory instruments are defined by the Statutory Instruments Regulations 1947 in a very clumsy and obscure fashion.

[76] The Index to the Statutes lists rule-making powers contained in the legislation on various subjects. The Statute Citator of *Current Law* also indicates whether regulations have been made under any statutory powers.

[77] S. 201 gives a general power to local authorities to make by-laws for the good rule and government of the council's area of authority. Ss. 202–204 provide a code of procedure for making by-laws, and authorise penalties for infringement of them.

[78] *Kruse* v. *Johnson* [1898] 2 Q.B. 91, 94.

this consequence, that if validly made it has the force of law within the sphere of its legitimate operation." By-laws can have force only within the area of the local authority in question and different local authorities may have different powers and may make different by-laws in the exercise thereof.

(4) *Public Corporations' Regulations.* Public corporations, such as the British Railways Board, are empowered by the Acts constituting them to make by-laws and other regulations regulating the performance of their functions and the rights and duties of the public when dealing with the corporation, and these by-laws, if validly made, similarly have the force of law in the places and circumstances and over the persons to which they apply.

(5) *Acts of Sederunt, Acts of Adjournal and Rules Committees' Rules.* Power is conferred by various statutes on various judicial committees to make rules for procedure in court. This power is exercised in the Court of Session and sheriff court by the passing of an Act of Sederunt,[79] which is an ordinance made by the court for the regulation of judicial procedure under powers conferred on the court at its foundation and repeatedly recognised by statutes since. The High Court of Justiciary similarly has powers conferred on it by various statutes to make by Act of Adjournal rules regulating procedure in that and the inferior criminal courts. Unless the Act conferring the power otherwise provides, any document by which a power conferred in an Act passed after the commencement of the Statutory Instruments Act 1946 to make Acts of Sederunt or Acts of Adjournal is exercised is a statutory instrument, and the provisions of the 1946 Act apply to it.[80] Similarly in England procedure is regulated by the Rules of the Supreme Court made under the authority of the Judicature Acts. These rules again have the force of law in the circumstances to which they apply. Their practical importance is great, since the details of litigation and court procedure are regulated by them more than by Acts of Parliament.

(6) *Autonomous Bodies' Rules.* Autonomous bodies such as professional associations, trade unions, societies and clubs may issue rules which bind their members, but these rules are binding on the individual only by agreement and by reason of his contractual membership of the body in question. A person who joins submits himself to the rules of that body by the contract of membership. Such rules are accordingly not legislation at all and have no force or effect on

---

[79] The Rules Council (Court of Session) is authorised by the Administration of Justice (Scotland) Act 1933, s. 18, and it recommends to the court changes in the Rules of Court. The power of the court to make Acts of Sederunt was conferred at the foundation of the court (Act 1532, c. 36) but modern Acts of Sederunt are usually passed under specific authority of some particular statute.

[80] Law Reform (Miscellaneous Provisions) (Scotland) Act 1966, s. 10.

individuals who are not members. Some such bodies sometimes have powers under statutory authority to make rules binding on their members, such as, *e.g.* the Solicitors Accounts Rules made under the Solicitors (Scotland) Act 1949.

Publication of Subordinate Legislation

The law on this matter is in a confused and unsatisfactory state. The substance of it can now [81] be stated as follows:

(1) If in an Act passed *before* 1948 (a) power to *make* subordinate legislation is conferred on a rule-making authority,[82] or (b) power to *confirm or approve* subordinate legislation is conferred on a rule-making authority and expressed to be exercised by Order in Council or Order, or (c) power to *confirm or approve* subordinate legislation is conferred on a rule-making authority, and that legislation has to be laid before Parliament or the House of Commons, *and* the power is exercised *after* 1947 in a document which is legislative rather than executive in character, then the document is a statutory instrument.[83]

(2) If in an Act passed *after* 1947, power to *make*, confirm or approve subordinate legislation is conferred on a rule-making authority, which is expressed to be exercisable by Order in Council, statutory instrument, Act of Sederunt or Act of Adjournal, and the document is either legislative or executive in character, then the document is a statutory instrument.[84]

Statutory instruments as so defined [85] must be sent to the Queen's Printer, numbered, and, unless otherwise provided by statute or regulations made under the Act of 1946, copies must be printed and put on sale to the public. The Statutory Instruments of each year are bound up in volumes and issued as the *Statutory Instruments*. But, however legislative in character a document issued under authority of a post 1947 Act may be, if the power of issue is not expressed to be exercisable by Order in Council, statutory instrument, Act of Sederunt or Act of Adjournal, the document is not a statutory instrument within the meaning of the Act or liable to be published as such.

---

[81] Prior to 1948 the law depended on the now repealed Rules Publication Act 1893.

[82] Defined by s. 4 of the Rules Publication Act 1893 as including every authority authorised to make statutory rules.

[83] Statutory Instruments Act 1946, s. 1 (2), as amplified by Statutory Instruments Regulations 1947, reg. 2 (1), and Statutory Instruments (Confirmatory Powers) Order 1947.

[84] Statutory Instruments Act 1946, s. 1 (1); Law Reform (Miscellaneous Provisions) (Scotland) Act 1966, s. 10.

[85] The definitions are constructed from the Statutory Instruments Act 1946 and the Statutory Instruments Regulations 1947 made thereunder. They came into force on January 1, 1948. See further, Griffith and Street, *Principles of Administrative Law*, 44–59; Allen, *Law and Orders*, 2nd. ed., 118–137; Craies, *Statute Law*, 5th ed., 275–276.

Publication of other Subordinate Legislation

The foregoing arrangements for publication of statutory instruments clearly do not cover all categories of subordinate legislation. Many schemes and orders emanating from Ministers or other authorities are executive rather than legislative and many circulars and instructions issued are intended as guidance and not as binding or laying down general rules of law. Such subordinate legislation other than statutory instruments may be published under particular statutory requirements or by custom and practice, but it may not, and in at least some cases ministerial circulars or letters may have legislative force yet need not be published.[86]

Citation

Statutory instruments normally contain provision for their own citation by short titles, e.g. The Students' Allowances (Scotland) Amendment Regulations 1974.

Statutory instruments are numbered within the calendar year by the Queen's Printer and may accordingly be cited by year and number, *e.g.* S.I. 1974 No. 1187.

Proof

Statutory instruments do not require to be proved.[87] In the absence of provision requiring judicial notice to be taken of it, other subordinate legislation must be pleaded and proved by the party relying on it. The method of proof depends on any special provision made as to legislation made in exercise of the particular power [88] and, failing such provision, on the general law of evidence.

Amendment and Repeal of Subordinate Legislation

A power in a statute to make subordinate legislation includes, unless the contrary intention is apparent in the Act, a power to rescind, revoke, amend or vary the subordinate legislation, and the latter power is exercisable in the same manner as the original power.[89] A specific power of revocation or amendment is usually conferred by empowering statutes.

Subordinate legislation normally remains in force indefinitely until revoked or superseded. If the empowering Act is repealed the delegated legislation will fall with it but rules may be expressly saved by the repealing Act and continued in force under it, with the same force and effect as under the former Act.

---

[86] *Blackpool Corporation* v. *Locker* [1948] 1 K.B. 349; *Patchett* v. *Leathem* (1948) 65 T.L.R. 69. See de Smith, " Subdelegation and Circulars " (1949) 12 M.L.R. 37.

[87] *Macmillan* v. *McConnell*, 1917 J.C. 43.

[88] *e.g.* by certificate: Agricultural Wages (Scotland) Act 1949, s. 15.

[89] Interpretation Act 1889, s. 32 (3).

Sub-delegated Legislation

In the normal case legislation effected by Parliament authorises subordinate legislation by its delegate only. But in some cases sub-delegation arises where the " parent " Act is very general, giving rise to general delegated legislation and more specific sub-delegated legislation. Thus under the Emergency Powers (Defence) Act 1939, passed at the outbreak of war, Defence Regulations were made; under these Regulations orders were issued; under the orders directions appeared and these in turn authorised the issue of licences in particular and specific cases, so that there were five levels in the hierarchy of legislation. In consequence while the immediate authority for a piece of subordinate legislation is normally an Act of Parliament it may be found in something which is itself an exercise of delegated power, such as the Regulations made under an Act.

It is a disputed question whether documents containing sub-delegated legislation are statutory instruments or not. The practice seems to have been to publish some sub-delegated legislation as statutory instruments [90] though the view has been expressed that the 1946 Act does not apply to sub-delegated legislation.[91]

A question which may also arise in a particular case is whether the delegate of Parliament has been authorised to sub-delegate all or any part of his subordinate legislative powers. It probably depends in each case on the generality of the main statute and the terms in which the delegate's powers are defined as against which may be adduced the fundamental common-law maxim *delegatus non potest delegare*.[92] The presumption is accordingly against any power to delegate further a delegated legislative power.

Validity of subordinate legislation

Subordinate legislation is valid only if the maker is duly authorised and exercises the authority within the limits authorised and not *ultra vires*.[93] It may be challenged in the courts and held invalid on such grounds as that the power to legislate was not operative, or the exercise of the power was formally defective, or the legislation was defective in substance. But modern statutes frequently contain provisions purporting to limit the jurisdiction of the courts to challenge the validity of subordinate legislation and acts done thereunder.

---

[90] The orders made under the Defence Regulations, which were made under the Emergency Powers (Defence) Act 1939, were so published.

[91] *Blackpool Corporation* v. *Locker* [1948] 1 K.B. 349, 369, *per* Scott L.J. Contrary views have been expressed: *Lewisham B.C.* v. *Roberts* [1949] 2 K.B. 608; see also *Falmouth Boat Construction Co.* v. *Howell* [1950] 2 K.B. 16, 25; *Simms Motor Units Ltd.* v. *Minister of Labour* [1946] 2 All E.R. 201, 204.

[92] See further, Griffith and Street, *Principles of Administrative Law*, 63–69; Willis, " Delegatus non potest delegare " (1943) 21 Can. Bar Rev. 257; Garner, " Delegation of Administrative Discretion " (1949) 27 *Public Administration*, 115.

[93] *e.g. A.-G.* v. *Brown* [1920] 1 K.B. 773; *Chester* v. *Bateson* [1920] 1 K.B. 829; *Malloch* v. *Aberdeen Corpn.* 1974 S.L.T. 253.

Authority of subordinate legislation

If validly made, subordinate legislation has the full force and effect of statute, whether or not the authorising statute provides expressly that it is to have effect as if enacted therein.[94]

Administrative Quasi-legislation

In addition to these recognised forms of legislation and subordinate legislation, various administrative Departments sometimes issue notices, circulars, practice notes and other literature which sometimes state the way in which the Department concerned proposes to apply or interpret certain statutes or orders or as to certain arrangements made as to the operation of various matters of law. Some such statements may be of general application and affect in material degree the working of the law,[95] but they are not strictly legislative at all and would be unenforceable in the courts.[96] Yet, without any legal force, these modifications may in practice have an important effect, an effect not really distinguishable from that of delegated legislation.

FURTHER READING

European Community Law
Halsbury's *Laws of England*, Supplement Vol.
Lasok and Bridge: *Introduction to the Law and Institutions of the European Communities.*
Parry and Hardy: *EEC Law*

United Kingdom Law
Craies: *Statute Law*
Eskine May: *Parliamentary Practice*
Hood Phillips: *Constitutional and Administrative Law*
Ilbert: *Legislative Methods and Forms*
      Mechanics of Law Making
Wade & Phillips: *Constitutional Law*

---

[94] *Institute of Patent Agents* v. *Lockwood* (1894) 21 R.(H.L.) 61; *Kruse* v. *Johnson* [1898] 2 Q.B. 91; *Willingale* v. *Norris* [1909] 1 K.B. 57.

[95] Thus the Inland Revenue periodically announce " concessions," that some item or other will not be counted or valued at its full value for taxation purposes.

[96] See further, Megarry, " Administrative Quasi-Legislation " (1944) 60 L.Q.R. 125, 218; Allen, *Law and Orders*, 2nd. ed., 221.

CHAPTER 6

THE EXECUTIVE AGENCIES OF SCOTS LAW

THE executive agencies comprise all the persons who give effect to, apply and use principles and rules of law in their work or everyday life. They include not only legal officials such as inspectors of taxes and the police but ordinary persons who, frequently unconsciously, are constantly involved in legal relationships and apply principles and rules of law in their daily lives, as when they travel by train or bus (contracts of carriage) or buy food in the supermarket (contract of sale).

Public law

The implementation and execution of government policy, a process which involves in many cases the application of rules of law, is the function of officers of four main groups of administrative agencies, namely, departments of state, such as the Department of Trade and Industry, the Department of Employment and the Scottish Office, which are staffed by civil servants, local authorities, namely the elected regional, islands and district authorities,[1] which are staffed by local government officers, many kinds of statutory authorities, boards, commissions, committees and other bodies, such as the Local Health Boards, the Countryside Commission for Scotland and the Highlands and Islands Development Board and public corporations, such as the National Coal Board and the British Steel Corporation.[2] The first two groups have very wide legal powers, including delegated legislative powers to make rules of law and, in certain spheres, quasi-judicial powers to decide disputes. But their major functions are to implement national government policy and, in the case of elected local authorities, also the policy of the local authority within the limits within which Parliament has allowed local authorities to form their own policies. The third group of bodies have much more restricted powers and bodies within the last group, while subject to general control by departments of state, are allowed some measure of freedom to act like large commercial and industrial undertakings.

Thus officials of the Department of Health and Social Security administer the national insurance and national insurance (industrial injuries) schemes, officials of the Department of Trade and Industry exercise oversight of companies, administer the patents, design and trade-marks legislation and have numerous functions in relation to shipping, exports and industrial development, and officials of the Board of Inland Revenue assess individuals

---

[1] Local Government (Scotland) Act, 1973, s. 1.
[2] For lists of such bodies see the annual *Whitaker's Almanack*.

and companies to tax. Similarly local authority officers grant or refuse planning permission for development of land, regulate the erection or alteration of buildings, issue compulsory purchase orders, enforcement notices under various statutes, and notices for payment of rates, manage as landlords large numbers of rented houses, promote public health and perform a great variety of other functions. Increasingly local authorities are being involved in the protection of consumers against unfair trading practices. The exercise of many of these functions fall within and are governed by rules of branches of public law. They may raise problems of the control by Parliament, the courts or the general body of citizens of the exercise of particular powers, and problems of the means of obtaining redress of grievances against public authorities.

But apart from executing the policy of Parliament and, in some cases, of local authorities, these numerous bodies also become legally involved in countless ways with private individuals, firms and companies. They employ staff, buy and sell property, contract with private persons and contractors, do them legal wrongs and in numerous ways get involved with them in legal disputes raising problems of private law. Thus an accident on British Railways or in a National Coal Board pit has to be decided by the same rules of private law as an accident involving a private car.

Criminal law

The application and execution of the criminal law is mainly effected by the police, by traffic wardens, factory inspectors, inspectors of trading standards and many other officials, who may frequently in trivial cases deal with the case by a warning themselves or, in some cases, by fixed penalties, but in all serious cases by report to the procurator-fiscal for prosecution. In all cases of any materiality the execution of the criminal law is effected by the Crown Office and locally by the procurators-fiscal, acting on information from the police, public officials and private persons.

Private law

Officers of central and local government, public boards and public corporations invoke and apply private law very extensively in their work, and it is also very extensively used by managers, administrators and secretaries of commercial and industrial organisations. Buying and selling, employing, securing payment and the like are their work and all these are effected in legal modes and according to legal rules. But a very great deal of the application and utilisation of private law in particular circumstances is in fact done by private persons themselves, by acting in conformity with principles and rules of law, as when individuals marry and support their spouses and children, do work, make and duly perform contracts, send for the plumber, lodge money in the bank, hold, use and transfer property, make wills, administer estates and so on. Sometimes in doing so they require to take, and take, or sometimes fail to take, legal advice and assistance, but in many cases they need not and do not do so. The vast majority of such applications of law, as in the case of sales in a shop, do not give rise to any difficulty or dispute or controversy, or any dispute which arises is resolved by agreement or compromise. Thus in most cases contracts are duly performed, parties pay their debts and otherwise act in conformity with precepts and standards of law. But in a minority of such relationships there is a dispute or difficulty which cannot be settled without litigation or other application to a court, as where a debtor delays or refuses to pay. Such cases accordingly require the application to and the decision of the dispute by one or other of the judicial organs of the community.

FURTHER READING

Bennett Miller: *Outline of Administrative and Local Government Law in Scotland.*
Garner: *Administrative Law.*
Grove: *Government and Industry in Britain.*
H.M.S.O.: *Handbook on Scottish Administration.*
Milne: *The Scottish Office.*
Mitchell: *Contracts of Public Authorities.*
Robson: *Nationalised Industry and Public Ownership.*

CHAPTER 7

THE MODERN JUDICIAL SYSTEM

THE judicial system consists of all the agencies which exist to adjudicate on disputes, to resolve controversies as to legal rights and conflicts of interests and claims, and to enforce legally recognised claims in case of recalcitrance or refusal to conform to law.

The salient features of the modern administration of the law are the existence of separate sets of courts and tribunals for civil, administrative and criminal business, though in fact all Scottish judges may at different times sit in either civil or criminal courts and many English judges may do so too. The civil and criminal courts are mainly of considerable antiquity but many of the administrative courts and tribunals are much more modern and they have not yet attained anything like the settled nature, composition or system exhibited by the civil and criminal courts.

A further distinction of courts is into superior and inferior; the former have jurisdiction over the whole country, the latter over only a district; thus the House of Lords, the Court of Session, the High Court of Justiciary and, in England, the Supreme Court of Judicature (comprising the Court of Appeal, the High Court and the Crown Court) are superior courts. The sheriff court and, in England, the county court and magistrates' courts are inferior courts. In England a distinction is also drawn between " courts of record " and " courts not of record," depending historically on whether or not the court, superior or inferior, maintained a record of its proceedings and now on whether it has power to punish for contempt.

It is impossible in modern times to confine the judicial system, the organs for the decision of disputes and the resolution of controversies, to the traditional courts of law. In modern Britain many kinds of issues are justiciable and by many different kinds of persons and bodies. It is accordingly necessary to consider individually the various civil, administrative, criminal and other tribunals which exist and to ascertain generally their spheres of competence and the limitations on their powers. In respect of the administrative tribunals it is difficult, if not impossible, to enumerate or describe them all, since they are constantly changing and developing.

The Judicial Function

A notable characteristic of litigation in Scotland is that it is contentious rather than inquisitorial. The function of the judge is not to act as inquisitor and himself to make an investigation, or even to inquire into a claim or complaint initiated by a party, but to preside at a forensic contest between two parties, to ensure that the rules of law are applied and followed and to arbitrate between the contending cases. The contentious nature of proceedings is further indicated by the fact that in criminal proceedings the Crown may drop a charge at any stage and that the judge may not pronounce sentence on a finding of guilt unless the prosecutor moves him to do so, and that in civil proceedings it is for the aggrieved party to determine whom to pursue, on what ground of law, on what issues of fact the action is to be fought, whether the action is to be compromised or settled, and whether any of the rules of evidence or of procedure are to be waived. Above all, in both civil and criminal proceedings, the overriding rule is that it is for the parties to determine what evidence they will produce and elicit from witnesses; the judge will not summon other or fresh witnesses or examine them himself, apart from sometimes putting a few supplementary questions to clear up a matter on which he is still in doubt. But his task is to supervise the contending parties and to arrive at a decision on the facts submitted to him, not to engage himself in the search for evidence or information.

The judicial function is not, however, by any means wholly passive, since the judge may take notice of principles of law even though they are not brought to his notice by the parties. He can, for example, dismiss an action founded on an illegal contract even though the parties take no notice of the fact. " In the system of trial which we have evolved in this country, the judge sits to hear and determine the issues raised by the parties, not to conduct an investigation or examination on behalf of society at large, as happens, we believe, in some foreign countries. Even in England, however, a judge is not a mere umpire to answer the question ' How's that? ' His object, above all, is to find out the truth, and to do justice according to law." [1]

The existence of the jury system is another element indicating the contentious character of litigation. Where there is a jury,[2] the parties set out to convince the jury and the judge has merely to explain the relevant law to the jury, take their answer to the questions of fact and law raised by the case, and give effect to their verdict.

I.—SCOTLAND

CIVIL COURTS

The Sheriff Court

The inferior, but very useful and important, civil court is the sheriff

---

[1] *Jones* v. *N.C.B.* [1957] 2 W.L.R. 760.
[2] Jury trial is confined to criminal trials on indictment and certain kinds of civil claims, so that 98 per cent. of cases are tried without a jury.

court.[3] Scotland is divided into six sheriffdoms based on groupings of the local government areas.[4] Each has a sheriff-principal appointed from senior members of the Bar; the appointment is a full-time one.[5] The office is one of great antiquity and prestige. The modern sheriff principal is the successor of the sheriff-depute, who was the trained deputy appointed by the former hereditary sheriffs and who became the permanent functionaries when the hereditary and titular sheriffs were replaced in 1747.[6] The sheriffs-depute formerly appointed sheriffs-substitute at their own hand but since 1825 the sheriff-substitute has had to be a lawyer and since 1877 the office has been a separate Crown appointment. The sheriff-substitute was renamed sheriff in 1971.[7] The sheriff-principal still retains, in addition to judicial functions, considerable administrative powers and duties.[8]

The Secretary of State for Scotland is responsible for the organisation and administration of the sheriff courts, a function discharged since 1971 by the Scottish Courts Administration, a body which is also responsible for a variety of other functions in the field of law.

Each sheriffdom is divided into several sheriff court districts centred on a town where the sheriff court is held, there being 50 districts in all. In most cases the sheriff court district comprises one or more local government districts but in five local government districts there are two or more sheriff court districts and sheriff court towns.[9]

Each sheriffdom similarly has a force of several sheriffs who are qualified lawyers of experience permanently resident in the principal towns of the sheriffdom, the number varying according to the place and

[3] Sheriff court, *not* sheriff's court. An idea of the amount of business can be gathered from the annual *Civil Judicial Statistics*.

[4] The number, names and sizes of the sheriffdoms have varied at different times. The present Sheriffdoms are: (1) Lothian and Borders; (2) South Strathclyde, Dumfries and Galloway; (3) Glasgow and Strathkelvin; (4) North Strathclyde; (5) Tayside, Central and Fife; and (6) Grampian, Highlands and Islands.

[5] Until 1975 there were 12 sheriffdoms but only two of the sheriffs-principal (Edinburgh and Glasgow) were full-time judges; the others continued in practice at the Bar, visiting the sheriffdoms as required to hear appeals and deal with other business.

[6] See further, *Glasgow Corpn.* v. *Glasgow Churches' Council*, 1944 S.C. 97, 126; Philip, in *Source Book of Administrative Law*, 74–76; McDonald, " The Sheriff Court and its Judges," 1952 S.L.T.(News) 121; Malcolm, in *Introduction to Scottish Legal History*, Chap. 26.

[7] Sheriff Courts (Scotland) Act, 1971, s. 4.

[8] *Ibid.* 76–78; Dobie, *Sheriff Court Practice*, Chap. 25; Grant Committee *Report*, Chap. 8.

[9] Western Isles: Stornoway and Lochmaddy; Ross and Cromarty: Dingwall and Tain; Banff and Buchan: Peterhead and Banff; Angus: Forfar and Arbroath; Argyll and Bute: Dunoon, Campbeltown, Oban and Rothesay. Certain parishes of Skye and Lochalsh District are in Dingwall court district and certain parishes in Kirkcaldy District are in Cupar court district.

the amount of business.[10] As a rule they hold courts only in one place but in some cases they hold courts in more than one town.[11] In addition there are several " floating " sheriffs who may be sent to any court if the regular sheriff is ill, or the post vacant. All these persons are salaried. The Scottish Courts Administration also appoints a number of legally qualified persons as temporary sheriffs, who are called on to sit as and when necessary to assist with pressure of work. They receive a daily fee when employed. The sheriff principal may also, however, appoint a few honorary sheriffs, either laymen or lawyers. Unqualified honorary sheriffs are appointed mainly as an honour and sit only exceptionally for formal business. Legally qualified honorary sheriffs are appointed partly as an honour and partly to assist when there is pressure of court business; they may deal with any kind of case. Apart from the civil appellate jurisdiction and certain administrative powers of the sheriff principal, the powers of sheriff principal and sheriff are the same. Honorary sheriffs have the same powers. The sheriff principal has the general responsibility of securing the speedy and efficient disposal of business in the courts of his sheriffdom.

In civil business the sheriff court is both a court of first instance and a court of appeal, in that cases heard first by a sheriff may be appealed to the sheriff principal. This provision for appeal from a single judge to another single judge is anomalous but it does provide for an appeal being heard locally without undue expense, and though sometimes abused by being used merely for delay, the system gives general satisfaction.

Jurisdiction

The civil jurisdiction of the sheriff court is wide. It extends to actions of debt or damages *without any pecuniary limit whatever* so that cases involving thousands of pounds may be and sometimes are dealt with by the sheriff.[12] Neither party can require a case to be remitted to the Court of Session on account of the magnitude of the sum involved, except in cases of actions involving questions of heritable right or title, or divisions of commonty or division of common property, where the amount involved exceeds £1,000 or £50 per annum, or actions relating to succession to

---

[10] Thus Glasgow has fourteen (with assistance from Lanark); Edinburgh five (one sitting also at Haddington); Hamilton three; Aberdeen, Dundee, Dumbarton and Ayr two each, while such places as Lanark, Banff, Falkirk, Inverness, Greenock and Dumfries have one each.

Sheriffs principal and Sheriffs are addressed as " My Lord " in court and " sheriff " when off the bench. No judicial robes have ever been prescribed for sheriffs-principals or sheriffs, and they wear counsel's robes.

[11] *e.g.* Forfar and Arbroath, Stirling and Alloa, Elgin and Nairn, Dingwall, Tain and Dornoch, Dunoon and Rothesay, For a full list, see the *Parliament House Book.* The Grant Committee *Report,* Chap. 10, discussed the possibility of closing some courts and opening new courts in areas of increasing population.

[12] But 95 per cent. of pecuniary claims are for less than £1,000. See also Grant Committee *Report,* Chap. 4.

moveables where the value of the subjects exceeds £1,000.[13] Actions of separation and aliment, adherence and aliment, interim aliment, and for regulating the custody of children may be remitted at any stage to the Court of Session on the sheriff's own motion, or on cause shown by either party.[14] Actions for damages in excess of £250, with certain exceptions, may be remitted to the Court of Session for jury trial.[15] The sheriff court also deals with many other kinds of cases, such as landlord and tenant, rent restriction, separation, affiliation and aliment, contract, succession and so on.

At the other end of the scale the sheriff's jurisdiction is exclusive and his decision final in cases where the value of the cause does not exceed £250.[16] Special procedure applies to claims not exceeding £50 brought under the Small Debt Acts [17] and the sheriff's decision can in this case be reviewed only by the High Court of Justiciary on the ground of corruption, incompetency, malice or oppression.[18]

The subjects excepted from the sheriff's jurisdiction and reserved to the Court of Session are actions involving status (marriage, nullity of marriage, divorce and legitimacy), reductions, petitions for the winding up of companies whose paid-up capital exceeds £10,000, and actions for proving the tenor of a lost document.

Trial is normally by the sheriff alone but actions of damages brought by workmen against employers for personal injuries claiming more than £250 may be tried by a jury of seven.[19]

In certain cases appeal lies to the sheriff principal or sheriff from decisions of other tribunals and authorities,[20] such as children's hearings.

The sheriff court also exercises important administrative functions, such as dealing with petitions for adoption of children and bankruptcy proceedings. The commissary offices are departments of the sheriff-clerk's offices which deal with the inventories of the estates of deceased persons and issue confirmation of appointments of executors. The office of commissary clerk, formerly separate, is now merged in that of sheriff clerk, except in Edinburgh, though even there they are held by the same person. The Sheriff Court of Chancery has functions in respect of the completion of title to land by the heirs of deceased persons. The office of Sheriff of Chancery is now held by the sheriff of the Lothians.

[13] Sheriff Court (Scotland) Act 1907, s. 5.   [14] *Ibid.*

[15] *Ibid.* s. 30, amended by Sheriff Courts (Scotland) Act 1971, s. 39.

[16] *Ibid.* s. 7, amended by 1971 Act, s. 31.

[17] Sheriff Court (Civil Jurisdiction and Procedure) (Scotland) Act 1963, s. 2. Down to 1975 there was a separate Justice of the Peace Small Debt Court with a very limited jurisdiction. It was abolished by the District Courts (Scotland) Act 1975.

[18] Small Debt (Scotland) Act 1837, ss. 30–31.

[19] Sheriff Courts (Scotland) Act 1907, s. 31, amended 1971 Act, s. 40. For criticism of this, see 1954 S.L.T.(News) 25, 57. The Grant Committee *Report* recommended the abolition of civil jury trial in the sheriff court.

[20] *e.g. Moore v. Clyde Pilotage Authority*, 1943 S.C. 30; *Arcari v. Dumbartonshire County Council* 1948 S.C. 62.

Appeals

Appeal lies in civil matters from the sheriff to the sheriff principal, or to the Inner House of the Court of Session, or to the sheriff principal and then from his decision to the Inner House of the Court of Session. This multiplicity of possible appeals is theoretically undesirable though the system works satisfactorily in practice. The tendency is for defenders to take the long course where delay is of value, as in the case of a tenant's appeal from an order for possession under the Rent Acts. The appeal does not involve a rehearing of the evidence, but only argument on the sheriff's findings as to the facts on the basis of the evidence already heard and on the relevant law. The sheriff principal may affirm, vary or reverse the decision of the sheriff.

The Court of Session

The Court of Session, the superior civil court, is likewise both a court of first instance and a court of appeal. It is, however, notionally still a unitary collegiate court; all judges have the same rank and title.[21] It sits only in Edinburgh, in the Parliament House,[22] and judges do not take civil business when on circuit.[23] From 1532 to 1808 the court sat as a group—the " haill fifteen "—but one or two of the judges went out in turn, a week at a time, to hear the preliminary stages of cases in the Outer House. In 1808 the court was divided into two Divisions presided over by the Lord President and the Lord Justice-Clerk respectively, and in 1825 the First and Second Divisions were reduced to four judges each (including the Lord President and Lord Justice-Clerk), the remaining seven judges becoming permanent Lords Ordinary sitting only in the Outer House. The total number of judges is now 20.[24]

Apart from the cases in which the Court of Session has exclusive jurisdiction, such as actions involving status, the pursuer has the choice of initiating his claim in the appropriate sheriff court or in the Court of Session and the choice may be determined by such factors as the value or importance of the cause, the availability of jury trial, or the desire to obtain a more authoritative ruling on the issue in dispute than that of a sheriff.

---

[21] The judges are designated Senators of the College of Justice and sometimes Lords of Council and Session, titles reflecting the origin of the court. They wear dark blue worsted robes with maroon facings and scarlet crosses on the facings.

[22] An interesting illustrated account of the Parliament House is in *The Pictorial History of Parliament House, Edinburgh* (Pitkin, " Pride of Britain " Books); see also Malcolm, in *Introduction to Scottish Legal History*, Chap. 34.

[23] For circuits, see p. 240, *infra*.

[24] Administration of Justice Act 1968, s. 1; Maximum Number of Judges Order 1972.

The Outer House—The Lords Ordinary

The Outer House consists of the 12 [25] junior Lords of Session who sit singly,[26] sometimes with, sometimes without, a jury of 12, to determine cases at first instance. The jurisdiction is extensive and extends to all kinds of civil claims unless jurisdiction is expressly excluded by statute. In particular it extends to actions of contract and debt, reparation, property and personal status, such as divorce, various kinds of petitions, the appointment of trustees, judicial factors and curators and many matters of succession and trusts.

The Outer House is exclusively a court of first instance in which most Court of Session business is initiated and adjudicated on for the first time. Much of the business does not proceed any further in that the parties rest content with an Outer House judgment; this is particularly so in the case of undefended divorce and other uncontested actions. The Outer House judges also deal with many petitions of an administrative nature, such as for the appointment of new trustees, or a judicial factor, for sequestration or for the winding up of a company.

Jury trial,[27] despite extensive criticism, is still utilised in certain classes of cases, mainly claims of damages for injuries occurring in industrial or street accidents. While favoured by speculative litigants it is an uncertain and doubtfully just mode of trial, and many jury verdicts seem questionably satisfactory. In certain cases actions of damages commenced in the sheriff court may be remitted to the Court of Session for jury trial in the Outer House.

The Inner House

The Inner House consists now of two divisions, the First and the Second Division, of equal authority, importance and jurisdiction. The Lord President and three Lords of Session comprise the First Division while the Lord Justice-Clerk and three Lords sit in the Second Division. Decisions are by a majority and the presiding judges have one vote only and no casting vote, so that in the event of equal division, a rehearing is necessary, usually before a larger court. In each Division three judges are a quorum, except in certain exceptional cases.[28] Either

---

[25] One judge is at present (1975) seconded as full-time chairman of the Scottish Law Commission and does not sit judicially.

[26] Until the Administration of Justice Act 1933, a pursuer might choose his judge and his Division for appeal, which produced some remarkable inequalities between the rolls of different judges, as can be traced in the periodical reports in the *Scots Law Times* (News) prior to that Act.

[27] A committee set up in 1957 under the chairmanship of Lord Strachan to examine the question of the retention or abolition of jury trial recommended, by a majority, that it be retained in a limited sphere.

[28] Hence when there is pressure of business one judge of the Division can, and frequently does, sit in the Outer House to deal with business there. Similarly, the absence of one judge on criminal circuit does not upset the working of the Division.

Division may call in a judge from the Outer House or from the other Division to make up a quorum. Any three judges may be constituted by the Lord President an Extra Division to assist in dealing with Inner House business; in such a case the senior judge of the Extra Division presides. In cases of importance and difficulty the two Divisions may sit together as a Court of Seven Judges, or may even summon additional judges to make a fuller court.[29]

While in practice certain kinds of cases are sometimes appropriated to one Division rather than the other, the two are of co-ordinate authority and there is no formal distinction between the sphere of the one and that of the other. Nor can the litigant now [30] choose to which Division to carry his case.

The Inner House is a court of first instance in respect of special cases,[31] certain petitions, revenue stated cases, and various particular appeals against decisions of tribunals and committees, but it is also and is mainly a court of appeal, reviewing judgments of the sheriff court and of the Lords Ordinary in the Outer House.

Only exceptionally is evidence heard in a case before the Inner House, in which case it is heard before one judge of the Division [32]: normally Inner House business is disposed of by consideration of the transcript of evidence heard in a lower court and by hearing argument thereon, while much of the business involves only argument on law applicable to proved or admitted or undisputed facts and no question on hearing evidence arises.

The House of Lords

The House of Lords has original jurisdiction only in cases of impeachment, breach of privilege and, acting on the recommendation of its Committee of Privileges, in relation to disputed claims to a peerage.

The House of Lords as an appellate body exercises the jurisdiction to deal with appeals to the Queen in Parliament, and in theory appeals are heard by the whole House.[33] In modern practice, however, appeals

---

[29] Thus in *Wright* v. *Bell* (1905) 8 F. 291, all the judges (then 13 in number) sat.
[30] He could prior to 1933.
[31] A special case is a written case setting forth certain facts as admitted and not in controversy and seeking a decision of the legal difficulty raised by those facts. It is frequently adopted in cases of disputes on the interpretation of a will or trust instrument.
[32] *e.g. Pirie* v. *Leask*, 1964 S.L.T. 107.
[33] The Judicature Act 1873 abolished the House of Lords as final court of appeal. The operation of the Act was suspended till 1875 and this provision was repealed before it took effect. See Stevens, " The Final Appeal: Reform of the House of Lords and Privy Council, 1867–76 " (1964) 80 L.Q.R. 343; Stevens, " The Role of the Final Appeal Court in a Democracy: The House of Lords Today " (1965) 28 M.L.R. 509; Bevan, " The Appellate Jurisdiction of The House of Lords " (1901) 17 L.Q.R. 155, 357; Blom-Cooper and Drewry, " House of Lords: Reflections on the Social Utility of Final Appellant Courts " (1969) 32 M.L.R. 262. For a detailed study of the working of the House see Blom-Cooper and Drewry, *Final Appeal*.

are heard only by the legally qualified members of the House, namely, the Lord Chancellor, the Lords of Appeal in Ordinary [34] and peers who hold or have held high judicial office. There is a convention that peers who are not legally qualified should not sit at the hearing of appeals. [35] The quorum is three [36] but appeals are frequently heard by five and sometimes, in cases of importance, by seven Law Lords; decision is by a majority. [37] In modern times it has been customary to have two of the Law Lords at any time of Scottish origin [38] while other Scottish judges who were peers have from time to time assisted with the hearing of appeals. [39] There is, however, no rule that a Scottish Law Lord must be present to hear a Scottish appeal, still less that a majority of those sitting should be Scottish Law Lords, so that in the last resort Scottish appeals may be decided by judges a majority (or even all) of whom have no training in or experience of Scots law. [40]

Appeals were formerly heard in the House of Lords chamber, but are now heard in one of the committee rooms. The Lords do not wear wig or gown, but counsel are robed. [41] The Lords sit in the chamber when they vote on the motion put by the Lord Chancellor or senior Lord that the appeal be allowed or dismissed. Their judgments are technically speeches in support of or against the motion and were formerly delivered orally. Now they are as a rule not delivered orally but are

---

[34] The Appellate Jurisdiction Acts 1876–1947 authorise the appointment of at first two, later four, later (1929) seven, then (1947) nine and since 1968 eleven Lords of Appeal in Ordinary. They are Life Peers and are entitled to sit in the House of Lords, at first during their tenure of office, and since 1887 for life and have the same rights as other peers, but in practice sit on the cross-benches and participate in political debates only on matters concerning law and the administration of justice. They must be barristers or advocates of 15 years' standing or persons who have for two years held high judicial office. For personal information about Law Lords since 1876 see Blom-Cooper and Drewry, pp. 152–183.

[35] *O'Connell* v. *The Queen* (1844) 11 Cl. & Fin. 155; see also Lord du Parcq in (1949) *Current Legal Problems* 5, and Megarry, *Miscellany-at-Law*, 11–13.

[36] In *Rylands* v. *Fletcher* (1868) L.R. 3 H.L. 330 only two Law Lords are reported as being present: see [1945] K.B. 242 and 86 L.Q.R. 160. Since 1960 two Committees of Law Lords may sit simultaneously to hear appeals, and this happened in the autumn of 1962.

[37] In consequence, the unanimous judgments of a Lord Ordinary and of four (or more) Lords in the Inner House may be reversed by a majority of one in the House of Lords. There are instances, *e.g. Commercial Union Assurance Co.* v. *Waddell*, 1919 S.C.(H.L.) 38, where the House has been equally divided in which case the appeal has failed. See also *Kennedy* v. *Spratt* [1972] A.C. 99.

[38] The Scottish Law Lords since 1876 have been Lords Gordon, Watson, Robertson, Shaw of Dunfermline, Dunedin, Macmillan, Thankerton, Normand, Reid, Keith of Avonholm, Guest, Kilbrandon and Fraser.

[39] *e.g.* Lords Shand, Kinnear and Alness.

[40] Thus *A/B Karlshamns Oljefabriker* v. *Monarch SS. Co.*, 1949 S.C.(H.L.) 1. was heard by five English Law Lords, and *Grant* v. *Sun Shipping Co. Ltd.*, 1948 S.C.(H.L.) 73 by four.

[41] Since 1965 senior counsel wear full-bottomed wigs only when the House is sitting in the Lords' chamber for the hearing of appeals or for the delivery of judgments: see [1965] C.L.Y. 3063.

issued in typescript and the Lords merely announce that the appeal will be allowed or dismissed for the reasons stated separately.[42] Dissenting opinions have always been allowed and are frequently uttered. If the House should be equally divided the appeal fails. The view of the House is not an operative judgment, but the case is returned to the Court of Session with the House's opinion, which must be translated into an operative decree by a petition to the Court of Session to apply the judgment of the House.

Appeal to the House of Lords is competent both on fact and on law though appeals on fact are not regarded favourably and great weight is attached by the House to the views on the evidence of the trial judge who saw and heard the witnesses.[43] If the case originated in the sheriff court the right of appeal is limited to questions of law. Appeal may be taken against final judgments of the Inner House, which dispose of the action, or against interlocutory judgments, which dispose of some part or stage of the action, if the Court of Session has given leave to appeal, or if the judges were not unanimous, and in certain other cases. In view of the delay and expense of an appeal to the House of Lords such appeals are usually taken only where a large sum or an important issue is at stake, or where an important or difficult point of law is in issue. Only a dozen or so cases are appealed from Scotland to the House of Lords in a year, and the majority of Scottish cases do not go beyond the Inner House.

By a legal fiction the House of Lords, as the final Court of Appeal from England, Scotland and Northern Ireland, has judicial knowledge of all the legal systems involved so that it can take cognisance of points of the law of each of these systems even though they have not been pleaded or established by evidence before it.[44] This is, however, the sheerest fiction, to ascribe to members of the English Bar and Bench, on their promotion to be Lords of Appeal, a sufficient knowledge of Scots law to correct the judges of the Court of Session.[45] In the past there have been some remarkable confessions of ignorance in the House and some scandalous impositions of foreign law on Scotland.[46] The House of Lords has been responsible for some of the worst misunderstandings and confused law in the Scottish books; over and over again English doctrines have been forced into Scots law by English Law Lords who did not know or realise the fundamental differences of principle

---

[42] [1963] C.L.Y. 2777.

[43] *Thomas* v. *Thomas*, 1947 S.C.(H.L.) 45.

[44] *Elliott* v. *Joicey*, 1935 S.C.(H.L.) 57.

[45] The converse is, of course, true in the case of Scottish Law Lords sitting in English appeals with the difference that the Scots are most unlikely to be in a majority, if indeed they sit at all. It is fair, however, to add that Lord Watson and Lord Reid won golden opinions for their judgments in English cases while Lord Birkenhead delivered some outstanding judgments in Scottish cases. See also (1956) 19 M.L.R. 95.

[46] Gibb, *Law from Over the Border, passim.*

and reason which frequently underlie apparent similarities of result, as where remedies are granted in circumstances similar to those justifying the corresponding remedy in English law.

Courts of special jurisdiction are courts of law as much as are the ordinary civil and criminal courts but differ in that they have jurisdiction in particular kinds of claims only.

The Court of the Lord Lyon

The Lord Lyon King of Arms is one of the Officers of State of the Kingdom of Scotland, and the Queen's counsellor in matters armorial, genealogical and ceremonial. The office is very ancient but appeared in its modern form in 1318. He exercises the whole Crown jurisdiction in armorial matters, enforces the laws of arms, and adjudicates in questions of name, family representation and chiefship. He is official adviser to the Secretary of State for Scotland in matters relating to the Scottish Honours and ceremonial and, as controller of messengers-at-arms, is head of the department of Scots law relative to execution and diligence.[47]

The Court of the Lord Lyon [48] exercises both a civil and criminal jurisdiction, both at common law and under statute, and almost all heraldic business is conducted therein on judicial lines, legal representation being allowed though not usually necessary. The court is concerned with the establishment of rights to arms and pedigrees which when established are recorded in the Public Register of all Arms and Bearings in Scotland or in the Public Register of All Genealogies and Birthbrieves in Scotland, and with protecting the rights of individuals and of the Crown in Scottish armorial bearings, and over messengers-at-arms. Lyon has, however, no jurisdiction to determine rights of precedence,[49] nor a disputed question of chieftainship.[50] The Lyon Court has a procurator-fiscal who acts as public prosecutor, and has powers of fine and imprisonment, power to erase unwarrantable arms, to break unwarrantable seals and to seize goods on which arms are unwarrantably represented. It may also interdict usurpers of arms.[51] Appeal lies to the Court of Session and to the House of Lords,[52] since arms are incorporeal heritable property.

---

[47] Innes of Learney, *Scots Heraldry*, revised ed., Chap. 2, and references therein; Innes, " The Style and Title of Lord Lyon King of Arms " (1932) 44 J.R. 197.

[48] It sits in H.M. Register House, Edinburgh. See also *Introduction To Scottish Legal History*, pp. 397–398.

[49] *Royal College of Surgeons* v. *Royal College of Physicians*, 1911 S.C. 1054.

[50] *Maclean of Ardgour* v. *Maclean*, 1938 S.L.T. 49; 1941 S.C. 613.

[51] Innes of Learney, *supra*. See also Adam, *Clans, Septs and Regiments of the Scottish Highlands* (ed. Innes), *passim*; Milne, *The Scottish Office*, 189–190. Reports of selected cases in Lyon Court are published in the *Scots Law Times*.

[52] *e.g. Stewart Mackenzie* v. *Fraser Mackenzie*, 1922 S.C.(H.L.) 39.

Lyon also enforces Royal Warrants of Precedency in Scotland, makes Royal Proclamations and acts as Secretary of the Order of the Thistle. He is assisted by Lyon Clerk, three heralds and three pursuivants.

Court of Teinds

The Court of Teinds is in fact merely a function of the Court of Session, since in statutes the judges have been nominated as Lords Commissioners of Teinds, but having distinct procedure and a separate Teind Clerk. The court now consists of the eight Inner House judges along with the second junior Lord Ordinary, five, including the last-named, to be a quorum. Teinds were originally the tenth part of the fruits of land and labour assigned for the maintenance of church and clergy.[53] In recent years the whole basis and substance of teind law has been much changed and the business of the court is almost entirely formal and carried through by the Lord Ordinary and the Teind Clerk, without opposition. An appeal lies to the House of Lords.[54]

The Scottish Land Court

The Land Court was established in 1911 in succession to the Crofters Commission set up in 1886.[55] Its work is entirely linked with agriculture and the four members of the court, other than the chairman, are practical agriculturists. The chairman is an experienced lawyer having the status and tenure of a judge of the Court of Session. The court makes an annual report which is laid before Parliament.

Its jurisdiction is entirely statutory[56] and has been greatly extended by the increased modern statutory control of agriculture, so that it has to decide a great variety of questions of considerable scope and value relative to agriculture. Some of its administrative duties have now been transferred to the (new) Crofters Commission.[55]

Resort may also be had to it, by agreement of parties, instead of to an arbiter, to decide questions arising between landlord and tenant, to deal with questions of valuation of sheep stocks, payment of grants under the Hill Farming Act 1946 and sundry war-time provisions. It is also the only court of appeal against certain decisions of the local Agricultural Executive Committees, giving or withholding consent to the dispossession of the occupier of a farm.

---

[53] See further, Bell's *Law Dictionary*; Black and Christie, *Parochial Ecclesiastical Law*, 395–446, 523–534; Church of Scotland (Property and Endowments) Act 1925. The development of the law is traced in *Galloway* v. *Earl of Minto*, 1920 S.C. 354; 1922 S.C.(H.L.) 24.

[54] *Galloway, supra.*

[55] A new Crofters Commission was set up in 1955 with duties of reorganising and developing crofting in the crofting counties. The judicial functions of the old Commission (1886–1911) were transferred to the Land Court.

[56] Small Landholders (Scotland) Act 1911. See further, Lamb: "The Scottish Land Court," 1958 S.L.T.(News) 129.

A party to a dispute decided by the Land Court may require a case to be stated on a point of law to one of the Divisions of the Inner House of the Court of Session.

Restrictive Practices Court

This court was established by the Restrictive Trade Practices Act 1956. It consists of five judges, one being a judge of the Court of Session nominated by the Lord President,[57] and not more than ten other persons (laymen) holding office for not less than three years. It may sit as a single court or in two or more divisions, in Scotland, England or Northern Ireland. The quorum is three, including at least one judicial member. Proceedings may be taken in this court by the Director General of Fair Trading to have certain restrictions, which have been disclosed to and registered with him, found to be contrary to the public interest and the relevant agreement held void to that extent. Restrictions are presumed to be contrary to the public interest unless the court is satisfied that certain general conditions are satisfied. Under the Resale Prices Act 1964 this court also considers claims for exemption of goods from the rule abolishing resale price maintenance. An appeal from the decision of this court lies, in Scotland, to the Court of Session.[58]

Transport Tribunal

Though designated a tribunal this body is a " court of record." It consists of an experienced lawyer as president and four other members with experience of transport, commercial affairs and financial matters or economics. It sits in two divisions, the London Fares and Miscellaneous Charges Division and the Road Haulage Appeals Division, dealing respectively with transport charges and facilities and with road carriers' licences. The president may appoint a person from a special panel, alone or with a member of the Road Haulage Appeals Division, to deal with the Division's business. It reports annually to Parliament. Appeal lies to the Court of Session,[59] but not on questions of fact or *locus standi*, and that court's decision is final, though if there is a difference of opinion either court may give leave to appeal to the House of Lords.[60]

---

[57] The other judicial members are three judges of the High Court in England, nominated by the Lord Chancellor, and one judge of the Supreme Court of Northern Ireland nominated by the Lord Chief Justice of Northern Ireland. The Lord Chancellor nominates one of the judicial members to be President of the court. See further, Grunfeld and Yamey, " The Restrictive Trade Practices Act 1956 " [1956] 1 P.L. 313; Korah, " The Restrictive Practices Court " (1959) 12 C.L.P. 76; Stevens and Yamey, *The Restrictive Practices Court*.

[58] Cases are reported in the ordinary series of reports and also in *Law Reports*, Restrictive Practices series (1958–). See, *e.g. Re Wholesale and Retail Bakers of Scotland Association's Agreement*, 1960 S.L.T. 130; (1959) L.R. 1 R.P. 347.

[59] *e.g. Russell* v. *B.R.S. (Caledonian) Ltd.*, 1964 S.C. 334.

[60] Transport Act 1962, s. 57 as amended and Sched. 10.

Dean of Guild Court

The Dean of Guild was originally the head of the Merchants' Guild which had a practical monopoly of trade and commerce in the Scottish burghs.[61] The Dean and his council originally had an extensive jurisdiction in mercantile and maritime disputes but this jurisdiction gradually fell into disuse. The Dean also had at common law a jurisdiction over buildings, nuisances and questions of neighbourhood, and under it he granted or withheld permission to erect or alter buildings, but this later came to be principally the regulation and control of building operations within the burghs to prevent obstruction or encroachment on private or public property, to ensure conformity with local and general legislation, and to promote public health and safety, so that no building operations could be undertaken without a warrant of the Dean of Guild Court. This court was abolished in 1975.

ADMINISTRATIVE COURTS AND TRIBUNALS

The development of administrative law in Britain has been empirical and unsystematic and this is reflected particularly in the courts and tribunals which adjudicate on claims and disputes. Their composition, jurisdiction and procedure are varied and individualistic and there is no clear hierarchy of authority or line of appeal. All that can be done is accordingly to discuss various important and representative courts and tribunals, subject to the general observations that the powers, composition, functions and procedure of every tribunal depend on the statute which created it,[62] and that changes are frequent.

The function of so-called administrative tribunals is in fact not administrative but judicial, consisting in the decision of conflicts of view and disputes which arise incidentally out of the functioning of public administration, usually between the citizen and a state department or agency, and in many cases resort to the tribunal is itself an appeal from the preliminary adjudication by the official dealing with the case or the claim in the first instance. Their practical importance can be appreciated from the fact that in 1960 at least 122,000 cases were decided by administrative tribunals.[63]

---

[61] See generally, Irons, *Law and Practice of the Dean of Guild Court*; Murray, *Early Burgh Organisation in Scotland*; Mackenzie, *The Scottish Burghs*; McKechnie in *Source Book and History of Administrative Law in Scotland* (ed. McLarty), 95; *Introduction to Scottish Legal History*, pp. 390–392.

[62] The best modern account is Wraith and Hutcheson, *Administrative Tribunals*. See also the Report of the (Franks) Committee on Administrative Tribunals and Enquiries (Cmnd. 218, 1957) and the Annual Reports of the Council on Tribunals, 1959–.

[63] Council on Tribunals, *Report*, 1960, p. 1. (In 1960 civil proceedings before the Court of Session and Sheriff courts totalled about 45,000, together with 150,000 small debt cases, but the great majority of these cases were uncontested or did not go to trial.)

It is difficult to classify these courts and tribunals and impossible to describe them all.[64] They can be classified functionally, according to the subject dealt with, or by their nature and composition. The latter method would merely indicate an infinite gradation of types from formality and procedure similar to that of a court in the ordinary sense to considerable informality and lack of method.

Another grouping would be into cases justiciable by a committee or tribunal, cases justiciable by a permanent legally qualified official, and cases determinable by a Minister of the Crown himself. In some cases appeal lies from one kind of body to another. Moreover there are differences as between England and Scotland and some bodies have different counterparts in the other country while some tribunals act for the whole United Kingdom.

The Tribunals and Inquiries Acts 1958 and 1966,[65] which put into effect some of the recommendations of the Franks Committee, made some badly needed reforms in a chaotic situation. Since 1959 the chairmen of specified tribunals have been selected from panels of persons appointed by the Lord President, and the removal of members of certain tribunals requires his concurrence. Appeal to the courts on a point of law is now permitted from a large number of tribunals and many are required on request to give reasons for their decisions.

The Council on Tribunals

This body was constituted by the 1958 Act to exercise a general supervision over tribunals and inquiries and it keeps under review the constitution and working of some 2,000 bodies and from time to time reports on their working. It consists of 10 to 15 members, with a Scottish Committee of two or three members, with three or four non-members added by the Secretary of State for Scotland, and has power over the whole United Kingdom. The Parliamentary Commissioner for Administration is *ex officio* a member both of the Council and of the Scottish Committee.[66] Its functions are purely advisory and consultative, and are confined to the constitutional and procedural aspects of the work of tribunals. It is not an appellate body. It must be consulted before procedural rules are made for specified tribunals, or for any statutory inquiry, and members visit tribunals to watch their operation. It also issues a valuable Annual Report.

---

[64] A list of tribunals subject to the supervision of the Council on Tribunals and its Scottish Committee is in Tribunals and Inquiries Act 1971, Sched. 1.

[65] Now replaced by Tribunals and Inquiries Act 1971.

[66] Parliamentary Commissioner Act 1967, s. 1 (5).

PARTICULAR ADMINISTRATIVE COURTS AND TRIBUNALS

Lands Valuation Appeal Court

This is a court consisting of three judges of the Court of Session which is constituted as and when necessary to dispose of appeals against the determination of the local Valuation Appeal Committees (which are established in each region and islands district) as to the value to be set on heritable property for the purpose of the raising of local rates.[67] The appeal is taken by way of a stated case setting out the facts held by the Committee to be established and the questions of law in issue, and argument is heard on the principle of law in issue. The actual monetary valuation set on a building or set of premises by the assessor is not usually challenged, but problems of statutory interpretation frequently arise, such as whether certain premises are a " retail shop " and entitled to be treated as such,[68] questions of whether certain subjects should be entered in the valuation roll at all or not, and problems of the proper principle is to be applied in arriving at a valuation. This court is final and there is no appeal to the House of Lords.

Court of Exchequer

The jurisdiction of the Court of Exchequer in Scotland, remodelled in 1708,[69] was in 1856 transferred to the Court of Session, and that court sits as Court of Exchequer in Scotland when dealing with revenue cases and for long exchequer causes were subject to procedural specialties.[70] The business consists chiefly of appeals on law by way of stated case from the determination of the Special Commissioners of Income Tax on issues of liability to tax. A further appeal lies to the House of Lords.[71]

Registration of Voters Appeal Court

An appeal on a matter of registration as a parliamentary elector lies from the registration officer to the sheriff and from him to a court of three judges of the Court of Session, whose decision is final. Business only occasionally arises for this court.[72]

---

[67] Decisions are reported in *Session Cases* and *Scots Law Times* and there is a considerable volume of case-law. Some of the older authorities are superseded by the Valuation and Rating (Scotland) Act 1956, which made revolutionary changes in the system. On older bases of valuation, see McKechnie, in *Source Book of Administrative Law*, 213–219.

[68] *Perth Assessor* v. *Shields Motor Car Co.*, 1956 S.C. 186.

[69] See further, Clerk and Scrope's *Historical View of the Court of Exchequer in Scotland* (1820).

[70] See *Inland Revenue* v. *Hood Barrs*, 1959 S.C. 273; and Bennett Miller, " Certiorari and the Scottish Courts " (1962) 25 M.L.R. 423.

[71] For an example, see *Inland Revenue* v. *Glasgow Police Athletic Association*, 1952 S.C. 102, reversed by H.L., 1953 S.C.(H.L.) 13.

[72] See *e.g. Edinburgh Electoral Registration Officer* v. *Robertson*, 1965 S.L.T. 14.

Election Petition Court

Petitions presented against the election of Members of Parliament on the ground of illegality or improper practices at the election are heard by a court of two judges of the Court of Session whose decision is final.[73] This court also rarely requires to be constituted.

National Health Service Tribunals

Within the National Health Service [74] the area Health Boards which are responsible for providing general medical, dental and other services in their areas have also to deal with complaints referred to them by the various Service Committees, which are investigated in private and informally, and they have wide disciplinary powers over practitioners, with a right of appeal to the Secretary of State for Scotland.

At the national level, apart from advisory and other committees, there is a Medical Practices Committee charged with the proper distribution of practitioners throughout the country, from which appeal lies to the Secretary of State, and a National Health Service Tribunal which deals only with disciplinary matters and serious complaints, usually referred to it by an area Health Board. There is again an appeal to the Secretary of State. The Secretary of State has these, and other, appellate duties, but from him no appeal lies to any court. The whole apparatus of tribunals is governed by a great mass of subordinate legislation, and is very complicated, so as to have incurred considerable criticism as " tribunalism run mad." [75]

In certain cases also complaints may be made to the Health Service Commissioner for Scotland.[76]

Mental Welfare Commission

The Mental Welfare Commission for Scotland [77] exists to exercise protective functions in respect of persons who, by reason of mental disorder, are incapable of adequately protecting their persons or their interests, to inquire into cases of ill-treatment or deficiency of care or treatment or improper detention, and to bring cases to the attention of hospital boards of management or local authorities, and advise the Secretary of State on any matter he may refer to them. It may summon witnesses and take evidence on oath.

---

[73] See, *e.g. Grieve* v. *Douglas-Home*, 1965 S.C. 313, 315.

[74] National Health Service (Scotland) Act 1972.

[75] Allen, *Administrative Jurisdiction*, 8; *cf.* Robson, *Justice and Administrative Law*, 3rd. ed., 143.

[76] On him see further p. 265, *infra.*

[77] Mental Health (Scotland) Act 1960, ss. 2, 4, amended by National Health Service (Scotland) Act 1972, s. 52.

Social Security.

In the sphere of National Insurance a dissatisfied claimant for benefit may appeal to an insurance officer, then to a local appeal tribunal of three.[78] The procedure is very informal and legal representation, though allowed, is not usual. There is no appeal to the courts but instead to the Chief National Insurance Commissioner or one of his Commissioners. These persons are full-time, legally qualified officers, and they issue reasoned judgments some of which are published and which are tending to develop into a body of case-law on the subject.[79] Some justiciable issues are, however, reserved for the determination of the Minister of Social Security himself with an appeal on a point of law to the Court of Session.[80]

Under the Social Security Acts, which are concerned with insurance against death or disablement caused by injury or industrial disease arising out of and in the course of employment, a claim is made in the first place to the local insurance officer, from whom appeal lies to local tribunals[81] and to the Chief National Insurance Commissioner and his Commissioners,[82] who are permanent and legally qualified experts. Certain matters may be appealed to the Minister himself and such a question may be referred or appealed to the Court of Session.[83] There are also Medical Boards, consisting of two or more medical practitioners, which deal with disablement cases and make provisional assessments of disablement benefits,[84] and from these appeal lies to Medical Appeal Tribunals,[85] which consist of a legally qualified chairman and two medical practitioners, with a further appeal on a point of law to the Commissioner. Cases before local appeal tribunals or the Commissioner will generally be heard in public. There are elaborate provisions for the review of decisions on the emergence of fresh evidence or on a change of circumstances.

Disputed claims under the Child Benefit Act are decided by the Minister of Social Security, from whom appeal lies to the National Insurance adjudicating authorities.[86] Certain issues are reserved for decision by the Minister.

The Supplementary Benefit scheme administered by the Supplementary Benefits Commission (formerly National Assistance Board) is administered

---

[78] Social Security Act 1975, ss. 97–100.
[79] Safford, " The Creation of Case Law under the National Insurance and National Insurance (Industrial Injuries) Acts "(1954) 17 M.L.R. 197; " Jurisdiction and Procedure of the National Insurance Commissioner " 1964 S.L.T. (News) 129.
[80] Social Security Act 1975, ss. 93–96.
[81] *Ibid.* ss. 97–100, 107–117.
[82] *Ibid.* s. 107.
[83] *Ibid.* ss. 93–96.
[84] *Ibid.* s. 108.
[85] *Ibid.* s. 109.
[86] Child Benefit Act 1975, s. 7.

by local officers, from whom appeal lies to a local Appeal Tribunal of three, from which there is no further appeal.[87]

Questions as to rights to or amount of family income supplement under the Family Income Supplements Act 1970 are determined by the Supplementary Benefits Commission, with a right of appeal to the same Appeal Tribunal as in the case of Supplementary Benefit.[88]

Pensions

Pensions Appeal Tribunals [89] deal with appeals against rejection of claims by members of the forces for war pensions. An appeal lies on a point of law to the Court of Session.[90]

Lands Tribunal

The Lands Tribunal for Scotland consisting of a President, legally qualified, and a number of other members all appointed by the Lord President of the Court of Session,[91] is the tribunal for assessing compensation in respect of land compulsorily acquired.[92] This tribunal also deals with applications under the Conveyancing and Feudal Reform (Scotland) Act 1970, for variation or discharge of conditions in feu-charters under which land is held.[93]

Valuation

In respect of valuation of land and buildings for rating purposes local Valuation Appeal Committees, of 15 to 20 persons appointed for each valuation area by the sheriff principal, deal with appeals against the valuation of land and buildings for local rates, fixed by the local assessor, and from which appeal lies to the Lands Valuation Appeal Court.[94]

Rents

The relationship of landlord and tenant of house-property falls within the jurisdiction of the sheriff court so far as relating to disputes about rent and ejection, but local authorities have the semi-judicial power of issuing certificates of disrepair which prevent an increase of rent being allowed, while in respect of furnished houses there are Rent Tribunals of three persons appointed by the Secretary of State, sometimes

---

[87] Ministry of Social Security Act 1966, s. 28 and Sched. 3.

[88] Family Income Supplements Act 1970, ss. 6–7.

[89] War Pensions (Administrative Provisions) Act 1919; Pensions Appeal Tribunals Act 1943.

[90] *Muir* v. *Minister of Pensions*, 1951 S.L.T. 18; *Macmillan* v. *Minister of Pensions*, 1952 S.C. 450.

[91] Lands Tribunal Act 1949, ss. 1–4.

[92] Land Compensation (Scotland) Act 1963, Pt. II.

[93] Decisions are reported in Scots Law Times (Lands Tribunal).

[94] Valuation and Rating (Scotland) Act 1956, s. 5.

of entirely non-legal composition, from which there is appeal only on a point of law to the Court of Session,[95] and where the tenancy of houses is regulated under the Rent (Scotland) Act 1971, the fair rent may be determined by a local rent officer, whose decision may be referred to a rent assessment committee constituted from a panel of persons appointed by the Secretary of State, and a further appeal to the Court of Session and House of Lords on a point of law.[96]

Agricultural marketing

The growth of marketing boards and governmental regulation of agriculture has given rise to numerous bodies to deal with complaints, applications, inquiries and so on. Thus a producer of wool has it valued by a marketing board appraiser and, if aggrieved by his decision, has a right of appeal to a tribunal of five members.[97]

Local authorities as controllers of building works

Certain local authorities[98] have jurisdiction and functions in relation to authorising building works and enforcing standards. An appeal lies in certain cases to the sheriff.[99]

Licensing Courts

The sale of excisable liquors may be effected only in premises licensed for that purpose.[1] There are different kinds of licences, for hotels, for public houses and for grocers or dealers.

There are separate licensing courts for each islands area and district or licensing division of an islands area or district. A licensing court consists half of J.P.s for and residing in the area which constitutes or includes the court area and half of councillors for the islands area or district whose area constitutes or includes the area of the court. The number of each is related to population. A licensing court of appeal consists as to half of J.P.s and as to half of councillors, but includes three more of each than the licensing court for the same area or the most populous licensing division.[2] There are two half-yearly meetings of the licensing courts. Courts of Appeal meet half-yearly after the meeting of the licensing court.

---

[95] Rent (Scotland) Act 1971, s. 84.

[96] Rent (Scotland) Act 1971, Sched. 5; see also *Stewart's J.F.* v. *Gallagher*, 1967 S.C. 59; *Skilling* v. *Arcari's Exrx*, 1974 S.L.T. 46.

[97] *Barrs* v. *British Wool Marketing Board*, 1957 S.C. 72.

[98] Defined by Local Government (Scotland) Act 1973, Sched. 15, para. 18.

[99] Building (Scotland) Act 1959, amended by Local Government (Scotland) Act 1973, Sched. 15.

[1] For the whole law, see Licensing (Scotland) Acts 1959 and 1962, and Purves, *Scottish Licensing Laws*.

[2] Licensing (Scotland) Act 1959, ss. 1–5 as substituted by Local Government (Scotland) Act 1973, s. 185.

Licensing courts also deal with applications for bookmaker's permits, betting agency permits and betting office licences. An appeal against refusal lies to the sheriff court, which is final.[3]

Licensing of credit and hire businesses

Licences are required to carry on a consumer credit (including money lending, pawnbroking or hire-purchase) business. These are issued by the Director General of Fair Trading, who may revoke or suspend them. Appeal against refusal to issue a licence, variation, suspension or revocation, lies to the Secretary of State for Consumer affairs with a further appeal on a point of law to the Court of Session.[4]

Road Traffic

The grant of licences for passenger road services and for goods vehicles [5] is in each area [6] in the hands of three Traffic Commissioners, the chairman of whom is a permanent official and the other two are drawn from panels nominated by local authorities. They sit in public and legal representation is permitted and common. The three commissioners sit as Licensing Authority for Public Service Vehicles and issue Public Service Vehicles Licences, Road Service Licences and the Drivers' and Conductors' Licences which are specially required for public service vehicles. Appeal lies from a refusal to the Minister of Transport, or, in the case of a driver's or conductor's licence, to the sheriff court.

The chairman sits alone as Licensing Authority for Goods Vehicles and may issue operator's licences for vehicles authorised thereby to be used for road haulage, or the carriage of the applicant's goods, special authorisation for the use of large goods vehicles, and also the necessary Heavy Goods Vehicle Driver's Licence. Objections may be raised and the Licensing Authority may hold any inquiries necessary. An aggrieved person may appeal to the Transport Tribunal, or in the case of a Heavy Goods Vehicle driver's licence to the sheriff.[7]

Aviation

The Civil Aviation Authority is responsible for granting air transport licences to British Airways and independent air-lines for the operation of

---

[3] Betting, Gaming and Lotteries Act 1963, ss. 2, 9 and Sched. 1; Gaming Act 1968; *Murphy* v. *Alloa Licensing Authy.* 1973 S.L.T. (Sh.Ct.) 2; *Jack* v. *Edinburgh Corpn.* 1973 S.L.T. (Sh.Ct.) 64; *W.M.T. Entertainments* v. *Glasgow Licensing Court*, 1974 S.L.T. (Sh.Ct.) 76; *Fehilly and Hope* v. *Stirling Licensing Court*, 1975 S.L.T. (Sh.Ct.) 16.

[4] Consumer Credit Act 1974, ss. 21–42.

[5] These licences are required as part of the regulation of services and are quite distinct from (a) vehicle excise licences; and (b) driving licences. See Road Traffic Act 1960, Parts III and IV.

[6] Scotland constitutes one area of the 11 in the U.K.

[7] *Crawford* v. *Scottish Area Licensing Authy.* 1974 S.L.T. (Sh.Ct.) 11.

air services. It is also charged with certification of operators of aircraft and the licensing of air crews and accommodation, regulation of noise from aircraft, operation of certain aerodromes and other matters.[8] Its decisions are subject to appeal to the Secretary of State. An Airworthiness Requirements Board makes recommendations to the Authority on matters of standards of design, construction and maintenance.

Performing Right Tribunal

This tribunal consists of a legally qualified chairman appointed by the Lord Chancellor and two, three or four other members appointed by the Department of Trade. Its function is to determine disputes between bodies licensing the performance of copyright works, such as music or plays, and persons requiring licences. A question of law may at the request of any party to the proceedings be referred to the Court of Session.[9]

Patents, Designs and Trade Marks

The Comptroller-General of Patents, Designs and Trade Marks as head of the Patent Office has the duty of granting or refusing applications for grant of a patent or for registration of a design or trade mark.[10] Appeal lies from his decision in patent cases to the Scottish Appeal Tribunal, who is a judge of the Court of Session nominated by the Lord President, from whom appeal lies by leave to the Court of Session in certain cases.[11] In design cases appeals lie to the Appeal Tribunal who is a judge of the High Court of England nominated by the Lord Chancellor.[12] In trade mark cases appeal lies to the Department of Trade or to the Court of Session.[13] Petitions in certain other patents and design matters may be presented in the Court of Session.[14]

Plant Varieties and Seeds Tribunal

This tribunal consists of a legally qualified chairman appointed by the Lord Chancellor or, in Scotland, the Lord President and one member selected from each of two panels of experts. Its function is to hear appeals from the decisions of the Controller of the Plant Variety Rights Office granting or refusing plant breeder's rights or licences thereof. The tribunal's decisions are final and conclusive.[15]

---

[8] Civil Aviation Act 1971, Pt. II.

[9] Copyright Act 1956, ss. 23–30.

[10] Patents and Designs Act 1907, ss. 62 (3), 63.

[11] Patents Act 1949, ss. 84–87, amended Courts Act 1971, s. 46.

[12] Registered Designs Act 1949, ss. 28, 45.

[13] Trade Marks Act 1938, ss. 17, 18, 22, 25, 28, 34.

[14] R.C. 250–257.

[15] Plant Varieties and Seeds Act 1964, s. 10 and Sched. 4; Tribunal Rules 1974.

Social Work

An appeal against refusal or cancellation of registration of residential or other establishments to accommodate persons for the purposes of the Social Work Act 1968, may be made to an appeal tribunal consisting of the sheriff principal of the county and two other members appointed from a panel set up by the Secretary of State.[16]

The Industrial Arbitration Board

The Industrial Arbitration Board was set up in 1919 [17] as the Industrial Court, a standing body, composed partly of independent persons, partly of representatives of employers and representatives of employees, appointed by the Secretary of State for Employment. It was intended as a permanent independent tribunal for industrial arbitration. It was renamed in 1971. In practice the Board is composed on each occasion of one representative from each of the panels. Any trade dispute may be reported to the Minister by or on behalf of the parties, and he may, with the consent of the parties, refer the matter for settlement by the Industrial Arbitration Board, or to arbitration, or for settlement by a Board of Arbitration. Some voluntary procedure agreements establish the Board as the final stage of the machinery and it also deals with references under certain statutes. The Minister may also refer other matters to the Industrial Arbitration Board for advice. Where, however, there are arrangements in a trade for conciliation or arbitration, the Minister may bring the matter before the Industrial Arbitration Board only by the consent of both parties and if the existing arrangements have failed to produce a settlement.

Industrial Tribunals

Under the Industrial Training Act 1964, s. 12, tribunals were established to determine whether persons assessed to a levy to meet the expenses of the training board for the industry in which they are engaged are liable to that levy or only to a reduced assessment.[18] To these tribunals have been assigned also questions arising under the Contracts of Employment Act 1963 (now 1972), questions whether an employee dismissed by reason of redundancy, or laid off or kept on short time, is entitled to redundancy payment under the Redundancy Payments Act 1965, s. 9, questions of unfair dismissal under the Trade Union and Labour Relations Act 1974, appeals against improvement notices and prohibition notices under the Health and Safety at Work Act 1974, and questions directed by various statutes [19] to be determined by a referee or board of

---

[16] Social Work (Scotland) Act 1968, s. 64 and Sched. 5.

[17] Industrial Courts Act 1919; Industrial Relations Act 1971, s. 124. See further, Sharp, *Industrial Conciliation and Arbitration in Great Britain*, 347–360.

[18] See *e.g. Road Transport Industry Trg. Board* v. *John Duncan Removals*, 1975 S.L.T. (Sh.Ct.) 2.

[19] Listed in the Redundancy Payments Act 1965, Sched. 7.

referees.[20] A tribunal consists of a legally qualified chairman and two members drawn from panels established by employers and employees respectively.[21] Appeal lies in certain cases to the Inner House and the House of Lords.[22]

Revenue

The Special Commissioners of Income Tax [23] are officials of the Inland Revenue Department, appointed by the Treasury to hear appeals against assessments for income tax and surtax. They usually sit in twos to hear appeals. The General Commissioners of Income Tax [23] are unpaid laymen appointed by and holding office during the pleasure of the appropriate local authority, together with sheriffs-principal and salaried sheriffs *ex officiis*, who also have a limited appeal jurisdiction in income tax assessments. The findings of the commissioners are final as to the facts but appeal lies by way of case stated on points of law to the Inner House of the Court of Session as the Court of Exchequer in Scotland, and thence to the House of Lords.[24]

Betting Levy Tribunal

An appeal tribunal for Scotland, consisting of a legal chairman appointed by the Lord President and two other members appointed by the Secretary of State for Scotland, was established by the Betting, Gaming and Lotteries Act 1963, ss. 28–29 to deal with appeals by bookmakers against assessments to pay bookmaker's levy imposed by the Horserace Betting Levy Board under ss. 24–27 of that Act.

Independent Schools Tribunal

Under the Education (Scotland) Act 1962, s. 113 and Sched. 7, independent schools tribunals exist to hear appeals against complaints that an independent school is inadequate in specified respects.

Immigration appeals

Under the Immigration Act 1971, Pt. II, a person refused leave to enter the United Kingdom may appeal to an adjudicator appointed by the Secretary of State, or may appeal against conditions attached to a limited leave to enter or remain in the U.K., or against a deportation order or

---

[20] Decisions of Industrial Tribunals are published by H.M.S.O. in a series of *Industrial Tribunals Reports*, in *Knight's Industrial Reports*, and in some of the ordinary reports.

[21] For procedure see Industrial Tribunals (Labour Relations) Regulations 1974.

[22] *e.g. Minister of Labour* v. *Reliant Tool Co.*, 1968 S.L.T. 101; *Lord Advocate* v. *De Rosa*, 1974 S.L.T. 214.

[23] Taxes Management Act 1970, Pts. I and V and Sched. 2.

[24] For examples, see any recent volume of *Session Cases*. Decisions are also reported in a special series, *Reports of Tax Cases*, 1875 to date, and in various privately published reports.

certain other directions. Appeal lies from an adjudicator's decision to an Immigration Appeal Tribunal appointed by the Lord Chancellor. The Secretary of State may refer any matter relating to a case for further consideration by an adjudicator or the Appeal Tribunal. No further appeal lies to the ordinary courts but a decision might be challenged if contrary to natural justice.[25]

Forestry

A person given by the Forestry Commissioners a direction to fell trees may have the matter referred to a committee of reference; the same course is open to a person adversely affected by felling directions.[26]

Milk and Dairies

Tribunals exist to hear appeals against revocation or suspension of a licence as an authorised milk producer.[27]

Nurses' Training Institutions

A person aggrieved by the decision of the General Nursing Council for Scotland to refuse to approve an institution for training nurses, or withdrawing approval or varying or revoking a scheme for training nurses may require the matter to be referred to two persons appointed by the Lord President.[28]

Iron and Steel

The Iron and Steel Arbitration Tribunal exists to determine any question or dispute assigned to it under the Iron and Steel Acts, 1949 and 1967.

Mines and Quarries

The fitness of a person to continue to hold a certificate of competency granted by the Mining Qualifications Board may be inquired into by a tribunal appointed by the Lord President.[29]

Criminal Injuries Compensation Board

A body which is neither a court nor a tribunal and indeed stands somewhat outside the legal system altogether but was established to give a remedy where it might otherwise not be obtained is the Criminal Injuries Compensation Board. It was set up in 1964 on an experimental and non-statutory basis and is composed of a chairman and five members, all legally qualified, two being members of the Scottish Bar, appointed

---

[25] *cf. Schmidt* v. *Home Office* [1969] 2 Ch. 149.
[26] Forestry Act 1967, ss. 20, 21, 27.
[27] Milk (Special Designations) Act 1949, s. 11.
[28] Nurses (Scotland) Act 1951, s. 24.
[29] Mines and Quarries Act, 1954, s. 150 and Sched. 3, Part I.

by the Home Secretary and the Secretary of State for Scotland.[30] It is based in London but may have offices elsewhere and may sit in London, Edinburgh or elsewhere as necessary. It submits an annual report and accounts to Parliament.

The Board exists to deal with claims for compensation for injuries or death suffered in circumstances amounting to criminal violence, where in many cases the assailant is not identified or is not worth suing for damages. Compensation is payable *ex gratia*, and the government does not accept any legal liability for injuries caused to persons by the criminal acts of other persons. The Board is solely and entirely responsible for determining what compensation, if any, is payable in particular cases and its decisions are not subject to appeal or ministerial review.

A claim is competent where the applicant or his deceased relative suffered personal injury or death directly attributable to a criminal offence or an arrest or attempted arrest of an offender or suspected offender or to the prevention or attempted prevention of an offence or to the giving of help to any constable who is engaged in arresting or attempting to arrest an offender or suspected offender or preventing or attempting to prevent an offence where such injury occurs in Great Britain or on a British vessel or aircraft, and the injury gave rise to at least three weeks' loss of earnings or is an injury for which not less than £50 compensation would be awarded, and the circumstances of the injury have been reported to the police without delay or have been the subject of criminal proceedings in the courts. Certain crimes are excluded from the scheme. Adjudication is by one member of the Board but there is a right of appeal to a larger Board. Compensation is assessed on the basis of common law damages subject to certain limits. Where damages are recovered at common law the compensation is repayable to the Board. Since the scheme was started a large number of claims have been made and numerous awards made.[31]

CRIMINAL COURTS

Criminal jurisdiction is divided into solemn and summary jurisdiction, the former being exercised by trial on indictment before a judge or sheriff sitting with a jury of fifteen [32] and the latter by trial on complaint by sheriff or magistrate alone, or by one or more justices of the peace sitting without

---

[30] The scheme under which the Board operates is printed in 1964 S.L.T.(News) 134 and discussed in Walker, *Law of Delict in Scotland*, II, 1062.

[31] Brief reports of awards made are given in *Current Law, s.v.* Criminal Law. See also *R.* v. *Criminal Injuries Compensation Board* [1967] 2 All E.R. 770, which indicates that at least in England the ordinary courts have a supervisory jurisdiction over the Board, though there is no appeal to them.

[32] Notice that the Scottish criminal jury numbers 15, the Scottish civil (like the English) jury 12.

a jury. The determination whether a case is to be prosecuted under solemn or under summary procedure depends on any statutory prescription which is applicable to the offence in question and on the gravity of the offence. If statute is silent the prosecutor has a discretion, but that discretion is limited by the fact that procedure in the sheriff's summary and in magistrates' courts is regulated by the Criminal Procedure (Scotland) Act 1975, which excludes from the jurisdiction of these courts a number of the more serious crimes, and limits the powers of these courts to punish offenders. Furthermore it is a general principle that justices of the peace cannot deal with statutory offences unless jurisdiction is conferred on them expressly or by implication in the statute in question.[33] There are accordingly four modes of trial: (i) magistrate or one or more justices alone (summary offences); (ii) sheriff alone (summary offences); (iii) sheriff [34] and jury; (iv) judge of the High Court and jury.

The prosecution of crimes and offences is almost exclusively in the hands of the Lord Advocate in the High Court and of procurators-fiscal, acting on instructions from the Lord Advocate, in the sheriff and district courts. Private prosecution, though possible, is practically unknown,[35] and while certain officials, such as factory inspectors, may prosecute summary offences in their own names, they do so in the public interest. The police do not in any circumstances prosecute in Scotland. Crimes are reported to the local procurator-fiscal in the first place and he decides, in serious cases in consultation with the Crown Office in Edinburgh, whether to prosecute and in what form. In High Court cases the indictment is settled by the Lord Advocate, the Solicitor-General or one of the advocates-depute appointed by the Lord Advocate, and one of these conducts the case for the Crown in the High Court and in important cases in the sheriff court. In other sheriff court cases and in summary offences the procurator-fiscal conducts the prosecution case.[36]

The District Court

A court consisting of a stipendiary magistrate or one or more justices of the peace has a criminal jurisdiction extending to all breaches of the peace and certain petty charges under statute and extending over the area having

---

[33] *McPherson* v. *Boyd*, 1907 S.C.(J.) 42. The sheriff's summary court is accordingly the commonest forum for prosecutions in Scotland.

[34] Sheriff principal or sheriff.

[35] *J. & P. Coats* v. *Brown*, 1909 S.C.(J.) 29; *McBain* v. *Crichton*, 1961 J.C. 25. The concurrence of the Lord Advocate must be sought though the High Court may permit the prosecution without his concurrence. It is wholly incompetent for a private prosecutor to prosecute on indictment in the sheriff court: *Dunbar* v. *Johnston* (1904) 7 F. 40. A county council has no title to institute a private prosecution: *McKinstry* v. *Lanark C.C.*, 1962 J.C. 16. Certain public bodies such as British Railways have statutory powers to bring what are technically private prosecutions; see, *e.g. British Railways Board* v. *Dick*, 1965 S.L.T.(Sh.Ct.) 25.

[36] See further, Milne, *The Scottish Office*, 206–208; Gordon, in *Source Book of Administrative Law*, Chap. 5. For statistics, see the annual *Criminal Statistics, Scotland.*

a distinct commission of the peace for which the justices are appointed.[37] The sheriff has jurisdiction within his sheriffdom concurrent with the justices in regard to all offences triable by them. Prosecutions are conducted by the procurator-fiscal and procedure is summary, there being no jury.

Appeal lies to the High Court of Justiciary by way of a stated case, which sets out the facts admitted or proved and raises a question of law only, or by bill of suspension. As a criminal court the district court is very much less important in Scotland than are magistrates' courts in England; it deals only with the most ordinary cases and not even with the bulk of them.

A local authority has power [38] to secure the appointment of a stipendiary magistrate, who must have been legally qualified for five years and also has the same jurisdiction as the sheriff in his summary court in respect of offences committed within the district. Only in Glasgow has this power been used, where three stipendiaries sit in the Central, Marine and Govan Police Courts.

The powers of punishment of these courts are strictly limited [39] so that numerous but not serious cases only are brought before them.

The Sheriff Court

As in civil matters, the sheriff court is the most generally important lower criminal court and it can try any crime or offence committed within the sheriffdom not reserved to the High Court, including cases which might be heard in the district court.[40] In criminal cases no distinction need be taken between the sheriff principal and the sheriffs since their powers are co-extensive and no appeal lies from the one to the other. The sheriff principal or sheriff may, sitting alone, deal with cases prosecuted on complaint under the Criminal Procedure (Scotland) Act 1975, and when sitting with a jury of 15, deal with cases prosecuted on indictment.[41] In the latter case the procedure followed is identical with that followed in the High Court of Justiciary. The selection of the mode of trial appropriate is determined by the prosecutor, and the accused has no right to elect jury trial. In either case the prosecution is prepared and conducted

---

[37] The District Court was created in 1975 and replaced the former Burgh Police Courts (in burghs) and Justice of the Peace Courts (in counties): District Courts (Scotland) Act 1975. For history of the justices' jurisdiction see *Wright* v. *Bell* (1905) 8 F. 291.

[38] District Courts (Scotland) Act 1975, s. 5.

[39] Criminal Procedure (Scotland) Act 1975.

[40] If a statute speaks of an offence being prosecuted in " a court of summary jurisdiction," jurisdiction is conferred on District and sheriff courts, but if it speaks of the offence being punishable " on summary conviction," or does not name the court, jurisdiction is conferred only on the sheriff court: *McPherson* v. *Boyd*, 1907 S.C.(J.) 42.

[41] About 90 per cent. of prosecutions on indictment and more than 50 per cent. of prosecutions on complaint are dealt with in the sheriff courts.

by the procurator-fiscal or one of his deputes, though in difficult cases an advocate-depute may appear for the Crown. Counsel may always, and frequently do, appear for the accused. In other cases the accused is normally represented by a solicitor, but he may defend himself. As compared with the High Court, however, the sheriff's power of punishment is limited, in cases on indictment, to two years' imprisonment or an unlimited fine, unless the offence is under a statute which imposes a limit on the fine, and in summary cases to three months' imprisonment unless there are previous convictions or a particular statute confers wider powers, or a fine of £150, unless a particular statute confers wider or narrower powers.[42] In cases on indictment the sheriff may remit a convicted person to the High Court for sentence if he regards his powers inadequate in the circumstances.[43] The sheriff court has concurrent jurisdiction with other lower courts within the sheriffdom in regard to all offences which can be tried in such courts and its jurisdiction is practically universal in that it need not be expressly conferred by the statute creating the offence, but it is limited in that the most serious crimes of all, such as murder and rape, may be tried only in the High Court, and by the fact that its powers of punishment are limited. Nevertheless the sheriff court, either summarily or on indictment, deals with an immense number of offenders and with practically every kind of crime and offence, and it is by far the most important of the inferior criminal courts.

An appeal from the sheriff sitting summarily lies to the High Court of Justiciary by way of stated case or bill of suspension and, from the sheriff sitting with a jury, under solemn procedure, to the High Court of Justiciary in its capacity as Court of Criminal Appeal under the Criminal Appeal (Scotland) Act 1926 (now the Criminal Procedure (Scotland) Act 1975).

The High Court of Justiciary

The High Court was established in 1672, replacing the Court of the Justiciars, and consisted till 1887 of seven judges—the Lord Justice-

---

[42] Criminal Procedure (Scotland) Act 1975, s. 289.

[43] Criminal Procedure (Scotland) Act 1975, s. 104. In such a case the High Court is not bound to impose a heavier sentence than the sheriff could have imposed. The sheriff cannot remit if the maximum penalty for the offence charged is within the sheriff's competence: *H.M.A.* v. *Stern*, 1974 S.L.T. 2. An accused may also notify his intention to plead guilty and ask for his case to be expedited, in which case the sheriff may sentence him or remit him to the High Court for sentence: Criminal Procedure (Scotland) Act 1975, s. 102.

General, Lord Justice-Clerk and five Lords Commissioners of Justiciary.[44]
The office of Lord Justice-General was long hereditary, becoming vested
in the sixteenth century in the Dukes of Argyll. In 1628 the Duke resigned
this office to the King, retaining the office of Justice-General for Argyll
and the Isles. The office of Lord Justice-General was held from 1628
to 1836 by various noblemen, but since 1836 has been held by the Lord
President of the Court of Session.

The Lord Justice-Clerk was originally the clerk of the criminal court
but became the normal president since the Act of 1672 provided that
he should preside when the Lord Justice-General did not sit, which
regularly happened down to 1836, while the latter office remained honorary.[45]

Since the Criminal Procedure (Scotland) Act 1887, the court consists
of the Lord Justice-General, Lord Justice-Clerk, and all the other (18)
Lords of Session as Lords Commissioners of Justiciary.[46]

It has jurisdiction over all Scotland and in respect of all crimes, unless
its jurisdiction is expressly or impliedly excluded by the terms of a statute.
It has exclusive jurisdiction to try the most serious crimes, such as treason
and murder, and in practice deals with all the more serious cases of
crime even though some of these might also have been tried by sheriff
and jury.

The High Court as Court of Trial

The High Court is both a court of first instance and a court of appeal.
As a court of first instance sittings of the High Court are held in Edinburgh and also on circuit as required. Scotland is divided into four
circuits, Home, West, North and South, and courts are held for these
districts at (i) Edinburgh; (ii) Glasgow, Stirling and Oban (formerly
Inveraray); (iii) Inverness, Aberdeen, Dundee and Perth; and (iv) Dumfries, Jedburgh and Ayr. Sittings are not, however, restricted to these
towns and a sitting may be held in any town which is convenient to or
near the locality of a crime. Sittings on circuit are appointed to be held

---

[44] When sitting as Lords Commissioners of Justiciary the judges wear scarlet
robes faced with white, decorated with scarlet crosses. The Lord Justice-General's
robe is faced with ermine and the Lord Justice-Clerk's robe has rows of square holes
in the white satin facings to give the appearance of ermine. The judges always wear
their justiciary robes for state functions, and public occasions.

[45] See further, *Introduction to Scottish Legal History*, Chap. 31; Malcolm, " The
Lord Justice-Clerk of Scotland " (1915) 27 J.R. 342, 375; Hannay, " The Office of
the Justice-Clerk " (1935) 47 J.R. 311.

[46] This gave rise in *H.M.Adv.* v. *Sugden*, 1934 J.C. 103, to the interesting question
whether a decision of a Full Bench of 1773 of seven judges could be overruled by that
of a Full Bench of 1934 consisting of 12 judges (the total strength being then 13, and
one being absent). It was held that it could. So, too, in *Muir* v. *Hart* (1912) 6 Adam
601 the question was raised whether a Full Bench of seven judges could overrule a
decision of a Full Bench of five judges of 1855, when five judges was the usual bench
to consider cases of difficulty.

quarterly but no circuit need be held if there is no business.[47] On the other hand, the volume of business at Glasgow requires monthly sittings there. As a rule only one judge needs to go on circuit but in Glasgow two courts sit concurrently and two judges go on the West circuit. They may be replaced at a convenient stage in the sittings by colleagues. The Lord Justice-General does not go on circuit and the Lord Justice-Clerk only for exceptionally important cases. As a rule only one judge sits at a trial but in cases of difficulty or importance two or more, usually three, may sit.[48] Procedure is always solemn (on indictment) and with a jury.

The jurisdiction of the court extends to all cases of crime except where its jurisdiction has been excluded by statute and it is exclusive in the case of the most serious crimes, namely, treason, murder and rape, incest, certain offences under the Official Secrets Act, deforcement of messengers-at-arms and breach of duty by magistrates. In practice, all the most serious cases are tried in the High Court, particularly since its powers of punishment are greater than those of any inferior courts.

The prosecution is invariably conducted by one of the Law Officers or one of the Advocates-Depute, and the accused is invariably defended by counsel (unless, as sometimes happens, he refuses or dismisses counsel).

The High Court as Appellate Court

Appeals from courts of summary criminal jurisdiction lie to the High Court of Justiciary in Edinburgh and are heard by three or more Lords Commissioners of Justiciary. The normal modes of appeal are by way of stated case or bill of suspension.

In a stated case the sheriff or other judge of the inferior court is requested to prepare a statement of the facts found by him to be admitted or proved and to formulate a question or questions of law raising the issue the accused wishes to have argued. The appeal is thus only on points of law and in this way authoritative rulings are given on many points, particularly of the interpretation of statutes and instruments creating offences. Thus the phrase, " in charge of " a vehicle, has been elucidated several times, when the High Court has held in stated cases that a sheriff was or was not entitled in particular circumstances to hold that an accused was " in charge of " a vehicle, so as to render him liable

---

[47] Lord Cockburn's *Circuit Journeys* gives a delightful picture of the circuit system in the early nineteenth century.
[48] *e.g.* trial of Madeleine Smith, where L.J.-C. Hope, Lords Handyside and Ivory all sat. Three or more judges also sit to dispose of any difficult or important point raised before trial, for deciding points raised at trials on circuit and certified to the High Court (see *e.g. H.M. Advocate* v. *Bickerstaff*, 1926 J.C. 65), and for disposing of petitions to the *nobile officium* of the court. In *H.M. Advocate* v. *Hay*, 1968 S.L.T. 334, three judges sat to dispose of a point of admissibility of evidence arising during a trial in Edinburgh.

to certain penalties. The question in such a case is not whether the inferior court was *correct* in its decision, which is a matter for it on the evidence, but whether the lower court was *entitled in law* to do what it did. Questions of evidence and matters of fact and the inferences therefrom are for the inferior court and cannot be raised in a stated case.

Appeal by bill of suspension is appropriate to raise an issue of jurisdiction, incompetency of proceedings or another matter extrinsic to the complaint or the facts adduced, or where the appeal is an attack on the judicial character of the proceedings, such as an allegation of oppression, or irregularity or radical defect in the proceedings. A Bill is prepared by the accused's advisers, narrating the conviction and the objections to it, and served on the procurator-fiscal as respondent; he usually lodges written answers and appears by counsel at the hearing to uphold the conviction. The High Court may pass the Bill and suspend the sentence, or refuse the Bill, or amend the conviction and sentence. At such sittings of the High Court the presiding judge has no vote unless the other judges are equally divided in opinion,[49] and if the court consists of four judges who are equally divided the judgment will be contrary to that of the presiding judge.[50]

Down to 1926 no appeal lay to the High Court from trials on indictment (*i.e.* under solemn procedure, with a jury, whether before a judge or a sheriff), but in that year in consequence of the miscarriage of justice in the case of Oscar Slater [51] the Scottish court of criminal appeal was established. It consists of three or more [52] judges of the High Court of Justiciary and is consequently another aspect of the appellate work of the High Court.[53] Appeal may be brought against conviction on a question of law, or against conviction on a question of fact or of mixed fact and law if the appellant obtains the leave of the High Court or the certificate of the judge who presided at the trial, or against conviction on any other ground which appears to the High Court or to the trial judge to be a sufficient ground of appeal. Appeal may further be taken against the sentence, unless it is one fixed by law,[54] with the leave of the High Court. The appellant, or counsel on his behalf, may present argument and a law officer or advocate-depute will appear for the Crown.

---

[49] *Campbell* v. *Maclennan* (1888) 1 White 604; *Muir* v. *Hart* (1912) 6 Adam 601.
[50] *Ross* v. *Johnston* (1886) 1 White 171.
[51] See *Trial of Oscar Slater*, ed. Roughead (Famous Trials Series) and *Slater* v. *H.M. Advocate*, 1928 J.C. 94.
[52] *e.g.* in *H.M. Advocate* v. *Kirkwood*, 1939 J.C. 36, 13 judges sat.
[53] In practice what usually happens is that every three or four weeks either the First or the Second Division of the Court of Session does not sit as such but three of its members (the Lord President or Lord Justice-Clerk and two others) don their justiciary gowns and sit as the High Court and then, having disposed of the Criminal Appeal Roll, sit on for disposal of the Justiciary Roll, *i.e.* appeals from summary cases. The fourth judge of the Division may be absent or unwell or on circuit, but, if available, is usually set to assist the Outer House judges in civil business.
[54] *e.g.* the penalty of death for treason.

The court decides by a majority, including the vote of the presiding judge; it may allow the appeal if it thinks the verdict of the jury was unreasonable and cannot be supported having regard to the evidence, or that there was improper admission or rejection of evidence, or misdirection of the jury by the judge or that on any ground there was a miscarriage of justice. In such a case the conviction is quashed. Or the court may refuse the appeal, or may modify the sentence. The court has no power to order a retrial save that it may do so when sitting as Courts-Martial Appeal Court.[55]

There is also provision for the Secretary of State referring a case to the High Court or referring a point to the court for their opinion.[56] No further appeal lies from the High Court to the House of Lords,[57] so that this court has final responsibility for disposing of cases and for settling the law, and has given many judgments of great importance and value for the development of Scottish criminal law.

SPECIAL CRIMINAL COURTS

Children's Panels

Under the Social Work (Scotland) Act 1968, children under 16 alleged to have committed offences are no longer dealt with in juvenile courts nor prosecuted at all except on the instructions of the Lord Advocate or at his instance.[58] Districts have to maintain panels of persons, selected by the Secretary of State with the advice of local committees. Cases are brought before the panels, each of which comprises three persons, including at least one woman, at children's hearings, by a local authority officer called the Reporter. He investigates the case and decides whether or not to bring the case before a hearing.[59] If the child " accepts the grounds stated by the Reporter for the referral, " *i.e.* admits the offence, the panel proceeds to disposal; if he does not the sheriff sitting in chambers must determine whether the grounds for the referral are established, and, if the allegation is substantiated, remit the case to the panel for disposal. Appeal may be taken by stated case to the Court of Session against the sheriff's finding.[60]

---

[55] Courts-Martial (Appeals) Act 1968, s. 19.

[56] For an example, see *Gallacher* v. *H.M. Advocate*, 1951 J.C. 38, footnote to p. 49.

[57] *Bywater* v. *Lord Advocate* (1781) 2 Pat. 563; *Mackintosh* v. *Lord Advocate* (1876) 3 R.(H.L.) 34; Criminal Procedure (Scotland) Act 1887, s. 72; but appeal lies from the High Court sitting in the capacity of Courts-Martial Appeal Court: Courts-Martial (Appeals) Act 1968, Part III. The House did consider an appeal in *Elgin Magistrates* v. *Elgin Ministers* (1713) Robert. 69. In 1773 two sheep-stealers appealed to the House of Lords but a Committee of the Lords ruled that the House of Lords could not receive appeals from the High Court of Justiciary: *Boswell for the Defence*, 1769–1774, ed. Wimsatt and Pottle, p. 156.

[58] See *M.* v. *Dean*, 1974 S.L.T. 229.

[59] A children's hearing is technically not criminal proceedings but is so in effect and the majority of, though not all, cases, brought before a hearing arise from the commission of offences. [60] *D.* v. *Kennedy*, 1974 S.L.T. 168.

The panel may discharge the reference, or make a supervision requirement,[61] or require residence in a residential establishment,[62] possibly subject to conditions. Every order must be reviewed annually and the child's parent can require review after six, or sometimes three, months. The Secretary of State may terminate a supervision requirement.

An appeal lies to the sheriff from the panel's decision, with a further limited right of appeal to the Court of Session by stated case on a point of law or in respect of any irregularity in the conduct of the case, at the instance of the child, his parent or the reporter.

In the case of serious offences children may still be dealt with in the sheriff court or High Court.

Courts-Martial and the Courts-Martial Appeal Court

Offences against naval, military or air force law are dealt with either summarily, by the accused's commanding officer, or in more serious cases by courts-martial constituted under the respective codes of discipline for the several forces.[63] The offences in question are mostly " service " ones, such as mutiny, desertion or other breach of discipline, but include also offences punishable by the ordinary law,[64] though the most serious crimes, unless committed on active service, must not be tried by a court-martial if they can with reasonable convenience be tried by an ordinary court.[65]

While it is no doubt desirable to have a common code of service law for all personnel, it is unfortunate that the code adopted is based entirely on English criminal law, which may cause difficulties for Scottish counsel or solicitors defending and may give rise to problems of great difficulty on appeal, since Scottish judges do not profess to know English criminal law.

If preliminary investigation within the unit discloses a prima facie case, a court-martial will be convened by an authorised convening officer.

In the Navy, commanding officers of ships have very extensive powers of summary punishment and there is only one type of court-martial—Naval Court-Martial—which deals with all offences under the Naval Discipline Act which cannot be dealt with summarily. The Naval Discipline Act does not extend to the W.R.N.S. The minutes of every defended court-martial and any legal questions of importance are always referred

---

[61] Equivalent to the former probation order; see *K.* v. *Finlayson,* 1974 S.L.T.(Sh. Ct.) 51.

[62] Formerly called an approved school.

[63] Naval Discipline Act 1957; Naval Disciplinary Courts (Procedure) Orders 1958; Army Act 1955; Rules of Procedure (Army) 1956; Air Force Act 1955; Rules of Procedure (Air Force) 1956. See further, Halsbury's *Laws of England,* tit. " Courts."

[64] *i.e.* the criminal law of *England.*

[65] Thus murder or assault in Britain, especially if perpetrated on a civilian, would be tried by the ordinary criminal courts. But murder committed on a foreign station would be tried by court-martial at that station; *e.g. R.* v. *Page* [1953] 3 W.L.R. 895.

to the Judge-Advocate of the Fleet, who advises the Board of Admiralty as to the validity of procedure, evidence, finding and sentence, whereupon the Board decide whether to uphold or quash the conviction and to uphold or reduce the sentence. An officiating judge-advocate is appointed at each court-martial to advise on law and procedure and to protect the accused.

In the Army and Air Force there are General Courts-Martial, consisting of not fewer than five officers, which try officers and also other ranks in the most serious cases, and District Courts-Martial, consisting of not fewer than three officers, which try other ranks. The president is usually of the rank of colonel or brigadier and the members are drawn, so far as possible, from different corps and units. Women officers must be represented on the court if a member of the women's forces is being tried. No member of the court need have any legal experience but must have certain minimum periods of commissioned service. On service the Field General Court-Martial, consisting of three officers, is the usual tribunal.

The prosecution is conducted by an officer but counsel [66] may be instructed on his behalf, and the accused may be represented by an officer or by counsel or solicitor. A judge-advocate [67] must, in the case of general courts-martial, and in other cases may, be appointed by the Judge-Advocate General of the Army and Air Force to attend to advise the court on law, procedure and powers of punishment. He sums up the evidence and advises the court before it deliberates on its finding. Courts-martial normally sit in public and the procedure, which is based on English criminal procedure, is largely regulated by the printed form used to record the proceedings, which sets out the stages of the trial. Findings of guilt and sentence are subject to confirmation by the convening authority.[68]

A person convicted by court-martial may petition the confirming or reviewing authority to quash or vary his conviction or sentence before or even after confirmation and in some cases the proceedings may be submitted to Her Majesty or to the Army Council. Apart from these prerogative petitions a convicted person must petition to have his conviction quashed before he may apply for leave to appeal; he is entitled to apply for leave to appeal within ten days of the dismissal of his petition or the end of the period for disposing of his petition.

The Courts-Martial (Appeals) Act of 1951 (now the Courts-Martial (Appeals) Act 1968) constituted a Courts-Martial Appeal Court con-

[66] In this context " counsel " includes Scottish advocates and solicitors, and they may appear wherever the trial be held; *e.g.* a Scottish advocate may appear at Aldershot.

[67] Judge-advocates are advocates or barristers employed whole-time in the legal branches of the services.

[68] As to powers of confirming authorities, see Criminal Appeal Act 1966, Sched. 1, Part II.

sisting, in Scotland,[69] of such Lords Commissioners of Justiciary as the Lord Justice-General may nominate, being uneven in number and not less than three. The Lord Chancellor may appoint other persons of legal experience to be judges of the Court. A person convicted by court-martial in any of the services may, with the leave of the Appeal Court, and subject to certain conditions, appeal against his conviction.

The practice of the High Court of Justiciary sitting as Court of Criminal Appeal is followed [70] and the powers of the court are similar except that it has no jurisdiction to deal with sentences.[71] The court will allow an appeal if it thinks that the finding of the court-martial under all the circumstances of the case is unsafe or unsatisfactory, or involves a wrong decision on a point of law, or that there was a material irregularity in the course of the trial, but the court may dismiss an appeal on a technical point if they consider that in the circumstances no miscarriage of justice has occurred. In certain cases the court may authorise a retrial. The court's decision is final but appeal lies to the House of Lords by leave of the court or of the House of Lords, which shall be granted only if the Appeal Court certifies that a point of law of general public importance is involved and that it appears to the court or the House of Lords that the point ought to be considered by the House of Lords.[72]

ECCLESIASTICAL COURTS [73]

Since there is no Church in Scotland established as part of the state, Church courts have jurisdiction only over their own members and in matters affecting church discipline, ritual and membership. But the courts of the Church of Scotland are legally established courts of the realm within their own field whereas courts of other Churches have

---

[69] When this court sits in England the judges are the *ex officio* and ordinary members of the Court of Appeal and certain judges of the Queen's Bench Division nominated by the Lord Chief Justice, and when it sits in Northern Ireland the judges are such of the judges of the Supreme Court of Judicature in Northern Ireland as the Lord Chief Justice of Northern Ireland may nominate. The Act also makes provision for " such other persons, being persons of legal experience, as the Lord Chancellor may appoint " being appointed judges of the court for such term as may be determined by the Lord Chancellor.

[70] See *R.* v. *Houghton* [1952] C.L.Y. 159; *R. v. Condon* (1952) 36 Cr.App.R. 130; *Hendry*, 1955 S.L.T.(Notes) 66.

[71] Powers are regulated by the Statutes regulating the powers of the [English] Court of Appeal, Criminal Division, *viz.* Criminal Appeal Act 1968; Courts-Martial (Appeals) Act 1968.

[72] Administration of Justice Act 1960, ss. 1, 10 and Sched. 1; now Courts-Martial (Appeals) Act 1968, s. 39.

[73] See further, Donaldson, " The Church Courts," in *Introduction to Scottish Legal History*, Chap. 27; Cox, *Practice and Procedure in the Church of Scotland*, 5th ed.; the *Church of Scotland Year Book*; Taylor, " Church and State in Scotland," 1957 J.R. 121; King Murray, " Constitutional Position of the Church of Scotland " [1958] Pub.L.155.

jurisdiction only so far as conferred by their own constitutions and the adherence of their members.[74]

The constitution and powers of the courts of the Church of Scotland are founded on the General Assembly Act 1592, c. 116, confirmed by the Confession of Faith Ratification Act 1690, c. 5, which in turn was ratified by the Act of Security which is incorporated into the Treaty of Union with England. These courts are supreme, and independent of the civil and criminal courts in matters ecclesiastical and spiritual,[75] so that no claim of damages lies against a Church court for a judgment in a proper case of discipline duly brought before it.[76] The civil courts are bound to assist the Church courts in making their decrees effectual, but cannot review their decisions in matters falling within their jurisdiction.

The courts of the Church are the Kirk-Session, composed of the minister and elders of the parish, which has a general power of discipline over members; the Presbytery, which consists of all the ministers of parishes within its bounds and an elder from each kirk-session and has a general supervisory responsibility, power to censure, suspend or depose ministers after due trial, and the duty of hearing appeals and references from inferior courts; the Synod, which consists of the members of the several presbyteries within its bounds and hears appeals and complaints against decisions of inferior courts; and the General Assembly.

The General Assembly is both the legislature [77] and the Supreme Court of the Church. It consists of ministers and elders elected by presbyteries, universities and royal burghs. It is presided over by the Moderator, who is elected annually, and the Queen is represented by a Lord High Commissioner who has no voice in the deliberations of the Assembly but is the official medium of communication between the Sovereign and the Assembly.[78]

The judicial functions consist of hearing and deciding appeals and complaints from inferior courts and adjudicating on petitions from members and congregations. Legal representation is permitted. Forms of libels in the Church courts are similar to those of indictments in the High Court. The procedure is regulated by Acts of Assembly.[79]

[74] *McMillan* v. *General Assembly of the Free Church of Scotland* (1859) 22 D. 290; (1861) 23 D. 1314.

[75] *Lockhart* v. *Presbytery of Deer* (1851) 13 D. 1296; *Wight* v. *Presbytery of Dunkeld* (1870) 8 M. 921.

[76] *Sturrock* v. *Greig* (1849) 11 D. 1220.

[77] The legislation is printed in the Acts of Assembly. *The Booke of the Universall Kirk of Scotland* (Peterkin, 1839) contains many Acts 1560–1616. Other volumes contain Acts of Assemblies of 1638–49, 1690, 1692, 1694–1895 while the printed Acts of each year are maintained in many libraries.

[78] In 1969 the Queen attended personally and there was no Lord High Commissioner.

[79] Acts of Assembly 1707, XI and 1889, XIX.

DOMESTIC TRIBUNALS

The various organisations and associations established by individuals for various purposes, social, economic, intellectual, professional and otherwise, may, and frequently do, establish their own adjudicating and disciplinary bodies to regulate the rights and duties of members *inter se* and, in some cases, also *vis-à-vis* the outside world. The law in general permits such organisations to manage their own affairs, but sometimes interferes where the individual member's rights, which are at stake, are of vital importance to him. Again some domestic jurisdictions are almost entirely internal, while others are recognised by statute and even provision made for appeal to the courts.

The bodies exercising most completely " internal " domestic jurisdiction are the Faculty of Advocates and the Inns of Court which each have jurisdiction over their members in matters of discipline and professional conduct to the extent, if need be, of disbarring counsel. At least in England there is, by custom, an appeal to the judges.[80] So too the committee of the London Stock Exchange is complete master over the members. But in all these cases it is likely that the courts would interfere to ensure that the requirements of natural justice [81] are complied with, though not further.

In the case of disciplinary committees of trade unions and associations to which the individual submits himself contractually by joining the body in question, provided the association acts within its own constitution and rules, the interpretation of which is a matter for the courts,[82] the courts will interfere only if there is an alleged contravention of the rules of actual justice.

But in other cases the disciplinary body is set up by statute, and there may even be prescribed appellate procedure. Thus the General Medical Council has disciplinary jurisdiction in respect of infamous professional misconduct, with an appeal to the Privy Council.[83] Solicitors are subject, in England, to the Disciplinary Committee, with an appeal to three judges, and subsequently, by leave, to the Court of Appeal and the House of

---

[80] *Re Marrinan* [1957] C.L.Y. 2747; see also *R.* v. *Gray's Inn* (1780) 1 Doug.K.B. 353. In 1874 E. V. H. Kenealy, Q.C., was disbenched and disbarred by Gray's Inn. In 1961 Mr. Victor Durand, Q.C. was suspended from practice for three years by the Benchers of the Inner Temple. On appeal five judges reduced this to one year. See further, Halsbury's *Laws of England,* tit. " Barrister."

[81] The requirements of natural justice are vague and undefined, but certainly cover the requirements that the person charged should be acquainted with the charge against him, be allowed to hear the evidence against him, and be heard in his own defence, and that the members of the tribunal be not biased or personally interested in the outcome of the dispute.

[82] See further, Morris, " The Courts and Domestic Tribunals " (1953) 69 L.Q.R. 318; *Lee* v. *Showmen's Guild* [1952] 2 Q.B. 329; *Birch* v. *N.U.R.* [1950] Ch. 602; *Baker* v. *Jones* [1954] 1 W.L.R. 1005.

[83] Medical Act 1956, s. 20 (this was first established by the Medical Act 1858); and see *G.M.C.* v. *Spackman* [1943] A.C. 627.

Lords. In Scotland solicitors are subject to the Solicitors' Discipline Committee and it may censure or fine or suspend the solicitor from practice or order his name to be struck off the roll of solicitors.[84] An appeal against the decision of the Discipline Committee lies to the Court of Session.

Similar disciplinary bodies have been established under statute for architects,[85] dentists,[86] pharmacists,[87] midwives,[88] registered nurses,[89] and veterinary surgeons,[90] and some other professions. All partake of some of the characteristics of courts, with defined procedures and, in some cases, statutory rights of appeal.

AD HOC TRIBUNALS

An *ad hoc* tribunal is one set up for a particular investigation only and having no permanent existence.

Public Inquiries [91]

A public local inquiry is required under many statutes for many different purposes but commonly to ascertain facts and local opinion, objections and grievances, so that a particular Minister or Department may be fully conversant with the state of local feeling in relation to certain proposals, such as a housing, town planning or development scheme, or with the opinions in a particular industry or trade, such as a proposed marketing scheme for some commodity.[92]

In Scotland the person appointed to hold the inquiry is frequently an experienced member of the Bar. The chief reporter is a full-time officer ranking as an under-secretary in the Scottish Office. Legal representation is allowed and evidence is led and submissions made very much as in a court of law. In England such inquiries are usually held by an official of the Department concerned. Hitherto the reports of the persons holding such inquiries have not been published.[93]

---

[84] See further, Solicitors' Discipline (Scotland) Committee Rules in *Parliament House Book*. See also *Solicitors' Discipline (Scotland) Committee v. B.*, 1942 S.C. 293; *X. v. Y.*, 1948 S.L.T.(Notes) 72; *E. v. T.*, 1949 S.L.T. 411; *Council of the Law Society of Scotland v. Docherty*, 1968 S.L.T. 133.

[85] Architects Registration Act 1938.

[86] Dentists Act 1956.

[87] Pharmacy Act 1954.

[88] Midwives (Scotland) Act 1951.

[89] Nurses (Scotland) Act 1951.

[90] Veterinary Surgeons Act 1966.

[91] See further, Robson, "Public Inquiries as an Instrument of Government" (1954) 1 B.J.A.L. 71.

[92] Whether the Minister is affected by anything in the report of the inquiry may be doubtful: see *Franklin v. Minister of Town and Country Planning* [1948] A.C. 87. As to procedure see *Hamilton v. Secretary of State for Scotland*, 1972 S.L.T. 233.

[93] See the observations of the Franks Committee on this (Report, paras. 344–345) and the Tribunals and Inquiries Act 1971, s. 12. Statutory inquiries are also under the supervision of the Council on Tribunals.

Tribunals of Inquiry

The Tribunals of Inquiry (Evidence) Act 1921 empowers Parliament, by resolution of both Houses, to establish an *ad hoc* tribunal to investigate any matter of urgent public importance. The purpose of such an inquiry is to investigate and report its findings, it being for Parliament to take any action thought fit. Such a tribunal has most of the powers of a court [94]; it usually sits in public and legal representation is allowed, and its report is usually published.[95]

Departmental Inquiries

A Minister may at any time institute an inquiry, frequently by a committee, into any matter which seems to him to require special investigation. The report is usually published. Thus the Secretary of State for Scotland set up a Departmental Committee to inquire into the law of succession in Scotland and propose changes, and this committee produced a valuable report [96] on which Parliament eventually took action.[97]

Fatal Accidents Inquiries

One of the commonest of the *ad hoc* tribunals is the Fatal Accidents Inquiry held to inquire into cases of death of a person engaged in any industrial employment or occupation due, or reasonably believed to be due, to accident occurring in the course of the employment or occupation,[98] and cases of sudden or suspicious death.[99] The inquiry is held before a sheriff principal or sheriff and a jury of seven, and the evidence is collected and presented by the procurator-fiscal. Persons interested may appear personally or by counsel or solicitor, take part in and lead evidence at the inquiry. These include the deceased's relatives, employer, fellow-employees, trade union representatives, and inspectors of mines or of factories. The inquiry is held in public and conducted on the lines of a criminal jury trial, the evidence being recorded. Parties may address the jury and the sheriff usually delivers a short charge indicating the form of verdict desired, after which the jury deliberate and return their verdict, by a majority or unanimously. The verdict may not be used in evidence

---

[94] As to power of punishing witnesses for contempt of court, see *Att.-Gen.* v. *Clough* [1963] 1 Q.B. 773; *Att.-Gen.* v. *Mulholland* [1963] 2 Q.B. 477.

[95] See, *e.g.* the " Lynskey " Inquiry into budget leaks (Cmd. 7616, 1949) and the " Parker " Inquiry into leakage of information about bank rate (Cmnd. 350, 1958), the " Waters " Inquiry into alleged assault on a boy by the police at Thurso (Cmnd. 718, 1959) and the " Vassall " Inquiry into offences under the Official Secrets Act (Cmnd. 2009, 1962) and generally, Keeton, *Trial by Tribunal*, and the Report of the Royal Commission on the Tribunals of Inquiry (Evidence) Act 1921 (Cmnd. 3121, 1966).

[96] Cmd. 8144, 1951.

[97] Succession (Scotland) Act 1964.

[98] Fatal Accidents Inquiry Act 1895.

[99] Fatal Accidents and Sudden Deaths Inquiry Act 1906.

or founded upon in subsequent civil or criminal proceedings arising out of the same accident and no witness may be required to answer questions tending to show him guilty of any crime or offence. Verdicts are usually in fairly formal terms and seldom include any finding of fault against anyone. They may include riders or recommendations as to the adoption of safety measures in future.

Department of Trade Shipping Inquiries

A sheriff may also have to hold an inquiry into the circumstances attending a shipping casualty[1] to answer questions raised by the Department of Trade. The sheriff sits with one or more nautical assessors, and parties may appear by counsel or solicitor. Department of Trade witnesses are heard, the questions in regard to the casualty and the conduct of the ship's officers on which the Department of Trade desires the court's opinion stated, and each party may be heard on the questions, and lead evidence thereon, the witnesses being subject to cross-examination and re-examination. After the evidence parties may address the court and then the Department of Trade representative may be heard in reply on the whole case. The judgment of the court is given in the form of answers to the questions proposed by the Department of Trade. Ship's officers, if in fault, may be penalised by having their certificates cancelled or suspended, and the sheriff reports his findings to the Department of Trade, with a confidential annexation setting out the circumstances, the court's opinion of the cause of the casualty and of the conduct of persons involved. A party found in fault may appeal to either Division of the Court of Session, which hears the appeal with nautical assessors, in the same way as an ordinary appeal from the sheriff court, and in certain circumstances the Department of Trade may direct a rehearing before the same court, or before a wreck commissioner or a judge of the Court of Session.

An analogous inquiry may be held by the sheriff with two assessors, sitting as a Court of Survey, in a dispute between a Department of Trade surveyor and a shipowner as to whether a ship is unsafe, unseaworthy or undermanned, or a passenger vessel so constructed as to be entitled to a passenger certificate.[2] The court may uphold or refuse the appeal and in either case reports to the Department of Trade.

Inquiry may also be ordered by the Department of Trade into the conduct of ship's officers, their incompetency, misconduct or failure in duties, and this may be held by a sheriff, or a person designated, or the local Marine Board.[3] The procedure is as in the case of an inquiry into a shipping casualty, and there is a report to the Department of Trade.

---

[1] Merchant Shipping Act 1894, ss. 466 (12), 479; Shipping Casualties Rules 1923.
[2] Merchant Shipping Act 1894, ss. 274–275, 459.
[3] *Ibid.* s. 471.

II.—ENGLAND

While the courts and legal system of England have no direct or immediate jurisdiction over transactions or legal problems arising entirely in and affecting Scotland only, the Scot may frequently have to consider whether legal action should or must be taken in England, while the references to English courts and procedure in legal books, documents and statutes are so common that he must be cognisant of the main features of the English system of courts and their respective competence in broad outline.[4]

CIVIL COURTS

Magistrates' Courts

A court of summary jurisdiction consisting of two or three justices of the peace has limited civil as well as substantial criminal jurisdiction.[5] They authorise recovery of certain civil debts such as income tax and electricity charges and may make adoption orders, affiliation orders in bastardy cases, grant judicial separation between husband and wife, grant a wife a maintenance order as well as exercising many ministerial functions particularly with regard to licensing. Domestic proceedings are heard separately from other business and the public is excluded.[6] Appeals in these cases generally lie to a Divisional Court of the Family Division, to the Court of Appeal and the House of Lords but certain appeals are heard by the Crown Court.

County Court

The main local courts for small causes are the county courts instituted in 1846.[7] England and Wales are divided into 63 circuits each with one or more circuit judges, formerly called county court judges.[8] These are full-time salaried judges who have had considerable experience at the Bar. Every judge of the Court of Appeal or High Court and every Recorder is, *ex officio*, capable of sitting as a judge for any county court district. County court judges hold courts regularly in the principal towns of the circuit, about 350 places in all.[9] They may sit with, but nearly always sit without, a jury of eight and have jurisdiction in actions founded on contract or tort where the claim does not exceed £1,000, and in certain other cases, and in cases under the Housing, Landlord and Tenant, and Rent Restriction Acts. Divorce jurisdiction has been conferred on certain designated county courts, to hear any undefended matrimonial cause.[10] They have no criminal jurisdiction.

---

[4] On these, see generally, Halsbury's *Laws of England*, tit. " Courts."
[5] The principal statute is the Magistrates' Courts Act 1952.
[6] Matrimonial Proceedings (Magistrates' Courts) Act 1960.
[7] For the modern jurisdiction, see County Courts Act 1959.
[8] The full title is His Honour Judge X, and they are addressed as Your Honour.
[9] For the circuits, judges and court towns, see the annual (English) *Law List*.
[10] Matrimonial Causes Act 1967, s. 1.

In the City of London the county court is called the Mayor's and City of London Court, replacing a special court of that name. The judge is known as the judge of the Mayor's and City of London Court.

The county court registrar has limited jurisdiction to try cases, subject to appeal to the circuit judge.

Appeal lies to the Court of Appeal on a matter of law, or, in cases involving the larger sums of money, on matters of fact or law except in bankruptcy matters, where appeal lies to a Divisional Court of the Chancery Division. The amount of work dealt with in the county courts is very great, as procedure is relatively simple and inexpensive. Both solicitors and counsel have the right of audience in county courts.

High Court

The superior civil courts are the High Court of Justice and the Court of Appeal which are both branches of the single Supreme Court of Judicature.[11] The High Court in 1875 replaced, and assumed the jurisdiction possessed by, the former separate Courts of King's Bench, Common Pleas, Exchequer, Chancery, Admiralty, and Probate, Divorce and Matrimonial Causes,[12] together with that of certain others, such as the Assize Courts and the Courts of Common Pleas at Lancaster and Durham, but excepting the Chancery Courts of the Counties Palatine of Lancaster and Durham. The High Court was for convenience divided in 1875 into five Divisions, Queen's Bench, Common Pleas, Exchequer, Chancery, and Probate, Divorce and Admiralty Division; in 1881 the first three were amalgamated into the Queen's Bench Division, and in 1971 the P.D. & A. Division was renamed the Family Division. Also in 1971 the Chancery Courts of the Counties Palatine of Lancaster and Durham were merged in the High Court. All Divisions are empowered to grant all remedies and to try all kinds of actions, but certain matters were originally assigned to each Division, corresponding roughly to the jurisdiction of the courts they had replaced, and in practice work is distributed among the Divisions according to subject-matter, the Queen's Bench dealing with actions of contract and tort, the recovery of land and commercial litigation, and Admiralty and prize jurisdiction, the Chancery Division with trusts, mortgages, wills and estates, partnership, companies and bankruptcy, contentious probate business, revenue matters, town and country planning and landlord and tenant cases, and the Family Division dealing with matrimonial causes, legitimacy, adoption, guardianship, maintenance orders and related topics. The Admiralty Court is

---

[11] The main Acts are the Judicature Acts 1873–75, substantially re-enacted by the Supreme Court of Judicature (Consolidation) Act 1925 and later amended in detail, notably by the Courts Act 1971. The Supreme Court also includes the Crown Court, which is the superior criminal court, on which see p. 258, *infra*.

[12] This is why pre-1875 English reports are of cases decided in one or other of these courts.

now part of the Queen's Bench Division. The Commercial Court, formerly only a list of cases dealt with by a particular judge, is now a part of the Queen's Bench Division, dealing with matters entered in the commercial list. A judge of the Commercial Court may, in a dispute of a commercial character, accept appointment as a sole arbitrator, or as umpire, under an arbitration agreement. In certain cases the jurisdictions of the Divisions overlap. There are no minimum or maximum pecuniary limits to High Court jurisdiction. The Divisions are staffed by judges [13] under the presidency respectively of the Lord Chief Justice of England (Q.B. Division), the Lord Chancellor [14] (who very seldom sits in the High Court at all, the working president of the Division being the Vice-Chancellor) (Chancery Division), and the President (Family Division). The main sittings are at the Royal Courts of Justice in the Strand, but the High Court may sit anywhere in England and Wales. The places at which the High Court and the Crown Court (for criminal business) sit regularly are divided into first tier, second tier and third tier centres. At the first tier centres the High Court and the Crown Court together exercise civil and criminal jurisdiction. At the second and third tier centres the Crown Court exercises criminal jurisdiction, the judges being respectively High Court and circuit court judges, and circuit court judges only.

Divisional Courts

Divisional Courts are constituted of such number of the judges of the Division as the president of the division with the concurrence of at least two other judges thinks expedient. The number is normally two.

A Divisional Court of the Queen's Bench Division is a tribunal of two or more judges of that Division which has a jurisdiction partly original and partly appellate. Its original jurisdiction includes the issue of the writ of habeas corpus and orders of certiorari, mandamus and prohibition, which are important in the judicial control of inferior courts and certain administrative bodies,[15] and the appellate jurisdiction covers the decision of questions of law raised by cases stated by magistrates' courts, the decision of appeals from the justices of the peace in landlord and tenant cases and certain other appeals from a judge sitting in chambers.

---

[13] The proper title is, *e.g.* Mr. Justice Smith, notwithstanding that on appointment they receive knighthoods, and the printed contraction is Smith J. The plural is, *e.g.* Smith and Jones JJ. A female High Court judge is known as Mrs. Justice X. Judges other than the heads of the three Divisions are known as " puisne " (pronounced " puny ") judges. The maximum number is now (1975) 75, but the number may be increased by Order. A Circuit judge or Recorder may be requested to sit as a judge of the High Court. For the current number and names of the judges, see the (English) *Law List.*

[14] This is a relic of the historical fact that the system of equity, which is the basis of the jurisdiction of the Chancery Division, was developed by successive Lord Chancellors in their courts of Chancery.

[15] See Griffith and Street, *Principles of Administrative Law*; de Smith, *Judicial Review of Administrative Action.*

The work of the Queen's Bench Divisional Court is, however, mainly criminal or administrative rather than civil.[16] A Divisional Court of the Chancery Division deals with appeals from county courts in bankruptcy matters, and a similar court of the Family Division hears appeals from magistrates' courts, in separation and maintenance orders and in certain other civil cases.

In all these civil cases there is an appeal from the Divisional Court to the Court of Appeal, and, with leave, to the House of Lords. There is no appeal from a decision on an application for a writ of habeas corpus or one of the other prerogative orders if the application arises out of a criminal cause or matter.

The Court of Appeal (Civil Division)

The Court of Appeal consists, apart from certain *ex officio* judges who rarely sit, of the Master of the Rolls and 14 Lords Justices of Appeal [17] sitting normally in four or five courts each of three judges [18]; the courts all have the same powers and are not related to particular subject-matter. A judge of the High Court may sit to make up a quorum and conversely a Lord Justice may sit as an extra judge in the High Court. The civil jurisdiction extends to hearing appeals from all Divisions of the High Court, county courts, the Restrictive Practices Court, the Lands Tribunal and certain local courts and various tribunals.[19] Further appeal lies to the House of Lords, but only with the leave of the Court of Appeal or of the House of Lords. For the great majority of cases the Court of Appeal is the final stage and its judgments command great respect as authoritative statements of the law of England.

House of Lords

The House of Lords as the supreme court of appeal from English courts in civil business is the same court and constituted in the same way as the House sitting as the supreme court of appeal from Scottish courts in civil business, and it acts subject to the same rules and conventions. Scottish Lords of Appeal may sit even for the hearing of English

---

[16] On this see p., 258 *infra*.

[17] The titles are, *e.g.* Lord Blank, Master of the Rolls, abbreviated as Blank M.R., and, *e.g.* Lord Justice Smith, printed as Smith L.J. The plural is, *e.g.* Smith and Jones L.JJ. They are appointed by the Queen on the recommendation of the Prime Minister and are sworn of the Privy Council. For the names of the present judges, see the (English) *Law List.*

[18] A " full court " of five or more members may hear appeals on novel or difficult points: see, *e.g. Young* v. *Bristol Aeroplane Co.* [1944] K.B. 718.

[19] On the work of the courts, see Lord Evershed M.R., *The Court of Appeal in England*; Asquith L.J., " Some Aspects of the Work of the Court of Appeal " (1950) 1 J.S.P.T.L.(N.S.) 350; Cohen L.J., " Jurisdiction, Practice and Procedure of the Court of Appeal " (1951) 11 Camb.L.J. 3.

appeals.[20] There is now, in certain circumstances, with the consent of all parties, a right of appeal direct from the High Court to the House of Lords, the so-called " leap-frog " appeal.[21]

COURTS OF SPECIAL JURISDICTION;
ADMINISTRATIVE COURTS AND TRIBUNALS;
ECCLESIASTICAL COURTS

Some of the special courts and many of the administrative tribunals found in Scotland are found also in England. In some cases there is no parallel and in other matters England has special courts of her own. These include a number of anomalous survivals of old local courts, distinct ecclesiastical courts, the jurisdiction of which is now limited to causes affecting the Church of England, and Coroners' Courts, which deal principally with ascertaining the causes of sudden deaths. Most of the Scottish administrative tribunals, domestic and *ad hoc* tribunals, have their English counterparts with corresponding jurisdiction.[22]

CRIMINAL COURTS

The essential distinction is into courts which may deal only with petty offences punishable on summary conviction (tried on information without a jury) and indictable offences, tried on indictment before a jury. Many criminal offences are of one kind or the other, but in some cases an offence, colloquially known as a " hybrid " offence, may be tried either on indictment or by summary proceedings. Summary trial requires the defendant's consent. Magistrates' courts deal with summary proceedings only. Judged by the number of cases dealt with, the magistrates' courts are by far the most important in the country, though the more serious crimes can be tried only by higher courts. All proceedings on indictment are brought before the Crown Court which, along with the Court of Appeal and the High Court, forms the Supreme Court of Judicature. Reorganisation of the courts in 1971 abolished the former courts of quarter sessions and assizes. In most cases there is no restriction on private prosecution but in practice most prosecutions are initiated and conducted by the police. The Director of Public Prosecutions is concerned with prosecutions in the more serious cases of indictable offences only.

---

[20] This gives rise to the complaint among English lawyers that Scottish Lords have sometimes mishandled the law of England. But it has to be remembered that the Scottish Law Lords are hardly ever in a majority in the House, particularly when dealing with English appeals, so that the chance of their ever affecting English law detrimentally is small.

[21] Adminstration of Justice Act 1969, ss. 12–16. For an example of its use see *Ealing London Borough* v. *Race Relations Board* [1972] 1 All E.R. 105. On the practice see Drewry, " Leapfrogging—and a Lords Justices' Eye View of the Final Appeal " (1973) 89 L.Q.R. 260.

[22] See generally Halsbury's *Laws of England*, tit. " Courts."

Magistrates' Courts

Justices of the peace are appointed in every county in England and Wales and the counties are divided into petty sessional divisions.[23] Certain persons are also *ex officio* justices. One such magistrate sitting alone has very limited powers; he may grant a prisoner bail, act as " examining justice " to determine whether to commit a prisoner for trial on indictment, or discharge him if there is insufficient evidence to justify committing him for trial, but he may not act as a court of trial. The function of the examining justice or justices is to conduct a preliminary inquiry to decide whether or not there is sufficient evidence against the accused to justify committing him for trial, and the justices must commit for trial if there is evidence on which a reasonable jury could convict. Only if there is no such evidence can the justices discharge him. If the offence is a hybrid one the examining justices must ask the defendant if he consents to summary trial. If he does not the court must commit him for trial on indictment or discharge him; if he consents the court will proceed to summary trial. If the offence is triable summarily but carries a maximum penalty of more than three months' imprisonment, the accused may claim the right to be tried by jury, in which case the court conducts the preliminary inquiry and commits or discharges the defendant.

A magistrates' court as a court of trial of offences tried summarily is constituted by from two to seven justices of the peace, one of whom acts as chairman, The court is assisted and advised by their legally qualified clerk. It tries criminal cases of minor importance, such as road traffic offences. The power of punishment is in general limited to six months' imprisonment and to a fine of £400. The court has power to commit the defendant to the Crown Court for sentence if it thinks the case warrants such disposal and in certain other cases.

Young persons charged with crimes other than homicide, needing care or protection, or truants, or beyond control are dealt with summarily in " care proceedings." [24]

Stipendiary and Metropolitan Magistrates

Cities may obtain the appointment of a legally qualified stipendiary magistrate who, sitting alone, has all the powers of a magistrates' court. He may also sit with, and act as chairman of, a bench of justices. In London there are a number of metropolitan stipendiary magistrates who sit in the various courts while additional acting magistrates may be appointed when there is pressure of business.

---

[23] The office of justice dates from 1361 in England, and is now regulated by the Justices of the Peace Act 1949. Jurisdiction and procedure are regulated by the Magistrates' Courts Act 1952 and rules made thereunder.

[24] Children and Young Persons Act 1969.

Appeals from Magistrates' Courts

Appeal lies at the instance of the accused to the Crown Court against conviction or sentence, or if he pleaded guilty, against sentence only. There is no right of appeal against a conviction or order unless it is specifically conferred by statute. For hearing an appeal the Crown Court is composed of a judge of the High Court, or a Circuit judge or Recorder sitting with at least two and not more than four justices of the peace. Where justices sit the decision of the court is by a majority, the regular judge having in case of equal division a casting vote.

Queen's Bench Divisional Court

A Divisional Court of the Queen's Bench Division, consisting of two or three judges of the Division, exercises appellate jurisdiction in respect of the proceedings of magistrates' courts by hearing and deciding cases stated on points of law for its opinion. Either prosecutor or defendant may ask for a case to be stated. The Divisional Court will hear counsel and may reverse, affirm or amend the determination of the lower court in respect of which the case was stated, or remit the matter to the justices with the court's opinion thereon, or make such other order as may seem just. Either party to any order, judgment or other decision of the Crown Court, other than one relating solely to trial on indictment, may also apply for a case to be stated to the Divisional Court on the ground that the decision is wrong in law or in excess of jurisdiction. The Divisional Court may deal with such an appeal in the same way as an appeal from a magistrates' court. In criminal matters the decision of the Divisional Court may be appealed by either party to the House of Lords, with the leave of that court or of the House of Lords, if a point of law of general public importance is involved in the decision and it appears that the point ought to be considered by the House.

The Crown Court

The Crown Court may sit at any place in England or Wales.[25] The judges are (a) all the judges of the High Court; (b) persons holding the office of Circuit judge or Recorder; and (c) a judge of the High Court, a Circuit judge or Recorder sitting with justices of the peace. A judge of the Court of Appeal may sit as a judge of the Crown Court at the request of the Lord Chancellor. Circuit judges must be barristers of ten years' standing or have held the office of Recorder for five years. They are capable *ex officio* of sitting as judge for any county court district.[26]

---

[25] It sits at about 90 centres, classified as first tier centres, where High Court and Circuit judges sit and where the High Court also takes civil business; second tier centres where High Court and Circuit court judges sit; and third tier centres where circuit judges and Recorders sit.

[26] Holders of various existing judicial offices abolished by the Court Act 1971, automatically became Circuit judges thereby.

Recorders are legally qualified persons (barristers or solicitors) appointed to act as part-time judges of the Crown Court for limited periods. Justices of the peace must sit in the Crown Court for the hearing of any appeal or of proceedings on committal by a magistrates' court to the Crown Court for sentence, but any jurisdiction or power of the Crown Court may be exercised by a regular judge sitting with not more than four justices.

For the purposes of trial in the Crown Court offences are classified [27] into (1) offences such as treason or murder, which must be tried by a High Court judge and jury; (2) offences such as manslaughter or rape, which must be tried by a High Court judge and jury unless a particular case is released by the High Court judge with special responsibility for the circuit; (3) all other indictable offences, which may be tried by a High Court judge or Circuit judge or Recorder, in each case with a jury, and (4) offences which may be tried either on indictment or summarily and which, if tried on indictment, will normally be tried by a circuit judge or recorder, in each case with a jury.

At the trial a jury is empanelled and evidence led, counsel address the jury and the presiding judge sums up. The jury give their verdict and, if the accused is found guilty on any part of the indictment, sentence is passed. The defendant may ask the court to take into consideration other offences still untried or even unknown.

Central Criminal Court

The Central Criminal Court, popularly known as the " Old Bailey," is a sitting of the Crown Court. Sessions are held at the Old Bailey in London four times a year, which in practice means continuous session, for the disposal of criminal cases from Greater London or committed on the high seas. The Lord Mayor and Aldermen of London may sit as judges with any judge of the High Court or Circuit judge or Recorder in this court but cases are tried by one of the judges of the High Court, the Recorder of London,[28] the Common Serjeant [28] or one of the judges of the Mayor's and City of London Court, always with a jury. A panel of counsel known as Treasury Counsel prosecute in cases directed by the Director of Public Prosecutions.

Court of Appeal (*Criminal Division*)

Prior to 1907 criminal appeals were heard by the Court for Crown Cases Reserved or by appeal by writ of error to the Queen's Bench Division. From 1907 to 1966 the Court of Criminal Appeal, consisting of the Lord Chief Justice and all the judges of the Queen's Bench

---

[27] Practice Note [1971] 3 All E.R. 829.
[28] These are ancient offices of the City of London and now rank as Circuit judges.

Division, heard appeals.[29] Since 1966 appeal against conviction on indictment lies to the Criminal Division of the Court of Appeal.[30] This is composed of the Lord Chief Justice and the Lords Justices of Appeal. The Lord Chief Justice may call on any judge of the Queen's Bench Division to sit as a member of the Criminal Division of the Court of Appeal. Two or more courts of the Criminal Division may sit simultaneously; each consists of three or a greater, uneven, number of judges usually including at least one judge of the Queen's Bench Division.[31] A " full court " of five or more judges may sit to hear especially difficult points, but has no wider powers than a normal court. Appeal may be brought by a person convicted on indictment against conviction, on any question of law, or under certain conditions on a question of fact, or a mixed question of fact and law, or against sentence. The court must allow an appeal if they think the verdict of the jury should be set aside on the ground that it is unsafe or unsatisfactory or that there was a material irregularity in the course of the trial, but may dismiss the appeal if they consider that no miscarriage of justice has actually occurred. The court may substitute a verdict of guilty of an alternative offence. It may reduce or vary the sentence passed. It may receive fresh evidence unavailable at the trial, quash the conviction and order a new trial. The Crown cannot appeal against an acquittal. Normally only one judgment is delivered by the court except in the case of a question of law where, in the presiding judge's opinion, it is convenient that separate judgments should be pronounced. Many of the judgments of this court are of great importance. The court acts also as Courts-Martial Appeal Court for England and Wales.

House of Lords

Any case brought on appeal to the Court of Appeal (Criminal Division) or a Divisional Court of the Queen's Bench Division in a criminal matter may be appealed by either prosecutor[32] or defendant to the House of Lords with the leave of the court below or of the House of Lords, if it is certified by the court below that a point of general public importance is involved and that court or the House gives leave on the ground that the point is one which ought to be considered by the House.[33] Appeal

---

[29] See Goddard, " The Working of the Court of Criminal Appeal " (1952) 2 J.S.P. T.L.(N.S.) 1; Knight, " The Court of Criminal Appeal and Binding Precedent " (1963) 113 L.J. 589.　　　　　　　　　　　　　　　　[30] Criminal Appeal Act 1966.

[31] A single judge may hear applications for leave to appeal.

[32] Thus in *D.P.P.* v. *Beard* [1920] A.C. 479, the Court of Criminal Appeal reduced a conviction of murder to one of manslaughter and the House of Lords restored it to one of murder. (The death penalty was not carried out.)

[33] Administration of Justice Act 1960, ss. 1–10. Cases heard under this provision include *Joyce* v. *D.P.P.* [1946] A.C. 347 (the trial of Lord Haw-Haw). Till 1960 appeal required the certificate of the Attorney-General that the decision involved a point of law of exceptional public importance. This was not always granted as a matter of course. The jurisdiction of the House of Lords in criminal cases is discussed in Blom-Cooper and Drewry, *Final Appeal*, Chap. 13.

lies also from the Courts-Martial Appeal Court for England and Wales under the same conditions. The House is constituted as for the hearing of civil appeals.

III.—NORTHERN IRELAND
CIVIL COURTS

The courts are in general organised on the English model. Resident magistrates hold courts for minor civil cases but the main inferior court is the county court which has a limited jurisdiction in common law, equity and probate matters. There are no juries. Appeals may be taken by way of civil bill appeal to a visiting judge of assize, when the case is reheard, or appeal may be made on a point of law to a Divisional Court of the Supreme Court.

The Supreme Court of Judicature of Northern Ireland consists of the High Court and the Court of Appeal.[34] The High Court is divided into a Queen's Bench Division, which also has probate, divorce and admiralty jurisdiction, and a Chancery Division, and there are circuit courts. Appeal lies to the Court of Appeal and a further appeal from the Court of Appeal to the House of Lords, and there is also an appeal on the constitutionality of a Northern Ireland statute to the Judicial Committee of the Privy Council, whose decision on such a point is binding on the House of Lords.

CRIMINAL COURTS

The resident magistrates, like stipendiary magistrates, try summary offences at petty sessions and also act as examining magistrates in more serious crimes. Lay magistrates have no criminal jurisdiction. Appeal lies from the petty sessional court to the county court. The county court judge in counties and the recorder in boroughs are also the chairmen of quarter sessions and, as such, sit with a jury to try all but the most serious indictable offences. There is a Director of Public Prosecutions who initiates criminal proceedings in certain circumstances.

The judges of the Supreme Court go on circuit to hold assizes (at which appeals from county courts are also heard) for the trial of serious crimes; appeal from assizes lies to the Court of Criminal Appeal, which consists of all the judges of the Supreme Court, with a further appeal to the House of Lords.

---

[34] The High Court consists of the Lord Chief Justice of Northern Ireland and not less than two nor more than four puisne judges, and the Court of Appeal of the Lord Chief Justice and three Lords Justices of Appeal. The puisne judges may be called on to serve as extra judges of the Court of Appeal, and the three Lords Justices of Appeal frequently sit in the High Court and go on assize. See further, MacDermott, " The Supreme Court of Northern Ireland—Two Unusual Jurisdictions " (1954) 2 J.S.P.T.L.(N.S.) 201, and " Law and Practice in Northern Ireland," 10 N.I.L.Q. 47.

IV.—JUDICIAL COMMITTEE OF THE PRIVY COUNCIL

This body [35] consists of the Lord Chancellor, the Lord President of the Council, ex-Lords President, the Lords of Appeal in Ordinary and all Privy Councillors who hold or have held high judicial office in the United Kingdom together with certain distinguished colonial judges. In practice the Lords of Appeal in Ordinary usually sit so that the judicial composition of this body is very much the same as that of the House of Lords. Appeals are heard at the bar of the Privy Council by at least three and usually five members of the Judicial Committee, who sit unrobed. The Committee is still in theory a branch of the Privy Council so that its decisions are tendered, not as judgments, but in the form of humble advice to Her Majesty to allow or dismiss an appeal. By convention this advice is accepted and implemented by an Order in Council. Till recently dissents were not voiced and only one opinion was delivered, but dissenting opinions may now be delivered in open court. [36]

It is not a court of appeal in the usual way from the United Kingdom but only in certain matters from the English ecclesiastical courts, from the Admiralty Court of the Queen's Bench Division of the High Court in prize cases, from the courts of the Channel Islands and the Isle of Man, and in certain constitutional matters from Northern Ireland. Any other disputed matter may be referred to it by the Crown for hearing and opinion. [37]

As an appellate court it hears appeals from the Dominions and colonies, a jurisdiction now considerably reduced since many parts of the Commonwealth, on attaining independence, have abolished appeals to the Privy Council from their own Supreme Courts. [38] The Privy Council does not consider it proper to interfere with the decision of the High Court of a Commonwealth country on a matter of policy, such as whether or not to follow a previous decision, as opposed to substantive law, when the High Court sitting in its own country, is better qualified than the Privy Council to assess the effect of its decision and the national attitude in the country concerned. [39] Nevertheless in view of the personal eminence of its judges, decisions of the Judicial Committee are entitled to careful consideration in so far as they seem relevant to any matter of United Kingdom law. Their authority is, however, never more than highly persuasive.

---

[35] It is regulated by the Judicial Committee Acts 1833 and 1844, the Appellate Jurisdiction Acts 1876–1947 and other statutes. See also, Normand, " Judicial Committee of the Privy Council " (1950) 3 C.L.P. 1.

[36] Judicial Committee (Dissenting Opinions) Order in Council 1966. See *e.g. Madzimbamuto* v. *Lardner-Burke* [1968] 3 All E.R. 561.

[37] *e.g. Re Macmanaway* [1951] A.C. 161.

[38] *Cf. Att.-Gen. for Ontario* v. *Att.-Gen. for Canada* [1947] A.C. 127.

[39] *Geelong Harbour Trust* v. *Gibbs Bright and Co.* [1974] 2 W.L.R. 507.

V.—THE EUROPEAN COURT

The Court of Justice of the European Communities sitting at Luxembourg consists of nine judges appointed by agreement among the member states for renewable six-year terms. The judges themselves elect the President of the Court from among themselves for renewable three-year terms. The Court is assisted by four Advocates-General who must possess the same qualifications as the judges and whose function is, acting impartially and independently, to make reasoned submissions in open court on cases brought before the Court, to assist the Court in the performance of its functions.[40]

The Court's function is to ensure that, in the interpretation and application of the Community Treaties, the law is observed. It may hear a complaint made by the Commission on its own initiative, or by a member state (which must first bring the matter before the Commission), that another member state has failed to fulfil any obligation under the Treaties. It has jurisdiction to review the legality of acts of the Council and the Commission, other than recommendations and opinions. Actions for such review may be initiated by the Council or by the Commission, by a member state, or by any person in respect of a decision addressed to him, and the Court may declare the act concerned to be void. It also has jurisdiction to give preliminary rulings on the interpretation of the Treaties, the validity and interpretation of acts of the Community institutions and the interpretation of the statutes of bodies established by an act of the Council. A court or tribunal of a member state, if any such question is raised before it and it considers that a decision on the question is *necessary* before it can give judgment, may request the Court to give a ruling thereon.[41] A court or tribunal must do so if it exercises final jurisdiction under national law.[42] The Court also has jurisdiction in disputes between member states relating to the subject matter of the Treaties if the dispute is submitted under a special agreement between the parties and in various other cases.

An institution whose act has been declared void or whose failure to act has been declared by the Court to be contrary to the Treaties must take the necessary measures to comply with the Court's judgment. Judgments of the Court are enforceable by the courts of the countries concerned and enforcement may be suspended only by a decision of the Court.

In United Kingdom courts judicial notice must be taken of any decision of, or expression of opinion by, the Court on any question as to the mean-

---

[40] On the functions of the Advocates-General see Warner, " The Role of the Advocate-General " (1975) 20 J.L.S.S. 47.

[41] See *e.g. Bulmer* v. *Bollinger* [1974] 2 All E.R. 1226; *Van Duyn* v. *Home Office* [1974] 3 All E.R. 178. The trial judge has complete discretion to refer or not to refer. Guidelines for the exercise of his discretion are set out in *Bulmer, supra.*

[42] Hence in a case raising interpretation or validity of a European Communities Treaty the House of Lords *must* refer it to the European Court; see *Bulmer, supra.*

ing or effect of any of the Treaties or the validity, meaning or effect of any Community instrument. For the purpose of proceedings in any United Kingdom court, any such question must be treated as a matter of law and, if not referred to the European Court, be treated as a question of law in accordance with the principles laid down by any relevant decision of the Court.[43] " That court is moulding the law of Europe into a single whole which every country of the nine must obey." [44]

The important distinction in practice is between interpreting a provision of the Treaties, the supreme tribunal for which is the European Court, and applying the treaties to a case arising, which remains the function of Scottish and English courts, which have to find the facts, state the issues in dispute, give judgment and see that the judgment is enforced.[45]

VI.—THE PARLIAMENTARY COMMISSIONER

The Parliamentary Commissioner for Administration is not a judge nor does he hold a court but he should be considered in the context of courts and tribunals as his function is equally to provide redress for grievances. The office was created by the Parliamentary Commissioner Act 1967 on the general model of that of the Ombudsman of the Scandinavian countries.[46] Under the Act the Queen may appoint a person to be Parliamentary Commissioner for Administration. He may not be a member of the House of Commons, nor of either House of the Parliament of Northern Ireland, but is *ex officio* a member of the Council on Tribunals and of the Scottish Committee thereof.

He may investigate any action [47] taken by or on behalf of any of the government departments or other authorities listed in Schedule 2 to the Act,[48] including the Ministers, members or officers of that department or authority, being action taken in the exercise of administrative functions of that department or authority, in any case where (a) a written complaint is made to a member of the House of Commons by a member of the public who claims to have sustained injustice in consequence of maladministration [49] in connection with the action so taken, and (b) the complaint is referred, with the complainer's consent, to the Commissioner by a member of the House with a request to conduct an investigation thereon. The Commissioner is not, however, to conduct an investigation

---

[43] *Bulmer, supra,* 1237.

[44] *Application des Gaz* v. *Falks Veritas* [1974] 3 All E.R. 51, 57, *per* Lord Denning M.R.

[45] *Bulmer, supra,* 1232.

[46] On these, see Rowat, *The Ombudsman.*

[47] " Action " includes failure to act: 1967 Act, s. 12 (1).

[48] The list may be amended. As framed the list does not include all the central government departments, and does not include public corporations or local authorities or departments thereof.

[49] Not defined by the Act.

in respect of any action in respect of which the aggrieved person has or had a right of appeal, reference or review to or before a tribunal, or a remedy by way of proceedings in any court of law, unless he is satisfied that in the particular circumstances it was not reasonable to expect the complainer to have resorted to it, and he may not investigate any of the actions or matters described in Schedule 3 to the Act.[50] He may use his own discretion whether to initiate, continue or discontinue any investigation.

Complaints may be made by any individual or body of persons, but not by local authorities or bodies constituted for the public service, or by a personal representative or member of the aggrieved person's family, and must be made to a member of the House of Commons within twelve months of the date when the person first had notice of the matters alleged in his complaint. Investigations are to be conducted in private in such manner as the Commissioner thinks fit, and he has wide powers of calling for information and witnesses. Where the Commissioner investigates or decides not to investigate he must report the results to a member of the House of Commons, and where he has investigated he must report to the head of the department or authority concerned. If after investigation it appears to the Commissioner that injustice has been done to the person aggrieved in consequence of maladministration and that the injustice has not been, or will not be, remedied, he may lay before each House of Parliament a special report on the case. He must report annually to Parliament on the performance of his functions generally.

Nothing in the Act authorises or requires the Commissioner to question the merits of a decision taken without maladministration by a government department or other authority in the exercise of a discretion vested in it.

Health Service Commissioner for Scotland

Under the National Health Service (Scotland) Act 1972, Pt. VII, there is a Health Service Commissioner for Scotland, a salaried officer who may not be an M.P. but may be the same person as the Parliamentary Commissioner. He may investigate any action taken by or on behalf of health authorities where a complaint is made that a person claims to have sustained injustice or hardship in consequence of maladministration in connection with the action so taken or in consequence of a failure in a service or in consequence of having been unfairly or unreasonably treated. Excluded are matters in respect of which there is a right of appeal or review before a tribunal, or a remedy by way of court proceedings, and

---

[50] These include matters involving the royal prerogative, the commencement or conduct of civil or criminal proceedings before any court in the United Kingdom, matters relating to contractual or other commercial transactions of a department or authority, and matters relating to the armed forces.

certain specified kinds of matters.[51] Procedure for complaints is laid down and the results of an investigation must be reported to the complainer, the body investigated, the person complained against and the Secretary of State. The Commissioner must also make a general report annually.

Commissioner for Local Administration in Scotland

Under the Local Government (Scotland) Act 1975, Part II, there is a Commissioner for Local Administration in Scotland who may investigate complaints in relation to local authorities, committees and joint committees and other specified bodies by a member of the public who claims to have suffered injustice in consequence of maladministration in the exercise of the authority's administrative functions. Certain matters are excepted. He investigates privately and reports to the complainer and to the authority, The report is normally made public, and he makes an annual report.

VII.—ARBITRATION

Arbitration is the submission by parties of any controversy or matter in dispute between them to the decision of a third party.[52] Reference to arbitration is commonly contractual, where the parties bind themselves by contract to refer disputes of any particular kind arising between them to the decision of a particular third person. The reference may also be made by a statutory provision that disputes arising in certain specified circumstances are to be determined not by resort to the courts but by arbitration. Thus the Workmen's Compensation Acts provided for disputes as to compensation between employer and employee being decided by the sheriff-substitute as arbitrator. Under the Agricultural Holdings (Scotland) Act 1949, questions and differences between landlord and tenant of an agricultural holding arising out of the tenancy fall to be determined by arbitration. Again the reference may be made by deed, expressing the agreement of parties to have their dispute decided by a person as arbiter rather than by the ordinary courts.

The advantages of arbitration are that in many cases the reference may be to an expert in the subject-matter of dispute, the procedure can be less formal and suited to the controversy, and not bound by rules of court procedure, that the issue may be determined more quickly than in the courts, and in private. The expense, however, may be greater in that the arbiter and his clerk have to be remunerated, while counsel and solicitors are required as for a court and witnesses may have to be called

---

[51] 1972 Act, s. 45 and Sched. 5.

[52] Questions of crime, personal status and issues involving the public interest cannot be the subject-matter of arbitration. Apart from that practically any issue can be referred to arbitration, though contractual and commercial issues are the commonest topics.

as to a court. Nevertheless commercial men frequently prefer quick arbitration by an expert to the lengthy process of a court action and various chambers of commerce and professional and trade associations have established arbitration panels to deal with disputes arising in their trade or business.

Effect of Submission

The effect of the contractual or statutory submission of any matter to arbitration is that the jurisdiction of the ordinary courts is excluded as to that matter, and if one party does appeal to the courts, the other may object; the court will decline to consider the merits of the dispute and will sist the action to await the result of the arbitration.[53] In case of doubt as to the interpretation of the reference, it is for the court to decide,[54] as a problem of the interpretation of the deed or statute in question, whether the dispute is one covered by the reference to arbitration or not, in which case the court may proceed to deal with the merits of the dispute. The scope of the submission depends on the terms used; it may be of specified or incidental matters only or of all questions arising between those parties out of their contract. If one party repudiates the contract completely, that does not exclude the jurisdiction of the arbiter if there was a reference to arbitration of all questions that may arise under the contract, and it will be for the arbiter to say whether the repudiation was justified or not. But the arbiter's jurisdiction will be excluded if the contract referred only specified matters to arbitration.[55]

Who may Arbitrate

Parties may submit their disputes to the arbitration of whomever they care to name. It is competent [56] in the contract to provide for arbitration by a specified and named person, or by the holder for the time being of a particular office, or by a person nominated by the holder for the time being of a particular office, or by a person designated in any similar way. Sometimes the reference is to a sole arbiter, or to two arbiters, one chosen by each party, in which case the two arbiters have power, unless there is provision to the contrary, to appoint an oversman. If the parties cannot agree as to the choice of a single arbiter, or if one party does not nominate an arbiter where the reference is to two, the court may make an appointment on the application of any party interested.[57] So too the court may appoint an oversman if the two

---

[53] *Hamlyn* v. *Talisker Distillery* (1894) 21 R.(H.L.) 21.

[54] See, *e.g. Brodie* v. *Ker*, 1952 S.C. 216.

[55] *Sanderson* v. *Armour*, 1922 S.C.(H.L.) 117; *Heyman* v. *Darwins* [1942] A.C. 356; *Mauritzen* v. *Baltic Shipping Co.*, 1948 S.C. 646.

[56] Prior to the Arbitration (Scotland) Act 1894, the rule was that reference to an unnamed arbiter was not binding.

[57] Arbitration (Scotland) Act 1894, ss. 1–3.

arbiters cannot agree in nominating one.[58] The person designated must be fair and unbiased, and have no interest in the subject-matter in dispute or in the outcome of the arbitration. He may stipulate for a fee and a man acting in a matter involving his professional knowledge and experience is in practice recognised as entitled to a fee.

Powers of Arbiter

In statutory arbitrations the powers of the arbiter, including any matter of appeal to the courts from his decision, are regulated by the relevant statute. In non-statutory arbitrations the decision of the arbiter, or of the oversman if two arbiters differ, is final both on questions of fact and of law. An arbiter has no power to find either party liable in damages unless there is express provision for that,[59] and he has no power to enforce his decision by civil diligence, though it is usual to insert in deeds providing for arbitration a clause consenting to the registration for preservation and execution of the award, and diligence may in such a case proceed on an extract of the award from the register. If there is no such clause, an action in court for decree conform is necessary. An arbiter has an implied power to award expenses.

FURTHER READING

Scottish Courts
Dobie: *Sheriff Court Practice.*
Gibb: *Law from Over the Border.*
Hannay: *The College of Justice.*
Mackay: *Practice of the Court of Session.*
Maclaren: *Court of Session Practice.*
Renton and Brown: *Criminal Procedure.*

English Courts
Archer: *The Queen's Courts.*
Blom-Cooper and Drewry: *Final Appeal.*
Cornish: *The Jury.*
Devlin: *The Criminal Prosecution in England.*
　　　　Trial by Jury.
Halsbury's *Laws of England*, tit. " Courts."
Holdsworth: *History of English Law*, Vol. 1.
Jackson: *The Machinery of Justice in England.*
Plucknett: *Concise History of the Common Law.*
Potter: *Historical Introduction to English Law.*
Radcliffe and Cross: *The English Legal System.*
Walker and Walker: *The English Legal System.*

---

[58] *Ibid.* s. 4.
[59] *Mackay & Son* v. *Leven Police Commissioners* (1893) 20 R. 1093.

Special Courts and Administrative Tribunals
Allen: *Law and Orders.*
           Administrative Jurisdiction.
Bell: *Tribunals in the Social Services.*
Denning: " Courts and Tribunals " (1954) 1 B.J.Adm.L. 107.
Forster: " The Industrial Court " (1954) 1 B.J.Adm.L. 35.
Hene: " Domestic Tribunals of Great Britain " (1956) 2 B.J.Adm.L. 24.
Mitchell: " Domestic Tribunals and the Courts " (1956) 2 B.J.Adm.L. 80.
Robson: *Justice and Administrative Law.*
de Smith: *Judicial Review of Administrative Action.*
Street: *Justice in the Welfare State.*
Wraith and Hutcheson: *Administrative Tribunals.*

CHAPTER 8

THE PERSONNEL OF THE LAW

THE personnel of the law comprise many classes and grades of persons all concerned with some function of administering justice through law.

The Judiciary

The office of judge is one of great honour and dignity as well as of immense constitutional and legal importance, and calls for the noblest moral and mental qualities and the highest standards of intelligence, scholarship and diligence.

The judicial function

The judicial function is to apply principles and rules of law to issues brought before the court or tribunal to the effect of deciding the issue and ordering the legal consequences, remedy, penalty or other. In case of doubt or dispute this frequently involves determining what principle or rule applies and what in the circumstances it means and directs or forbids or authorises. In many cases also the judicial function involves exercising discretion, in determining what it seems right to do in the circumstances.

The College of Justice

The College of Justice in Scotland, established in 1532, comprises the judges of the Court of Session, who are designated Senators of the College, and advocates, Writers to the Signet, clerks of session, keepers of the rolls, macers and certain other persons, who are members of the College.[1] The judges and sheriffs principal are invariably, and sheriffs are usually, chosen from among the senior advocates, but on appointment to the Bench, apart from temporary appointments as sheriff, members of the judiciary become public officers and cease to be practising members of the legal profession, though they do not relinquish their membership of their professional organisation.

Appointment as a judge of the Court of Session and a Lord Commissioner of Justiciary is made [2] by selection from the practising bar, usually of a

---

[1] See further, Mackay's *Practice*, Chap. 3. Though designated Senators of the College of Justice the judges are officially addressed, *e.g.* in petitions, as Lords of Council and Session, a title reflecting the origins of the court. The Law Society of Scotland and its members are not members of the College of Justice: see *Law Society of Scotland*, 1955 S.L.T.(Lyon Ct.) 2.

[2] The appointment is made by the Queen on the nomination of the Prime Minister, who doubtless consults the Secretary of State for Scotland and the Lord Advocate. The Lord Advocate may, and frequently does, propose himself for promotion to the Bench.

Law Officer or ex-Law Officer or senior Advocate-Depute or the Dean or Vice-Dean of the Faculty of Advocates.[3] The person appointed has frequently had previous judicial experience as a part-time sheriff principal; there seem, at least in modern times, to be no instances of the promotion of a sheriff [4] still less of an academic jurist.[5] The judges are accorded the courtesy title of Lord ——, the title being either taken from their estates or, more frequently today, merely their family names. They are not peers [6] nor are they knighted on appointment.[7] A judge may, however, have been knighted previously for public services. There is now a retiring age of seventy-five.[8] All judges have the same rank and title and promotion to the Inner House from the Outer House is by seniority on a vacancy occurring and no judge is appointed direct or promoted to the Inner House over his brethren,[9] except in the cases of the chairs of the two divisions.

The Lord President presides in the First Division. Since 1830 the formerly separate offices of Lord President and of Lord Justice-General of Scotland have been held by the same person. The latter office under the name of Justiciar goes back to the thirteenth century. The Lord Justice-

---

[3] Of the present (1975) twenty, eight had held the offices of Lord Advocate or Solicitor-General; four of Dean of Faculty; and eight were promoted from the senior Bar, and of these several had previously been Advocates-Depute. Two were serving with the Scottish Law Commission when appointed to the Bench.

[4] T. D. King Murray was a sheriff-substitute but later returned to practice and took silk. In 1938 he became Chairman of the Scottish Land Court as Lord Murray. He resigned in 1941, became Solicitor-General and became a judge of the Court of Session in 1945 as Lord Birnam. H. S. Wilson was a sheriff-substitute but resigned in 1965 to become Solicitor-General and later (1967) Lord Advocate. He was made a Life Peer in 1969. In 1970 on a change of government he resumed duty as a sheriff-substitute and in 1972 became Director of the Scottish Courts Administration. In 1975 he became sheriff principal of Glasgow and Strathkelvin. Now that, since 1975, all sheriffs principal and sheriffs (except temporary sheriffs) are full-time judges, it remains to be seen whether any are ever promoted to the Court of Session; it would be a good thing if some persons with substantial experience of the sheriff court were promoted. In England several county court judges have been promoted to the High Court, including Mrs. Elizabeth Lane, the first lady to be either a county court or a High Court judge.

[5] There were one or two cases of this in the eighteenth century but in those days professorships were not full-time posts. Appointment of an academic jurist has occasionally been made in America, Canada and elsewhere.

[6] A judge may be made a peer, before or after promotion to the Bench, but he does not become one by becoming a judge. Judges promoted to be Lords of Appeal in Ordinary, *i.e.* to the House of Lords, receive a life peerage, and occasionally a Lord of Session receives a peerage; instances are Lord President Balfour (1899–1905), created Lord Kinross, in 1902, Lord President Cooper (1947–55), created Lord Cooper of Culross in 1954, and Lord Wheatley (1954–) created a life peer in 1970. Interlocutors and correspondence are signed by the judges in their personal names unless they have been made peers. An index of territorial titles of judges is in Grant: *The Faculty of Advocates in Scotland*, 1532–1943 (Sc. Record Socy.) and in Brunton and Haig, *Senators of the College of Justice*, Appendix. The courtesy title of Lady was conferred on judges' wives and widows only by Royal Warrant of 1905, which also allowed retired judges to continue to use the style of, *e.g.* The Honourable Lord Blank.

[7] All English judges are knighted on appointment to the High Court bench.

[8] Judicial Pensions Act 1959.

[9] In these respects the court differs markedly from the High Court and Court of Appeal in England.

Clerk ranks next to the Lord President in judicial status and presides in the Second Division. His title is derived from the office of Clerk and assessor to the criminal court prior to 1663, when the Justice-Clerk was added to the judges. In 1672 when the Court of Justiciary was instituted the Justice-Clerk was made the deputy of the Justice-General. Appointment as Lord President [10] or Lord Justice-Clerk [11] is usually made direct from the Bar, usually by the promotion of a Law Officer.[10,11] Only occasionally has the Lord Justice-Clerk been promoted Lord President [12] and it is rare for a judge already on the Bench to be promoted Lord President or Lord Justice-Clerk.[13]

The two places among the Lords of Appeal in Ordinary usually filled by Scottish lawyers are filled by the Queen on the advice of the Prime Minister. They are normally filled by promotion from the Court of Session Bench, from the office of Lord President [14] or from the Inner House [15] or Outer House,[16] but may be filled by promotion direct from the Bar.[17] They must now retire at seventy-five.[18]

Since 1800 only four out of 47 holders of the office of Lord Advocate have failed to ascend the bench of the Court of Session or go to the House of Lords, and only a few of those holders of the office of Solicitor-General for Scotland who did not later become Lord Advocate have failed to do so.

---

[10] Thus in the present century Alexander Ure, Lord Strathclyde (1913–20), was Lord Advocate 1909–13; James Avon Clyde (1920–35) was Lord Advocate 1916–20 and also Dean of the Faculty of Advocates; Wilfrid Guild Normand (1935–47) was Lord Advocate 1933–35; Thomas Mackay Cooper (1947–54) was Lord Advocate 1935–41 and Lord Justice-Clerk 1941–47; James Latham Clyde (1955–72) was Lord Advocate 1951–55. A list of Lords President is in *Introduction to Scottish Legal History*, Appx. 2, and 1972 S.L.T.(News) 233.

[11] *e.g.* L.J.C. Aitchison (1933–41) was Lord Advocate 1929–33; L.J.C. Cooper (1941–47) was Lord Advocate 1935–41; L.J.C. Moncrieff (1947) was promoted from the Bench; L.J.C. Thomson (1947–62) was Lord Advocate 1945–47; L.J.C. Grant (1962–72) was Lord Advocate 1960–62; L.J.C. Wheatley (1972–) had been a Lord of Session since 1954. A list of Lords Justice-Clerk is in *Introduction to Scottish Legal History*, Appx. 3, and 1972 S.L.T.(News) 233. See also, Malcolm, " The Lord Justice-Clerk of Scotland " (1915) 27 J.R. 342, 375.

[12] The only instances are: Thomas Miller of Barskimming and Glenlee (L.J.C. 1766–87, L.P. 1787–89); Charles Hope (L.J.C. 1804–11, L.P. 1811–41); David Boyle (L.J.C. 1811–41, L.P. 1841–52); John Inglis (L.J.C. 1858–67, L.P. 1867–91); T. M. Cooper (L.J.C. 1941–47, L.P. 1947–55).

[13] Duncan McNeill (later Lord Colonsay) was appointed in 1851, promoted Lord President in 1852 and elevated to the House of Lords as Lord Colonsay in 1867; Alexander Moncrieff, appointed in 1926, was promoted Lord Justice-Clerk in 1947. He retired later in the same year. George Emslie was appointed in 1970 and promoted Lord President in 1972. John Wheatley was appointed in 1954 and promoted Lord Justice-Clerk in 1972.

[14] *e.g.* Lord Robertson (1899); Lord Dunedin (1913); Lord Normand (1947).

[15] *e.g.* Lord Keith (1953); Lord Fraser (1975).

[16] *e.g.* Lord Guest (1961); Lord Kilbrandon (1971).

[17] *e.g.* Lord Gordon (1876); Lord Watson (1880); Lord Shaw (1909); Lord Thankerton (1929); Lord Macmillan (1930); Lord Reid of Drem (1948); he was then Dean of Faculty and an M.P., and had previously been Lord Advocate, 1941–45.

[18] Judicial Pensions Act 1959.

These offices are political appointments given, save exceptionally, to supporters or at least adherents of the party in power, though it is fair to say that promotions of Law Officers or ex-Law Officers have not always been made by their own party. Since 1800 only six out of 45 holders of the office of Dean of Faculty have not attained the Bench, though only a few of the holders of the office of Vice-Dean have done so. As these offices are filled by election by the Faculty of Advocates, this road to the Bench is a means whereby professional standing and esteem among his peers are recognised in judicial appointments.

It is apparent that promotion to the Bench is commonly the reward for political service or support, and there is too little chance of promotion to the Bench for the advocate who is politically inactive, unless he should attain the office of Dean or Vice-Dean of Faculty, though it is undeniable that the system has brought to the offices of Lord President and Lord Justice-Clerk and to the Bench some outstanding lawyers whose contributions to the development of Scots law have been of permanent value. Some others have been merely adequate and legal ability does not always reach the Bench.[19]

Appointment as a sheriff principal is made from Q.C.s or advocates or sheriffs of at least ten years' standing, and as sheriff from Q.C.s, advocates or solicitors of at least ten years' standing. Sheriffs principal are sometimes transferred from one sheriffdom to another and sheriffs are sometimes moved from one town to another. Retirement of full-time sheriffs principal and sheriffs on pension is now compulsory at seventy-two.[20]

Women are eligible for all judicial appointments equally with men. In England Mrs. Elizabeth Lane became the first lady county court judge and later (1965) the first lady High Court judge: she is known as Mrs. Justice Lane. In Scotland Miss M. H. Kidd Q.C. became the first lady part-time Sheriff Principal in 1960, and Miss I. L. Sinclair Q.C. the first lady full-time sheriff in 1965. No lady has yet attained the Court of Session Bench.

Stipendiary magistrates and justices of the peace

Stipendiary magistrates are appointed by a local authority from among qualified legal practitioners. Justices of the Peace are appointed by the Secretary of State for Scotland on the recommendation of local committees; they need have no qualifications.[21]

---

[19] See also, Wilton, " The Scottish Judiciary " (1923) 35 J.R. 73; Willock " Scottish Judges Scrutinised," 1969 J.R. 193; " The Judiciary " 1972 S.L.T.(News) 217; Campbell, " Judicial Selection and Judicial Impartiality " 1973 J.R. 255. For personal memories see Lord Walker, " The Scottish Judiciary in the first half of the Twentieth Century," 1968 S.L.T.(News) 9.

[20] Sheriffs' Pensions (Scotland) Act 1961.

[21] District Courts (Scotland) Act 1975, ss. 5, 9.

Legal Practitioners

In Scotland the legal profession is sharply divided into advocates and solicitors,[22] each body having exclusive functions, rights and privileges in certain respects and concurrent functions and rights in others. While an individual may move from the one branch to the other, no one may belong to or practise simultaneously in both.[23] The two branches of the profession have developed separately[24] and each has its own governing body, qualifications for entry, *esprit de corps* and etiquette. As compared with countries where the legal profession is undivided, the terms " counsel " (both denoting the singular and as a collective noun) and " the Bar " are properly used in United Kingdom countries of advocates and their counterparts only, and not of the whole legal profession.

The distinction between the two branches is broadly that between the specialist or consultant, particularly in relation to possible or actual litigation, or other disputed issue, and the general adviser. The advocate specialises in advice on complicated issues of law, the framing of pleadings and the conduct of proceedings, oral and written, before courts and tribunals on behalf of the client. In England to a substantial extent, but in Scotland to a much lesser extent, particular counsel specialise in particular branches of law and acquire reputations for expertise in those areas of law. The solicitor alone comes into personal contact with the client and concerns himself generally with advice, business negotiations, commercial work such as the formation of companies, taxation questions, conduct of the legal formalities relating to the sale and transfer of property, the drawing up of wills, and pleading in the inferior courts as well as much preliminary work in cases coming before superior courts. The solicitor is to a large extent the general legal practitioner, the primary adviser, the negotiator and the man of business, whereas the advocate is called in in cases of difficulty, for advice in tricky or important business, and in all cases where there is litigation of any consequence in prospect or in train.[25] The two branches of the profession call for slightly different training, and appeal to different types of men. The advocate has to be the legal expert, the quick thinker, the fluent and persuasive debater, usually involved in matters of controversy, whereas the solicitor has much more routine work to do and spends much time in consulting clients, negotiating and carrying through business, frequently non-contentious, and attending to everyday affairs.

---

[22] This division of the profession is not found in the U.S.A. nor in some Commonwealth countries. It is arguable whether division or fusion is theoretically better: see Sweet, " Fusion in the Legal Profession " (1890) 2 J.R. 147; Walker, " Fusion of the Profession " (1956) 72 S.L.R. 25; Jackson, *Machinery of Justice in England*, Chap. 4.

[23] It is, of course, also incompetent to be a Scottish solicitor and an English barrister simultaneously and vice versa, though one may be enrolled simultaneously in the *same* branch of the profession in two or more countries of the United Kingdom.

[24] See further, Henderson Begg, *Treatise on Law Agents*, Chap. 1.

[25] The distinction is not unlike that between medical specialist or consultant, particularly connected with a hospital, and general medical practitioner.

Many solicitors are employed by other solicitors, by local authorities, and by large commercial and industrial concerns, to attend to business having legal connections and implications.

Advocates

The Faculty of Advocates [26] is the Scottish Bar and members of Faculty have a status and function corresponding to that of barrister in England or Northern Ireland.[27] With the exception of a party to the cause, the only person permitted to appear and plead a case in the superior courts in Scotland is an advocate.[28] They also have the right, equally with barristers, to appear before the House of Lords, Privy Council and Parliamentary Committees. Advocates and barristers are not, however, interchangeable in that neither may in general appear before the courts of the other country unless he has qualified in the other system of law and been called to the Bar in the other country also.[29] Advocates have the right of audience, unless it is expressly excluded by statute, before every court, civil, criminal and ecclesiastical, and before all courts of special jurisdiction, tribunals, and quasi-judicial bodies in Scotland. In the inferior courts, however, and before special tribunals the right of audience is concurrent with that of solicitors. Most papers and pleadings in the Court of Session must be signed by counsel; the most important exception is a summons, which is signed by a solicitor, but it is customary to have all papers and pleadings for the superior courts prepared or revised by counsel.

The Faculty is by prescriptive right an autonomous corporation and as such dates from at least the early sixteenth century, having its origin in the group of pleaders who regularly appeared before the courts which preceded the foundation of the Court of Session.[30] Admission is by election

---

[26] See Wilson, " The Faculty of Advocates Today," 1965 *Acta Juridica*, 227. The Society of Advocates in Aberdeen is a local body of solicitors and quite distinct from the Faculty.

[27] In England persons are called to the Bar, *i.e.* become barristers, after passing examinations and " keeping terms " at one or other of the four Inns of Court (Lincoln's Inn, The Middle Temple, The Inner Temple and Gray's Inn). In Northern Ireland there is an Inn of Court of Northern Ireland. On the Inns, see further, Jackson, *Machinery of Justice in England*, Chap. 4, and generally, Halsbury's *Laws of England*, tit. " Barrister."

[28] *Longworth* v. *Yelverton* (1867) L.R. 1 Sc.App. 218, 220. A firm (*Macbeth & Maclagan* v. *Macmillan*, 1914 S.C.(J.) 165) and a company (*Equity and Law Life Assce. Socy.* v. *Tritonia Ltd.*, 1943 S.C.(H.L.) 88) must always be represented by counsel. One spouse may not represent another: *Gordon* v. *Nakeski-Cumming*, 1924 S.C. 939.

[29] Some advocates do in fact possess the additional qualification of barrister and could therefore appear in both Scottish and English courts. Apart from that a barrister cannot appear in the Court of Session or an advocate in the High Court in England.

[30] The right of advocates to plead was secured by law in the time of Alexander III: A.P.S. I, 425; and there is frequent mention in records from the thirteenth century onwards of forespeakers (*prolocutores* or *praelocutores*) and advocates. See, *e.g.* Acts 1318, c. 17 and c. 18; 1320, c. 28; 1425, c. 45; 1429, c. 125; Bankton IV, 3, 1 *et seq.*; Mackay's *Practice of the Court of Session*, I, 102 *et seq.*; Henderson Begg, *Treatise on Law Agents*, 5 *et seq.*

after the intrant has petitioned the court, paid certain fees, and satisfied the Faculty Examiners as to his qualifications in both general scholarship and in law.[31] The principal officer of the Faculty is the Dean, who takes precedence over all members of the Bar except the Lord Advocate for the time being.[32] He is assisted by a Vice-Dean [33] and other officers, all being elected annually at the anniversary meeting of the Faculty held in January, and in practice usually re-elected so long as they are willing to serve. The Dean and his Council of senior members of Faculty exercise strict control over the professional discipline and etiquette of all members of Faculty and may censure or even disbar a member guilty of professional or other serious misconduct.[34]

The Law Officers

The Crown has two official advisers or Law Officers for Scotland, the Lord Advocate and the Solicitor-General for Scotland.[35] Nowadays they are appointed by the Prime Minister and go out of office with the government.[36] Either or both may be M.P.s and, if in the House, assist the Secretary of State for Scotland in handling government business.[37] They advise the Crown and represent it in civil cases and the Lord Advocate is the head of the system of public prosecution in the criminal courts, and he or the Solicitor-General appears for the Crown in important cases. He has full power over and complete discretion in the prosecution of crimes in any court in Scotland.

To assist him in the ordinary business of prosecuting in the High Court the Lord Advocate appoints a number of Advocates-Depute (at present

---

[31] Much information about " devilling," as pupillage is often miscalled in Scotland, about the formalities of call to the Scottish Bar, and life and work thereat, is in Lord Macmillan's *A Man of Law's Tale*, 26 *et seq.* See also, Guthrie, " R. L. Stevenson " (1920) 32 J.R. 7.

[32] A list of Deans of Faculty from 1698 is in 1972 S.L.T.(News) 233.

[33] A list of Vice-Deans of Faculty from 1754 is in 1972 S.L.T.(News) 233.

[34] For an example, see 1968 S.L.T.(News) 47; sequel to *Lee* v. *H.M. Advocate,* 1968 S.L.T. 155.

[35] Their English counterparts are the Attorney-General and the Solicitor-General. Lists of the holders of the offices of Lord Advocate and Solicitor-General are in 1972 S.L.T.(News) 233 and in Milne, *The Scottish Office,* 218–221. See also, Mackay, *Practice,* I, 119; Omond, *The Lord Advocates of Scotland,* 3 vols; Green's *Encyclopaedia, s.v.* Criminal Administration; " Law Officers of Scotland " 1924 S.L.T.(News) 43; Malcolm, " The Solicitor-General for Scotland " (1942) 54 Jur.Rev. 67, 125; *King's Advocate* v. *Lord Dunglas* (1836) 15 S. 314, 318 (discussing history of the office); *Dumfries C.C.* v. *Phyn* (1895) 22 R. 538; *McBain* v. *Crichton,* 1961 J.C. 25; *Hester* v. *Macdonald,* 1961 S.C. 370.

[36] A person may be appointed Lord Advocate, or Solicitor-General, on a non-political basis, in which case he advises the Government but is not committed to supporting it in any political context. The office of Lord Advocate was held on this basis by H. P. Macmillan in 1924–25 (appointed a Law Lord in 1930) and I. H. Shearer in 1962–64 (appointed a judge as Lord Avonside in 1964) and that of Solicitor-General by D. P. Blades in 1945–47 (appointed a judge as Lord Blades in 1947).

[37] In 1969 the Lord Advocate (H. S. Wilson, Q.C.), not being an M.P., was made a Life Peer, so as to assist the then Government in Parliament.

seven). One of these, the " Home Depute," is a Q.C., and deals with Edinburgh cases. The others may be senior or junior counsel, and exchange circuits every six months so as to share the work evenly. These appointments formerly fell when the Lord Advocate went out of office, but in 1970 the rule was established that the appointments of advocates-depute should not fall automatically with a change of Lord Advocate, but that they would be continued by the new incumbent.

Various advocates are also appointed to be standing junior counsel to various government departments and boards, such as the Inland Revenue and the Post Office, and act as advisers to and counsel for these offices. These appointments are non-political, but a standing junior counsel resigns office when he takes silk.

The Lord Advocate's Department

The Lord Advocate's Department [38] is a small group of advocates employed in the Civil Service to assist the Lord Advocate and Solicitor-General and to advise the staff of any Government department which has no Scottish legal adviser of its own. They are known as Legal Secretaries and also act as Parliamentary Draftsmen, drafting Bills and parts of Bills applicable to Scotland for consideration and enactment by Parliament and consulting with the Parliamentary Counsel to the Treasury on Scottish aspects of legislation to be applicable throughout the United Kingdom. Their work includes work, under the direction of the Scottish Law Commission, on Law Reform Bills and Bills for the consolidation or revision of statute law affecting Scotland.

Senior and Junior Counsel

An advocate or junior counsel remains a junior from the date of his call to the Bar until he becomes a Queen's Counsel, otherwise known as senior counsel.[39] Senior counsel thus consist of such members of the Bar as have, after a number of years of practice and the acquisition of considerable experience and legal skill, been appointed by the Queen, on the recommendation of the Lord Justice-General, to the rank and dignity of Her Majesty's Counsel learned in the law.[40] Queen's Counsel take precedence *inter se* according to the dates of their respective patents, except that the Lord Advocate for the time being has precedence over all others and is entitled to a seat " within the Bar," *i.e.* in the well of the court, at the clerk's table on the right side. The Dean of Faculty ranks next in precedence and has his seat at the centre of the Bar. The Solicitor-General for the

[38] The main office of the Department is in London.

[39] In England also sometimes called " leading counsel," or " leaders."

[40] A roll of Queen's Counsel in Scotland was created only in 1897; till then the dignity was conferred only on Law Officers and the Dean of Faculty. For the full story, see " The Faculty of Advocates and Queen's Counsel " (1896) 4 S.L.T. 47, 51, 55, 60, 143, 169, 254.

time being ranks third and has his seat within the Bar, at the left side of the clerk's table. Thereafter rank ex-law officers of the Crown and other Q.C.s according to the dates of their patents. As in England, a Q.C. wears a silk gown,[41] and he is entitled in court to lead any other counsel not of that rank, whatever may be his date of call to the Bar. A Q.C. may not draw or revise pleadings, nor appear in any " court," nor before a Provisional Order Inquiry, Board of Trade Inquiry, a Royal or Parliamentary Commission or a Departmental Inquiry unless accompanied by a junior counsel. Accordingly a party who wishes to instruct a Q.C. *must* in these cases instruct a junior as well, and this is customary in the House of Lords, the Inner House and in all cases of importance. In cases not covered by the general rule senior counsel may appear alone provided that junior counsel has neither drawn nor revised pleadings or that junior counsel has not previously advised as to the preparation of the case. The rule requiring that a junior be instructed along with a Q.C. does not apply to criminal cases or arbitrations, nor to written opinions. A senior may, for not more than one year after taking silk, continue to write in any case in which he was previously instructed as a junior, and be instructed to appear in court unaccompanied by a junior.[42] In exceptional cases several counsel may be instructed for one party, but there must always be at least one junior among them. In some cases two juniors are instructed, one of whom acts as senior counsel, or a senior counsel may be assisted by two juniors.

It was originally the rule, at least in England, that senior counsel must not be employed against the Crown without special licence, which was refused only if the Crown desired to be represented by the Q.C. concerned.[43]

Function of Counsel

The major function of counsel is to represent a party in proceedings before any court or tribunal, unless representation is barred by statute. Representation includes advising on whether to bring a claim, in what court and for what remedy, or whether to defend, drafting and revising all necessary pleadings and papers for the court or tribunal, advising on what evidence is necessary and should be sought, advising on procedure, appearing at all necessary stages, arguing points of law orally, examining and cross-examining witnesses and generally presenting the client's case to the court, advising on appeal, negotiating a settlement of a claim and generally seeking to safeguard the client's interests.

---

[41] Hence the phrase " taking silk," signifying promotion to the rank of Q.C.

[42] Rulings by the Dean of Faculty: 1970 C.L.Y. § 3405.

[43] With the great increase in litigation against the Crown and Crown Departments in modern times this rule was abrogated in 1920, and Q.C.s were granted a general dispensation to appear against the Crown without a licence. For the development of the status of Q.C. in England, where it originated in the 16th century, see Plucknett, *Concise History of the Common Law,* 5th ed., 230; Holdsworth, " Rise of the Order of King's Counsel " (1920) 36 L.Q.R. 212.

Counsel is also frequently consulted in matters not, or not yet, the subject of litigation, as when he is asked to give his opinion on certain documents or issues. This opinion may be accepted as a basis for action or as settling a controversy without litigation. In such cases a Memorial is prepared by a solicitor, setting out the facts which raise the legal problem, and sent with all the relevant documents and information to one or more counsel with certain questions formulated to which answers are desired. The answers are returned in the form of a written Opinion, which deals *seriatim* with the questions, usually giving reasons for the answers with references to cases and statutes.

Relations between Counsel

No form of partnership or sharing of work or profits is permitted among counsel, so that every counsel, both junior and senior, works entirely independently, and is dependent for his income on his own exertions and ability. Hence there is no such thing as standing partnerships between any two or more counsel, or between senior and junior. The collaboration which exists between a senior and the junior instructed by a party in one case subsists in respect of that case only, and the two counsel may simultaneously be instructed to appear on opposite sides in another case. Hence every counsel is alone personally and solely responsible for the whole work of his practice and for every opinion, note or pleading which he writes. It says much for the sense of honour and *camaraderie* of the Bar that such a system works smoothly and is not productive of personal enmities. The settled tradition is that disagreement and opposition are confined to the court room and are never carried over into personal relationships.

In the conduct of a litigation the junior counsel is responsible for all drawing and adjusting of pleadings,[44] incidental motions and procedure, and advice on evidence, and generally all steps leading up to the trial of the action, though on all matters he may consult with his senior, and the senior will frequently in complicated cases revise the pleadings before they are finally closed. At a hearing in court the senior counsel normally conducts the examination and cross-examination of most of the witnesses and certainly of all the important and difficult witnesses, while the junior counsel is noting the substance of the evidence, taking care that his senior is supplied with any maps, books or documents to which he may be referring, and trying to ensure that no point of substance is overlooked in the examination. There are, however, no rigid rules about the apportionment of work at a hearing and the two counsel may divide it as they choose.

---

[44] Hence, in Scotland, prior to the introduction of a roll of Queen's Counsel, an advocate was said to " give up writing " (*i.e.* pleadings) when he began to undertake only senior practice.

Instruction of Counsel

A client may instruct counsel only through an enrolled solicitor, and if he has a consultation with counsel the solicitor will be present.[45] The choice of counsel lies with the client, but he normally leaves the choice to the solicitor, who is usually better acquainted with the personality and experience of the different counsel in practice and with their special experience in particular fields. Instructions should always be in writing and counsel is not bound to appear unless properly instructed. Exceptionally an advocate may accept instructions from persons not practising solicitors, namely from patent agents, in matters relating to patents or trade marks and designs, Parliamentary agents, clerks to local authorities, in non-contentious matters or for the purposes of appearance at local inquiries, or lawyers furth of Scotland in matters in which no litigation in Scotland is contemplated or in progress.[46]

An advocate is presumed to have a mandate to appear for a person from the bare fact of his appearance [47] and this can be rebutted only by a disclaimer.[48] He is not responsible for the consequences if he acts on the instructions of a practising solicitor.[49] Once he has accepted instructions to act in a case he must remain free to act according to his judgment and discretion [50] so that he may take a particular course of action or even abandon or compromise a claim on his own responsibility,[51] unless he has been expressly instructed not to, though it is advisable to consult the client before taking any drastic step. " The nature of an advocate's office makes it clear that in the performance of his duty he must be entirely independent and act according to his own discretion and judgment in the conduct of the cause for his client. His legal right is to conduct the case without any regard to the wishes of his client, so long as his mandate is unrecalled, and what he does bona fide according to his own judgment will bind his client and will not expose him to any action for what he has done, even if the client's interests are thereby prejudiced." [52]

Special rules apply to " retainers," *i.e.* to instructions with reference to any particular cause (special retainer), or retainer by virtue of instructions to draw or revise pleadings or to appear for a party in court (implied retainer), or retainer whereby the services of a particular counsel are secured in all cases in Scottish courts, but not in arbitrations or in the House of

---

[45] A country agent may put before counsel a Memorial for opinion without the intervention of an Edinburgh agent: *Journal of Jurisprudence*, XIV, 148, 206.
[46] Ruling by Dean of Faculty [1970] C.L.Y. § 3405.
[47] Ersk., III, 3, 33; Maclaren's *Practice*, 16; *Ballantine* v. *Edgar* (1676) Mor. 348; *Marchmont and Morison* v. *Home* (1715) Mor. 358.
[48] *Ogston* v. *Turnbull* (1875) 13 S.L.R. 69.
[49] *Wallace* v. *Miller* (1821) 1 S. 40.
[50] *Batchelor* v. *Pattison and Mackersy* (1876) 3 R. 914.
[51] *Mackintosh* v. *Fraser* (1860) 22 D. 421; *Duncan* v. *Salmond* (1874) 1 R. 329; *Ballach* v. *Kelly* (1900) 8 S.L.T. 52. *Cf. Strauss* v. *Francis* (1866) L.R. 1 Q.B. 379.
[52] *Batchelor* v. *Pattison and Mackersy* (1876) 3 R. 914, 918.

Lords, in which the person retaining him is concerned as a party (general retainer). A general retainer endures for the lifetime of the client and the counsel, but falls if the client instructs another counsel. General retainers rank according to their dates so that if a counsel holds retainer from two parties who come together on opposite sides in a case he must act for the one whose retainer is earlier in date, provided that party sends a special retainer for that case. Detailed rules have been formulated from time to time by the Dean of Faculty.[53]

Since mutual confidence is of the essence of the professional relationship, the client remains free at any time to instruct another counsel and the counsel to return his papers at any stage in the course of employment. The advocate is not bound to disclose information which he has obtained in the course of the employment, unless the client waives the privilege.

On grounds of public policy and by long-settled custom an advocate is not liable in damages for wrong advice in law, negligence, mistake, indiscretion, error of judgment, or the mismanagement of a cause,[54] unless in case of an express agreement, or if he has acted fraudulently or treacherously[55]; nor is a solicitor liable who acts upon the advice of counsel in matters connected with the conduct of a suit.[56]

Solicitors

The other branch of the legal profession in Scotland consists of solicitors, formerly known as writers or law agents.[57] While many solicitors practise individually or in partnership, many also are employed by large businesses or public or local authorities, as full-time employees, to conduct their legal transactions, or in managerial or secretarial capacities.[58] Admission to the Roll of Solicitors kept by the Registrar of Solicitors is by petition following the taking of a law degree at a Scottish university or the passing of professional examinations in lieu thereof and a period of practical training with a practising solicitor.[59] A solicitor in practice must take out a practising certificate annually.[60]

---

[53] Printed in *Parliament House Book*, Division A.

[54] *Fell* v. *Brown* (1791) 1 Peake 131; *Purves* v. *Landell* (1845) 12 Cl. & F. 91, 103; *Burness* v. *Morris* (1849) 11 D. 1258; *Swinfen* v. *Lord Chelmsford* (1860) 5 H. & N. 890; *Batchelor* v. *Pattison and Mackersy* (1876) 3 R. 914; *Rondel* v. *Worsley* [1969] 1 A.C. 191.

[55] *Swinfen, supra,* at p. 920.

[56] *Megget* v. *Thomson* (1827) 5 S. 275; *Dixon* v. *Rutherford* (1863) 2 M. 61.

[57] Some individuals and firms adhere to the older designations, but since the Solicitors (Scotland) Act 1933, " solicitor " has been the correct term. On the history of the profession, see Henderson Begg, *Treatise on Law Agents*, Chap. 1. See also Cooper, " The Future of the Legal Profession," in *Selected Papers*, 153.

[58] See further, Lynex, " The Role of the Employed Lawyer in Industry " (1954) 2 J.S.P.T.L.(N.S.) 214.

[59] See Admission as Solicitor (Scotland) Regulations 1969, printed in *Parliament House Book*, Section D.

[60] See Solicitors (Scotland) Acts 1933 to 1965 and Solicitors (Scotland) Practising Certificate Rules 1951, printed in *Parliament House Book*, Section D.

The professional organisation is the Law Society of Scotland, established in 1949, which comprises all practising solicitors in Scotland, conducts the professional examinations, acts as Registrar of Solicitors, and controls the Legal Aid Scheme. In addition there are various smaller professional societies of considerable antiquity and high professional status of which the principal are the Society of Writers to the Signet,[61] the Society of Solicitors in the Supreme Courts,[62] the Royal Faculty of Procurators in Glasgow, and the Society of Advocates in Aberdeen [63] (which last is a body of solicitors and is not to be confused with the Faculty of Advocates).[64]

The employment of a solicitor is regulated by the general principles of the law of agency and a formal mandate is seldom necessary.[65] The extent of the solicitor's authority depends on the kind of work he has been instructed to perform.[66] He is entitled to a measure of discretion in the conduct of litigation, subject to the directions of counsel where one has been retained,[67] though he may not abandon a claim without authority from the client,[68] and various extraordinary steps, such as entering into a judicial reference, require express authority. His actings are binding on the client so long as they do not go beyond what is necessary for the accomplishment of the work he was employed to perform, or what is usual in the exercise of the authority conferred.[69] The nature of solicitors' work is very varied. It includes general business advice, sale and purchase of land and houses, income tax affairs, winding up of the estates of deceased persons, administration of trusts, representation of clients in sheriff courts and tribunals, preparation of cases for the Court of Session and practically any kind of work which has legal implications.

By accepting employment solicitors undertake to perform the business entrusted to them with due diligence and skill [70] and will be liable in damages for loss sustained by the client in consequence of breach of this duty.[71] There are many decisions on what constitutes professional negligence in various circumstances.[72] A solicitor will not, however, be

---

[61] See *History of the Society of Writers to H.M. Signet* (revised ed., 1936); Haldane, "The Society of Writers to H.M. Signet " (1970) 15 J.L.S.S. 35.
[62] Anon., "The Society of Solicitors in the Supreme Courts " (1971) 16 J.L.S.S. 66.
[63] Anon., "The Advocates of Aberdeen " (1969) 14 J.L.S.S. 325.
[64] On these bodies, see further, Mackay, *Practice*, I, 128 *et seq.* On their precedence, see *Law Society of Scotland*, 1955 S.L.T. (Lyon Ct.) 2.
[65] For the cases where one is necessary, see Begg on *Law Agents*, pp. 75–78.
[66] See further, Begg, *op. cit.*, Chaps. 8 and 9.
[67] *Buchanan* v. *Davidson & Stevenson* (1877) 14 S.L.R. 233.
[68] *Thoms* v. *Bain* (1888) 15 R. 613.
[69] *Sanderson* v. *Campbell* (1833) 11 S. 623.
[70] *Frame* v. *Campbell* (1839) McL. & Rob. 595; *Bell* v. *Ogilvie* (1863) 2 M. 336; See Bell's *Prin.* §§ 153–154.
[71] *Evans* v. *Stool* (1885) 12 R. 1295; *Stewart* v. *McLean, Baird & Neilson*, 1915 S.C. 13. See also *Rondel* v. *Worsley* [1969] 1 A.C. 191.
[72] See Begg on *Law Agents*, Chap. 18; cases in *Faculty Digest, s.v.* " Agent and Client," and in *Scots Digest, s.v.* " Agency." See also, Eddy, *Professional Negligence.*

held liable in damages for giving incorrect advice on a doubtful point of law where there has been no clear rule or practice, since that is properly the function of counsel.[73] Nor will he be held liable if he follows the usual course of practice even if it should be held in the end to be incorrect.[74] Advice on doubtful or difficult matters of law is properly the province of counsel and the proper course in such a case is to submit such points to counsel in a Memorial containing a full and accurate statement of facts and to act upon the opinion obtained. Neglect to obtain counsel's opinion may in some cases be enough to render a solicitor liable in damages for breach of duty and he is protected against such a claim by bona fide reliance on counsel's opinion, at least in matters which do not fall within the exclusive province of the solicitor.[75]

Solicitors' Discipline Committee

The Solicitors' Discipline (Scotland) Committee consists of five, six, or seven solicitors recommended by the Law Society as representative of the profession throughout Scotland, and appointed by the Lord President.[76] It investigates complaints of professional misconduct by a solicitor, and may strike a solicitor off the roll of solicitors or suspend him from practice, or fine or censure him. An appeal against the decision of the Discipline Committee lies to the Court of Session.[77] Convictions of solicitors in the criminal courts for fraud or dishonest appropriation of property are reported to the Committee for consideration. Complaints may be lodged by a client, the Council of the Law Society, the Lord Advocate, judges, sheriffs and auditors of court. A solicitor struck off the roll may subsequently petition to be restored and may be restored to the roll on proof of a substantial period of trustworthy conduct subsequent to the offence for which he was struck off. Apart from the statutory jurisdiction the Court of Session probably still has a common law jurisdiction *ex proprio motu* to censure or suspend a solicitor for misconduct.[78]

Notaries Public

The office of notary public is very ancient and has survived as a distinct office in some legal systems.[79] In Scotland his functions were and are the

---

[73] *Cooke* v. *Falconer's Reps.* (1850) 13 D. 157; *Blair* v. *Assets Co.* (1896) 23 R.(H.L.) 36.   [74] *Hamilton* v. *Emslie* (1868) 7 M. 173,
[75] Mackay's *Practice of the Court of Session*, I, 138. The practical aspects of conveyancing are possibly the only subject which is peculiarly the solicitor's province.
[76] Solicitors (Scotland) Act 1933, ss. 24–40, as extended by Solicitors (Scotland) Act 1949, ss. 20 (3), 25 (3), and Solicitors (Scotland) Act 1958, s. 5. See also Scottish Solicitors Discipline Committee Procedure Rules 1959, printed in the *Parliament House Book*, Section D.   [77] See, *e.g. Law Society* v. *Docherty*, 1968 S.C. 104.
[78] Maclaren, *Court of Session Practice*, 28–29.
[79] See, *Ars Notariatus; or the Art and Office of a Notary Public as practised in Scotland* (1740–1821); Murray, *Law of Scotland relating to Notaries Public* (1890); Brown, " Origin and Early History of the Office of Notary " (1935) 47 J.R. 201, 355; " The N.P.," 1923 S.L.T.(News) 103; " Mottoes of Notaries Public," 1926 S.L.T. (News) 54; " The Notary Public," 1970 S.L.T.(News) 77; see also *Sources and Literature of Scots Law* (Stair Society), 289–300.

authentication of various categories of formal deeds, particularly in relation to the title to heritable property, notes of which were formerly made in his protocol book.[80] In mercantile matters the noting and protesting of bills of exchange, the execution of maritime protests, and the swearing of affidavits in bankruptcy, are all notarial business, while deeds executed in Scotland for use abroad have frequently to be executed before and authenticated by a notary public. In modern times, in consequence of legal changes, his services have increasingly been dispensed with and the powers conferred also on enrolled solicitors, while since 1896 admission to the roll of notaries public has been restricted to enrolled solicitors. Admission is by petition to the First Division of the Court of Session.

The Crown Agent

The Crown Agent is the permanent head of the Crown Office, Edinburgh, solicitor to the Lord Advocate's department and chief permanent official of the system of criminal administration. To his office come reports from procurators-fiscal in each sheriffdom and in reply go instructions, requests and general guidance on prosecutions. He also acts in certain civil actions where the Lord Advocate is a party in the public interest, but not where he appears on behalf of a Government department.

The Scottish Courts Administration

This is a small office established in 1971 responsible for the general oversight of the sheriff courts, their administration, staffing and efficient operation.

The procurator-fiscal service

The procurator-fiscal service is a body of lawyers, a few advocates, mostly solicitors, employed full-time as civil servants and located at the various sheriff courts throughout Scotland and responsible for investigating and instituting proceedings for criminal offences within their districts, and for presenting the cases in court. They also prosecute in the district courts. The more serious crimes are reported to the Crown Office for the consideration and instructions of Crown Counsel. They are also responsible for inquiry into sudden and suspicious deaths and conduct Fatal Accident Inquiries and have other miscellaneous functions. In country districts procurators-fiscal are local solicitors, employed part-time only on procurator-fiscal duties. Young lawyers are also frequently employed as temporary procurators-fiscal in busy courts.

Solicitor to the Secretary of State for Scotland

The Solicitor's Office which has a large staff of solicitors, who are civil

---

[80] These accordingly frequently contain valuable information about lands, families and legal practice and some have been edited and published by the historical clubs.

servants, is based in St. Andrew's House and acts in legal matters for all the departments of the Scottish Office and for numerous other Government departments and offices, including United Kingdom departments such as the Treasury which have functions in Scotland. The functions are general legal advice, drafting and submission to Parliament of Scottish delegated legislation, instructions for Bills to be drafted by the Lord Advocate's Department, conveyancing and reparation work and management of land and other property belonging to departments for which the Solicitor acts. Members of the staff appear before the Scottish Land Court, tribunals, arbitrations and in some sheriff courts.

The Accountant of Court

The Accountant of Court is an officer of the Court of Session appointed by the Secretary of State on the nomination of the Lord Advocate. He supervises the conduct of persons judicially appointed by the Court of Session or Sheriff Court to be judicial factor or *curator bonis* to administer the estates of persons incapable of doing so themselves, and annually audits and reports on their accounts and fixes their remuneration. He also supervises persons appointed trustees on sequestrated estates.

The Queen's and Lord Treasurer's Remembrancer

This officer is the Treasury representative in Scotland and the Accounting Officer for the Vote for Law Charges and Courts of Law, Scotland. He makes payments from the Consolidated Fund of legal salaries and from the various Votes of Parliament administered by the Scottish Departments and carries out functions relating to banking and receipts and payments such as the Paymaster-General does in England. He audits the criminal accounts of procurators-fiscal and sheriff clerks and the expenses of returning officers at elections, and has certain functions of examining Court of Session and Sheriff Court books. He is *ex officio* administrator of treasure trove and of estates which fall to the Crown by reason of failure of heirs or as *bona vacantia*. By warrant of the Department of Trade he is Registrar of Companies, Registrar of Limited Partnerships and Registrar of Business Names. He is also Keeper of the *Edinburgh Gazette* and responsible on behalf of the Great Officers of State for the custody of the Regalia of Scotland in Edinburgh Castle.

The Keeper of the Registers of Scotland

The Keeper is appointed by the Secretary of State with the consent of the Lord President and is head of the Department of the Registers of Scotland which is concerned with the maintenance of fifteen separate registers and with the registration therein of a large variety of deeds and documents relating to various legal processes. The registers are the General Register of Sasines, the Register of Inhibitions and Adjudications, of Hornings, of

Deeds, of Entails, Protests, of Service of Heirs, of the Great Seal, of the Quarter Seal, of the Prince's Seal, of the Cachet Seal, of Crown Grants, of Sheriffs' Commissions, of English and Irish Judgments, and of European Court Judgments. The most important of these is the General Register of Sasines in which are registered all writs relating to rights in land. Legal registers, together with the records of the Court of Session, are periodically transmitted to the Scottish Record Office for preservation along with other public records and many private collections of material of historical interest.

The police

The police is not a national force but separate forces administered by regional councils as police authorities. The Scottish Home and Health Department is responsible for police legislation and generally guides and co-ordinates the work of the police forces; it administers the police grant, maintains a central establishment for the training of police officers and maintains contact through Her Majesty's Inspectors of Constabulary who report to the Secretary of State on the efficiency of police forces. The function of the police is to preserve law and order, to enforce a great volume of legislation, to search out and apprehend criminals and to report crimes detected to the appropriate procurator-fiscal. In Scotland the police do not themselves decide whether to prosecute, nor do they initiate or conduct prosecutions.

The prison service

The Scottish Home and Health Department, acting through the Director of the Scottish Prison Service, administers prisons, borstal institutions and other penal establishments in Scotland. The probation service has since 1968 been part of local authority social work service.

Juries

In various kinds of legal investigations a part is played by a jury.[81] The main cases are criminal trials under solemn procedure (jury of 15), civil trials of certain actions, mainly for damages for personal injuries or death, in the Court of Session (jury of 12), civil trials of actions of damages by employee against employer in the Sheriff Court (jury of 7) and Fatal Accident Inquiries (jury of 7). The jurors are persons chosen by lot from a larger number of qualified persons summoned for the purpose by the Clerk of Justiciary, Principal Clerk of Session or Sheriff-Clerk from those named in the General Jury Book of the District. The qualifications are to be between 21 and 60 owning lands of the yearly value of £5 or goods of the value of £200. Both men and women are eligible to serve but many

---

[81] For a modern evaluation of jury trial, particularly in England, see Cornish: *The Jury.*

categories of persons, *e.g.* doctors in practice, are exempted and women may apply to be exempted on medical grounds.

In criminal cases the prosecutor or the accused may challenge five jurors peremptorily and any number on cause shown. But there should be no general questioning by judge or on behalf of either party to ascertain whether any person cited could or should be excused from a particular trial. It is not a sufficient cause for a juror to be excused that he is of a particular race, religion, political belief or occupation, or that he might be prejudiced either way. The essence of the jury system is of a number of individuals chosen at random.[82]

In all cases the function of the jury is to have regard to the evidence and, subject to the directions in matters of law of the presiding judge or sheriff, to return a verdict on one or more questions of fact, or of mixed fact and law, *e.g.* in a criminal case, the question: Are you satisfied beyond reasonable doubt that the accused committed the crime charged? Or in a civil case: Are you satisfied on the balance of probabilities that the accident to the pursuer was caused by the fault of the defender? If so, at what sum do you assess the damages?[83] In all cases a majority verdict is competent. The jury verdict is announced orally by the chancellor, chosen from among themselves by the jurors, in response to a question from the clerk of court. Jurors are entitled to compensation for loss of earnings and to travelling and subsistence allowances.

PROFESSIONAL ETHICS AND ETIQUETTE

Both branches of the legal profession have a profound *esprit de corps* and regard for the ethics of the profession, and also a distinct code of professional etiquette. Most of these rules are rules dictated by prudence and the desire that justice should, so far as humanly possible, both be done and be manifestly seen to be done. Some matters of professional etiquette, relating to the relations between the two branches of the profession, have already been touched on. No comprehensive code of professional ethics exists and much of it is simply absorbed by experience[84]; nevertheless the administration of justice depends in large part on the integrity and honour of the profession.

---

[82] *M.* v. *H.M. Advocate*, 1974 S.L.T.(Notes) 25.

[83] A jury may, exceptionally, be directed to bring in a special verdict, *i.e.* answers to specific questions, the legal effect of which is later decided by the court after argument.

[84] The American Bar Association has adopted a code of Canons of Professional Ethics for the guidance of its members and in some states an oath must be taken on admission to the Bar to observe the highest moral principles in the practice of the profession. The " Canons of Professional Ethics " are printed in Moreland, *Equal Justice Under Law*. The Annual Statements of the [English] Bar Council, summarised in *Current Law Year Books*, contain rulings on points of ethics and etiquette. See also, Lord Macmillan, " The Ethics of Advocacy," in *Law and Other Things*, p. 36; Stone, *Law and its Administration*, 162–165; Rogers, " Ethics of Advocacy " (1899) 15 L.Q.R. 259; Boulton, *Conduct and Etiquette at the [English] Bar*, 1975; Solicitors' (Scotland) Practice Rules, 1964, in *Parliament House Book*, Section D.

It is difficult to generalise but the overriding consideration, applicable equally to both branches of the profession, is that an advocate or solicitor, if consulted or instructed, must invariably apply his whole mind and devote his fullest energies to the business entrusted to him, and seek to use his ability, ingenuity and knowledge towards achieving by honest means a fair and just conclusion of the issue without regard to his personal advantage or belief. He must retain his own professional integrity and opinions and not subordinate them to the client's opinions or interests, and if a client should insist on doing what the legal adviser believes is imprudent or wrong or unjust or illegal he must be free to withdraw from the employment; he is not bound to aid in some foolish or wrongful escapade, still less to advise or abet some unjust or illegal enterprise. " An advocate in undertaking the conduct of a cause in this court enters into no contract with his client, but takes on himself an office in the performance of which he owes a duty, not to his client only, but also to the court, to the members of his own profession, and to the public . . . The position of an agent is somewhat different. There is a contract of employment between him and his client, by virtue of which the client, for certain settled rates of remuneration, is entitled to require from the agent the exercise of care and diligence, and professional skill and experience. . . . The agent, of course, cannot be asked to follow the client's instructions beyond what is lawful and proper. For the agent, as well as the counsel, owes a duty to the court. . . . He is also bound by that unwritten law of his profession which embodies the honourable understanding of the individual members as to their bearing and conduct towards each other." [85]

Duties to the Court

A lawyer owes to any court of law or tribunal a duty to treat it with proper respect and to make any criticisms in a moderate and respectful manner. Disrespectful or insulting conduct in the face of a court is punishable as contempt of court. Any attempt to exert personal influence on the court, or even to discuss privately with a judge any pending matter is very improper.

The lawyer, moreover, is present in court not merely to present his client's case but to assist the court, by argument and criticism of opposing contentions, to arrive at a just and legally correct decision. Hence his conduct must be characterised by candour and fairness. It is professionally disgraceful to resort to or be a party to any fraud, deception or trickery,[86] such as fabricating documents or deliberately withholding evidence, or knowingly to misquote the substance of a document, a witness's testimony, an opposing argument, or a decision or textbook. An advocate is bound

---

[85] *Batchelor* v. *Pattison and Mackersy* (1876) 3 R. 914, 918, *per* Lord President Inglis.
[86] *Cf.* Annual Statement of the [English] Bar Council, 1953, p. 16, quoted in [1954] C.L.Y. 2514.

to bring to the notice of the court authorities known to bear on the subject of a debate, whether or not they are in his client's favour.[87] He must not cite a decision known to have been overruled or a statute repealed or amended, nor assert as fact what has not been proved. Nor should pleading or argument include any scandalous or irrelevant matter [88] or matter merely prejudicial or statements designed to sway a jury emotionally or on grounds other than legal.

Counsel must accept a brief offered " and do all he honourably can on behalf of his client. I say ' all he honourably can ' because his duty is not only to his client. He has a duty to the court which is paramount. It is a mistake to suppose that he is the mouthpiece of his client to say what he wants; or his tool to do what he directs. He is none of these things. He owes allegiance to a higher cause. It is the cause of truth and justice. He must not consciously mis-state the facts. He must not knowingly conceal the truth. He must not unjustly make a charge of fraud, that is, without evidence to support it. He must produce all the relevant authorities, even those that are against him. He must see that his client discloses, if ordered, the relevant documents, even those that are fatal to his case. He must disregard the most specific instructions of his client, if they conflict with his duty to the court. The code which requires a barrister to do all this is not a code of law. It is a code of honour. If he breaks it, he is offending against the rules of the profession and is subject to its discipline; but he cannot be sued in a court of law." [89]

Both the court and the other parties must be able to rely on the honesty and to trust the word of legal advisers. Moreover in some cases issues are decided on the *ex parte* statements of one party,[90] so that it is important that only such statements be made as are true to the best of the adviser's belief and knowledge. It is quite improper to assert in argument a personal belief in the innocence of the client or the justice of his cause.

It is part of the duty to the court to treat opposing parties and witnesses with fairness and consideration, and not to indulge in abuse, to suggest improprieties, or to make any personal attack, even at the instance of the client, except in so far as any such conduct may be necessitated by the circumstances of the case. Thus sometimes one has to put to the other side's witnesses the suggestion that they are lying.

When initiating proceedings in court counsel and solicitors owe a duty to the court and also to the other party involved to consider seriously whether there is any prospect of success. It is professional misconduct, at least on a solicitor's part, to raise and maintain an action without belief

---

[87] *Glebe Sugar Refining Co.* v. *Greenock Harbour Trustees*, 1921 S.C.(H.L.) 72.
[88] See, *Wardrope* v. *Hamilton* (1876) 3 R. 876; *A.* v. *B.* (1895) 22 R. 402; *H.* v. *P.* (1905) 8 F. 232; *M.* v. *S.*, 1909, 1 S.L.T. 192; *A.* v. *C.*, 1922 S.L.T. 34.
[89] *Rondel* v. *W.* [1966] 3 All E.R. 657, 665, *per* Lord Denning M.R.
[90] *e.g.* the granting of *interim* interdict.

that it has any reasonable prospect of success,[91] but counsel and agents need not go so far as to be fully convinced of the rightness or substantial justice of the client's case.[92] So, too, in presenting appeals to the High Court from conviction by a jury it has been observed that where counsel considers there are no statable grounds of appeal, he acts properly in performance of his duty to the court as well as to his client, in refusing to act further in the case.[93]

Counsel or procurator-fiscal engaged in conducting a criminal prosecution has the primary duty not of securing a conviction but of assisting the court and trying to secure that justice is done. Hence he must not press the prosecution case unduly and may properly afford the defence reasonable facilities to prepare their defence.[94] " The Crown counsel is a representative of the State, ' a minister of justice '; his function is to assist the jury in arriving at the truth. He must not urge any argument that does not carry weight in his own mind, or try to shut out any legal evidence that would be important to the interests of the person accused. ' It is not his duty to obtain a conviction by all means; but simply to lay before the jury the whole of the facts which compose his case, and to make these perfectly intelligible, and to see that the jury are instructed with regard to the law and are able to apply the law to the facts.' [95] ' It cannot be too often made plain that the business of counsel for the Crown is fairly and impartially to exhibit all the facts to the jury. The Crown has no interest in procuring a conviction. Its only interest is that the right person should be convicted, that the truth should be known, and that justice should be done.' [96] " [97]

When defending on a criminal charge a lawyer is entitled to act independently of his personal opinion as to the guilt of the accused and he is entitled and even bound to present every legal defence which he can reasonably rely on, so that no person shall be convicted save after due process of law and after guilt has been satisfactorily proved by competent evidence, to a competent tribunal. As regards confessions of guilt, if the confession is made before proceedings have commenced, no harm can be done by requesting the accused to retain another advocate. But if the confession is made during proceedings, the advocate should continue and must continue the defence by all legitimate means, though he may not set

---

[91] *X Insurance Co.* v. *A. and B.*, 1936 S.C. 225.

[92] So, too, a litigant is not liable in damages to his opponent for judicial proceedings which are unsuccessful or unfounded so long as there is no malice or fraud: *Ormiston* v. *Redpath* (1866) 4 M. 488; *Davies* v. *Brown* (1867) 5 M. 842; *Kinnes* v. *Adam* (1882) 9 R. 698.

[93] *Scott, J. N.* v. *H.M. Advocate*, 1946 J.C. 68. *Cf. Monteath* v. *H.M. Advocate*, 1965 J.C. 14.

[94] *Cf. Smith* v. *H.M. Advocate*, 1952 J.C. 66.

[95] Sir J. Holker, Att.-Gen. (*The Times*, Feb. 25, 1880).

[96] Lord Hewart C.J. (1941) 25 Cr.App.R. at p. 115.

[97] Kenny, *Outlines of Criminal Law*, 16th ed., 504–505.

up an affirmative case inconsistent with the confession as by suggesting that another person committed the crime.[98]

Duties to the Profession

A lawyer owes it to his profession, to the abstract idea of Law and all that it stands for, and to the ideal of Justice, that he does nothing in his professional practice of which a moral, skilful, diligent and upright man need be ashamed. Advertisement, direct or indirect, is forbidden,[99] though this does not extend to the insertion of names and addresses in the recognised Law Lists, nor giving name and qualifications as the author of legal books and articles, but it does cover articles in the press or broadcasts in which the person is named or given his professional designation.[1] The sharing of fees with, or partnership with, an unqualified person is also forbidden.[2]

It is a duty to the profession to take a share in assisting individuals in need of legal assistance even though they may be unable to pay, or may require Legal Aid,[3] and to accept instructions in a cause from the first person who tenders instructions to him with the customary fee, even though he might prefer to act on the other side or not to be involved in that case at all. The duty to defend on a criminal charge takes priority over a competing engagement in a civil case.[4]

Other members of the profession must be treated as gentlemen of honour and not abused, ridiculed or condemned, and undertakings, promises and assurances given one to another must be fulfilled. Thus if counsel's fees are paid by the client to the solicitor it is a debt of honour to remit them to counsel. Again any ill feeling between parties should not be allowed to affect or influence their advisers in their conduct towards one another or the parties.

Duties to the Client

The lawyer's first duty to his client is to perform with requisite skill and due diligence the business entrusted to him [5] and the solicitor, though not the advocate, will be liable to the client in damages for breach of duty, negligence, or gross ignorance or want of professional skill.[6] The relationship of advocate and client is that of mandatory and mandant and the fee paid is theoretically an honorarium, and is not recoverable by law. The

---

[98] Annual Statement of the [English] Bar Council, 1915, p. 14, approved by the then Attorney-General.

[99] Solicitors' (Scotland) Practice Rules 1964, r. 1.

[1] Annual Statement of the [English] Bar Council 1954, p. 21.

[2] Solicitors' (Scotland) Practice Rules 1964, r. 2.

[3] On Legal Aid, see p. 298, *infra.*

[4] *Cf.* Denning, *The Road to Justice,* 53.

[5] *Bell* v. *Ogilvie* (1863) 2 M. 336. For details, see Begg on *Law Agents,* Chaps. 18 and 24.

[6] *Landell* v. *Purves* (1845) 4 Bell 46; 12 Cl. & F. 91.

relationship of solicitor and client is that of agent and principal, the fee is impliedly due under the contract and it is recoverable by law.[7] Beyond the general duty to perform business with due diligence it is difficult to state duties in detail.

It is not, however, a lawyer's duty to do whatever may enable him to win his client's case, but only to utilise any remedy, claim or defence which is permitted by law and which may be used honourably and honestly, and he is entitled, and indeed bound, to prevent his client from taking any action which he himself ought not to do, such as fabricating or suppressing evidence or suborning witnesses. If a client does anything disgraceful or improper the lawyer should terminate his employment.[8]

The fiduciary character of the relationship between solicitor and client necessarily imposes restrictions on their transacting one with another in view of the possible conflict of interests. Contracts between them are liable to reduction, as contrary to public policy, and in any such transaction the client should be advised by another and independent solicitor.[9] Even gifts [10] or bequests [11] to the solicitor are scrutinised closely and suspiciously while he may not make any secret profit at the client's expense in dealing with third parties.[12] So too if a solicitor acts as a trustee he may not, unless expressly authorised by the trust deed or all the beneficiaries,[13] take any remuneration for his services. Nor may a lawyer divulge secrets or confidences obtained during employment or act subsequently for others utilising knowledge gained in a previous professional connection.

Again it is quite improper to accept instructions from a client if there is any conflict of interest between that client and another client. Accordingly one advocate or solicitor should not act for two persons whose interests do, or even may, conflict.[14] Thus it is bad practice for one solicitor to act for both buyer and seller of property; he can properly protect the interests of one or other only. He cannot act for both in settling the price.[15] If he acts for both lender and borrower (which is undesirable) he is responsible to both parties for any failure in duty [16] and may be liable for recommending

---

[7] *Cf. Rondel* v. *W.* [1966] 3 All E.R. 657; [1967] 3 All E.R. 993.

[8] Bankton, IV, 3, 13.

[9] *McPherson's Trustees* v. *Watt* (1877) 5 R.(H.L.) 9.

[10] *Long* v. *Taylor* (1824) 2 Sh.App. 233.

[11] *Grieve* v. *Cunningham* (1869) 8 M. 317.

[12] *Tyrrell* v. *Bank of London* (1862) 10 H.L.C. 26.

[13] *Lewis's Trustees* v. *Pirie* 1912 S.C. 574. This even extends to the solicitor-trustee's partner: *Mitchell* v. *Burness* (1878) 5 R. 1124.

[14] *Oastler* v. *Dill, Smillie & Wilson* (1886) 14 R. 12; *McClure, Naismith, Brodie & MacFarlane* v. *Stewart* (1887) 15 R.(H.L.) 1; *Ellis's Trustees* v. *Ellis* (1898) 1 F. 4 (two parties to a special case); *Stewart* v. *McLean, Baird & Neilson,* 1915 S.C. 13; *Dunlop's Trustees* v. *Farquharson,* 1955 S.L.T.(Notes) 80.

[15] *McPherson's Trustees* v. *Watt* (1877) 5 R.(H.L.) 9.

[16] *McLeod* v. *McDonald* (1835) 13 S. 287; *Haldane* v. *Donaldson* (1840) 1 Rob.App. 226; *Oastler, supra.*

a security which turns out inadequate, quite apart from any failure in the legal validity of the security.[17]

Privilege

Neither advocate nor solicitor can be obliged to disclose information obtained by him in his professional capacity unless the client consents,[18] and it is a breach of professional confidence to do so voluntarily. Memorials to and the opinions of counsel are protected.[19] But anything which is part of the events in a crime or fraud is not protected.[20] The privilege certainly covers communications having reference to a contemplated action or an action in progress and probably also all communications made in a professional capacity, whether or not any dispute has yet arisen.[21]

Advocates and solicitors are absolutely privileged in their written and oral pleading in court, in commenting on the evidence and the conduct of parties and in all other matters relevant to the cause,[22] while litigants have qualified privilege only and will accordingly be liable to an action for defamation if personal malice can be proved.[23] But counsel and solicitors are liable to censure for improper or insulting conduct in court and the Court of Session may punish by censure, suspension or even deprivation of the office of advocate.[24] Counsel and agent are also privileged in respect of matters alleged or put in pleadings with the authority and on the instructions of the client so long as pertinent to the matter in issue.[25]

PROFESSIONAL FEES

An advocate's fees are, as in the Roman law, regarded as honoraria, not as fees, and used to be presumed to have been paid at the time he is instructed.[26] The practice used to be for the solicitor to send the appropriate fee with each letter instructing a particular step to be taken,[27] but fees were sometimes noted and paid in a lump sum afterwards.[27] There are no fixed scales of fees for counsel though in practice the fees for various standard types of business are conventionally fixed within limits, depend-

---

[17] *Cleland* v. *Brownlie, Watson & Beckett* (1892) 20 R. 152; *Wernham* v. *McLean, Baird & Neilson*, 1925 S.C. 407.

[18] *Forteith* v. *Earl of Fyfe* (1821) 2 Mur. 467; *Noble* v. *Scott* (1843) 5 D. 723; *Hay* v. *Edinburgh & Glasgow Bank* (1858) 20 D. 701.

[19] Bell, *Prin.* § 2254; *Thomson's Trustees* v. *Clark* (1823) 2 S. 262; *Clark* v. *Spence* (1824) 3 Mur. 454.

[20] *McCowan* v. *Wright* (1852) 15 D. 229, 494.

[21] *Ibid.*; *Munro* v. *Fraser* (1858) 21 D. 103.

[22] *Drew* v. *Mackenzie* (1862) 24 D. 649, 662; *Williamson* v. *Umphray and Robertson* (1890) 17 R. 905.

[23] *Williamson, supra.*

[24] A.S. Dec 21, 1649; July 26, 1699; June 23, 1756.

[25] *Ramsay* v. *Nairne* (1833) 11 S. 1033. *Cf. Bayne* v. *Macgregor* (1862) 24 D. 1126; (1863) 1 M. 615.

[26] *Batchelor* v. *Pattison and Mackersy* (1876) 3 R. 914.

[27] Mackay's *Practice*, I, 115.

ing largely on the value and importance of the cause, on its complexity, and on the time involved.[28] There is no rule in Scotland that the fee of junior counsel should be two-thirds of the fee of any senior counsel with whom he is instructed to appear.[29] It is always open to a client to pay counsel more than the conventional fee though a successful litigant, if awarded expenses against his opponent, will be allowed by the Auditor of Court to recover from his opponent not what he may have paid but what was reasonably necessary in the circumstances to secure the services of competent counsel.[30]

Fees cannot be recovered by action since they are honoraria,[31] unless in the exceptional case where a solicitor has received payment of his professional account from the client and has failed to transmit counsel's fee to him,[32] or in the case of a salary as standing counsel, which may be sued for.[33] An advocate is probably entitled to retain a fee sent to him even though he has not had to render any services.[34] It is illegal to take a proportion of the subject of a litigation in lieu of a fee, or to buy up any debatable rights which are still in dependence,[35] but quite legitimate to act on the basis that there will be no remuneration unless in the event of success.[36]

In 1971 a new system was adopted. A company, Faculty Services Ltd., was formed to obtain payment of counsel's fees.[37] When work has been done, it sends to the instructing solicitor a note of the work done and the fee counsel proposes to charge. If solicitor and counsel's clerk are unable to agree on a fee the Auditor of the Court of Session adjudicates on what is a reasonable fee. In case of failure to pay counsel's fee the Dean of Faculty may request the Law Society to take disciplinary action against the solicitor.

In the case of the solicitor on the other hand fees are in the same category as the fees of other professional men in that the fact of employment implies an undertaking by the client to pay professional fees at the ordinary rate [38] and they may be recovered by action.[39] Fees in most cases are

---

[28] For examples, see cases in *Faculty Digest, s.v.* " Expenses." It should be observed that, over all, counsel are not highly paid for their work and much of it, particularly of the kind given to young junior counsel, is very poorly renumerated, and there are many instances where counsel gets no fee at all, or only a token fee. See also, Lord Macmillan, *A Man of Law's Tale*, pp. 130–140 (an exceptionally successful advocate).

[29] Ruling by Dean of Faculty [1970] C.L.Y. § 3405.

[30] See, *Elas* v. *Scottish Motor Traction Co.*, 1950 S.C. 570; *Macnaughton* v. *Macnaughton*, 1949 S.C. 42.

[31] *Batchelor* v. *Pattison and Mackersy* (1876) 3 R. 914.

[32] *Cullen* v. *Buchanan* (1862) 24 D. 1132; *Keay* v. *A.B.* (1837) 15 S. 748n.

[33] *McKenzie* v. *Town of Burntisland* (1728) Mor. 11421.

[34] Mackay, *Manual of Court of Session Practice*, 28.

[35] Land Purchase Act 1594, c. 220.

[36] *X Insurance Co.* v. *A. and B.*, 1936 S.C. 225, 238–239, 250–251.

[87] See 1971 S.L.T.(News) 197.

[38] Bell, *Prin.* § 226; *Manson* v. *Baillie* (1855) 2 Macq. 80; *Goodsir* v. *Carruthers* (1858) 20 D. 1141; *Bell* v. *Ogilvie* (1863) 2 M. 336; *Winton* v. *Airth* (1868) 6 M. 1095.

[39] *Bell* v. *Ogilvie* (1863) 2 M. 336.

regulated by the Table of Fees for Professional Services of 1970,[40] the Fees for Solicitors in the Supreme Courts of Scotland, 1970,[41] and the Fees of Solicitors and Others in the Sheriff Court [42] which are based generally, in the case of conveyancing and property transactions, on a percentage of the value of the property concerned, and in the case of litigious business, on the complexity and time occupied. The client is always entitled to have the account remitted for taxation to the Auditor of the Court of Session or of the local Sheriff Court before paying it. Solicitors are also, of course, entitled to recover all outlays and expenses properly incurred on account of the client.[43] A solicitor may charge less than is permitted by the Table of Fees and he may act gratuitously for a poor client, taking his chance of recovering his fees and outlays from any award of damages and expenses made against the opposite party.

It is doubtful whether the Roman law rule of *pactum de quota litis* (the prohibition on a legal adviser taking as fee a share of the property in dispute) is applicable in Scotland,[44] but the principle seems to be followed, as the practice is highly undesirable.[45] But a non-professional man may advance money to carry on a litigation on the basis of receiving a share of any sum recovered.

Transacting with Clients

A solicitor is not debarred from transacting with a client so long as he is not acting as legal adviser in that same transaction, but he must show that he made full disclosure and gave full value,[46] and it is desirable to have the client separately advised by a completely independent solicitor. A bequest in a will to the solicitor who drew up the will is valid [47] but the onus is on the solicitor to show that the testator was in full possession of his faculties and made the bequest freely and in knowledge of its effect.[48] If a solicitor has been instructed by a client to find a purchaser for property, he may not purchase himself without the client's express authority and without divesting himself of the character of agent for sale.[49] The same applies in a case of agency to purchase. Again the notarial execution of a will by a

---

[40] Printed in *Parliament House Book*, Section A, and separately.
[41] A.S. (Rules of Court Amendment No. 5) 1970: printed in *Parliament House Book*, Section A.
[42] A.S. January 14, 1971: printed in *Parliament House Book*, Section A.
[43] *Carrick* v. *Manford* (1854) 16 D. 410; *Dingwall's Trs.* v. *Earl of Kintore* (1862) 24 D. 427.
[44] Contrast Stair I, 10, 8; Bell, *Prin.* § 36; with *Johnston* v. *Rome* (1831) 9 S. 364.
[45] *Farrell* v. *Arnott* (1857) 19 D. 1000; Land Purchase Act 1594, c. 220.
[46] *McPherson's Trustees* v. *Watt* (1877) 5 R.(H.L.) 9; *Cleland* v. *Morrison* (1878) 6 R. 156; *Gillespie & Sons* v. *Gardner*, 1909 S.C. 1053; *Aitken* v. *Campbell's Trustees*, 1909 S.C. 1217.
[47] *Rooney* v. *Cormack* (1895) 22 R. 761.
[48] *Weir* v. *Grace* (1899) 2 F.(H.L.) 30; *Rigg's Exrx.* v. *Urquhart* (1902) 10 S.L.T. 503; *Stewart* v. *Maclaren*, 1920 S.C.(H.L.) 148.
[49] *Cunningham* v. *Lee* (1874) 2 R. 83.

solicitor on behalf of a client is invalid if the solicitor or a partner of his takes any benefit thereunder or is nominated as executor or trustee.[50]

All these limitations arise from the policy of the law that there must be no conflict of interest between legal adviser and client and there must be no suspicion of the one gaining improper benefit for himself at the other's expense.[51]

Accounts

Solicitors are under strict obligations with regard to the care of clients' money which comes into their hands in the course of their actings on behalf of the clients. Under the Solicitors' (Scotland) Accounts Rules 1952,[52] made by the Law Society of Scotland, money in excess of £50 received from or held on behalf of a client must be paid into a client account, and books and accounts must be kept showing all dealings with the money of each separate client. The Law Society is empowered to institute the investigation of any solicitor's books by an accountant to discover whether the rules are being complied with.

Regular and accurate books must be kept and business accounts, which should be rendered periodically or, in the case of employment for one transaction, at the conclusion of that transaction, must be fair transcripts of the entries therein,[53] and give all the information necessary to enable the client and the auditor to examine it.[54]

The Law Society has power [55] to withdraw the practising certificate of a solicitor who is failing to comply with the Accounts Rules. Every solicitor must balance his books at least once in every practice year and within six months thereof deliver an accountant's certificate that the books appear to be in order.[56]

Provision is made [57] for a guarantee fund from which to compensate persons who suffer pecuniary loss by reason of dishonesty on the part of a solicitor. It is improper to do anything which can reasonably be regarded as touting, advertising or calculated to attract business unfairly, or to share profits with an unqualified person, with certain exceptions.[58]

Expenses in Litigation

Every civil court has an inherent common-law discretionary right to

---

[50] *Ferrie* v. *Ferrie's Trustees* (1863) 1 M. 291; *Finlay* v. *Finlay's Trustees*, 1948 S.C. 16.
[51] See further, cases discussed in Begg on *Law Agents*, Chap. 21.
[52] Printed in *Parliament House Book*, Section D.
[53] *Stewart* v. *Scott* (1844) 6 D. 889.
[54] *Grant* v. *Alcock* (1870) Guthrie's Sel.Shf.Ct.Cas. 11.
[55] Solicitors (Scotland) Act 1958, s. 3, amended 1963 and 1965.
[56] *Ibid.* s. 13; Solicitors' (Scotland) Accountants' Certificate Rules 1964, amended 1966.
[57] Solicitors (Scotland) Act 1949, s. 22, and Scottish Solicitors' Guarantee Fund Rules 1951, printed in *Parliament House Book*, Section D.
[58] Solicitors' (Scotland) Practice Rules 1964.

award expenses in any cause which comes before it, unless that right has been qualified or abrogated by statute.[59] In practice a pursuer usually includes an express conclusion for expenses in his summons, the justification for this being that he has been put to the expense and trouble of litigation by the defender's failure spontaneously to satisfy the pursuer's requests. The award of expenses is in the discretion of the court and accordingly, while an appeal may be taken on the question of expenses, an appellate court will not interfere unless it be shown that the judge making the award had erred in principle.

While the award of expenses is always in the discretion of the court, the court usually exercises its discretion in accordance with principles worked out in previous cases, and a large volume of case-law has developed on the subject.[60] Expenses can be awarded even if not claimed. Counsel moves for an award of expenses when judgment has been given after any hearing.

Accordingly as a rule expenses will be awarded to the successful party against the unsuccessful party, but sometimes expenses are modified or refused, sometimes no expenses are found due to or by either party and, commonly in cases arising out of a will or the disposal of an estate, all parties' expenses are made payable out of the estate. There are many special rules affecting particular categories of litigants and particular kinds of cases.

To say, however, that the court may award the successful party expenses does not mean that he will be reimbursed by the unsuccessful party to the full extent of his expenditure in the litigation. Where expenses are awarded the solicitor for the party awarded expenses must make up his itemised account and submit it to the Auditor of the Court of Session [61] for taxation. The purpose of taxation is to strike out and disallow all items of expenditure considered to have been unnecessary or excessive for the prosecution of the claim. Hence, if a party chooses to employ an unnecessary number of counsel, or pay higher fees than are warranted by ordinary practice, the extra expense will not be allowed against the other party. The auditor will allow only such expenses as are necessary for conducting litigation in a proper manner but with due regard to economy. Parties' solicitors may attend before the auditor and contend that certain items of expenditure were justifiable, and appeal may be taken to the court against the auditor's decision.

In taxing an account, the auditor may proceed on any one of three bases, expenses as between party and party,[62] which allows only such expenses as

---

[59] *Rooney* v. *Cormack* (1895) 23 R. 11; *Thomson* v. *Kerr* (1901) 3 F. 355.

[60] See Maclaren on *Expenses*, and cases in the Digests *sub voce* " Expenses."

[61] Or, in the sheriff court, the Auditor of the Sheriff Court.

[62] When expenses are awarded without qualification by the court, the taxation is between party and party.

are absolutely necessary for conducting the litigation in a proper manner with due regard to economy; expenses between solicitor and client chargeable against the opposite side, which is rather more generous; and expenses between solicitor and own client, which is still more generous and allows all expenses reasonably incurred by the solicitor for the protection of his client's interest, even though such expenses could not be recovered from the opposite party, and any extraordinary expenses specially authorised by the client.[63]

LEGAL AID AND ADVICE

A system of free legal aid for the poor has existed in Scotland since 1424. Latterly the practice was for the Faculty of Advocates annually to appoint a number of advocates as counsel for the poor, while the W.S. and S.S.C. Societies appointed agents for the poor. A committee of reporters on *probabilis causa litigandi* considered applications, which had to be supported by certificates of poverty, and could admit to the benefit of the poor's roll, which conferred the privileges of obtaining the services of counsel and solicitors for the poor gratuitously and the right to litigate without payment of any court dues.[64]

Civil Cases

This scheme was superseded in the civil courts by the establishment of the Legal Aid Scheme in 1950,[65] intended to make legal aid more readily available for persons of small or moderate means. The general administration of the scheme is in the hands of the Law Society of Scotland, which acts through a Central Committee as supervisory and accounting body, a Supreme Court Committee of advocates and solicitors which determines whether applicants have a *probabilis causa* for litigation in the Court of Session and what contribution to the expenses they must themselves pay, and a number of Local Committees of solicitors which have similar functions in respect of their local sheriff courts. The various committees maintain lists of counsel and solicitors who hold themselves as willing to act for assisted persons in various types of cases. No counsel or solicitor need participate in the scheme but nearly all do.

Legal aid is available for civil proceedings in the House of Lords, Court

---

[63] Apart from the question of paying another party's expenses, every client is entitled to have his solicitor's account of judicial expenses taxed by the auditor and need not pay any more than the taxed amount.

[64] See further, Maclaren, *Court of Session Practice*, 274 *et seq.*; Dobie, *Sheriff Court Practice*, 491.

[65] Legal Aid and Solicitors (Scotland) Act 1949, later amended, now Legal Aid (Scotland) Act 1967, as amended, and Legal Advice and Assistance Act 1972. The Acts, the Legal Aid (Scotland) Scheme 1958 (replacing the 1950 Scheme), the Legal Advice (Scotland) Scheme 1970 and other schemes and certain other regulations, are printed in the *Parliament House Book*, Section E, and in the Law Society of Scotland's *Compendium of Legal Aid and Advice*.

of Session, Lands Valuation Appeal Court, Restrictive Practices Court, Scottish Land Court, Lands Tribunal for Scotland and sheriff court, and before any person to whom a case is referred by any of these courts; but certain kinds of proceedings are excepted.[66]

An applicant for assistance must have his " disposable income " and " disposable capital," both of which are defined from time to time by regulations, assessed by the Department of Health and Social Security, which fixes a maximum contribution to be required of him. He must also show to the satisfaction of the appropriate committee that he has a *probabilis causa litigandi*. If the committee is satisfied that he has a statable case it fixes the actual contribution required and issues a legal aid certificate, which entitles him to the services of counsel (if authorised) and solicitor as an " assisted person." The litigation proceeds in the normal way but all papers are marked to the effect that the party is an assisted person, and moneys payable to an assisted person under any judgment, settlement or agreement must be paid into the Legal Aid (Scotland) Fund and only the receipt of the Law Society is a good discharge. The Law Society retains any sum due to the fund in respect of the assisted person's liability to the fund and pays him the balance.

Expenses in a legal aid case are awarded and taxed according to the ordinary rules and as between solicitor and client. The solicitor recovers his fees from the Legal Aid Fund and must pay counsel, counsel's clerk and other outlays. Counsel and solicitors receive as fees 90 per cent. of the amount of fees allowed by the Auditor on taxation. An unsuccessful legally aided litigant is responsible for any award of expenses made against him, though the court in making such an award must have regard to his means, and even if successful, the balance of the expenses of the proceedings, so far as not covered by any contribution made by him or by any award of expenses from his opponent, will be deducted from the money payable to him. The scheme is accordingly one for the assistance of litigants and is not intended to be " free."

Criminal Cases

In criminal matters the Legal Aid Scheme did not apply till 1964. It was enacted in 1587 that those accused of crime should be represented by counsel and solicitors and from the establishment of the High Court of Justiciary advocates and solicitors assumed the duty of providing representation for poor persons.[67] In each sheriff court a number of young solicitors were appointed to the Poor's Roll and were responsible for advising and defending those who could not afford to instruct a solicitor in the normal way. The Faculty of Advocates continued to appoint, at each anniversary meeting, six young advocates to act as counsel for the poor,

---

[66] 1967 Act, Sched. 1.
[67] For history see *Graham* v. *Cuthbert*, 1951 J.C. 25.

who gave their services without remuneration. It was the tradition of the Faculty that all advocates of less than three years' standing put down their names for circuits, volunteering to go to the circuit towns if required to defend poor persons, and the solicitors for the poor in the circuit towns got in touch with juniors attending the circuit as required. For long counsel for the poor undertook these duties entirely at their own expense, or for a purely nominal fee, but latterly the Exchequer paid the railway fare to the trial town and the overnight hotel expenses at a prescribed rate, but no fee for the work done.

In the case of murder trials, the solicitor approached junior counsel, whose duty it was to approach the senior Bar and to ascertain from a roster which Q.C.s were next for duty in work of this kind. Only if the Q.C. approached was actually involved in a case extending into the period in which the murder trial would be held was he excused. If the junior could not find a Q.C. who was available, the Dean of Faculty would assign a senior counsel to the case and might even take it himself. It was an obligation of honour on the Faculty that senior and junior counsel would be found to defend a person thus accused.

Legal aid now applies to proceedings in any of the High Court, the sheriff court and any court of summary jurisdiction,[68] but not for children's hearings apart from referrals or appeals.

Under the Criminal Proceedings Scheme lists of counsel and solicitors willing to act are maintained. " Duty solicitors " take it in turn to attend at courts to assist those who wish their assistance. Persons charged may also apply to a particular solicitor to have him act for them. Application is made to the court for the grant of legal aid by completion of a form giving required information and the court may inquire further from the accused or the solicitor before granting or refusing legal aid. It is not to be given in summary proceedings unless the court considers that in all the circumstances of the case it is in the interests of justice that legal aid be available, but is to be available if the court is satisfied that he is unable without undue hardship to meet the expenses of the case. It is available without inquiry into resources where the prosecution is under solemn procedure until he is allowed bail or committed for trial. There is no appeal if the court refuses legal aid. The grant entitles the solicitor to fees settled by Act of Adjournal for his work. His work includes preparation of and conduct of defence and, in indictment cases, arranging for employment of counsel. In sheriff court cases the employment of counsel requires prior sanction. A separate application must be made for an appeal. A solicitor acting for a person under the Legal Aid Scheme is not bound to carry on a defence if satisfied that it is dishonest, and may withdraw from the case.[69]

---

[68] 1967 Act, Sched. 1.
[69] *Monteath* v. *H.M. Advocate,* 1965 J.C. 14.

Legal Advice and Assistance

Legal advice in the form of oral or written advice on legal questions by a solicitor or, if necessary, by counsel is available in accordance with a scheme administered by the Law Society. The cost of the advice must not exceed £25 or a larger sum prescribed. Contributions may be required from persons receiving advice or assistance. The Law Society may employ solicitors to assist local organisations concerned with advising or guiding persons. The solicitor's account, less contributions, is paid by the Legal Aid Fund.

CONTEMPT OF COURT

Contempt of court includes a wide variety of acts insulting to the court or prejudicial to the fair administration of justice. It includes disorderly or unseemly behaviour in court by members of the public, witnesses, parties or their agents or counsel, including refusal to answer competent questions [70] or prevarication by a witness,[71] though not necessarily an inadvertent failure to attend court.[72] It includes also attempts to exert improper influence on the course of justice, including verbal attacks on judges, intimidation of witnesses [73] and particularly the publication of reports, articles or letters in the press or elsewhere which may tend to prejudice the fair trial of any pending cause [74] (though it is not contempt to report,[75] or comment subsequently, even in unfavourable terms, on, the merits or conduct of proceedings then completed) or the publication of pleadings or documents in cases before the court.[76] Contempt also covers disobedience to orders of the court, such as breach of interdict,[77] and refusal to give up or state the whereabouts of children.[78]

The court itself must determine whether conduct amounts to a contempt of its authority [79] and contempt committed in face of the court is usually dealt with summarily by the judge himself. The power to punish contempt is inherent in every court, civil or criminal, superior or inferior,[80] and may be exercised by admonition, fine or imprisonment, or in the case of legal

---

[70] *Kerr* (1822) Shaw Just. 68.

[71] *Macleod* v. *Speirs* (1884) 11 R.(J.) 26; *Wylie* v. *H.M. Advocate*, 1966 S.L.T. 149.

[72] *Pirie* v. *Hawthorn*, 1962 J.C. 69.

[73] *Forbes* v. *Weir* (1897) 5 S.L.T. 194.

[74] *Watson* v. *Murray* (1820) Shaw Just. 9; *Henderson* v. *Laing* (1824) 3 S. 384; *McLauchlan* v. *Carson* (1826) 5 S. 147; *Miller* v. *Mitchell* (1835) 13 S. 644; *Smith* v. *Mitchell* (1835) 14 S. 172; *Smith* v. *Ritchie* (1892) 20 R.(J.) 52; *Cowie* v. *Outram*, 1912 J.C. 14; *MacAlister* v. *Associated Newspapers*, 1954 S.L.T. 14. See also *Att.-Gen.* v. *Times Newspapers* [1973] 3 All E.R. 54; *Att.-Gen.* v. *London Weekend Television* [1972] 3 All E.R. 1146.

[75] But see Judicial Proceedings (Regulation of Reports) Act 1926.

[76] *Richardson* v. *Wilson* (1879) 7 R. 237; *Young* v. *Armour*, 1921 1 S.L.T. 211.

[77] *Johnston* v. *Grant*, 1923 S.C. 789; see also *Stark's Trs.* v. *Duncan* (1906) 8 F. 429.

[78] *Leys* v. *Leys* (1886) 13 R. 1223.

[79] *McLeod* v. *Lewis J.P.'s* (1892) 20 R. 218.

[80] Stair, IV, 36, 7; Ersk. I, 2, 8.

practitioners, suspension from office.[81] It should be exercised with care and discretion.[82] Sentences for contempt may be appealed to the Court of Session,[83] High Court of Justiciary,[84] or House of Lords.[85]

FURTHER READING

Boulton: *Conduct and Etiquette at The Bar*, 6th ed.
Cardozo: *Nature of the Judicial Process.*
　　　Growth of the Law.
　　　The Paradoxes of Legal Science.
Drinker: *Legal Ethics.*
Forsyth: *Hortensius: Historical Essay on the Duties of an Advocate.*
Halsbury's *Laws of England*, tit. "Barrister."
Hannay: *The College of Justice.*
Henderson Begg: *Treatise on Law Agents*, 2nd ed.
Hilbery: *Duty and Art in Advocacy.*
Keeton and Lloyd: *The British Commonwealth*, Vol. I, 1—England.
Law Society of Scotland: *Compendium of Legal Aid and Advice*, 3rd ed.
Mackay: *Practice of the Court of Session*, Vol. I.
Muirhead: "From Attorneys to Solicitors," 68 S.L.R. 25.
Singleton: *Conduct at the Bar and Some Problems of Advocacy.*
Slesser: *The Art of Judgment.*
　　　The Judicial Office and Other Matters.
Wasserstrom: *The Judicial Decision.*
W.S. Society: *History of the Society of Writers to H.M. Signet*, 1936.

---

81 *Hamilton* v. *Anderson* (1856) 18 D. 1003.
82 *Royle* v. *Gray*, 1973 S.L.T. 31.
83 *Hamilton, supra*; *Munro* v. *Matheson* (1877) 5 R. 308.
84 *Macleod* v. *Speirs* (1884) 11 R.(J.) 26; *Graham* v. *Younger*, 1955 J.C. 28; *Cordiner* 1973 S.L.T. 125.
85 *Hamilton* v. *Caledonian Ry.* (1850) 7 Bell 272.

CHAPTER 9

THE STRUCTURE OF SCOTS LAW

THE great body of doctrines, principles and rules which comprise Scots law form a logical structure with major divisions, sub-divisions, branches, headings and sub-headings and an understanding of this logical structure is an aid to study and understanding of the principles and rules and important in finding and applying the law. In its structure Scots law accords generally with the common pattern of modern Western legal systems,[1] though differing in details and having its own nomenclature for many of the categories.

Public and Private Law

The fundamental division between public and private law, recognised in Roman law and in Continental legal systems, is recognised in Scotland. According to Stair [2]: " Rights . . . are divided into public and private rights. Public rights are those which concern the state of the commonwealth. Private rights are the rights of persons and particular incorporations. . . ." Similarly, Erskine [3] wrote: " The public law is that which hath more immediately in view the public weal and the preservation and good order of society; as laws concerning the constitution of the State, the administration of the government, the police of the country, public revenue, trade and manufactures, the punishment of crimes, etc. Private law is that which is chiefly intended for ascertaining the civil rights of individuals." The distinction accordingly is generally one of whether the interests of the state, the community or society, are involved or not.

In Scotland, as in England, no clear or rigid division can be drawn between those two major bodies of law, largely because of the absence of any written constitution and of special courts or procedure for dealing with issues of public law generally. Public law issues may arise in the context of purely private law disputes in the civil courts [4] as much as in administrative tribunals or criminal courts, and government departments and public bodies commonly sue and are sued in the civil courts like private persons.[5] Only to a limited extent are there special courts charged

---

[1] Chap. 3, Branch 6, *supra*.   [2] I, 1, 23. Similarly Bankton, I, 1, 53.

[3] I, 1, 29. The distinction is also found in Art. 18 of the Articles of Union of 1707, and is used by William Forbes in his *Institutes* (1722) and Gilbert Stuart's *Observations concerning the Public Law of Scotland* (1779).

[4] *e.g. McKie* v. *Western S.M.T. Co.*, 1952 S.C. 206; *Whitehall* v. *Whitehall*, 1957 S.C. 30.

[5] *e.g. Palmer* v. *Inverness Hospitals Board*, 1963 S.C. 311; *Holmes* v. *Secretary of State for Scotland*, 1965 S.C. 1; *Bulkeley-Gavin* v. *Inland Revenue*, 1965 S.C. 232; *Ayr Town Council* v. *Secretary of State for Scotland*, 1965 S.C. 394.

with matters of public law, in that some controversies of specified kinds are determined not by ordinary civil courts but by administrative tribunals, and even then appeal sometimes lies to the superior civil courts.[6] Moreover the growth of governmental interference with many kinds of private law relationships, such as employment and leases, and the all-pervading effect of taxation make it impossible to regard the two bodies as self-contained or clearly distinguished.

Criminal law is particularly appropriately classified as public rather than private law in Scotland since the prosecution of criminal charges is almost invariably carried through in Scotland by officials acting in the public interest and not by wronged individuals. In England on the other hand private prosecution is common.[7] But the sources and literature of criminal law are distinct from those of the rest of public law and criminal law is usually regarded as a separate branch of public law.

Civil, Administrative and Criminal Law

The divisions between civil, administrative and criminal law are also well recognised in Scots law but are hard to define. They depend fundamentally on the purpose and methods of application of the particular rules, civil law existing to define the mutual rights and duties of persons with each other and to provide remedies where one has failed to implement his legal duties to the other, administrative to define and apply principles of public policy, *e.g* in relation to housing, planning or social security, in particular cases, and criminal to define what kinds of conduct are deemed objectionable or harmful to the community as a whole and to repress infringements thereof by the punishment of the offenders. There are distinct sets of civil, administrative and criminal courts and tribunals with their separate bodies of procedure.[8] Though the line of division is frequently clear, being determined by the purpose of the proceedings, the courts in which and the procedure by which matters fall to be decided, there are difficult cases,[9] and anomalies such as the rule that the only review of a decision in the (civil) Small Debt Court may be by the (criminal) High Court of Justiciary.[10]

In general much of the public law and all of the private law is civil or administrative in character and only some of the public law is criminal. In so far as this distinction depends on the courts and procedure whereby cases are decided, it is confused because today many issues of a civil

---

[6] Chap. 7, *supra.*

[7] *Cf.* Bankt. I, 1, 53; Ersk. I, 1, 29 " . . . that part of the public law that relates to crimes. . . ."

[8] See Chap. 7, *supra.*

[9] *e.g. Wright* v. *Kennedy,* 1946 J.C. 142; *Berkeley* v. *Finnie,* 1949 J.C. 118; *Haldane* v. *Allan,* 1956 J.C. 41. Many questions of administrative law arise in civil courts. See *e.g. Hamilton* v. *Roxburghshire C.C.,* 1970 S.C. 248.

[10] Small Debt (Scotland) Act 1837, s. 31.

character are decided by courts of special jurisdiction and special tribunals, and issues of administrative character decided by, or by appeal to, civil courts, so that one must think, at least procedurally, of civil and administrative, as opposed to criminal law.

Civil and Commercial Law

No distinction exists or has ever existed in Scots law between bodies of civil and of commercial law, in that there are no distinct codes or statutes dealing with the one as distinct from the other, and the same rules apply to a transaction such as sale or carriage whether the parties are private citizens or merchants or traders, and whether it is a private one or one done in the course of trade or in implement of government policy. As in England doctrines of the laws merchant and maritime have long since been absorbed into the general body of the private law rather than being kept apart in a separate body of law.[11] " This general law merchant is in England said to form part of the common law; and it is so much a part of that law that it requires not to be proved by witnesses, like matter of foreign regulation, but is noted judicially by the court . . . the same principle operates as in England; and our courts are daily in the habit of proceeding on this law-merchant as fully authoritative in Scotland, and of allowing the decisions of courts and the writings of lawyers to be cited in illustration of it." [12] In Continental systems on the other hand civil and commercial law are frequently distinct bodies of law, regulated by distinct codes and statutes, with distinct courts.

Common Law and Equity

The distinction drawn in English law and systems in the English-speaking world based thereon between courts and principles of common law and courts and doctrines of equity has never existed in Scotland. But it does not follow either that doctrines and principles founded on the idea of equity, of natural justice, reason and fairness are absent from Scots law, or that the doctrines which were and are the subject-matter of Chancery or equity proceedings in England are without their Scottish counterparts. The Court of Session has always been a court of both law and equity and the law of Scotland a mixed body of rules of strict law and of principles founded on equity.[13] It was observed by Lord Kames, and it is still true, that pleas and defences and remedies founded on equity, and in many cases closely comparable to those developed by the Chancery in England, have long been administered by the Scottish courts as part of their ordinary jurisdiction and so are interwoven into the fabric of the ordinary Scots law. " In England, where the courts of equity and common law are

---

[11] For the meaningful use of the term " commercial law," see p. 335, *infra.*
[12] Bell, *Commentaries*, Preface, xi.
[13] Bankt. IV, 7, 19 and 23.

different, the boundary between equity and common law, where the legislature doth not interpose, will remain always the same. But in Scotland and other countries where equity and common law are united in one court, the boundary varies imperceptibly; for what originally is a rule in equity, loses its character when it is fully established in practice; and then it is considered as common law: thus the *actio negotiorum gestio*, retention, salvage, etc., are in Scotland scarce now considered as depending on principles of equity." [14]

The ordinary equitable jurisdiction of the Court of Session includes, in the sphere of contract: application of the principles of retention, compensation, rescission and rectification of contracts, relief against penalty and irritancy clauses, the insistence on fiduciary duties in many relationships, the obligations of restitution, various principles in the law of succession, many doctrines of the law of trusts, and, in the sphere of remedies, specific implement and interdict, and the defences of personal bar. This ordinary equitable jurisdiction, being treated as part of the common law, is not exclusive to the Court of Session but may be exercised by all courts. [15]

In addition to its ordinary equitable jurisdiction the Court of Session has a *nobile officium*, or extraordinary equitable power to do justice in case of necessity or strong expediency, where ordinary procedure would provide no remedy. [16] The chief categories of cases where this power is now exercised are where there are omissions or defects in statutes or statutory procedure, particularly in bankruptcy, or omissions or defects in deeds or writings which frustrate their true purpose, particularly in the sphere of trusts, and the grant of remedies on petition to the Inner House in cases not competent to the Outer House or the Sheriff court. [17] The court is slow to exercise this power unless there is exact or closely analogous precedent for its exercise.

The High Court of Justiciary has a similar, though more restricted, *nobile officium*, exercised by three or more of the Lords Commissioners of Justiciary, and an inherent jurisdiction to prevent injustice and provide a remedy for all extraordinary occurrences in criminal business not otherwise provided for. [18]

---

[14] Kames, *Principles of Equity*, 17.

[15] Walker, " Equity in Scots Law " (1954) 66 J.R. 103.

[16] Stair, IV, 3, 1; Bankt. IV, 7, 24; Ersk. I, 3, 22; Kames, *Historical Law Tracts*, 231. See also *Gibson's Trustees*, 1933 S.C. 190, 198, *per* L. P. Clyde.

[17] Mackay, *Practice of the Court of Session*, 1209; MacLaren, *Court of Session Practice*, 100, 828.

[18] Hume, II, 59; Alison, II, 23; see also, *e.g. Sweeney* (1894) 1 Adam 392; *Graham Hunter* (1904) 4 Adam 523; *Lamond Lowson* (1909) 6 Adam 118; *Wylie* v. *H.M. Advocate*, 1966 S.L.T. 149; *Wan Ping Nam* v. *Federal German Republic Minister of Justice*, 1972 S.L.T. 220; *Lloyds & Scottish Finance* v. *H.M. Advocate*, 1974 S.L.T. 3. See also " Nobile Officium of the High Court of Justiciary," 1974 S.L.T. (News) 37.

Common Law and Statute Law

The distinction between common law [19] and statute law depends on the source of the particular rules in question and this distinction is met with in public and private, civil, administrative and criminal law. Common law was originally the body of law common to the whole country, based on ancient customs, practices, moral stands and beliefs and worked out and built up in the courts by the process of authoritative declaration of the rules and their application in specific cases. It is judge-made law. Statute law or legislation, enacted by Parliament, was long thought of as an alien source of rules breaking in upon the established doctrines of the law. In consequence rules and principles tend to be distinguished according as their source is in case law worked out and declared by the courts on the basis of ancient custom and practice, or in the statutes of the legislative body. This distinction corresponds to that mentioned in older books between consuetudinary and statutory, or unwritten and written law.[20]

In consequence of this distinction mention will be found in the books of common law crimes and statutory crimes or offences, common law rights and statutory rights, and so on.[21] The difference is not merely in the origin and source of the crime or right in question but in that in the former case the definition and conditions attaching to the right or claim or power in question have to be gathered mainly from the decisions in which the courts recognised, defined and restated the right or claim in question, while in the latter the definition and conditions are laid down in authoritative form in the statute, though subsequent decisions may be of value in showing the interpretation put by the courts on the verbal formulation adopted in the statute.

Substantive and Adjective Law

In both public (including constitutional, administrative and criminal)

---

[19] The term " common law " is used in various senses with different counterparts. Of these the principal are (i) the common law or Anglo-American system of law as contrasted with civil law systems, deriving from the law of Rome; (ii) common law (in England) as distinct from equity; (iii) common law of the realm as distinct from particular local or customary law; (iv) common law as contrasted with statute law, as here discussed. See further Salmond, *Jurisprudence*, 81–99; Ersk., I, 1, 28. In old Scottish books and statutes the term " common law " is occasionally used as meaning the civil, or civil and canon, law of Rome, as being the basic common rules of Scotland, distinct from the statutory law.

[20] Ersk., I, 1, 30 and 43. *Cf.* Mackenzie, *Inst.* I, 1, 9–10.

[21] Thus the claim of one person to damages for the loss caused by the death of a spouse, parent or child, is a common law claim, in that it has no other origin than ancient custom, recognised and defined in authoritative decisions of which the leading case is *Eisten* v. *N.B. Ry.* (1870) 8 M. 980. The claim of a person to Industrial Injury Benefit is statutory in that it was conferred by and is obtainable only under conditions specified in what is now the Social Security Act, 1975, as amended by later Acts and amplified by subordinate legislation made thereunder. Again, murder is a common law crime; to be in charge of a vehicle while under the influence of drink is a statutory crime.

and private law the distinction between substantive and adjective law is material. The substantive law of each branch sets out the principles and rules defining in administrative law the rights and duties of persons and authorities, in criminal law the kinds of conduct which are punishable, and in private law what rights, powers and privileges attach to legal persons in various circumstances and what duties, liabilities and disabilities are incumbent on them in other circumstances, such as the mutual rights and duties of husbands and wives, buyers and sellers, landlords and tenants, employers and employees, careless drivers and their victims, and so on, and also what secondary or remedial rights and duties comes into being on a primary right being violated or a primary duty not being implemented, such as the right to recover damages when a contract is not properly performed. In administrative law the adjective law deals with the constitution and powers of administrative bodies and tribunals, the mode of proceedings, and the awards they may make. In criminal law it deals with the jurisdiction of the various criminal courts, their procedure, the evidence competent in them, the punishments they may award and the rights of appeal therefrom. In private law the adjective law comprises the rules as to the modes of effectuating rights, the rules as to the jurisdiction of the courts, the rules of evidence, the rules as to the machinery of procedure and diligence whereby claims may be brought before courts for determination and the decrees of those courts enforced. Remedies and procedure are separate though closely connected; not every civil remedy requires that any formal legal step or approach to the court be made, and the recognised classes of legal remedies do not correspond exactly with the recognised categories of legal action.

Adjective law is not synonymous with, but wider than, law of procedure. Similarly the antithesis sometimes referred to between " right " and " remedy " is a false one; substantive rights, such as not to be injured, and remedial rights, such as to be compensated if one has in fact been injured by another's fault, are both equally legal rights, but the former is logically prior to the latter, and the latter right is contingent, and comes into existence only if the former right has been infringed. Actions and procedure come into play if need be to declare a claimant's entitlement or not to a remedy and to enforce his claim. Substantive and adjective law are constantly overlapping and interacting and no study or statement of either can avoid consideration of the other.

PUBLIC LAW

The public law of Scotland comprises all the bodies of principles and rules dealing with the legal organisation of the community and its control and direction of the affairs of individuals. These bodies of rules have greatly increased in bulk, scope and importance in the present century on account of the increased and still increasing power of the state and the greater extent to which it controls, supervises and interferes in matters with which it previously had little or no concern. State regulation, initiative, control and management, state or public enterprises and agencies abound in modern Britain and all tend to increase the importance of public law.

The General Part

The term " General Part " is better known in continental codes than in uncodified British law. The General Part deals with those matters common to the whole of the Public Law, such as the authoritative litera-ture, the sources of the principles, their authority and interpretation, and the most fundamental and general concepts and ideas which run through all the specific and particular branches and rules. Salmond [22] called it the Introductory Portion—" all those rules which by their preliminary character or of the generality of their application cannot be appropriately relegated to any special department."

Constitutional Law

The body of legal principles which determines the constitution or legal structure of a state, the essential and fundamental elements of its organisation, make up its constitutional law.[23] It deals with the structure, powers and functions of the supreme power in the state together with those of all the more important of the subordinate departments of govern-ment.[24] More specifically it deals with the head of the state and his powers; the composition and powers of the legislative body; the status and powers of Ministers, the executive and of the civil service; the courts and their judges; the armed forces; the relations of Church and state and the legal position and powers of the established Church; the relations between central government and local or subordinate authorities; relations with foreign countries, the Commonwealth and the colonies; the public revenue and the law of taxation; citizenship and its rights, such as those to personal liberty, freedom of speech and of association, and public duties, such as of jury service and assistance in the maintenance of order.[25]

Constitutional law is made up of two main elements, rules of law derived from statute, decided cases and custom, and a body of rules, understandings, habits or practices which are not in strictness rules of law, in the sense that they will not be enforced by the courts, commonly

---

[22] *Jurisprudence*, Appx. III.
[23] Salmond, *Jurisprudence*, 138; *cf*. Dicey, *Law of the Constitution*, 10th ed., Chap. 1.
[24] *Ibid*. 506.
[25] Hood Phillips, *Constitutional and Administrative Law*, 12. The whole of Chaps. 1 and 2 is enlightening. The subject-matter of constitutional law can be discerned also from the bibliography in Chap. 11.

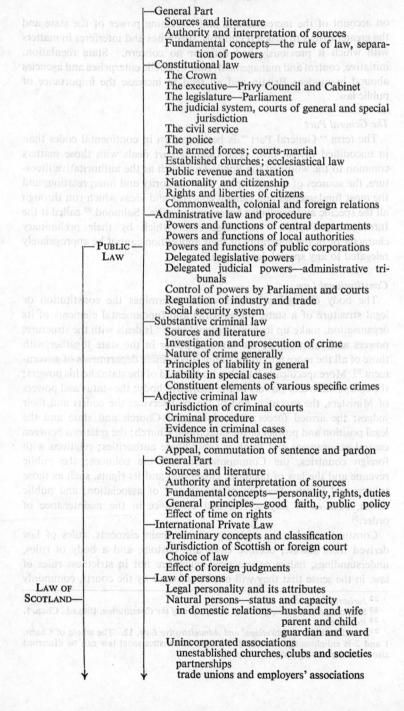

PUBLIC LAW

—General Part
    Sources and literature
    Authority and interpretation of sources
    Fundamental concepts—the rule of law, separation of powers
—Constitutional law
    The Crown
    The executive—Privy Council and Cabinet
    The legislature—Parliament
    The judicial system, courts of general and special jurisdiction
    The civil service
    The police
    The armed forces; courts-martial
    Established churches; ecclesiastical law
    Public revenue and taxation
    Nationality and citizenship
    Rights and liberties of citizens
    Commonwealth, colonial and foreign relations
—Administrative law and procedure
    Powers and functions of central departments
    Powers and functions of local authorities
    Powers and functions of public corporations
    Delegated legislative powers
    Delegated judicial powers—administrative tribunals
    Control of powers by Parliament and courts
    Regulation of industry and trade
    Social security system
—Substantive criminal law
    Sources and literature
    Investigation and prosecution of crime
    Nature of crime generally
    Principles of liability in general
    Liability in special cases
    Constituent elements of various specific crimes
—Adjective criminal law
    Jurisdiction of criminal courts
    Criminal procedure
    Evidence in criminal cases
    Punishment and treatment
    Appeal, commutation of sentence and pardon

LAW OF SCOTLAND

—General Part
    Sources and literature
    Authority and interpretation of sources
    Fundamental concepts—personality, rights, duties
    General principles—good faith, public policy
    Effect of time on rights
—International Private Law
    Preliminary concepts and classification
    Jurisdiction of Scottish or foreign court
    Choice of law
    Effect of foreign judgments
—Law of persons
    Legal personality and its attributes
    Natural persons—status and capacity
        in domestic relations—husband and wife
                parent and child
                guardian and ward
    Unincorporated associations
        unestablished churches, clubs and societies
        partnerships
        trade unions and employers' associations

friendly societies
Juristic persons or corporations
    public corporations and boards
    local authorities
    chartered and incorporated institutions
    companies
    building societies
    industrial, provident and co-operative societies
—Law of obligations
    Natural obligations
    Voluntary and contractual obligations

—PRIVATE—
LAW

      General principles
      specific and particular contracts
    Quasi-contractual obligations
      General principles
      Particular cases
    Delictual obligations
      General principles
      Particular delicts
    Obligations arising from statute, decree or other
      source
—Law of property
    Divisions of property—conversion; fixtures
    Rights in objects of property—ownership,
      possession
    Corporeal heritable property
      subjects thereof and rights therein
    Incorporeal heritable property
      subjects thereof and rights therein
    Corporeal moveable property
      subjects thereof and rights therein
    Incorporeal moveable property
      subjects thereof and rights therein
    Trusts, public and private, and trustees
    Judicial factors
    Succession on death
      Legal rights
      Intestacy—devolution of property by law
      Testacy—making and interpretation of wills
      Other modes of transfer of property on death
      Powers and duties of executors
    Bankruptcy, trust deeds and arrangements with
      creditors
—Law of civil remedies
—Adjective law
    Conveyancing
      Authentication of deeds
      Requisites of various kinds of deeds
      Examination and completion of title
      Registration of deeds
    Jurisdiction of civil courts
    Civil procedure
    Pleading and practice
    Evidence in civil cases
    Diligence and enforcement of decrees
    Appeal
    Legal profession, expenses
    Representation and Legal Aid
    Arbitration

termed conventions of the constitution.[26] Yet these conventional rules and practices, while of very particular interest to the historian and political scientist, cannot be ignored by the lawyer in that they complete the structure, the bare bones of which are supplied by the law. Without the conventions the constitutional machinery would probably be unworkable, while many of the conventions could be ignored or flouted only at the expense of causing sooner or later a breach of the law or the breakdown of the machinery of government. Hence constitutional law has been defined as the rules of law, including binding conventions, "which regulate the structure of the principal organs of government and their relationship to each other, and determine their principal functions." [27]

Constitutional law, possibly more than any other branch of law, requires to be studied with constant reference to its history and development. Many of its institutions and fundamental rules can be explained only by reference to the past circumstances which gave rise to them or caused the evolution to take a particular course. In consequence constitutional, legal and political history must regularly be prayed in aid for explanation, while many of the problems of the constitutional lawyer are equally pressing problems of the political scientist, because the organisation of the state is both a legal and a political conception and form of association or institution. The very haphazard historical development of the British Constitution, coupled with the fact that it has never been reduced as a whole to writing in the form of a single comprehensive legal document, as is customary in other countries, is one reason for the tangled and illogical nature of many of the rules of constitutional law. The close connection between law and politics in the sphere of constitutional law may be seen from the fact that the working of the British Constitution must be explained not merely in terms of rules of law but also of practices or conventions of political origin.

Administrative Law and Procedure

Administrative law has been recognised as a distinct branch of law and topic of legal study in Britain only in the last sixty years or so, owing to the enormous growth of its manifestations during that period, though the subject is really much older. There is no rigid line between it and constitutional law since the difference is mainly one of convenience and degree, constitutional law dealing with structure and with the broader rules which regulate function, while the details of function are left to administrative law.[28]

---

[26] The term was invented by A. V. Dicey in his *Law of the Constitution* (1885, 10th ed. 1960) and has been generally accepted since. See his discussion of the distinction at pp. 24–30.
[27] Wade and Phillips, *Constitutional Law*, 3.
[28] Maitland, *Constitutional History*, 526–539.

It is the law of public administration, that part of public law which prescribes the nature of the activities of the executive and administrative portions of government, the powers and duties of executive departments, agencies and officials and their relations with individuals, the forms and instruments in and through which the lower ranges of government operate.[29]

Thus it deals with the organisation and functions of the various departments of the central government, such as the Treasury and the Scottish Office, the various authorities of local government, such as district councils, which exercise functions within particular limited areas only, and of the public corporations and statutory bodies set up by the state yet not departments thereof, for the exercise of various specific social or economic functions, such as the National Coal Board, Health Boards, Agricultural Marketing Boards, the British Broadcasting Corporation. The first execute the policy of Parliament, under the directions of the Ministers of the Crown, the second the policy of representatives elected by local government electors within the framework set by Parliament, but the third are neither government departments under the control of Ministers of State nor are they elected by the electorate.[30] The functions of central departments, local authorities and public corporations are very numerous and the law is bulky and complicated: it covers such matters as police and fire services, public utilities, roads and bridges, public education, housing, social services, public health, licensing, town and country planning, the regulation of industry, trade and agriculture, supervision of factories and mines, valuation and rating, compulsory purchase of land and compensation therefor, and all the great variety of circumstances in which the state exercises control or guidance over people's lives in the general interest, or, directly or indirectly, provides some benefit or service for them.

Departments, local authorities and public bodies, moreover, have delegated to them by Parliament certain limited legislative powers, of making rules binding within limited spheres only in the form of rules, orders, by-laws, and so on, and the scope of and limitations on these powers also fall to be studied.

While administrative agencies and officials work to some extent through the ordinary civil and criminal courts and processes, of great importance are the special administrative courts, tribunals and procedures frequently

---

[29] Salmond, *Jurisprudence*, 506–507; *cf.* Jennings, *The Law and the Constitution*, 3rd ed., 194. See also Chap. 11, *infra*.

[30] See generally Campion (ed.), *British Government since* 1918; Greaves, " Public Service Boards " (1944) 7 M.L.R. 25; Friedmann, " The New Public Corporations and the Law " (1947) 10 M.L.R. 233, 377; Wade, " The Constitutional Aspect of the Public Corporation," 1949 *Current Legal Problems*, 172; Robson, "The Public Corporations in Britain To-day " (1950) 63 H.L.R. 1321; Robson, *Nationalised Industry and Public Ownership*; Friedmann, *Law and Social Change*, Chap. 9.

set up to determine matters of controversy arising in the course of administering some particular service or body of administrative controls, so that to some extent along with each branch of the public administration one must study the particular machinery provided for enforcement or the resolution of disputes in connection therewith. Thus the system of National Insurance set up in 1946 brought into existence not merely a new Ministry [31] and a mass of new legal rights and duties, but a special system of tribunals for determining disputes concerning entitlement to a payment of National Insurance benefits.

The problems of administrative law are amongst the most interesting of the present day, not least because they are frequently politico-economic-legal and not purely legal, in that they raise fundamental problems of social policy and of government as well as of pure law. The salient problems of administrative law can probably be said to be:

(1) The extent to which and the powers under which Ministers and departments of state enjoy authority delegated by Parliament to make rules, regulations and orders, filling in with details the gaps left by skeleton legislation, and the control of this delegated legislative power by the courts. [32]

(2) The extent to which and the ways in which the individual may, either through the ordinary civil courts or by administrative means, inquire into, question and challenge the exercise of administrative powers and in some cases check and limit such executive action. [33]

(3) The extent to which the ordinary courts can review and control the proceedings of administrative tribunals and officials exercising a judicial power or right to determine disputes. [34]

(4) The way in which adequate supervision and control of public corporations may be exercised by Parliament in the interests of the consumer and taxpayer, while allowing the authority freedom from detailed control and avoiding excessive centralisation. [35]

(5) Special rules relative to litigation against executive officials and departments, a topic sometimes conveniently entitled Crown Proceedings. [36]

---

[31] Now the Ministry of Social Security: Ministry of Social Security Act 1966.

[32] See generally Carr, *Delegated Legislation*; *Concerning English Administrative Law*; Allen, *Law and Orders*; *Law in the Making*; Sieghart, *Government by Decree*; Kersell, *Parliamentary Supervision of Delegated Legislation*; Report of the Committee on Ministers' Powers (Cmd. 4060, 1932).

[33] The above books and Report of the Committee on Administrative Tribunals and Enquiries (Cmnd. 218, 1957).

[34] See Griffith and Street, *Administrative Law*; Allen, *Law and Orders*; de Smith, *Judicial Review of Administrative Action*.

[35] See Morrison, *Government and Parliament*, Chap. 12; Friedmann, *Law and Social Change in Contemporary Britain*, Chap. 9.

[36] See Bickford Smith and Middleton, *The Crown Proceedings Act*, 1947; Glanville Williams, *Crown Proceedings*.

Administrative law exhibits equally with constitutional law the defects of unplanned historical development, lack of coherent system, and a welter of individual cases, each facet of public administration having a system of its own.[37] The law is developing rapidly and is constantly undergoing change, though much remains to be done to fashion it into a coherent body of doctrine. Public dissatisfaction with aspects of it has twice given rise to investigations of aspects of the subject by strong committees[38] which recommended many changes, not all of which have been carried into effect.[39] It is in the sphere of administrative law more than any other that the rights and liberties of the subject are involved in modern times and most of the important cases illustrate one facet or another of the constant struggle between the state and the individual, between government and freedom.

Substantive Criminal Law

While constitutional and administrative law overlap and run into one another, criminal law stands rather apart from the rest of Public Law with a considerable literature of its own. The criminal law consists of the body of rules relative to crimes and offences, that is, to such human acts and omissions as the supreme authority in the state wishes to prevent and suppress, and consequently declares illegal, deserving to be repressed, and punishable. The distinction between wrongs which are criminal and those which are rated by the legal system as merely civil wrongs or delicts, giving a civil remedy in damages only, depends not on the essential nature of the act or omission in question but simply on whether the government policy of the time deems the activity to deserve repression by punishment on the ground that its doing or repetition would be harmful to the community. Some wrongful conduct, such as assault, may be both a crime and a delict; conversely, adultery was once a crime and is now only a delict[40]; while modern social policy requires many kinds of conduct to be made criminal and repressed though they were previously innocent. Accordingly the main distinguishing mark of criminal law is that the state rather than an individual initiates proceedings, which

---

[37] The principal discussions, analyses and criticisms are Allen, *Law and Orders*; Robson, *Justice and Administrative Law*; Schwartz, *Law and the Executive in Britain*; Carr, *Concerning English Administrative Law*.

[38] Committee on Ministers' Powers (Donoughmore Committee), 1931–32 (Report— Cmd. 4060), and Committee on Administrative Tribunals and Enquiries (Franks Committee), 1955–57 (Report—Cmnd. 218).

[39] See Tribunals and Inquiries Acts 1958 and 1966, now Tribunals and Inquiries Act 1971.

[40] The confusion between criminal wrongs and civil wrongs (delicts) is very marked n early systems of law; see, *e.g.* Maine's *Ancient Law*, Chap. 1; Walker, " The Development of Reparation " (1952) 64 J.R. 101; Robson, *Civilisation and the Growth of Law*, Chap. 8.

have as their object the punishment of the wrongdoer and the repression of such conduct, rather than compensation for a person harmed.

So, too, classification as criminal does not necessarily follow from the inherent wrongness or wickedness or immorality of an act; thus it is no crime to commit fornication, nor, in general, to let a person drown unassisted. In some cases abortion is criminal; in some cases it is innocent. Unless the activity has been condemned by common law or statute as criminal it may be done with impunity so far as the criminal law is concerned, however immoral or potentially harmful it may be.

A distinctive characteristic of those activities declared criminal is that they are dealt with by legal proceedings of a special kind, in distinct courts and by distinct procedure, and for practical purposes an important classification of crimes is into those triable by a judge and jury in the superior criminal courts, carrying a heavy penalty, and those triable by a sheriff or magistrate, without a jury, in the inferior criminal courts and carrying only a limited penalty. There is also a substantial area of overlap between the two in that some crimes may according to circumstances be dealt with either in the superior or inferior courts.

In the study of substantive criminal law there are three main topics for consideration: there is the general problem of criminal liability, that is, the question of what physical acts or omissions and what concomitant mental states will import criminal liability [41]; secondly, there is the problem of variations in liability, that is, of what differences from the normal rules of liability exist in the case of individuals who are in some respect abnormal, either temporarily or permanently, as by reason of youth, insanity, intoxication, pregnancy or amnesia. Lastly, there is the problem of what factual and mental elements are required to constitute various specific and individual types of crimes: this is really the application in detail of the general conditions of criminal liability to particular crimes. When dealing with these specific crimes they are frequently conveniently grouped into crimes against the state, such as treason and breach of the peace, which are harmful to the peace and order of the community, crimes against the person, such as murder, rape, and assault, which are infringements of some individual's personal integrity, and crimes against persons' property, such as fire-raising, malicious damage, theft and reset.[42]

Adjective Criminal Law

In adjective criminal law the main topics are the constitution and

---

[41] See further Allen, " The Nature of a Crime," in *Legal Duties*, 221; Kenny, " The Nature of a Crime," in his *Outlines of Criminal Law*, 16th ed., Appx. I; Hall, *General Principles of Criminal Law, passim*; Williams, *The Criminal Law—The General Part*; Brett, *Inquiry into Criminal Guilt*, Chap. 2. *Cf.* also Hall Williams, " The Proper Scope and Function of the Criminal Law " (1958) 74 L.Q.R. 76.

[42] Crimes against property are by far the most numerous.

competence or jurisdiction of the different courts dealing with criminal cases, the means of investigating crimes, of apprehension of suspects, and of initiating criminal proceedings, the steps which have to be gone through before, at and after trial, the course of procedure at trial, specialties of the rules of evidence in criminal cases, the protection of the accused, the provision for appeal and the modes of punishment or treatment of the convicted which may be ordered in different circumstances.[43] The discussion of the purposes of punishment and treatment and of the most appropriate methods for various kinds of criminals and crimes is so important as to be a subject in itself, and one nowadays attracting greater attention more commensurate with its importance.

Criminology and Penology

The body of criminal law and procedure is necessarily closely connected with those other branches of social studies which are concerned with the volume of socially harmful conduct in the community.[44] The criminal law and its procedure is the instrument of the criminal policy of the state in its task of repressing and punishing socially harmful conduct. That policy leans heavily on criminology, the study of the causes of crime and criminality, both those causes which may be traced to the mental and physical constitution or abnormalities of the delinquent, such as his heredity and innate defects of character, and those which may be ascribed to the effects of social environment, such as bad housing, evil companions, poverty or unemployment, poor conditions of work and so on. " Criminology is the body of knowledge regarding crime as a social phenomenon . . . The objective of criminology is the development of a body of general and verified principles and of other types of knowledge regarding this process of law, crime, and treatment or prevention." [45]

Further knowledge of the causes of crime naturally leads to the study of suitable measures to remove or neutralise them and also, so long as criminal conduct continues to take place, study must similarly be devoted to methods of education, deterrence, repression and punishment, the suitability of particular sanctions for particular individuals, the institutions in which offenders should be treated and the methods of training and reformation which can best be employed to bring home to the offender the wrongness of his conduct and lead him on release to live an honest life.[46] This is the science of penology, which increasingly influences state criminal policy.

---

[43] See further Chap. 14, *infra.*
[44] See Radzinowicz and Turner, " The Meaning and Scope of Criminal Science," in *Modern Approach to Criminal Law* (1948), 12 *et seq.*
[45] Sutherland and Cressey, *Principles of Criminology*, 6th ed., 3.
[46] See further Fox, *English Prison and Borstal System*; Walker, *Crime and Punishment in Britain.*

While neither criminology nor penology is a branch of law in the strict sense, both are so bound up with criminal law that the study of the latter inevitably leads to the former and it is from the criminal policy of the country, informed by the discoveries of criminology and penology, that guidance can be found for the reform and development of criminal law.[47] These sciences in turn lean heavily on sociology, statistics, psychology and psychiatry.

PRIVATE LAW

Private law is the other major branch of Scots law, dealing in the main with the legal relations of individuals with other individuals or with state departments and agencies in matters wherein the latter have no special privileges, but only the rights and powers, duties and liabilities of private individuals. It defines what interests, claims or demands are recognised and protected by rules of law and how they may be vindicated against other individuals. Despite the growth of state intervention it is the private law which is of greatest concern to the layman and his legal adviser and most of the personal and economic relationships a man has with other men are regulated by private law.

The fundamental and best-known division of private law is still that of the Roman lawyers,[48] into law of persons, law of things, and law of actions, and this, with its subdivisions, is the basis for most later classifications. Another classification formerly employed was into personal rights, that is, claims against another individual only, and real rights, that is, claims enforceable against some object of property such as a man's house.[49] The division here adopted, based on the Roman one, is convenient for study and understanding as well as for practical purposes.

The General Part

For academic purposes it is again useful to segregate for separate study the most general ideas which apply throughout the whole of private law, such topics as the recognised sources of law,[50] their respective authority and the accepted principles for their interpretation, the most fundamental conceptions, such as legal personality, status, rights and duties, obligation, and so on, principles of wide general application such as good faith, public policy and personal bar, and the effect of lapse of time on rights, as by cutting them off, altering the rules of proof, or limiting the right to sue on those rights. These general ideas have to be gathered from their

---

[47] A good general introduction to this subject are the volumes of the *English Studies in Criminal Science* (now *Cambridge Studies in Criminology*) series, especially Vol. I: *Penal Reform in England*; Vol. II: *Mental Abnormality and Crime*; and Vol. IV: *Modern Approach to Criminal Law*.

[48] Inst., I, iii, 12. Omne autem jus quo utimur, vel ad personas pertinet, vel ad res vel ad actiones. *Cf.* Ersk., I, 2, 1.

[49] See, *e.g.* Ersk., IV, 1, 10.

[50] For the term " sources of law," see Chap. 10, *infra.*

piecemeal examination in books on diverse specific topics and in Scots and common law systems are largely relegated to books on Jurisprudence, whereas in civil law systems they belong to the General or Introductory Part of the Civil Code.[51]

International Private Law

It has been pointed out already that in general every state or national territory has a distinct system of law, and the courts and other agencies for enforcing that law. It follows that a group of facts raising a legal problem may involve a foreign element, in that one of the parties may live under another legal régime, or that some material fact, such as the performance of a contract, may take place in a foreign country. In recent years the extension of business and commercial relations throughout the world, of foreign travel and service abroad, of intermarriage and migration, have increased this tendency and swelled the number of cases in which a foreign element arises. Accordingly in every case involving any non-Scottish element three preliminary problems fall to be determined, namely, what country's courts have jurisdiction, or the legal power of determining this controversy; secondly, once that has been decided, what system of law falls to be applied to determine the controversy; and, thirdly, what effect is to be given to any foreign judgment in existence on the matter in issue.[52]

The rules which exist for resolving these preliminary problems are the rules of international private law, conflict of laws, or private international law. All three names have found support yet none is specially felicitous.[53] The first is probably best as indicating what the topic truly covers, namely, private law so far as it has an international or extra-national character or has to take account of extra-national factors.[54]

It is to be noted that, despite the similarity of names, these rules have no connection with, or even similarity to, Public International Law,[55]

---

[51] These topics are to some extent dealt with in the opening sections of the works of the institutional writers: see, *e.g.* Stair, I, 1; Erskine, I, 1.

[52] While logically the possibility that a problem raises an issue of International Private Law has in every case to be considered first, it is in fact convenient to postpone the study of the principles of International Private Law to a late stage in legal studies, dealing with cases having a foreign element only after the principles applicable to cases not thus complicated have been studied.

[53] The name " conflict of laws " is supported by the Bills of Exchange Act 1882, s. 72; see also *Ewing* v. *Orr-Ewing* (1885) 13 R.(H.L.) 1.

[54] Notice that for the purposes of the Scottish rules of International Private Law, England is a foreign country as much as France or Peru. The converse is equally true.

[55] See further Stevenson, " Relationship of Private International Law to Public International Law " (1952) 52 Col.L.R. 561; Gutteridge, " Comparative Law and the Conflict of Laws " (1944) Trans. Grotius Society, 119; Schmitthoff, " The Science of Comparative Law " (1939) 7 Camb.L.J. 107; Starke, " The Relation between Private and Public International Law " (1937) 52 L.Q.R. 395; Beckett, " What is Private International Law? " (1926) 7 B.Y.I.L. 73.

and that unlike that body of law, the rules of international private law
are not common to all or many legal systems, but are bodies of rules
which are part of each particular legal system and vary from one state
to another as do the other parts of the several legal systems. International
private law or private international law is therefore that part of the private
law of a particular state which determines, in a case involving a foreign
element, whether the courts of that state have jurisdiction to determine
the issue and, if so, what system of law falls to be applied, and what
effect given to any foreign judgment there may be. It is in a sense a series
of appendices to the main branches of private law, in that a question of
conflict of laws may arise in any and every branch of private law.[56]
Thus marriage is a matter of private law: if it involves a foreign element,
e.g. if one of the parties is a foreigner, or it is celebrated abroad, the international private law rules relative to marriage come into play. So too
there are conflict of laws rules applicable to contracts, property, and so
on. Moreover, it is noteworthy that the rules of international private
law do not solve the actual problems which arise, but simply answer
the preliminary questions which will enable the Scottish courts to decide
whether it is their duty or not to decide the case, by directing them to
deal with or to decline to handle the controversy, and in the former
case, to apply Scots law or another system, as may be required in the
circumstances. It is then for the rules of the Scots law or other system
chosen to determine the rights and duties of the parties.

It further follows that in some cases the appropriate answer given by
this country's rules of international private law will be that this country's
courts have no jurisdiction to deal with the case, or that they have jurisdiction but must apply another country's rules of private law to the matter
in issue; it is therefore not in every case that a country's courts will adjudicate upon a case brought before them, or will apply their own system of
private law to that case. The justification for this possible declinature
of jurisdiction, or application of another country's rules of law, by a court
is fundamentally the interests of justice, and the general practice of
civilised countries in recognising, by the comity of nations, and giving
effect to, rights acquired under another legal system or properly enforceable
by other courts. Difficulties may arise, however, as to the determination
of what foreign rules may be applied by a state since the domestic private
law of some states might be unsuitable for application or recognition
by another state. The tendency is to recognise all rights acquired under
the law of another country unless their recognition is flatly contradictory
of fundamental principles of British law.[57]

---

[56] Such questions do not arise in public law since it is concerned only with transactions within the frontiers of the country in question.

[57] On the history of the subject, see Yntema, " The Historic Bases of Private
International Law " (1953) 2 Am.Jo.Compar.L. 297; Sack, " Conflict of Laws in
the History of English Law," in *Law, A Century of Progress*, III, 342.

Law of Persons

Law deals with the rights and duties of legal persons, and duties and rights attach to legal persons. But there are " persons " in law who are not individual human beings, who are groups of individuals collectively personified by law as artificial or juristic persons and also groups which are treated as entities for some purposes yet not fully recognised as legal persons. Personality is in law the attribution by the legal system of legal existence, of the ability to have legal rights and to be subject to legal duties, and it is for the law itself to lay down what kinds of human beings, of groups of beings and of institutions, have legal personality.[58]

The law of natural persons deals with all the rights, privileges and powers which attach by law to an individual as such, independently of rights acquired by contract or rights arising from the possession of property. It relates first to the recognition of an individual's legal personality, or his existence in the eyes of the law, and of his legal status and capacity, as being a minor or a person of full age or an incapax, and as having various rights, powers and immunities, and being subject to various duties, liabilities and disabilities.[59]

Secondly, the law of persons deals with the law of domestic relations, those legal rules which affect an individual by reason of his membership of a family group and govern his interactions with others of that group. This branch falls into three main topics concerned respectively with relations flowing from marriage, parenthood, and guardianship, frequently called the law of husband and wife, parent and child, and guardian and ward respectively.[60] In each of these spheres one is concerned with the constitution and termination of the relationship, the mutual rights and duties which flow from it during its subsistence, and the regulation of the matrimonial or family property rights of the parties.

At the centre of all these relationships lies the cardinal social, moral and religious institution of marriage of which the root conception is a lasting and permanent, though possibly not lifelong, union of one male and one female for cohabitation, as distinct from a merely temporary association.[61] This idea of lasting union has been recognised by every legal system in varying degrees; in Christian countries monogamous marriage alone is fully recognised though polygamous or potentially

---

[58] On the concept of personality see further Salmond, *Jurisprudence*, Chap. 15.

[59] Much of the detail of this branch of the law of persons is, for reasons of convenience, discussed also in connection with constitutional law (*e.g.* the right to become an M.P. or a naturalised subject), or contract (*e.g.* power to make a contract), or reparation (*e.g.* rights to liberty, reputation and freedom from harm), or property (*e.g.* right of landowner to cut timber).

[60] The name " Family Law " is being increasingly given to this branch of the subject, as a convenient compendious term for its main topics.

[61] On marriage generally see Westermarck's *History of Human Marriage*; James, *Marriage and Society*; Lecky, *History of European Morals*.

polygamous marriages contracted under other legal and religious regimes are not necessarily wholly devoid of recognition and effect.

The nature of marriage and the conditions under which it may be contracted and under which, if indeed at all, it may be dissolved, is a difficult modern social, moral and religious as well as legal problem.[62] The rules of law on the subject at any time can only be those which commend themselves as a compromise solution to a large proportion of the community. The legal rules, it should be noted, are those of the state and not of the individual's Church, so that the state law may permit a person to do what his religious beliefs and his Church will not permit him to do, and conversely. The legal rules are those which seem best, having regard to marriage primarily as a social institution, though they naturally tend to correspond fairly closely with the general view of the principal Churches. But there are many matters on which the law is silent and the Churches may exert their influence on their own members unhindered.

It follows that there are bodies of legal rules regulating the contracting of marriage and the dissolution of marriage and the consequences which result in various departments of law from the fact that two individuals are husband and wife. Formerly, the fact that a woman was married placed her under numerous and serious legal disabilities, but over the last hundred years the movement has been towards the emancipation of women and these disabilities are now greatly diminished.[63]

In the same way legal consequences, mutual rights and duties, follow from the birth of children, and these differ according as the children are legitimate or illegitimate, while there must also be considered the intermediate categories of those who are born illegitimate but later legitimated, or who are adopted by individuals as their children though not born as such.

The last topic of family law, guardianship, arises from the natural incapacity of young persons and persons of defective mental capacity to look after themselves or exercise the judgment required in legal transactions. Accordingly there is a body of rules laying down the extent of legal incapacity of various categories of persons too young or mentally too weak to be allowed to act on their own behalf and prescribing what persons may act on their behalf and by what means the appropriate person may be selected and appointed and authorised to act on behalf of the ward, and what the mutual rights and duties of guardian and ward shall be.

Guardianship, it should not be overlooked, is not merely a matter

---

[62] See Report of the Royal Commission on Marriage and Divorce (Cmd. 9678, 1956).

[63] See *A Century of Family Law, 1857–1957* (ed. Graveson and Crane). The details belong to English Law only, but the general parts apply substantially to Scotland also.

between the parties, but is today of increased social importance as part of the complex legal machinery for the care and protection of children and others unable to look after themselves, and it is now regarded as increasingly important that these persons should have as good opportunities as other individuals of growing up and developing their potentialities.

The law of natural persons also covers the capacities and powers of individuals in extra-domestic relations, that is, *vis-à-vis* persons outside the family, the status, capacity and powers of exceptional persons such as aliens, bankrupts, convicts, and persons of unsound mind, in their relations with other persons, and the special capacities and powers attaching to persons by virtue of professional qualifications.

It has been pointed out that legal persons include not only human beings or natural persons; there are also groups of persons who come together for particular purposes and form voluntary associations. These associations are to some extent and for limited purposes treated by the law as legal entities, but are unincorporated, *i.e.* not fully recognised as legal persons in themselves.[64] The device of association is rather a collective name for the group of members, though in some cases such associations come very close to being legal persons or corporations. Of this kind are churches other than the legally established church, friendly societies, trade unions, partnerships, trustee savings banks and many clubs, societies and professional bodies.

Thirdly, however, there are those other cases where the groups formed by the association of individuals for specific purposes are treated by the law as themselves legal entities or juristic persons, with legal powers and capacities, liabilities and duties, quite independent and separate from those attaching to the persons who form the group. This arises only where the group is incorporated in a manner recognised by law; the corporation, not the members, owns the property, sues and is sued, can contract, do wrong, and even commit crime, and it will still exist if all the members die.[65] The main examples of juristic persons are public corporations incorporated by statute, such as the National Coal Board, and municipal corporations, both considered in their private capacities, *e.g.* as employers or buyers of goods, chartered bodies such as Universities, Royal Colleges and professional institutions, companies incorporated under the Companies Acts, building societies, and industrial and provident societies.

---

[64] See generally Lloyd, *Unincorporated Associations*.

[65] See further Geldart, " Legal Personality " (1911) 27 L.Q.R. 90; Wolff, " On the Nature of Legal Persons " (1938) 54 L.Q.R. 494; Gray, *Nature and Sources of the Law*, Chap. 2; Hallis, *Corporate Personality*; Salmond, *Jurisprudence*, Chap. 15; Maitland, " Trust and Corporation " in *Collected Papers*, III, 321, and *Selected Essays*, 141. See also Gower, *Modern Company Law*, 3rd ed., Chaps. 1–4 and 11.

In the cases of voluntary associations and of corporations the law of persons defines the way in which the association or corporation comes into being, its powers and capacities, its duties and liabilities, the relations between the body and its members and outsiders, the position of the representatives who act in its name, and the way in which the association or corporation may be ended and dissolved. While in many respects associations and corporations can act like natural persons in other respects they cannot, nor are the different kinds of associations and of corporations all alike.[66]

Law of Obligations

The law of obligations covers all those sets of circumstances when two persons come to be so placed that the law imposes a legal link or bond of obligation between them, from which flow rights, duties, liabilities, privileges, disabilities and powers as between one and another.[67] This department of law falls into five branches.

The first branch deals with natural obligations arising by force of law from the natural relations of spouses, parents and children.

The second is the law of voluntary obligations and contracts, which deals with the rules whereby individuals may voluntarily bind themselves by promises or may contract or agree in legal and binding form to create certain rights and duties, claims and liabilities between themselves and exigible from each other only. Thus where A and B agree, the one to buy and the other to sell, there is a legal contract of sale, and the law imposes duties on one to deliver the goods and on the other to pay the price, or grants remedies for defective performance or non-performance. The general principles of the law of contract deal with the capacity of individuals to contract, the illegality of some contracts, the form requisite for contracts, the effect of such factors as error or fraud on the making of a valid contract, performance, and remedies for breach of contract. These general principles of the law of contract have been determined inductively by jurists from the examination of the particular cases. The law of contract also includes the particular and specific kinds of contracts such as sale, hiring, carriage, lease and others, which, as well as being regulated by the general principles applicable to all or at least most kinds of contracts, frequently have specialties and peculiarities applicable only to contracts of those particular kinds. In many cases, too, there are statutory provisions applicable to particular kinds of contracts only. The main specific contracts are agency, banking contracts, building and engineering contracts, cautionry and guarantee, carriage by land, by sea, and by air, custody, deposit, employment or

---

[66] See further bibliography in Chap. 11, *infra*.
[67] *Cf*. Inst. 3, 13, *pr*. Obligatio est juris vinculum, quo necessitate adstringimur alicuius solvendae rei, secundum nostrae civitatis jura.

service, hire, hire-purchase, insurance, lease, loan, moneylenders' contracts, partnership, pledge, sale of goods, of land, and of incorporeal rights.

The third branch of obligations, usually known as quasi-contract or restitution, covers various miscellaneous cases of obligation which are neither truly contractual, despite the name, nor truly delictual, but which resemble contract in that they might have arisen from contract and may even fictionally be supposed to have done so, and resemble reparation or delict in that the obligation is imposed by force of the general law rather than undertaken by agreement of the parties. The circumstances giving rise to a quasi-contractual obligation all have the common element that, if the law did not impose in these circumstances an obligation to make restitution, one party would benefit unjustifiably and the other would lose. Thus quasi-contractual obligations of restitution are imposed by law where one man pays by mistake money which he did not owe, or where one comes into possession of another's property not intended for him.

The fourth branch of obligations is the law of delict or reparation, whereby the law by its own force and independently of any agreement imposes on one individual a legal obligation to make compensation for, or otherwise to remedy, a legal wrong he has done to another, which has constituted an infringement of a legal right vested in that other person by a general principle of law. Thus the law invests individuals generally with a right to freedom from bodily harm; if X injures Y unjustifiably, that is a delict and the law creates an obligation of reparation, imposing on X the duty to compensate Y, and giving Y a right of legal action to recover reasonable reparation from X for his injuries. The law of delict defines the circumstances in which and conditions under which such a claim to reparation arises. There is again a body of general principles applicable generally to all or at least most delicts, dealing with such matters as title to sue, the liability of one person for another, the general grounds of liability, defences and exemptions from liability, the effect of insurance and contributory negligence, the remedies, and so on. In addition there are principles applicable to specific delicts, to harm done in particular ways. The main specific delicts recognised are assault, damage to property, defamation, fraud, negligently causing personal injury or death, infringement of copyright or patent rights, nuisance, passing-off, trespass, and wrongful imprisonment or use of legal process, but the list is not closed and new modes of wrongs may yet call for recognition and remedy.

The final branch of obligations deals with obligations imposed on parties by statute, such as the duties on employers to have care for the safety of employees, obligations imposed by decree of court, such as to pay another money or refrain from conduct injurious to him, and obligations arising from other grounds such as from the relationship of trust.

These bodies of law are of enormous practical importance. Contract is obviously of great importance in business and trade, and commercial undertakings engage every day in numerous contracts, of employment of men, of hiring of plant, of purchase of material, of sale of finished products, of carriage of goods to consignees, and so on. The individual likewise enters into and performs contracts every time he buys a newspaper, travels on public transport, orders coal, instructs the plumber to repair his water-taps and so on. Quasi-contract or restitution is much less common or important yet arises not infrequently. Delict or reparation is similarly of widespread and everyday importance. Every accident in the street or at work may give rise to a claim of damages in reparation for the breach of duty, *i.e.* the legal duty or obligation, imposed on each of us by the legal system, not unjustifiably to injure or do harm to our neighbour.

The law of obligations in one branch or another accordingly regulates a great deal of our relations with one another in the normal life of society and it covers a very extensive body of principles and rules of law. It is important to remember that the number of cases of breach of contract or cases where contracts fail of their intended effect are enormously outnumbered by the cases where legal contracts are made, duly performed on both sides, and terminated to the complete satisfaction of both parties, all in accordance with the rules of the law of contract, but without the legal system being formally invoked at all. So, too, in the great majority of cases persons avoid doing unjustifiable harm to others and avoid coming under the duty to pay damages in compensation for wrong, that is, they manage to observe the legal obligation not to do wrong to others.[68]

Law of Property

The law of property [69] consists of all the rules conferring, defining and regulating legal rights vested in individuals over material and immaterial things, rights of ownership, possession, use, alienation and disposal. It is a large and important subject of law because of the great number, importance, utility and value of the kinds of property recognised, and of the number and variety of the kinds of legal rights which may be exercised in relation thereto. For various reasons, partly historical, partly rational, various kinds of objects of rights of property have special sets of rules

---

[68] See further bibliography in Chap. 11, *infra.*

[69] Note that the word " property " may mean either the legal right of property, of owning, holding, using and disposing of a thing, or the thing itself over which legal rights subsist (*e.g.* " desirable property situated at ..."). The former is the more correct legal meaning of the word.

applicable to them. Moreover, in modern times legislative intervention in property law has been common, the underlying notion being to limit or prevent the use of property for personal or selfish ends and to encourage and even require its use in the interest of the general welfare. Thus disposal on death is limited by taxation and the rules of succession, and use during life is regulated by requirements of licences, planning permission, requisition or compulsory purchase by public authorities and so on.

Objects of property, however, take many forms and a distinction must be drawn at once between heritable and moveable objects of property,[70] which, in general, comprise land and buildings on the one hand and goods, such as clothes, furniture and vehicles, on the other hand. This distinction, moreover, is close to but does not quite coincide with the physical distinction between immoveable and moveable property, which is a distinction important where problems of conflict of laws arise. This is not a distinction drawn entirely on logical grounds but stems from the dualism of rules of succession on death whereby for reasons explicable only by legal history some property (heritable property) descended to the person designated by the law as heir, and some (moveable property) descended to the persons designated by the law as next-of-kin. Difficult questions sometimes arise as to whether some thing is in the circumstances heritable or moveable, and it must be noted that a thing may shift from one category to the other: thus trees are heritable, but when cut the timber is moveable.

Cutting across this division into heritable and moveable property is the distinction of corporeal and incorporeal objects of property, according as there is a corporeal, visible and tangible object over which the property-rights subsist, such as land, buildings or goods, or only an incorporeal right, such as patent rights and copyrights, shares in companies, leases or servitudes. In the latter case all that exists is the legal right, which may, however, be represented by some tangible object such as a deed, certificate or other piece of paper; but in such a case the paper is evidence only of the right, and is not itself the object of the proprietary right.

A further distinction of importance applicable to all kinds of objects of property is that between *jura in re propria*, or the rights which an individual may exercise over or in relation to objects of his own property, whether material or immaterial, such as enjoying, using, selling or bequeathing them, and *jura in re aliena*, or those rights which an individual may possess and exercise in or over objects of the property of another, whether material

---

[70] This corresponds, in general though *not* exactly, to the distinction in English law between real and personal property; land is real property, books, money and shares personal property. In neither system does the distinction correspond *exactly* to that between moveables and immoveables. Note also that " moveable " in this connotation is spelled with an " e." On the distinction between heritable and moveable property, see further Erskine, *Inst.* II, 2; Bell's *Commentaries*, II, 1–10.

or immaterial, such as using a servitude or holding a security right over it, or enjoying a lease of it. The rights, *jura in re propria* or proprietary rights, which a man has over his own property are those of ownership and possession. The full rights of ownership include the power to use the property, deal with its fruits or produce or earnings, and to use up or consume or destroy; the power to possess in person or by another; the power to sell or to give or burden as security for debt; and the power to bequeath or give by will. These rights are not by any means unqualified; thus the common law rules of nuisance limit the uses to which land may be put while statutory regulations restrict building or development, and the power of bequest is restricted by the doctrine of legal rights.[71] The modern tendency is to limit very much by statute the exercise of the rights of ownership in the general interest of the community. Social and political theory and the economic exigencies of modern times have played havoc with property rights and there is as much law, and more complicated law, dealing with what one is not now allowed to do than with what one may do at common law.

Jura in re aliena, on the other hand, are created by the transfer by an owner to another of certain of the mass of rights which he enjoys by virtue of his ownership; in consequence the other party comes to have certain defined and limited rights in property which he does not himself own. *Jura in re aliena* are always incorporeal. The commonest forms of such rights are first, the taking of a lease of land or buildings, whereby a tenant acquires the right to possess and occupy certain property for a defined period and on conditions defined partly by the general law, both of statute and of common law, and partly by the terms of the lease or tenancy agreement. The comparable transaction in moveable property is that of letting on hire. The second important kind of *jus in re aliena* consists of the transfer of property, heritable or moveable, to another in security for the repayment of money borrowed by the owner from that other. This has various forms, some applicable to heritable property[72] and some to moveable property[73]; in some the title is transferred to the lender[74] but in others, particularly of moveable property, only possession and not full title of ownership is transferred.[75] The third main item under this heading is the servitude or right of another to put an owner's property to a certain class of definitely limited uses[76] or to prevent the owner from putting it to a certain class of determined uses.[77] A servitude right is

---

[71] See under Succession, *infra.*

[72] *e.g.* standard security; floating charge.

[73] *e.g.* pawn or pledge; floating charge; assignation in security (for incorporeals).

[74] *e.g.* in disposition or assignation in security.

[75] *e.g.* in pledge.

[76] *e.g.* right of way, *i.e.* right to pass over X's land by a determined path.

[77] *e.g.* right *altius non tollendi*, to prevent X's raising his building higher and thereby cutting off light and air.

normally real, *i.e.* attaching to and exercisable over a piece of land, but there is a small class of personal servitudes, of which the only important example is liferent, or the right of one person to occupy or use certain property during his lifetime only, and not as absolute owner, and for that period to be a burden or encumbrance on the rights of the owner. The last kind of *jus in re aliena* is the trust, where the holder of property as trustee has his rights qualified by the claims of the beneficiary, for whose benefit he holds the property.[78]

These distinctions may be summed up in tabular form [79]:

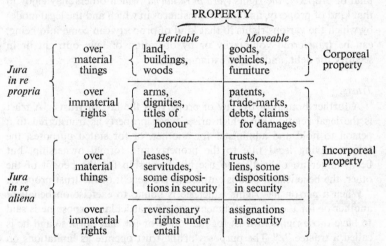

PROPERTY

		Heritable	Moveable	
Jura in re propria	over material things	land, buildings, woods	goods, vehicles, furniture	Corporeal property
	over immaterial rights	arms, dignities, titles of honour	patents, trade-marks, debts, claims for damages	
Jura in re aliena	over material things	leases, servitudes, some disposi- tions in security	trusts, liens, some dispositions in security	Incorporeal property
	over immaterial rights	reversionary rights under entail	assignations in security	

Accordingly, the law of property falls naturally into a preliminary part and four main branches. The preliminary part deals with the classification of things and rights as heritable or moveable, corporeal or incorporeal, with " fixtures," that is, with the circumstances in which a thing moveable by nature may be treated in law as so affixed to heritage as to be heritable, and with the doctrines of conversion and reconversion, that is, with the circumstances in which a claim to heritable property may be changed in law to a claim to moveable property and vice versa, as where for example, land bequeathed by will has been converted into money before the will takes effect. The four branches are (i) corporeal heritable property, such as land, buildings, growing timber and crops; (ii) incorporeal heritable property, such as titles and rights to arms, leases of land, servitudes over land and some security rights secured over land; (iii) corporeal moveable property, such as vehicles, furniture, books, animals,

---

[78] On trusts, see further, p. 330, *infra*.
[79] The items of property listed in the two columns are examples of each class only, not a complete enumeration.

trading stock and machinery; and (iv) incorporeal moveable property, such as claims of debt or for damages, patents and trade-marks, commercial goodwill, shares in companies and some security rights. The rules of law are not always the same for the four branches: thus sale of land differs in certain respects from sale of goods, such as vehicles, and the mode of taking security over land for the repayment of money differs from the mode of taking security over trading stock or company shares. Under each of the branches have to be considered the kinds of property covered, the rights (*jura in re propria*) conferred by ownership and possession of that kind of property, the rights (*jura in re aliena*) which others may enjoy in that kind of property, and the circumstances in which and the legal modes by which the various rights in that kind of property can come into being, can be transferred voluntarily or by operation of law, outright or in security for debt, and can be extinguished.

Trusts

A further branch of the law of property is the law of trusts. A trust is the legal relationship which arises when property is transferred to a person to hold and administer for another, or for stated purposes, the trustee having legal title to the property and formal ownership, but being under an obligation to use his ownership for the benefit of the other, the beneficiary, who is entitled to the benefit of the trust property. " When a person has rights which he is bound to exercise on behalf of another or for the accomplishment of some particular purpose he is said to have those rights in trust for that other or for that purpose and he is called a trustee." [80] The purposes of the trust operate as limitations on the trustee's ownership and powers of disposal and are commonly declared in a deed or will under which the truster creates the trust.[81]

The trust conception has many and varied uses; it has been and is of social importance in protecting inexperienced, absent or incapable owners whose property is held and managed by trustees on their behalf. It is the normal way in which endowments for charitable, religious and educational purposes are held and administered. Again, the property of unincorporated groups and communities such as some clubs, churches, trade unions, is commonly held by trustees on behalf of their body of members. In the international sphere the concept has been applied to the protection and supervision of less developed communities by more advanced ones.[82]

---

[80] Maitland, *Lectures on Equity*, 44.

[81] Bell, Prin. § 1991. The trust has been greatly developed in English law: a classic passage is Maitland's *Lectures on Equity*, lects. III–IV. But history and practice in Scotland have not followed English models entirely.

[82] The Trusteeship Council of the United Nations operating under the United Nations Charter, Chaps. 11–13.

Private law trusts are classified as private or public, private where the property is held for individuals, public where it is held for charitable, educational or other public purposes. There is a great mass of law dealing with trustees' powers and duties in different circumstances, the most striking feature of which is the strict insistence by the court that the trustee must always take care, be diligent in his duties, and never make any personal profit from his trusteeship or otherwise permit a conflict to arise between his personal interests and those of the funds under his care. Trusteeship is an onerous responsibility, but the high standards exacted have played a considerable part in the maintenance of public morality, probity and honour, while the courts have extended this by treating company directors and others having charge of property not their own as trustees, and thus enforced a generally high standard of commercial morality.

The Judicial Factor is a kind of trustee; he is appointed by the court and answerable thereto, but his functions are similar to those of the trustee in that they normally consist in holding, administering or otherwise dealing with property on behalf of another, who is absent, or incapax, or bankrupt or otherwise cannot be allowed to handle it himself. While he is an officer appointed by the court he is usually an accountant or other man of business and is not a permanent court official.

Succession

An important branch of the law of property, both in heritable and moveable objects, consists of the rules of succession, which determine the way in which property devolves on other persons on the death of its owner. It falls into three sections. In the first place there are certain claims existing at common law in Scotland known as " legal rights," conferring on certain relatives of a deceased rights to succeed to specified proportions of the moveable property of the deceased. These claims are of the nature of debts against the estate and may be claimed whatever the deceased may have wanted or prescribed by his will and even against his wishes. Accordingly it is not possible in Scotland completely to disinherit the relatives protected by these provisions.

Secondly, there is the body of rules of intestate succession, which apply in the cases where there is no will, or no will which is valid and effectual, or where any will left has failed in part or has left part of the estate undisposed of; these rules prescribe to what persons and in what proportions the estate should be distributed. There are also certain statutory preferences under which in particular cases certain relatives have preferential claims on the property of the deceased. Till 1964 separate sets of rules existed for heritable property and for moveable property and further rules dealt with the interaction of the two sets of rules where the deceased left both kinds of property. Since 1964 a common set of rules deals with both heritable and moveable property, save in certain special cases.

Thirdly, there are the rules of testate succession, covering the case where the deceased leaves a will. These rules prescribe the requirements for the form and validity of a will or testamentary declaration by the owner on how he wishes his property to devolve or be distributed on his death, and there are various principles of construction and presumptions which have been developed to assist the courts in interpreting the various forms of written expressions which are found in wills.

A pendant to the law of succession is the body of rules governing the rights and duties of executors, who are the individuals appointed by the deceased, or by the court, to ingather the deceased's estate, pay his debts, and distribute it according to his will or the rules of succession.

Succession is in practice materially affected by the incidence of capital transfer tax prescribing what percentage of a deceased person's estate falls to the government on his death. This is itself a substantial body of statutory law and of the interpretations placed on the various statutory provisions in particular circumstances, and the effect of taxation has always to be considered in framing wills and settlements of property.

Bankruptcy

Bankruptcy is the proceedings taken to declare bankrupt a person who cannot pay his debts, to take his property, heritable and moveable, out of his hands and administer it for the benefit of his creditors, distributing it rateably among them. The court may in appropriate circumstances sequestrate the estates of an insolvent person and appoint a trustee in bankruptcy to administer the property. The debtor is bound to assist in the realisation and distribution of his estates and, when he is discharged, he is freed from liability for his debts. As an alternative to going through the procedure of bankruptcy, an insolvent person may voluntarily sign a trust deed, making over his property to a trustee who administers it for behoof of the creditors, or make an arrangement with his creditors, called a composition contract, whereby he agrees to pay each so much in the pound of his debt.

Law of Civil Remedies

The law of civil remedies defines what remedial rights may be claimed by a person aggrieved by an infringment of his rights, and in what circumstances one remedy or another is competent or appropriate. Remedies include judicial declarator of rights, interdict against infringement of rights, damages in compensation for harm done, divorce and many others.

Adjective law

This is a compendious term for the bodies of law governing the means of giving effect to rights, and the rules governing civil actions to obtain these remedies. The older books, following the Roman law, call it the law of actions, but this is too limited.

Conveyancing

The topic of conveyancing is an adjunct to the law of property. " Conveyancing is the art which deals with the transfer of property by writing . . . transfer includes every kind of right in and over property which can be originated, conveyed, or extinguished by writing." [83] It accordingly covers the requisites of deeds in general and the form of the particular deeds appropriate to create, transfer or extinguish all the different kinds of rights which may subsist in and over the various kinds of property, in particular their transfer on sale or by succession from one person to another. Rules of the law of property define what rights may subsist in various kinds of property and who may hold them and what the incidents of his enjoyment of those rights are: conveyancing law and practice prescribe how the rights may be created, transferred or extinguished. Hence conveyancing covers the examination of the written title-deeds to land to ascertain a person's rights therein and the framing of the deeds requisite to convey those rights to a buyer, the preparation of dispositions in security, wills, leases, and similar documents affecting property rights.

The handling of conveyancing occupies a large part of the time and attention of many solicitors, and it involves drafting and practical techniques and rules of professional practice as well as law and requires practical instruction as much as study. [84]

Other branches of Adjective Law

Other branches of adjective law prescribe the circumstances in which and the manner in which actions to obtain remedies may be brought and carried through in the various civil courts. It is plain that it is of no advantage to a man to have a legal right or claim against another if he cannot in case of necessity vindicate that right speedily and cheaply, and the importance of a simple and inexpensive method of bringing disputes before a court and having them determined and enforced can hardly be stressed too much. It is equally true that for the legal practitioner knowledge of procedure is important so that he will know in what way best to obtain the remedy required by his client.

Firstly there are rules prescribing the structure and the competence or

---

[83] Wood, *Lectures on Conveyancing*, 1; *cf.* Bell's *Law Dictionary, s.v.*; Jowitt's *Dictionary of English Law, s.v.*
[84] See further, bibliography in Chap. 11, *infra.*

jurisdiction [85] of the various civil courts in different kinds of civil cases, the kinds of claims which may be made in different circumstances, and rules governing procedure or the steps to be taken to initiate the claim and the stages it must or may go through before hearing, the course of events at the hearing, and the rules regulating appeals. Procedure is constantly in danger of being treated as an end in itself rather than as merely a means to facilitate the ascertainment of rights and the adjudication of disputes. It is today less possible than it formerly was to lose a good case through mistakes in procedure but mistaken procedure may still waste much time and money.

An adjunct of civil procedure is the art of pleading,[86] of framing properly and accurately the written statements which are necessary steps in litigation. This is something of an art in itself, requiring an extensive knowledge of law and of procedure, a ready pen, and a subtle and even crafty insight into the strategy and tactics of litigation. In the past pleading has sometimes been practised rather as an intellectual exercise for its own sake than for its proper function, which is to bring before the court as shortly and accurately as possible the litigant's version of what events happened, his contentions as to what legal result should follow, and to afford his opponent fair notice of the case the latter has to meet.

The law of evidence is likewise intimately connected with procedure and pleading. Evidence comprises the facts, documents and testimony which may legally be adduced at a judicial inquiry to prove or disprove the existence or happening of some matter in dispute. The principles of the law of evidence define, first, what matters the judge is expected, as an intelligent and educated man, to know,[87] and in what cases the judge must [88] or may [89] presume some fact. Then there are principles regulating the admissibility or competency of particular kinds of evidence, as whether certain persons may give evidence, whether oral evidence may be given or only written, whether evidence of what the witness was told

---

[85] Notice that jurisdiction means (1) the *power* of issuing an enforceable decree or order, and also (2) the *area* within which a particular court may issue valid and enforceable decrees or orders. Thus the Court of Session alone has jurisdiction in divorce cases (sense 1) but actions for debt may be brought in Edinburgh Sheriff Court only against individuals residing within the jurisdiction thereof (sense 2).

[86] The art of advocacy or oral pleading and argument is a further more remote adjunct, which is, however, almost completely unrestrained by rules of law, depending almost entirely on the arts of rhetoric and logic, yet requiring an extensive underlying knowledge of procedure and evidence as well as of law. It is a subject by itself, best learned by experience and following good exemplars. See further, Munkman, *The Technique of Advocacy.*

[87] *e.g.* the main facts of geography, history, physical science, social and commercial life, etc.

[88] *e.g.* that a child under eight is incapable of committing crime; in such cases no evidence to the contrary is allowed.

[89] *e.g.* that a person confined in a mental hospital for five years is incurably insane; presumptions of this latter kind may be rebutted by evidence to the contrary.

by another may be given and so on; there are other principles relating to the relevancy of evidence, or its pertinency to the matter under inquiry, such as whether previous incidents similar to that under investigation may be adduced as evidence, or whether actings or statements should be proved as tending to establish intention or other state of mind, and principles regulating the mode of proof of particular kinds of facts, such as that trust may be proved only by writing or the defender's admission on oath.

There are numerous other topics important to evidence such as oaths and affirmations, questions of onus of proof, identification of persons, authentication of documents, sufficiency of evidence and corroboration, and the weight of evidence and its evaluation.

While pleading and procedure may tend to be technical and somewhat arid, the study of evidence is valuable for developing the logical and reasoning faculties, and is of great importance in legal practice since points of evidence frequently crop up and, if objection is not taken instantly, some damaging statement may be made.

Diligence deals with the various ways of enforcing a decree obtained against a defender and is a topic of some size and complexity.

Closely connected with procedure are the rules regulating the representation of litigants and prescribing what litigants may be granted Legal Aid, *i.e.* financial assistance from public funds to litigate, and the principles of expenses, defining who must bear the cost of particular steps of litigation.

Arbitration is the determination of a dispute, not by resort to the courts, but by an arbiter or arbiters. Any matter, except an issue relating to the status of an individual or of a criminal nature, may be referred to arbitration. In some cases statute directs that certain disputes are to be referred to arbitration. Arbitration may be preferable to litigation in some circumstances, as being quicker, less formal and more private, and permitting the parties to choose an arbiter familiar with the technicalities of the subject in dispute. Commercial contracts frequently provide for the settlement of disputes by arbitration in accordance with rules framed by a trade association. The London Chamber of Commerce maintains a Court of Arbitration which has great experience in settling commercial disputes.[90]

Mercantile, Commercial or Business Law; Industrial or Labour Law; Agricultural Law

In Scots law, as in Anglo-American legal systems generally, mercantile or commercial or business law is not a distinct branch of law applicable to a particular class of persons or transactions, but is only a compendious

---

[90] See further, bibliography, in Chap. 11, *infra.*

name for a group of topics of the general law of the land.[91] The same is true of industrial law and agricultural law.[92] Any special rules applicable to merchants or traders under the law merchant or the general maritime law have long since been absorbed into the general body of the law,[93] and the legal principles applicable to sale, insurance, cheques, patents, bankruptcy and so on apply equally to all persons, whether merchants or not, whether in any particular kind of business or not, whose activities or transactions fall under that legal heading.

These names therefore do not denote distinct branches of law or logical divisions of the legal system, but are at most cross-divisions, merely convenient compendious names for groups of specific topics selected from all the recognised branches of law and brought together because of common relevance to particular professions and aspects of business life. Books bearing these titles are manuals only, usually for persons whose concern is only with the topics of law relevant in their particular business or profession; the lawyer finds his law applicable to commercial or industrial relations under the general branches and analytic headings of the law and in the detailed treatises on particular heads thereof.[94] In consequence the scope and boundaries of these groups are very vague and indefinite.

Books on mercantile law usually deal with partnerships and companies (from the law of persons), contract generally and the specific contracts of sale, carriage and insurance (from the law of obligations), moveable property, including bills and cheques, securities and bankruptcy (from the law of property), and arbitration (from the law of actions).

In modern times the law on certain mercantile topics has been restated and modified by statute but the statutes have been more concerned to

---

[91] Pound, *Jurisprudence*, V, 73; Keeton and Lloyd, *The British Commonwealth—England*, 232, 347; Paton, *Jurisprudence*, 216–217; Keeton, *Jurisprudence*, 228, 416. It is otherwise in French, German and some other systems of law founded closely on the Roman law, which have separate commercial codes, the rules based on the law merchant not having been absorbed into the general law. Hence French private law is divisible into *droit civil* and *droit commercial*, but there is a movement to integrate commercial law with *droit civil*. See further, Schlesinger, *Comparative Law*, 186; Van Mehren, *The Civil Law System*, 43–54.

[92] The same is also true of banking law, engineering law, medical, dental, veterinary and nursing law (commonly miscalled " medical jurisprudence," etc.), and any other similar collection of legal principles relevant to the work of a particular profession.

[93] For England, see Holdsworth, *History of English Law*, V, 60; VII, 99; Plucknett, *Concise History of the Common Law*, 657. For Scotland, see Bell's *Commentaries*, Preface, where he says: " The same principle operates as in England; and our courts are daily in the habit of proceeding on this Law-merchant as fully authoritative in Scotland, and of allowing the decisions of courts and the writings of lawyers to be cited in illustration of it. . . . The English books afford valuable aid in cultivating the subject of Mercantile Law." But Bell's Commentaries was not meant to be, and is not, a treatise on mercantile law alone.

[94] Such headings as mercantile law, industrial law and so on are not found in encyclopedias, digests of cases, or other reference books; the particular branch of law in question must be looked for.

achieve a settled formulation of the rules than to innovate so that reference is still frequently necessarily made to older cases and practice.[95] The law of companies is, however, entirely a modern statutory creation. Prior to the nineteenth century trading enterprises were either partnerships or set up by Royal Charter,[96] private Act of Parliament [97] or by contract between the members.[98] Private Act became common but was expensive and inconvenient and the principle of limited liability, that each shareholder was to be liable to the amount of the nominal value of his shares and no more, was conceded in 1862. The law has been periodically restated and modified since then with increased stress on the disclosure of information to the public and the present or prospective shareholder.

Characteristics of topics included in mercantile law have been relative informality, a large degree of freedom to the parties to make what bargains they chose, and steady change and development. Thus in recent years carriage by air and the financing of transactions by commercial credits have developed very much. The volume of commercial transactions taking place in the United Kingdom and with persons abroad is large and the problems which arise are numerous, frequently involving large sums of money and great commercial reputations, and interesting, while every change in commercial practice or technique is liable to react on the law.[99]

The study of industrial or labour law commonly covers trade unions and industrial associations (from the law of persons), contract generally and the specific contract of employment (traditionally known as the law of master and servant), and the employer's delictual liability for wrongs by or to the employee (from the law of obligations), industrial property, such as patents and trade-marks (from the law of property), and arbitration and the settlement of industrial disputes (from the law of actions). The fundamental topic is the contractual relationship of master and servant,[1] employer and employee, a relationship which gives rise to numerous contractual and delictual rights between the parties and between them and third parties. On this stem there has been grafted since 1800 an enor-

---

[95] Some of the principal statutes are the Bills of Exchange Act 1882; the Partnership Act 1890; the Sale of Goods Act 1893; the Merchant Shipping Acts 1894–1960; the Marine Insurance Act 1906; the Bankruptcy (Scotland) Act 1913; the Carriage of Goods by Sea Act 1924; the Carriage by Air Act 1961.

[96] *e.g.* The Bank of Scotland, The East India Company.

[97] *e.g.* The Royal Bank of Scotland, early railway companies.

[98] The standard work is W. R. Scott, *Constitution and Finance of English, Scottish and Irish Joint Stock Companies to 1720* (3 vols., 1910–12); see also Carr, *Select Charters of Trading Companies* (Selden Society); Causton and Keane, *Early Chartered Companies, 1296–1858*; Davis, *Corporations* (2 vols.); Formoy, *Historical Foundations of Modern Company Law*; Hunt, *Development of Business Corporation in England, 1800–67.*

[99] See Lord Devlin, " Commercial Law and Commercial Practice," in *Samples of Lawmaking,* 28.

[1] In the older books the law of master and servant was usually dealt with as part of the law of persons, or of domestic relations, but this treatment is appropriate only to domestic servants now.

mous growth of statute law and subordinate legislation regulating wages and holidays, hours and conditions of work, and providing in great detail for the safety, health and welfare of the employee. The complexity of modern industry requires separate provisions for many particular kinds of industrial enterprises. In modern times, as part of the national system of social security,[2] there have developed provisions for unemployment insurance[3] and for insurance against the loss caused by industrial injuries.[4] Again, one of the significant modern social and economic developments has been the development of freedom to associate in trade unions for the purpose of collective bargaining[5] and the legal aspects of trade union activity, industrial disputes and their settlement are of profound importance. Elements of public law, such as the control of monopolies may also be considered in the context of industrial law, and some relevant elements in the total situation such as collective bargaining between employers and trade unions are very little regulated by law at all.

Agricultural law deals with contract generally, the particular contracts of sale, hiring and employment, delictual liability to and for employees and for animals, the law of landownership, leases and smallholdings, compensation and arbitration. It may include partnerships and even companies and many topics of public law such as farm subsidies, and taxation.

These titles accordingly connote functional selections of topics which are useful for particular groups of students and particular professions, but the student of the law and of the legal system as a whole must regard them as divisions cutting across the logical and analytical classification of the law and not as distinct branches of law. In the same way books can bring together all the principles of law relevant to the theatre, or engineering operations, or any other species of activity.[6]

---

[2] The history, background and development of this may be studied in the (Beveridge) Report on Social Insurance and Allied Services, 1942 (Cmd. 6404), Appx. B.

[3] Social Security Act 1975, superseding legislation which originated with the National Insurance Act 1911.

[4] Social Security Act 1975, replacing the Workmen's Compensation Acts 1897–1943.

[5] This can be studied in such books as Cole's *Short History of the British Working Class Movement, 1789–1947*, and in books on social and economic history such as Gregg's *Social and Economic History of Britain, 1760–1965*.

[6] It is noteworthy also that the institutional writers and main text-writers deal with the topics sometimes brought under the headings of mercantile, industrial or agricultural law in the context of their general expositions of the private law as a whole. Thus, *e.g.* Bell's *Principles* deals with all the different kinds of commercial contracts in Book First, with industrial property in Book Second, and with bankruptcy in Book Fifth. So, too, do Erskine's *Principles*, Hume's *Lectures* and More's *Lectures*. Furthermore, the study of law under such titles as commercial and industrial law is overlapping and very repetitive, and it is not possible on any such basis to construct a convenient or satisfactory classification of the whole legal system, because much of the law would have to be restated for each of the types of human relations. Similarly,

Forensic Science, Medicine and Psychiatry

These subjects are not branches of the law at all, but are applications of science, medicine and psychiatry to the purposes of the law and the ends of justice. In many sets of circumstances, both in civil but even more so in criminal law, the lawyer has to call on the scientist, doctor [7] or psychiatrist for assistance in the elucidation or interpretation of facts, particularly where difficult issues as to the state of mind or body of some person arise for determination. Thus scientific knowledge is called on in questions involving forgery, poisons and weapons, medical knowledge in cases of wounding, homicide, sexual offences and the like, and psychiatric knowledge in regard to cases of mental deficiency or abnormality, diminished responsibility and other difficult mental states. There is no good reason why there should not equally be subjects of forensic engineering or forensic architecture where equally the knowledge of experts in other branches of learning must be called on to assist legal purposes, but the three branches referred to have legal importance with particular frequency because the law is always dealing with human beings and their actings, and has so often to answer the questions Who, When, How and Why, about these human beings before it can seek to apply a legal rule. These branches of knowledge, and indeed all expert testimony from persons skilled in sciences other than law, supply evidence of states of fact and the bases for inference of fact, so that they are adjuncts of the law of evidence. They do not themselves answer problems of law. Much of the confusion and dispute between legal and medical approaches to insanity would be avoided if it were remembered that the function of the forensic physician or psychiatrist is to supply expert evidence from which a judge or jury may, as tribunal of fact, determine whether or not the person under examination is insane within the legal definition thereof, which is concerned with responsibility for conduct and liability to the legal consequences thereof, rather than with insanity in a medical sense.

Scots Law and English

Having now surveyed the main departments of the law it may be of value, in view of the proximity of English law and of its constant tendency to encroach on Scots law, to consider the points of contact and distinctness between the two systems. It is too often assumed that Scots law is much the same as English, or a pale reflection, or substantially the same with different terminology, or with a few minor variations.[8] In fact it is

the grouping of cases or rules under topic-headings arranged alphabetically, as in legal encyclopedias and other reference works, is useful only to the person who understands the analytical arrangement. For purposes of exposition, study and understanding, analytical classification remains the only satisfactory basis.

[7] Forensic medicine is sometimes called Medical Jurisprudence but, despite the name, it has no connection at all with Jurisprudence in the sense of legal theory.

[8] Lawson, *The Rational Strength of English Law*, persistently underestimates the differences.

radically different,[9] has developed differently under the influence of different agencies and frequently arrives at results not dissimilar to those of English law but from very different premisses and by a very different train of reasoning.[10] It is all too common to find in judgments, even of the highest courts,[11] statements or assumptions that the laws of Scotland and of England are the same on the matter in issue; these are frequently unjustified and frequently made by persons with no real qualification to say so.

Quite apart from terminology and procedure of enforcement the principles and content of the rules of Scots law are different from English. This is most noticeable in property law where the two systems are poles apart in their land law.[12] The differences are lesser in family law, in reparation and in contract, and least in mercantile and industrial topics. In public law, the difference is quite substantial in constitutional and administrative law, very material in criminal law, and at its least in taxation. Pleading and procedure are quite different in both civil and criminal matters, but evidence rather less so, though not by any means the same in the two systems.

In its reliance on broad principles the Scots law shows affinity with civil law systems of the Continent rather than with the Anglo-American common law. " The civilian naturally reasons from principles to instances, the common lawyer from instances to principles. The civilian puts his faith in syllogisms,[13] the common lawyer in precedents. . . . The civilian thinks in terms of rights and duties, the common lawyer in terms of remedies. The civilian is chiefly concerned with the policy and rationale of a rule of law, the common lawyer with its pedigree. The instinct of the civilian is to systematise. The working rule of the common lawyer is *solvitur ambulando.* . . . The differences in methods are fundamental and far more significant than the apparent similarity of the end products of widely different processes of thought." [14]

Accordingly while Scots law operates in an environment very similar to that of English law and is subject to a common court of final appeal [15]

---

[9] René David, *Introduction à l'Etude du Droit Privé de l'Angleterre,* 164, considers Scots law as " très different du droit anglais."

[10] Untold harm has been done to Scots law by lawyers and judges, even of the House of Lords, who have assumed that because Scots and English law both give a remedy for the same wrong, they do so for the same reasons. See further, Walker, " Some Characteristics of Scots Law " (1955) 18 M.L.R. 321.

[11] Gibb, *Law from Over the Border, passim.*

[12] See Farran, *Principles of Scots and English Land Law.*

[13] On this mode of legal reasoning in Scotland, see Walker, " The Theory of Relevancy " (1951) 63 J.R. 1.

[14] Cooper, " The Common and the Civil Law—A Scot's View " (1950) 63 H.L.R. 468, 471.

[15] Except that no Scottish criminal appeals go to the House of Lords.

and a common legislative body and higher executive, it is, in varying degrees in different topics, a distinct system with principles and methods of legal thought of its own which are not necessarily inferior to English. It can never safely, and should never, be assumed that any principle or rule of English law either is or should be the law of Scotland, and the Scottish rule should always be sought independently.

FURTHER READING

Hall: *Readings in Jurisprudence,* Chap. 14—Classification.
Cooper: *The Scottish Legal Tradition.*
Gibb: *Preface to Scots Law.*
Mitchell: *Constitutional Law.*
Smith: *British Justice—The Scottish Contribution.*
   Studies Critical and Comparative.
   Short Commentary on the Law of Scotland.

CHAPTER 10

THE SOURCES OF SCOTS LAW

THE term " sources of the law " has several meanings which have to be carefully distinguished.[1] There are, firstly, historical sources, which are the events and incidents in legal history which have given rise to the principle or rule in question. Thus historical sources of various rules may be that the rule was laid down by Justinian and adopted into Scots law,[2] or enacted by Parliament in response to certain needs of that time, or developed by the courts over a particular period.[3] Common historical sources include the Roman law, the Bible, the canon law, the medieval law merchant and maritime law and many of the major events in constitutional and legal history. Every principle and rule of law has an historical source somewhere, even though it may not be known, but the principle or rule does not draw any validity or binding force from that source. The historical source merely explains when and how that rule came to be established. It frequently helps also to explain why the rule took a particular form. Secondly, every principle and rule has a social, political, economic, moral or religious source in that some fact or set or state of facts, moral, political, economic and so on, have provoked or given rise to that rule.[4] Thus some rules of law were enacted or developed for social reasons, such as the legislation on race relations, others for political reasons, such as the law regulating trade unions, others for economic reasons, such as the law of companies, others for moral reasons, such as those relating to punishment of cruelty and neglect of children, and so on. Again, every principle and rule has such a philosophical source, though it may be forgotten or difficult to discover, but the philosophical source also does not give the rule any legal validity but merely gives a justification for the rule, and that justification, moreover, may later disappear or seem unsound or inadequate to a later generation, but the rule is not thereby abrogated.[5] Thirdly, the statements in enactments, decisions, books and documents and the usages of persons from which a court may derive a principle for the decision of a case are sometimes spoken of as material sources, and again

---

[1] See further, Salmond, *Jurisprudence*, Chap. 6; Allen, *Law in the Making*, Introduction; Pound, *Jurisprudence*, Chap. 16; Smith, " Sources of Scots Law " (1904) 16 J.R. 375; Dove Wilson, " Sources of Scots Law " (1892) 4 J.R. 1.

[2] See, *e.g.*, *Central Motors* v. *Cessnock Garage Co.*, 1925 S.C. 796.

[3] Many examples of historical sources of the latter two kinds may be found in Chap. 4.

[4] See, *e.g.* the Incest Act 1567, adopting the substance of Leviticus, c. 18, into Scots law.

[5] See further, Dicey, *Lectures on the Relation between Law and Public Opinion in the Nineteenth Century, passim.*

every principle or rule has such a source, but these are better described as the materials for formulating a decision and which determine the content of a principle or rule derived from them. Thus if a judge adopts a principle from Roman law or a textbook that is the material source of his decision; it supplies the material for his decision. It would be better if the term " sources " were not used in all these senses and instead one talked of historical origins of rules, philosophical bases of rules and material grounds of rules.

Legal or formal sources from which are drawn authoritative precepts of law

The only true " sources " of legal principles and rules are the legal or formal sources. The legal sources of the law are the answer to the question: where do I find authoritative statements of the principles and rules which the courts must apply to determine my rights and duties, my remedies and penalties, in various circumstances? Legal validity, and authority compelling obedience, attach to a principle or rule of law only by virtue of its being drawn from a legal source, one recognised by the legal system itself as an authoritative reservoir of valid and binding principles and rules of law, and it is with these legally authoritative sources that this chapter is concerned. It is to these legal sources only that one may resort to find a rule or principle of law for the application to and solution of a legal controversy or problem raised by certain facts. To put it another way: how does one distinguish a precept of law from a precept of non-law? The answer is that the first issues from a legal source, the second from what is not recognised as a legal source. Thus if a precept of conduct such as: You must give up your seat on a bus to a lady, can be shown to be drawn from a legal source, it is a precept of law; if it is drawn from a non-legal source such as generally accepted good manners, it is a precept of non-law. The importance of identifying the legal sources of principles and rules of law is that this furnishes the criterion of identification of valid statements of law.

The ultimate legal source of all Scots law, that which confers the authority on all principles and rules to make them determinative of rights and decisive of controversies, is the power of the state, that is, of the legally organised community of the United Kingdom. The state issues authoritative statements of principles and rules through its legislature and courts, and the immediate practical sources of principles and rules recognised in Scots law as legally authoritative are the Treaties establishing the European Communities and rules made thereunder, the statutes of the Parliament of the United Kingdom, and of the former Parliaments of Scotland and of Great Britain, subordinate legislation authorised by such statutes, judicial decisions of the superior courts of the United Kingdom, certain books recognised by the courts as of authority, accepted customs, and principles of equity and certain other extraneous sources. No other sources give rise to principles and rules having legal validity and authority recognised by the courts of this country. The recognised forms of law in Scotland are accordingly legislation, case-law, statements in certain recognised books, accepted customs, and principles drawn from equity and other extraneous sources. The facts that rules embodied in statute-law and case-law themselves have historical origins, philosophical bases, and material grounds are matters of interest and concern to historical and philosophical legal study, but do not by themselves confer any validity or authority on the rules. Thus the condemnation of the slave trade gave rise to valid and authoritative rules of law only when and because Parliament proscribed it by statute, not because of the historical steps towards or the moral justifications for the abolition of slavery. The principle that an employer must take reasonable care for the safety of his employees is a valid principle only because the superior courts have said so in many cases, not because such a principle is socially, economically or morally justifiable. The legal sources, moreover, are the only sources from which new principles or rules can be added to the body of law.

Sources of knowledge of the law—legal literature

These legal sources must be sharply distinguished from legal literature, books on the law. Books on law are, in general, *not* authoritative sources of the law on any matter but only means of our knowledge of the law, to which we turn to discover not what the principles of law are, but what the author of the book believes the principles and rules to be, having regard to the statutes and cases which appear to him applicable to his subject-matter. Certain books, as has been indicated and as will appear later, are in a privileged position, have substantial authority and may be described as literary sources of law, as distinct from the general body of legal literature (legal encyclopedias, textbooks, periodicals, legal histories, etc.), but in general any court may quite freely ignore what is written in a textbook as unauthoritative.[6] The function of the textbook is to collect and present in logical form a statement of the rules of law on a given topic, drawn from the authoritative sources, the relevant statutes and scattered cases, and to suggest their cumulative effect and how they appear to the author to apply in different circumstances. Textbooks are of great value for their synthesis and reasoned statement of the rules drawn from different legal materials and for their criticism of rules and their conjectures of suitable developments to solve problems which have not yet arisen. They may supply, or help to supply, materials for a decision. If a court accepts

---

[6] Lord Wrenbury, who, when still young Mr. Buckley at the Bar, had written a book on Companies, once remarked from the Bench when Buckley's *Companies Acts* was cited to him: " You must not substitute for the judgments of the court the irresponsible conjectures of a textbook writer." This emphasises that textbooks are not infrequently written by comparatively young and inexperienced men, and many contain statements which are tentative, conjectural or even simply wrong.

the view of a text-writer that view becomes authoritative, not because the text-writer wrote it but because the court has adopted and approved it, and it thereby acquires the authority of case-law; in future the rule is authoritative because of the case and the judicial adoption, and not because of being stated in the book. Parliament and the courts are always entirely free to ignore formulations of legal principle or doctrine in a textbook, however highly esteemed it or its learned author may be. Textbooks are, in general, therefore, only secondary authorities and useful in so far as they completely and accurately present rules laid down in the primary authorities, *i.e.* the statutes and cases, on any topic.

" *The authorities* "

The sources which yield authoritative statements of principle and rules for application in a particular case are generally referred to as " the authorities." Thus: " Counsel referred us to a number of authorities including . . . Counsel said that these authorities showed that . . . The authorities, both the writers of the textbooks and the decided cases, now accept it." [7] In this sense an " authority " is a statement in a source having legal authority and requiring, or at least influencing, a judge or lawyer to the view that the rule of law on the point in question is to a particular effect.

The problems in relation to legal sources

Having determined what are the legally recognised sources of authoritative rules of law it will be evident that two problems exist in relation to each class of legal source, namely, how and where to recognise and find the expressions of rules of law which come from these various sources, and, secondly, how to interpret the statements therein so as to draw from them a rule suitable for the resolution of the particular problem or controversy which is in issue, or for advice on that issue.

A—LAW COMMON TO COUNTRIES OF THE EUROPEAN COMMUNITIES

In certain spheres, mainly economic, there is a body of law common to all the countries which are members of the European Communities. The sources of this body of law are (1) (a) the Treaties which established the European Communities and certain subsidiary Conventions and treaties, and (b) the bodies of administrative Regulations, Directives and Decisions made by the Council and the Commission of the Communities in pursuance of their powers under the Treaties and for the furtherance of policies agreed upon to give effect to the purposes of the Communities; and (2) rulings and decisions of the Court of Justice of the Communities interpreting the Treaties and administrative legislation and filling the gaps left by them

---

[7] *Dundee Corpn.* v. *Marr,* 1971 **S.C.** 96, 102–103.

in the law. The general principles of the law common to the member states and general principles of international law may be referred to as subsidiary sources.

B—LAW APPLICABLE TO SCOTLAND

I—LEGISLATION

As has been explained [8] legislation comprises statutes or Acts of Parliament, prerogative legislation, and subordinate or delegated legislation made by Ministers of the Crown, local authorities, courts and other bodies.

A statute is an authoritative declaration of the will of the Queen in Parliament as to some matter of law, usually prescribing some general rule for the future regulation of conduct. It may, however, be specific and relate to only one or a few limited cases only. The body of statute law which is of relevance in Scotland comprises the body of statutes or Acts of the Scottish Parliaments down to 1707, of the Parliament of Great Britain from 1707 to 1800, and of the Parliament of the United Kingdom since 1801, in all cases so far as these statutes are still in force and have been amended but not repealed or cancelled by subsequent legislation.

To use legislation as a source from which possibly to find a rule resolving a doubt or deciding a dispute it is necessary first to discover what statutory provisions, if any, are relevant to the matter under consideration and then to resort to the process of construction or interpretation to determine what the words thought to be relevant mean in the circumstances.

DISCOVERY OF RELEVANT LEGISLATION

The discovery of what, if any, provisions of statute law are relevant to a particular matter is part of the problem of legal method.[9] It includes the discovery of whether each piece of legislative material has or has not been brought into force, is or is not applicable to Scotland, has or has not been amended or repealed or has expired.[10]

CONSTRUCTION OR INTERPRETATION OF LEGISLATION

The process of construction [11] or interpretation is that whereby a legal adviser or a court seeks to discover, in a particular factual context, whether a given statutory provision is applicable to the set of facts, and, if so, what meaning and effect has to be given to it.[12] It is in essence the problem of finding the meaning of certain statutory expressions in the context of

---

[8] Chap. 5, *supra.*

[9] Chap. 12, *infra.*

[10] Chap. 5, *supra.*

[11] From the verb " construe," not from " construct."

[12] A distinction has sometimes been drawn between " construction " or the process of resolving uncertainties or ambiguities in a statute, and " interpretation " or the process of assigning a meaning to the words in a statute.

certain circumstances. This is a problem which arises very frequently, raises many and difficult issues, and is one of the most thorny with which any adviser or court can be faced. It is always a question of law, not of fact, to be decided by the court, not the jury, to be decided after legal argument, not on evidence.[13] It arises frequently, not only in contentious proceedings in court, but in the course of advising or deciding on the legality or competency of some projected course of action, and in seeking to predict the legal consequences of certain action, past or proposed. Construction or interpretation are necessary because the words used in statutes may be ambiguous *i.e.* susceptible of two meanings,[14] or be indefinite or uncertain in scope and application. Thus it has been said[15]: " The word ' office ' is of indefinite content. Its various meanings cover four columns of the New English Dictionary, but I take as the most relevant for purposes of this case the following . . ." A considerable volume of principles of construction, presumptions and guides has grown up in practice and much depends on which is followed, since the application of different guides may produce diametrically opposite consequences.[16] As has been observed: " The English language is not an instrument of mathematical precision. Our literature would be much poorer if it were. This is where the draftsmen of Acts of Parliament have often been unfairly criticised. A judge, believing himself to be fettered by the supposed rule that he must look to the language and nothing else, laments that the draftsmen have not provided for this or that, or have been guilty of some or other ambiguity. It would certainly save the judges trouble if Acts of Parliament were drafted with divine prescience and perfect clarity. In the absence of it, when a defect appears a judge cannot simply fold his hands and blame the draftsman. He must set to work on the constructive task of finding the intention of Parliament, and he must do this not only from the language of the statute, but also from a consideration of the social conditions which gave rise to it and of the mischief which it was passed to remedy and then he must supplement the written word so as to give force and life to the intention of the legislature." [17] It has to be remembered that Parliament in enacting any provision, or a Department

---

[13] *Mason* v. *Bibby* (1864) 2 H. & C. 881.

[14] For an example of ambiguity see *Renfrewshire Assessor* v. *Hendry*, 1969 S.C. 211, 213.

[15] *McMillan* v. *Guest* [1942] A.C. 561, 566 quoted in *I.R.C.* v. *Brander & Cruickshank*, 1970 S.C. 116, 121.

[16] The principal guides are Craies' treatise on *Statute Law* (7th ed., 1971); Maxwell on *The Interpretation of Statutes* (11th ed., 1961) and Odgers, *The Construction of Deeds and Statutes* (4th ed., 1956). See also, Willis, " Statute Interpretation in a Nutshell " (1938) 16 Can.Bar Rev. 1; Davies, " Interpretation of Statutes in the Light of Their Policy by the English Courts " (1935) 35 Col.L.R. 519; Friedmann, " Statute Law and its Interpretation in the Modern State " (1948) 26 Can.Bar Rev. 1277.

[17] *Seaford Court Estates Ltd.* v. *Asher* [1949] 2 K.B. 481, 499, *per* Denning L.J. criticised on appeal ([1950] A.C. 508, 530) as stated much too widely.

or local authority in enacting subordinate legislation, cannot foresee every contingency or set of circumstances which may arise, and may never have considered at all the kind of case which has arisen, so that it is not surprising that the language used seldom fits every possible case. Indeed the perversity of circumstances is such that, as soon as a carefully phrased piece of legislation comes into force, a case seems to arise which the words do not seem particularly apt to cover. Thus it is an offence to be in charge of a vehicle while under the influence of drink.[18] Do the words " in charge of " cover a drunken person put in the back seat of his car in a car-park, the car having been immobilised,[19] a drunken person in the front passenger seat while another person, who held only an expired provisional licence, had started the engine,[20] a drunken person in the driving seat of a stationary car but who had arranged for another person to drive it to that person's garage,[21] or a drunken person sitting beside a " learner " who was driving?[22]

The work of interpreting a statute is not a mechanical function: " the duty of the courts is to ascertain and give effect to the will of Parliament as expressed in its enactments. In the performance of this duty the judges do not act as computers into which are fed the statute and the rules for the construction of statutes and from which issue forth the mathematically correct answer. The interpretation of statutes is a craft as much as a science and the judges, as craftsmen, select and apply the appropriate rules as the tools of their trade. They are not legislators, but finishers, refiners and polishers of legislation which comes to them in a state requiring varying degrees of further processing."[23]

The two Approaches to Interpretation

There are two general approaches or attitudes discernible in statutory interpretation, the one favouring a literal, strict or narrow construction, and the other a more liberal or broader construction. The choice between them is a matter for the individual judge and much depends on his general attitude to the law and legal development, and more particularly on his subjective view of the case and the Act and on whether he thinks that the statute should cover the circumstances of the case before him or not. This renders prediction of the court's attitude to a particular provision difficult, may give rise to inconsistencies between similar cases or similar statutory provisions, and has given rise to accusations of judicial bias against certain

---

[18] Road Traffic Act 1972, s. 5 (2) (formerly Road Traffic Acts 1930, s. 15 and 1960 s. 6).
[19] *Dean* v. *Wishart*, 1952 J.C. 9.
[20] *Winter* v. *Morrison*, 1954 J.C. 7.
[21] *Macdonald* v. *Kubirdas*, 1955 S.L.T.(Sh.Ct.) 50.
[22] *Clark* v. *Clark*, 1950 S.L.T.(Sh.Ct.) 68. It has been observed (*Fraser* v. *Caledonian Ry.* 1911 S.C. 145, 159) that some older statutes were badly drafted, with contempt, or ignorance, or both, of Scots Law.
[23] *Corocraft Ltd.* v. *Pan-American Airways* [1969] 1 Q.B. 616, per Donaldson J.

kinds of legislation, as of giving an unduly narrow construction to some social welfare legislation. These criticisms seem quite unjustified, but the analysis of this belongs to jurisprudence, and need not be pursued further here.

The Literal Approach

The literal approach stresses the need for close and careful scrutiny of the actual words enacted by the legislature and has little regard for anything but the relevant words or phrases, the context and any other relevant provision of the Act itself. The general effect of adopting this approach is that an Act will not be held to affect, or to be intended to have affected, anything not dealt with expressly or by clear implication even if the result of this attitude may be obviously absurd or inconsistent with the commonsense idea of what Parliament meant to do.[24] This approach is frequently buttressed with such arguments as that if Parliament had meant to cover this case it could and should have said so, that it is not for the courts to legislate or to usurp the function of Parliament or to speculate what Parliament might have intended and to write this into the Act. For example, at common law a wife was entitled to exact a share of her husband's moveable estate, called *jus relictae*, when he died or she divorced him. The Married Women's Property (Scotland) Act 1881 gave a husband a corresponding right of *jus relicti*, but it was held exigible only on death, not on divorce, because the Act says " the husband of any woman who may *die*," [25] and the court declined to apply the fiction that divorce had the same effect as death in view of the literal terms of the Act, though this was commonly quoted as the basis for the wife's claim. The result was a legal anomaly; it is likely that Parliament had merely overlooked the case of divorce and had not intended to exclude it.

The Liberal Approach

The liberal approach lays stress on the need for the courts to try to appreciate the overriding intention of the legislation, the general policy behind the Act, and the need to further remedies and not to take refuge in pettifogging verbal objections. The discovery of the general purpose and intention of legislation is, however, difficult and subject to two serious handicaps. The court can most easily and readily discover Parliament's intention from what Parliament has enacted, that is, from an examination of the literal form and wording of the enactment, and, secondly, the court is not at liberty to read into a statute phrases or provisions which are quite clearly not there, however much the general policy might seem to render them desirable. Thus in *Taff Vale Ry.* v. *A.S.R.S.*,[26] the House of

---

[24] *Glasgow Court House Commrs.* v. *Lanarkshire C.C.* (1900) 3 F. 103.
[25] *Eddington* v. *Robertson* (1895) 22 R. 430.
[26] [1901] A.C. 426.

Lords examined the policy of successive Trade Union Acts as a means of deciding that Parliament must have meant that trade unions could be sued in their registered names for tort.

The desire to give effect to the general policy expressed in literal terms in the Act underlies what is sometimes called " the golden rule " of statutory interpretation. " The only rule for the construction of Acts of Parliament is that they should be construed according to the intent of the Parliament which passed them. If the words of the statute are in themselves precise and unambiguous, then no more can be necessary than to expound these words in their natural and ordinary sense. The words themselves alone do in such case best declare the intention of the lawgiver." [27] " It is a very useful rule in the construction of a statute to adhere to the ordinary meaning of the words used, and to the grammatical construction, unless that is at variance with the intention of the legislature to be collected from the statute itself or leads to any manifest absurdity or repugnance, in which case the language may be varied or modified so as to avoid such inconvenience, but no further." [28] It remains of course difficult in many cases to say what the intention of Parliament seems to have been, and it may well be a matter of opinion whether the ordinary meaning does or does not lead to absurdity or repugnance, so that this rule does not take the discussion much further.

Another version of the liberal approach is what is sometimes called the " mischief rule," that where a statute was passed to remedy some mischief and defect in the law, the interpretation should be adopted which corrects the mischief.

Interpretation Act

Some guidance is given by the Interpretation Act 1889,[29] which assigns meanings to a number of words commonly found in statutes and provides, for example, that words importing the masculine shall include the feminine, that words in the singular shall include the plural and vice versa,[30] that " person " includes any body of persons corporate or unincorporate, and so on. These definitions, however, may always have to give way to contrary indications in the context of a particular Act, and this Act is accordingly far from providing a comprehensive code of interpretation. Its only real value is in fact to abbreviate statutes by permitting the omission of such phrases as " he or she," " person or persons or body of persons."

---

[27] *Sussex Peerage Case* (1844) 11 Cl. & F. 85, 143, *per* Tindal C.J.

[28] *Becke* v. *Smith* (1836) 2 M. & W. 191, 195, *per* Parke B. *Cf. Caledonian Ry.* v. *N.B. Ry.* (1881) 8 R.(H.L.) 23; *Campbell's Trs.* v. *O'Neill*, 1911 S.C. 188; *I.R.C.* v. *Luke*, 1963 S.C.(H.L.) 65, 80.

[29] Printed as an appendix to Craies' *Statute Law,* and to Maxwell, *Interpretation of Statutes.* The whole Act should be read carefully.

[30] See *e.g. Griffith* v. *Ferrier*, 1952 J.C. 56, and generally *20 Cannon St.* v. *Singer* [1974] 2 All E.R. 577.

A few definitions of general application are contained in Acts other than the Interpretation Act 1889.

Interpretation Sections

In many modern Acts there is, usually near the end, an interpretation section which gives definitions of certain words used in the Act and provides that they shall have in the Act the particular meaning thereby assigned to them, which may be wider or narrower than the ordinary dictionary meaning of the word.[31] The section may provide that certain words shall " mean " something, which explains, defines and limits the words used, or it may provide that certain words shall " include " or " exclude " particular cases, in which case the definition is extensive or restrictive of the usual meaning. The meanings thus statutorily assigned to particular words hold for that Act only, though subsequent legislation may refer back to that definition by providing in another context that a word shall bear the meaning assigned to it in a specified prior Act. An interpretation section which extends the meaning of a word does not thereby abolish the ordinary, popular and natural sense of the word where that is properly applicable but merely enables the word, when there is nothing in the context or subject-matter to the contrary, to be applied to some things to which it would not ordinarily be applicable.[32] Moreover the interpretation section is not to be taken as defining the terms mentioned in all circumstances but only as defining what may be comprehended by the term where the circumstances require that it should be so comprehended.[33]

Subsidiary Principles

It is apparent that courts get little assistance in the task of interpretation from the Interpretation Act and any interpretation section in the Act under consideration and that they have to draw a meaning out of the statutory passage in the circumstances which have given rise to the controversy primarily by reference to the words enacted and also to what the court or judge thinks, on a consideration of the whole legislation in issue, Parliament intended. Sometimes one factor rather than the other weighs more with the court. But numerous subsidiary principles have been developed to assist the court in its scrutiny of the language employed.

In the first place the usual dictionary meaning of a word is taken, as at the time when the statute was passed, and if the word has a legal or technical connotation the usual technical meaning is taken. Parliament is presumed to be familiar with, and to use, the ordinary and, if applicable,

---

[31] For these, see Stroud's *Judicial Dictionary* and Saunders' *Words and Phrases Legally Defined.*
[32] *Robinson* v. *Barton Eccles Local Board* (1883) 8 App.Cas. 798.
[33] *Meux* v. *Jacobs* (1875) L.R. 7 H.L. 481; *Strathern* v. *Padden,* 1926 J.C. 9.

usual legal or technical meanings of words.[34] Any unusual or restricted or extended sense of a word calls prima facie for a mention in the interpretation section. Words which are permissive or empowering may be shown in particular circumstances to be really imperative, and it has been said that prima facie where powers are conferred by statute for the public benefit they must be exercised.[35]

Secondly, the usual meaning is taken subject to the context in which the word is used, so as to attribute to the word or phrase a meaning consistent with the rest of the section and even of the whole Act or series of Acts on the subject.

Reference to Context

The fact that a particular word or phrase has to be construed does not justify ignoring the verbal context in which the word is used and three principles have been recognised in this connection:

(a) *Noscitur a sociis*, that is, a vague word takes a shade of meaning from the accompanying words; thus in the context of " houses for public refreshment, resort and entertainment," the last word was held to be limited to physical and not mental gratification,[36] because that meaning, it was felt, agreed better with the earlier part of the phrase than the other or wider meaning which might have covered a theatrical or musical performance.

(b) *Expressio unius est exclusio alterius*. Under this the express mention of one thing or category and not of another similar or related thing or category tends to indicate the implied exclusion of the latter. It is inapplicable to a situation other than one where there is only a choice between two persons or objects.[37] But the exclusion of the other may be the result of inadvertence or accident, so that the principle cannot be rigidly applied,[38] and is indeed of very limited value.

(c) *Ejusdem generis*. Where several things or specific items are enumerated, all of the same kind or having some distinct characteristic in common, and this enumeration is followed by general words such as " or otherwise," " or other things," " or other person," it has to be presumed that the general words are limited to other things or items or persons having the same common characteristic or of the same kind or class or category as the items specifically mentioned.[39] It is clear accordingly that the rule has no application where the

---

[34] *Clerical Assurance Co.* v. *Carter* (1889) 22 Q.B.D. 444.
[35] *Walkinshaw* v. *Orr* (1860) 22 D. 627; *Julius* v. *Bishop of Oxford* (1880) 5 App.Cas. 214; *Black* v. *Glasgow Corpn.*, 1958 S.C. 260.
[36] *Muir* v. *Keay* (1875) L.R. 10 Q.B. 594.
[37] *R.* v. *Palfrey* [1970] 2 All E.R. 12.
[38] *Stevenson* v. *Hunter* (1903) 5 F. 761. *Cf. Dean* v. *Wiesengrund* [1955] 2 Q.B. 120.
[39] *Mortimer* v. *Samuel B. Allison Ltd.*, 1959 S.C.(H.L.) 1.

specific words have no common category or characteristics,[40] or if the concluding general words are so very general as to include every other case or, at least, the case under discussion, *e.g.* " any other place *whatsoever*." Thus in a provision that traffic signs should include " all signals, warning signposts, direction posts, signs or devices," it was held that " devices " must be *ejusdem generis* with the previous words and could not cover a painted white line.[41] A prohibition on " all houses and every other building whatever " did not extend to a low parapet wall and iron railing.[42] Before the rule can be applied, accordingly, one must be able to discover a *genus* common to all the specific words and also to assign a meaning to the concluding general words consistent with their limitation to that same *genus*.

Reference to Whole Act

Interpretation must have regard, moreover, not merely to the immediate verbal context, but to the whole of the Act in which the phrase under construction appears, because regard to the whole Act may reveal an underlying scheme or legislative purpose which helps to give a meaning to a particular phrase. Sections of Acts frequently refer back and forward to other sections and even without express reference one interpretation of a word may be more consistent with another section of the Act than is the alternative interpretation. Thus if one section provides for notice being " given " and another for the notice being " served on or left with " a person, it is apparent that written notice was contemplated and that this meaning will fit both sections while oral notice would fit only the earlier section; one does not " serve " or " leave " an oral notice with a person. Reference to the whole Act, or at least the whole of that part of the Act, will therefore tend to give an interpretation consistent with the rest of the Act. Moreover where there is a series of Acts dealing with the same subject-matter they should be looked at as a continuous code.[43]

Further indications of the appropriate shade of meaning to give to a word may sometimes be gathered from one or more of two sets of indications, which are distinguished as internal and external aids to construction.

Internal Aids to Construction

Internal aids are those indications which may be drawn from the statute

---

[40] *e.g. Crichton Stuart* v. *Ogilvie*, 1914 S.C. 888.

[41] *Evans* v. *Cross* [1938] 1 K.B. 694.

[42] *Partick Police Commrs.* v. *G.W. Steam Laundry Co.* (1886) 13 R. 500; see also *Moss' Empires* v. *Glasgow Assessor*, 1917 S.C.(H.L.) 1.

[43] *Hamilton* v. *N.C.B.*, 1960 S.C.(H.L.) 1.

under construction itself to assist in arriving at a true interpretation of its provisions. The principal are:

(a) *Title.* It is now accepted that the long title is part of an Act and may legitimately be used to assist in interpreting the Act as a whole and in ascertaining its scope.[44] The short title cannot be used as an aid to construction.[45]

(b) *Preamble.* This again is part of the Act and may be resorted to, to explain the meaning of an Act.[46] But a preamble cannot cut down or control or qualify a clear and unambiguous provision in the body of the Act.[47]

(c) *Headings.* Headings prefixed to groups of sections or parts of an Act may, like preambles, be taken as a guide but only for the purpose of explaining doubtful expressions or ambiguities in the body of the sections or part of the Act.[48]

(d) *Marginal notes.* These have been said to be not part of a statute and the courts cannot look at them,[49] or to be part of the Act but a most unsure guide to construction.[50]

(e) *Punctuation.* Modern statutes are punctuated, but punctuation is regarded not as forming part of the statute but rather as a kind of *contemporanea expositio.*[51] Sometimes it has been referred to,[52] but punctuation is not authoritative.

(f) *Schedules.* These are part of the Act and may be looked at to resolve ambiguities,[53] though mere forms contained in a schedule cannot limit or qualify words of enactment in the Act.

External Aids to Construction

External aids are those sources of information outside the Act under construction which may be sought to be invoked to assist interpretation.

---

[44] *Fielden* v. *Morley Corpn.* [1899] 1 Ch. 1, 3; *Fenton* v. *Thorley* [1903] A.C. 443, 447; *Millar & Lang* v. *Macniven & Cameron* (1908) 16 S.L.T. 56; *Vacher* v. *London Socy. of Compositors* [1913] A.C. 107, 128; *Mags. of Buckie* v. *Dowager Countess of Seafield's Trs.,* 1928 S.C. 525; *Kelly* v. *Nuttall,* 1965 S.C. 427, 438, 449.

[45] *Re Boaler* [1915] 1 K.B. 21.

[46] *L.C.C.* v. *Bermondsey Bioscope Co.* [1911] 1 K.B. 445, 451; *Vacher, supra*; *Renfrewshire C.C.* v. *Orphan Homes of Scotland* (1898) 1 F. 186.

[47] *Powell* v. *Kempton Park Racecourse Co.* [1899] A.C. 143, 157, 184; *Att.-Gen.* v. *Prince Ernest of Hanover* [1955] Ch. 440; [1957] A.C. 436.

[48] *Martins* v. *Fowler* [1926] A.C. 746, 750; *Buckie Magistrates* v. *Seafield's Trustees,* 1928 S.C. 525; *R.* v. *Surrey (N.E. Area) Assessment Committee* [1948] 1 K.B. 28, 32; *D.P.P.* v. *Schildkamp* [1969] 3 All E.R. 1640.

[49] *Nixon* v. *Att.-Gen.* [1930] 1 Ch. 566, 593.

[50] *D.P.P.* v. *Schildkamp, supra.*

[51] *Duke of Devonshire* v. *O'Connor* (1890) 24 Q.B.D. 468, 478; *I.R.C.* v. *Hinchy* [1960] A.C. 748.

[52] *Alexander* v. *Mackenzie,* 1947 J.C. 155; *D.P.P.* v. *Schildkamp, supra.*

[53] *Ellerman Lines* v. *Murray* [1931] A.C. 126; see also *Jacobs* v. *Hart* (1900) 2 F.(J.) 33.

The principal external aids are:

(a) *Prior state of the law.* Parliament must be presumed to know the state of the law existing when the Act in question was passed, and the intention of the later legislation may sometimes be discovered by examination of the previous state of the law. This includes the previous common law, any prior Acts, and the known defects of the previous state of the law.[54] This is sometimes comprehensively called the parliamentary history of the Act. Only prior statutes *in pari materia* relating to the same subject-matter can be regarded, so closely related that they can fairly be said to form one system of legislation, and not other statutes or other statutes vaguely relating to kindred topics.[55] Reference to prior statutes is particularly appropriate in the case of a group of Acts relating to one topic, such as housing or merchant shipping, where the legislation is practically a code in itself.[56] Even subsequent legislation *in pari materia* may be looked at in the same way.

(b) *Earlier statutes repealed and consolidated by statute under construction.* Prior statutes repealed but reproduced in substance in consolidated form may be looked at [57] and judicial decisions on a repealed statute are treated as applicable to substantially identical provisions in the repealing Act.[58] This is justifiable on the basis that consolidation and re-enactment are both designed to restate rather than to change the law. Earlier legislation is of much less value as an aid to construction if the later legislation is professedly amending or clearly makes extensive changes, since there is then no presumption that Parliament intended the earlier interpretations to be continued.

(c) *Subsequent Acts.* Subsequent legislation may be looked at in order to find the proper construction to be put on an earlier and ambiguous Act [59] since Parliament may in a later Act on the same subject-matter expressly give a meaning to what was doubtful in an earlier Act, or may, more commonly, do so by implication, as by making further provision which is consistent with or inconsistent with the construction of the earlier Act proposed by the court.

---

[54] *Bank of England* v. *Vagliano* [1891] A.C. 107, 144; *Re Mayfair Property Co.* [1898] 2 Ch. 28, 35; *Eastman Photographic Co.* v. *Comptroller-General of Patents* [1898] A.C. 571, 575; *Macmillan* v. *Dent* [1907] 1 Ch. 107, 120; *Keates* v. *Lewis Merthyr Consolidated Collieries* [1911] A.C. 641, 642; *Avery* v. *N.E. Ry.* [1938] A.C. 606, 612, 617.

[55] *Sharp* v. *Morrison*, 1922 S.L.T. 272.

[56] *Lord Advocate* v. *Sprot's Trustees* (1901) 3 F. 440.

[57] Thus in interpreting the Companies Act 1948, reference may be made in many cases to decisions on similar sections of the 1929, 1908 and earlier Companies Acts.

[58] *Smith* v. *Baker* [1891] A.C. 325; *Boyle* v. *Wilson* [1907] A.C. 45, *sub nom.* *Walsh* v. *Pollokshaws Magistrates*, 1907 S.C.(H.L.) 1.

[59] *Att.-Gen.* v. *Clarkson* [1900] 1 Q.B. 156, 163; *Re Macmanaway* [1951] A.C. 161; *Att.-Gen.* v. *Prince Ernest Augustus of Hanover* [1957] A.C. 436.

(*d*) *Cases.* Decided cases which construe the words of an Act of Parliament [60] establish principles and rules of law whereby its scope and effect may be interpreted.[61] This principle is not without its defects as some statutory provisions have been interpreted in many cases, and the task in a subsequent case may be more obscured by the quest for a meaning consistent with the earlier cases than helped by them. But it is only if the actual words under construction have been previously construed in the same or a closely analogous statute that there is any scope for case-law doing any more than lay down general principles. The law is contained in the Act, not in what previous judges have said the Act meant.[62] Reference to cases where a similar question has arisen on Acts differently framed is of little value, since they merely illustrate a general principle.[63] Moreover, when Parliament uses in an Act a term which has already received judicial interpretation in a case, it is presumed that the term is used in the sense in which it has been judicially interpreted, unless a contrary intention appears.[64] But while a court will be slow to differ from a decision when Parliament has re-enacted a statutory provision in the same terms, it may do so, and is not *bound* to apply the same meaning as before.[65] This presumption has been heavily criticised by some judges and is not very strong.[66]

In connection with cases interpreting particular statutory words and phrases it should be noted that the courts take the view that statutes common to Scotland and England should be interpreted to the same effect in both countries, so that cases from the other jurisdiction are relevant guides to interpretation. So too a phrase in a Scottish Act may sometimes be elucidated by a case construing the corresponding provision in the equivalent English Act, though here there may be more room for diversity, but English cases construing the same word or phrase in a statute not also applicable to Scotland and not the counterpart of the Scottish provision may be of very little value indeed. The value of interpretative cases from the other

---

[60] Many of the interpretations put in past cases on particular words in particular statutory and factual contexts are collected in Stroud's *Judicial Dictionary*, Saunders' *Words and Phrases Legally Defined* and in *Current Law, s.v.* " Words and Phrases."

[61] *Re Aeronautics in Canada* [1932] A.C. 54, 70.

[62] *Hochstrasser* v. *Mayes* [1960] A.C. 376, 391; *Ogden Industries Ltd.* v. *Lucas* [1970] A.C. 113.

[63] *Reid* v. *Reid* (1886) 31 Ch.D. 402, 405.

[64] *Webb* v. *Outrim* [1907] A.C. 81; *Barras* v. *Aberdeen Steam Trawling Co.*, 1933 S.C.(H.L.) 21; Winder, " Interpretation of Statutes subject to Case Law " (1946) 58 Jur.Rev. 93; *Zimmerman* v. *Grossman* [1971] 1 All E.R. 363.

[65] *Royal Crown Derby Porcelain Co.* v. *Russell* [1949] 2 K.B. 417; *R.* v. *Bow Road Domestic Proceedings Court* [1968] 2 All E.R. 89.

[66] *Paisner* v. *Goodrich* [1955] 2 Q.B. 353; 358, [1957] A.C. 65.

jurisdiction is greatest in such matters as taxation, where parity of application throughout the United Kingdom is clearly desirable.[67]

(e) *Usage and contemporanea expositio.* Where it appears that a statutory provision has long been understood and acted upon in a certain sense the court will adopt that sense unless it appears manifestly wrong.[68] If the meaning of the statute is clear no usage to the contrary will prevail [69] and any such understanding or practice or usage must have been generally accepted, not merely prevalent.[70] These aids are particularly relevant to the construction of ancient statutes but have much less weight in more modern statutes.[71] The principle is accordingly relevant in the construction of old Scots Acts.[72] Similarly in interpreting the older Scots statutes, equitable considerations have been admitted.[73]

(f) *Textbooks.* A statement in an established textbook as to the meaning of a statutory provision has no binding force on any court but if there is doubt and the view of the text-writer has been accepted as law for a substantial period of time the court will probably accept it as correct. This is particularly true of very old statutes commented on by text-writers of high repute.[74]

(g) *Dictionaries.* In case of doubt as to the ordinary scope or sense of particular words standard dictionaries may be consulted. Their definitions are not authoritative but are valuable evidence of the ordinary and accepted connotation of particular words and accordingly may be of assistance, but the court is quite free to hold that Parliament has used a word with another meaning than that which is usual.[75]

(h) *International law.* If legislation is clear it must be given effect to even

---

[67] *Income Tax Commrs.* v. *Pemsel* [1891] A.C. 531; *Lord Advocate* v. *Earl of Moray's Trs.* (1905) 7 F.(H.L.) 116; *Inland Revenue* v. *Glasgow Police Athletic Assocn.*, 1953 S.C.(H.L.) 13; *Secretary of State for Employment* v. *Clarke Chapman & Co.* [1971] 2 All E.R.798.

[68] *Gorham* v. *Bishop of Exeter* (1850) 15 Q.B. 52, 73; *Migneault* v. *Malo* (1872) L.R. 4 P.C. 123; *Welham* v. *D.P.P.* [1961] A.C. 103.

[69] *Magistrates of Dunbar* v. *Duchess of Roxburghe* (1835) 3 Cl. & F. 335, 354; *Northam Bridge Co.* v. *R.* (1886) 55 L.T. 759; *Walker Trs.* v. *Lord Advocate*, 1912 S.C.(H.L.) 12.

[70] *Bank of Ireland* v. *Evans' Charity* (1855) 5 H.L.C. 389, 405.

[71] *Clyde Navigation Trustees* v. *Laird* (1883) 10 R.(H.L.) 77.

[72] *Montrose Peerage Case* (1853) 1 Macq. 401; *Graham* v. *Irving* (1899) 2 F. 29; cf. *Middleton* v. *Tough*, 1908 S.C.(J.) 32.

[73] *Mill's Trs.* v. *Mill's Exrs.*, 1965 S.C. 384, 388, 393.

[74] *Mayor of Newcastle* v. *Att.-Gen.* (1845) 12 Cl. & F. 402; *Bastin* v. *Davies* [1950] 1 All E.R. 1095.

[75] *Camden* v. *I.R.C.* [1914] 1 K.B. 641. Cf. *McVittie* v. *Bolton Corpn.* [1945] 1 K.B. 281; *Mills* v. *Cooper* [1967] 2 Q.B. 459; *Thornton* v. *Fisher and Ludlow Ltd.* [1968] 2 All E.R. 241; *I.R.C.* v. *Brander & Cruickshank*, 1970 S.C. 116, 121. In *Lord Advocate* v. *Mirrielees' Trs.* 1945 S.C.(H.L.) 1, when considering the words " common soldier " the House was led by the O.E.D. to discuss Shakespeare's use of the phrase.

if that conflicts with general international law or with treaty obligations.[76] But if the legislation is not clear it is presumed that Parliament did not intend to legislate in breach of international law or of specific treaty obligations, and the meaning consonant with the treaty obligations is to be preferred.[77]

(*j*) *International conventions.* When a statute is passed to give effect in the United Kingdom to an international convention to which the United Kingdom has become a party, the convention may be referred to if scheduled to the Act [78] and, even if not expressly referred to in the Act, may be looked at for the purpose of resolving ambiguities and obscurities, certainly where the terms of the convention and of the Act are similar so that there is an irresistible inference that the statute was intended to embody the convention.[79]

(*k*) *Royal Commission and other Reports.* Reference may not be made to Royal Commission or other Reports, on the subject-matter of the legislation, since these are merely proposals put before Parliament and there is no certainty that Parliament has accepted the recommendations in whole or in part or intended to accept or enact any part of the suggestions. Parliament has sometimes accepted a minority report and rarely accepts and enacts everything exactly as recommended by a Commission or Committee.

(*l*) *Hansard, White Papers, etc.* Similarly no reference is permitted to *Hansard* (the Parliamentary Debates), or to White Papers [80] or memoranda circulated in Parliament, since these have no authoritative verbal form, nor do they necessarily represent the finally agreed will of Parliament, while, particularly in the case of *Hansard*, the volume of words is considerable, there is no certainty which speech could be taken as authoritative since the speeches are argument rather than expression of will, and each argument can usually be matched by a counter-argument.

(*m*) Schemes made under authority of a statute and to give effect to it are not part of the statute and may not be consulted, except to confirm an interpretation of the words of the statute itself.[81]

Presumptions

There is also a considerable body of presumptions which can be invoked in various cases and which have greater or lesser weight depending on the

---

[76] *Mortensen* v. *Peters* (1906) 8 F.(J.) 93; *Ellerman Lines* v. *Murray* [1931] A.C. 126
[77] *Salomon* v. *Commissioners of Customs and Excise* [1966] 3 All E.R. 871.
[78] *e.g.* Carriage by Air Act 1961.
[79] *Salomon, supra*; *P.O.* v. *Estuary Radio Ltd.* [1968] 2 Q.B. 740; *The Banco* [1971] 1 All E.R. 524.
[80] *Viscountess Rhondda's Claim* [1922] 2 A.C. 339; *McCormick* v. *Lord Advocate*, 1953 S.C. 396.
[81] *Howgate* v. *Att.-Gen.* [1951] 1 K.B. 265.

statute in question and the composition of the court. These are only, be it noted, presumptions which may be applied in the absence of contrary indications but they must give way to any clear indication that they should not apply. The principal ones are:

(*a*) The Crown, Crown officials, and Crown Departments are not bound by statute unless that is expressly laid down.[82] Hence some modern statutes provide that the Act shall bind the Crown.[83]

(*b*) It is presumed that fundamental principles of constitutional law or of the common law of the land will not be altered by implication but only expressly.[84] It is difficult to say what are " fundamental principles " in this sense and it might be more helpful to phrase the presumption in the form that extensive and far-reaching changes in the law require to be made expressly, or that there is a presumption against interference with existing common law rights.[85]

(*c*) It is to be presumed that a British statute does not intend to infringe international law.[86] It may do so, but for reasons of international peace and comity the presumption is to the contrary.

(*d*) It is presumed that the jurisdiction of the ordinary courts applies and that an individual aggrieved may resort thereto and bring actions and appeals in the usual way.[87] Hence if appeal to the ordinary courts is to be limited or excluded that should be stated expressly.

(*e*) An interpretation is to be preferred which makes a statutory provision meaningful, purposeful and operable, rather than one which renders it nugatory and inoperable. Nothing short of impossibility should allow the court to declare a statute unworkable.[88]

(*f*) Statutes are presumed to have prospective effect only and not retrospective, *i.e.* to deal with future cases and not past ones.[89] A provision may, of course, be expressed to be retrospective, and indeed

---

[82] *Cooper* v. *Hawkins* [1904] 2 K.B. 164; *Tamlin* v. *Hannaford* [1950] 1 K.B. 18; *Somerville* v. *Lord Advocate* (1893) 20 R. 1050; *Schulze* v. *Steele* (1890) 17 R.(J.) 47; *Edinburgh Magistrates* v. *Lord Advocate* 1912 S.C. 1085.

[83] *e.g.* Crown Proceedings Act 1947; Road Traffic Act 1960, s. 250. *Cf. Salt* v. *MacKnight*, 1947 J.C. 99.

[84] *e.g. Nairn* v. *University Courts of St. Andrews and Edinburgh*, 1909 S.C.(H.L.) 10 (decided when women did not have the vote and had just been admitted to university degrees, but university graduates had a vote: argued that women could be graduates, and graduates could vote, *ergo* women graduates could vote. *Held* that if Parliament meant to confer the franchise on any woman it must do so expressly); *Nokes* v. *Doncaster Amalgamated Collieries* [1940] A.C. 1014; *National Assistance Board* v. *Wilkinson* [1952] 2 Q.B. 648.

[85] *Rendall* v. *Blair* (1890) 45 Ch.D. 139; *Central Control Board (Liquor Traffic)* v. *Cannon Brewery Co. Ltd.* [1919] A.C. 744.

[86] *Mortensen* v. *Peters* (1906) 8 F.(J.) 93.

[87] *Dunbar* v. *Scottish County Investment Co.*, 1920 S.C. 210; *Chester* v. *Bateson* [1920] 1 K.B. 829; see also *Portobello Mags.* v. *Edinburgh Mags.* (1882) 10 R. 130.

[88] *Murray* v. *Inland Revenue*, 1918 S.C.(H.L.) 111; *Nokes* v. *Doncaster Amalgamated Collieries* [1940] A.C. 1014; *Kelly* v. *Nuttall*, 1965 S.C. 427, 438.

[89] *Gardner* v. *Beresford's Trustees* (1878) 5 R.(H.L.) 105.

a statute may be passed deliberately to abrogate rights declared by a court decision,[90] or it may be held that such must have been the intention of Parliament, and this presumption is much weaker in the case of statutes extending remedies or rights than in the case of statutes limiting liberty or imposing penalties.[91]

(g) A strict construction will be given to penal statutes, which impose a prohibition or a penalty, and they will not be held to extend to cases not clearly covered by the words used.[92] So, too, there is a presumption against any interference with individual liberty.

(h) In penal statutes or those creating criminal offences it is presumed that *mens rea* (intention, guilty knowledge) is required for the commission of the offence and not merely the ignorant or inadvertent doing of the prohibited thing.[93] But the words used frequently rebut this presumption and many modern statutes have infringed it.[94]

(j) A strict construction is to be given to statutes restrictive of personal liberty or encroaching on the property rights of individuals. This presumption is weaker in times of national emergency[95] and weaker than it used to be in view of the impact of social welfare legislation. So, too, the intention to take away property from an individual without compensation is not to be imputed to Parliament unless that intention is clearly expressed.[96]

(k) A strict construction is to be given to statutory provisions imposing taxes on the public; such imposts must be clearly imposed, if at all,[97] though the courts are not keen to stretch this to the length of letting evasive transactions escape if they are within the spirit if not the exact words of the section.[98]

(l) Unless they do so clearly statutes should not be construed so as to take away the jurisdiction of superior courts[99] or to enlarge it by giving a right of appeal from inferior courts[1] or to confer jurisdiction on inferior courts, government departments or *ad hoc* authorities.[2]

---

[90] *e.g.* War Damage Act 1965, overruling retrospectively *Burmah Oil Co. Ltd.* v. *Lord Advocate*, 1964 S.C.(H.L.) 117.
[91] *Wilson* v. *Wilson*, 1939 S.C. 102.
[92] *I.R.C.* v. *Hinchy* [1960] A.C. 748; *H.M. Advocate* v. *R.M.*, 1969 J.C. 52, 59; *Zimmerman* v. *Grossman* [1971] 1 All E.R. 363.
[93] *Younghusband* v. *Luftig* [1949] 2 K.B. 354; *Sweet* v. *Parsley* [1970] A.C. 132.
[94] *e.g. Mitchell* v. *Morrison*, 1938 J.C. 64.
[95] *Liversidge* v. *Anderson* [1942] A.C. 206.
[96] *Central Control Board* (*Liquor Traffic*) v. *Cannon Brewery Co. Ltd.* [1919] A.C. 744.
[97] *I.R.C.* v. *Wolfson* [1949] 1 All E.R. 865.
[98] *Howard de Walden* v. *I.R.C.* [1942] 1 K.B. 389, 397; contrast *I.R.C.* v. *Levene* [1928] A.C. 217, 227. See also *Ross and Coulter* v. *Inland Revenue*, 1948 S.C.(H.L.) 1; *Edinburgh Life Assce. Co.* v. *Solicitor of Inland Revenue* (1875) 2 R. 394.
[99] *Pyx Granite Co.* v. *Ministry of Housing* [1960] A.C. 260.
[1] *Edwards* v. *Roberts* [1891] 1 Q.B. 302.
[2] *R.* v. *Board of Education* [1910] 2 K.B. 165.

Other presumptions of greater or lesser weight are sometimes enumerated but the foregoing are the principal ones.

Conclusions on Statute Law

It will be apparent that statutory interpretation is neither a mechanical task nor an exact science. It is more of an art and many factors enter into the final decision, the inherent vagueness and inexactness of the ordinary words of the English language, grammatical difficulties, the draftsman's human failure to foresee all possible cases, the immense variety and complexity and unusual character of the circumstances which may arise, the temperament of the judge or court before whom the matter comes, the judges' philosophy and their social, moral and other beliefs, their sympathy or lack of it for the parties, their judicial caution in adhering to a safe interpretation or valour in boldly extending a provision to cover a new case.

Too much attention should not be devoted to so-called rules of construction since " it must be remembered that the courts have laid down, indeed, not rigid rules, but principles which have been found to afford some guidance when it is sought to ascertain the intention of Parliament," [3] and so conflicting are these in many cases that one is driven to the view that " a court invokes whichever of the rules produces a result that satisfies its sense of justice in the case before it." [4] It cannot be pretended that statutory interpretation is a satisfactory part of British law.[5]

The Scottish and English Law Commissions made a joint study of the interpretation of statutes [5] and proposed that reference be permitted to a wider range of materials to ascertain Parliament's intention, and that specially prepared material be provided to ascertain the context in which statutory provisions were to be read, explanatory statements issued with the Act. The proposals seem as likely to complicate the process of interpretation as to facilitate it and have not been acted on.

II.—JUDICIAL PRECEDENTS OR CASE-LAW

The reasons or principles underlying the decisions of judges of the superior courts in past cases are also important sources of principles and rules of law.[6] A judicial decision embodying a principle capable of subsequent application is a judicial precedent. Judicial precedents have an authority as sources of principles and rules of law for application in later cases second only to relevant statutory provisions and of highest authority in the absence of relevant statutory provisions. Every judicial decision is in the

---

[3] *Cutler* v. *Wandsworth Stadium* [1949] A.C. 398, 410, *per* Lord du Parcq.

[4] Willis, " Statute Interpretation in a Nutshell " (1938) 16 Can. Bar Rev. 1, 16.

[5] Law Com. No. 21; Scot. Law Com. No. 11, 1969.

[6] See generally, Gardner, *Judicial Precedent in Scots Law*; and " Judicial Decisions as a Source of Scots Law " (1941) 53 J.R. 33; Smith, *Judicial Precedent in Scots Law*; Cross, *Precedent in English Law*.

first place the determination of a litigated controversy between two parties; secondly, it is an example of the application of some principle of law to certain facts, and as such, apart from its value to students and jurists, will naturally be looked at as a guide when a court again has to deal with a similar problem, since judges naturally wish to utilise the wisdom and experience of their predecessors and to give decisions consistent with those previously given in like cases. Thirdly, under the modern system of *stare decisis*, discussed later, it may in certain circumstances provide an authoritative ruling on the law which *must* be applied in a subsequent case raising a similar problem of law. The acceptance of even single decisions as settling the law and binding later courts to adopt the same principle is, in Scotland, a modern development under English influence, superseding the native rule that a train of decisions was very persuasive but that one decision was merely an example.[7]

Reference to previous decisions makes for consistency of treatment of similar cases and permits extension and development of principles by analogy. " Our common law system consists in the applying to new combinations of circumstances those rules of law which we derive from legal principles and judicial precedents; and for the sake of obtaining uniformity, consistency and certainty, we must apply those rules where they are not plainly unreasonable and inconvenient, to all cases which arise; and we are not at liberty to reject them, and to abandon all analogy to them, in those to which they have not been judicially applied, because we think that the rules are not as convenient and reasonable as we ourselves could have devised." [8]

Precedents are prior decisions embodying statements of principles of *law*, or rulings on disputed points of *law*. Previous decisions on questions of fact, *e.g.* that X was negligent in driving at 30 m.p.h. in fog, are not precedents to be followed in later similar cases,[9] because the facts of every case are unique and must be examined individually,[10] but decisions on some matters of fact, such as the sum of damages which may reasonably be awarded, are sometimes assisted by the citation of other decisions where similar injuries have been sustained.[11] So, too, previous decisions as to criminal penalties may give guidance, but are never binding authorities which have to be followed. A jury verdict on certain facts is never a precedent, even where very similar facts recur. Earlier cases on similar facts can only show how a basic rule has been applied to situations of a particular class.[12]

---

[7] Smith, *Judicial Precedent in Scots Law*, 1–14.

[8] *Mirehouse* v. *Rennell* (1833) 1 Cl. & F. 527, 546.

[9] *L. & Y. Ry.* v. *Highley* [1917] A.C. 352; *G.W. Ry.* v. *S.S. Mostyn* [1928] A.C. 57; *cf. Beith's Trs.* v. *Beith*, 1950 S.C. 66.

[10] *Qualcast (Wolverhampton) Ltd.* v. *Haynes* [1959] A.C. 743, 757–759; *Cavanagh* v. *Ulster Weaving Co.* [1960] A.C. 145; *Brown* v. *Rolls-Royce Ltd.*, 1960 S.C.(H.L.) 22.

[11] *Waldon* v. *War Office* [1956] 1 W.L.R. 51.

[12] *Hazell* v. *B.T.C.* [1958] 1 W.L.R. 169.

The use of judicial precedents as a source of law depends on several factors, the general practice in the superior courts, at least in cases of any difficulty or complexity or legal interest, of the judge or judges not merely issuing a decision but delivering an opinion explaining how and why they have reached their decision and what rules or principles of law they have applied [13]; the long-established practice of reporting judicial decisions and the judges' reasons and in later times the existence of a system of publishing reliable reports of the decisions of the superior courts; and the existence of a settled hierarchy of courts, in which the decisions of the higher courts carry greater weight than those of the lower.

Judicial opinions

In the superior courts it is customary in all but the simplest cases for the judge or judges to deliver or issue an opinion stating the relevant facts and explaining why he or they have found for the one party rather than the other, with references to the statutes and cases relied on as justifying the decision. The practice is very valuable as affording the parties the legal justification for the actual decision, and affording lawyers generally an explanation and discussion of the principles and rules of law thought applicable to the case and others raising the same issue of law. " It is not the function of noble and learned Lords or indeed of any judges to frame definitions or to lay down hard and fast rules. It is their function to enunciate principles and much that they say is intended to be illustrative or explanatory and not to be definitive. When there are two or more speeches they must be read together and then it is generally much easier to see what are the principles involved and what are merely illustrations of it." [14]

Reports

There is no official series of law reports, though *Session Cases* in Scotland and the *Law Reports* in England enjoy a rather more favoured status than do other series in that the printed opinions are revised by the judges, which is not always the case with other reports. There is nothing, however, to prevent other reports being published or cited in court [15] and sometimes

---

[13] Note that in the sheriff court in civil cases, the sheriff is bound by the Sheriff Courts Act 1907, Sched. 1, rule 82, to make findings in fact and in law separately, and to add a note giving his reasons. For examples, see the Sheriff Court Reports. In higher courts the practice is only customary. Note also that in the Privy Council the opinion, or majority opinion, is couched in the form of advice from the Privy Council to Her Majesty to dismiss or allow the appeal. See Privy Council cases in the volumes of *Appeal Cases. Cf. Jacobs* v. *L.C.C.* [1950] A.C. 361, 369: " While it is the primary duty of a court of justice to dispense justice to litigants, it is its traditional role to do so by means of an exposition of the relevant law."

[14] *Cassell* v. *Broome* [1972] 1 All E.R. 801, 836, *per* Lord Reid.

[15] *Renshaw* v. *Dixon* [1911] W.N. 40; Megarry, " Reporting the Unreported " (1954) 70 L.Q.R. 246; Allen, *Law in the Making*, 6th ed., 257, 355. In the House of Lords the *Law Reports* should normally be cited if the case is in that series; there is no practice in revenue cases to cite *Tax Cases* instead: *National Bank of Greece* v. *Westminster Bank Executor Co.* [1970] 1 W.L.R. 1400.

reports in other series are preferable or include cases or points omitted from the main series.[16] Not all cases are reported; probably on average only about 5 per cent. to 10 per cent. of cases decided in the Inner House,[17] so that an unreported decision can sometimes be found useful.[18] A report, moreover, may deal with only one aspect or one stage of a case, and other points, the ultimate result and the disposal of a case may remain unknown.[19] At least in England there is a salutary rule that only reports prepared and initialled by a member of the Bar may be cited [20] but there are instances of cases being cited from newspapers,[21] textbooks,[22] a shorthand report of the judgment,[23] and the personal recollection of the judge.[21] Mere notes of cases are of little use.[24]

The Form of Reports

The standard modern form of report consists of several parts.[25] There are first certain head-words or catch-words chosen to indicate very briefly by reference to recognised legal headings and sub-heads what legal topics

---

[16] Thus *Robertson's Tutor* v. *Glasgow Corpn.* is reported in 1950 S.C. 502, but not in S.L.T.; *Donnelly* v. *Glasgow Corpn.* is in 1949 S.L.T. 362 and not in S.C.; in *Lawrence* v. *Scott*, 1965 S.C. 403, 406, a passage is referred to which is omitted from the S.C. report of the precedent cited. *Cf.* also *Coats's Trs.* v. *Lord Advocate*, 1965 S.C.(H.L.) 45, 66, *per* Lord Guest; *Duke of Buccleuch* v. *I.R.C.* [1967] 1 All E.R. 129, 133.

[17] Walker, " The Mass of Reports " (1953) 69 S.L.R. 222. Decisions unreported at the time may subsequently be exhumed and reported either fully, *e.g. Walker* v. *Walker* (1949) in 1953 S.C. 297; or as a note appended to the report of a later case: see, *e.g. McNamara* v. *Laird Line* (1924), reported in a note to *McKay* v. *Scottish Airways*, 1948 S.C. 254, 265; *Robertson* v. *Lord Advocate* (1950), reported in a note to *Ayr Town Council* v. *Secretary of State for Scotland*, 1965 S.C. 394, 400.

[18] The proportion of cases decided by a single judge in the Outer House or in the sheriff court and not reported is much higher: so also in England. In *Leighton* v. *Harland & Wolff*, 1953 S.L.T.(Notes) 36, it was observed that it was counsel's duty to refer the court to unreported as well as reported cases on the point in issue. But the discovery of unreported decisions on a point may be fortuitous.

[19] Thus *McGhie* v. *B.T.C.* is reported at one stage and on one point in 1964 S.L.T. 25. The Lord Ordinary's unreported decision on another point is referred to and printed in part, in *Russell's Exrx.* v. *British Railways Board*, 1965 S.C. 422, 424.

[20] *Rivoli Hats* v. *Gooch* [1953] 1 W.L.R. 1190; *Birtwistle* v. *Tweedale* [1954] 1 W.L.R. 190.

[21] *R.* v. *Labouchere* (1884) 12 Q.B.D. 320, 328; *Barras* v. *Aberdeen Steam Trawling Co.*, 1933 S.C.(H.L.) 21; *Overstone Ltd.* v. *Shipway* [1962] 1 All E.R. 52; but on the dangers of this, see *Mahon* v. *Osborne* [1939] 2 K.B. 14.

[22] *Bush* v. *Whitehaven Trustees*, reported only in Hudson on *Building Contracts*, cited in *Davis Contractors Ltd.* v. *Fareham U.D.C.* [1956] A.C. 696; *Cowe* v. *Millar*, reported only in Connell on *The Agricultural Holdings Act*, cited in *Smith* v. *Grayston Estates Ltd.*, 1960 S.C. 349, 354.

[23] *Renshaw* v. *Dixon* [1911] W.N. 40; *Perez* v. *C.A.V. Ltd.* [1959] 2 All E.R. 414.

[24] *Birtwistle* v. *Tweedale* [1954] 1 W.L.R. 190 (*Estates Gazette* rejected); *Rivoli Hats Ltd.* v. *Gooch* [1953] 1 W.L.R. 1190 (*Current Law* rejected); see also, *Mahon* v. *Osborne* [1939] 2 K.B. 14; *Chapman* v. *Chapman* [1954] A.C. 429. In *Re Alsopp* [1967] 2 All E.R. 1056, it was said to have been the practice to ignore reports in *Weekly Notes* on matters of construction of wills. In *Maitland*, 1961 S.C. 291, and *McLaughlin*, 1965 S.C. 243, a prior case reported without opinions only in S.L.T.(Notes) was said to be valueless as a precedent in future.

[25] *Cf.* Newark, " Anatomy of a Law Report " (1965) 16 N.I.L.Q. 371.

are dealt with in the case, mentioning first the principal ones and then the subordinate or more detailed matters,[26] and what statutes have been discussed or interpreted in the case. This is followed by the rubric or headnote, which is a concise statement of the facts, of the point of law in issue, and of the court's decision, which last element is usually preceded by the word " Held." There is also an indication of any dissenting or divergent opinions by particular judges and of any specially noteworthy remarks or observations, and sometimes a mention of the attitude adopted to certain previous cases.[27] It has to be noticed that the head-words and rubric are compiled by the reporter under the supervision of the editor of the series of reports, and they have no authority at all. They may contain mistakes or misleading statements [28] and judges sometimes have occasion to criticise the rubric of previous reports.[29] The rubric is only the reporter's summary, his view of what the case decided. There may be two or more sets of head-words and rubrics where the case has raised two or more distinct matters for argument and decision, as where there have been debatable points on procedure, on law and on evidence.

Then follows a narrative of the facts of the case and of the material steps in the litigation, sometimes with quotations from the written pleadings of the parties or from the evidence heard at an earlier stage. Sometimes this is done by incorporating that part of a judge's opinion which states the facts, or by reference to his opinion which, in the reporter's view, adequately states the facts. This information should make clear what the controversy is about, and everything that has gone before in its progress through the courts. It should, but may not, contain all factual information about the case which enables the reader to understand it and to evaluate or criticise the decision and judicial opinions. But some facts are sometimes tantalisingly omitted.

This is followed by a brief account of the arguments put forward by counsel on each side with a note of the cases, statutes and books referred to by them. Sometimes important or valuable statements are made in argument, or made by the Bench in reply to an argument. Moreover it may be very important in a later case to know whether the court was referred in argument to a particular case or statute as there have been instances of decisions arrived at in ignorance of a case or statute in point, and a

---

[26] These catch-words are of great importance for determining where the case will be placed in the Digests.

[27] *e.g.* that some precedent case has been " applied," or " followed " or " not followed " or " distinguished " or " overruled." For the significance of these terms, see p. 395, *infra.*

[28] Thus in *Victoria Laundry* v. *Newman* [1949] 2 K.B. 528 it was pointed out that the rubric in *Hadley* v. *Baxendale* (1854) 9 Ex. 341 was incorrect in a material respect.

[29] Thus in *Hamilton* v. *Hamilton*, 1954 S.L.T. 16, the report of *Robb* v. *Robb*, 1953 S.L.T. 44, was severely criticised.

decision is of lesser authority for the future if relevant prior cases were not cited in argument.[30]

Lastly there are printed the opinions of the judges, usually in full, but sometimes with omissions. It should be noted that another series of reports may include passages omitted in one report,[31] or may give a slightly different version of a passage.[32]

Some reported decisions are merely instances of the application of an existing rule of law, reported for the interest of the circumstances or the value of the judicial expression of an old and settled principle of law, while others are really creative of new law, as where a new rule is laid down or an existing rule reformulated, modified, extended or limited, or applied to a fresh set of circumstances. The former kind of cases are merely applications of law, the latter in some measure create new law or define or delimit the applicability of some principle or rule of law in a sphere previously vague. Cases of the former sort may be, but are rather unlikely to be, authoritative or binding in a future case, but cases of the latter sort are much more likely to be authoritative in future.

The Principle of Stare Decisis

While, as has been pointed out, it is a natural and common-sense practice to have regard, when deciding a case, to reported decisions in prior cases raising the same issue of law, the modern British system goes further by its insistence on *stare decisis*, that is, on the principle of abiding by authorities or decided cases, so that in certain circumstances the doctrine derived from a precedent case or series of cases *must* be followed and applied, even though the judge in the subsequent case might not have been disposed of his own accord to apply that doctrine. The habit of referring to precedents in point and applying them has grown into the rule that a precedent in point *must* be applied.[33]

This principle of *stare decisis* may be justified on the ground that it makes for certainty and consistency of the law, that it makes for the disposal in the same way of similar cases (and equality of treatment is a commonly accepted element in justice), that it tends to limit or exclude judicial mistakes, prejudices and faulty formulations of an appropriate rule of law to apply to the facts, and that it tends to make the law predictable, so as to enable a legal adviser to forecast what rule a court would probably apply to a given set of facts.

---

[30] *Penrikyber Navigation Colliery Co.* v. *Edwards* [1933] A.C. 28.

[31] Thus the report of *Leadbetter* v. *N.C.B.* in 1952 S.L.T. 179 deals with a matter omitted from 1952 S.C. 19. *Cf. Barras, supra,* at p. 50, *per* Lord Macmillan and *Lawrence* v. *Scott*, 1965 S.C. 403, 406, *per* L.P. Clyde, in each case quoting a passage from one report of a case, absent from another report.

[32] Thus there are four different reports of *Holmes* v. *Mather* in 1875 (L.R. 10 Ex. 261; 44 L.J.Ex. 176; 33 L.T. 361; 23 W.R. 869) which show important verbal differences: two are set out in parallel columns for comparison in Pollock on *Torts*, 15th ed., 132.

[33] See also Salmond, " Theory of Judicial Precedents " (1900) 16 L.Q.R. 376.

On the other hand, as will appear later, there are countervailing disadvantages: adherence to *stare decisis* may make the law rigid, inflexible and impervious to social change; the discovery of the doctrine enunciated by a precedent is difficult and may be impossible; judicial distaste for, or disinclination to be regulated by, a particular precedent produces much verbal juggling, sophistry, casuistry and the drawing of fine, or even invisible, distinctions; and a decision may come to depend too much on the finding or not finding of an apt precedent in the reports.

Nevertheless this is the modern British rule [34]: a precedent which is both *in point and binding must* be applied; a precedent which is *in point and persuasive* should be considered and *may be adopted* and applied; a precedent which is *not in point may be ignored.* Much accordingly depends on the criteria for deciding whether a particular precedent is in point or not and, in the circumstances before a particular court, whether it is binding or merely persuasive.

When is a Precedent " in point " ?

A prior decision is a precedent in point when there was raised, argued and decided in it as applicable to a certain set of facts some issue of law which is the same issue of law as arises in the instant case in relation to a different set of facts of the same general kind. Similarity of facts between the precedent and the instant case is not enough and may, indeed, matter very little. One case about sale of a car may have no relation in law to another case about sale of a car. But a decision about the sale of a car or a book may contain a statement of principle on an issue of law relevant to a later case about the sale of a car or a horse raising the same issue of law. Decisions on questions of fact do not make precedents though they may give some guidance in a later case.[35] What is important is the raising in a subsequent case of the same issue of law as was decided in the precedent case, as, for example, whether artificial insemination by a donor amounts to legal adultery or not,[36] or what amounts in law to fraudulent misrepresentation inducing a contract.[37] Thus the precedent about fraudulent misrepresentation is in point in a later case of a contract of sale or of hiring, even though the precedent related to the contract to take shares in a company, but is not necessarily in point in relation to fraudulent misrepresentation inducing a marriage, since marriage is a relationship legally distinct from a commercial contract.[38]

As will be seen later, much ingenuity is sometimes devoted to arguing that a precedent is not " in point " or not " on all fours with " the instant

---

[34] The rule is English in origin and has been accepted in Scotland only since 1800, largely under the influence of the House of Lords: see Smith, *Judicial Precedent*, 10–17.
[35] *Waldon* v. *War Office* [1966] 1 All E.R. 108.
[36] *MacLennan* v. *MacLennan*, 1958 S.C. 105.
[37] *Derry* v. *Peek* (1889) 14 App.Cas. 337.
[38] *Lang* v. *Lang*, 1921 S.C. 44.

case, on the ground that the precedent dealt with a different legal issue or that the facts are sufficiently different from those of the precedent to make the issue of law materially different. When it is remembered that facts never exactly reproduce themselves and that possible combinations of facts raising legal issues are limitless, it will be apparent that it is frequently difficult to say whether a given prior case is really in point or not, and that in most cases it is really a matter of degree, the decision being that the prior case is or is not sufficiently similar in the legal issue raised to the instant case to be treated as having raised the same point of law and accordingly to be a precedent for the decision of the instant case.

Binding and Persuasive Precedents

Even of prior decisions which are in point, not every one is binding on a subsequent court, or authoritative. Some are merely persuasive.

A precedent in point is authoritative or binding when judges in a subsequent case raising the same issue of law *must* follow and apply it to the facts before them, irrespective of their views as to its soundness.

A precedent in point is persuasive when judges in a subsequent case will take it into consideration, when they will attach such weight to it as they think the precedent deserves, having regard to its value, the personal eminence of the judges who decided it, the place in the judicial hierarchy from which it comes, and the extent to which it is in point in the later case, but which they are *not bound* to follow and apply. It may persuade them to apply it, but if it does so, it does so on its merits, and not because it is authoritative.

The question whether any given precedent which is " in point " is authoritative or merely persuasive in a subsequent case depends primarily on where it emanated from in the hierarchy of courts and, secondly, on certain factors affecting its evaluation. These two elements must now be considered.

The Hierarchy of Courts

The regular courts of the United Kingdom form a systematic hierarchy in which appeals generally lie from inferior courts to courts superior to them in their own line of ascent. In considering whether any given court is bound or subject to persuasion by a precedent emanating from another court in the hierarchy it is essential to have in mind the place of each court in the hierarchy. The authority of a prior decision does not depend on whether an appeal lies from the court considering the precedent to the court which issued judgment in the precedent case. It depends on the place in the hierarchy held by the court from which the precedent came relative to the place of the hierarchy held by the later court considering the precedent.

The hierarchy of United Kingdom regular courts consists of six parallel lines, comprising respectively the civil and criminal courts of Scotland, England and Wales, and of Northern Ireland. These are set out in the following table, in which courts shown on the same horizontal line are of generally corresponding standing and authority. The lowest courts can be omitted from consideration since their decisions are very seldom reported and are of negligible value as precedents.

The general principle is that any court is bound by prior decisions in point pronounced by courts superior to it in its own vertical line of authority, and that prior decisions in point of courts of equal or higher rank in other vertical lines of authority are persuasive in varying degrees.[39] Decisions of courts of lower rank in any vertical line of authority may be ignored but may sometimes be of some persuasive value. But this general statement must now be examined in more detail in relation to the main courts since practice is not uniform in all courts. Moreover the practice in Scotland is less strict and rigid throughout than in England.

SCOTLAND		ENGLAND & WALES		N. IRELAND	
Civil	*Criminal*	*Civil*	*Criminal*	*Civil*	*Criminal*
H.L. Ct. of Session (Inner Ho.)	— High Court (appeals)	H.L. Ct. of Appeal [40] (Civil Division)	H.L. Ct. of Appeal [41] (Criminal Division)	H.L. Ct. of Appeal	H.L. Ct. of Crim. Appeal
Ct. of Session (Outer Ho.)	High Court (trials)	⎰ Divisional Court ⎱ High Court [42]	⎰ Divisional Court Crown Court [43]	High Court	Assizes
Sheriff Principal	Sheriff and jury		Crown Court		Quarter Sessions
Sheriff	Sheriff (summarily)	County Court		County Court	

The Principle of stare decisis in Operation

The way in which the principle of *stare decisis* operates varies slightly in different courts and must be examined in relation to the different Scottish and English courts separately.

[39] " In the hierarchical system of courts which exists in this country, it is necessary for each lower tier . . . to accept loyally the decisions of the higher tiers " : *Cassell* v. *Broome* [1972] 1 All E.R. 801, 809, per Lord Hailsham.

[40] Including the Court of Exchequer Chamber which was the predecessor of the Court of Appeal.

[41] Including the former Court for Crown Cases Reserved (1846–1906) and Court of Criminal Appeal (1906–66).

[42] Including the pre-1875 separate Courts of Queen's Bench, Common Pleas, Exchequer, Admiralty and Matrimonial Causes.

[43] Including the Central Criminal Court.

SCOTLAND

House of Lords

The House of Lords, when sitting as the final court of civil appeal from Scotland, sits as a Scottish court [44] and normally considers itself bound by precedents of its own pronounced in Scottish appeals,[45] but not by its own precedents pronounced in English or Irish appeals,[46] nor by dicta on questions of Scots law raised incidentally in such appeals,[46] nor by precedents in such appeals relating to questions of general jurisprudence and not turning on specialties of English law.[47] Such precedents will, however, be persuasive.[48] Decisions of the House in English appeals on statutes common to England and Scotland are probably binding,[49] but otherwise if the statute is peculiar to England.

The Lord Chancellor announced on behalf of himself and the Lords of Appeal in Ordinary in July 1966 [50] that their Lordships regarded the use of precedent as an indispensable foundation upon which to decide what is the law and its application to individual cases, and providing at least some degree of certainty upon which individuals can rely in the conduct of their affairs, as well as a basis for orderly development of legal rules. Their Lordships nevertheless recognised that too rigid adherence to precedent might lead to injustice in a particular case and also unduly restrict the proper development of the law, and they therefore proposed to modify their previous practice and, while treating former decisions of the House as normally binding, to depart from a previous decision when it appeared right to do so. In this connection they would bear in mind the danger of disturbing retrospectively the basis on which contracts, settlements of property and fiscal arrangements had been entered into and also the especial need for certainty as to the criminal law.[51] The announcement was stated as not intended to affect the use of precedent elsewhere than in the House.

The House has, so far, been very hesitant to overrule any of its own previous decisions.[52]

---

[44] *Concha* v. *Murietta* (1889) 40 Ch.D. 543, 550; *cf. Cooper* v. *Cooper* (1888) 15 R.(H.L.) 21; *Elliot* v. *Joicey*, 1935 S.C.(H.L.) 57.

[45] *Gordon* v. *Marjoribanks* (1818) 6 Dow 87, 112; *Houldsworth* v. *City of Glasgow Bank* (1880) 7 R.(H.L.) 53, 62; *Oliver* v. *Saddler*, 1929 S.C.(H.L.) 94, 97; as to England, see *London Street Tramways Co.* v. *L.C.C.* [1898] A.C. 375; Landau, " Precedents in the House of Lords " (1951) 63 J.R. 222.

[46] *Glasgow Corpn.* v. *Central Land Board*, 1956 S.C.(H.L.) 1; and see discussion in 19 M.L.R. 427.

[47] *Orr Ewing's Trustees* v. *Orr Ewing* (1885) 13 R.(H.L.) 1.

[48] *Virtue* v. *Alloa Police Commissioners* (1873) 1 R. 285; *Blacks* v. *Girdwood* (1885) 13 R. 243; Henderson, " English Cases as Scots Authorities " (1900) 12 J.R. 304.

[49] *Inland Revenue* v. *Glasgow Police Athletic Association*, 1953 S.C.(H.L.) 13.

[50] Note [1966] 3 All E.R. 77.

[51] The House does not deal with criminal appeals from Scotland, save from the Courts-Martial Appeal Court.

[52] It declined to do so in *Jones* v. *Secretary of State for Social Services* [1972] A.C. 944 but did so in *British Railways Board* v. *Herrington* [1972] A.C. 877.

Decisions of the House in Scottish appeals are binding on all civil courts in Scotland, but decisions of the House in other appeals, on statutes not common to the United Kingdom, and on grounds of general jurisprudence raised in non-Scottish appeals are persuasive only, though in a high degree.[53] It is always difficult to determine what are questions of " general jurisprudence " particularly in view of the tendency of English Lords of Appeal to assume that much English law is general, and that the same principles apply in Scotland.

Court of Session, Inner House

Either Division of the Inner House of the Court of Session is normally bound by decisions of the House of Lords in Scottish appeals, by a decision of seven or more judges of the Court of Session, and by a previous decision of either Division.[54] There is no fixed rule that even the whole court is bound by its own previous decisions, and it is certainly not the rule that decisions of a Division have the same weight as decisions of the full court.[55] A court of seven judges may quite freely overrule a precedent of either Division.[56] In exceptional cases a precedent in point of either Division may not be followed and doubtful precedents or conflicts of precedent are normally resolved by convening a fuller court of seven or more judges.[57] There are also expressions of the view that a Division is not necessarily bound by a single decision of either Division.[58] Moreover even when a precedent is directly in point it may be disregarded if the social and economic background has so changed that the precedent is quite outmoded.[59]

---

[53] *Virtue* v. *Alloa Police Commrs.* (1873) 1 R. 285; *Orr Ewing's Trs.* v. *Orr Ewing* (1885) 13 R.(H.L.) 1.

[54] *e.g. Garden's Exor.* v. *More*, 1913 S.C. 285; *Heavyside* v. *Smith*, 1929 S.C. 68; *Cameron* v. *Glasgow Corpn.*, 1935 S.C. 533; *Galloway* v. *Galloway*, 1947 S.C. 330; *Marshall* v. *Scottish Milk Marketing Board*, 1956 S.C.(H.L.) 37, 39; (revd. by H.L., *ibid.* 40–48). In *Hargrave's Trs.* v. *Schofield* (1900) 3 F. 14 there were expressions of dissent from this principle. On whether the whole court can review a decision of seven judges, see *Yuill's Trs.* v. *Thomson* (1902) 4 F. 815.

[55] As is the case in England under *Young* v. *Bristol Aeroplane Co.* [1944] K.B. 718. In *Yuill's Trs.* v. *Thomson* (1902) 4 F. 815, 819, it was said to be contrary to practice for the whole court to reconsider a question considered by seven judges, seven judges having the same authority as the whole court, but not all the judges accepted that proposition.

[56] *e.g. Cochrane's Exrx.* v. *Cochrane*, 1947 S.C. 134; *McElroy* v. *McAllister*, 1949 S.C. 110; *Smith* v. *Stewart & Co.*, 1960 S.C. 329.

[57] In *Drummond* v. *Inland Revenue*, 1951 S.C. 482, it was doubted whether it was competent for the court, when sitting as Court of Exchequer, to convene a larger court to reconsider a precedent, and the view was expressed that this should be done by the House of Lords.

[58] *Lord Advocate* v. *Young* (1898) 25 R. 778; *Earl of Wemyss* v. *Earl of Zetland* (1890) 18 R. 126, 130.

[59] *Beith's Trustees* v. *Beith*, 1950 S.C. 66. *Cf.* Lord Carmont's reasons in *Macdonald* v. *Glasgow Western Hospitals*, 1954 S.C. 453, 484 for refusing to hold the First Division bound by the First Division's decision in *Reidford* v. *Aberdeen Magistrates*, 1933 S.C. 276. In *Donnelly* v. *Donnelly*, 1959 S.C. 97, Lord Justice-Clerk Thomson (p. 102) refused to regard a case of 1561, however much in point, as binding, but Lord Patrick (p. 103) accepted the case as an authority.

Decisions of the House of Lords in English or Irish appeals are very strongly persuasive, and of the English or Irish Courts of Appeal strongly persuasive, the degree of persuasion depending largely on the similarity of Scots to English or Irish law on the point in issue.[60] Decisions of lower English or Irish courts are weakly persuasive, though rather more so when construing a statute common to Scotland and to England or Ireland.

High Court of Justiciary as Court of Criminal Appeal

The High Court is not bound by decisions of the House of Lords in a criminal matter, even when dealing with a United Kingdom criminal statute, still less by the (English) Court of Appeal, Criminal Division, or the predecessors of that court, though such decisions are persuasive if the matter is one common to United Kingdom law. Nor is it bound by a previous decision of a similar quorum of the High Court, though the practice is to follow such decisions,[61] but a larger court would probably be convened to reconsider a difficult precedent.[62] There is no rule which prevents a bench of the High Court from reversing an unfortunate precedent, even of the full court, if the requirements of justice make this desirable, but normally any precedent doubted is reviewed by a larger, or even a full, bench.[63] A full bench probably can overrule a precedent decided by a prior full bench.[64] Decisions of the High Court are normally binding on High Court judges presiding at trials and on sheriffs.

Court of Session, Outer House

A Lord Ordinary sitting alone in the Outer House normally considers himself bound by decisions of the House of Lords in Scottish appeals, by decisions of seven or more judges, or of either Division of the Inner House. He is not bound by decisions of another Outer House judge, though he treats such decisions with respect. But he may decline to follow them, leaving it to a higher court at a later date to decide which view is right.[65] Decisions of the House of Lords in English or Irish appeals are very persuasive,[66] of the English or Irish Courts of Appeal strongly persuasive, and of the English or Irish High Courts mildly persuasive, the degree depending on the similarity of the legal systems on the point in issue.

---

[60] *e.g. Inland Revenue* v. *Ferguson*, 1968 S.C. 135, 151 (revd. 1969 S.C.(H.L.) 103).
[61] *McAvoy* v. *Cameron*, 1917 J.C. 1.
[62] *Macmillan* v. *McConnell*, 1917 J.C. 43; *Marshall* v. *Clark*, 1957 J.C. 68.
[63] *e.g. Kirkwood* v. *H.M. Advocate* 1939 J.C. 36 (11 judges).
[64] *Sugden* v. *H.M. Advocate*, 1934, J.C. 103. A " full bench " may be any court larger than the essential quorum of three, and may consist of five (*e.g. McFadyen* v. *Stewart*, 1951 J.C. 164), seven (*e.g. Mitchell* v. *Morrison*, 1938 J.C. 64), 11 (*e.g. Kirkwood, supra*), 12 (*e.g. Sugden, supra*), or other, normally uneven, number.
[65] *Blackwood* v. *Andre*, 1947 S.C. 333, not following *McDaid* v. *Clyde Navigation Trustees*, 1946 S.C. 462; *Blackwood* was later approved by the House of Lords in *B.T.C.* v. *Gourley* [1956] A.C. 185. *Cf. McKenzie* v. *McKenzie*, 1960 S.C. 322 and *Breen* v. *Breen*, 1961 S.C. 158, 175, 188.
[66] See *Spencer* v. *Macmillan's Trs.*, 1958 S.C. 300, 303.

High Court of Justiciary (as court of trial)

A single Lord of Justiciary usually accepts the law laid down previously on appeal by a bench of the High Court, but single-judge rulings, though very persuasive, are not binding on other single judges.[67] Decisions of the English superior criminal courts are highly persuasive and of English trial judges mildly persuasive, if the legal systems are similar on the point in issue.

Sheriff Principal and Sheriff (civil)

Sheriffs principal and sheriffs are bound by decisions of the House of Lords and Inner House of the Court of Session and regard English and Irish decisions as persuasive in varying degrees, depending on the rank of the court and the subject-matter. They are not bound by decisions of the Outer House, though they treat them with respect, nor are they bound by one another, though a sheriff will usually follow the decisions of his sheriff principal.

Sheriff and Jury; Sheriff's Summary Court (criminal)

A sheriff presiding at a trial by jury or trying a case summarily must accept law laid down by the High Court sitting as Court of Criminal Appeal but is not necessarily bound by previous rulings of a single trial judge, whether Lord of Justiciary or sheriff, though he will normally follow such rulings. English and Irish criminal decisions are persuasive, depending on the status of the court which pronounced them and on the similarity or difference between Scots and English or Irish law on the matter.

District courts

A magistrate sitting in a district court is probably bound by rulings of any superior criminal court or of a single judge or sheriff.

Special Courts

In the Scottish Land Court, the court does not seem to hold itself bound by a single prior decision.[68] The Lands Valuation Appeal Court retains the power to review its own previous decisions.[69] The Courts-Martial Appeal Court follows the practice of the High Court of Justiciary as Court of Criminal Appeal. The Transport Tribunal is successor to the Railway Rates Tribunal and treats previous decisions as persuasive only.[70] The

---

[67] *H.M. Advocate* v. *Higgins* (1914) 7 Adam 229.

[68] See, *e.g. Niven* v. *Cameron*, 1939 S.L.C.R. 23; *Chisholm* v. *Campbell Orde*, 1920 S.L.C.R. 36; *Georgeson* v. *Anderston's Trustees*, 1945 S.L.C.R. 44.

[69] *Inverness Assessor* v. *Cameron*, 1938 S.C. 360. It has followed the House of Lords in preference to one of its own previous decisions, even though no appeal lies: *Aberdeen Assessor* v. *Collie*, 1932 S.C. 304.

[70] *B.T.C.* v. *Bristow Ltd.* (1955) 30 Traf.Cas. 217, 232.

Restrictive Practices Court is empowered to discharge its own previous declarations and orders.[71]

In administrative tribunals the rules of precedent do not apply and to some extent administrative tribunals have been resorted to, to avoid this feature of British judicial technique. But where decisions are published, as of the Commissioner in National Insurance cases, there seems to be developing a tendency to have regard to prior cases in decision. Where an appeal lies from the tribunal to the ordinary courts it seems probable that the tribunals hold themselves bound by precedents in those courts. Tribunals such as the Commissioners of Income Tax in fact regard themselves as bound by reported decisions of the courts in tax cases. This was also the case with the Pensions Appeal Tribunal and in one case [72] it was held that the English tribunal should follow a later Court of Session decision on appeal in preference to an earlier High Court decision on a similar appeal. But where there is no appeal to the ordinary courts tribunals seem to be free from the doctrine of *stare decisis*.

ENGLAND

House of Lords

Decisions of the House of Lords when pronounced in an English appeal are normally binding on the House itself for the future [73] and that even though the House were equally divided so that the decision appealed against stands unreversed.[74] " This House has debarred itself from ever reconsidering any of its own decisions. It matters not how difficult it is to find the *ratio decidendi* of a previous case, that *ratio* must be found. And it matters not how difficult it is to reconcile that *ratio* when found with statutory provisions or general principles; that *ratio* must be applied to any later case which is not reasonably distinguishable." [75] A binding precedent cannot be disregarded merely because it was inadequately argued or considered, nor because their Lordships disagree with it,[76] nor even can it be disregarded on the ground that it was based on industrial

---

[71] Restrictive Trade Practices Act 1956, s. 22 (1).

[72] *Minister of Pensions* v. *Higham* [1948] 2 K.B. 153.

[73] *Beamish* v. *Beamish* (1861) 9 H.L.C. 274, 338; *London Street Tramways Co.* v. *L.C.C.* [1898] A.C. 375; *Radcliffe* v. *Ribble Motor Services* [1939] A.C. 215; *Nash* v. *Tamplin* [1952] A.C. 231. On history of this, see Salmond on *Jurisprudence*, 11th ed., 175–184. See also Dworkin, " *Stare Decisis* in the House of Lords " (1962) 25 M.L.R. 163; Cross, " *Stare Decisis* in Contemporary England " (1966) 82 L.Q.R. 203. The Lord Chancellor's announcement (p. 370) that the House will exceptionally consider itself free to disregard its own precedents applies to English and Irish appeals also.

[74] *Att.-Gen.* v. *Dean of Windsor* (1860) 8 H.L.C. 369; *R.* v. *Millis* (1844) 10 Cl. & F. 534; *Beamish* v. *Beamish* (1861) 9 H.L.C. at 338; *I.R.C.* v. *Walker* [1915] A.C. 509, 519. As to other courts equally divided, see *The Vera Cruz* (1884) 9 P.D. at 98.

[75] *Nash* v. *Tamplin & Sons Brewery* [1952] A.C. 231. This dictum is now qualified by the Lord Chancellor's announcement in 1966 (*supra*).

[76] *London Transport Executive* v. *Betts* [1959] A.C. 213.

and social conditions which have changed.[77] The decision is probably not binding if decided *per incuriam*, in ignorance of the terms of a statute or statutory instrument.[78] The House was formerly forced in many cases to resort to " distinguishing " its own previous decisions if it wished not to be bound to follow them.[79] It seems probable also that, if a conflict be found between two previous decisions of the House, the House could follow either and would not be bound to follow one because it was earlier or later.[80] But a dictum patently wrong and unnecessary to the decision of the precedent may be disapproved,[81] and it has been suggested that when a particular precedent, even of the House, conflicts with a fundamental principle, also of the House, the latter must prevail.[82] It has also been said *obiter* [83] that there are at least three classes of cases where the House can question or limit the *ratio decidendi* of a previous House of Lords decision: (a) where it is obscure; (b) where the decision is out of line with other authorities or established principles; and (c) where it is much wider than was necessary for the decision so that it becomes a question of how far it is proper to distinguish the earlier decision. Nor is the House bound to follow a previous decision of its own, merely because it is indistinguishable on the facts; the decision is binding only because it lays down some principle of law or for its reasoning on particular facts.[84]

The House has stated that the power to depart from its own previous decisions should only be sparingly exercised, and rarely on a matter of statutory interpretation.[85] The power should not be used where the effect would be to abolish an offence; certainty being important in the criminal law and abolition the function of Parliament.[86]

In respect of decisions pronounced in Scottish or Irish appeals the House is clearly technically not bound in a subsequent English case, but it has been accepted that it will normally be so bound where the Scottish case was decided in the House on the same principles as apply in English law.[87]

---

[77] *Radcliffe* v. *Ribble Motor Services* [1939] A.C. at 245–246. But on this, see Lord Evershed M.R., *The Court of Appeal in England*, p. 18.

[78] *London Street Tramways, supra*, at p. 379. " *Per incuriam* " has been said (*Morelle* v. *Wakeling* [1955] 2 Q.B. 379) to cover only decisions given in ignorance or forgetfulness of some inconsistent statutory provision or of some authority binding on the court concerned.

[79] On " distinguishing," see p. 395, *infra*.

[80] This is the rule in the Court of Appeal.

[81] *Public Trustee* v. *I.R.C.* [1960] A.C. 398.

[82] *London Transport Executive, supra*, 247, *per* Lord Denning.

[83] *Scruttons* v. *Midland Silicones Ltd.* [1962] 1 All E.R. 1, *per* Lords Reid and Keith.

[84] *Chancery Lane Safe Deposit Co.* v. *I.R.C.* [1966] A.C. 85.

[85] *Jones* v. *Secretary of State for Social Services* [1972] 1 All E.R. 145.

[86] *Knuller* v. *D.P.P.* [1972] 2 All E.R. 898.

[87] *R.* v. *Minister of Health, ex p. Yaffé* [1931] A.C. at 502; *Heyman* v. *Darwins Ltd.* [1942] A.C. at 401. In the leading case (*London Street Tramways, supra*) the House held itself bound by its previous decision in a Scottish appeal, *Edinburgh Street Tramways* v. *Edinburgh Mags.* (1894) 21 R.(H.L.) 78.

Thus it has always been accepted in England that *Donoghue* v. *Stevenson* [88] is binding on the House and on lower English courts, but strictly it is not, being a Scottish appeal. And the House can, in an English appeal, choose between previous decisions of its own in a Scottish and in an English appeal, and elect to follow the Scottish one, where the law is or is assumed to be the same in both countries.[89] The decisions of the House of Lords are binding on all inferior English courts,[90] and must be loyally observed by the Court of Appeal and all lower English courts.[91] An inferior court can justifiably refuse to follow what has been said in the House if what was said was *obiter*, or where there are two clearly inconsistent decisions of the House and the lower court has then to choose which to follow.[92]

Court of Appeal (Civil Division)

The Court of Appeal is bound by decisions of the House of Lords in English civil appeals,[93] even if it were decided *per incuriam*,[94] but not if the House of Lords decision discloses no discernible *ratio decidendi*.[95] The Court of Appeal also has held that it is bound by its own previous decisions [96] unless the prior decision was arrived at *per incuriam*, *i.e.* in ignorance or forgetfulness of some inconsistent statutory provision or of some authority binding on the court,[97] or without full citation of authorities,[98] or is inconsistent with and expressly or impliedly overruled by a later decision of the House of Lords.[99] Moreover, it has the right, when referred to several conflicting previous decisions of its own, to select and follow one of them, and this selection probably binds later Court of Appeal cases.[1] Full binding force attaches even to unreported decisions of the

---

[88] 1932 S.C.(H.L.) 31. In that case the Lords said that the principles applicable were common to Scots and to English law. But this is a dangerous doctrine.

[89] *Heyman* v. *Darwins Ltd.* [1942] A.C. 356.

[90] *Att.-Gen.* v. *Dean and Canons of Windsor* (1860) 8 H.L.Cas. 369; *G.W.Ry.* v. *SS. Mostyn* [1928] A.C. 57.

[91] *Cassell* v. *Broome* [1972] 1 All E.R. 801, 809, 835.

[92] *Cassell, supra,* 854.

[93] *Conway* v. *Rimmer* [1967] 2 All E.R. 1260.   [94] *Cassell, supra.*

[95] *Harper* v. *N.C.B.* [1974] 2 All E.R. 441.

[96] *Young* v. *Bristol Aeroplane Co.* [1944] K.B. 718; affd. [1946] A.C. 163, 169; *Gallie* v. *Lee* [1969] 1 All E.R. 1062, 1076, 1082; affd. [1970] 3 All E.R. 961, and see Goodhart, " Precedents in the Court of Appeal " (1947) 9 C.L.J. 349; Gooderson, "Precedents in the Court of Appeal " (1950) 10 C.L.J. 432; Mason, " *Stare Decisis* in the Court of Appeal " (1956) 19 M.L.R. 136.

[97] *Morelle Ltd.* v. *Wakeling* [1955] 2 Q.B. 379. *Per incuriam* is relevant only to the right of an appellate court to decline to follow one of its own previous decisions not to its right to disregard a decision of a higher court: *Cassell* v. *Broome* [1972] 1 All E.R. 801, 874.

[98] *A. & J. Mucklow Ltd.* v. *I.R.C.* [1954] Ch. 615. *Cf. Bryers* v. *Canadian Pacific Steamships Ltd.* [1957] 1 Q.B. 134.

[99] *Noble* v. *Southern Ry.* [1940] A.C. 583, 598; *Williams* v. *Glasbrook Bros.* [1947] 2 All E.R. 884. See also *Worcester Works Finance* v. *Cooden Eng. Co.* [1971] 3 All E.R. 708.

[1] *Craddock* v. *Hampshire C.C.* [1958] 1 W.L.R. 202; *Tiverton Estates Ltd.* v. *Wearwell* [1974] 1 All E.R. 209.

court,[2] and a full court of five judges has no greater powers than the usual court of three.[3] The court must follow its own previous decisions even though a point was less fully argued in the previous case,[4] though it be argued that in the previous decision it had misunderstood a House of Lords precedent,[5] and even though another case on the same point is under appeal to the House of Lords,[6] but it can overrule one of the grounds of a prior Court of Appeal decision, leaving that decision to stand on its other ground.[7]

A decision arrived at by the court being equally divided is not binding [8] and a ruling by a court of two lords justices is not binding on the court.[9] Decisions of the Court of Appeal are binding on judges of the High Court in civil cases, on the Divisional Court in cases where an appeal lies from it to the Court of Appeal, and on county court judges.[10] Similar weight attaches to decisions of the former Court of Exchequer Chamber and Court of Appeal in Chancery, which were superseded by the Court of Appeal in 1875.

Court of Appeal (*Criminal Division*)

This court is bound by decisions of the House of Lords in English criminal appeals. Decisions of the old Court for Crown Cases Reserved, which was the predecessor (to 1906) of the Court of Criminal Appeal, are entitled to similar weight.[11] This court also will normally follow decisions of its predecessor, the Court of Criminal Appeal (1906–66) and its own decisions [12] but, since the liberty of the subject is at stake in its decisions, it does not apply the doctrine of *stare decisis* with the same rigidity as in its civil jurisdiction [12] and may, if sitting as a full court, reconsider a previous decision, if it finds that the law was misunderstood or misapplied in the earlier case.[13] Accordingly it is not always or absolutely bound by a prior decision.[14] It may also reconsider a decision which was not argued on

---

[2] *Gibson* v. *South American Stores* [1950] Ch. 177; *cf. King* v. *King* [1943] P. 91.

[3] *Morelle Ltd.* v. *Wakeling* [1955] 2 Q.B. 379; *Tiverton Estates Ltd., supra.*

[4] *Critchell* v. *Lambeth B.C.* [1957] 2 Q.B. 535.

[5] *Williams* v. *Glasbrook Bros.* [1947] 2 All E.R. 884.

[6] *Re Yates' Settlement Trusts* [1954] 1 W.L.R. 564.

[7] *Betty's Cafés Ltd.* v. *Phillips Furnishing Stores Ltd.* [1959] A.C. 20, 53.

[8] *The Vera Cruz* (1884) 9 P.D. 96.

[9] *Boys* v. *Chaplin* [1968] 2 Q.B. 1, 11.

[10] *Consett Industrial Socy.* v. *Consett Iron Co.* [1922] 2 Ch. 135.

[11] *R.* v. *Cade* [1914] 2 K.B. 209, 211; *R.* v. *Porter* [1949] 2 K.B. 128, 132.

[12] *R.* v. *Gould* [1968] 1 All E.R. 849.

[13] *R.* v. *Taylor* [1950] 2 K.B. 368, overruling *R.* v. *Treanor* (1939) 27 C.A.R. 35. In this case seven judges sat instead of the usual three. It is not certain whether it needs the larger court to exercise this power or whether the number was summoned simply to obtain the benefit of extra opinions. A court of five judges may, certainly in relation to the discretion as to sentencing, depart from a recent earlier view of a court of three: *R.* v. *Newsome* [1970] 3 All E.R. 455, 458.

[14] See Winder, " The Rule of Precedent in Criminal Courts " (1941) 5 J.Crim.L. 242.

both sides.[15] Its decisions are binding on the Queen's Bench Divisional Court in criminal matters, even though no appeal lies,[16] and certainly bind judges of the Crown Courts and Central Criminal Court.

Differences may arise between the Civil and Criminal Divisions of the Court of Appeal, and did between the former Court of Appeal and the former Court of Criminal Appeal, since they are of equal status and the same problem may arise in civil and in criminal proceedings. Thus in one case [17] the Court of Criminal Appeal held that to demand money from a member of a trade protection association as an alternative to blacklisting him was a criminal offence, but in another [18] the Court of Appeal held that an agreement by such a trader to pay a sum to have his name deleted from a blacklist was a valid contract. The House of Lords eventually held [19] that the latter view was the correct one and no crime had been committed.

Divisional Courts

A Divisional Court of the High Court is certainly bound by decisions of the House of Lords and by decisions of the Court of Appeal in civil matters,[20] though it has held itself free [21] to disregard a precedent in the Court of Appeal [22] in which two prior decisions, of the House of Lords and the Privy Council, respectively, had not been cited. The Divisional Court is bound in criminal matters by House of Lords decisions in criminal cases and by the Court of Criminal Appeal, and now by the Court of Appeal, Criminal Division.[23] It seems now to hold itself bound by its own decisions,[24] whether exercising civil or criminal jurisdiction, unless, probably, the prior decision was inconsistent with the decision of a higher court or obviously reached by mistake.[25] It may, however, exceptionally, depart from a previous decision.[26]

In civil matters the Divisional Court probably ranks no higher than a single judge of the High Court and its decisions cannot bind him, though

---

[15] *R.* v. *Ettridge* [1909] 2 K.B. at 27; *R.* v. *Norman* [1924] 2 K.B. at 322.
[16] *Ruse* v. *Read* [1949] 1 K.B. 377, 384; *Russell* v. *Smith* [1958] 1 Q.B. 27.
[17] *R.* v. *Denyer* [1926] 2 K.B. 258.
[18] *Hardie and Lane* v. *Chilton* [1928] 2 K.B. 306.
[19] *Thorne* v. *Motor Trade Association* [1937] A.C. 797.
[20] *Read* v. *Joannon* (1890) 25 Q.B.D. 300, 302.
[21] In *R.* v. *Northumberland Compensation Tribunal* [1951] 1 K.B. 711; *cf. Nicholas* v. *Penny* [1950] 2 K.B. 466.
[22] *Racecourse Betting Control Board* v. *Secretary of State for Air* [1944] Ch. 114.
[23] *Carr* v. *Mercantile Products Ltd.* [1949] 2 K.B. 601. In *Hawke* v. *Mackenzie* [1902] 2 K.B. 225, 232, 233 the D.C. took the view that it was bound by decisions of the former Court for Crown Cases Reserved, the predecessor of the C.C.A., and in *Russell* v. *Smith* [1958] 1 Q.B. 27 a D.C. held itself bound by the C.C.A.
[24] *Huddersfield Police Authority* v. *Watson* [1947] K.B. 842 (civil); *Younghusband* v. *Luftig* [1949] 2 K.B. 354; *Russell* v. *Smith* [1958] 1 Q.B. 27 (criminal): see further, Winder, " Divisional Court Precedents " (1946) 9 M.L.R. 257; Stone, " *Stare Decisis* in the Divisional Court " (1951) 14 M.L.R. 219.
[25] *Melias Ltd.* v. *Preston* [1957] 2 Q.B. 380; *Cogley* v. *Sherwood* [1959] 2 Q.B. 311.
[26] *R.* v. *Fulham Rent Tribunal* [1951] 1 T.L.R. 423.

only exceptionally would a single judge differ from the Divisional Court's view of the law.[27] In criminal matters its rulings probably bind inferior criminal courts.

High Court

Judges of the High Court are certainly bound by decisions of the House of Lords and the Court of Appeal,[28] but probably not by Divisional Court decisions. If a single judge is faced with a series of decisions of higher courts which are difficult to reconcile, he must follow any one which is indistinguishable, failing which he must try to apply the principles which can be extracted from the reported decisions as a whole.[29]

A decision of one High Court judge does not bind another [30] and a High Court judge may even decline to follow a previous decision of his own.[31] It is, however, unusual, for reasons of judicial comity, to refuse to follow a decision of another High Court judge unless there seems good reason for doing so,[32] particularly in such a matter as the interpretation of a statute or a common commercial document,[33] and that even though the previous single-judge decision has been doubted in a dissenting judgment in the Court of Appeal.[34] Even where the matter is one for the exercise of judicial discretion there is a strong tendency to conform to practice and give decisions consistent with those of other judges. In the event of one judge declining to follow another, two contradictory precedents stand in the books until a superior court in a later case resolves the conflict by approving one and overruling the other. Decisions of High Court judges are probably binding on county court judges in civil cases, though appeal lies not to the High Court but direct to the Court of Appeal.

Crown Court

Judges of the Crown Court are bound by rulings of the House of Lords, the Court of Appeal (Criminal Division), and probably by the Divisional Court in its criminal jurisdiction. The decisions of judges of the Crown Court in criminal matters probably bind magistrates' courts, though no appeal lies. In cases of any consequence appeal is usually taken by case

[27] *Chandris* v. *Isbrandtsen-Moller Inc.* [1951] 1 K.B. 240, 243; but see *Huddersfield Police Authority* v. *Watson* [1947] K.B. 842, 848, *per* Lord Goddard C.J.

[28] *Cackett* v. *Cackett* [1950] P. 253, 258.

[29] *Re House Property and Investment Co. Ltd.* [1954] Ch. 576.

[30] *Forster* v. *Baker* [1910] 2 K.B. 636, 638; *Green* v. *Berliner* [1936] 2 K.B. 477, 493; *Alma Shipping Co.* v. *Salgaoncar* [1954] 2 Q.B. 94, 104; *Receiver for Metropolitan Police* v. *Croydon Corpn.* [1957] 2 Q.B. 154.

[31] *Andrews* v. *Styrap* (1872) 26 L.T. 704, 706.

[32] *Receiver for Metropolitan Police District* v. *Croydon Corpn.* [1956] 1 W.L.R. 1113; contrast *Monmouthshire C.C.* v. *Smith* [1956] 1 W.L.R. 1132; *The Makedonia* [1958] 1 Q.B. 365.

[33] *Alma Shipping Co.* v. *V. M. Salgaoncar E. Irmaos Ltda.* [1954] 2 Q.B. 94.

[34] *Re Cohen* [1960] Ch. 179.

stated from magistrates' courts to the Queen's Bench Divisional Court for a ruling on the law.

County Courts

County court judges are bound by decisions of the House of Lords and Court of Appeal, and probably by decisions of single judges of the High Court, but probably not by other county court decisions, of which only a few are reported. In practice other single-judge decisions are followed, unless they appear unsound.

Magistrates' courts

Magistrates' courts are bound by decisions of all courts higher in the judicial hierarchy.

Scottish and Irish decisions

Decisions of Scottish and Irish courts are not binding on English courts, though treated with respect, particularly in matters where the law is the same or very similar to English law.[35]

NORTHERN IRELAND

The doctrine of binding precedent is accepted in Northern Ireland so that decisions of the House of Lords in Northern Ireland cases, of the Court of Appeal, Court of Criminal Appeal and of the High Court of Northern Ireland are binding on lower courts. The Court of Appeal is bound by its own previous decisions [36] under the principles laid down in *Young* v. *Bristol Aeroplane Co.*[37] Decisions of the English and Scottish superior courts have persuasive value and decisions of the Irish courts prior to 1921 have high persuasive value. Decisions of the Irish courts are entitled to the highest respect but are never binding on Scottish or English courts.[38]

PRIVY COUNCIL

Judgments of the Privy Council, except in those few cases where it sits as a court of appeal from a United Kingdom court,[39] are not binding on any United Kingdom court,[40] though highly persuasive and entitled to great weight because of the personal eminence of the lawyers who form the

---

[35] *Kahn* v. *Newberry* [1959] 2 Q.B. 1; *Andrew* v. *Philby* [1960] Ch. 27; *Westward Television* v. *Hart* [1969] 1 Ch. 212.

[36] *Parkinson* v. *Watson* [1956] N.I. 1.

[37] [1944] K.B. 718.

[38] *Re Parsons* (1890) 45 Ch.D. 51.

[39] *Combe* v. *Edwards* (1877) 2 P.D. 354.

[40] *Dulieu* v. *White* [1902] 2 K.B. 669; *Venn* v. *Tedesco* [1926] 2 K.B. 227; *Lynn* v. *Bamber* [1930] 2 K.B. 72; *Brown* v. *John Watson Ltd.*, 1914 S.C.(H.L.) 44; *Duncan* v. *Cammell Laird & Co.* [1942] A.C. 624.

Judicial Committee.[41] The Privy Council is, moreover, not bound by its own previous judgments and may reconsider points decided in previous appeals to the Board.[42]

EVALUATION OF PRECEDENTS

Binding Precedent

The foregoing paragraphs indicate that of prior decisions in point in a later case the category of binding precedents is determined for any given court primarily by the place in the hierarchy of the court which decided the precedent case in relation to the place held by the court which subsequently has to consider the applicability of the prior decision to a case before it. The only precedents absolutely binding are those decided by a higher court in the same vertical line of the hierarchy.

Persuasive Precedent

The category of persuasive precedents includes all precedents other than those which may be held binding under the foregoing principles. Thus any case decided by a court in another vertical line of the judicial hierarchy will be persuasive in greater or less degree, depending on the status of the court which decided it. So will a case from a court of equivalent or even lower status, in the same or another line, though but little weight attaches in the latter case.

Other persuasive precedents include judgments of the Privy Council when sitting as the final court of appeal from the colonies, and formerly from the dominions [43] ; judgments of superior courts in Ireland [44] and countries of the Commonwealth [45] ; judgments of superior courts in America [46] ; judgments of foreign courts [47] ; while rather similar persuasive force attaches to judicial dicta,[48] to statements in reputable books [49] and

---

[41] *Leask* v. *Scott* (1877) 2 Q.B.D. 376, 380. Thus the decision of the Privy Council in *Overseas Tankship* (*U.K.*) *Ltd.* v. *Morts Dock & Engineering Co.* [1961] A.C. 388, has been repeatedly treated by English courts as authoritative as to English law.

[42] *Re Transferred Civil Servants* (*Ireland*) *Compensation* [1929] A.C. 242; *Mercantile Bank of India* v. *Central Bank of India* [1938] A.C. 287; see also Raney, " The Finality of Privy Council Decisions " (1926) 4 Can.B.R. 307.

[43] *Leask* v. *Scott* (1877) 2 Q.B.D. 376, 380.

[44] *Re Parsons* (1890) 45 Ch.D. 51.

[45] *Chester* v. *Waverley*, 62 C.L.R. 1 (Australia) cited in *Bourhill* v. *Young*, 1942 S.C.(H.L.) 78; *cf. Hughes and Vale Pty. Ltd.* v. *State of N.S.W.* [1955] A.C. 241, 307; *Midland Silicones Ltd.* v. *Scruttons Ltd.* [1961] 1 Q.B. 106, 128; *Conway* v. *Rimmer* [1967] 2 All E.R. 1260, 1262–1263.

[46] *Castro* v. *R.* (1881) 6 App.Cas. at 249; *Scaramanga* v. *Stamp* (1880) 5 C.P.D. at 303; *Cory* v. *Burr* (1882) 9 Q.B.D. at 469; *Donoghue* v. *Stevenson*, 1932 S.C.(H.L.) 31; *Haynes* v. *Harwood* [1935] 1 K.B. at 156–157, 163, 167; *Walsh* v. *Lord Advocate*, 1956 S.C.(H.L.) 126; *Midland Silicones Ltd.* v. *Scruttons Ltd.*, *supra.* But see cautions voiced in *Re Missouri* (1889) 42 Ch.D. at 330; *Fender* v. *Mildmay* [1938] A.C. at 25; *A/B Karlshamns Oljefabriker* v. *Monarch S.S. Co.*, 1949 S.C.(H.L.) 1.

[47] *Sugden* v. *H.M. Advocate*, 1934 J.C. 103.

[48] As to judicial dicta, see p. 392, *infra.*

[49] *e.g.* Dicey, *Conflict of Laws.*

articles in standard legal periodicals,[50] and to the civil [51] and canon laws [52] and the opinions of the standard commentators thereon.[53] Judgments of the Scottish courts are persuasive in England and elsewhere, particularly when interpreting a United Kingdom statute or discussing a point of general jurisprudence.[54] In matters of commercial law it is particularly desirable that there should be uniformity of decision in common law jurisdictions.[55]

Factors affecting the Evaluation of Precedents

Quite apart from the formal questions whether a precedent is authoritative and binding or merely persuasive, its value as a guide in a future case is affected by various other factors which are all of relevance when one has to evaluate a precedent. The importance of the factors affecting evaluation arises particularly when a court is trying to find a reason for not holding itself bound or is dealing with persuasive authority.

A precedent in general gains authority from its antiquity and the lapse of time since it was decided. This is particularly so if it has been approved, followed and applied in other cases, but even if it has stood unquestioned and unreversed for a substantial time, a precedent may have acquired such authority that a later court will hesitate to overrule it, even though it could, in view of the upset to the law and to expectations and transactions founded on the precedent.[56] If it has been considered as establishing the law and been acted upon, a later court will not interfere with it.[57]

---

[50] *e.g. Gold* v. *Essex C.C.* [1942] 2 K.B. 293.

[51] *e.g. Taylor* v. *Caldwell* (1863) 3 B. & S. 826; *Cantiere San Rocco* v. *Clyde Shipbuilding Co.* 1923 S.C.(H.L.) 105.

[52] *e.g. Annan* v. *Annan,* 1948 S.C. 532.

[53] *e.g.* Pothier: *McLean* v. *Clydesdale Bank* (1883) 11 R.(H.L.) 1.

[54] *Minister of Pensions* v. *Higham* [1948] 2 K.B. 153, 155; *Murdoch Lownie* v. *Newman* [1949] 2 All E.R. 783; *Newman* v. *Lipman* [1951] 1 K.B. 333, 337; *Regional Properties* v. *Frankenschwerth* [1951] 1 K.B. 631; *Trickers (Confectioners)* v. *Barnes* [1955] 1 W.L.R. 372; *Cording* v. *Halse* [1955] 1 Q.B. 63; *R.* v. *Minister of Agriculture* [1955] 2 Q.B. 140; *Watson* v. *Nikolaisen* [1955] 2 Q.B. 286; *Wiseburgh* v. *Domville* [1956] 1 W.L.R. 312; *Kahn* v. *Newberry* [1959] 2 Q.B. 1; *Abbott* v. *Philbin* [1960] Ch. 27 (revd. [1961] A.C. 352); *see also McLean* v. *Clydesdale Bank, supra.*

[55] *Midland Silicones Ltd.* v. *Scruttons Ltd.* [1961] 1 Q.B. 106, 128.

[56] *West Ham Union* v. *Edmonton Union* [1908] A.C. 1; *Baird* v. *Baird's Trs.,* 1956 S.C.(H.L.) 93, 107–108; *Brownsea Haven Properties Ltd.* v. *Poole Corpn.* [1958] Ch. 574; *cf. Fortington* v. *Lord Kinnaird,* 1942 S.C. 239, 266: " [The precedent] has been cited and quoted too often down to very recent times to be open to challenge." So, too, in *Baird* v. *Baird's Trs.,* 1956 S.C.(H.L.) 93, 107, it was said that it was too late to reconsider *Alves* v. *Alves* (1861) 23 D. 712, but it was distinguished; *Shand's Trs.* v. *Shand's Trs.,* 1966, S.C. 178, 184.

[57] *Pugh* v. *Golden Valley Ry.* (1880) 15 Ch.D. at 334; *Smith* v. *Keal* (1882) 9 Q.B.D. at 352; *Bourne* v. *Keane* [1919] A.C. 815, 857; *Admiralty Commissioners* v. *S.S. Valverda* [1938] A.C. 173, 194; *see also Ridsdale* v. *Clifton* (1877) 2 P.D. 306; *Foakes* v. *Beer* (1884) 9 App.Cas. 630; *Queen* v. *Edwards* (1884) 13 Q.B.D. 590; *Re Wallis* (1890) 25 Q.B.D. 180; *Admiralty Commissioners* v. *S.S. Amerika* [1917] A.C. 38, 55; *Weld Blundell* v. *Stephens* [1920] A.C. 956, 987; *French Marine* v. *Compagnie Napolitaine* [1921] 2 A.C. 494, 511; *Gibaud* v. *G.E. Ry.* [1921] 2 K.B. 426, 432; *Triefus & Co.* v. *Post Office* [1957] 2 Q.B. 352.

Conversely, however, an older precedent may be of small value if inadequately reported,[58] repeatedly criticised,[59] not followed or distinguished, or if in the course of time it becomes inconsistent with modern views and doctrines or is inconsistent with or superseded by later legislation. It may thus become practically obsolete and inoperative.[60]

Something depends too on whether the court in the precedent case was unanimous or divided and, in the latter case, whether the dissents were substantial and on weighty grounds.[61] Approval by a subsequent court, especially if a higher one, affirmation on appeal, approval by academic jurists, consultation with other judges [62] or the presence of a larger bench,[63] and the passage of a subsequent statute which does not interfere with the decision,[64] all tend to strengthen it.

The personal eminence of the judges has also to be borne in mind. Some decisions can be characterised as of a " strong bench," not so much in number of judges as of high judicial quality. Other cases are of the converse.[65] In modern times judgments of Lord President Inglis,[66] Lord Dunedin (both as Lord President and later as Lord of Appeal) [67] and Lord President Cooper [68] are always entitled to especial respect. In the House of Lords judgments of Lords Cairns, Halsbury, Watson, Macmillan, Atkin, Wright and Reid have similarly had special value and are not lightly to be disregarded.

Precedents are of less value if it appears that the case was not fully argued,[69] as where only one party appeared, or if some points passed un-

---

[58] *Stirling* v. *Lauderdale* (1733) disregarded in *Glasgow Corpn.* v. *Lord Advocate*, 1959 S.C. 203, 231; *Logan* v. *Wood* (1561) regarded as not binding in *Donnelly* v. *Donnelly*, 1959 S.C. 97; *Bell's Exor.*, 1960 S.L.T.(Notes) 3 said not to be binding in *McLaughlin*, 1965 S.C. 246.

[59] *Cf. Barras* v. *Aberdeen Steam Trawling Co.*, 1933 S.C.(H.L.) 21, 38.

[60] *Rawlence* v. *Spicer* [1935] 1 K.B. at 435; *Matthews* v. *Kuwait Bechtel Corpn.* [1959] 2 Q.B. 57. *Cf.* also the observations in *R.* v. *Jackson* [1891] 1 Q.B. 671, that a husband's right to chastise his wife is now obsolete, and *Winchester* v. *Fleming* [1958] 1 Q.B. 259. *Cf.* also *Beith's Trustees* v. *Beith*, 1950 S.C. 66.

[61] *Cf.* Lord Blanesburgh in *Barras, supra*, at p. 42, evaluating *Ex parte Union Bank of Manchester* (1871) L.R. 12 Eq. 354.

[62] *e.g.* where the judges of one Division of the Court of Session consult with the other Division before giving their judgment, as in *Connell* v. *Connell*, 1950 S.C. 505.

[63] As in cases argued before seven judges.

[64] *Cf. Thorne* v. *Motor Trade Association* [1937] A.C. 797, 806.

[65] *Cf.* Kennedy, " The Second Division's Progress " (1896) 8 J.R. 268, where he criticises the Second Division of his day.

[66] See Crabb Watt, *John Inglis*, Chap. 13.

[67] " Dunedin, the greatest master of the principles of Scots Law in our time": *per* Lord Macmillan, *Stewart* v. *L.M.S. Ry.*, 1943 S.C.(H.L.) 19, 38.

[68] See Smith, "The Contribution of Lord Cooper of Culross to Scottish Law " in (1956) 67 J.R. 249 and in Lord Cooper's *Selected Papers*, xxix.

[69] *R.* v. *Ettridge* [1909] 2 K.B. at 27 (C.C.A.); *Edwards* v. *Jones* [1947] 1 All E.R. 830 (D.C.); *Nicholas* v. *Penny* [1950] 2 K.B. 466. *Cf. Sagar* v. *Ridehalgh* [1931] 1 Ch. 310. In *Bell* v. *Bell*, 1941 S.C.(H.L.) 5, an undefended divorce case, in view of the importance of the principle of law in issue, the Solicitor-General appeared in the

noticed or were not argued [70] or conceded,[71] or if it appears from the printed arguments of counsel in the report that certain relevant cases or statutes were not cited or considered in the precedent,[72] particularly if they were to a contrary effect, or if no reasoned judgments are delivered,[73] or if there are powerful dissenting judgments, or if the case were compromised or settled,[74] or if the report is defective,[75] or if the judges differ as to their reasons or if these seem defective, or the decision has been criticised in textbooks [76] or if the decision has apparently been reached on some specialty, such as to avoid hardship or injustice, or on the particular terms of a deed or contract or statute.

What is it that is binding or persuasive?

Decisions are cited in textbooks for various reasons, sometimes as examples, sometimes for the form of action chosen, sometimes for points which are implicit in the case, sometimes for the interest of the decision reached, and sometimes for other reasons. But all these reasons are of little or no value when the matter in issue is whether a later court is in the circumstances bound to follow or is subject to persuasion to follow the principle of law enunciated or developed in the precedent, because the importance of precedents as a source of law is that earlier cases lay down and develop principles, rules and doctrines of law capable of future application.[77] The problem is: what is it in a precedent that a later court must, or should consider carefully whether to, follow and apply?

A reported case is of value as a precedent for guidance in future cases, whether authoritative or persuasive, only in respect of the principle of law, if any, which can be derived from it, as that on which it was decided,[78]

House of Lords, at the House's request, and was heard, so that the House had the benefit of argument on both sides. In *Aldridge* v. *Simpson-Bell,* 1971 S.C. 87, the Lord Ordinary refused to follow a precedent when the point in question had not been argued in it.

[70] *Rahimtoola* v. *Nizam of Hyderabad* [1958] A.C. 379.

[71] *O'Shea* v. *O'Shea and Parnell* (1890) 15 P.D. 59, 64; *Young* v. *Sealey* [1949] 1 All E.R. 92, 108.

[72] *e.g. Racecourse Betting Control Board* v. *Secretary of State for Air* [1944] Ch. 114, not followed in *R.* v. *Northumberland Compensation Appeal Tribunal, ex p. Shaw* [1952] 1 K.B. 338.

[73] As in some old cases.

[74] *Sagar* v. *Ridehalgh* [1931] 1 Ch. 310.

[75] Some reports prior to 1800 are so brief and defective that it is not really possible to say what the basis for the decision was: such a precedent is of little value.

[76] *Cochrane's Exrx.* v. *Cochrane,* 1947 S.C. 134, 140, 147.

[77] " The only use of authorities or decided cases is the establishment of some principle, which the judge can follow out in deciding the case before him," *Re Hallett* (1879) 13 Ch.D. 696, 712, *per* Jessel M.R.; *cf. Smith* v. *Harris* [1939] 3 All E.R. 960, 965.

[78] " The only thing in a judge's decision binding as an authority upon a subsequent judge is the principle on which the case was decided ": *Osborne to Rowlett* (1880) 13 Ch.D. 774, 785, *per* Jessel M.R. *Cf. Craig* v. *Glasgow Corpn.,* 1919 S.C.(H.L.) 1, 10.

and which must, or may, be used again to decide a later case. Not every reported case contains a statement of a principle; it may be reported for the interest of the factual situation, or simply as an example of how the court applied a particular principle in certain circumstances, or because of a ruling on evidence or pleading or procedure, or because of the application of an accepted principle to a new or unusual set of facts. Again it may not be apparent on what principle the judges proceeded, but in many cases a statement of a principle of law can be discerned as expressed or implied in the decision reached in the circumstances, and it is this statement of principle alone which is valuable in subsequent cases. " When any tribunal is bound by the judgment of another court, either superior or co-ordinate, it is, of course, bound by the judgment itself. And if from the opinions delivered it is clear—as is the case in most instances—what the *ratio decidendi* was which led to the judgment, then that *ratio decidendi* is also binding." [79] " The inevitable first question, then, with which the court must deal necessarily is:—Is a certain general *ratio* laid down and at the root of [the precedent]; and is it to be approved and applied? " [80]

The Ratio Decidendi

This underlying principle of a judicial decision is termed the *ratio decidendi* and it is only this element of the decision which is binding upon a subsequent judge. It has been defined as " the reason or ground on which a judgment is rested," [81] " the underlying principle which forms the authoritative element [of a judicial decision]," [82] or " the conclusion reached by the judges on the basis of the material facts and on the exclusion of the immaterial ones," [83] or " the proposition of law which was necessary for the decision, or can be extracted from the decision," [84] or " the enunciation of the reason or principle on which a question before a court has been decided is alone binding as a precedent," [85] or " that part of [any judgment of any court] . . . which is considered to have been necessary to the decision of the actual issue between the litigants," [86] or " any rule of law expressly or impliedly treated by the judge as a necessary step in reaching his conclusion, having regard to the line of reasoning adopted by him, or a necessary part of his direction to the jury . . . [It] is

[79] *G.W. Ry.* v. *Owners of S.S. Mostyn* [1928] A.C. 57, 73, *per* Lord Dunedin, quoted in *Beith's Trs.* v. *Beith*, 1950 S.C. 66, 70 and *Douglas Hamilton* v. *Duke and Duchess of Hamilton's Trs.*, 1961 S.C. 205, 229.

[80] *Fortington* v. *Lord Kinnaird*, 1942 S.C. 239, 269, *per* Lord Mackay; *cf.* Lord Wark at 281.

[81] Bell's *Law Dictionary*, 884; *cf.* Fraser Tytler's *Memoirs of Lord Kames*, I, 114; ". . . the *ratio decidendi*, or rule of law on which the judgment rests."

[82] Salmond, *Jurisprudence*, 11th ed., 223.

[83] Paton, *Jurisprudence*, 2nd ed., 160, following Goodhart, *Essays*, 22.

[84] Dias & Hughes, *Jurisprudence*, 72.

[85] Halsbury's *Laws of England*, tit. " Judgments," para. 1682.

[86] Allen, *Law in the Making*, 6th ed., 247.

generally the proposition of law for which that case may be cited as authority, but it is the practice of the judges to interpret a decision in the light of the facts of the case and the decisions in other cases." [87] Finding the *ratio* of a case is a process of abstracting principle from a mass of allegations, facts, arguments, opinions and judgment. *Ratio* should *not* be translated as " the reason *for* the decision," because a decision yielding a sound *ratio* may be reached, overtly or tacitly, for a bad reason, *e.g.* because the judge disapproved of the pursuer's morals, or felt sorry for him. " The reason which the judge gives for his decision is never the binding part of the precedent." [88]

The *ratio* of a precedent is distinct from the facts of and the actual decision of the precedent case, and from the judgments or judicial opinions delivered by the judges when justifying their decision, because these are all concerned with the actual circumstances of the particular case, whereas the *ratio* is the underlying principle which was used in and is exemplified by the decision and opinions. The *ratio*, though distinct from, must be a proposition of law which supports the actual decision. Thus in *Bourhill* v. *Young* [89] Mrs. B. claimed damages from Y's executor, alleging that while removing her basket from the platform of a tram-car Y had passed the tram-car on the other side on his motor-cycle, had collided with a car and killed himself, and had caused Mrs. B. shock by the noise and the sight of blood on the road. It was decided that her claim failed. According to the opinions this was because in the place where she had been Y could not have realised or foreseen that, if he was involved in a collision, Mrs. B. might in consequence be injured or shocked. The *ratio* or general proposition derivable from the decision is probably: one person is not entitled to damages from another for injuries or shock unless the other should, as a reasonable person, have realised or foreseen that his conduct [90] was liable to harm a person in the claimant's place; or it may be expressed as: the range of liability of an alleged causer of harm is limited to those whom he should reasonably have foreseen were liable to be harmed by his wrongful conduct.[91]

The determination of the *ratio decidendi* of a precedent is the task of the judge in a subsequent case, or of the legal adviser when trying to discover the law applicable to a problem before him. He has to try to determine

---

[87] Cross, *Precedent in English Law*, 75–76.

[88] Goodhart, " Determining the *Ratio Decidendi* of a Case " in *Essays in Jurisprudence and the Common Law*, 1, and (1930) 40 Yale L.J. 161.

[89] 1942 S.C.(H.L.) 78.

[90] In this case the wrongful conduct was riding recklessly and crashing into the car. It should be noted that while Mrs. B.'s claim failed it was observed that a claim by the persons in the car would have succeeded, because injury or shock to them should reasonably have been foreseen.

[91] In strict logic a general proposition can only be inferred from at least two particular propositions or decisions; many general propositions may justify one particular proposition or decision.

what general proposition of law the precedent expressly or impliedly stated, apart from the court's application of that proposition in the circumstances of the prior case to produce the court's actual disposal of the case.[90] It is a task of extreme importance and considerable difficulty for which unfortunately no settled formula or rules of thumb can be suggested; it cannot be done mechanically; it is an art rather than a science.[92]

Finding the Ratio Decidendi

It should be noted first that the *ratio* of a decision is not necessarily contained in the rubric of the report, since that is compiled by the reporter and is not authoritative, nor is it necessarily to be found in any phrase or passage of any of the opinions delivered in the case. It is the proposition of law which is the ground or basis of the decision, or was necessary for the decision of the precedent, necessarily underlying and inherent in the decision reached on the facts alleged or found proved,[93] a generalised statement of law which justifies the decision on the facts of the precedent case, neither more nor less.[94] A judgment must always be read as applicable to the facts of the case in which it was delivered and the generality of expressions used are qualified by the facts of the case and are not necessarily more widely applicable.[95] Every judgment, that is, is to be read *secundum subjectam materiam.*[96]

According to Wambaugh [97] the *ratio* is a general rule without which the case must have been decided otherwise, but he gives little guidance on how to extract the *ratio* from the actual decision and the opinions.

---

[92] There is a considerable periodical literature on this topic. The most important are: Goodhart, " Determining the *Ratio Decidendi* of a case," in *Essays in Jurisprudence and the Common Law,* 1; Paton and Sawer, " *Ratio Decidendi* and *Obiter Dictum* in Appellate Courts " (1947) 63 L.Q.R. 461; Gooderson, " *Ratio Decidendi* and the Rules of Law " (1952) 30 Can.B.R. 892; Montrose, " *Ratio Decidendi* and the House of Lords " (1957) 20 M.L.R. 124; Montrose, " *Ratio Decidendi* of a Case " (1957) 20 M.L.R. 587; Simpson, " *Ratio Decidendi* of a Case " (1957) 20 M.L.R. 413; (1958) 21 M.L.R. 155; Goodhart, " *Ratio Decidendi* of a Case " (1959) 22 M.L.R. 117; Simpson, " *Ratio Decidendi* of a Case " (1959) 22 M.L.R. 453; Stone, " The *Ratio* of the *Ratio Decidendi* " (1959) 22 M.L.R. 597.

[93] In Scottish practice when the precedent is of a decision on relevancy (as to which see p. 456, *infra*) the facts averred and accepted for the purposes of argument are material, but when the precedent is of a decision arrived at after proof or trial the material facts are those which have been held proved.

[94] In logic, of course, an indefinitely large number of general propositions can be thought of, all of which would justify the particular decision on the actual facts of the precedent. No general proposition can be deduced from one particular proposition. But, in fact, the possible general propositions are limited by the court's opinion and by the accepted context of that branch of the law and other cases on related points. On this point, see further, Stone, *The Province and Function of Law,* 186 *et seq.;* Patterson, *Jurisprudence,* 306 *et seq.*

[95] *Quinn* v. *Leathem* [1901] A.C. 495, 506, *per* Lord Halsbury.

[96] *Neilson* (1890) 17 R. 608, 613; *Fortington* v. *Kinnaird,* 1942 S.C. 239, 271; *Price* v. *Watson,* 1951 S.C. 359; *Inverurie Mags.* v. *Sorrie,* 1956 S.C. 175, 181.

[97] *The Study of Cases.*

According to Goodhart [98] one must first determine what facts were averred for the purposes of the argument (in a debate on pleadings) or were found to have been proved (in a decision after proof) and segregate these facts into facts necessary for or material to the decision and facts immaterial to the decision. It is impossible to lay down in the abstract what averments or facts can be treated as immaterial. Any averment or fact may be material but normally such averments or facts as the name, age, sex, status or condition of the parties, time, date, place, or weather conditions of the happenings, and all merely coincident and concomitant circumstances will be immaterial, though in particular cases any one or more of these factors may be material. If the judge treats any factor as material, either expressly or impliedly, in his opinion, then it must be accepted as material. The material averments or facts must then be set down in relation to the actual decision of the court and the *ratio* formulated in terms of a general proposition of law which takes account of all, but no more than, the material averments or facts and of the ultimate decision. Thus the *ratio* of *Donoghue* v. *Stevenson* [99] might be expressed as follows: A person who claims to have suffered injury in consequence of drinking a bottled drink containing an impurity is entitled to claim damages direct from the manufacturer thereof where there was no reasonable possibility of intermediate inspection of the product between manufacture and consumption.

The more averments or facts are held to be material and therefore necessarily incorporated in the *ratio*, or the more narrowly they are stated, the narrower will be the resulting *ratio* and the more limited its scope of application in future cases.[1] Conversely the fewer the essential material averments or facts, or the more broadly they are stated, the wider will be the principle and the more readily available for later cases. It follows also from this insistence on material facts that a case may yield a *ratio* even if there is only a judgment on certain facts with no opinion delivered and no reasons given.

---

[98] " Determining the *Ratio Decidendi* of a Case," *supra.*

[99] 1932 S.C.(H.L.) 31. It has to be remembered that *Donoghue's* case was decided, even in the House of Lords, on the basis of facts averred to have happened, and not proved to have taken place. The main averments were that Mrs. D. was bought a ginger-beer (manufactured and put out in an opaque bottle by S.) by a friend in a café. She drank some of it and when emptying the rest of the bottle into her glass, the remains of a decomposed snail floated out of the bottle. She was shocked and made sick, and sued S. for damages. In law, could she recover? This was the question for debate, it being necessarily assumed for the purposes of that debate that Mrs. D. could, if called on, prove by evidence that there had in fact been a decomposed snail in the bottle. As the case was finally settled by agreement, Mrs. D. was never called on to try to prove the existence of the snail, and that it had caused her sickness. The case is familiarly known as the " Snail in the bottle " case.

[1] Thus a *ratio* which starts " A married person . . ." is narrower than one starting " A person . . ." and one including the fact of sex, *e.g.* " A married female person . . ." is narrower still. A formulation of the *ratio* of *Donoghue* which says " a bottled drink " is narrower than one which says " food or drink," and narrower still than one which says " manufactured product " (which could include clothing, vehicles, etc.).

This technique of seeking to determine material facts and elicit a *ratio* therefrom may also tend to produce a statement of a *ratio* which is very closely related to the facts of a case and dependent on its specialties. Also, relating the *ratio* so closely to the material facts of a case means that the *ratio* is not strictly applicable to any future case unless it has the same material facts or averments, and this theory of *ratio* may produce a state in which every case has its own *ratio*, which is not necessarily applicable to any other case.

Alternatively one can approach the problem by searching the opinions of the judges for a statement of principle which that judge held to subsume and to justify his decision on the facts or averments of the case before him. This depends on a close analysis of the opinions and no more detailed guidance than that can be given. On this basis examination of the opinions in *Donoghue* v. *Stevenson* shows that Lord Macmillan considered the case to fall within this principle: " A person who for gain engages in the business of manufacturing articles of food and drink intended for consumption by members of the public in the form in which he issues them is under a duty to take care in the manufacture of these articles," and Lord Atkin under this: " A manufacturer of products which he sells in such a form as to show that he intends them to reach the ultimate consumer in the form in which they left him with no reasonable possibility of intermediate examination, and with the knowledge that the absence of reasonable care in the preparation or putting up of the products will result in an injury to the consumer's life or property, owes a duty to the consumer to take that reasonable care."

This kind of approach to the problem of finding the *ratio* implies that there is no *ratio* where a case is decided without opinions being expressed,[2] and it tends to produce *rationes* which are broader than required for, or sometimes justified by, the circumstances of the case argued and decided, and which may in literal terms cover sets of circumstances never contemplated by the judges, since judges commonly express their opinions more generally than the facts of the case demand. In fact, even if no opinions are delivered, a *ratio* may exist and can be inferred from the facts taken along with the actual judgment or disposal of the case. It is essential to remember that no proposition can ever be said to be the *ratio* if the court's actual decision and disposal of the case is not consistent with or does not follow from that proposition.

Any formulation of the *ratio* of a precedent must moreover be construed in the light of cases subsequent to the precedent and what may appear to

---

[2] Lord Dunedin in *G.W. Ry.* v. *S.S. Mostyn* [1928] A.C. 57, 73 suggested that in such a case the judgment on the facts might be binding, apart from any *ratio* or principle discoverable. So, too, if there are opinions delivered which do not seem to yield any clear statement of the principle on which the case was decided.

be, or even be clearly indicated as, part of the *ratio*, may have been explained in later cases as inaccurate or unnecessary.[3]

Multiple Rationes

It is, of course, apparent that one precedent may contain decisions and rulings on several separate points of dispute, and any one of these separately may be a valuable precedent in a later case, even though the other points decided in the precedent may have no relevance. Thus if a precedent contains rulings on (i) the jurisdiction of the court, (ii) a matter of pleading, (iii) the merits of the claim, (iv) the kind of remedy, and (v) the expenses of the cause, the *ratio* on point (iii) may be extracted and used in a subsequent case for which the precedent is in point, even though the other points argued and decided in the precedent did not arise in the subsequent case. One case may, that is, be authority for several points of law on widely different topics, and may consequently be referred to in a textbook in several different contexts. It follows also that a decision may be superseded or overruled on one point but remain good law on another.

But even on a single point a judge sometimes gives two or more reasons for his decision or formulates his ruling on the law in two or more ways. Each formulation is regarded as a separate *ratio decidendi* and both are binding; a later court cannot pick one and ignore the other [4] ; but one may be *obiter* or merely tentative, and merely tentative indications of opinion do not amount to *ratio*.[5] One ground of decision may subsequently be overruled, leaving the decision to rest on the other ground.[6] If a court gives two reasons for its decision and later finds that one of the reasons was right and the other wrong, they are entitled to accept the right reason and reject the wrong, and the case is authority for the right reason.[7] It is also difficult where a judge discusses several possible grounds of decision and finally, looking at the case as a whole, arrives at a decision without making clear which ground is really the basis of decision. Probably in such a case a subsequent court must accept each of the grounds of decision as being the *ratio* of the case. " It is well established that if a judge gives two reasons for his decision, both are binding. It is not permissible to pick out one as being supposedly the better reason and ignore the other one; nor does it matter for this purpose which comes first and which comes second. But the practice of making judicial observations *obiter* is also well established. A judge may often give additional reasons

---

[3] See, *e.g.* the explanation of the *ratio* of *Barwick* v. *English Joint Stock Bank* 1866) L.R. 2 Ex. 259 in *Lloyd* v. *Grace, Smith & Co.* [1912] A.C. 716.

[4] *Behrens* v. *Bertram Mills Circus Ltd.* [1957] 2 Q.B. 1, 24.

[5] *Jacobs* v. *L.C.C.* [1950] A.C. 361, 369. " There is no justification for regarding as *obiter dictum* a reason given by a judge for his decision because he has given another reason also." *Cf. London Jewellers* v. *Attenborough* [1934] 2 K.B. 206, 222.

[6] *Betty's Cafés Ltd.* v. *Phillips Furnishing Stores Ltd.* [1959] A.C. 20, 53.

[7] *Re Holmden's Settlement Trusts* [1966] 2 All E.R. 661, 666.

for his decision without wishing to make them part of the *ratio decidendi*; he may not be sufficiently convinced of their cogency as to want them to have the full authority of precedent, and yet may wish to state them so that those who later may have the duty of investigating the same point will start with some guidance. This is a matter which the judge himself is alone capable of deciding and any judge who comes after him must ascertain which course has been adopted from the language used and not by consulting his own preference." [8]

A rather similar problem arises in the event of discrepancy or conflict between the opinions delivered and the interlocutor pronounced as the operative part of the court's decision. On principle the *ratio* has to be consistent with the operative decision, whatever the opinions may appear to say. [9]

Ratio in Appellate Courts

It is likewise obviously a problem of great difficulty to determine the *ratio* of the decision of an appellate court, where several opinions may be delivered (apart from any dissents), and different judges may formulate principles differently or proceed on the basis of different facts being material. [10] If a majority apply one *ratio* and a minority another, the majority *ratio* is that of the court. It is possible for several judges of an appellate court each to arrive at the same decision and to concur in the disposal of the case but for different reasons, and each judge's opinion may yield a quite distinct *ratio*, possibly inconsistent with the others. [11] In such a case there cannot be said to be any *ratio*, and the case is not authority for any more than its actual decision.

If the *ratio* common to all, or at least to the majority, of the judges is obscure, a subsequent court is probably entitled to consider itself influenced by the decision itself and to choose for itself the *ratio* of the precedent. [12]

Cases where there is no useful Ratio

There are some few cases which are decided entirely on their own facts and which are not authority for anything more than the particular decision of that case. Among such cases are decisions on matters of fact, on the

---

[8] *Behrens* v. *Bertram Mills Circus* [1957] 2 Q.B. 1, 25, *per* Devlin J.

[9] See, however, *Pollock School* v. *Glasgow Town Clerk*, 1946 S.C. 373 and 1947 S.C. 605.

[10] Paton and Sawer, " *Ratio Decidendi* and *Obiter Dictum* in Appellate Courts " (1947) 63 L.Q.R. 461.

[11] *e.g. Republica de Guatemala* v. *Nunez* [1927] 1 K.B. 669; *Boys* v. *Chaplin* [1971] A.C. 356.

[12] *G.W. Ry.* v. *S.S. Mostyn* [1928] A.C. 57, 73, where the House of Lords abandoned the attempt to discover the *ratio* of *River Wear Commrs.* v. *Adamson* (1877) 2 App.Cas. 743. See further, Paton and Sawer, " *Ratio Decidendi* and *Obiter Dictum* in Appellate Courts " (1947) 63 L.Q.R. 461. See also the observations of L.-P. Cooper in *Macdonald* v. *Glasgow Western Hospitals*, 1954 S.C. 453, 474 on *Reidford* v. *Aberdeen Magistrates*, 1933 S.C. 276.

sentence or measure of damages appropriate in the circumstances, on the way judicial discretion is being exercised in the particular case, or those decided on the terms of a particular trust deed or will, or on the precise terms of particular pleadings, or in the precise factual circumstances of a particular case. They are decisions on their own facts and do not purport to lay down any general rules or principles, and are unlikely to be of any value at all as precedents unless in the very unlikely event of precisely similar circumstances arising again. The decisions are merely choices between one of two or more possible interpretations of words or facts and proceed on no legal basis capable of wider application. Every such case has, of course, its own individual *ratio*, but it is so special to the terms and circumstances of that case that it is of little or no use as a precedent for the future. Thus in *Mair's Trustee* v. *Aberdeen Royal Infirmary* [13] a testatrix made certain bequests and directed finally that " what money is left over " was to go to a charity. It was held that, while the word " money " might sometimes cover heritable property, it did not do so *in the will under construction*, and accordingly that a bequest of heritage which had lapsed did not fall under this residuary bequest of " money."

There is again no useful *ratio* where the judgments delivered are so unclear that a subsequent court cannot find the *ratio*,[14] and where a case has been so frequently distinguished or doubted that it cannot be taken as more than a decision on its own special facts.[15] If no *ratio* is discernible the decision for or against the pursuer may be binding.[16]

Ratio and Obiter Dictum

All statements by the judges which are outwith the *ratio* or are not necessary for the *ratio* fall to be classed as *obiter dicta*. Such dicta thus include all statements of law which go beyond the occasion, as where a rule is laid down for " animals " in a case dealing with a horse; or which lay down a rule irrelevant to the problem before the court, as where in the case of a limited company a judge says, " It would be competent for a local authority . . ."; or which are stated as analogies, as where a judge remarks, " Similarly in cases of . . . the same would apply "; or which deal with the opposite case, as where a judge remarks, " Conversely, the rule would not apply to . . ."; or which deal with hypothetical cases, as where a judge

---

[13] 1946 S.L.T. 88.

[14] The famous example is *River Wear Commrs.* v. *Adamson* (1877) 2 App.Cas. 743; in *G.W. Ry.* v. *S.S. Mostyn* [1928] A.C. 57 the House of Lords abandoned the attempt to find its *ratio*. In *Harper* v. *N.C.B.* [1974] 2 All E.R. 441, the Court of Appeal held that there was no discernible *ratio* in the House of Lords decision in *Central Asbestos Co.* v. *Dodd* [1973] A.C. 518.

[15] Thus *McLachlan* v. *McLachlan*, 1945 S.C. 382 has been distinguished in *Swan* v. *Swan* [1953] P. 258; *Jamieson* v. *Jamieson*, 1951 S.C. 286; *Scott* v. *Scott*, 1960 S.C. 36 and *Breen* v. *Breen*, 1961 S.C. 158 and can now be regarded as limited to its own special circumstances, if not indeed wrongly decided.

[16] *Harper* v. *N.C.B.* [1974] 2 All E.R. 441.

states the law: " if the pursuer had proved . . . then I should have been prepared to hold that . . ."; or which are mere observations made in the course of argument.[17] Other kinds of *obiter dicta* are statements of law by a judge who dissents, and statements leading to one conclusion which the court then does not adopt for a particular reason.[18] There can be no complete catalogue of what will be dicta rather than part of the *ratio* and these are only examples. Subsequent judges sometimes condemn as mere dicta statements which others have thought were part of the *ratio* of a prior decision.[19]

Dicta are of varying weights and varying value, from mere casual observations, possibly unconsidered, possibly even erroneous, to carefully considered statements which are not, however, part of the *ratio* as going outside or beyond the circumstances of the case before the court.[20] They may be highly important as persuasive precedent in future,[21] but they are never binding.[22] A distinction has also been drawn [23] between *obiter dicta*, judicial *dicta*, and other *dicta*.

Drawing the distinction between *ratio* and *obiter dictum* is clearly also an art rather than a science; different men may differ as to what is *ratio* and what is dictum in a precedent, and while to stigmatise something as merely dictum is one of the easiest ways to avoid being bound by an inconvenient precedent, that is not always practicable. All that can be said is that the *ratio* is the central and essential part of the decision while the dicta are collateral and inessential, but in certain cases have to be weighed and regarded carefully. Cross [24] sums it up as follows: " The *ratio decidendi* of a case is any rule of law expressly or impliedly treated by the judge as a necessary step in reaching his conclusion, having regard to the line of reasoning adopted by him, or a necessary part of his direction to the jury. In arriving at it regard must be had to the facts of the case, the issues raised by the pleadings and arguments, and the previous state of the law. Further guidance may sometimes be obtained from the observations in prior and subsequent cases by judges who were members of the

---

[17] Practice Note [1942] W.N. 89.

[18] Thus in *Hedley Byrne & Co.* v. *Heller* [1964] A.C. 465 the House of Lords laid down that the maker of a statement in certain cases owed a duty of care to persons relying on it, but then held the defendants not liable, because they were protected by their disclaimer of liability. See discussion of this in *Rondel* v. *Worsley* [1967] 1 Q.B. 443.

[19] A great judicial luminary once told a Lord Justice: " The rule is quite simple: if you agree with the other bloke you say it's part of the *ratio*, if you don't you say it's *obiter dictum* with the implication that he is a congenital idiot ": (1950) 1 J.S.P.T.L (N.S.) 359.

[20] *Slack* v. *Leeds Industrial Co-operative Society* [1923] 1 Ch. 431, 451.

[21] *Cf. Re House Property and Investment Co.* [1953] 3 W.L.R. 1037.

[22] " A dictum of a judge of first instance is not binding even upon himself ": *Kwei Tek Chao* v. *British Traders and Shippers* [1954] 3 W.L.R. 496, *per* Devlin J.

[23] *West* v. *Dick* [1969] 1 All E.R. 289, 292, *per* Megarry, J.

[24] *Precedent in English Law*, pp. 75–76.

court in the case the *ratio decidendi* of which is to be determined. It is open to question whether the decision of any issue in a case in favour of the party against whom the court order is made can constitute part of the *ratio decidendi* of that case. The *ratio decidendi* of a case is generally the proposition of law for which that case may be cited as authority, but it is the practice of the judges to interpret a decision in the light of the facts of the case and the decisions in other cases. Accordingly, in order to ascertain the proposition of law for which a case is authority at a later date, regard must be had to subsequent cases in which it has been considered."

Ratio and Principles of Law

The *ratio* of a case is accordingly the proposition of law necessary to the decision of the case. It is not the same as a general principle of law but is an example and application of such a principle, and general principles of law have in fact been, particularly in England, largely built up by the generalisation from a number of specific *rationes* or principles of particular cases, whereas in Scotland *rationes* have also been frequently deductions from overriding general principles of law. The *ratio* or principle of a case is thus related to but distinct from those broader and more general principles. Thus to say that a man is entitled to recover damages from one who has caused him loss, injury or damage without legal justification is a general principle from which may be deduced, in the circumstances of an actual case, the *ratio* that if a defender has caused another person loss and damage by knocking him down with his car, an action lacking legal justification, the other person may recover damages from the defender. The *ratio* of *Donoghue* v. *Stevenson*[25] is distinct from, and a specific instance of, the more general principle that a person is liable in damages to another if it was foreseeable that his act or omission might cause injury to that other, and if his act or omission has actually so caused injury.

The possibility exists of conflict between a binding precedent and a fundamental principle, in which case it has been said that the fundamental principle must prevail,[26] but this involves the difficult task of formulating verbally the fundamental principle as well as the *ratio* of the precedent.

The Application of Precedents in Later Cases

When a precedent is cited in a later case the later court has several things to do before it can accept and apply it or reject it. It has to decide first of all what the *ratio* of the precedent is and then, comparing the material facts of the precedent with those of the instant case, to decide whether the precedent is in point or not. If it is not in point, if the material

---

[25] 1932 S.C.(H.L.) 31.
[26] *London Transport Executive* v. *Betts* [1959] A.C. 213, *per* Lord Denning.

facts do not coincide in all respects, the precedent is not exactly in point and is not decisive, though it may remain highly persuasive. Now it has to be accepted that precedents are hardly ever absolutely in point, exactly on all fours, agreeing in all material facts. They will always differ, if only in point of time, and usually in some other respects too, from the instant case, and this question comes to be whether a particular precedent is, if not exactly, at least sufficiently close in point to be treated as relevant. Secondly, the court must consider from what place in the judicial hierarchy the precedent has come and whether it is binding under the rules of *stare decisis* or merely persuasive, and in the latter case, how highly persuasive it is, having regard to the status of the court and the other factors affecting evaluation. Thirdly, the court must decide how far the precedent is to be influential in its decision. Is the later court going to accept it as binding and apply it to the case before the court or to try to avoid that course?

The court may *apply* the precedent by accepting the *ratio*, if it is binding on that court, and applying it to the material facts of the instant case, in effect saying that the rule of case X (the precedent) shall govern the present facts also.[27] Or the court may *follow* the precedent, if it is merely persuasive, applying it by analogy or by extension to the instant case, or adopting its reasoning as leading to the decision of the instant case.

A court may also *not follow* a precedent. This can be done only in the case of a precedent which is not binding or proceeds from a court of co-ordinate jurisdiction.[28] It is a plain indication that the second court has serious doubts about the correctness of the precedent. In such a case the precedent and the later case both stand in the reports as representing divergent views as to the law and this divergence can be solved only by a later superior court accepting one and overruling the other decision,[29] or possibly by reconciling both by means of an explanation or formula which allows each to stand as correct in its own circumstances. Even plainer is the action of a superior court when it *reserves its opinion on the soundness of* a decision not binding on it.[30]

Alternatively, the court may *distinguish* the precedent by pointing to differences between the precedent and the instant case in certain material facts. It may decline on that ground to consider the precedent to be in point and to be either binding or even persuasive.[30] The technique of distinguishing is much resorted to where a judge or court does not in fact wish

---

[27] See, *e.g. Lockhart* v. *Barr*, 1943 S.C.(H.L.) 1.

[28] Thus in *Blackwood* v. *Andre*, 1947 S.C. 333 a judge of the Outer House did not follow another judge of the Outer House in *McDaid* v. *Clyde Navigation Trustees*, 1946 S.C. 462.

[29] In *British Transport Commission* v. *Gourley* [1956] A.C. 185, *McDaid* was approved and *Blackwood* disapproved.

[30] Thus the House of Lords in *O'Hanlon* v. *Stein*, 1965 S.C.(H.L.) 23 reserved its opinion on *Sinclair* v. *N.C.B.*, 1963 S.C. 586.

to be bound by or to follow or apply a particular precedent.[31] It tends to produce hair-splitting distinctions when courts point to slight or even imaginary differences in facts to avoid being required to follow the precedent.[32]

If a court *approves* a precedent, the precedent must have been one accepted on its merits as a valuable guide though not binding, either because it comes from an inferior court or one in a different line of descent.[33] If the court *disapproves* a precedent, the precedent must be one not binding in the circumstances and not so closely in point as to require the court either not to follow or to overrule it.[34] Weaker than disapproval is the action of a court when it *doubts* a precedent, which can be done only in the case of a merely persuasive precedent, or one not sufficiently in point to be binding but on an analogous point. The effect of this is to suggest that the doubted case may not be good law. A case which has been doubted may be overruled in a later case [35] or may be reconsidered and the doubts rejected as unjustified.[36]

Other modes of dealing with precedents, as where they are *considered, explained, discussed, questioned, observed upon* or *commented on*, are self-explanatory; all are appropriate to precedents which are not in the circumstances both in point and binding.

Lastly, a superior court may *overrule* a precedent of a lower court in the same line of descent by declaring expressly or impliedly that the precedent is bad law and no longer of any authority on the point in question.[37]

---

[31] " It must, however, in my opinion, always be open to a party to contend that the differences between the facts in the case then under discussion and those in the case on which the decision in the House of Lords proceeded are so material as to prevent his case from falling within the *ratio decidendi* of the House, even though the opinions of the noble and learned lords who decided the case in the House are so worded as to seem to apply equally to the facts in the case then under discussion ": *Houldsworth* v. *City of Glasgow Bank* (1880) 7 R.(H.L.) 53, 62 *per* Lord Blackburn.

[32] See *e.g. Donoghue* v. *Stevenson*, 1932 S.C.(H.L.) 31, Lord Atkin at pp. 49-56, Lord Macmillan at pp. 65-69.

[33] Thus the Inner House might approve an Outer House precedent or an English precedent but it is not for the Inner House to " approve " a House of Lords decision, whether it is binding or not, since it comes from a superior court. It could only apply it or follow it or distinguish it.

[34] Thus the Court of Session may disapprove an English Court of Appeal decision, and conversely. See, *e.g. Dempster's Trs.* v. *Dempster*, 1949 S.C. 92. In *National Commercial Bank* v. *Fife Assessor*, 1963 S.C. 197 the Lands Valuation Appeal Court disapproved *Simpson* v. *Selkirk Assessor*, 1948 S.C. 270.

[35] *e.g. Greig* v. *Macleod*, 1908 S.C.(J.) 14, doubted in *Thornley* v. *Hunter*, 1965 J.C. 22, and overruled in *Noble* v. *Heatly*, 1967 S.L.T. 26.

[36] *e.g.*, opinions were reserved on *Traill* v. *Dalbeattie* (1904) 6 F. 798 in *Smith* v. *Stewart*, 1960 S.C. 329, but it was approved as good law in *Cole-Hamilton* v. *Boyd*, 1963 S.C.(H.L.) 1.

[37] Thus, *Horn* v. *N.B. Ry.* (1878) 5 R. 1055 was overruled in *McElroy* v. *McAllister*, 1949 S.C. 110. In *H.M.A.* v. *Cunningham*, 1963 J.C. 80, the High Court of Justiciary overruled *H.M.A.* v. *Ritchie*, 1926 J.C. 45. In *I.R.C.* v. *Ferguson*, 1969 S.C.(H.L.) 103, the House of Lords overruled *Blount* v. *Blount* [1916] 1 K.B. 230. Notice that overruling a precedent is quite distinct from reversing a prior decision of the

A precedent overruled becomes of no value for the future so far as concerns the *ratio* on which it has been overruled, but other points decided in the same case may still continue to be accepted as good law, and the actual decision, as affecting the parties, is unaffected.

A court is sometimes faced with the difficult task of *reconciling* precedents, and trying to derive from two or more binding precedents a doctrine which subsumes them both or all. " What is the duty of a judge when he is confronted with a series of decisions which are difficult to reconcile? In my judgment it depends: if there is a decision which cannot be distinguished from the case before him, even if it is a decision of a judge of first instance, *a fortiori*, of course, if it is a decision of the Court of Appeal or House of Lords, he ought to apply it—expressing maybe his doubts whether it is still good law, but leaving a superior tribunal to overrule it." [38] Sometimes it is possible to reconcile, sometimes one decision or group of decisions can be distinguished and the other followed, sometimes one can be set aside as inconsistent with a later decision of a superior court, but sometimes a court or judge may be faced with two equally binding precedents of equal status which cannot be reconciled, in which case the only course open is to follow what appears the better or preferable.[39]

Conclusions on Case-law

Possibly even more than with statutory law it will be apparent that the handling of case-law is an art rather than a mechanical process. Lord Wright, indeed, observed that it was partly intuition.[40] Such rules as there are are not by any means settled or unchanging. In the last resort a great deal depends on judicial temperament, on whether the judge agrees with and wishes to follow a precedent or whether he disagrees with it, wants to avoid it, and can find a way of avoiding being bound, on whether he values more highly consistency of decisions or what he conceives to be the requirements of justice in the circumstances. It is undoubtedly true that the rigidity of some of the modern rules leads to much casuistry, narrow verbal distinctions, excessive refinements of rules and doctrines and hypocrisy in " distinguishing " cases when the truth is that the later court

---

instant case (not a precedent) by a lower court. Also, overruling a precedent does not affect the decision of the earlier case as between the parties to it, since it was decided on what was then believed to be the law, but is now found to have been an incorrect statement of the rule. Old cases cannot be reopened on this ground. In *Davie* v. *New Merton Board Mills* [1959] A.C. 604, the House of Lords, in an English appeal, purported to overrule *Donnelly* v. *Glasgow Corpn.*, 1953 S.C. 107. This is, strictly, a misstatement; all that the House could do in an English appeal was to disapprove a Scottish case.

[38] *Re House Property Investment Co.* [1953] 3 W.L.R. 1037.

[39] See, *e.g.* *Angus's Executrix* v. *Batchan's Trs.*, 1949 S.C. 335, where one prior decision was followed and the other overruled.

[40] " Precedents," 8 Camb.L.J. 138.

does not wish to apply the rule of the precedent. Nevertheless despite the rules there is still considerable scope for judicial discretion and the creative function of the judge, developing the law according to current trends, beliefs and policies.

But while these difficulties arise in marginal cases it has to be remembered that principles worked out and laid down in cases of the higher courts suffice for the decision of hundreds of cases in lower courts, in which those precedents are accepted as undoubtedly in point and equally undoubtedly authoritative, and, on the whole, the advantages of consistency, certainty and predictability of the law justify in large measure the existence of the rule of *stare decisis.* What is, however, very doubtful is whether not only the House of Lords but possibly also the Inner House and corresponding courts, should have the power to overrule their own previous decisions, and whether any binding force should ever attach to a single decision of a single judge. But the discussion of this belongs to jurisprudence.

III.—LITERARY SOURCES—BOOKS OF AUTHORITY

Statements as to the law made by legal writers have varying degrees of authority, but always less than that of statute or case-law in that in case of conflict the rule laid down by statute or worked out by the courts has undoubtedly to be given effect to, notwithstanding anything in the books. The highest degree of authority attaches to the writings of a small number of writers, all of bygone ages, who all treated in their works of the whole law of Scotland, or at least of very large tracts of it. These are known as the institutional writings,[41] and a statement in one of them, in default of other authority, will almost certainly be taken as settling the law.[42] Among the institutional writers are *always included*[43] Sir Thomas Craig (*Jus Feudale,* 1655); Viscount Stair (*The Institutions of the Law of Scotland,* 1681); Andrew McDouall, Lord Bankton (*An Institute of the Laws of Scotland,* 3 volumes, 1751–53); Professor John Erskine (*An Institute of the Law of Scotland,* 2 volumes, 1773); and Professor George Joseph Bell (*Commentaries on the Law of Scotland and the Principles of Mercantile Jurisprudence,* 1804,[44] and *Principles of the Law of Scotland,* 1829).

To these are sometimes added Sir George Mackenzie (*The Institutions of the Law of Scotland,* 1684) and Henry Home, Lord Kames (*Principles of Equity,* 1760), but not all authorities concede the privileged status of institutional writings to these works.

---

[41] Because most of them were modelled on the *Institutes* of Justinian and were entitled *Institutions, Institute* or *Institutes.* On the institutional writers see David, *Introduction à l'Etude du Droit Ecossais,* 295–380.

[42] " When on any point of law I find Stair's opinion uncontradicted I look upon that opinion as ascertaining the Law of Scotland ": *Drew* v. *Drew* (1870) 9 M. 163, 167, *per* Lord Benholme. See also, *Kennedy* v. *Stewart* (1889) 16 R. 421, 430 on Kames.

[43] The dates given are of the first publication of the books in question.

[44] First published in 1800–04 as *Treatise on the Law of Bankruptcy in Scotland.*

In criminal law, Sir George Mackenzie (*The Laws and Customs of Scotland in Matters Criminal*, 1678), Baron David Hume (*Commentaries on the Law of Scotland respecting Crimes*, 2 volumes, 1797) and, probably, Archibald Alison (*Principles of the Criminal Law of Scotland*, 1832, and *Practice of the Criminal Law of Scotland*, 1833) are also regarded as institutional writers.

The authority of a statement by an institutional writer [45] is probably about equal to that of a decision of either Division of the Inner House. It has been said,[46] " Stair, Erskine and Bell are cited daily in the courts, and the court will pay as much respect to them as to a judgment of the House of Lords, though it is bound to follow a judgment of the House of Lords whatever the institutional writers may have said." The authority of institutional writings does not, however, extend automatically to all the writer's works, so that Erskine's *Principles*, written as a textbook for students, is not institutional, and Hume's *Lectures on Scots Law*,[47] not finally revised or published by him, are not entitled to the same weight as his *Commentaries on Crimes*.[48] These other works are merely legal literature though valuable specimens of it in view of the personal eminence of the writer. The institutional writings have been immensely influential in the past and have guided many past decisions of the courts, so that their importance is not confined to the somewhat spasmodic reference to them today.

IV.—Standard Textbooks and other Legal Literature

Writers on law other than the institutional writers, whose writings are legal literature rather than literary sources of the law, are technically not authorities at all and, according to the older view, could not be quoted in court during their lifetimes,[49] unless possibly they were elevated to the Bench, and even then their writings were of less weight than their judg-

---

[45] A distinction may have to be taken between what the writer himself wrote and what a later editor may have added. Hence reference to the last edition *by the author* is sometimes made.

[46] Lord Normand, *The Scottish Judicature and Legal Procedure* (Holdsworth Club, Birmingham, address, 1941).

[47] *Ed.* Paton, Stair Society, 6 vols.

[48] *Fortington* v. *Kinnaird*, 1942 S.C. 239, 253; but Hume's *Lectures* have nevertheless frequently been cited since then; see also *Pettigrew* v. *Harton*, 1956 S.C. 67; *MacLennan* v. *MacLennan*, 1958 S.C. 105; *Thomson* v. *St. Cuthbert's Co-operative Assocn., Ltd.*, 1958 S.C. 380, 394, 398; *N.C.B.* v. *Thomson*, 1959 S.C. 353, 383; *Cole-Hamilton* v. *Boyd*, 1962 S.C. 247, 257; *Mill's Trs.* v. *Mill's Trs.*, 1965 S.C. 384, 394; *Balshaw* v. *Balshaw*, 1967 S.C. 63, 83. On More's *Notes on Stair*, see *Forrest* v. *Forrest* (1863) 1 M. 806.

[49] Hence Lord Wright, speaking of (the then still-living) Sir Frederick Pollock's *Law of Torts*, called it " fortunately not a work of authority ": *Nicholls* v. *Ely Beet Sugar Factory* [1936] 1 Ch. 343, 349. This restriction is not now observed in the Scottish courts.

ments.[50] Their writings are secondary and not primary sources of the law. Such writings can only be " adopted " in argument as representing part of the speaker's contention as to the law. " The law books give no assistance because the work of living authors, however deservedly eminent, cannot be used as authority, although the opinions they express may demand attention." [51] But in fact in modern practice many writers are nowadays cited in argument and judgment notwithstanding that in many cases they are neither dead nor have been on the Bench. Thus in one case [52] a judge said: " In support of their argument, pursuer's counsel relied mainly on (1) certain cases such as . . .; (2) certain English authority; (3) certain Scottish textbooks, including . . .; and (4) the case of . . ." and continued: " I turn, therefore, to the law . . . as expounded by text-book writers and judicially in Scotland. . . ." While many such books are referred to in argument and even sometimes quoted in judgments they are only statements of what the jurist in question *believes* the law to be, what he submits is the result of the statutes and decided cases, and any court is quite free to differ from him and to lay down the true rule otherwise.[53] Such books do not state the law as authoritatively as the institutional writings do, but are only persuasive and state what the writer thinks is the law, on a particular subject. There is further a gradation of books, from standard treatises on various branches of law with established reputations down to books with no reputation and no influence on the court. Some books are in fact highly regarded and their views usually accepted and followed, while approval of a decision by the text-writers may be taken as supporting its soundness,[54] or disapproval as shaking its authority [55] but it is important to remember that these books do not impose law on the Bench, but merely

---

[50] A distinction may also be taken between a work written by a judge when he was young and an inexperienced advocate at the Bar and a work written in the days of his maturity.

[51] *Donoghue* v. *Stevenson*, 1932 S.C.(H.L.) 31, 35, *per* Lord Buckmaster.

[52] *Stein* v. *Beaverbrook Newspapers*, 1968 S.C. 272, 278.

[53] Thus, in cases on vesting, the courts repeatedly have referred to Candlish Henderson's *Principles of Vesting* with approval. But textbooks may equally be criticised. See *e.g.* Bell v. *Blackwood Morton & Sons Ltd.*, 1960 S.C. 11, 23, disapproving a passage in Glegg on *Reparation*; *Carter* v. *Allison*, 1966 S.C. 257, approving some and disapproving other textbooks. *Cf. Bastin* v. *Davies* [1950] 2 K.B. 579, where Lord Goddard C.J. said: " If a statement has appeared in a well-known textbook for a great number of years and has never been dissented from by a judicial decision, it would be most unfortunate to throw doubt on it after it had been acted on . . . for so long." For criticisms of statements in textbooks, see also *Re H. L. Bolton Engineering Co. Ltd.* [1956] Ch. 577; *Beevis* v. *Dawson* [1957] 1 Q.B. 195, 207; *Bentley* v. *Macfarlane*, 1964 S.C. 76. See also *Leon* v. *Leon* [1967] P. 275, where the court disapproved a statement in one textbook but applied principles stated in two others.

[54] *Cf. Dempster's Trs.* v. *Dempster*, 1949 S.C. 92, 95, *per* Lord Jamieson: " The decision . . . has been accepted by the text writers as settling the law."

[55] Thus *Machado* v. *Fontes* [1897] 2 Q.B. 231 has been almost universally condemned by the text-writers: see *McElroy* v. *McAllister*, 1949 S.C. 110, 135, where L. P. Cooper noted this consensus of disapproval.

may be voluntarily accepted for their clarity and accuracy of statement. The precise degree of regard paid to a particular book depends on the writer's reputation,[56] the esteem in which the book is held in the profession, and its age, for on the one hand it takes some time for any book to acquire reputation and on the other all books tend to become out of date, and if not revised may become practically valueless by the passing of time and the progress of the law, as new statutes and cases arise. But, if in point, a statement in a standard treatise carries weight comparable to a single-judge decision. English textbooks have lesser weight unless the principles in question are the same in both legal systems.

Legal literature, of course, serves an invaluable purpose in presenting, either for student or practitioner or judge, a connected, coherent and systematic account of the law on its topic, and in collecting in its text and footnotes references to the main statutes, cases and other primary sources of the rules of law on the subject. It is only in legal literature that one can find a coherent systematised account of any branch of law; without the textbooks the law is a jumble of disconnected statutory provisions and decisions. Many textbooks have done much to clarify and systematise the law and by constructive suggestions, generalisations from cases, examina-tion of terms and doctrines, criticism of unsatisfactory decisions and interpretations of statutes, and indications of desirable developments have influenced courts and judges in subsequent cases.[57]

In the present century the influence of legal literature has extended also to the chief legal periodicals; courts and judges have shown themselves sensitive to criticism by academic jurists in these journals, and have with increasing frequency considered and paid respect and attention to opinions expressed therein. Everything depends on the personal standing and reputation of the writer, without which matter in a legal journal carries no weight.[58]

V.—Custom

Among other sources mention must be made of custom,[59] which now plays a much smaller part as a source than it formerly did, in that many older customs have now been embodied in legislation or cases or books of authority. Many general customs have accordingly been incorporated long ago in the common law of Scotland. Thus the " legal rights " of spouses on death and the common-law rules governing the relationship of

---

[56] See *e.g. Coats's Trs.* v. *Lord Advocate*, 1965 S.C.(H.L.) 45, 69 on an article in Green's *Encyclopaedia*. See also the reliance on, and discussion of, Gloag on *Con-tract* in *Errol* v. *Walker*, 1966 S.C. 93.

[57] Thus the completely unofficial *Restatement of the Law*, published by the American Law Institute, has considerable influence: it was cited in *e.g. McPhail* v. *Lanark C.C.*, 1951 S.C. 301.

[58] For an example of the influence of periodicals, see *Haynes* v. *Harwood* [1935] 1 K.B. 146.

[59] See Cameron, " Custom as a Source of Law in Scotland " (1964) 27 M.L.R. 306.

landlord and tenant are based on very old customs. But apart from these customs, now absorbed into the law, custom may still be alleged in a particular case and, if proved, will be a valid source of a new rule of law. Such a custom must be (*a*) in some sense an exception to or qualification of the ordinary rule of law, yet not run completely counter to or be contradictory of an already established rule of statute or case-law. It must, that is, be an exception to, yet still consistent with, the existing general body of law.[60] It may, for example, be confined to a locality. Also it must be (*b*) definite and certain. It cannot be a custom if it is not known what it is, or is vague or if it is not habitually observed. It must further (*c*) be fair and reasonable; hence a claim for an exaction by a landlord for which nothing was given in return has been held unreasonable.[61] It must (*d*) have been generally accepted for so long as to justify the inference that it has long been accepted as law, as the binding rule. No particular period of time must be proved.[62]

The basis on which the court in an appropriate case will enforce the custom as law is that it has been shown to have been so certain, settled and established that it was in fact accepted as law and treated as binding even though it had not previously been before the courts or obtained express judicial recognition. If it is proved that a particular custom is accepted as law it will rule notwithstanding that either party is ignorant of it; *ignorantia juris neminem excusat*.[63] The importance of this kind of custom as a source of new rules of law is clearly limited.

Quite distinct from this kind of custom is the kind of custom or usage, sometimes sought to be proved, particularly in mercantile matters, to assist in interpreting a contract or implying a term into one. In this case evidence may be allowed to explain or supplement a mercantile contract, not on the basis that the custom is a rule of law, but on the ground that parties must have known of and must be taken to have intended to act in accordance with some particular trade usage. Since the basis for this kind of custom is implied agreement of parties to be bound by the custom, notice to or knowledge of the usage on the part of the person against whom it is pleaded must be proved.[64] Such a usage must be reasonably fair [65] and at least generally recognised in the trade in question.[66] Thus under this rule it has been proved that by the custom of the rabbit trade " one thousand " means 1,200,[67] or that a provision in a contract for oil for the reference of

---

[60] *Walker Trustees* v. *Lord Advocate*, 1912 S.C.(H.L.) 12.
[61] *Bruce* v. *Smith* (1890) 17 R. 1000.
[62] Ersk., I, 1, 44; *secus* in England.
[63] *Learmonth* v. *Sinclair's Trustees* (1878) 5 R. 548.
[64] *Holman* v. *Peruvian Nitrate Co.* (1878) 5 R. 657.
[65] *Devonald* v. *Rosser* [1906] 2 K.B. 728.
[66] *Hogarth* v. *Leith Cottonseed Oil Co.*, 1909 S.C. 955; *Dick* v. *Cochrane & Fleming*, 1935 S.L.T. 432.
[67] *Smith* v. *Wilson* (1832) 3 B. & Ad. 728.

disputes to " arbitration in Glasgow " meant, by the custom of the oil trade, a reference to an arbiter appointed by each party with an oversman chosen by them.[68] Moreover, unless a contract is made expressly subject to some usage, proof of usage is not permitted to contradict the plain meaning of express words in the contract. Thus a contract to supply " the whole of the steel for [a bridge], the estimated quantity to be 30,000 tons," was held to be a contract for the whole amount of steel, despite an alleged usage of the steel trade that the words meant 30,000 tons only.[69]

Parties may also contract in general terms by reference to, *e.g.* the custom of a particular port, and in that case they will be bound by the custom even though they did not know of its precise terms.[70]

The importance of this kind of custom as a source of law is considerable and in many cases mercantile contracts still have to be interpreted in accordance with customs and usages of particular ports, or particular trades.

VI.—EQUITY

Scottish courts have always administered an undivided system of law and equity [71] and many of the principles commonly applied by the courts are as much equitable as legal in origin and justification.[72] Many doctrines of Scots law have been modified by equity, in the sense of the force of reason and natural justice, to rectify or avoid an excessive strictness or rigidity. In many fields of law this influence has so exercised itself in the past that the legal and equitable elements in the modern doctrine have been completely blended and the boundary is not perceptible. But equity remains a valid and unexhausted source of Scots law in that it is still open to a court to delimit a rule or interpret a principle in the light of what seems consistent with reason and natural justice.[73]

Apart from instances where the rule of law has been modified by equitable ideas in the course of its development, the Court of Session and, to

---

[68] *United Creameries Co.* v. *Boyd & Co.*, 1922 S.C. 617.

[69] *Tancred, Arrol & Co.* v. *Steel Co. of Scotland* (1887) 15 R. 215; (1890) 17 R.(H.L.) 31; *MacLellan* v. *Peattie's Trustees* (1903) 5 F. 1031. *Cf. Affréteurs Réunis* v. *Walford* [1919] A.C. 801.

[70] *Strathlorne S.S. Co.* v. *Baird*, 1915 S.C. 956; revd. 1916 S.C.(H.L.) 134. *Cf. Forget* v. *Baxter* [1900] A.C. 467.

[71] Until 1875 England had courts of common law which administered law and courts of equity which gave equitable remedies. The distinction still persists in some Commonwealth countries. Since 1875 all courts in England may give both legal and equitable remedies but it is doubtful how far law and equity have been merged; the merger is still incomplete. On English Equity, see further, Levy-Ullmann, *The English Legal Tradition*, Part 3; Plucknett, *Concise History of the Common Law*, 675 *et seq.*; Potter, *Historical Introduction to English Law*, 4th ed., 569 *et seq.*; Allen, *Law in the Making*, Chap. 5.

[72] See further, Brown, " Equity " (1914) 26 J.R. 338; Walker, " Equity in Scots Law " (1954) 66 Jur.Rev. 103; art. " Equity " in Green's *Encyclopaedia*; Lord Wark, " The Law of Nature," in (Stair Society) *Sources and Literature of Scots Law*, 249.

[73] As a factor in interpreting the old Scots prescription statutes, see, *e.g. Earl of Fife* v. *Duff* (1888) 15 R. 253; *Mill's Trs.*, 1965 S.C. 384, 388.

some extent, the High Court of Justiciary [74] retain an ultimate residuary
equitable power to provide a remedy where justice requires it and to
intervene to prevent unduly rigorous law working injustice. This power,
the *nobile officium*, has of late come to be much restricted and is, as a rule,
exercised now only in circumstances for which there is precedent or
analogy.[75]

Moreover, in many fields of law a judge is expressly or impliedly en-
joined to keep equitable considerations, the concepts of what is reasonable
and conform to natural justice, in mind. He is endowed with discretion,
which has to be exercised consistently with these principles and not
arbitrarily, though in practice the exercise soon tends to become limited by
the ways in which the exercise has been done in past cases, and repeatedly
he finds that he has to do what is " just and reasonable " or " fair," or
otherwise finds a standard fixed which has to be applied to the facts
of the case having in mind the equitable considerations of providing a
remedy for any obvious wrong, of avoiding the injustice of excessively
rigid application of law, and of rewarding care, diligence and honesty.

VII.—EXTRANEOUS SOURCES

Extraneous sources include all those other sources to which a judge may
resort, in default of guidance from the sources already discussed, and from
which he may draw or adapt a principle or rule to apply to a new problem
before him.

Other Systems of Law

If the sources from which rules and principles of Scots law are normally
drawn, those already discussed, yield nothing or nothing very satisfactory,
it is permissible and proper to look at other systems of law in which the
problem may have arisen and which may, accordingly, be able to suggest a
suitable rule. Among other systems regard should first be had to Roman
law, particularly in questions of obligations and moveable property.
Roman law has long been, and may still be, a good quarry for the material
of legal decisions and it would be consistent with the tradition of Scots
law if resort were made more to the Roman law instead of always running
to the English books.[76] Modern systems of law which have drawn heavily
on the Roman law, such as the Roman-Dutch law of South Africa, and
later commentators on the Roman law, such as Voet, may also usefully be
referred to.

In consistorial matters the old Roman canon law and the great mass of

---

[74] See, *e.g. Wylie* v. *H.M. Advocate*, 1966 S.L.T. 149.
[75] See Green's *Encyclopaedia*, art. " Nobile Officium."
[76] Ersk. I, 1, 41, speaks of the Roman law as " of great weight in all cases not
fixed by statute or custom, and in which the genius of our law will suffer us to apply
it."

learned commentaries thereon is likewise a traditional, and still valuable and highly reputable source.

Especially in matters of commercial and industrial law, the laws of England, the Commonwealth countries, and the United States may usefully be looked at. But one has always to keep in mind the very different history, development and working-out of English rules and doctrines. In particular the different approaches of common law and of equity to the same problems prior to 1875, and the continuing results of that dichotomy since then, make English law a very unsafe guide unless in the hands of a scholar who understands both systems. Immense harm has been done to Scots law by the uncritical culling from English law of decisions which appear applicable equally to Scotland but which have really been misunderstood. Moreover, the more remote the legal system from which guidance is being sought, the greater the danger of failing to appreciate the background of the decision or the rule and of importing an unsound principle. Continental law is also occasionally referred to.[77]

Dissenting judgments, *obiter dicta*, and argument by analogy from principles accepted in other contexts may also give assistance.

Ideals of Justice

In default of all other sources the judge is thrown back on his own moral conscience, his beliefs as to what is fair and right and reasonable in the circumstances, in short, on his idea of what justice requires.[78] In the House of Lords it has been said [79]: " In the end and in the absence of authority binding this House, the question is simply: ' What does justice demand in such a case as this? ' " Failing other authority the broad principles of justice, as the judge sees it, are not a bad basis for decision, and such principles can also sometimes be appealed to in support of a conclusion based also on another ground. Thus conduct has been stigmatised as " morally and socially wrong," [80] or it has been held that something was " contrary to natural justice," [81] or " opposed to the fundamental principles of justice." [82]

---

[77] For examples of reference to foreign law, see, *e.g. Donoghue* v. *Stevenson*, 1932 S.C.(H.L.) 31 (English and U.S. cases); *A/B Karlshamns Oljefabriker* v. *Monarch S.S. Co.*, 1949 S.C.(H.L.) 1 (U.S. case); *Drummond's J.F.* v. *H.M. Advocate*, 1944 S.C. 298 (English and French Law); *Cantiere San Rocco* v. *Clyde Shipbuilding Co.*, 1923 S.C.(H.L.) 105; *Glasgow Corpn.* v. *Lord Advocate*, 1959 S.C. 203 (Roman law); *Sugden* v. *H.M. Advocate*, 1934 J.C. 103 (Dutch jurists, French and Roman law); *Collins* v. *Collins* (1884) 11 R.(H.L.) 19; *Purves' Trustees* v. *Purves* (1895) 22 R. 513; *Annan* v. *Annan*, 1948 S.C. 532; *Imre* v. *Mitchell*, 1958 S.C. 439, 464 (all canon law); *Walsh* v. *Lord Advocate*, 1956 S.C.(H.L.) 126 (U.S. case); *Breen* v. *Breen*, 1961 S.C. 158 (Roman and canon law); *Burmah Oil Co.* v. *Lord Advocate*, 1965 S.C.(H.L.) 117 (international jurists, legal history and U.S. law).
[78] See further, Cardozo, *Nature of the Judicial Process*.
[79] *National Bank of Greece and Athens S.A.* v. *Metliss* [1958] A.C. 509, 525, *per* Viscount Simonds.   [80] *Wilson* v. *Glossop* (1888) 20 Q.B.D. 354.
[81] *Valentini* v. *Canali* (1889) 24 Q.B.D. 166.
[82] *Robinson* v. *Continental Insurance Co.* [1915] 1 K.B. 155.

Akin to ideals of justice, and indeed only facets of justice under other names are those considerations of morality and public policy sometimes invoked to justify a decision, reflecting the fact that an important characteristic of any acceptable system of law is that it will promote what is generally beneficial and good and discourage the contrary.[83]

Conclusions

These, then, are the sources, and it will be seen that the legal adviser must sometimes have to search long and deeply for the basis for his advice, and the judge at least as far and widely for the ground of his decision and its justification in the eyes of critical jurists and subsequent judges. Frequently no ready-made proposition of law can be found directly applicable to the facts in issue, and the search must be for the materials with which the court may fashion a proposition for application to those facts. Increasingly, moreover, the courts in their decisions put the stamp of authority on propositions which in part they work out and formulate themselves, but in large part they select and develop from doctrinal writings. New problems keep on turning up and every now and then a case arises which raises some quite fundamental point and requires for its solution long and careful research in these sources and sometimes outward from them into history or social science or some other branch of learning which might at first sight appear remote from the law. The inevitable conclusion is that nothing can be ignored by the lawyer as irrelevant to his main study and that the wider his background knowledge the better. Moreover, even when matter bearing on the problem can be found in the statutes or cases or books the matter must be interpreted to see what light it casts on the problem, and to decide whether it supplies the answer or merely a guide to the answer.

FURTHER READING

Sources Generally
Allen: *Law in the Making.*
Gray: *Nature and Sources of the Law.*
Holdsworth: *Sources and Literature of English Law.*
Holland: *Jurisprudence*, Chap. 5.
Paton: *Jurisprudence*, Chaps. 6–10.
Patterson: *Jurisprudence*, Chaps. 9–11.
Pound: *Jurisprudence*, Chap. 16.
Salmond: *Jurisprudence*, Chaps. 5–9.
Stair Society: *Sources and Literature of Scots Law.*
Sweet and Maxwell: *Guide to Law Reports and Statutes.*

---

[83] For cases where considerations of morality and public policy have been in issue, see *e.g. R.* v. *Bourne* [1939] 1 K.B. 687; *Steel* v. *Glasgow Iron & Steel Co.*, 1944 S.C. 237; *Fender* v. *Mildmay* [1938] A.C. 1; *Beresford* v. *Royal Insurance Co.* [1938] A.C. 586.

Sources of European Communities Law
Lasok and Bridge: *Introduction to the Law and Institutions of the European Communities.*

Legislation
Allen: *Law and Orders.*
Carr: *Delegated Legislation.*
Craies: *Treatise on Statute Law.*
Davies: " Interpretation of Statutes in the light of their policy by the English courts " (1935) 35 Col.L.R. 519.
Erskine May: *Treatise on the Law, Privileges, Proceedings and Usages of Parliament.*
Friedmann: " Statute Law and its Interpretation in the Modern State " (*Law and Social Change*, Chap. 2).
Graham-Harrison: " Criticisms of the Statute Book," 1935 J.S.P.T.L. 9.
Griffith and Street: *Principles of Administrative Law.*
Ilbert: *Legislative Methods and Forms*, 1901.
    Methods of Legislation, 1911.
Jennings: *Parliament.*
Maxwell: *The Interpretation of Statutes.*
Thring: *Practical Legislation.*
Willis: " Statute Interpretation in a Nutshell " (1938) 16 Can.B.R. 1.

Case-Law
Cross: *Precedent in English Law.*
Daniel: *History and Origin of the Law Reports.*
Ellis Lewis: " History of Judicial Precedent " (1930) 46 L.Q.R. 207, 341; (1931) 47 L.Q.R. 411; (1932) 48 L.Q.R. 230.
Frank: *Courts on Trial.*
    Law and the Modern Mind.
Gardner: *Judicial Precedent in Scots Law.*
    " Judicial Precedent in American and Scots Law " (1940) 52 J.R. 144.
Gibb: *Law from over the Border.*
Goodhart: " Precedent in English and Continental Law " (1934) 50 L.Q.R. 40.
Jensen: *The Nature of Legal Argument.*
Levi: *Introduction to Legal Reasoning.*
Moran: *The Heralds of the Law.*
Ram: *The Science of Legal Judgment*, 1871.
Smith: *Judicial Precedent in Scots Law.*
Stone: *The Province and Function of Law*, Chaps. 6 and 7.
    Legal System and Lawyer's Reasonings, Chap. 7.
Wallace: *The Reporters*, 4th ed., 1882.
Wambaugh: *Study of Cases*, 2nd ed., 1894

Institutional Writings
Black: " The Institutional Writers " in (Stair Society) *Sources and Literature of Scots Law.*
Cooper: " Some Classics of Scottish Legal Literature " in *Selected Papers.*
Fifoot: *Judge and Jurist in the Reign of Queen Victoria.*

Custom
Institutional writers.

Equity
Kames: *Principles of Equity.*
Walker: " Equity in Scots Law " (1954) 66 J.R. 103.

Extraneous Sources
Cardozo: *Nature of the Judicial Process.*
Frank: *Courts on Trial.*
Mackintosh: *Roman Law in Modern Practice.*
Oliver: " Roman Law in Modern Cases," in *Cambridge Legal Essays*, 243.
Stein and Shand: *Legal Values in Western Society.*

CHAPTER 11

THE REPOSITORIES OF SCOTS LAW

A DISTINCTION has been drawn between the legally authoritative sources
of the law and legal literature, or books about the law, which are sources
of our knowledge of the law, setting out only the author's view of what
the law is on the subject discussed in his work. Legal literature has no
binding authority at all and is only a secondary source of the law, though
some books may in fact enjoy a high reputation and exercise an influence
on a court not much, if at all, inferior to that of a judicial decision. The
whole corpus of books which contain the written law, both the authoritative sources, and the unauthoritative books about the law or literary or
secondary sources, forms the repositories of the law, to which the inquirer
must resort to search out the law applicable to some precise point. A
knowledge of these repositories is essential; the lawyer must know where
and how to look for the law.[1]

I. PRIMARY OR AUTHORITATIVE SOURCES

A—LAW COMMON TO COUNTRIES OF THE EUROPEAN COMMUNITIES

The primary sources are the foundation Treaties, supplementary conventions and treaties,[2] the Regulations, Directives and Decisions made by
the Council and the Commission in implement of the Treaties [3] and rulings
and decisions of the Court of the European Communities.[4]

B—LAW APPLICABLE TO SCOTLAND

Statutes

Scots Acts prior to 1707 are to be found in *The Acts of the Parliaments
of Scotland*, 1124–1707,[5] and also in Murray of Glendook's *Laws and*

---

[1] Every lawyer and student should become familiar with the Legal Bibliographies
and Reference Books listed on p. 425.

[2] Collected in Sweet & Maxwell's *European Community Treaties.*

[3] Published in the *Official Journal of the European Communities*, which appears
almost daily in each of the official languages of the Communities. There is an English
edition from January 1973. Since 1968 the *Journal* has appeared in two series, one
devoted to legislation, the other to other communications and information.

[4] Judgments of the Court are published periodically in each of the official languages
of the Communities. The French version, *Recueil de la Jurisprudence de la Cour*
is commonly used prior to 1973. There is an English version from 1973. Judgments
down to 1962 are also in Valentine: *Court of Justice of the European Communities*,
Vol. 2, and thereafter in the *Common Market Law Reports.*

[5] ed. Thomas Thomson and Cosmo Innes, 11 vols. in 12, and Index Vol., 1814–
75, cited, *e.g.* A.P.S. II, 345. This is known as the Record edition, having been published by the Commissioners on the Public Records.

Acts of Parliament, 1424–1681,[6] while Scots Acts still in force in 1908 were reprinted in Scots Statutes Revised, 1424–1707,[7] and those still in force in 1964 were reprinted in the *Acts of the Parliaments of Scotland*, 1424–1707.[8]

Statutes of the Parliament of England prior to 1707 are contained in the *Statutes of the Realm*, 1225–1713,[9] and in various editions of the *Statutes at Large*.[10] Legislation during the Interregnum is collected in the *Acts and Ordinances of the Interregnum*, 1642–60.[11]

Acts of the Parliaments of Great Britain, 1707–1800, and of the Parliaments of the United Kingdom since 1801 are also in the *Statutes at Large*. There is also an edition of statutes 1806–69 in 63 volumes, and since 1831 the Queen's Printer has published annually the *Public General Statutes*.[12]

The most convenient modern editions are the *Statutes Revised*, third edition (1235–1948)[13] which prints, in chronological, not classified, order, the statutes (excepting Acts of the pre-1707 Scottish Parliaments) so far as still in force and as amended to the end of 1948. Each volume has a chronological table which lists all Acts within the period it covers and gives the reason for omissions, and an index to subjects dealt with in the volume. This is continued to the present by annual volumes of *Public General Statutes*. The *Scots Statutes Revised*[14] includes only Acts applicable to Scotland, as amended to the date of each volume. This is continued by *Scots Statutes*[15] and *Scottish Current Law Statutes*.[16] There are other editions, such as the Blackwood edition,[17] while reprints of

---

[6] folio, 1681; duodecimo, two volumes, 1682; cited, *e.g.* Act 1449, c. 18. A third volume continues to the Union.

[7] 1908.

[8] Second revised edition, H.M.S.O., 1966. This edition gives also the short titles conferred on the surviving Scots Acts by the Statute Law Revision (Scotland) Act 1964, Sched. 2, and references to both the Record edition and Glendook's edition.

[9] Published by the Record Commissioners, 9 vols. in 10, large folio, 1810–22, with alphabetical index, 1824, and chronological index, 1828, reprinted, 1963. It includes private Acts to 1539 and the titles of private Acts thereafter, and there are valuable introductions and editorial notes.

[10] The best are Ruffhead's (1215–1764) in 9 vols. with 9 supplementary vols. covering 1763–1800; Runnington's new edition of Ruffhead (1215–1785) in 10 vols. with 4 supplementary vols, covering 1785–1800; Tomlins and Raithby's (1215–1800) in 10 vols. quarto, or 20 vols. octavo, continued by a Queen's Printer's edition 1801–69 in 29 vols.; and Pickering's (1215–1761) in 24 vols., continued to 1806 by 22 supplements.

[11] ed. Firth and Rait, 3 vols. 1911.

[12] The Statutory Publications Office also issues annually *Annotations to Acts*, in the form of adhesive slips containing substituted provisions which can be attached to older Acts affected by the year's new legislation.

[13] (1235–1948) in 32 vols. There is also a uniform volume of [English] *Church Assembly Measures Revised*.

[14] (1707–1900) in 10 vols.

[15] (1901–1948) in 12 vols.

[16] (1949–   ), annual volumes. Acts of Sederunt and Acts of Adjournal are also printed therein.

[17] (1707–1847) in 3 vols., and annual vols. 1848–1947.

statutes were issued with the *Scots Law Times* from 1901 to 1948 and with the [English] *Law Reports* from 1865 to 1950.

Publication commenced in 1972 of *Statutes in Force*, a new official revised edition of the statutes in which each Act (including Acts of the Parliaments of Scotland) in force is printed as a separate booklet. When an Act is heavily amended the booklet is replaced by a new one containing an amended print of the Act. A cumulative amendments booklet issued annually lists all the amendments not yet incorporated in the edition. In respect of some groups there are separate Scottish and English groups of Acts and in such cases Acts extending to both Scotland and England may be included in both groups. There will be indexes to groups or large sub-groups of the recommended arrangement, and there will ultimately be an index to the whole work. Cumulative lists of the Acts in the edition, both alphabetical and chronological, will be published from time to time. The booklets are held in loose-leaf binders and may be included therein in any order the user or library may choose, though there is a recommended arrangement prepared by the Editorial Board on the advice of a working party. Repealed Acts are simply removed from the binders. In this way this edition will be constantly self-renewing and once complete will be constantly substantially up-to-date.[18] It will supersede *Statutes Revised*.

Halsbury's *Statutes of England*[19] contains the public general Acts applicable to the United Kingdom and to England, classified under alphabetical subject-headings, and annotated. There are also various books containing statutes relevant to particular topics, and annotated editions of particular Acts.

None of the foregoing includes local or private Acts. There is a separate annual volume of *Local and Personal Acts* (with tables and index) and some cities have published volumes containing their own local Acts.

Subordinate Legislation

Orders in Council and Statutory Rules and Orders have been issued since 1890 in annual volumes, collected under the same headings of legal subjects as in the *Indexes to the Statutes in Force*. Since 1948 the annual volumes have been entitled *Statutory Instruments*.

The *Statutory Rules and Orders and Statutory Instruments Revised*[20] reprints all S.R. and O.s and S.I.s of a permanent nature and still in force, as amended, arranged, not numerically or chronologically, but

---

[18] Individual holdings of *Statutes in Force* may be complete, or contain Acts applicable to Scotland, or to England and Wales, or to Northern Ireland, or be limited to the particular groups or sub-groups of Acts which are of interest to the library or holder of the set in question.

[19] 3rd ed., 41 vols. (in progress).

[20] (1904–1948) 25 vols., continued by annual volumes of S.I.s.

under subject-headings. The last volume contains a list of subject-headings, a numerical table, and a table of effects.

Halsbury's *Statutory Instruments* [21] also collect the orders and instruments under subject-headings and include annotations but neglect purely Scottish matters, so that they must be used only cautiously.

Acts of Sederunt passed by the Court of Session to regulate procedure are collected in various older collections [22] but the *Codifying Act of Sederunt* of 1913 [23] collected those relative to procedure then in force, and was itself superseded by the *Rules of Court*, 1936, revised editions, 1948 and 1965.[24] Modern Acts of Sederunt, and Acts of Adjournal passed by the High Court of Justiciary to regulate criminal procedure [25] are also published in *Scottish Current Law Statutes*, the *Scots Law Times* and *Parliament House Book*.

Indexes to Legislation

Statutes can be traced through the *Index to the Statutes in Force, 1235–*,[26] and the *Chronological Table of the Statutes, 1235–*.[27] The *Index* groups under selected headings, arranged alphabetically, entries relating to the whole of the general statute-law in force. It is analytical within each heading, and provides a subject-matter index to every provision in any Act of Parliament in operation at the date of the Index; it has to be noticed that some headings are duplicated, such as Education (England) and Education (Scotland), where there are two distinct bodies of statute-law referring to the two countries. Headings are not duplicated where the statute-law is entirely or largely common to the two countries. The *Chronological Table* gives a list of public general Acts (since 1966 including Scots Acts) from 1235 to the date of the edition in chronological order showing, for repealed Acts, by what Act they were repealed, and, for Acts still in operation, the effect on each section of all subsequent amendments and modifications, both by Act of Parliament and by Statutory Instrument.[28]

---

[21] 24 vols. and supplements.

[22] See Sweet and Maxwell's *Legal Bibliography*, Vol. 5, for details. They are cited, *e.g.* A.S. 9th March, 1951.

[23] Cited by book, chapter and section, *e.g.* C.A.S., A, ii, 2.

[24] Reprinted, as amended to date, in the annual *Parliament House Book:* cited by book and number, or by number alone, *e.g.* R.C. II, 134 or R.C. 134.

[25] Cited, *e.g.* A.A. 2nd February, 1921.

[26] 2 Volumes, annually.

[27] Published annually. These volumes act as the general Table and Index of the *Statutes Revised*, as continued by the annual *Public General Statutes*.

There is also published annually *Annotations to Acts*, a volume of notes by means of which the effect of each year's legislation can be noted up briefly on any set of statutes to keep them up to date, and this includes gummed printed sheets, called " annexes," for lengthier entries, which can be stuck in at the appropriate places.

[28] The *Acts of the Parliaments of Scotland* (second revised edition, H.M.S.O., 1966) has a similar chronological table of the Scots statutes, 1424–1707.

There is a separate *Index to Local and Personal Acts, 1801–1947*, continued by an annual table and index.

Subordinate legislation

Subordinate legislation can be traced by recourse to the *Index* (formerly *Guide*) to *Government Orders*,[29] the *Numerical Table, S.R. & O.s and S.I.s as at December 31, 1958*,[30] and the *S.I. Effects*.[31] The *Index* shows all statutory powers to make subordinate legislation, under classified sub-headings with the references of the enabling Acts and of all amending Acts. There are cross-references and a Table of Statutes. With each power are given particulars of all instruments under it current at the stated date of the volume, showing the date, title and number of the instrument and a reference to where it can be found in the *S.R. & O.s and S.I.s Revised, 1948*, by volume and page or (in the case of a post-1948 exercise) to the annual volume and page of S.I. The *Numerical Table* shows in chronological order, with the exception of certain categories, the titles, numbers and volume references of all *S.R. & O.s and S.I.s* then in operation. The annual Supplement thereto lists the new instruments made during the year and still current and those earlier ones which fall to be deleted from the Table as now revoked or spent. The *S.I. Effects* gives a cumulative table showing revocations and changes.

Parliamentary and Command Papers

Parliamentary papers include documents, such as reports of Parliamentary committees, ordered to be printed by either or both Houses of Parliament and which are commonly known, according to the colour of the cover, as Blue Books and White Papers.[32] They include many documents important for the study of the law. Other official documents, such

---

[29] H.M.S.O. Published in alternate years. This acts as Index to the *S.R. & O.s and S.I.s Revised*, as continued by the annual *Statutory Instruments*.

[30] H.M.S.O., 1959, with annual Supplements.

[31] H.M.S.O., annually. This volume comprises a table showing the effect of the statutory instruments of the year on previous statutory rules and orders and statutory instruments, showing which have been revoked or amended, and which have become spent or have ceased to operate. It does not cover instruments made under emergency legislation. H.M.S.O. also publishes daily, monthly and annual lists of S.I.s.

[32] They are cited by the title, followed by, in brackets, the year, the House concerned and the serial number, *e.g.* (1950: H.C. 178). They are catalogued in the annual *Government Publications* and the *General Index to Parliamentary Papers*, 1900–49. There is also *Hansard's Catalogue and Breviate of Parliamentary Papers, 1696–1834*, a *General Index to the reports of Select Committees printed by Order of the House of Commons, 1801–52*, a *General Index to the Accounts and Papers printed by Order of the House of Commons and to the papers presented by command, 1801–52*, and a *General Index to the Bills, Reports, Estimates, Accounts and Papers printed by order of the House of Commons and to the papers printed by command, 1852–69.* See also P. and G. Ford's *Select List of British Parliamentary Papers, 1833–99, Breviate of Parliamentary Papers, 1900–54* (3 vols.) and *Select List of British Parliamentary Papers, 1955–64.* A classified reprint of the *British Parliamentary Papers* commenced in 1968.

as Reports of Royal Commissions, Departmental Committees and Law Reform Committees, are presented to Parliament by command of Her Majesty and are published usually in blue or white covers as Command Papers.[33] Many of these official papers contain valuable information about the working of government and of the law, interesting criticisms and proposals for amendment of the law, and they are sometimes the basis for legislation.

Case-Law—Scottish Reports

Down to the eighteenth century the only reports were notes of cases contained in volumes of *Practicks*, or notes made by private individuals, frequently judges, for their own use and subsequently published.

The published volumes of *Practicks* are:

Name	Vols.	Period	Citation
Spotiswoode's *Practicks* (1716)	1	1541–37	Spot.Prac.
Hope's *Minor Practicks* (1726, 1734)	1	1608–33	Hope, Min.Prac.
Balfour's *Practicks* (1754)[34]	1	1469–1579	Balf.Prac.
Hope's *Major Practicks* (1937–38)[35]	2	1608–33	Hope, Maj.Prac.

In the seventeenth century individuals, frequently judges, made collections of notes of decisions and later published them. These private reports are cited by volume and page with an abbreviation of the reporter's name. The following is a list of the old private reports:

Reporter	Vols.	Period	Citation
Sir Alexander Gibson, Lord Pres. Durie	1	1621–42	Durie
Decisions of the English Judges during the Usurpation	1	1655–61	Eng.Judg.
Sir John Gilmour, Lord Pres. Craigmillar	1	1661–66	Gil. & Fal.
Sir David Falconer, Lord Pres. Newton		1681–86	
Sir James Dalrymple, Lord Pres. Stair	2	1661–81	Stair

---

[33] They are cited by title, followed by, in brackets, the year, series and number therein. Command papers have been issued in five series, identified and numbered as follows: 1833–69, numbered 1 to 4222; 1870–99, C. 1 to C. 9550; 1900–18, Cd. 1 to Cd. 9239; 1919–56, Cmd. 1 to Cmd. 9889; November 1956 to date, Cmnd. 1 onwards. Some are commonly known by the name of the chairman of the committee reporting, *e.g.* the Beveridge Report is the *Report on Social Insurance and Allied Services* (1943: Cmd. 6404). A list of the reports commonly thus known is in *Where to Look for your Law.*

[34] Reprinted in facsimile by the Stair Society in 1962–63.

[35] Ed. Lord Clyde, Stair Society.

Reporter	Vols.	Period	Citation
Sir John Nisbet, Lord Dirleton	1	1665–77	Dirl.[36]
Sir John Lauder, Lord Fountainhall	2	1678–1712	Fount.
Sir Roger Hog, Lord Harcarse	1	1681–91	Harc.
Sir Hew Dalrymple of North Berwick, Lord Pres.	1	1698–1718	Dalr.
William Forbes, Faculty Reporter	1	1705–13	Forbes [37]
Alexander Bruce, Faculty Reporter	1	1714–15	Bruce [38]
Henry Home, Lord Kames	2	1716–28	Kames Rem.Dec.[39]
John Edgar, Faculty Reporter	1	1724–25	Edgar
Patrick Grant, Lord Elchies	2	1733–54	Elchies [40]
Alexander Home, Clerk of Session	1	1735–44	Cl. Home
Sir James Fergusson, Lord Kilkerran	1	1738–52	Kilk.[41]
David Falconer, Faculty Reporter	2	1744–51	D.Falc.
Henry Home, Lord Kames	1	1752–68	Kames Sel.Dec.[42]
Sir David Dalrymple, Lord Hailes	2	1766–91	Hailes
David Hume, Baron of Exchequer	1	1781–1822	Hume
Robert Bell, Clerk to the Signet	1	1790–92	Bell Oct.Cas.[43]
do.	1	1794–95	Bell Fol.Cas.[43]

In 1705 the Faculty of Advocates first appointed a reporter of decisions.[44] From 1752 there appeared three series of their reports, known as the *Faculty Collection* or *Faculty Decisions*, namely, the Old Series in fourteen

---

[36] These reports are normally bound up along with Dirleton's *Doubts*, but separately paginated.

[37] This volume is entitled *A Journal of the Session*. Some further reports by Forbes, 1713–14, were included in Lord Kames' *Folio Dictionary*.

[38] Bruce's *Decisions* are usually found bound with Vol. 1 of Kames' *Remarkable Decisions* and cited as Bruce and Home's *Decisions*. Further decisions reported by Bruce, 1716–17, are printed in Vol. 3 of the *Faculty Collection* (1760–64).

[39] The volume is entitled *Remarkable Decisions in the Court of Session*.

[40] Vol. 1 consists of reports of cases and was printed by Morison as Appendix II to his *Dictionary of Decisions*. Vol. 2 consists of notes of cases from which the reports were compiled.

[41] Additional cases noted by Kilkerran, 1735–59, are printed in Brown's *Supplement*, Vol. 5. On Kilkerran, see Fergusson, "Background to a Lord of Session," 1974 S.L.T.(News) 1.

[42] The volume is entitled *Select Decisions of the Court of Session*.

[43] These are known, from the sizes of the volumes, as Bell's Octavo and Folio cases, respectively.

[44] The Faculty reporters were in succession Forbes (later Professor of Law at Glasgow) (1705–13), Bruce (1714–15), Edgar (1724–25) and Falconer (1744–51), and from 1714 to 1744 the work was very inadequately done, but the collections of Lords Elchies, Kames and Kilkerran and of Clerk Home supply most of the defects.

volumes (1752–1808), the New Series in seven volumes (1808–25) and the Octavo Series in sixteen volumes (1825–41). The first two series are cited by the date of the decision with the letters F.C. added, *e.g.* 10th Jan., 1793, F.C., and the Octavo Series by volume and page, *e.g.* 9 Fac.Dec. 123.[45]

Most of the older cases are reprinted in Kames' and Woodhouselee's *Dictionary* (five vols. covering cases 1540–1796 and cited Fol.Dic. or K. & W.Dic.) and in Morison's *Dictionary of Decisions* (twenty-two vols.)[46] with Morison's *Synopsis* 1808–16 (two vols.) and *Indexes* (one vol.) and Tait's *Index* (one vol.).[47] Brown's *Supplement* in five volumes (1622–1794) includes most of the cases omitted by Morison, and also some not previously printed, and is cited *e.g.* 3 B.S. or Brown's Supp. Brown also published in four volumes Brown's *Synopsis of Cases, 1540–1827*, contained in Morison's *Dictionary*, Brown's *Supplement* and in some other reports down to 1827.

Session Cases

From 1821 to 1906 five series of *Session Cases* were issued, distinguished by the initial letter of the editor or chief reporter's name. These are:

First Series—	Shaw [48]	16 vols. 1821–38	*e.g.*	5 S. 390.[49]
Second Series—	Dunlop [50]	24 vols. 1838–62	*e.g.*	7 D. 436.
Third Series—	Macpherson	11 vols. 1862–73	*e.g.*	10 M. 120.[51]
Fourth Series—	Rettie	25 vols. 1873–98	*e.g.*	17 R. 931.
Fifth Series—	Fraser	8 vols. 1898–1906	*e.g.*	4 F. 297.

From 1907 the *Session Cases* were issued by the Faculty of Advocates.[52] In 1957 the Scottish Council of Law Reporting was formed to take over the responsibility for publishing *Session Cases*. From 1907 these reports are cited by the year and page of the annual volume, *e.g.* 1935 S.C. 471.[53]

---

[45] There are several editions of some of the volumes, and variations in binding. Halkerston's *Compendium* (1819, and Supplement 1820) contains indexes of the decisions in *Faculty Collection* (1752–1817).

[46] Vols. 20 and 21 consist of a Synopsis or Digest of the cases in the previous 19. This is distinct from Morison's *Synopsis* 1808–16. Vol. 22 is a Supplemental volume. Appendix I to the Dictionary is usually bound into it, each title after the title in the Dictionary, but sometimes bound as two separate volumes. The Dictionary is paginated consecutively throughout the work and cited *e.g.* (1540) Mor. 5932 or (1714) M. 12345. At some places the pagination is inaccurate.

[47] The notes at the end of Tait's *Index* supply much valuable bibliographical information about the older Scottish reports and reporters.

[48] Occasionally known as Shaw and Dunlop's reports and cited S. & D.

[49] There are two editions of the first five volumes of Shaw which do not coincide in pagination.

[50] The earlier volumes are sometimes known as Dunlop, Bell and Murray's reports, and cited as D.B. & M.

[51] Distinguish this reference from Morison's *Dictionary*. These volumes are sometimes cited *e.g.* 3 Macph. 617.

[52] Short notes of cases were also issued, 1925–48, as *Session Notes*. They were frequently, but not always, superseded by fuller reports in *Session Cases*.

[53] Where the date is an essential part of the reference to the volume (*i.e.*, since

House of Lords Cases

The older House of Lords decisions in Scottish appeals are in private reports. These are set out in the following list:

Reporter	Vols.	Period	Citation
David Robertson	1	1707–27	Rob. or Robert.
Thomas S. Paton	6	1726–1821	Pat.[54]
Patrick Shaw	2	1821–26	Sh.App.
James Wilson and Patrick Shaw	7	1825–35	W. & Sh.
Patrick Shaw and Charles H. Maclean	3	1835–38	Sh. & Macl.
Charles H. Maclean and Geo. Robinson	1	1839	Macl. & R.
Geo. Robinson	2	1840–41	Rob. or Robin.
Sydney S. Bell	7	1842–50	Bell
John F. Macqueen	4	1851–65	Macq.[55]
James Paterson	2	1851–73	Paters.[56]

From 1850 House of Lords decisions are reported and bound in with the annual volumes of *Sessions Cases* but separately paginated,[57] as follows:

Dunlop	12 vols.	1850–62	*e.g.* (1850) 13 D.(H.L.) 5.[58]
Macpherson	11 vols.	1862–73	*e.g.* (1862) 1 M. (or Macph.) (H.L.) 6.
Rettie	25 vols.	1873–98	*e.g.* (1874) 1 R.(H.L.) 21.
Fraser	8 vols.	1898–1906	*e.g.* (1898) 1 F. (H.L.) 7.
Session Cases (annual)		1907–	*e.g.* 1950 S.C.(H.L.) 17.

Some Scottish appeals are also reported in the English volumes covering the same period, in Law Reports (*Appeal Cases*) and *All England Reports*.[59]

1906), it is *not* in brackets. Where the date is not essential (*i.e.* before 1907), it is put, if at all, in round brackets. Square brackets are *never* used in references to Scottish but only in references to English reports, for which see *infra*.

[54] Craigie and Stewart collaborated with Paton in the first volume and it is sometimes cited as Craigie, Stewart and Paton.

[55] These reports are contemporaneous with reports in 13 D.(H.L.) to 3 M.(H.L.).

[56] This series is a revised reprint of the House of Lords reports in the *Scottish Jurist*. It is also contemporaneous with reports in 13 D.(H.L.) to 11 M.(H.L.).

[57] It follows that since 1874 volumes of Scottish reports contain three sets of reports, each separately paginated (House of Lords, Justiciary and Court of Session). Hence 1958 S.C.(H.L.) 1; 1958 J.C. 1 and 1958 S.C. 1 are all different reports, in different series, but contained in the one volume.

[58] House of Lords decisions are included in Dunlop's reports only from Vol. 13.

[59] Information on which of the older series of English House of Lords cases contain Scottish appeals may be found in Stair Society, *Sources and Literature of Scots Law*, pp. 57–58.

Justiciary (Criminal) Cases

Some early criminal reports have been published independently.[60]
Separate series of criminal reports by private reporters appeared from
1819 to 1916. They are set out in the following list:

Reporter	Vols.	Period	Citation
Patrick Shaw	1	1819–31	Shaw Just. or P. Shaw
David Syme	1	1826–29	Syme
Archibald Swinton	2	1835–41	Swin.
Archibald Broun	2	1842–45	Broun
Patrick Arkley	1	1846–48	Arkley
John Shaw	1	1848–51	J. Shaw
Alex. Forbes Irvine	5	1851–68	Irv.
Charles T. Couper	5	1868–85	Coup.[61]
James C. White	3	1885–93	White[61]
Edwin Adam	7	1893–1916	Adam[61]

From 1874 Justiciary cases have also been published in the annual
volumes of *Session Cases* but paginated separately,[57] as follows:

Rettie	25 vols.	1874–98	*e.g.* (1874) 1 R.(J.) 19.
Fraser	8 vols.	1898–1906	*e.g.* (1898) 1 F.(J.) 24.
Session Cases	11 vols.	1907–16	*e.g.* 1907 S.C.(J.) 17.[62]
Justiciary Cases (annual)		1917–	*e.g.* 1917 J.C. 8.[62]

Since 1917 these Justiciary cases, as well as being bound in with *Session
Cases*, are sometimes found bound separately, five years to a volume. The
citation remains the same.

Collateral Reports and Reprints

At various times other series of reports have been issued and are
frequently of value in reporting other cases and supplying information
on matters omitted from the reports already mentioned. These include
Murray's *Jury Court Reports* (five vols., 1815–30) and McFarlane's
Jury Court Reports (one vol., 1838–39), Shaw's *Teind Court Decisions*
(one vol., 1821–31), Deas and Anderson's reports (five vols., 1829–33),
Fergusson's *Consistorial Cases* (one vol., 1811–17) and Stuart, Milne

---

[60] Collections of earlier criminal cases, more used in legal history than in modern
law, are Pitcairn's *Criminal Trials*, 3 volumes bound in 7, 1488–1624; Arnot's *Celebrated Criminal Trials in Scotland*, 1536–1784; McLaurin's (Lord Dreghorn's) *Arguments and Decisions in Remarkable Cases before the High Court of Justiciary*, 1670–
1773; Scott-Moncrieff's *Justiciary Court Records*, 1661–78 (S.H.S., 2 vols.); *Justiciary
Cases*, 1624–50 (ed. Gillon and Irvine Smith, Stair Socy. 3 vols.) and *Argyll Justiciary
Records*, 1664–1705 (ed. Cameron, Stair Socy.).

[61] From 1874 reports of some of the same cases are also to be found in Rettie
(Justiciary), Fraser (Justiciary) and Session Cases (Justiciary) reports.

[62] The change in the abbreviated citation after 1916 should be noted.

and Peddie's *Reports* (two vols., 1851–53). More important are the *Scottish Jurist* (forty-five vols. and five parts, 1829–73, cited S.J. or Sc.Jur.), the *Scottish Law Reporter* (sixty-one vols., 1866–1924, cited S.L.R.),[63] and the *Scots Law Times*, since 1893. This last is cited from 1893 to 1908 by volume, *e.g.* (1900) 7 S.L.T., and thereafter by the year only.[64] The last three include House of Lords, Justiciary and Court of Session cases, while the S.L.T. now has also separately paginated sections of reports of Sheriff Court cases, Lyon Court cases, Land Court cases and notes of recent decisions.[65] Some Scottish appeals to the House of Lords are also reported in current English series of reports.

The *Scots Revised Reports* includes in forty-five volumes a reprint of the principal decisions down to 1873, as follows: Morison's *Dictionary*, two vols.; *Faculty Collection*, 1807–25, two vols.; House of Lords Appeals, ten vols.; Shaw, six vols.; Dunlop, thirteen vols.; Macpherson eleven vols.; cases reported only in the *Scottish Jurist*, vols. 1–37 (1829–65), one vol.

Selected sheriff court cases are found in Guthrie's *Select Cases in the Sheriff Courts*,[66] sheriff court reports printed in the *Scottish Law Review*,[67] and sheriff court cases in the *Scots Law Times*.[68]

Selected decisions of Lyon Court have been printed in the *Scots Law Times* since 1959.[69]

Decisions of the Scottish Land Court were published as a Supplement to the *Scottish Law Review*,[70] and now appear in the Land Court portion of the *Scots Law Times*.

Decisions of Scottish courts of special jurisdiction and administrative tribunals are only sometimes reported: some may be found in the ordinary series, some in the Administrative Law Reports published in the *British Journal of Administrative Law* (now *Public Law*) and others in series published by the Government. Reports of cases before Industrial Tribunals are reported in *Industrial Tribunals Reports*, cited (volume) I.T.R. (page), and in *Knight's Industrial Reports*, cited K.I.R.

English Reports

The practice of noting cases began early in England [71] and from the

---

[63] Distinguish references to the *S.L. Reporter* from those to the *S.L. Review*, which contains the Sheriff Court reports (1885 to 1963).

[64] From 1909 to 1916 there are two volumes in each year, cited, *e.g.* 1912, 1 S.L.T.— and 1912, 2 S.L.T.—.

[65] These notes are frequently but not always superseded by a full report issued in a later part.

[66] Two vols., 1861–78 and 1879–85.

[67] 1885 to 1963; cited, *e.g.* (1954) 70 Sh.Ct.Rep.—.

[68] Latterly these are separately paginated and cited, *e.g.* 1955 S.L.T.(Sh.Ct.)—.

[69] Cited, *e.g.* 1965 S.L.T.(Lyon Ct.).—.

[70] 1913 to 1963: cited, *e.g.* (1951) 40 L.C.— or 40 S.L.C.R.—; contin ued since 1964 by S.L.T.(Land Ct.) Reports.

[71] On the older English reports and reporters, see Holdsworth, *Sources and Literature of English Law*, 74–104, and " Law Reporting in the Nineteenth and Tw entieth

later twelfth century to 1536 there is a series of Year Books, notes made in law-French of points of procedure and pleading, probably for the writer's own information, but later copied and printed. Reports proper begin in the sixteenth century. Down to 1865 reporting was in the hands of private reporters and the reports vary greatly in value [72]; they were usually printed some time afterwards, sometimes from inaccurate or even stolen notes. Round about 1800 the practice developed of judges revising copies of their judgments and even supplying copies to the reporters, and one reporter in each court tended to be favoured as the " authorised " reporter, though this was never official, and the practice of revising judgments was extended to other series also. The various series of private reports are usually cited by initials or abbreviations of the reporters' names, though in some instances other abbreviations, sometimes confusing, are used. [73] Three reprints of the older reports have to be noticed: *The Revised Reports* (1785–1865) in 149 volumes (plus Table of Cases (one vol.) and *Index-Digest* (two vols.)), which omits some obsolete cases, cited *e.g.* 110 R.R. 345, the *English Reports* (1220–1865) in 178 volumes, which is a literal reprint with a few annotations, [74] cited, *e.g.* 137 E.R. 234, and the *All England Reports Reprint* (1558–1935), which reprints only selected cases, and is cited, *e.g.* [1775–1802] All E.R. Rep. 266. All are generally reliable and very useful.

In 1866 the Incorporated Council of Law Reporting began to publish the *Law Reports*, and these quickly superseded all the old private reporters though not the series of reports issued by various legal journals. The *Law Reports* have no exclusive privilege of citation but are usually pre-

Centuries," in *Essays in Law and History*, 284; Wallace, *The Reporters*; Winfield, *Chief Sources of English Legal History*, 145–199; Bolland, *The Year-Books*; Pollock, *First Book of Jurisprudence*, Chap. 5; Veeder, " The English Reports," in (1901) 15 Harv.L.R. 1, 109, reprinted in part in *Select Essays in Anglo-American Legal History*, II, 123; Daniel, *History and Origins of the Law Reports*. On reporting, see also Moran's *Heralds of the Law*; Goodhart, " Reporting the Law " (1939) 55 L.Q.R. 29; O'Sullivan, " Law Reporting " (1940) 4 M.L.R. 104.

[72] This has given rise to many stories about reports and reporters, some of which can be read in Williams' *Learning the Law* and in Allen's *Law in the Making*.

[73] Lists of these abbreviations can be found in Sweet and Maxwell's *Where to Look for your Law*, in Sweet and Maxwell's *Guide to Law Reports and Statutes* and prefaced to Halsbury's *Laws of England*, Vol. I, volume I of the *English and Empire Digest*, or to Green's *Encyclopaedia of Scots Law*, Vol. I. The date is not an essential of the reference to a pre-1865 report, but if inserted it is put in round brackets, *e.g.* (1842) 10 M. & W. 546.

[74] A chart supplied with the set in a slim volume to itself shows in which volume is to be found any particular volume of the old reports. The spine of each volume of the E.R. lists which of the older volumes are reprinted within. This chart is not perfect and some of the old reports are known under variant names; this can be found in *Where to Look for your Law*. Volumes 177–178 contain a complete index of cases under the names of the parties. Lists in *Where to Look for your Law* and the *Guide to Law Reports and Statutes* indicate in which volumes of Revised Reports and/or English Reports private reports are reprinted. Another table in the *Guide* shows what volumes of what series relate to particular calendar years from 1810 onwards.

ferred for purposes of citation and references.[75] They have been issued in three series, 1866–75, 1876–90, 1891 to date.[76]

Other Series

Other series of reports now discontinued are the *Law Times Reports* (New Series, 177 volumes, 1859–1947, cited, *e.g.* (1934) 150 L.T. —), the *Law Journal Reports* (127 volumes, 1822–1949, cited, *e.g.* (1930) 99 L.J. —),[77] both now incorporated in the *All England Law Reports, The Times Law Reports* (71 volumes, 1884–1952, cited, *e.g.* (1910) 26 T.L.R. —),[78] and *Commercial Cases* (46 volumes, 1895–1941, cited, *e.g.* (1941) 46 Com.Cas. —).

Other series now current are the *All England Law Reports* (since 1936,[79] cited, *e.g.* [1950] 2 All E.R. —) and the *Weekly Law Reports* (since 1953, cited, *e.g.* [1953] 1 W.L.R. —), which replaced the earlier *Weekly Notes* (1865–1952, cited, *e.g.* [1945] W.N. —)[80] while brief reports and notes are to be found in many of the legal journals and periodicals.

[75] See *Fairman* v. *Perpetual Investment Building Socy.* [1923] A.C. 74; Practice Note [1931] W.N. 121.

[76] The series comprise the following; First Series: Admiralty and Ecclesiastical (4 vols.); Crown Cases Reserved (2 vols.); Common Pleas (10 vols.); Chancery Appeals (10 vols.); English and Irish Appeals [House of Lords] (7 vols.); Equity (20 vols.); Exchequer (10 vols.); Privy Council Appeals (6 vols.); Probate and Divorce (3 vols.); Queen's Bench (10 vols.); Scotch and Divorce Appeals (2 vols.). These are cited, *e.g.* (1875) L.R. 7 H.L.—; (1875) L.R. 10 Q.B.—.

Second Series: Appeal Cases (15 vols.); Chancery Division (45 vols.); Common Pleas Division (5 vols.); Exchequer Division (5 vols.); Probate Division (15 vols.); Queen's Bench Division (25 vols.). These are cited, *e.g.* (1890) 15 App.Cas.—; (1890) 25 Q.B.D.—.

Third Series: Appeal Cases; Chancery Division; Queen's (Kings, 1901–1952) Bench; Probate Division (1891–1971) and Family Division (1972–). These are cited, *e.g.* [1959] A.C.—. Sometimes there is more than one volume for each court in one year, *e.g.* [1958] 2 Q.B.—.

In 1958 a series of reports of the Restrictive Practices Court commenced (cited (1959) L.R. 1 R.P.—) and there was a series for the National Industrial Relations Court, 1971–74.

For correct abbreviations, see *Where to Look for your Law* and *Guide to Law Reports and Statutes.*

Note that L.R. precedes the volume number in the First Series only, and that D. after Q.B., Ch., C.P., Ex. and P. is found only in the Second Series.

Prior to 1891 the date is not an essential of the reference to the Law Reports and goes in round brackets. After 1890 the year is essential and is put in square brackets.

[77] From 1947 the volumes were cited, *e.g.* [1949] L.J.R.—. The Old Series covered 1822–31 in 9 volumes, the New Series 1831–1949 in 118 volumes. Many volumes of *Law Journal* are separately paginated within the volume for the different courts, *e.g.* for L.J.C.P. and L.J.Ch.

[78] The 1950 volume was cited 66 T.L.R. Part 1 and Part 2, and the 1951 and 1952 volumes, *e.g.* [1951] 1 T.L.R. and [1951] 2 T.L.R.

[79] Reports of selected cases 1558–1935 have now been published by All E.R. in a series called *All E.R. Reprints*, cited, *e.g.* [1904–7] All E.R.Rep. 438. The selection is based on the frequency of citation of the cases in later judgments and the cases are reprinted from the private reports down to 1843 and from the *Law Times* thereafter.

[80] On the authority of *Weekly Notes*, see *Re Loveridge* [1902] 2 Ch. 859; *Re Smith's Settlement* [1903] 1 Ch. 373; *Re Allsop* [1967] 2 All E.R. 1056, 1060.

Series of reports concentrating on particular topics include *Lloyd's Law Reports* (1919–   ), *Reports of Patent, Design, Trade Mark and Other Cases* (1884–   ), *Railway and Canal Traffic Cases* (1855–1934) continued by *Traffic Cases* (1935–   ), *Criminal Appeal Reports* (1908–   ), *Tax Cases* (1875–   ), *Annotated Tax Cases* (1922–   ), *Fleet Street Patent Law Reports* (1963–   ) and *Knight's Industrial Reports* (1967–   ).

Special series of reports and Irish and Commonwealth Series may be traced through *Where to Look for your Law* and *Guide to Law Reports and Statutes.*

Digests of Case-Law

The finding of case-law is greatly facilitated by the Digests of case-law which arrange the reported cases under main and subordinate subject-headings on an analytical basis, the main headings being arranged in alphabetical order. Each entry gives a brief account of the case and the legal propositions which can be inferred from it but the entries are so brief that they are not a substitute for the full reports. It is usually necessary to follow up a point by searching the relevant headings in the main part of the Digest and then in each supplementary volume down to the latest published. There is considerable variation in the headings and sub-headings used [81] so that a search must frequently be made under several different headings, but experience greatly increases familiarity with the system used.

The older Scottish cases are mostly to be found, grouped under alphabetical subject-headings, in Kames's *Folio Dictionary*, 1540–1728 (two volumes) Woodhouselee's continuation thereof to 1796 (two volumes) and McGrugar's Supplement thereto (one volume), Morison's *Dictionary of Decisions*, 1540–1808 (twenty-two volumes), Morison's *Synopsis* of the cases in the *Dictionary* (two volumes), Brown's *Supplement* to Morison's Dictionary, 1628–1794 (five volumes), Brown's *Synopsis* of the cases in Morison's *Dictionary*, Brown's *Supplement* thereto, the reports of Elchies, Hailes, Bell and the *Faculty Decisions* down to 1827 (four volumes), Halkerton's *Compendium*, digesting the cases in the *Faculty Decisions* 1752–1817 (one volume), and Bell's *Dictionary of Decisions*, 1808–33 (two volumes). Shaw's *Digest of Cases* (three volumes) [82] contains House of Lords decisions from 1726 to 1868 and decisions of the Scottish superior courts from 1800 to 1868. This is carried on by the *Faculty Digest* from

---

[81] Thus the *Faculty Digest* includes all criminal cases under the heading Justiciary; *Shaw's Digest* puts such cases under the heading Crime. There are, of course, many cross-references to assist the searcher, but much ingenuity and some luck is sometimes requisite for the search. Of course, there may not be any cases closely in point: the *Digest* only contains what has been reported in the main series of reports.

[82] This consolidates earlier Digests covering parts of the period.

1868.[83] The *Scots Digest* contains House of Lords cases from 1707–1947 and cases from the Scottish superior courts from 1800–1947.[84] The *Sheriff Court Digest* covers 1885–1944 in five volumes dealing with consecutive periods, and there is a *Digest of Sheriff Court Cases reported in S.L.T.*, 1893–1943.

English cases are digested in Mews' *Digest of English Case-law* (which includes a selection of Scottish cases),[85] in the *English and Empire Digest* which contains English cases from early times with Scottish and Commonwealth decisions in footnotes on each page,[86] and in the *Law Reports Digest of Cases*, 1865–1950.[87]

Modern Digests also contain such additional reference tools as an index of statutes, showing in what cases statutory provisions have been interpreted, an index of cases commented on in later cases, an index of words and phrases discussed in particular cases, and an index of parties' names whereby a case known by name can be traced to its classified subject. Very recent cases are found in *Current Law*.[88]

Institutional Writings

The standard editions in modern use are:

Craig's *Jus Feudale and the Books of the Feus*, translated by J. A. (Lord President) Clyde, 2 vols., 1934; Stair's *Institutions*, new (fifth) edition, with notes by Professor J. S. More,[89] 2 vols., 1832 [90]; Mackenzie's *Institutions*, eighth edition, 1758 and in his *Collected Works* (2 vols., 1716–22); Bankton's *Institute*, only edition, 3 vols., 1751–53 [91]; Erskine's *Institute*, new (eighth) edition, with notes by J. Badenach Nicolson,[92] 2 vols., 1871 [90]; Kames's *Principles of Equity*, fifth edition 1825; Bell's *Commentaries*, seventh edition, by John (later Lord) McLaren, 2 vols.,

[83] 1868–1922, 6 vols., supplementary volumes 1922–30, 1930–40, 1940–50, 1951–60, and supplementary parts thereafter. Superseded by *Scottish Current Law* thereafter.

[84] 1800–73, 4 vols.; 1873–1904, 2 vols.; supplementary volumes 1904–14, 1914–23, 1923–30, 1930–37, 1937–44, and supplementary parts to 1947. Superseded by *Scottish Current Law* thereafter.

[85] Second ed., 24 volumes (to end of 1924) and annual supplementary volumes.

[86] 48 volumes, with supplements, replaced by the " Blue-Band " edition in 56 volumes, which incorporates material in earlier supplements. This is being replaced by the " Green-Band " edition. There are also Continuation Volumes and Annual Cumulative Supplements.

[87] Twelve volumes, covering 1866–1950, continued by *Index to Law Reports*, 1951–60 and 1961–70.

[88] On this, see further, p. 436, *infra*.

[89] In *Fortington* v. *Kinnaird*, 1942 S.C. 239, 265. Lord Justice-Clerk Cooper attached importance to the views expressed in More's Notes and Lord Mackay (at p. 276) said that the Notes " carries almost the authority of a separate Institution."

[90] These books are cited by Book, title and section, *e.g.* Stair, I, 1, 16.

[91] Bankton is also cited by Volume, page and section.

[92] In *Fortington*, *supra*, Lord Cooper attached importance also to Lord Ivory's Notes to Erskine, which are printed in Lord Ivory's (sixth) edition of Erskine, and reprinted in Badenach Nicolson's edition.

1870 [93]; and Bell's *Principles*, tenth edition by Sheriff William Guthrie, 1899.[94]

On criminal law the standard editions are: Mackenzie's *Laws and Customs*, second edition, 1699, and in his collected *Works* (2 vols., 1716–22); Hume's *Commentaries*,[95] fourth edition with supplement by B. R. Bell, 2 vols., 1844 [93]; and Alison's *Principles* and *Practice*, only editions, 1832 and 1833.[93]

II. Secondary Sources—Legal Literature

These sources comprise all commentaries, books and other writings, about the law or any topic thereof, other than institutional writings, which may give a court, or an inquirer, valuable guidance on where to find the authoritative primary sources of a principle of law relevant to the problem before him, on the interrelation of several relevant primary sources, such as several statutes and cases, and on the interpretations which have hitherto been placed by the courts on the primary authorities. Legal literature is also valuable as giving a coherent account of all the law on a topic, with the legislation, case-law, views of the institutional writers, and later comment and criticism brought together into a related whole and presented, so far as possible, as a reasoned and systematic body of related principles and rules.

The writing of legal literature, of commentaries and treatises on the law and various branches of it, has from the time of Gaius been an important function of the academic jurists. The literary sources are the essential means of legal study, of research for the answer to some problem, and of obtaining a general conspectus of the law on any topic.

Some books are written expressly for students, or for different groups of students, others for legal practitioners as reference books and guides through the tangle of statutes and cases. A knowledge of what books there are on each subject and what they cover, their relative sizes and values, their standing, is a necessary part of a lawyer's knowledge, and with these books his investigation of any problem starts.[96]

The following list of books includes those which are reliable guides on their various subjects. The classification is systematic, corresponding to the systematic division of the Law of Scotland previously set out.[97] On every topic the distinction between Scottish and English books must be kept in mind, since the latter do not usually cite statutes applicable to Scotland or Scottish cases, ignore specialities of Scottish procedure, and are

---

[93] These books are cited by volume and page.

[94] This book is cited by the section number.

[95] In *H.M. Advocate* v. *Grant* (1848) J. Shaw, 17, 92, Lord Justice-Clerk Hope spoke of Hume as of great authority; see also Paton's Biography of Baron Hume (*Lectures* (Stair Society) VI) at 350.

[96] See further, Chap. 12, *infra*.

[97] Chap. 9, *supra*.

all, to a greater or less degree, depending on whether the topic is one on which Scots and English law diverge much or little, unreliable guides in Scottish practice. But many English books have to be considered, if only *faute de mieux*, in default of any, or any modern, Scottish book.[98]

A—EUROPEAN LAW

General
Campbell: *Common Market Law*, 2 vols. and supps.
Encyclopaedia of European Community Law.
Kapteyn and Verloren van Themaat: *Introduction to the Law of the European Communities.*
Lasok and Bridge: *Introduction to the Law and Institutions of the European Communities.*
Lipstein: *Law of the E.E.C.*
Parry and Hardy: *E.E.C. Law.*
Valentine: *Court of Justice of the European Communities*, 2 vols.
Wall: *Court of Justice of the European Communities.*

Periodicals
Common Market Law Review, 1963– .
Journal of Common Market Studies, 1962– .

B—SCOTS LAW

GENERAL BOOKS

Legal Bibliographies and Reference Books
Institute of Advanced Legal Studies: *Bibliographical Guide to U.K. Law.*
                                     Manual of Legal Citations, Part I.
Stair Society: *Sources and Literature of Scots Law.*
Sweet & Maxwell, Ltd.: *Guide to Law Reports and Statutes*, 4th ed., 1962.
                       Where to Look for Your Law, 14th ed., 1962.
                       Legal Bibliography of the British Commonwealth—
                               Vol. 1—*English Law to 1800.*
                               Vol. 2—*English Law 1800–1954.*
                               Vol. 5—*Scots Law and Roman Law, to 1955.*
Price and Bitner: *Effective Legal Research* (U.S.A.).

Dictionaries
      Bell: *Dictionary and Digest of the Law of Scotland.*
E   Wharton: *Law Lexicon.*
E   Jowitt: *Dictionary of English Law.*

---

[98] The list does not include books written wholly or primarily for students. Books written from the English standpoint but useful, if care be taken, in Scotland are listed with " E " prefixed to the title. There are very many other English books some of which may be useful on particular points in Scottish practice but which are not listed because they have no general utility in Scotland. This list does not attempt to deal with related social sciences, background legal subjects, international or supranational law, nor with books which are obsolete or of mainly historical interest, nor with the considerable literature of biography, legal essays, collected papers, studies in honour of distinguished jurists, famous trials, etc. These must be looked for in the legal bibliographies.

Maxims
　　Trayner: *Latin Maxims and Phrases.*
E　Broom: *Legal Maxims.*

Words and Phrases
　　Gibb and Dalrymple: *Scottish Judicial Dictionary.*
E　Stroud: *Judicial Dictionary of Words and Phrases*, 3rd ed., 4 vols. and 5 Supp.
E　Saunders: *Words and Phrases Legally Defined*, 5 vols. and Supp.

Interpretation
E　Beal: *Cardinal Rules of Legal Interpretation.*
E　Craies: *Statute Law.*
E　Maxwell: *Interpretation of Statutes.*
E　Odgers: *Construction of Deeds and Statutes.*

Encyclopaedias and General Textbooks
　　Green's *Encyclopaedia of the Laws of Scotland*, 16 vols. and suppls.
E　Halsbury's *Laws of England*, 3rd ed., 43 vols. and annual cumulative supplement, 4th ed. in progress.
　　Erskine: *Principles of the Law of Scotland*, 21st ed., 1911.
　　Gloag and Henderson: *Introduction to the Law of Scotland*, 7th ed., 1968.
　　Smith: *Short Commentary on Scots Law*, 1962.
　　Gow: *Mercantile and Industrial Law of Scotland*, 1964.
　　Walker: *Principles of Scottish Private Law*, 2nd ed., 1975.

Older Books, not Institutional, but still Valuable.[99]
Balfour: *Practicks or System of the More Ancient Law of Scotland*, 1754 and (Stair Society) 1962–63.
Dallas, George, of St. Martins: *Stiles of Writs*, 1697, 1774.
Dirleton (Sir J. Nisbet, Lord): *Doubts and Questions in the Law*, 1698.
Fergusson, James: *Consistorial Law of Scotland*, 1829.
Forbes, Prof. Wm.: *Institutes of the Law of Scotland*, 2 vols., 1722–30.
Hermand, George Fergusson, Lord: *Consistorial Decisions* (ed. Walton, Stair Society), 1940.[1]
Hope, Sir Thomas: *Minor Practicks*, 1726 and 1734.
　　　　　　　　　Major Practicks (ed. Lord Clyde, Stair Society), 1937–38.
Hume, Prof. (later Baron), David: *Lectures on the Law of Scotland* (ed. Paton, Stair Society) 6 vols., 1939–58.[2]
Kames (Henry Home, Lord)[3]: *Elucidations respecting the common and statute law of Scotland*, 1777.
　　　　　　　　　Historical Law Tracts, 1758.
　　　　　　　　　Principles of Equity, 1760.
　　　　　　　　　Statute Law of Scotland Abridged, 1757.
Mackenzie, Sir George: writings contained in his *Works*, 2 vols., 1716–22.
Menzies, A.: *Lectures on Conveyancing*, 1900.
Montgomery Bell, A.: *Lectures on Conveyancing*, 2 vols., 1882.
More, Prof. J. S.: *Lectures on the Law of Scotland*, ed. McLaren, 2 vols. 1864.

---

[99] The dates given are those of first publication and, where applicable, of a modern edition. In some cases there were several early editions, for which see the bibliographies.

[1] On the authority of this, see *Fortington* v. *Kinnaird*, 1942 S.C. 239, 277.

[2] On the authority of Hume's *Lectures*, see *Fortington* v. *Kinnaird*, 1942 S.C. 239, 253, 265.

[3] Kames also published various volumes of essays and decisions.

Regiam Majestatem, ed. Skene, 1597, 1609, 1774 and (ed. Cooper, Stair Society) 1947.

Skene, Sir John: *De Verborum Significatione*, 1597.[4]

Spotiswoode, Sir Robert: *Practicks of the Law of Scotland*, 1706.

Stuart, Gilbert: *Observations concerning the Public Law of Scotland*, 1779.

Stuart, Sir James, of Goodtrees: *Answers to Dirleton's Doubts and Questions in the Law of Scotland*, 1715.

Wallace, George: *System of the Principles of the Law of Scotland*, Vol. I, 1760.[5]

Wood, J. P.: *Lectures on Conveyancing*, 1903.

PUBLIC LAW

CONSTITUTIONAL LAW

General

Mitchell: *Constitutional Law.*

E   Dicey: *Introduction to the Study of the Law of the Constitution.*

E   Jennings: *The Law and the Constitution.*

E   Hood Phillips: *Constitutional and Administrative Law.*

E   Wade and Phillips: *Constitutional Law.*

E   de Smith: *Constitutional and Administrative Law.*

E   Campion: *British Government since 1918.*

E   Halsbury's *Laws of England*, Vol. 8.

The Crown

E   Anson: *Law and Custom of the Constitution*, Vol. 2.

The Executive

E   Jennings: *Cabinet Government.*

E   Keith: *The British Cabinet System.*

E   Mackintosh: *The British Cabinet.*

E   Wheare: *Government by Committee.*

The Legislature

E   Jennings: *Parliament.*

E   *Party Politics*, 3 vols.

E   Anson: *Law and Custom of the Constitution*, Vol. 1.

E   Erskine May: *Parliamentary Practice.*

E   Schofield: *Parliamentary Elections.*

The Judicial System

E   Jackson: *The Machinery of Justice in England.*

E   Walker and Walker: *The English Legal System.*

The Civil Service

E   Mackenzie and Grove: *Central Administration in Britain.*

---

[4] Reprinted in Skene's *Lawes and Acts of Parliament*, 1597, and in R. Bell's *Dictionary of the Law of Scotland*.

[5] No more ever published. On the authority of this book, see *Kerr* v. *Martin* (1840) 2 D. 752, 776, 792.

The Armed Forces
    HMSO: *Queen's Regulations for the Royal Navy.*
          Manual of Military Law.
          Queen's Regulations for the Army.
          Manual of Air Force Law.
          Queen's Regulations for the RAF.

Established Churches
    Mair: *Digest of Church Laws.*
    Cox: *Practice and Procedure in the Church of Scotland.*
    Black: *Parochial Ecclesiastical Law of Scotland.*
    Buchanan: *Law of Scotland on Teinds or Tithes.*
    Connell: *Law of Scotland respecting Parishes.*
          Law of Scotland regarding Tithes and Stipends, 3 vols.
    Elliot: *Teinds or Tithes, and Procedure in the Court of Teinds.*

Public Revenue and Taxation
E   Wheatcroft (ed.): *British Tax Encyclopaedia,* 8 vols.
E   Simon: *Simon's Taxes,* 9 vols.
E   Sophian: *Taxation of Capital Gains.*
E   Beattie: *Corporation Tax.*
E   Dymond: *Death Duties.*
E   Green: *Death Duties.*
E   Monroe: *Law of Stamp Duties.*

Nationality and Citizenship
E   Jones: *British Natiionality Law and Practice.*
E   Parry: *Nationality and Citizenship Laws of the Commonwealth.*

Rights and Liberties of Citizens
    See books on Constitutional Law—General.

Commonwealth, colonial and foreign relations
E   *Annual Survey of Commonwealth Law,* 1965—.
E   Halsbury's *Laws of England,* Vol. 6.
E   Jennings: *Constitutional Laws of the Commonwealth.*
E   Wheare: *The Statute of Westminster and Dominion Status.*
E   Roberts-Wray: *Commonwealth and Colonial Law.*
E   McNair: *Law of Treaties.*

ADMINISTRATIVE LAW

General
E   Griffith and Street: *Principles of Administrative Law.*
E   Wade: *Administrative Law.*
E   Garner: *Administrative Law.*

Central Departments
E   Mackenzie and Grove: *Central Administration in Britain.*
E   Chester: *Organisation of British Central Government.*
E   Griffith: *Central departments and local authorities.*
    Milne: *The Scottish Office.*
    HMSO: *Handbook on Scottish Administration.*

Local Authorities
    McLarty: *Source-Book and History of Administrative Law in Scotland.*
    Miller: *Outline of Administrative and Local Government Law in Scotland.*
    HMSO: *Local Government in Scotland.*
    Purves: *Scottish Licensing Laws.*
    Armour: *Law of Valuation in Scotland.*
    Guest: *Law of Valuation and Rating in Scotland.*
    Mill: *The Scottish Police.*
E   Chester: *Central and Local Government: Financial and Administrative Relations.*
E   Schofield: *Local Government Elections.*

Public Corporations
E   Robson: *Nationalised Industry and Public Ownership.*

Delegated Legislative Powers
E   Allen: *Law and Orders.*
E   Sieghart: *Government by Decree.*

Delegated Judicial Powers
E   Robson: *Justice and Administrative Law.*
E   Wraith and Hutchesson: *Administrative Tribunals.*

Control of Powers
E   Schwarz: *Law and the Executive in Britain.*
E   Robinson: *Public Authorities and Legal Liability.*
E   Street: *Governmental Liability.*
E   Bickford Smith and Middleton: *The Crown Proceedings Act.*
E   de Smith: *Judicial Review of Administrative Action.*
E   Kersell: *Parliamentary Supervision of Delegated Legislation.*

Social Services
E   Hall: *Social Services of Modern England.*
E   Ormrod and Walker: *The National Health Service.*
E   Speller: *The National Health Service Act* 1946.
E   Steele: *The National Assistance Act* 1948.
E   Potter and Stansfeld: *National Insurance.*
E   Potter and Stansfeld: *National Insurance (Industrial Injuries) Act* 1946.
E   Vester and Cartwright: *Industrial Injuries,* 2 vols.

CRIMINAL LAW AND PROCEDURE

Prosecution
    Gross: *Criminal Investigation.*
    Mill: *The Scottish Police.*

Jurisdiction and Procedure
    Alison: *Practice of the Criminal Law of Scotland.*
    Renton and Brown: *Criminal Procedure according to the Law of Scotland.*
    Trotter: *Summary Criminal Jurisdiction.*
E   Archbold: *Pleading, Evidence and Practice in Criminal Cases.*

Liability
    Hume: *Commentaries on the Law of Scotland respecting Crimes,* 2 vols.

Alison: *Principles of the Criminal Law of Scotland.*
Mackenzie: *Laws and Customs of Scotland in Matters Criminal.*
Burnett: *Treatise on Various Branches of the Criminal Law of Scotland.*
Gordon: *Criminal Law of Scotland.*
E   Smith and Hogan: *Criminal Law.*
E   Williams: *The Criminal Law; The General Part.*
E   Russell on *Crimes*, 2 vols.

Punishment
Walker: *Crime and Punishment in Britain.*
E   McClean and Wood: *Criminal Justice and the Treatment of Offenders.*
E   HMSO: *Prisons and Borstals—England and Wales.*

PRIVATE LAW

GENERAL

Sources and Literature
See Chap. 10, *supra.*

General Principles
See Encyclopaedias and General Textbooks, *supra.*

Lapse of Time
Walker: *Law of Prescription and Limitation in Scotland.*

Personal Bar
Rankine on *Personal Bar and Estoppel.*

INTERNATIONAL PRIVATE LAW

Jurisdiction
Gibb: *International Law of Jurisdiction.*
Duncan and Dykes: *Principles of Civil Jurisdiction as applied in Scotland.*
Maclaren: *Court of Session Practice.*
Anton: *Private International Law.*

Concepts, Classification, Choice of Law and Foreign Judgments
Anton: *Private International Law.*
E   Graveson: *The Conflict of Laws.*
E   Morris: *Conflict of Laws.*
E   Cheshire: *Private International Law.*
E   Dicey and Morris: *Conflict of Laws.*

LAW OF PERSONS

Natural Persons
Fergusson: *Consistorial Law.*
Lothian: *Consistorial Actions.*
Fraser: *Treatise on Husband and Wife*, 2 vols.
Walton: *Handbook of Husband and Wife.*
Clive and Wilson: *Husband and Wife.*
Fraser: *Treatise on the Law of Scotland relative to Parent and Child and Guardian and Ward.*
E   Bromley: *Family Law.*

Unincorporated Associations
E Lloyd: *Law relating to Unincorporated Associations.*
E Keeling: *Trusts and Foundations.*
   Bennett Miller: *Partnership.*
E Pollock: *Digest of the Law of Partnership.*
E Lindley: *Treatise on the Law of Partnership.*
E Vester and Gardner: *Trade Union Law and Practice.*
E Citrine: *Trade Union Law.*
E Grunfeld: *Modern Trade Union Law.*
E Fuller: *Law of Friendly Societies and Industrial and Provident Societies.*
E Daly: *Club Law and Unregistered Friendly Societies.*

Juristic Persons or Corporations
E Arnold: *Municipal Corporations.*
   Wilton: *Company Law and Practice in Scotland.*
   Palmer's *Company Law*, 21st ed.
E Gower: *Principles of Modern Company Law.*
E Pennington: *Principles of Company Law.*
E Gore-Brown: *Handbook on Joint-Stock Companies.*
E Buckley on *The Companies Acts.*
E Halsbury's *Laws of England*, Vol. 7.
E Wurtzburg and Mills: *Law relating to Building Societies.*
E Street: *Ultra Vires.*

LAW OF OBLIGATIONS

Law of Contract generally
   Gloag: *Law of Contract.*
   Walker: *Law of Civil Remedies in Scotland.*
E Anson: *Principles of the English Law of Contracts.*
E Cheshire and Fifoot: *Law of Contract.*
E Treitel: *Law of Contract.*
E Chitty: *Contracts*, 2 vols.
E Macgregor: *Law of Damages.*

Specific Contracts
Agency
E Fridman: *Law of Agency.*
E Powell: *Law of Agency.*
E Bowstead: *Digest of the Law of Agency.*

Banking Contracts
   Wallace and McNeil: *Banking Law.*
E Paget: *Law of Banking.*
E Hart: *Law of Banking.*
E Gutteridge: *Law of Bankers' Commercial Credits.*
E Megrah: *Bankers' Commercial Credits.*
E Davis: *Law relating to Commercial Letters of Credit.*
E Sheldon and Drover: *Practice and Law of Banking.*

Bills of Exchange
   Hamilton: *Bills of Exchange Act 1882.*
E Chalmers: *Bills of Exchange.*
E Byles: *Bills of Exchange.*

Building and Engineering Contracts
E   Hudson on *Building Contracts.*
E   Emden and Watson on *Building Contracts and Practice*

Carriage
  Deas: *Railways.*
E   Macnamara: *Law of Carriers by Land.*
E   Leslie: *Law of Transport by Railway.*
E   Bonner: *British Transport Law.*
E   Chorley and Giles: *Shipping Law.*
E   Temperley: *Merchant Shipping Acts.*
E   Maclachlan: *Treatise on Merchant Shipping.*
E   Carver: *Carriage of Goods by Sea.*
E   Scrutton: *Contract of Affreightment as expressed n charter-parties and bills of lading.*
E   Kennedy: *C.I.F. Contracts.*
E   Sassoon: *C.I.F. and F.O.B. Contracts.*
E   Tiberg: *Law of Demurrage.*
E   Kennedy: *Treatise on the Law of Civil Salvage.*
E   Norris: *Law of Salvage.*
E   Chalmers: *Marine Insurance Act.*
E   Stevens & Sons: *British Shipping Laws*, 14 vols.
E   Arnould: *Law of Marine Insurance and Average*, 2 Vols.
E   Lowndes and Rudolf: *Law of General Average.*
E   Marsden: *Law of Collisions at Sea.*
E   McNair: *Law of the Air.*
E   Shawcross and Beaumont on *Air Law.*
E   Cheng: *Law of International Air Transport.*

Caution and Guarantees
  Gloag and Irvine on *Rights in Security and Cautionary Obligations.*

Custody and Deposit
E   Paton: *Bailment in the Common Law.*
E   Beven: *Negligence*, Vol. 2.

Employment
  Fraser: *Law of Master and Servant.*
  Umpherston: *Law of Master and Servant.*
  Miller: *Industrial Law in Scotland.*
E   Cooper and Wood: *Outlines of Industrial Law.*
E   Batt: *Law of Master and Servant.*
E   Rideout: *Principles of Labour Law.*
E   Munkman: *Employer's Liability.*
E   Samuels: *Factory Law.*
E   Redgrave: *Factories and Truck Acts.*
    Offices and Shops.
E   Bowen: *The Mines and Quarries Acts.*
E   Temperley: *The Merchant Shipping Acts.*
E   Haslam: *Law relating to Trade Combinations.*
E   Clegg: *Industrial Relations in Great Britain.*
  HMSO: *Industrial Relations Handbook.*

Hiring
E   Paton: *Bailment in the Common Law.*
E   Beven: *Negligence*, Vol. 2.

Hire-Purchase
E   Guest on *Consumer Credit.*

Insurance
E   Preston and Colinvaux: *Insurance.*
E   Ivamy: *General Principles of Insurance Law.*
        Fire and Motor Insurance.
        Personal Accident, Life and Other Insurance.
E   Macgillivray on *Insurance Law*, 2 vols.
E   Houseman: *Law of Life Insurance.*
E   Shawcross on *The Law of Motor Insurance.*
E   Arnould on *Marine Insurance*, 2 vols.

Lease
        See under PROPERTY—Corporeal Heritable.

Loan
E   Paton: *Bailment in the Common Law.*
E   Beven: *Negligence*, Vol. 2.

Moneylender's Contracts
E   Stone and Meston: *Law relating to Moneylenders.*

Partnership
        See under PERSONS—Unincorporated Associations.

Pledge and Pawn
E   Paton: *Bailment in the Common Law.*
E   Beven: *Negligence*, Vol. 2.

Sale of Incorporeal Rights
        See books on PROPERTY—Incorporeal Moveable Property.

Sale of Land
        See books on PROPERTY—Conveyancing.

Sale of Moveables
        Brown (M. P.): *Treatise on the Law of Sale.*
        Brown (R.): *Sale of Goods Act.*
E   Chalmers: *Sale of Goods Act.*
E   Schmitthoff: *Sale of Goods.*
E   Benjamin: *Sale of Goods.*
E   Wilberforce, Campbell and Elles: *Restrictive Trade Practices and Monopolies.*

Securities
        Gloag and Irvine: *Rights in Security and Cautionary Obligations.*

Law of Quasi-Contract or Restitution
        Gloag on *Contract*, Chap. 18.
E   Goff and Jones: *Restitution.*

Law of Delict or Reparation Generally
    Walker: *Law of Delict in Scotland*, Vol. I.
        Law of Civil Remedies in Scotland.
E   Fleming: *Law of Torts.*
E   Salmond: *Law of Torts.*
E   Winfield and Jolowicz: *Textbook of the Law of Torts.*
E   Pollock: *Law of Torts.*
E   Street: *Law of Torts.*
E   Clerk and Lindsell: *Law of Torts.*
E   Williams: *Joint Torts and Contributory Negligence.*
E   Macgregor: *Law of Damages.*

Specific Delicts
    Walker: *Law of Delict in Scotland*, Vol. II.
    Borthwick: *Law of Libel and Slander in Scotland.*
    Cooper: *Law of defamation and verbal injury.*
    Broun: *Law of Nuisance in Scotland.*
E   Beven: *Negligence in Law*, 2 vols.
E   Charlesworth: *Law of Negligence.*
E   Gatley: *Libel and slander in a civil action.*
E   Marsden: *Collisions at Sea.*
E   Munkman: *Employer's Liability at Common Law.*

LAW OF PROPERTY

Classification and divisions of property
E   Adkin and Bowen: *Law of Fixtures.*

Corporeal Heritable Property
    Rankine: *Law of Landownership in Scotland.*
    Ferguson: *Law of Water and Water Rights in Scotland.*
        Law of roads, streets and rights of way.
    Stewart: *Laws and rights of fishing in Scotland.*
    Tait: *Game and fishing laws of Scotland.*
    Sandford: *History and Law of Entails.*
    Ross: *Law of Entail in Scotland.*
    Dobie: *Manual of the Law of Liferent and Fee.*
    Gloag and Irvine: *Rights in Security.*
    Hunter: *Landlord and Tenant*, 2 vols.
    Rankine: *Law of Leases in Scotland.*
    Paton and Cameron: *Law of Landlord and Tenant in Scotland.*
    Connell and Johnston: *Agricultural Holdings (Scotland) Acts.*
    Scott: *Law of Smallholdings.*
    Stewart: *Law relating to Mines, Quarries and Minerals in Scotland.*
    Fraser: *Rent and House-Letting Acts in Scotland.*
E   Megarry on *The Rent Acts.*

Incorporeal Heritable Property
    Gloag and Irvine: *Rights in Security.*
    Hewlett: *Jurisdiction in Scottish Peerage Cases.*
    Riddell: *Law and Practice in Scottish Peerages.*
    Innes: *Scots Heraldry.*
    Stevenson: *Heraldry in Scotland*, 2 vols.
    Wallace: *Nature and Descent of Ancient Peerages.*

Corporeal Moveable Property
    Dobie: *Liferent and Fee.*
    Gloag and Irvine: *Rights in Security.*
E   Vaines: *Personal Property.*
E   Paton: *Bailment in the Common Law.*
    also books on sale, hiring, etc.

Incorporeal Moveable Property
    Hamilton: *Bills of Exchange Act 1882.*
    McNeil: *Bills of Exchange, Cheques and Promissory Notes.*
E   Chalmers on *Bills of Exchange.*
E   Byles on *Bills of Exchange.*
E   Copinger and Skone James on the *Law of Copyright.*
E   Kerly: *Law of Trade Marks and Trade Names.*
E   Terrell: *Law of Patents.*
E   Blanco White: *Patents for Inventions.*
E   Russell Clarke: *Copyright in Industrial Designs.*
    For shares, see books on companies.

Succession and Executors
    McLaren: *Law of Wills and Succession,* 2 vols. and Supp. Vol. by Dykes.
    Meston: *The Succession (Scotland) Act 1964.*
    Murray: *Law of Wills in Scotland.*
    Henderson: *Principles of Vesting in the Law of Succession.*
    Macmillan: *Law of Bona Vacantia in Scotland.*
    Currie: *Confirmation of Executors in Scotland.*

Trusts, Trustees and Judicial Factors
    Menzies on *Trustees.*
    Mackenzie Stuart on *Trusts.*
    Wilson: *Trusts, Trustees and Executors.*
    Walker: *Judicial Factors.*

Bankruptcy
    Goudy: *Treatise on the Law of Bankruptcy in Scotland.*
    Wallace: *Law of Bankruptcy in Scotland.*

LAW OF CIVIL REMEDIES
    Walker: *Law of Civil Remedies in Scotland.*

ADJECTIVE LAW

Conveyancing
    Burns: *Handbook of Conveyancing.*
        Conveyancing Practice.
    Montgomery Bell: *Lectures on Conveyancing,* 2 vols.
    Menzies: *Lectures on Conveyancing.*
    Wood: *Lectures on Conveyancing.*
    Craigie: *Scottish Law of Conveyancing—Moveable Rights.*
                                  Heritable Rights.
    Ross: *Lectures on Conveyancing,* 2 vols.

Jurisdiction
>   Gibb: *International Law of Jurisdiction.*
>   Duncan and Dykes: *Principles of Civil Jurisdiction.*

Civil Procedure
>   Parliament House Book.
>   Maclaren: *Court of Session Practice.*
>   Maclaren: *Bill Chamber Practice.*
>   Thomson and Middleton: *Manual of Court of Session Procedure.*
>   Mackay: *Manual of Practice in the Court of Session.*
>   *Court of Session Practice,* 2 vols.
>   Lewis: *Sheriff Court Practice.*
>   Dobie: *Sheriff Court Practice.*

Pleading
>   Lees: *Handbook of pleadings in the sheriff court.*

Evidence
>   Lewis: *Manual of the Law of Evidence in Scotland.*
>   Dickson: *Treatise on the law of Evidence in Scotland.*
>   Walker and Walker: *Law of Evidence in Scotland.*
>   E   Cross: *Evidence.*
>   E   Phipson: *Treatise on the Law of Evidence.*

Diligence
>   Graham Stewart: *Law of Diligence.*

Expenses
>   Maclaren on *Expenses in the Supreme and Sheriff Courts.*

Legal Aid
>   Law Society: *Legal Aid and Advice Compendium.*

Arbitration
>   Bell: *Law of Arbitration in Scotland.*
>   Irons and Melville: *Law of Arbitration.*

There are also many books of forms and precedents to assist in the framing of pleadings and the drafting of every kind of legal document, and forms are appended to some treatises.

Legal Periodicals

Periodicals have various functions, to keep the jurist, practitioner and student acquainted with recent changes and developments in the law, and to enable him to bring his search for any matter of law right up to date, to keep members of the profession in touch with changes affecting them and matters of common interest, and to serve as an outlet for academic thinking and a forum for the discussion of doctrines and critical analysis of developments.

The first function is performed primarily by *Current Law*. This publication appears in pamphlet form each month and each monthly part contains, digested under subject-headings, notes of all British statutes, statutory instruments, cases and articles published during the previous month. The indexes are cumulative, including references to matter included in any of the monthly parts for the current year. It has to be noted that all matters applicable to the United Kingdom generally are included in the English section of *Current Law*, so that the Scottish lawyer cannot ignore that section of the publication entirely.

Each Summer the matter contained in the twelve monthly parts of the previous calendar year's *Current Law* is brought together, reprinted and issued in consolidated form as the *Current Law Year Book*.[6] There are indexes of cases, statutes and subjects. The volumes for 1956, 1961, 1966 and 1971 (Master Volumes 1948–56, 1957–61, 1962–66 and 1967–71) contain cumulative references to matters covered in detail in the annual volumes 1948–56, 1957–61, 1962–66 and 1967–71.

The *Current Law Citator Volume* lists all statutes passed, amended, applied, repealed or otherwise affected by legislation in the period 1948–, together with statutory instruments made under rule-making powers contained in statutes, and cases and articles relating to the statute. It also lists separately for England and for Scotland all the reports of each decided case and indicates by reference to paragraph numbers in what other cases the case under consideration was applied or distinguished or otherwise treated, or discussed in the periodicals. The references in the *Citator Volume* are to the *Current Law Consolidation* volume 1947–51,[7] which contains United Kingdom and English matter only, and for matters subsequent to 1951 to the annual volumes of the *Scottish Current Law Year Book*. The monthly parts of *Current Law* enable research to be continued from the date of the *Citator Volume* used down to the time of search.

The monthly supplement to Halsbury's *Laws of England—Current Service* includes a *Review* which notes developments under the headings of the articles in that encyclopedia. From 1974 the *Reviews* are consolidated in an *Annual Abridgment* volume.

The second function of the periodical, that of the professional journal,

---

[6] There are two editions of both monthly parts and Year Book, the Scottish and the English. The Scottish is a complete reprint of the English edition with the addition of pages, printed on green paper in the monthly parts, of exclusively Scottish material. The English pages contain (a) exclusively English matter, and also (b) United Kingdom matter also applicable in whole or in part to Scotland. Both sets of pages must accordingly be looked at.

[7] *Current Law* began in England in 1947 and in Scotland in 1948. The *Current Law Consolidation* deals with matter in the English *Current Law*, 1947–51, and has no Scottish equivalent, but United Kingdom and English matters for 1948–51 are found in the U.K. and English sections of the *Scottish Current Law Year Books*, 1948–49–50–51, and a paragraph reference to the C.L.C. (unless it relates to 1947) can be traced through the indexes to these years of the *Scottish Current Law Year Book*. The preface to each volume gives guidance on the use of these volumes.

is performed by several journals many of which include also notes, or full reports, of cases and reviews of legislation.[8]

Articles and notes in periodicals of the third kind, *fora* for scholarly discussion, may be persuasive authority and may have considerable influence on judicial thinking; articles vary from highly theoretical to very practical but the general theme is of scholarly analysis, discussion and criticism. There are many journals of this kind, both general [9] and specialised,[10] and a few of the major U.S. and other foreign periodicals also sometimes contain matter of interest in this country.

Articles in legal periodicals can be traced through the special indexes thereto.[11]

Apart from periodicals there are various annuals which frequently contain valuable information and articles [12] and many volumes of collected essays and studies, sometimes by one author, sometimes by several, and sometimes contributed by many hands to make a volume in honour of a distinguished jurist.[13]

---

[8] The main ones are the *Scots Law Times* (1893–   ); the *Scottish Law Review* (1885–1963); the *Scottish Law Gazette* (1933–   ); the *Journal of the Law Society of Scotland* (1956–   ) and the *Conveyancing Review* (1957–1963) now incorporated in the *Journal of the Law Society of Scotland*. In England there are the *Law Journal* (1822–1965); the *Law Times* (1843–1965) merged in the *New Law Journal* from October 1965; the *Solicitors' Journal* (1857–   ) and the *Law Society's Gazette* (1904–   ).

[9] The principal are the *Juridical Review* (1888–1955); the *Juridical Review*; *The Law Journal of Scottish Universities* (1956–   ), and in England, the *Law Quarterly Review* (1885–   ); the *Cambridge Law Journal* (1921–   ); the *Modern Law Review* (1937–   ); the *Journal of the Society of Public Teachers of Law* (1924–38 and, New Series, 1947–   ); the *British Journal of Law and Society* (1974–   ). Articles of legal relevance also appear in non-legal journals.

[10] The principal are *Public Administration* (1923–   ); the *British Journal of Administrative Law* (1954–57) merged with *Public Law* (1956–   ); *Justice: The Journal of the International Commission of Jurists* (1958–   ); the *Journal of Planning and Property Law* (1948–   ); the *British Tax Review* (1956–   ); the *Journal of Criminal Law* (1937–   ); the *Journal of Criminal Science* (1948–   ); the *Criminal Law Review* (1954–   ); *The British Journal of Delinquency* (1950–60) incorporated in the *British Journal of Criminology* (1960–   ); the *Howard Journal* (1921–   ); the *Medico-Legal Journal* (1901–   ); *Medicine, Science and the Law* (1960–   ); the *Business Law Review* (1954–   ); the *Journal of Business Law* (1957–   ); the *Industrial Law Review* (1946–60); the *Conveyancer and Property Lawyer* (1936–   ); the *Journal of Comparative Legislation and International Law* (1896–1951), combined with the *International Law Quarterly* (1947–51) into the *International and Comparative Law Quarterly* (1951–   ); also the annual *British Yearbook of International Law* (1921–   ); and *Current Legal Problems* (1948–   ).

[11] See Jones-Chipman, *Index to Legal Periodical Literature*, 1803–1937, 6 vols.; *Index to Legal Periodicals* (1908–   ); *Index to Foreign Legal Periodicals* (1960–   ); *International Index to Periodicals*, 1907–55; *International Index*, (1955–65); *Social Sciences and Humanities Index* (1965–74); *Social Sciences Index* (1974–   ) and *Humanities Index* (1974–   ); *Subject Index to Periodicals* (1915—61) and *British Humanities Index* (1962–   ).

[12] The chief are the *U.N. Yearbook;* the *European Yearbook*; and the *Yearbook of World Affairs.*

[13] These are more common in Germany, where they are known as *Festschriften* or *Festgaben*, in Italy, where they are usually entitled *Studi in onore di—*, and in France, where they are called, *Mélanges* or *Études*.

CHAPTER 12

LEGAL METHOD

THE utility of law in supplying guidance on the legality of proposed action or in resolving difficulties and controversies about legal rights or in determining a party's entitlement to some remedy or liability to some penalty consists in essence in the discovery of a general principle or rule of law appropriate to a set of facts and circumstances which fall within the range of circumstances to which that general principle or rule applies, and its application thereto, so as to make the legal conclusion of that principle determinative of the particular controversy or difficulty raised by the particular circumstances of the case. In short what are the facts and what legal category do they fall into? What is the rule applicable to that category? What is the result? In essence the situation is: principle of law A states that in cases X, Y and Z consequence Q follows; this case is an instance of case Y; therefore principle A applies and states that Q follows. But faced with a set of circumstances, how does one determine whether this is an instance of X or Y, or G or H, and how does one find what legal principle applies to X or Y, G or H?

The problem of legal method consists in ascertaining what methods can best or indeed should be adopted to find the principles of law relevant to the solution of some legal difficulty. As in other sciences, systematic inquiry is essential, though the difficulties thereof in legal contexts are numerous, frequently arising from uncertainty as to the precise state of the facts for which a rule of law is required but sometimes from difficulty of deciding what principle or rule of law applies and how it is verbally formulated. The task is essentially the same, whether the purpose of the search is to advise, on the basis of a prediction of what the court may be thought likely to do, the task of the legal adviser; or to find the material on which to base an argument designed to persuade a judge or arbiter, the task of the pleader; or to reach and justify a decision, the task of the judge; or to state and systematise the law, the task of the jurist.

It has to be remembered that in some cases there is no ready-made proposition of law applicable to the legal problem in question, and the search must be for the materials from which to develop a proposition of law, one which, in the last resort, the courts would hold to be properly applicable to the case.

Furthermore, problems usually come before the legal adviser as a confused narrative, full of irrelevancies and inconsistencies and with important facts ignored or unclear. Persons seeking legal advice rarely produce the facts relevant to their problem clearly, correctly, concisely or chronologically stated.

Analysis of Problem

The first step is to analyse the factual situation and diagnose the legal difficulties it discloses. Sometimes the facts are clear and undisputed. In other cases the facts must be discovered as fully and accurately as possible, though it may be necessary initially to assume some facts and formulate a legal answer on the basis that certain facts, still unknown or doubtful or unproved, can yet be discovered or proved. Frequently further factual information must be sought before an answer to the legal difficulty can be attempted. It has also to be remembered that one set of facts may involve several legal problems and that a particular answer to one problem may affect the answers to the others.

The facts known, or believed, or at least stated and assumed for the purposes of inquiry, to exist should be set down in chronological order and checked for discrepancies by reference to all other sources of information available, such as documents or other witnesses' evidence. Irrelevant facts and details should be eliminated, though what is irrelevant may depend on the particular legal issue involved. Sometimes it matters that the party concerned is female, or married; sometimes it does not; there is no invariable standard of relevancy of facts and only legal knowledge and experience can enable one to say what is relevant or irrelevant in a particular context.

The factual situation can best be stated under five headings, as follows: (i) the parties to the controversy, any peculiarities of status or capacity attaching to them, and any legal relationship between them; (ii) the events giving rise to the controversy; (iii) the course of action considered, remedy sought or other object of the legal quest; (iv) the legal basis for claiming the remedy, or proponing the defence; and (v) the point or points in doubt or dispute, which may relate to any one or more of the previous four heads. Thus in a simple matrimonial case the problem might be analysed thus:

(i)   W (Scot) and H (French), married in London on ——;
(ii) W left H on ——; H friendly with X; suspicious circumstances;
(iii) divorce of H by W;
(iv) adultery by H;
(v)   Were parties validly married? Have Scottish courts jurisdiction to grant divorce? Was W justified in leaving H, or herself in desertion? Has H committed adultery? Evidence? Corroboration? Has W any claim for money or allowance from H?

Only considerable legal study and experience enable a person to know what legal bases for claiming a remedy or proponing a defence must be considered, and to spot what legal difficulties may be raised by a given factual situation. The experienced legal mind will at once see difficulties not apparent to the layman. Thus in the example the lawyer will know that adultery is a possible ground of divorce and that jealousy of H because of his friendship with X is not. The lawyer also will think of the difficulties of jurisdiction and evidence which the layman might overlook. In other circumstances the lawyer will start considering whether a particular person has a title to sue for the remedy, or whether an alleged contract was ever properly constituted, or whether the deceased's will was properly executed, or other points which would escape the layman. Only extensive study of good textbooks and of decided cases develops this awareness of possible difficulties and the ability quickly to spot all the legal problems inherent in a factual situation.

Classification

The next stage is to classify each point of difficulty in terms of the legal concepts and categories involved, under such legal headings and sub-heads as the legal textbooks, encyclopaedias, indexes, digests and other reference books deal with particular topics, as if the situation raising the difficulty were having to be fitted into place in one of these publications.[1] Categorisation should be done by reference to main branch of law, main head thereof and sub-head, *e.g.* contract—formalities, need for writing—sale of heritage. This indicates both where to look and the means of narrowing down the search to the precise point in issue. This categorisation is by far the most important element in the legal analysis of a problem.[2] It requires extensive knowledge of the logical system of the law, of the classification of its principles and rules and of the most likely heads under which topics may be discussed. It is essential to note that the classification is *by legal categories*, *e.g.* divorce, hiring, defamation, etc., and that the factual element is subsidiary, though not irrelevant, since, *e.g.* sale of a house and sale of a car are regulated to a substantial extent by different rules. Also the answer to some difficulty may require further investigation of the facts. Thus the answer to the query about the jurisdiction of the Scottish courts should elicit the answer that in general it depends on whether W was or was not " domiciled " or " resident " in Scotland. It would then be necessary to investigate what is meant by " domicile " and " resident " and whether the facts indicate that W had or had not her " domicile or " residence " in Scotland. Again it may be necessary to investigate whether the facts about H's conduct assuming they can be proved, amount to adultery as legally understood, or merely to lesser misconduct.[3]

---

[1] These are the headings and sub-heads used in Chaps. 9 and 11, though the reference and search books break headings down into a much finer sub-classification.

[2] It is particularly important and difficult in cases raising issues of International Private Law.

[3] See *e.g. MacLennan* v. *MacLennan*, 1958 S.C. 105, and authorities cited therein.

Finding the Law—Primary and Secondary Authorities

In searching for correct principles and rules of law to apply to the problems formulated the distinction between primary and secondary authorities [4] is important. Primary authorities are those texts which state principles and rules of law in authoritative form: such are statutes, statutory instruments and other legislation, binding cases and judicial opinions, and passages in institutional writings. A statement of a rule by one of these authorities, if in point, may be binding and will be, at least, persuasive. Secondary authorities are those sources of information in which individuals of greater or lesser eminence and experience state with a greater or lesser degree of authority *their view* of what principles and rules of law are relevant to various topics and how they are expressed: such are passages in legal textbooks, encyclopaedias, dictionaries, articles in legal periodicals, and other expressions of opinion or suggestions as to the law. Secondary authorities are always of lesser authority than primary authorities, though some of them, such as some highly respected textbooks, have weight not far short of binding judicial opinions; but statements by one of these authorities, however much in point, will never be binding on a court.

Consulting the Secondary Sources

If the subject-matter of the problem is relatively unfamiliar it is advisable to start by reading the most general secondary authorities and proceeding only later to more detailed and specific secondary authorities and thence to primary authorities, proceeding, for example, from a chapter in a general textbook or an article in an encyclopaedia to a book more specifically related to the subject of inquiry alone, thence to relevant statutes and cases.[5] If the subject-matter is familiar in general terms, one may go at once to the specific detailed textbook, or even direct to the statutes and cases which may be remembered from previous study as relevant to such circumstances. It is accordingly necessary to know what books there are on the main topics.

It is always proper to start with the secondary authorities, since reference to the relevant articles and chapters will tend to refresh the mind as to the branch of law involved, or, if the topic is unfamiliar, it will place the problem in perspective in relation to and against a background of the rest of the law on that topic. This general scrutiny of the background sometimes uncovers hitherto unsuspected pitfalls and difficulties, such as the requirement of any proceedings being taken within a limited period or in a particular form. Every legal adviser is constantly in this way discovering points he was unaware of or had forgotten.

---

[4] Explained in Chap. 10, *supra*.
[5] For the main secondary authorities, see Chap. 11.

In searching the sources the proper approach is to work from the more general to the more particular and from that in turn to the specific statutes and cases, that is, from secondary authorities to primary authorities. The reason for this approach is that primary authorities such as statutes, statutory instruments and cases do not, in themselves, give any guide or indication to later changes or developments of the law, to other statutes or cases in point, to the amending, repealing or over-ruling effect of later legislation or cases, to the way in which the statement of law in question has been interpreted in the courts, nor to the explanations or criticisms of jurists. Only in the systematic treatise can one find a synthetic picture of the law, admittedly as understood by one particular legal writer, but taking account of all the statutes, amendments, orders, cases, discussion, criticism and so on down to the date at which he wrote. Even then text-writers are fallible and may overlook or misstate some points.

Accordingly research in secondary authorities in the first place is likely, quite apart from any guidance or statements of principle by the text-writer, to yield a list of statutes, orders and cases which seem relevant to the topic which embraces the instant problem. Research to ascertain the solution of a legal difficulty must *never*, however, stop at the text-books or other secondary authorities, because these represent merely what some legal scholar *thinks* is the legal position resulting from the various statutes and cases, and his view may be mistaken, or superseded by some later development. Passages in encyclopaedias and textbooks are sometimes criticised by judges as being inaccurate or mistaken.[6] Moreover secondary authorities are unauthoritative.

Even if a sentence in a textbook appears exactly to fit the circumstances of the instant problem the basis in statutes and cases for the writer's view *must* be examined to see if they appear to justify his view. If they do, the statutes and cases are the primary material for solving the instant problem and the text-writer's view is purely supplementary and confirmatory. If they do not, the text-writer's view may stand alone as a, possibly inaccurate, expression of opinion.

Method of Searching Secondary Authorities

The relevant secondary authorities must be searched systematically and the following principles should be followed in order: (i) search the table of contents of the volume for headings which may be relevant, having in mind both the legal categories involved and the salient facts of the problem-situation, *e.g.* divorce—cruelty—kicking, or negligence —car (automobile, vehicle, road traffic)—skidding; (ii) search the subject-

---

[6] *e.g. Bell* v. *Holmes* [1956] 1 W.L.R. 1359; *Sinclair* v. *Juner*, 1952 S.C. 35, 43, *per* L.P. Cooper.

index similarly; (iii) if any relevant case is already known, trace from the index of cases whether it is cited in the volume, and read each page whereon it is cited; (iv) if any relevant statute is known, check the index of statutes similarly; and (v) if any significant word or phrase is involved, check any index of words and phrases discussed, or the general index, and follow up any leads given thereby. Lastly, note the date of the edition being used, or the date stated in the preface as that down to which the writer has been able to take account of changes in the law, because information about subsequent changes must be sought elsewhere.

As each secondary authority is examined a brief note should be made of any passages which appear helpful and of all references given to primary authorities, so that these clues can be followed up, these notes being segregated according to the legal problem to which they seem to indicate an answer.

With any luck this process should accordingly yield, under the heading of each problem, a list of text-writer's statements, and of references to statutes, relevant cases, institutional writings, and other guides.

Research into Primary Authorities

Research into the secondary authorities in the way already discussed may be expected to yield at least some references to primary authorities which must next be followed up. It may, however, yield little or nothing, in which case equally the search must be carried to the primary authorities, and in any event a search must always be made for primary authorities which have come into being since the date of publication of the textbook or other secondary authority, such as new cases, statutes or orders, and for primary authorities which may have been overlooked or omitted from the textbooks.[7]

References culled from the encyclopaedias and textbooks should be followed up first and read carefully, since these are likely to be the most important statutes and cases on the subject and they will probably themselves contain other references backwards leading the inquiry to other statutes and cases. Beyond that comes the search in the primary authorities by means of the Indexes to legislation and Digests of case-law. The *Index to the Statutes in Force* must be searched under all topic-headings which it is thought might conceivably cover any statute relevant to the

---

[7] Even the most diligent compiler of a textbook may overlook some decision or other point and textbooks and encyclopaedias do not guarantee to, and, in many instances, do not even attempt to, refer to all the statutes and cases. They try as a rule to mention all the more interesting and important ones. It is the function of the textbook to explain the state of the law, not to list all the statutes and cases, and it is always open to argument whether particular cases are sufficiently relevant or important to deserve to be cited on a particular point.

problem. This Index groups " under selected headings,[8] index entries relating to the whole of the general statute law in force. Each item indexed is followed by a citation of any current supporting enactment in the form of a reference to the calendar year, chapter number, section, etc., of the appropriate Act which takes the place of page references in an ordinary index." [9] These citations lead to the relevant provisions (in any edition of the statutes). Most titles are divided and sub-divided, dealing with substantive law, adjective law, and miscellaneous provisions, or following the layout of the principal Act.

The *Digests* of case-law must similarly be searched using successively the analytical or topic-heading approach, which is similarly based on recognised branches, headings and sub-headings, the table of cases approach (where any analogous case is known), the table of statutes approach (where any relevant statute is known), and the index of words and phrases approach (where any word or phrase may have previously been discussed). This must be done for the main body of each Digest used, and for each supplement in turn.[10]

The institutional writers should be searched in succession, using the tables of contents and the general indexes to the standard editions, and the older non-institutional writings should also be searched. This is less necessary where the subject of inquiry is a matter of entirely modern law on which the institutional writers are likely to be silent.

Bringing Research up to date

It must be kept in mind that research in even the latest published edition or volumes of these tools of primary research can bring the statement of law down, at best, to a period a few months back, or sometimes a year or two back,[11] and sometimes a number of years back. The search must be carried on by the use of *Current Law*. The *Scottish Current Law Year Book*, the *Scottish Current Law Citator Volume*, and the monthly parts of *Current Law* enable search to be continued from the date of the authorities consulted down to the time of search.

---

[8] While these headings correspond generally to the branches and headings used in Chaps. 9 and 11 hereof, there are some " catch-all " titles, such as Animals and many statutes are relevant under several branches of the analytical classification of the legal system. The headings are arranged alphabetically, not grouped analytically under major heads and sub-heads as in Chap. 9.

[9] *Index to the Statutes in Force*, Preface. The whole Preface should be read for information on how to use the Index.

[10] The *Faculty Digest* Index volume contains a subject-index, indexes of cases referred to in other cases, of statutes commented on, of words defined, and of cases in the *Digest*. This last leads from a known case to the heads under which it appears and hence to similarly classified cases. There are similar indexes in each of the decennial Supplements.

[11] The time-lag required to print and publish these books alone makes them not quite up to date even when they are freshly published.

Utility of English and Foreign Authorities

In many cases it is desirable and even necessary to have recourse to authorities, both secondary and primary, which are not Scottish, most commonly to English authorities, such as Halsbury's *Laws of England*,[12] or English textbooks. On some topics the law is the same or nearly the same in both countries, on others the law is in a general way common to Scotland and to England, while on others rules applicable to Scotland have very similar English counterparts. In topics of the former kinds it is useful and indeed necessary to look at the English books, subject always to the caution that peculiarities of Scottish practice, of courts and procedure, are seldom discussed, that purely Scottish primary authorities are frequently not cited, and that one must always consider whether any statement made in the book is consistent with the general body of law and practice of Scotland; much harm has been done in the past by too-ready and uncritical acceptance of principles laid down in English books, even though they might appear to be entirely applicable in Scotland.[13] In topics of the latter kind resort to English books is much more difficult and dangerous and they should not be searched save in total default of any Scottish authority. On other topics again the laws of Scotland and of England are quite different and reference to English authorities is of little or no value.

Periodicals

Articles, discussion and criticism in legal periodicals [14] are of increasing importance and it is desirable to check the relevant periodicals to see if there are any articles on the subject and if any relevant cases have been criticised therein. These may be found through the *Index to Legal Periodicals* and *Current Law*.

Synthesis of Materials

The next step is to effect a synthesis of materials bearing on each problem under investigation in the case. In all but the simplest cases it should be done on paper by noting down in summary form all the relevant materials which have been discovered, in chronological order, thereby seeing how far each new factor affects the earlier ones.[15] This inevitably involves at every stage taking decisions on interpretation of

---

[12] Note that there is a cumulative annual Supplement to *Halsbury*, which includes all new material since each volume was published, and a further loose-leaf *Current Service* brought up to date every month.

[13] *Cf.* Lord Cooper's warning in *McLaughlan* v. *Craig*, 1948 S.C. 599, of the dangers of reliance on English authorities in negligence cases.

[14] For these, see Chap. 11, *supra*.

[15] For examples in judicial opinions of the tracing out of a long series of cases, see *Donoghue* v. *Stevenson*, 1932 S.C.(H.L.) 31, *per* Lord Atkin, *Candler* v. *Crane, Christmas & Co.* [1951] 2 K.B. 164, and *Re Diplock* [1948] Ch. 465. For examination of institutional writers and cases, see *Fortington* v. *Kinnaird*, 1942 S.C. 239.

statutory provisions, on the *rationes* and evaluation of cases, and on the applicability and weight of statements in institutional writers and legal literature.

In thus working towards an answer to any problem the weight to be given to the various sources of law is important. If there is a statutory provision which appears to cover the case, or as interpreted in other cases has been held to do so, that must rule. In default of statutory provision, if there is a *ratio* discoverable from a judicial precedent which is both in point and binding, that must rule. In default of statute or binding precedent, the answer may be supplied or suggested by a passage in an institutional writer, a passage in a textbook of greater or less authority, the *ratio* of a merely persuasive precedent, or of one not directly in point though closely analogous, an *obiter dictum* in a precedent, suggestion or criticism in a legal periodical, or other indication. Failing all else, an answer may be suggested by common sense, reason and personal ideas of the requirements of equity and justice.

This process of synthesis of materials determines the net consequence of all the various legal factors which are elements in making up the answer to the problem under consideration. The process is not an exact science but a difficult process of balancing and weighing, depending on tentative interpretation of possibly obscure and conflicting statutory phrases and provisions, on eliciting the *rationes* of cases and on the evaluation of materials from secondary sources. The synthesis in fact demands a prediction, a prophecy, a guess at what a court would decide on these materials. Sometimes no clear or decided view can be arrived at, but only a formulation that something " appears to be the law " or is " thought to be the rule."

It has to be noticed that in the case of some problems the answer may be wholly negative, in that each possibility is negatived, or the answer may contain two positive alternatives, in that each of two possible courses may be legally competent.[16] In this case the choice of which course to adopt may be determined by other factors, such as the availability of evidence, and the general convenience of making one claim rather than another.

The Process in Operation

One brief example may show how this process of finding the law appropriate to rule certain facts applies. Suppose the problem is: a coalman supplied to a householder a bag of coal which contained an explosive, and when some of the coal was put on the fire an explosion took place

---

[16] Thus investigation into whether divorce is possible for adultery or for desertion on certain facts may reveal that both are competent, as where a husband deserts and lives in adultery with someone else. After three years' desertion divorce is open on either ground or on both.

damaging the room. Has the householder any claim for the damage? Analysis and legal classification suggest that the problem is Contract— sale of goods—goods of defective quality—explosive coal, or Delict— dangerous goods—duty of care on producer for consumer—explosive coal.[17] Search in the books on Contract or Sale suggests as relevant the Sale of Goods Act 1893,[18] section 14 (3) of which imports an implied condition of fitness of goods sold for a particular purpose in certain cases. The books on sale in discussing this section mention *Duke* v. *Jackson*, 1921 S.C. 362, which seems almost exactly to fit these facts but to lead to an odd result, inconsistent with the common-sense interpretation of the section of the 1893 Act.[19] The index of statutes commented on in the *Faculty Digest* leads also to this case as the closest in point of several decided on that section. The annual *Current Law Case Citator*, under Scottish cases, reveals that this case was distinguished in a virtually identical Scottish case in 1948, where the opposite conclusion was reached, and that there was an article discussing the case of *Duke* in 1954 S.L.T. which in turn reveals that *Duke's* case was severely criticised in the English Court of Appeal in another exactly similar case [20] in 1954. The *Current Law Case Citator*, under English cases, indicates that *Duke* was " not followed " in the 1954 English case, and also indicates several comments on this English case in the periodicals, which, when read, seem to favour it as a true application of section 14 (1) and to condemn *Duke*. The *Current Law Statute Citator* (1948–71) under the heading of the 1893 Act, s. 14 (1), lists various other cases but none when examined is any more closely in point. The annual *Scottish Current Law Citator*, under the 1893 Act, reveals that section 14 (1) was amended in 1973 and again in 1974, and reference to the amending Acts brings out that it is now section 14 (3), with a different wording from that discussed in the cases of 1921 and 1954. But does the new wording make any difference?

Synthesis of these materials thus suggest that one answer to the problem is given by section 14 (1) (now section 14 (3)), as interpreted in the English case, and that *Duke* should not be followed but distinguished.

Search in the books on Delict under the head of " dangerous goods " would indicate numerous cases where it has been held that the producer of dangerous goods is under a legal duty to the consumer and liable if

---

[17] Note the importance of legal classification of the problem under legal headings and sub-heads. The layman might start to look under " Coal " or " Explosion " and would be unlikely to find the answer from such starting points.

[18] The relevant provision was s. 14 (1) in the 1893 Act but by virtue of the Supply of Goods (Implied Terms) Act 1973, s. 3 and the Consumer Credit Act 1974, Sch. 4, is now s. 14 (3) with different wording.

[19] The decision was that the householder had no ground for complaint because there was nothing wrong with the coal, but it contained a detonator which was a free gift from the coal merchant! The report indicates that there was an alternative claim founded on delict.

[20] *Wilson* v. *Rickett, Cockerell & Co.* [1954] 1 Q.B. 598.

the danger causes him, or his property, injury or damage. There are cases about bad food, poisonous drink, dangerous clothing and so on, but none specifically about coal. But the principle might seem to apply equally to coal with an explosive therein. The books, and all these cases, point to *Donoghue* v. *Stevenson* [21] as the basic statement of this principle of producer's liability to consumer for harm caused by defective product, provided there was no reasonable probability of examination of the product by an intermediary and discovery of the element which caused the harm. The general principle laid down in *Donoghue* v. *Stevenson* [21] suggests that a possible ground of action is provided by the *Donoghue* principle,[21] many of the applications of which are closely analogous to coal with an explosive therein, but in this case action lies against the producer of the coal rather than the coal-merchant.

The conclusion is that the householder has two alternative valid grounds of action, one against the coalman, under statute, for breach of contract, one against the producers of the coal, at common law, for delict (breach of a general duty of care).

Formulation of Solution

The materials discovered for answering each issue in doubt having been thus assembled, and a provisional view formed on each point, it remains to put them together and see how far, if at all, a complete legal answer has been found to the whole problem posed by the facts. Inconsistencies may be found, discrepancies or doubtful points, and much may have to be left on a hypothetical basis, depending on the view taken on some prior issue. The answer to one problem may exclude some possible answer on another problem, or may depend on the answer adopted to some logically prior problem.

The last stage in formulating the solution is to put it into shape for use, possibly drafting an opinion on the state of the law for information and future reference, possibly framing advice to a client on what should be done immediately, possibly drafting a summons or petition or other pleading so as to commence an action to obtain a remedy from a competent court, or defences so as to challenge another party's entitlement to what he claims.

It is important that a systematic process of research be undertaken at an early stage into all the legal problems which are apparent, as not infrequently in practice a view is formulated, advice is given or a claim made without considering subsequent difficulties, such as that of proving allegations made in a summons. It is not possible to foresee or take precautions against every eventuality, every defence, or every unexpected point which may emerge later, but every difficulty visible or readily

---

[21] 1932 S.C.(H.L.) 31, particularly *per* Lord Atkin at p. 44.

foreseeable should be taken into account from the start, since there is no point in embarking on a course of action or on litigation if there appears to be material risk of not being able to take it through all its stages successfully.

Testing the Solution

The only real test for a legal adviser's solution for any legal difficulty or problem in issue is to have the matter decided by the court, which can be done only if there is truly a controversy. The courts will not answer academic problems, where the rights of individuals are not affected by their decision. But, while the court's decision of any legal problem settles the matter as between the parties and may, under the doctrine of precedent, settle the law for the future, it does not follow that the court's decision is necessarily right. For there are many reported cases which have been subsequently overruled as wrongly decided, or have been so criticised and distinguished or not followed as to be devoid of authority and little regarded. The judgment of the court has, however, to be accepted by the parties as the answer and there is no other way of testing or verifying the solution, and the acid test of any legal advice comes when the claim, or refusal, based on that advice is scrutinised by the court. This does not mean that every time a court action fails the legal adviser has been wrong, because actions which involve any issue of evidence or fact may, independently of the law and legal advice, fail if the evidence does not measure up to expectations,[22] or if it does not impress the judge or jury as accurate, or if judge or jury decline to accept it or to draw any desired inference from it. In these respects very much depends on the manner and demeanour of witnesses, and the whole way in which the evidence comes out and the impact which it makes on the tribunal of fact. But in a purely legal issue, such as the debate on a plea to the relevancy of pleadings, an appeal on a point of law, or a stated case or special case, the court's decision, right or occasionally wrong, is the only real test of the validity of the legal adviser's solution to his problem.

FURTHER READING

Secondary Sources
Institute of Advanced Legal Studies: *Bibliographical Guide to United Kingdom Law*
Sweet & Maxwell: *Where to Look for Your Law.*
      Legal Bibliography of British Commonwealth, vols. 1, 2 and 5.
Green's *Encyclopaedia of Scots Law*, 16 vols. and Supps.
Halsbury's *Laws of England*, 3rd ed., 4th ed. in progress, with Cumulative Supplement and monthly Current Service.
General and specific textbooks, as in Chapter 11.

---

[22] Thus in *McKillen* v. *Barclay Curle & Co.*, 1967 S.L.T. 41, a pursuer claimed damages for injuries and for tuberculosis reactivated by the injuries. The court held that the second part of the claim was good in law, but that the pursuer had failed to prove that the reactivation had been caused by the injuries, *i.e.*, the second part of the claim succeeded on law, but failed on the evidence.

Primary Sources
Sweet & Maxwell: *Guide to Law Reports and Statutes* (4th ed.).
Chronological Table of Statutes (annual).
Index to the Statutes in Force (annual).
Index to Government Orders (bi-annual).
Scots Digest, 1800–1947, 11 vols.
Faculty Digest, 1868–1960, 10 vols.
Mews' Digest of English Case Law.
English and Empire Digest.
Index to Legal Periodicals.
Scottish Current Law Yearbooks,
Scottish Current Law Statute Citator, 1948–71,
Annual *Scottish Current Law Citator* volume and monthly parts.
Institutional writings, as in Chapter 11.

General reference books
Bell: *Dictionary and Digest of the Law of Scotland* (ed. Watson).
Broom: *Legal Maxims.*
Craies: *Statute Law* (7th ed.).
Gibb and Dalrymple: *Scottish Judicial Dictionary.*
Jowitt: *Dictionary of English Law.*
Saunders: *Words and Phrases Legally Defined.*
Stair Society: *Sources and Literature of Scots Law*, 1936.
Stroud: *Judicial Dictionary.*
Trayner: *Latin Maxims and Phrases.*
Wharton: *Law Lexicon.*

CHAPTER 13

THE RESOLUTION OF CIVIL DISPUTES

A CIVIL dispute arises whenever two or more parties are at issue on any matter of fact or of law or of both which affects their legal rights and duties. Such controversies may sometimes be resolved by compromise or agreement or by accepting the opinion of counsel or other third party. But in the last resort controversies as to legal rights or duties can be resolved only by application to the appropriate court or tribunal for a ruling, or, in certain cases, to arbitration. Such applications are regulated by the several bodies of law of procedure, civil and administrative, and the principles of pleading and the principles and rules of the law of evidence are accessory thereto. These subjects are too complicated to discuss here in detail. The following pages merely indicate in very broad outline the course of procedure followed in the commoner kinds of cases to obtain an authoritative ruling on matters in controversy and the main ways in which effect may be given to such rulings. An understanding of procedure is also important in that to understand the law stated in reported decisions it is necessary to understand how the issue had been raised before the court and what stage it had reached at the point at which it is reported.

In civil or administrative proceedings, where the individual has a grievance or claim, he must initiate and press the claim himself, because the failure to satisfy his grievance or claim is a harm to him alone, but in the case of conduct stigmatised as criminal, it is prejudicial to the general welfare of the community and the claim to have the wrongdoer punished will be taken up and pressed by a public officer on behalf of the community. In a few cases a question of choice may arise, but normally the questions of who is to initiate the claim, and by what procedure, civil, administrative or criminal, will depend on the nature of the claim involved and its legal classification.

In all cases it is important to observe how disputed issues of law and disputed issues of fact are elucidated and at what stages one or the other may be investigated.

I.—CIVIL PROCEEDINGS

In certain cases an individual may legally act at his own hand and need not invoke the help of the court. Thus a man may eject a trespasser, or rescind a contract if the other party is in breach thereof, in each case without the court's intervention. But in most cases he must seek a remedy from a court.

Civil proceedings are undertaken to obtain a civil remedy. Civil remedies may be classified according to their purposes into:

(i) declaratory judgments, whereby the court declares that particular rights do or do not exist, without necessarily making any order as to consequential action, as where it declares that a pretended marriage was null;

(ii) reduction, whereby the court reduces or sets aside as invalid a contract, will, decree or other writing which is prejudicial to the pursuer's rights;

(iii) prevention, whereby the court stops a threatened legal wrong, or the continuance of the perpetration of a legal wrong or some illegality, before any, or any further, harm is done to the pursuer, as where it issues an order of interdict against commission of a nuisance;

(iv) enforced performance, whereby the court gives redress by compelling the doing of what should have been done voluntarily by the defender in performance of his legal duty, as by ordering payment, delivery or other action;

(v) damages, or substitutional redress in the shape of pecuniary compensation, for loss caused or injury or harm done by the failure to implement some legal duty owed to the pursuer by the defender, as where the court awards damages in compensation for loss caused by the defender's breach of contract or for personal injuries resulting from the defender's fault;

(vi) consistorial remedies, as where it judicially separates two spouses or decrees dissolution of a marriage on the ground of the commission of a matrimonial offence;

(vii) admiralty remedies, being those peculiar to maritime cases;

(viii) remedies competent under particular statutes in particular cases;

(ix) administrative remedies, as where the court appoints a judicial factor, or new trustees, or sequestrates an estate; and

(x) miscellaneous remedies, such as applications to the *nobile officium*.

Before proceedings are initiated many preliminary problems have to be decided. Such problems include that of jurisdiction, *i.e.* which country's courts, and, within that country, which court or tribunal is appropriate and can issue a valid decree against the defender or otherwise deal with the case; that of choice of law, *i.e.* whether Scots or some other system of law falls to determine the rights and duties of parties; that of competency, whether that court can take account of the claim, or by way of the kind of proceedings contemplated; that of choice of remedy; that of relevancy, namely, what will have to be alleged and proved to justify the court in granting the remedy sought; and that of evidence, of what evidence must and can be adduced to establish any facts alleged but disputed or in doubt but which must be established if the claim is to succeed. Such preliminary consideration may convince the aggrieved person that he has no remedy, or is unlikely to be able to establish it. Nobody should rush into court without careful preliminary consideration.

In all proceedings the distinction between questions of fact and questions of law must be kept in mind.[1] Disputed questions of fact must be alleged in the written pleadings and are decided by the judge, or jury if there is one, after hearing and considering evidence.[2] Disputed questions of law must be raised by appropriate pleas-in-law and are decided by the judge after hearing legal argument.[3] Disputed questions of mixed fact and law are determined by the judge after hearing evidence of fact and legal argument as to the effect of the evidence being interpreted in one way or another, though sometimes a jury verdict is the decision of a mixed question of fact and law.

Court of Session Proceedings

Proceedings in the Court of Session are usually initiated in the Outer House by *summons*, occasionally by *petition* and more rarely by other forms of application to the court. A summons [4] is a writ running in the name of the Queen and passing the Royal Signet, prepared by the pursuer's legal advisers, setting out the demand of one party, the *pursuer*, against another, the *defender*, and summoning the defender to appear in court to answer the pursuer's demand, with the warning that the pursuer may proceed to take decree in absence against the defender if he does not appear to defend. The first page of a summons is a printed form with certain blanks completed in typewriting. The remainder consists of typewritten sheets setting out the substance of the claim.

After the formal printed introduction stating the parties and summoning the defender to appear, the summons contains *conclusions*, or brief statements of the remedies claimed,[5] a *condescendence*, or statement in numbered paragraphs of the facts which the pursuer alleges to exist and on which he relies as justifying his claim (but not of the evidence thereof nor of arguments on the relevant law), and *pleas-in-law*, which are brief proposi-

---

[1] See p. 28, *supra*.

[2] Thus if the pursuer alleges that the defender drove fast round the corner and knocked him down, and the defender alleges that he drove slowly and carefully round the corner and could not avoid hitting the pursuer who ran out in front of his car without looking, there is a disputed issue of fact, which must be determined after hearing evidence.

[3] Thus whether facts alleged *can* amount in law to cruelty justifying divorce, or to fraud justifying reduction of a contract, or to negligence justifying damages, are questions of law. If it is held that they *can*, whether they *do* is a question of fact.

[4] For form, see *Rules of Court*, 1965, Appx. form 1.

[5] See *R.C.* Appx. form 2, for specimens.

tions of law, stating the legal principles on which the pursuer rests his case.[6]

The summons is signeted at the court offices, and *citation* of the defender is effected by serving a copy of the summons on him by post or personally. The summons is then *called* by being published in the Rolls of Court and at the same time various papers known collectively as *the process* are lodged for the use of the court.

Pleadings

If the defender ignores the summons, the pursuer may take *decree in absence* against him. If he wishes to defend, he must *enter appearance* and lodge *defences*, which are a typed statement of facts, and which must answer, statement by statement, every material allegation in the pursuer's condescendence, and which are completed by *pleas-in-law for the defender*. The defences may be defences on the facts, in the form of statements contradictory of the pursuer's narrative in his condescendence, or defences in point of law, in the form of pleas-in-law challenging the legal basis of the pursuer's claim, or the defences may be both as to fact and law. A defender may also lodge a *counterclaim* with his defences.

An *open record*[7] is now made up, a duplicated pamphlet reproducing the summons, conclusions, the paragraphs of the pursuer's condescendence followed each by the corresponding paragraph of the defender's defences, the pleas-in-law for the pursuer and the pleas-in-law for the defender. Counsel now *adjust the record*[7] by each making alterations in their written pleadings to meet points made by the other, so as to narrow down the matters in dispute and focus clearly the matters of disagreement. The solicitors for the parties communicate to each other the adjustments made. New statements may be added to condescendence and defences, or existing statements altered, and pleas-in-law added or deleted. The pursuer may, for example, add a plea challenging the legal basis of the defences. The careful framing of written pleadings is an essential preliminary to proof or jury trial and evidence at proof or jury trial will be limited to issues raised in the pleadings and of which each party has thereby been given fair notice, so as to enable him to prepare his answer, and to plan his examination and cross-examination of witnesses.

When counsel have completed their adjustments, or earlier if delay is taking place, the Lord Ordinary will pronounce an *interlocutor*[8]

---

[6] For specimens of summons, see *Encyclopaedia of Scottish Legal Styles*, *sub voce* " Action."

[7] In this sense pronounced " recórd."

[8] An interlocutor is an order made by a judge giving effect to his ruling on any matter, and disposing of the whole or any part of a case.

closing the record[7] and appointing further procedure.[9] This completes the written pleadings.[10] A *closed record*[7] is then made up, which is a reprint of the open record but embodying all the adjustments made on the open record, and copies are duplicated.[11]

Debate

The next step depends on whether the parties are at issue as to law, or fact, or both.

If parties are at issue on a question of fact only, the court will order a *proof* (*i.e.* trial by judge alone) or *jury trial*,[12] so that the facts can be determined.

If parties are at issue on law, or on both fact and law, the court will send the case to the Procedure Roll[13] for discussion of the pleas-in-law raising legal points which have been tabled in the pleadings. This legal debate proceeds by way of legal argument only and the party challenging the legal sufficiency or basis of the other's case must, for the purposes of his argument, accept as true his opponent's narrative of the facts. His contention is that, even if the other party can prove the facts to be as he has alleged, he is not entitled in law to succeed. The debate may discuss the *jurisdiction* of the court to grant the remedy in the circumstances, whether the pursuer has a *title to sue* for the remedy sought, the legal *competency* of the remedy sought, the *specification* or adequacy of the averments or allegations of either party, or the *relevancy* or sufficiency in law of the averments of one party or the other to justify his claim or establish his defence, on the assumption that the facts stated by him are true.[14]

---

[9] This procedure was superseded in 1968 as an experiment: see Practice Note [1967] C.L.Y. 4581.

[10] Alterations to either party's written pleadings can thereafter only be made by *Minute of Amendment*, with the leave of the court. Amendment may be penalised by an award of expenses caused thereby to the other side, particularly if it has caused delay or wasted effort. Amendment may be attempted at a late stage, or even after proof or jury trial, and indeed at any stage till final judgment, but it is in the court's discretion whether to allow it or not; see *e.g. Thomson* v. *Glasgow Corpn.*, 1962 S.C.(H.L.) 36. The decision to allow or refuse an amendment may be appealed to the Inner House and to the House of Lords; *e.g. Thomson, supra*; *Duke of Argyll* v. *Duchess of Argyll*, 1962 S.C.(H.L.) 88.

[11] Portions of pleadings from the closed record are frequently reprinted in reported cases.

[12] Jury trial is competent only on defined and limited grounds, on which see *Robertson* v. *Bannigan*, 1965 S.C. 20, 28. The institution is much criticised.

[13] Formerly there were separate Procedure and Debate Rolls to which were assigned cases raising different kinds of legal issues.

[14] See *Jamieson* v. *Jamieson*, 1952 S.C.(H.L.) 44, 50, 63; Walker, " The Theory of Relevancy " (1951) 63 J.R. 1; and on the theory of pleading Michael and Adler, " The Trial of an Issue of Fact " (1934) 34 Col.L.R. 1224. A famous example of a debate on relevancy is *Donoghue* v. *Stevenson*, 1932 S.C.(H.L.) 31, where the legal question was whether, even if the pursuer's story could be proved true, she was entitled in law to the remedy sought; it was held that, if the pursuer's averments were

A debate in a civil action in an Outer House court, Court of Session. On the bench, the Lord Ordinary; at the table a Clerk of Session; in the front seat junior and senior counsel for the defender, senior and junior counsel for the pursuer; in the second row, the defender's solicitor.

Such debates proceed by counsel bringing to the judge's attention statutory provisions thought to be relevant, principles laid down in and dicta uttered in cases, passages in institutional writings and authoritative textbooks, and basing arguments thereon, trying to lead the judge to one view or the other on the issue or issues of law being debated. Such arguments frequently raise problems of the interpretation of statutory provisions, or of the discovery of the true *ratio* of one or more cases and sometimes of the effect on the *ratio* of one case of the *ratio* or of *dicta* in another, or the meaning or weight to be attached to a statement by an institutional or authoritative text-writer. The discovery of the materials for argument raises again the importance of knowing the sources of the law and of diligently digging out materials relevant to each point in debate. How to arrange and present an argument is a skill born of experience.

After the debate the judge may give judgment at once but will normally make *avizandum* [15] and subsequently give judgment when he will issue an *interlocutor* disposing of the points raised [16] and an opinion on the law involved, and, if the parties were at issue on law alone, grant the pursuer decree (if he holds that the defences, even if proved, would not be adequate in law), or dismiss the action, because the court has no jurisdiction to deal with the claim, or the pursuer no title to sue for it, or because it is incompetent, *i.e.* claims what cannot be granted, because it has been inadequately stated, or because it is irrelevant, *i.e.* insufficient in law, even if the facts were proved to be as stated.[17] But if the parties were at issue on both law and fact, he will rule as to the law and either dismiss the action on any ground of law, if convinced by the defender's argument, or, if convinced by the pursuer's argument on the law, order either a *proof* or *jury trial* to enable the pursuer to try to prove the facts he has averred, on the basis of which the judge has ruled as to the law, or he may order a *proof before answer*, if he cannot rule on the law without knowing the facts more fully and wishes to reserve all points of law, which will thus still be open for argument after the facts have been elucidated.[18]

---

proved true, she was entitled to the remedy claimed. In fact the case was compromised, so that the pursuer never required to prove by evidence that her narrative was in fact true, and it remains unknown whether the narrative could have been proved or not and consequently whether Mrs. Donoghue was or was not entitled to her remedy. But the House of Lords' ruling on the law, that such a claim was good in law, is a valid and valuable precedent for later similar cases, quite apart from the fate of that particular claim.

[15] That is, reserve the case for consideration; the word is derived from medieval Latin *avizare*, to consider.

[16] This normally takes the form of his upholding certain pleas-in-law for one party or repelling certain pleas-in-law for the other party. He may also grant decree, dismiss the action, or appoint further procedure.

[17] Appeal may be, and frequently is, taken at this stage, and this may finally dispose of the case, or it may come back to the Outer House, the judge's ruling having been upheld or reversed.   [18] See *Forbes* v. *Forbes's Trs.*, 1957 S.C. 325.

Proof

When the case is called in court on the date fixed for the diet of proof, counsel for both parties appear. There is no opening speech outlining the case and counsel for the pursuer [19] proceeds at once to call his witnesses. Each witness is in turn sworn by the judge, *examined-in-chief* by counsel, *cross-examined* by defender's counsel, and, if thought necessary, *re-examined* by pursuer's counsel to clear up any matter left in doubt. After all the witnesses for the pursuer have been heard the defender's witnesses are in turn sworn, *examined-in-chief* by the defender's counsel, *cross-examined*, and, if need be, *re-examined*. The rules of evidence determine what must be proved, and by what means, and incidental argument may arise as to the admissibility or pertinency of some of the evidence.[20]

There must be a basis in the pleadings of the parties for evidence led by them and parties will not be allowed to lead evidence on matters not made the subject of averment on record. Nor may a judge rely on evidence as to a matter not averred on record.[21] Evidence is of various kinds: *observation evidence*, given by the parties and independent witnesses of what they severally saw, heard and did at the material times; *opinion or expert evidence* by skilled persons such as physicians, engineers, architects, accountants, chemists and other persons of skill of what they observed, found, measured or tested and of what inferences they drew and what conclusions they reached on the basis of their measurements and tests as interpreted in the light of their professional knowledge and experience, *e.g.* as to cause, nature and extent of injuries, cause of explosion, effect of wind-pressure, and so on; *real evidence*, such as production of a broken support or a burst tyre; *circumstantial evidence*, of facts and circumstances bearing on a matter in dispute, as of the state of goods; *written evidence*, such as correspondence, invoices, contract notes, title-deeds, plans and other kinds of documents which tend to establish facts. Evidence of the first four kinds is given orally, sometimes supported by production of things, or photographs of them; written evidence, if probative or *in re mercatoria*, proves itself and need only be lodged in court, but the other kinds of written evidence must be proved by oral evidence to have been executed by the person who bears to have executed the writing.

In general, hearsay evidence, *i.e.* evidence of what the witness heard from another, is not admissible; the person who told him must be brought to tell the court himself; but exceptions exist, *e.g.* where the original informant has died.

The purpose of examination-in-chief is to ascertain from the witness what he knows favourable to the case of the party calling him as a witness.

---

[19] Exceptionally, the defender may be ordained to lead in the proof.
[20] *e.g. Young* v. *N.C.B.*, 1960 S.C. 6.
[21] *Robertson* v. *Cowe*, 1970 S.C. 29.

A proof in a defended civil action in the Court of Session. L. to R. The witness, the shorthand writer and the Lord Ordinary. At the table a Clerk of Session; in the front row, junior and senior counsel for the defender, senior and junior counsel for the pursuer; in the second row, the parties' solicitors.

The purpose of cross-examination is to test the veracity, accuracy of observation and correctness of the witness's evidence, to find whether he will qualify or retract it and to ascertain what he knows favourable to the other side's case. If the other side has a different explanation of any matter in dispute, this explanation must be put to the witness in cross-examination to see whether he agrees with it or not. Any point on which a witness is not cross-examined is taken as accepted. Leading questions, *i.e.* questions so framed as to indicate the answer desired, are allowed only in cross-examination. The evidence is recorded by a shorthand writer and the judge makes notes for his own use. Evidence is supplemented by *judicial knowledge, i.e.* those facts which judges are assumed to know without need for evidence, and may be affected by *presumptions, i.e.* rules to the effect that in certain circumstances some state of fact must, or may, be treated as if proved.

At the conclusion of the evidence, or at an adjourned *hearing on evidence,* counsel make their submissions to the judge on the effect of the evidence and on what inferences should be drawn from it. The assessment or weighing of evidence is a difficult job. It involves deciding which witnesses are honest, which lying, which exaggerating, which confused, or inaccurate, or forgetful, which truthful, accurate and reliable, and trying to build up from the whole body of evidence a coherent picture of what happened. This involves accepting some evidence, discarding some and trying to piece it all together. There may be gaps in the evidence, things not observed, periods as to which there is silence and so on, and questions may arise of how far a judge can draw an inference from incomplete evidence. The judge may give judgment at once or may make *avizandum,*[22] in which case the cause is called again a few days later for judgment, when junior counsel attend, the judge reads his judgment and, on the motion of counsel, awards or reserves expenses. While the judge's opinion contains his reasons, the operative part of his judgment is the *interlocutor,* which sustains and gives effect to one or more of the pleas in law for one party and repels contrary pleas, or the *decree* which he pronounces, determining the cause, granting the pursuer the remedy sought, or assoilzieing[23] the defender.

Procedure where proof before answer has been allowed is the same, save that legal issues are kept open for argument when counsel is heard on the evidence, and they will then make submissions both on the law and on the evidence. Each party will argue to the judge that on the evidence he should hold it proved that certain facts were, or were not, established, that the facts established did, or did not, amount to legal cruelty or breach of contract or negligence or whatever be the case, and that in consequence

---

[22] *i.e.* take the case for private consideration.
[23] The " z " is not pronounced. The word means " absolving " and the decree is called " absolvitor."

the judge should find the defender liable, or not liable. In such cases evidence and legal argument are closely interwoven. Thus in *B. S. Brown* v. *Craiks* [24] B sued C for damages for breach of a contract of sale of cloth by delivery of defective cloth. At a proof evidence was led of the contract, the delivery, the quality of the cloth and its defects, and the pursuers argued that the cloth supplied with the defects proved was not of " merchantable quality " within the meaning of the Sale of Goods Act 1893, s. 14 (1), and that the sellers were therefore in breach of contract and should be held liable in damages. The Lord Ordinary found the facts [25] and reached the conclusion [26] that the pursuers had failed to prove the facts necessary to establish their claim under section 14 (1) and also, after examination of the cases to determine what " merchantable quality" in section 14 meant, held [27] that the pursuers had failed to prove that the cloth was not of " merchantable quality." He therefore assoilzied the defenders. The case was appealed on the legal issue only to the First Division [28] and to the House of Lords [29] and both courts agreed with the Lord Ordinary.

Jury Trial

Jury trial is normally done with Issues. An *Issue* is a question of fact precisely formulated in writing by the pursuer for the jury to answer; there may also be a *Counter-Issue* for the defender.[30] Issue and counter-issue, if any, are designed to obtain an answer from the jury to the major matters of fact on which the parties are in dispute, such as whether the pursuer's injuries were caused by the defender's fault.

The jury numbers twelve and both sexes are usually represented. The members are drawn by lot from a larger number cited for the purpose. The jury are sworn and junior counsel for the pursuer makes an opening speech to the jury outlining the case.[31] Evidence for the pursuer is then led as in a proof. As at a proof, the evidence is recorded in shorthand and the judge makes his own notes. At the conclusion of the pursuer's case counsel for the defence may submit that there is no case to answer and that the case should be withdrawn from the jury.[32] Unless this is acceded to, the defence case is opened by junior counsel and evidence for the

---

[24] 1970 S.C.(H.L.) 51.
[25] p. 53.
[26] p. 55.
[27] p. 61.
[28] pp. 61–70.
[29] pp. 71–80.
[30] For specimens, see *Hayden* v. *Glasgow Corpn.*, 1948 S.C. 143; *McLean* v. *The Admiralty*, 1960 S.C. 199.
[31] On this speech, see *Robertson* v. *Federation of Iceland Co-operative Societies*, 1948 S.C. 565; *Lawrie* v. *Glasgow Corpn.*, 1952 S.C. 361.
[32] *McDonald* v. *Duncan*, 1933 S.C. 737; *Grant* v. *W. Alexander & Sons*, 1937 S.L.T. 572.

A civil jury trial in the Court of Session. L. to R. The jury, the presiding judge, the shorthand writer and the witness; at the table a Clerk of Session; in the front row, junior and senior counsel for the pursuer, senior and junior counsel for the defender; behind them the parties' solicitors.

defence led in the same way. If the motion to withdraw the case from the jury is acceded to, the pursuer may move the Inner House to allow a new trial.[33]

After the conclusion of the evidence senior counsel for the pursuer and for the defender successively address the jury, each trying to commend his client's case to the jury. Each counsel must, after addressing the jury, make any special requests or submissions in law to the judge, such as requests for a particular direction to the jury in point of law.

The judge then charges the jury; he instructs them that they are sole masters of the facts and judges of the credibility of witnesses, of the cogency, value and weight to be attached to their evidence, and of the inferences which may be drawn from conduct, circumstantial evidence or the absence of evidence or explanations. He will explain to them as simply as possible the points of law which are involved [34]: he will indicate the main points in the evidence, to assist the jury to have the evidence clearly before their minds; he must point out the necessity for corroborative testimony. Lastly he will indicate what elements have to be taken into account if the jury come to consider damages, and what principles should be followed in their assessment, and he will refer to the Issue, and Counter-Issue, if there is one, indicating the possible answers according to the possible views of the evidence.

If counsel for either party objects to any part of the charge or wishes any further or other direction to be given to the jury, he must say so at the end of the charge. The jury is directed to withdraw and counsel addresses the judge, indicating the direction desired, and if the judge refuses to give it, counsel must there and then tender a *Note of Exceptions*, formulating the exception taken by him and stating the substance of the direction desired and this note, recording the judge's determination thereon is certified by him.[35] The judge may accept counsel's proposition and give further or other directions to the jury in the sense requested.

At the conclusion of the charge the jury may at once give its verdict but usually retires to the jury room to deliberate before doing so. They may return to court to request further directions from the judge on any point, or to request that some portion of evidence be read over to them from the notes.

The verdict may be given unanimously or by a majority at any time, but if after three hours the jury has been unable to agree upon some verdict, the judge may order them to be discharged and order the case

---

[33] *Mulligan* v. *Caird* (*Dundee*), 1973 S.L.T. 72.

[34] The jury must accept his view of the law: *Gelot* v. *Stewart* (1871) 9 M. 957.

[35] For an example, see *Power* v. *Central S.M.T. Co.*, 1949 S.C. 376; see also *Bain* v. *Fife Coal Co.*, 1935 S.C. 681; *Robertson* v. *Federation of Iceland Co-operative Societies*, 1948 S.C. 565; *Glacken* v. *N.C.B.*, 1951 S.C. 617; *Douglas* v. *Cunningham*, 1964 S.C.(H.L.) 112; *McArthur* v. *Weir Housing Corpn.*, 1970 S.C. 135.

to be tried afresh with another jury. The verdict is normally a *General Verdict, i.e.* such answers to the Issue, and Counter-Issue, if any, as amount to a general finding for or against the pursuer, but do not answer specific points as to grounds of liability or otherwise. A *Special Verdict, i.e.* a series of answers to specific questions on points of fact formulated by the trial judge, is competent but rare. The verdict is recorded and the jury discharged. Subsequently counsel for the party favoured by the verdict moves the court to apply the verdict, *i.e.* convert it into a decree, and to deal with expenses. Difficulties occasionally arise when juries return self-contradictory or incomprehensible verdicts.

Settlement of action

At any stage the parties may settle the action, as when the defender offers a sum in settlement of the pursuer's claim and the pursuer accepts it. When this happens the action is abandoned or the court grants decree in terms of a joint minute agreed by the parties.

Abandonment of action

A pursuer who sees no prospect of success may abandon his action.

Petitions

Petition is the proper mode of approaching the court and seeking its authority for some action, or some administrative remedy, or some appointment which only the court can make. Petitions are frequently non-contentious and uncontested. Thus a petition is appropriate for the appointment of a judicial factor, for the appointment of new trustees, to obtain power for trustees to sell heritage, to wind up a company or effect an arrangement between a company and its creditors and in various other cases.

Some petitions are presented to the Outer House, some to the Inner House. The authority of the court is necessary before the petition is served on the persons who may wish to object or advertised or otherwise intimated. If no answers are lodged by the respondents called, the petition appears on the rolls, counsel appears before the court and may have his petition granted at once. In some cases the court remits to a member of the Bar or to a solicitor of experience [36] to inquire into the facts alleged and to report before it disposes of the petition. In other cases a proof is ordered, which proceeds in the same way as the proof in an action.

If the petition should be opposed, *Answers* are lodged and the court may hear parties, have a proof, or remit to a reporter and hear parties on his report before disposing of the application. A party affected by

---

[36] See *e.g. Scotstown Moor Children's Camp*, 1948 S.C. 630; *City Property Investment Trust Corpn. Ltd.*, 1951 S.C. 570.

the petition but not desiring to oppose it may lodge a Minute and crave to be heard on some point.

Motions

Incidental applications to the court are made by *motion*, which may be opposed, argued, and appealed.[37]

Special forms of action

Certain kinds of actions have special procedural features.

Report to the Inner House

An Outer House judge, faced with a point of general importance or particular difficulty, may report the case to the Inner House with an opinion. The point is then argued before one of the Divisions which delivers an opinion, giving guidance to the Lord Ordinary, and returns the case to him.[38]

Appeal to the Inner House—Reclaiming Motion

The decision of a judge pronounced in the Outer House after debate or proof may be appealed to the Inner House by way of *reclaiming motion*, which brings under the review of the Inner House the whole or any part of the cause as decided down to that point. Only exceptionally need the leave of the Outer House judge be obtained. Copies of the pleadings and documents used in the Outer House and of the Lord Ordinary's opinion are lodged for the court, and, where appropriate, duplicated transcripts of evidence extended from the shorthand-writer's notes. In due course the case appears in the rolls assigned to either the First or the Second Division and is argued. If the reclaiming motion is from the decision of an Outer House judge on a point debated in Procedure Roll, there is purely legal argument on the pleadings, there being no evidence. In this case the pleadings and the Lord Ordinary's opinion are read and criticised by the reclaimer and supported by the respondent. If the reclaiming motion is against a Lord Ordinary's decision after proof, the evidence which has been heard in the Outer House is not reheard but the judges and counsel have duplicated copies of the shorthand-writer's transcript of the evidence and this, or the relevant parts of it, is read to the court. Junior counsel for the reclaimer opens the case and is replied to by junior counsel for the respondent. Thereafter senior counsel for the reclaimer and for the respondent respectively address the court.

At the end of the hearing judgment may be given at once. One of the judges may deliver extempore a leading opinion and the others concur or add short opinions. In more difficult cases the court will *make*

---

[37] *e.g. Harley* v. *Kinnear Moodie & Co.*, 1964 S.C. 99.
[38] *e.g. Kerr* v. *John Brown & Co.*, 1965 S.C. 144.

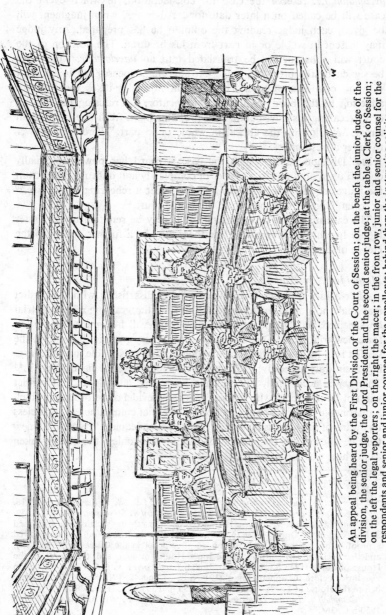

An appeal being heard by the First Division of the Court of Session; on the bench the junior judge of the division, the senior judge, the Lord President and the second senior judge; at the table a Clerk of Session; on the left the legal reporters; on the right the macer; in the front row, junior and senior counsel for the respondents and senior and junior counsel for the appellants; behind them the instructing solicitors.

avizandum i.e. reserve the case for consideration, in which event the case will be called on a later date for " Advising," when judgment will be given, each judge reading the opinion he has prepared. Any judge may dissent in whole or in part from his brethren. The decision of the court will subsequently be translated into an *interlocutor*, which will be signed by the presiding judge. At advising, expenses fall to be dealt with on counsel's motion. The decision normally takes the form of adhering to the Lord Ordinary's interlocutor, *i.e.* refusing the appeal, or of recalling his interlocutor and pronouncing a fresh one in different terms, *i.e.* allowing the appeal in whole or in part. There is no power to order a fresh proof.

The Division before which the case is heard has power, if equally divided or in doubt as to a matter of complexity and difficulty, to consult the judges of the other Division,[39] or to order a rehearing before five [40] or seven judges,[41] or even before the whole court.[42]

The case may now be at an end, or it may be remitted to the Outer House for further procedure,[43] or there may be a further appeal to the House of Lords.

Motion for New Trial

After a jury trial has taken place a party dissatisfied with the verdict may make a motion in the Inner House for the granting of a new trial on specified and limited grounds. The court will not grant the motion for a new trial merely if it disagrees with the jury's verdict but only if the verdict is in its view so flagrantly wrong that no reasonable jury discharging their duty honestly under proper direction would have given it.[44] The jury is accordingly allowed a considerable latitude and its verdict will not be interfered with if there was some evidence before it on which a reasonable jury could have reached the verdict complained of, or unless its award of damages is grossly excessive or inadequate.[45] Nor will a new trial be allowed on the ground of misdirection unless the charge taken as a whole was misleading.[46]

---

[39] *e.g. Connell* v. *Connell,* 1950 S.C. 505.

[40] *e.g. Houston* v. *Buchanan,* 1937 S.C. 460.

[41] *e.g. Yuill's Trustees* v. *Thomson* (1902) 4 F. 815; *Brodie* v. *Ker,* 1952 S.C. 216.

[42] *e.g. Lang* v. *Bruce* (1832) 10 S. 777; see also *Baird* v. *Stevenson,* 1907 S.C. 1259.

[43] Thus in *Bourhill* v. *Young,* 1941 S.C. 395, the pursuer's claim was dismissed as irrelevant in the Outer House (p. 398), reclaimed to the Inner House, which allowed a proof before answer (p. 403), dismissed after proof in the Outer House (p. 405), and this decision was affirmed in the Inner House (p. 407), and, on appeal, in the House of Lords (1942 S.C.(H.L.) 78). In *Boyd and Forrest* v. *G.S.W. Ry.* the action was thrice before the Inner House (1911 S.C. 37 and 42, 1914 S.C. 472) and twice before the House of Lords (1912 S.C.(H.L.) 93 and 1915 S.C.(H.L.) 20).

[44] *Campbell* v. *Scottish Educational News Co.* (1906) 8 F. 691; *McGinley* v. *Pacitti,* 1950 S.C. 364.

[45] *Elliot* v. *Glasgow Corpn.,* 1922 S.C. 146; *McKinlay* v. *Glasgow Corpn.,* 1951 S.C. 495.   [46] *McArthur* v. *Weir Housing Corpn.,* 1970 S.C. 135.

The case is heard before either of the Divisions of the Inner House, and the judge who presided at the jury trial in the Outer House formerly also sat with the Division for the hearing of the motion. As in the case of reclaiming motions, any evidence necessary is read from duplicated transcripts of the shorthand-writer's notes. While two counsel are usually instructed, only one speech is heard from each side.

The court delivers judgment in the usual way, allowing or refusing a new trial and remitting the case to the Outer House for the verdict to be entered up, or to have a fresh jury summoned and the case retried.[47] Sometimes, by consent of parties, the court itself decides the issue instead of allowing a new trial, and in certain circumstances it may set aside the verdict and enter judgment for the party unsuccessful at the trial.[48] The exercise of the court's discretion in allowing or refusing a new trial, or setting aside the verdict and entering judgment for the other party, may be challenged by way of appeal to the House of Lords,[49] which may itself exercise similar powers.[50]

Appeals from the Sheriff Court

Appeals from the sheriff court are heard by the Inner House and disposed of in very much the same way as reclaiming motions. The case appears in the rolls of either Division of the Inner House and the judges have before them prints of the sheriff court record, the interlocutors of the sheriff, and of any evidence heard and documents produced in the sheriff court. Argument is heard from one or two counsel on each side and the sheriff's interlocutor appealed from may be adhered to, or recalled and a different interlocutor substituted, or the court may make different or additional findings in fact or in law. The appeal may thus be allowed or dismissed, and the action may, if necessary, be remitted to the sheriff court. The court may order additional proof to be heard.

Other Inner House Appeals

Other Inner House Appeals brought under particular statutes commonly proceed in the same general manner as appeals from the sheriff court. In some cases, particularly appeals to the Court of Session as Court of Exchequer, the appeal is by way of *stated case*, in which procedure the parties frame a case setting forth the facts found or agreed and formu-

---

[47] Sometimes a third trial is necessary, and there is theoretically no limit, but the court rarely grants a third trial and there seems to be no record of a fourth ever being granted: see *Watson* v. *N.B. Ry.* (1904) 7 F. 220; *McKnight* v. *General Motor Carrying Co.*, 1936 S.C. 17; *McCallum* v. *Paterson*, 1969 S.C. 85.

[48] Jury Trials (Scotland) Act 1910, s. 2: *Mills* v. *Kelvin & White*, 1913 S.C. 521; *Collum* v. *Carmichael*, 1957 S.C. 349; *Potec* v. *Edinburgh Corpn.*, 1964 S.C.(H.L.) 1. For an unusual example of practice, see *Moyes* v. *Burntisland Shipbuilding Co.*, 1952 S.C. 429.

[49] *e.g. Potec, supra*; *Douglas* v. *Cunningham*, 1964 S.C.(H.L.) 112.

[50] Administration of Justice (Scotland) Act 1972, s. 2.

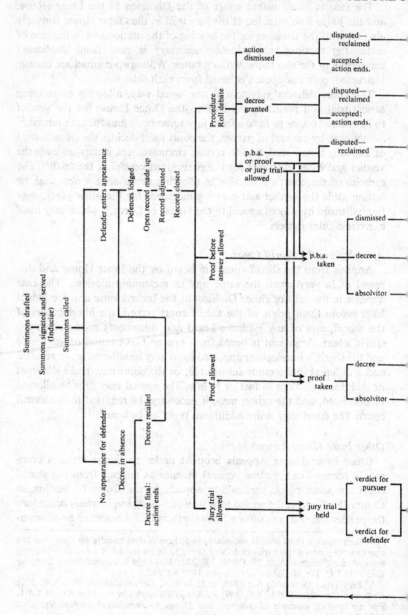

COURT OF SESSION ACTION

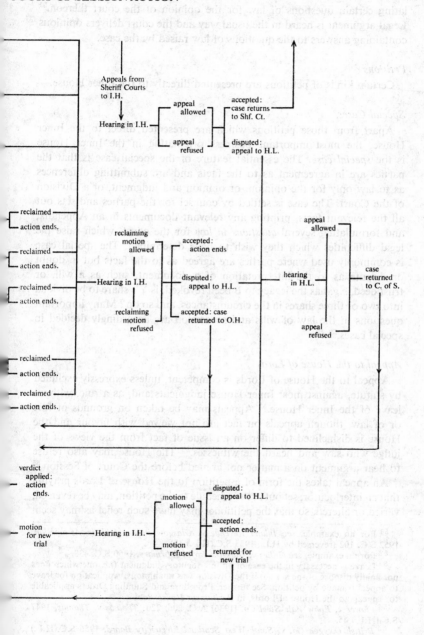

INNER HOUSE STAGES   H.L. STAGE

lating certain questions of law for the opinion of the court thereon.[51] Legal argument is heard in the usual way and the court delivers opinions containing answers to the questions of law raised by the case.

Petitions

Certain kinds of petitions are presented directly to the Inner House.

Special Cases

Apart from those petitions which are presented direct to the Inner House, the most important business originating in the Inner House is the *special case*. The essential feature of the special case is that the parties are in agreement as to the facts and are submitting differences as to law only for the opinion, or opinion and judgment, of a Division of the Court. The case is settled by counsel for the parties and sets out all the relevant facts, printing any relevant documents in an Appendix, and formulating several *questions in law* for the court, which raise the legal difficulties which they wish to have determined. The special case is commonly used where parties are agreed as to the facts but in doubt or dispute as to the interpretation of a document, such as a will, or trust deed, *e.g.* has the legacy to B been revoked, is Y's share to be divided into two or three shares in the circumstances, and so on? Many important questions in the law of wills and succession are accordingly decided in special cases.[52]

Appeal to the House of Lords

Appeal to the House of Lords is competent, unless expressly excluded by statute, against most Inner House judgments and, as a rule, without leave of the Inner House.[53] Appeals may be taken on grounds of fact or of law, though appeals on fact are not viewed with favour and the House is disinclined to differ on an issue of fact from the views of the judge who saw and heard the witnesses.[54] The House may also refuse to hear argument on a matter not argued before the Court of Session.[55]

An appeal takes the form of a petition to the House of Lords praying that an interlocutor, set out in the schedule to the petition, may be reversed, varied or altered, so that the petitioner may have such relief as may seem

---

[51] For an example, see *Inland Revenue* v. *Glasgow Police Athletic Association,* 1952 S.C. 102 (reversed by H.L., 1953 S.C.(H.L.) 13).

[52] For an example, see *Gillies* v. *Glasgow Royal Infirmary,* 1960 S.C. 438.

[53] Leave is necessary in the case of an interlocutory judgment (*i.e.* one which does not finally dispose of the action) if the Division was unanimous. Application for leave to appeal is made by petition. See further, Procedure and Standing Orders applicable to Appeals to the House of Lords, in *Parliament House Book.*

[54] *Flower* v. *Ebbw Vale Steel Co.* [1936] A.C. 206, 220; *Thomas* v. *Thomas,* 1947 S.C.(H.L.) 45.

[55] *British Oxygen Co.* v. *South-West Scotland Electricity Board,* 1956 S.C.(H.L.) 112, 120.

right. It must be signed by two counsel as being a proper case to be heard by way of appeal. Each party lodges a printed or duplicated case, or a joint case with reasons *pro* and *con*, and the appellant lodges an Appendix of all the documents in the case, including pleadings, interlocutors, correspondence, etc. The opinions of the judges in the courts below are also printed or, if the case has been reported, copies of the reports are lodged. Copies of the printed cases are exchanged between the agents and copies are bound in a volume containing both cases.[56]

The case is heard by at least three, and usually by five, Law Lords sitting formerly in the same legislative chamber as is used by the full House of Lords and nowadays in one of the committee rooms. Only the Lord Chancellor on the Woolsack is robed. At least two counsel are instructed but the argument is normally sustained by one senior counsel on each side (who for this appearance formerly had to wear full-bottomed wigs), but in cases of great length and complexity the argument on each side is divided, one counsel arguing certain points, the other following on other topics. Not more than two counsel will be heard on each side. Counsel for the appellant opens, and may reply briefly after the respondent has made his submissions.[57]

The House usually takes time to consider and gives judgment later. Since the sitting is nominally a sitting of the House as a legislative body, the question is put and the peers present (*i.e.* the Law Lords who heard the appeal) speak for or against the motion. In modern practice judgments are not usually delivered orally but are issued later in typescript.[58]

After judgment in the House the case returns to the Inner House, which *applies the judgment*, but if the judgment of the Inner House has not been simply affirmed, a petition must be presented to the Inner House craving it to apply the judgment of the House of Lords and to deal with expenses.

SHERIFF COURT PROCEEDINGS

Ordinary Causes

The main principles of the procedure already discussed in relation to the Court of Session apply also to the sheriff court, with certain variations of terminology and practice. Thus, for example, an action is commenced by an Initial Writ, Petition or Summons[59] but it cannot be served on the defender without a warrant obtained from the sheriff-clerk: it does not pass the Signet. But the principles of pleading, the Open and

---

[56] See *Practice Direction* [1964] 2 All E.R. 509.

[57] As to submitting in advance lists of authorities to be cited in argument, see *Practice Direction* [1967] 1 All E.R. 128.

[58] See *Practice Direction* [1963] 1 W.L.R. 1382; [1963] C.L.Y. 2777.

[59] There is no fixed name for the first writ in a sheriff court action; it is sometimes called Initial Writ and sometimes Summons or Petition or Statement of Claim.

A proof in a defended civil action in a Sheriff Court. L. to R. The witness, the shorthand writer and the Sheriff. At the table the defender, his solicitor, the sheriff-clerk depute, the pursuer's solicitor and the pursuer.

Closed Records, the hearings on Procedure Roll and the conduct of proof follow closely Court of Session procedure. Jury trial in the sheriff court is very limited and is uncommon,[60] but in certain cases an action commenced in the sheriff court may be removed to the Court of Session for jury trial there. The sheriff must append a note to all interlocutors, except those of a formal nature, setting forth the grounds on which he has proceeded, and in a final judgment on the merits he must set out his findings in fact and in law separately.

Summary Causes

More material variations arise in respect of summary causes, that is, actions where the value of the cause does not exceed £250, or where the parties consent to summary trial. A summary cause is commenced by the ordinary form of Initial Writ but thereafter the sheriff orders such procedure as he thinks fit. Formal defences are usual but not essential; the record is not usually made up or closed; and the evidence is not usually recorded. The procedure is intended to be carried through without delay, and the case may be heard and decided within a very short time. There is appeal to the sheriff principal on fact and law only if the evidence is recorded, but otherwise on law only, and further appeal is competent only with the sheriff principal's leave.

Small Debt Causes

Claims not exceeding, or restricted to, £50 may be pursued in the Sheriff's Small Debt Court, which deals with the recovery of debts, demands and penalties, and a few other special kinds of cases.[61]

A small debt action is commenced by completing the blank portions of a printed form, giving a brief statement of the claim and the grounds for it. The form is signed by the sheriff-clerk, who thereby grants warrant for its service on the defender and assigns a date for the defender to appear[62]: it is served personally or by recorded delivery service. A copy of any statement of account issued is attached to the summons.

On the trial date the cases are called in succession and decree commonly passes in absence. If the defender appears, he frequently agrees to pay by instalments, and decree is granted accordingly. If a proof is necessary it is conducted summarily, the only note of the evidence being that taken by the sheriff himself. The proceedings are summary, and the only record is that made in the statutory book of causes. Judgment is

---

[60] See Sheriff Courts (Scotland) Act 1907, Sched. 1, rr. 133–150.

[61] See Dobie, *Sheriff Court Practice*, Chap. 22, and Sheriff Courts (Civil Jurisdiction and Procedure) (Scotland) Act 1963.

[62] In the larger sheriff courts the Small Debt Court is held once or twice each week, or even daily, and numerous cases come up at each court. The *induciae* (period of notice) is usually six days, so that the defender will be cited to appear at the first court more than a week ahead.

pronounced orally but the case may be adjourned for judgment. The decree is usually endorsed on the summons form and signed by the sheriff-clerk. Written defences may be ordered and such a case is then automatically transferred to the Ordinary Court roll.[63]

Judgments in the small debt court are appealable only to the High Court of Justiciary on the grounds of corruption, malice or oppression on the sheriff's part, deviation from the due form, or incompetency of the proceedings (which includes defect in jurisdiction). There is no appeal in the normal sense of that term on the ground either of fact or of law.

Appeal from Sheriff to Sheriff Principal

Appeal is competent from the judgment of the sheriff to the sheriff principal in many cases, including all final judgments, without leave, and in other cases with the leave of the sheriff.

The sheriff principal hears oral argument on behalf of parties, based on the Record and transcript of evidence, if any, and may allow amendment of the Record, or further proof in the action. He will dispose of the appeal by adhering to the interlocutor of the sheriff, or recalling it and pronouncing a fresh one. As in the case of the sheriff, the sheriff principal must append to his interlocutor a note setting forth the grounds on which he has proceeded. There is no appeal on the merits in small debt cases.

Appeal from Sheriff Court to Court of Session and House of Lords

Appeal is competent to the Court of Session against final judgments of either sheriff or sheriff principal or against certain interlocutors, or in any case with leave,[64] save that in a case tried as a summary cause no appeal is competent unless the sheriff principal after final judgment by him on appeal, certifies the cause as suitable for appeal to the Court of Session.[65] Further appeal to the House of Lords is competent, but only on grounds of law, and that even if further proof has been heard in the Court of Session.

DILIGENCE

When one party obtains a decree against another, as for payment of money as debt or damages, the decree may not be satisfied voluntarily, in which case resort must be had to one or more of the forms of diligence. Some forms of diligence may be used at an early stage in an action to

---

[63] *Ailardice* v. *Wallace*, 1957 S.L.T. 225.

[64] See *e.g. Kearney's Exrx.* v. *MacLeod and Parker*, 1965 S.C. 450.

[65] Thus, *e.g.* in *White & Carter (Councils) Ltd.* v. *McGregor*, 1962 S.C.(H.L.) 1 an action was brought in the sheriff court and dismissed after debate; appeal was taken to the Court of Session which allowed a proof before answer; after proof the sheriff-substitute dismissed the action, and the Court of Session on appeal affirmed his decision. The House of Lords by 3 to 2 reversed the Court of Session and the sheriff-substitute. See also *Grant* v. *N.C.B.*, 1956 S.C.(H.L.) 48; *Designers and Decorators (Scotland) Ltd.* v. *Ellis*, 1957 S.C.(H.L.) 69.

force a debtor to appear, or to compel him to find security for the sum claimed against him pending the decision of the action, but diligence is most commonly used in execution of a judgment. The forms of diligence vary according as it is done against the person or the property of the debtor and according to the kind of property.

The usual basis for diligence is an *extract* of the decree of court, containing a warrant for execution, but diligence may also follow on any writ containing a clause of consent to registration for execution and recorded in the books of a court, which is equivalent to an extracted decree.

Imprisonment for civil debt or failure to obey a decree is the only form of diligence against the person and is now very limited in application.

Moveable property belonging to the debtor but in the hands of a third party, such as money in a bank, may be attached by *arrestment* and may be taken by a subsequent action of *furthcoming*. Moveable property in the debtor's own hands may be taken in satisfaction of a decree by *poinding* [66] followed by sale by auction. As a preliminary to poinding the defender must receive a *charge*, or formal requisition to pay, served by a messenger-at-arms (for a Court of Session decree) or sheriff-officer (for a sheriff court decree).[67]

Adjudication is the means of attaching heritable property and requires a special action in the Court of Session. Other forms of diligence which are less common are *inhibition* which prevents a party transacting to the creditor's prejudice, *poinding of the ground*,[66] which attaches moveables on land belonging to the proprietor of the lands; *maills and duties*, which attaches the rents payable by a debtor's tenants to him, and *sequestration for rent* which entitles a landlord to have a tenant's goods sequestrated, valued and sold. Bankruptcy (or more properly *sequestration*) is not strictly a form of diligence but may be resorted to by a creditor who presents a petition for the sequestration of the debtor as a means of exacting payment of at least part of a claim. It is the legal process whereby a person who is unable to pay his debts in full may surrender, or have all his property transferred by the court, to a trustee, who realises the property and pays creditors proportionately to their claims, after certain preferential claims have been met.

II—Proceedings in Special Courts and Administrative Tribunals

It is impossible to discuss briefly and generally the characteristic features of proceedings before special courts and administrative tribunals since they differ so very much *inter se*. They vary from special courts such as

---

[66] Pronounced " pinding."
[67] For procedure see *New Day Furnishing Stores Ltd.* v. *Curran,* 1974 S.L.T. (Sh.Ct.) 20; *Cantors* v. *Hardie,* 1974 S.L.T. (Sh.Ct.) 26; *Scottish Gas Board* v. *Johnstone,* 1974 S.L.T. (Sh.Ct.) 65.

service courts-martial and the Scottish Land Court, which have formal rules of procedure, to tribunals where the greatest informality prevails. In every case the rules and practice of the particular judicial body must be looked for and followed.

III.—ARBITRATIONS

Procedure

The procedure in an arbitration is such as the parties may agree, and the degree of formality or informality will depend largely on whether issues of fact or of law bulk larger in the case. Counsel or solicitors may be instructed, there may be pleadings, written or oral argument, a proof, an inspection of the premises or subject-matter of dispute or otherwise as may be required. The arbiter may consult an expert, such as an engineer, if such assistance is necessary.

The arbiter may submit a draft award or proposed findings to the parties, and allow them to lodge, and be heard on, representations regarding these proposed findings. He may also make an interim award. The final award or decree arbitral narrates the circumstances, the submission, and the procedure which followed, and then makes the final finding and decree, which once issued and delivered to the parties, is beyond recall and binding on them and their successors.

Appeal to the Courts

By accepting arbitration parties voluntarily exclude the jurisdiction of the courts. In statutory arbitrations there may be an appeal to the courts by case stated,[68] and, subject to express provision to the contrary in an agreement to refer to arbitration, an arbiter or oversman may, on the application of a party, and must, if the Court of Session directs, at any stage in the arbitration state a case for the opinion of that court on a question of law arising in the arbitration.[69] Apart from that the courts will not interfere on the merits, however wrong the arbiter's decision may appear to be in fact or in law or in both, and there is no appeal. The whole object of arbitration is to exclude resort to the courts.

An arbiter's award may however be reduced by an action of reduction in court on the ground that he had an interest, unknown to one party, in the case, or if he proceeds *ultra fines compromissi*, that is, deals with a point beyond the scope of the reference to him, or if he has mistaken the point in issue, or has not exhausted the questions submitted to him, or if there has been corruption, bribery or falsehood, or such a serious error in procedure as amounts to a denial of a principle of natural justice, as, for example, failing to hear one party.[70]

---

[68] *e.g.* under the Agricultural Holdings (Scotland) Act 1949; see *e.g.*, *MacNab of MacNab* v. *Willison*, 1960 S.C. 83; *Forsyth-Grant* v. *Salmon*, 1961 S.C. 54.
[69] Administration of Justice (Scotland) Act 1972, s. 3.
[70] On the need for an arbiter to be impartial, see *Fleming's Trs.* v. *Henderson*, 1962 S.L.T. 401.

FURTHER READING

Remedies
Walker: *Law of Civil Remedies in Scotland.*

Court of Session Procedure
Mackay: *Practice of the Court of Session.*
         Manual of Practice in the Court of Session.
MacLaren: *Court of Session Practice.*
Thomson and Middleton: *Manual of Court of Session Procedure.*
Annual Reports: *Civil Judicial Statistics (Scotland).*

Sheriff Court Procedure
Dobie: *Sheriff Court Practice*
       Sheriff Court Styles.
Lees: *Handbook of Pleading in the Sheriff Court.*
Lewis: *Sheriff Court Practice.*

Evidence
Walker and Walker: *Law of Evidence in Scotland.*

Diligence
Graham Stewart: *Law of Diligence.*

Expenses
Maclaren: *Expenses in the Court of Session and Sheriff Court*

Legal Aid
Law Society of Scotland: *Legal Aid (Scotland) Compendium.*

Special Courts and Administrative tribunals
Allen: *Administrative Jurisdiction.*
Robson: *Justice and Administrative Law*
Annual Reports of the Council on Tribunals

Arbitration
Irons and Melville: *Arbitration.*

CHAPTER 14

THE ADMINISTRATION OF CRIMINAL JUSTICE

THE purpose of criminal proceedings is not so much to obtain a remedy for an injured person as by the exercise of the power of organised society to vindicate and enforce law and order, to maintain minimum standards of conduct and to prevent and suppress anti-social, amoral, dangerous, harmful or other detrimental conduct by punishing those who have infringed the code of conduct maintained by the criminal law.

The salient feature of criminal proceedings in Scotland is that public prosecution is the rule and private prosecution uncommon,[1] except in such cases as factory inspectors, who are prosecuting in the public interest.[2] Government departments do not prosecute but in case of need the Lord Advocate acts on their behalf. Nor do the police conduct prosecutions, but transmit information and evidence to the procurator-fiscal with a view to prosecution by him.

The system of public prosecution is directed by the Lord Advocate [3] who is assisted by the Solicitor-General for Scotland and seven Advocates-Depute appointed by the Lord Advocate from members of the Bar. There is a small permanent staff in the Crown Office in Edinburgh, headed by the Crown Agent, and permanent officials, the procurators-fiscal, are appointed in each sheriffdom to be responsible for the investigation and prosecution of crime in the sheriffdom, subject to the overriding control of the Crown Office.[4] It is ultimately the responsibility of the Lord Advocate in practically all cases to decide whether to prosecute, in what court, whether on indictment or summarily, and on what charge, though most everyday offences can be dealt with without need to refer to him for instructions. Cases reported by procurators-fiscal are sent to the Crown Office and there is a code of instructions issued to all P.F.s to secure uniformity of practice, and all High Court indictments are prepared in the Crown Office.

Solemn and Summary Procedure

The important distinction in criminal proceedings is that between solemn procedure (trial on *indictment* before a judge of the High Court

---

[1] *J. & P. Coats* v. *Brown*, 1909 S.C.(J.) 29 and the account thereof by Lord Macmillan (who was counsel in the case) in *A Man of Law's Tale* at pp. 110–114; *McBain* v. *Crichton*, 1961 J.C. 25; *Trapp* v. *M.*, 1971 S.L.T.(Notes) 30.

[2] *e.g. Griffith* v. *Ferrier*, 1952 J.C. 56.

[3] On powers and duties, see *Dumfries C.C.* v. *Phyn* (1895) 22 R. 538. See also Normand, " The Public Prosecutor in Scotland " (1938) 54 L.Q.R. 345.

[4] On the privileged position of Lord Advocate and procurators-fiscal in conducting prosecutions, see *Hester* v. *Macdonald*, 1961 S.C. 370.

of Justiciary and a jury, or before a sheriff principal or sheriff and a jury), and summary procedure (trial on *complaint* before a sheriff principal or sheriff, or magistrate, or one or more justices of the peace, in each case without a jury). This distinction depends mainly on the gravity of the particular crime in question and on whether the limited powers of sentence of a sheriff or magistrate seem adequate, if a conviction is obtained. Some serious crimes are triable on indictment only, but most may be tried in either manner depending on the circumstances and gravity of the case. The decision whether to prosecute on indictment or summarily is vested in the Crown officers. The course of procedure followed and the measure of punishment competent differs in the two cases. Crimes created by statute are frequently prescribed as being " punishable on summary complaint " or " punishable by a court of summary jurisdiction " only.

The High Court has exclusive jurisdiction in cases of treason, murder, rape, incest, deforcement of messengers, breach of duty by magistrates, and cases of certain statutory offences, and may try all crimes unless its jurisdiction is expressly or impliedly excluded by statute. Other serious crimes may be tried in the High Court or before a sheriff and jury. The sheriff court has jurisdiction over all crimes not within the exclusive competence of the High Court. District courts may try cases only if jurisdiction is conferred on them by statute expressly or by implication.[5]

SOLEMN PROCEDURE

Petition

Solemn procedure is initiated by the procurator-fiscal presenting a petition to a magistrate (in practice a sheriff) naming the accused, stating the charge and craving warrants to arrest the accused, search him and his premises, cite witnesses and, after examination, to commit the accused for further examination or until liberated in due course of law. The police also have common law and statutory powers of arrest without warrant in various circumstances. The Crown authorities may obtain warrant to have a special examination made of a suspect,[6] or a search of his house,[7] and—in emergency—examination may be made without warrant.[8]

Judicial examination

On being arrested an accused is entitled to have a solicitor summoned and to have an interview with him. A person arrested on a serious criminal charge must be brought before a magistrate, usually a sheriff, as soon as possible, for examination. Judicial examination is now normally a brief and formal appearance. The proceedings are private. The charge is read and he is cautioned. Normally he makes no *plea* or *declaration* but,

---

[5] *McPherson* v. *Boyd* (1907) 5 Adam 247; *Torrance* v. *Robertson*, 1946 J.C. 135.
[6] *Hay* v. *H.M. Advocate*, 1968 J.C. 40.
[7] *Stewart* v. *Roach*, 1950 S.C. 318.
[8] *Bell* v. *Hogg*, 1967 J.C. 49.

if he does, it is taken down and signed by him and by the sheriff and some
of those present as witnesses. He may then be committed to prison for
further examination, or committed for trial, or released on bail. An accused,
in all cases except treason and murder, is entitled to release on bail unless
the Crown objects. It is then a question for the court's discretion whether
to grant or refuse release on bail having regard to the nature of the crime.
The danger of the accused absconding or tampering with witnesses or
committing further offences, and his criminal record are all factors to be
considered.[9] The grant or refusal of bail may be appealed to the High
Court.[10] The case is then reported to the Crown Office and the accused's
release ordered or the suitable mode of trial ordered, and an *indictment*[11]
is then prepared. It is at the instance of Her Majesty's Advocate, and must
be served on the accused.[12] It sets out the crimes charged and lists the
witnesses and productions *i.e.* documents and articles to be produced, to be
adduced at the trial. To enable him to prepare his defence an accused may
apply to the court for a commission and diligence to enable him to recover
documents in the hands of third parties.[13] There are statutory provisions
to ensure that an accused may only be detained for a limited time in
custody after committal for trial and before his trial is brought to conclusion. The Lord Advocate may apply for an extension of the period.[14]
An accused who wishes to plead guilty and have the disposal of his case
expedited may do so by letter to the Crown Agent.[15] The accused may then
be sentenced.[16]

The Pleading Diet

A person indicted must appear at two diets of trial, the first or pleading
diet and the second or trial diet. At the first, which is normally called
in the sheriff court before which the accused appeared for judicial examination, the accused is called on to plead guilty or not guilty. If he pleads
guilty he may be sentenced or remitted to the High Court for sentence.
The accused may object to the competency of the proceedings or to the
relevancy or legal sufficiency of the charge.[17] These objections raise issues
of law only.[18] He must at this stage tender any *plea in bar of trial* he wishes

---

[9] *A.B.* v. *Dickson*, 1907 S.C.(J.) 111; *Mackintosh* v. *McGlinchy*, 1921 J.C. 75;
MacDonald v. *Clifford*, 1952 J.C. 22; *MacLeod* v. *Wright*, 1959 J.C. 12.

[10] *Mackintosh, supra*; *MacLeod, supra*.

[11] Pronounced " inditement."

[12] Specimen form in Renton and Brown, *Criminal Procedure*, 4th ed., 56.

[13] *H.M. Advocate* v. *Hasson*, 1971 J.C. 35.

[14] Criminal Procedure (Scotland) Act 1975, s. 101; see *e.g.* *H.M.A.* v. *Park*, 1967
J.C. 70; *Hartley* v. *H.M. Advocate*, 1970 J.C. 17; *H.M.A.* v. *McTavish*, 1974 S.L.T. 246.

[15] Criminal Procedure (Scotland) Act 1975, s. 102.

[16] *e.g.* *H.M.A.* v. *Cairns*, 1967 J.C. 37; *Mackie* v. *H.M.A.*, 1969 J.C. 20.

[17] *e.g.* *H.M.A.* v. *Mannion*, 1961 J.C. 69; *H.M.A.* v. *Cairns, supra*; *H.M.A.* v.
R.M., 1969 J.C. 52; *Cameron* v. *H.M. Advocate*, 1971 J.C. 50.

[18] Debates on difficult cases of competency or relevancy may be heard by three
judges of the High Court, *e.g.* *H.M.A.* v. *Cairns*, 1967 J.C. 37; *H.M.A.* v. *McKenzie*,
1970 S.L.T. 81.

to put forward; these include that he was under the age of criminal responsibility, that he is presently *insane*, unable to plead and to give instructions for his defence, that a libel in the same form as the indictment and based on the same facts has previously been held irrelevant, or that he already *tholed an assize, i.e.* been tried for the same offence. He must also at this stage render any *special defence* which he wishes to rely on.[19] Special defences are probably limited to the pleas of *insanity at the time of committing the crime, alibi, i.e.* that he was not there but at another stated place, *incrimination, i.e.* that the crime was not committed by him but by another named person, and *self-defence.*[20] If the accused intends to attack the character of the person he is alleged to have attacked he must give notice of his intention. If he intends to call witnesses, or put in evidence productions not listed in the indictment, he must give written notice at least three days before the second or trial diet.

The Trial Diet

At the trial diet, which is always called in the court which has jurisdiction to try the accused, unless the panel, as the accused is now called, when called on to plead, pleads guilty, a jury of fifteen is empanelled, and the substance of the indictment read to it. There should be no questioning of prospective jurors as to facts which might prejudice them.[21] It is then sworn and any special defence read to the jury. There is no opening speech and Crown counsel (High Court) or the procurator-fiscal (sheriff and jury court) proceeds at once to examine his witnesses. Each is in turn sworn by the presiding judge, examined-in-chief by the Crown counsel or procurator-fiscal, cross-examined by defence counsel and, if need be, re-examined by Crown counsel or the procurator-fiscal. Cross-examination may be selective and the defence need not cross-examine every witness on material points.[22] If the accused on judicial examination emitted a declaration, it is read to the jury at the end of the Crown evidence. The Crown must prove the facts necessary to convince the jury *beyond reasonable doubt* that the accused did the things charged. As in civil actions the evidence may be oral evidence of observation, expert evidence, real or circumstantial evidence [23] or written evidence, but the rules as to admission or rejection of evidence are more strictly applied than in civil cases. Importance attaches to corroboration; by Scots law every essential fact must be corroborated *i.e.* the evidence must be supported by independent evidence from another

---

[19] On preparation for trial and the practice of the Crown to give a measure of assistance to the defence, see *Smith* v. *H.M. Advocate*, 1952 J.C. 66; *Hasson* v. *H.M. Advocate*, 1971 J.C. 35.

[20] On special defences see *H.M. Advocate* v. *Hayes*, 1973 S.L.T. 202; *Lambie* v. *H.M. Advocate*, 1973 S.L.T. 219.

[21] *H.M. Advocate* v. *Stern*, [1975] Crim.L.R. 110.

[22] *McPherson* v. *Copeland*, 1961 J.C. 74.

[23] See *e.g. H.M. Advocate* v. *Kidd*, 1960 J.C. 61; *Ryrie* v. *Campbell*, 1964 J.C. 33.

witness or from facts and circumstances justifying an inference to the same effect.[24]

At the conclusion of the Crown case the presiding judge may, with the consent of the Lord Advocate or his representative prosecuting, if satisfied that there is no evidence to support a conviction, withdraw the case from the jury, but otherwise the defence witnesses are called and examined by defence counsel, cross-examined and, if need be, re-examined. If the panel gives evidence, he usually does so first, and from the witness-box, on oath. If the panel has put forward a special defence he must support it by evidence but it is enough if he satisfies the jury *on balance of probabilities*. If his defence is a mere denial he need not give evidence at all but merely argue that the Crown has failed to prove its case beyond reasonable doubt. A question which frequently causes difficulty in identification of the accused; is the man in the dock the one who was seen or heard to do the crime? [25] Neither panel nor witness may make any unsworn statement, nor make any statement except by way of evidence.[26] The evidence is recorded by a shorthand-writer and the judge makes notes for his own use.

Thereafter prosecuting and defence counsel successively address the jury, and the judge charges the jury, instructing them in the relevant law and on the points in issue.[27] He must instruct the jury that the onus of proof is throughout on the Crown, that all material factors in the evidence must be corroborated, that the jury must evaluate the evidence and decide which evidence to accept and which to reject, that before convicting the jury must have been satisfied beyond reasonable doubt [28] of the panel's guilt, and as to the possible verdicts. He may have to instruct them as to a defence plea of insanity, diminished responsibility or alibi, or other special defence, as to treating the evidence of certain witnesses with particular care, and may have to instruct them to return a verdict of not guilty on a count on which no legally adequate evidence has been adduced.[29] The panel may at any stage change his plea to one of " guilty as libelled " or to a modified plea of guilty, in which case the judge directs the jury to return a verdict of guilty in terms of the confession. The prosecutor may at any stage abandon the prosecution in whole or in part, in which case the judge directs the jury to return a verdict of not guilty.

---

[24] *e.g. Sinclair* v. *MacLeod*, 1964 J.C. 19; *H.M. Advocate* v. *W.B.*, 1969 J.C. 72. There are exceptions; see *e.g. Gerber* v. *B.R. Board*, 1969 J.C. 7.

[25] On identification see *Cameron* v. *H.M. Advocate*, 1959 J.C. 59; *Patterson* v. *Nixon*, 1960 J.C. 42; *Sinclair* v. *MacLeod*, 1964 J.C. 19; *Hay* v. *H.M. Advocate*,1 968 J.C. 40; *Muldoon* v. *Herron*, 1970 J.C. 30; *Temple* v. *H.M. Advocate*, 1971 J.C. 1.

[26] *Gilmour* v. *H.M. Advocate*, 1965 J.C. 45.

[27] For specimens of presiding judge's charge to a jury, see, *e.g., Bird* v. *H.M. Advocate*, 1952 J.C. 23; *H.M. Advocate* v. *Kidd*, 1960 J.C. 61.

[28] In civil cases the onus is on the pursuer to satisfy the court or jury on the balance of probabilities only: *Hendry* v. *Clan Line Steamers*, 1949 S.C. 320.

[29] On charging juries, see *McKenzie* v. *H.M. Advocate*, 1959 J.C. 32; *McPhelim* v. *H.M. Advocate*, 1960 J.C. 17; *McCann* v. *H.M. Advocate*, 1960 J.C. 36.

A criminal trial in the North Court, Justiciary Buildings, Glasgow. On the bench the shorthand writer and the presiding judge; facing the judge, in the dock, the panel, between two officers; in the centre the witness, the advocate-depute and his assistant, the Clerk of Justiciary, counsel for the defence, and the panel's solicitor, and, behind them, the jury.

At the conclusion of the charge the jury may give a verdict at once, or retire to consider it. The jury verdict may be returned by a majority and may, unless they have been specially directed in law that one or another is not open to them, be any one of "guilty," "not guilty," or "not proven." [30] It is announced in reply to a question from the clerk of the court, by the chancellor (more commonly called foreman) of the jury. The verdict discloses whether the jury was unanimous or divided, but the size of the majority is not disclosed. Some jurors may have voted for each of these possible verdicts, [31] but the panel is liable to be convicted only if at least eight jurors vote for "guilty." [32] The verdict is recorded, read over to the jury and their assent to its terms recorded. Thereafter the verdict cannot be amended. [33] If there are several counts in the indictment the jury must bring in a verdict on each count.

If the verdict is one of "not guilty" or "not proven" the accused is at once assoilzied from the charge and discharged. If the verdict is one of "guilty" prosecuting counsel moves his Lordship to pass sentence, without which no sentence can be passed, [34] and, if any previous convictions are relied on, lays before the presiding judge a copy of the notice of previous convictions previously served on the accused. If these are disputed they will have to be proved. Defending counsel may make a plea in bar of sentence, such as that the verdict is ambiguous, or that the accused has become insane. He then addresses the court in mitigation of punishment and may adduce witnesses (who should be sworn) [35] in support of his plea in mitigation, after which the presiding judge pronounces sentence. He may adjourn the case, but not for more than three weeks at a time, to consider what sentence is suitable or to permit of inquiries being made as to the accused's physical or mental condition or his suitability for particular kinds of punishment or treatment. If the trial has been before a sheriff and jury the sheriff may remit the panel to the High Court for sentence if he thinks that any sentence which he can pronounce is inadequate. [36]

Appeal

A person convicted on indictment in the High Court or sheriff court [37] may appeal to the High Court of Justiciary sitting as Court of Criminal Appeal. [38] Appeal may be taken (a) without leave, against conviction, on any question of law alone, or (b) with the leave of the High Court or upon

---

[30] On the Not Proven verdict, see J. G. Wilson, *Not Proven*; *McNicol* v. *H.M Advocate*, 1964 J.C. 25.

[31] See *Lord Advocate* v. *Nicholson*, 1958 S.L.T.(Sh.Ct.) 17.

[32] *McPhelim* v. *H.M. Advocate*, 1960 J.C. 17, 22.

[33] *McGarry* v. *H.M. Advocate*, 1959 J.C. 30.

[34] See *Noon* v. *H.M. Advocate*, 1960 J.C. 52.

[35] *Forbes* v. *H.M. Advocate*, 1963 J.C. 68.

[36] See, *e.g. H.M. Advocate* v. *Churchill*, 1963 J.C. 6.

[37] *i.e.* after trial before a sheriff and jury.

[38] Criminal Procedure (Scotland) Act 1975, s. 228.

A criminal appeal in the High Court of Justiciary, Edinburgh. On the bench the Lord Justice-General or Lord Justice-Clerk and two Lords Commissioners of Justiciary; on the left, the legal reporters; on the right, the Justiciary macer; at the table, on the left, one of the Law officers and an advocate-depute; in the centre, the Clerk of Justiciary; on the right, senior and junior counsel for the appellant. Behind the appellant's counsel is the unoccupied dock.

the certificate of the judge who presided at the trial that it is a fit case for appeal, on a ground of fact, or of mixed fact and law, or on any other ground which appears to the court or the trial judge to be a sufficient ground of appeal, or (c) with the leave of the court, against sentence, unless the sentence is fixed by law.[39] The appeal is initiated by completing and lodging within ten days a note of application for leave to appeal [40] stating the grounds of appeal. Full specification of the grounds of appeal must be stated and not merely a vague objection to the conviction.[41] The appellant may be released on bail pending the appeal but such applications are not regarded favourably. If released on bail the period of liberation is not counted towards his period of sentence.

Sessions of the High Court are held in Edinburgh every few weeks for the disposal of appeals and the Bench normally consists of the Lord Justice-General or Lord Justice-Clerk and two other Lords Commissioners of Justiciary, though a larger Bench may be convened to hear cases of particular importance.[42] The appellant may present a written case but usually oral argument is presented by counsel. The appellant may be present in court, in the custody of two warders, except in the case of appeals on law alone. The Crown is represented by one or more of the Advocates-Depute and sometimes by one of the Law Officers.

The court have before them the trial judge's notes and his report giving his opinion on the case or on any point arising therein and, if necessary, a transcript of the shorthand-writer's notes of the evidence and proceedings at the trial. They may order the production of documents or the attendance of further witnesses for examination, so long as the witnesses could not have been examined at the trial.[43] If fresh evidence is admitted the court must consider whether the jury verdict would necessarily have been different if it had heard both the evidence now adduced and that put before it at the trial.

Where the appeal is on a matter of law alone and leave is consequently not required, counsel for the appellant proceeds at once with his argument, after which Crown counsel replies. But where leave to appeal is required counsel must first outline the circumstances of the case down to its present stage and satisfy the court that there is a prima facie case or an arguable point before they will grant him leave to develop his argument in full.[44] In

---

[39] This applies only to treason and murder and formerly to capital murder.

[40] The forms are specified in the Schedule to Act of Adjournal, October 27, 1926.

[41] *Boyd* v. *H.M. Advocate*, 1939 J.C. 6; *Reilly* v. *H.M. Advocate*, 1950 J.C. 52.

[42] A notable instance is *Sugden* v. *H.M. Advocate*, 1934 J.C. 103.

[43] As, for example, when it has only later been discovered that those witnesses had any knowledge of the facts in issue. See further, *Lowson* v. *H.M. Advocate*, 1943 J.C. 141; *Lennie* v. *H.M. Advocate*, 1946 J.C. 79; *Gallacher* v. *H.M. Advocate*, 1951 J.C. 38.

[44] *Leighton* v. *H.M. Advocate*, 1931 J.C. 1; *Fox* v. *H.M. Advocate*, 1950 J.C. 64.

considering any criticism of the trial judge's charge the court will have regard to the whole of it, not merely to some phrase.[45]

The court is empowered [46] to allow the appeal if they think that the verdict of the jury should be set aside on the ground that it is unreasonable or cannot be supported having regard to the evidence,[47] or that the judgment of the trial court should be set aside on the ground of a wrong decision of any question of law,[48] or that on any ground there was a miscarriage of justice.[49] If the court allow the appeal they quash the conviction and discharge the accused. The court may also allow an appeal but substitute a verdict of guilty of another charge, and impose a sentence therefor.[50] In other cases they dismiss the appeal, and the court may dismiss the appeal even if of the opinion that the point raised in the appeal might be decided in favour of the appellant, if they consider that no substantial miscarriage of justice has actually occurred.[51] If the appeal is dismissed the court may reduce or increase the sentence.[52] The court has no power to order a retrial, save when sitting as Courts-Martial Appeal Court,[53] but may allow fresh evidence to be led.[54] A case may also be referred to the High Court by the Secretary of State.[55]

Where the appeal is against sentence counsel's statement applying for leave to appeal is treated as the hearing of the appeal, and in practice Crown counsel do not exercise their right of reply, unless called on by the

---

[45] *Reynolds* v. *H.M. Advocate*, 1928 S.N. 103; *McEwan* v. *H.M. Advocate*, 1939 J.C. 26; *McPhelim* v. *H.M. Advocate*, 1960 J.C. 17.

[46] Criminal Appeal (Scotland) Act 1926, s. 2 (1).

[47] This covers cases where the jury convicted on inadequate evidence, *e.g. Morton* v. *H.M. Advocate*, 1938 J.C. 50. The test is not whether the court agrees or disagrees with the jury's verdict, but whether the jury's verdict was so flagrantly wrong and unreasonable that no reasonable jury acting honestly under proper direction could have given it: *Webb* v. *H.M. Advocate*, 1927 J.C. 92.

[48] This includes irrelevancy of the indictment, wrongful admission or exclusion of evidence, and misdirection of the jury by the presiding judge, as by laying down the wrong rule of law, or failing to direct them on some matter.

[49] Under this head the appellant must show that but for the irregularity complained of, it is reasonably probable that the jury would not have convicted him. *Cf. Scott* (*A. T.*) v. *H.M. Advocate*, 1946 J.C. 90. It covers cases of improper evidence being admitted, and other irregularities such as allegations that a witness had talked to a juror.

[50] *McKenzie* v. *H.M. Advocate*, 1959 J.C. 32.

[51] This is known as " the proviso." It is intended to prevent convictions having to be quashed because of some trivial objection, which is valid, but does not at all disturb the rightness of the conviction. For the rather differently worded powers which regulate the court when sitting as Courts-Martial Appeal Court, see Courts-Martial Appeal Act 1968, s. 12.

[52] *Connelly* v. *H.M. Advocate*, 1954 J.C. 90.

[53] Criminal Appeal Act 1964, s. 6 (5) and Sched. 1.

[54] *Slater* v. *H.M. Advocate*, 1928 J.C. 94; *Lowson* v. *H.M. Advocate*, 1943 J.C. 141; *Thompson* v. *H.M. Advocate*, 1968 J.C. 61; *Henderson* v. *H.M. Advocate*, 1970 J.C. 52; *Temple* v. *H.M. Advocate*, 1971 J.C. 1.

[55] *e.g. Gallacher* v. *H.M. Advocate*, 1951 J.C. 38; *Higgins* v. *H.M. Advocate*, 1956 J.C. 69.

court. The court may quash the sentence and pass any other sentence legally allowed, whether more or less severe, or dismiss the appeal.

Appeal procedure does not affect the royal prerogative of mercy which may be exercised on the recommendation of the Secretary of State for Scotland.

SUMMARY CRIMINAL PROCEDURE

Summary criminal procedure is followed by all courts in Scotland having criminal jurisdiction, other than the High Court of Justiciary,[56] when criminal jurisdiction is exercised by the sheriff or other inferior judge sitting alone and without a jury.[57] The sheriff court has jurisdiction to try all common law offences except murder, rape, incest and wilful fire-raising, and also statutory offences, except where that jurisdiction is expressly or impliedly excluded,[58] and certain crimes must be tried by the sheriff. Courts other than the sheriff court have jurisdiction to try minor common law crimes, but statutory offences only if the statute clearly confers such jurisdiction.[59] Apart from that principle and from the provisions of any relevant statute, it rests with the Lord Advocate and the procurators-fiscal to decide in which court a summary prosecution is to commence.

Prosecution

Most prosecutions in the sheriff court are initiated by the procurator-fiscal in the public interest, but some are initiated by other persons prosecuting in the public interest such as factory inspectors,[60] and some by private persons statutorily authorised to prosecute for statutory offences; this includes such as British Railways Board.[61] Prosecutions in the district court are initiated by the district prosecutor or procurator-fiscal.

Initiation of Proceedings

In some cases an accused has been arrested but he has frequently merely been reported by the police as having committed an offence and never been in custody. There is no petition to a magistrate, judicial examination, declaration or committal for trial.

The accused may be in custody, but is usually on bail or has merely been ordained to appear, sometimes under penalty.

Complaint

Summary criminal proceedings are instituted by the service on the

---

[56] These courts are the sheriff court and district courts. Procedure is uniform for all these courts.

[57] The main procedural statute is the Criminal Procedure (Scotland) Act 1975, replacing earlier Acts in similar terms.

[58] *Wilson* v. *Hill*, 1943 J.C. 124.

[59] *McPherson* v. *Boyd*, 1907 S.C.(J.) 42; *Czajkowski* v. *Lewis*, 1956 J.C. 8.

[60] e.g. *Griffith* v. *Ferrier*, 1952 J.C. 56; *Simpson* v. *Hardie & Smith, Ltd.*, 1968 J.C. 23.

[61] e.g. *Gerber* v. *British Railways Board*, 1969 J.C. 7.

accused of a *complaint* [62] and, in the case of a statutory offence, a relative notice of the penalties to which the accused is liable on conviction. This runs in the name of the procurator-fiscal or other prosecutor [63] and states the substance of the charge against the accused, adding, in the case of a statutory contravention, that it is contrary to a specified section of a particular Act. If previous convictions are to be laid before the court by the prosecutor, notice is served separately of those which it is intended to rely on, and they are not disclosed to the judge till after conviction. The complaint is signed by the prosecutor.

In many cases of statutory contraventions the accused pleads guilty by letter, in which case sentence may be pronounced in his absence.

Trial

When the complaint is called in court, the accused must plead to it, if he has not already done so by letter, and the trial may take place then but, as a rule, if he pleads not guilty, an adjourned diet is fixed for trial.

Prior to pleading the accused may state objections to the competency or relevancy of the complaint,[64] or pleas in bar of trial. The complaint may accordingly be dismissed [65] or amended at this stage.

At the adjourned diet of trial the accused, who may be represented by counsel but usually is represented by a solicitor, or may elect to defend himself, is again called on to plead and many accused, at this stage, change their plea to one of guilty, or of guilty to a modified charge. If the accused pleads guilty and his plea is accepted by the procurator-fiscal the sheriff proceeds to consider previous convictions, hears any plea in mitigation offered, and pronounces sentence. If the accused adheres to his plea of not guilty the trial proceeds; the proceedings are conducted fairly informally and summarily and only brief notes of the evidence are taken by the sheriff. The witnesses for the prosecution are called by the procurator-fiscal, and examined, cross-examined and re-examined in the usual way. Then the accused himself, if he wishes, and any witnesses for the accused, give evidence. The rules of evidence are the same as in trials under solemn procedure. Thereafter procurator-fiscal and counsel or solicitor for the accused address the court. Objections to evidence may be taken in the course of the trial and must be noted, if requested, so as to be available for appeal. No previous conviction should be disclosed, even by implication, until the judge is satisfied that the charge has been proved.[66]

---

[62] For specimen, see Summary Jurisdiction (Scotland) Act 1954, Sched. 2.

[63] Certain officials, such as factory inspectors, may prosecute in their own names. A local authority has no title to institute a private prosecution: *McKinstry* v. *Lanark C.C.*, 1962 J.C. 16.

[64] See *e.g. McLennan* v. *MacMillan*, 1964 J.C. 1.

[65] See *e.g. Aitchison* v. *Bartlett*, 1963 J.C. 27.

[66] *Bryce* v. *Gardiner*, 1951 J.C. 134; *McGregor* v. *Macdonald*, 1952 J.C. 4; *Clark* v. *Connell*, 1952 J.C. 119.

A summary criminal trial in a Sheriff Court. On the bench the Sheriff. L. to R. The procurator-fiscal depute, the witness, the accused, the sheriff-clerk depute, and the accused's solicitor.

The judge must himself determine the credibility and veracity of witnesses and decide whether he finds the charge proved beyond reasonable doubt or not. The judge normally pronounces his finding at once; if it is " not guilty " or " not proven," the accused is liberated at once; if " guilty " any previous convictions, notice of which has been served on the accused, if they are admitted or proved, are laid before the sheriff; the accused or his counsel or solicitor may address the court in mitigation before sentence is pronounced.

The sentence is usually one of fine or imprisonment, and a fine is sometimes paid on the spot, but an accused is entitled, save exceptionally, to have time to pay or to be allowed to pay by instalments. In many road traffic cases the sheriff must order the offender's driving licence to be endorsed and may, or must, order him to be disqualified from driving for a period. In some cases the court is required to, and in other cases the sheriff decides to, defer sentence for a period, not exceeding three weeks, to obtain a social inquiry report from the local authority social work department to assist him in determining what sentence is appropriate,[67] and possibly also to obtain reports on the offender's suitability for detention centre or Borstal training. In certain cases the court must state and record in the minutes its reasons for imposing or refraining from imposing certain penalties.[68] The court may in its discretion fix any punishment within the limits of its competency, or may dismiss with an admonition, or without recording a conviction, or may make a probation order. There is no power to remit to the High Court for sentence. If the accused fails to pay the fine or any instalment he is cited to the court again and a means inquiry held, that is, he is questioned by the sheriff as to the reasons for non-payment and he may be committed to prison or another arrangement made for payment, such as smaller instalments.

Review of Summary Trial Verdicts

There are five methods whereby the proceedings of courts of summary criminal jurisdiction may be reviewed. Of these one is obsolete,[69] two uncommon [70] and only two regularly employed. These are appeal by Stated Case, and Bill of Suspension.

Stated Case

Either party [71] may, on the final determination of a summary prose-

---

[67] See *e.g. Auld* v. *Herron,* 1969 J.C. 4.

[68] *e.g. Bruce* v. *Hogg,* 1966 J.C. 33.

[69] Appeal to the Circuit Court under the Heritable Jurisdiction (Scotland) Act 1746.

[70] Appeal to the Court of Session as Court of Exchequer (competent only in Customs and Excise prosecutions); and Advocation, appropriate to the review of irregularities in the preliminary stages. It is usually resorted to by the prosecution: see *McFadyean* v. *Stewart,* 1951 J.C. 164.

[71] For an instance of stated case requested by the procurator-fiscal, see *Macdonald* v. *Cassidy,* 1959 J.C. 1.

cution, apply to the court to state a case for the opinion of the High Court of Justiciary. A stated case may be obtained on very varied grounds, so as to cover practically every question likely to be raised on appeal, including objections to jurisdiction, competency, relevancy, the admission or rejection of evidence, irregularities in procedure, oppressive conduct by the sheriff,[72] and the competency of sentence [73] (but not the amount of sentence). The question may be raised whether a sentence was harsh and oppressive in the circumstances.[74]

It is competent for either party to ask for a stated case, so that the prosecutor may appeal against an acquittal.[71] The party dissatisfied with the legal determination of the court applies to the judge to state and sign a case for the opinion of the High Court of Justiciary. The applicant, unless he is a person prosecuting in the public interest or obtains a dispensation from the judge, must find caution [75] for or consign a sum of money fixed by the judge.

The stated case [76] is prepared by the clerk of court [77] and each party may intimate any adjustments desired, the case being finally settled by the judge. Review does not cover questions of fact but only questions of law (which includes legal inferences drawn from findings in fact). The case narrates the circumstances and what facts the judge found to be admitted or proved,[78] and states the judge's decision and disposal of the case on the basis of these findings of fact. It then states for the opinion of the High Court one or more questions of law [79] such as: " On the facts stated, was I entitled to convict the accused? " or " On the facts stated, was I entitled to reject the evidence of . . . ? " The question whether the inferior court was *right* in convicting is not a question of law for appeal, but a matter which the inferior court had to determine on the facts. The question really is whether the summary court erred in applying the law to the facts it had found admitted or proved, not whether it was right in finding those facts. In some cases it has been difficult to decide whether a question was one of fact, on which the summary court was final, or one of law and open to reconsideration by the High Court on appeal.

Stated cases are heard by the High Court of Justiciary, similarly composed as for a sitting as Court of Criminal Appeal.[80] The appellant is

---

[72] *e.g. McClung* v. *Cruickshank*, 1964 J.C. 64.

[73] *e.g. Kesson* v. *Heatly*, 1964 J.C. 40.

[74] *e.g. Stewart* v. *Cormack*, 1941 J.C. 73; *Fleming* v. *Macdonald*, 1958 J.C. 1; *Geddes* v. *Copeland*, 1962 J.C. 51; *Lockhart* v. *Macdonald*, 1962 J.C. 53.

[75] *i.e.* security: pronounced " kayshun."

[76] For specimen, see Summary Jurisdiction (Scotland) Act 1954, Sched. 2.

[77] In the sheriff court it is in practice done by the sheriff himself.

[78] It is incorrect, as is sometimes done, to narrate some of the evidence; the inferior court should have made up its mind on what it held, on the evidence, to have been established. [79] See *Drummond* v. *Hunter*, 1948 J.C. 109.

[80] In practice the judges of one or other of the Divisions of the Inner House of the Court of Session sit as High Court for about a week, hearing first criminal appeals and then stated cases and bills of suspension.

represented by counsel, and the procurator-fiscal by one or more Crown counsel. Legal argument is heard from both sides, one speech on each side and the court usually disposes of the case at once. It may, however, remit the case with an opinion, or for amendment or clarification of the findings or the point in issue.

The High Court has wide powers [81] to affirm, reverse or alter the decision of the inferior court, to substitute a fine for imprisonment, to reduce either fine or imprisonment, to convict and sentence an accused or remit the case to the inferior court with instructions to convict and sentence, to quash the conviction, and so on. There is no further appeal and application to the *nobile officium* of the High Court is incompetent.[82]

Bill of Suspension

Suspension is the procedure whereby an illegal or improper warrant, conviction or judgment issued by an inferior judge acting under summary criminal procedure [83] may be reviewed and set aside by the High Court. If the complainer is in custody the process becomes one of suspension and liberation. It is a remedy open to the person accused or convicted only and not to the prosecutor.[84] It is not a means of having reviewed the rightness of a conviction [85] but a means of having stopped proceedings in excess of jurisdiction, illegal or unwarrantable, or where there is oppression or injustice or irregularity in the proceedings.[86]

The Bill of Suspension runs in name of the aggrieved party as complainer against the prosecutor as respondent and resembles a civil petition in form, having a prayer for the suspension of the sentence complained of, and, where appropriate, for liberation from prison, a statement of facts in numbered paragraphs, and pleas-in-law.[87] The prosecutor normally lodges answers in the form of corresponding paragraphs and pleas in law. The facts in the Bill must aver relevantly grounds on which the sentence is challenged, and it is competent even though the sentence has been carried out.

The Bill is put out for hearing by three or more members of the High Court of Justiciary and legal argument is heard from counsel for the suspender and from Crown counsel. The facts are not investigated except so

---

[81] Criminal Procedure (Scotland) Act 1975, s. 452.

[82] *Anderson* v. *H.M. Advocate*, 1974 S.L.T. 239.

[83] It has no application to trials on indictment.

[84] The prosecutor's remedy is by advocation, *e.g. MacLeod* v. *Levitt*, 1969 J.C. 16, though this may be invoked by both parties.

[85] *Moffat* v. *Skeen*, 1963 J.C. 84.

[86] Full list of grounds in Renton and Brown, 313–315: see also *Henderson* v. *Forster*, 1944 J.C. 91; *Blair* v. *Hawthorn*, 1945 J.C. 17; *Gray* v. *Morrison*, 1954 J.C. 31; *McGinley and Dowds* v. *MacLeod*, 1963 J.C. 11; *Auld* v. *Herron*, 1969 J.C. 4. Exceptionally, in *Loch Lomond Sailings Ltd.* v *Hawthorn*, 1962 J.C. 8, the court considered a bill of suspension brought by one other than the accused, whose property had been used in the crime and been forfeited.

[87] For specimen, see Renton and Brown, 484.

far as admitted by the respondent, but a remit may be made to the inferior court to report on some matter. It is not a suitable process to challenge the sufficiency of the evidence for conviction or the admissibility of evidence, or otherwise to challenge the merits of a conviction, but only a means to object where some miscarriage of justice is alleged.

The High Court may pass the Bill, suspend the sentence and order repayment of any fine paid, or repel the reasons of suspension, refuse the Bill and let the sentence take effect, or amend the conviction and sentence and, if necessary, remit the case to the inferior court. Expenses may be awarded, in full or modified.

Offences Committed by Children

A child under the age of eight cannot in law be guilty of any offence. Special provision is made for dealing with children under sixteen.[88] No child may be prosecuted for any offence save on the instructions of the Lord Advocate or at his instance, and even then only in the High Court or sheriff court.[89] If a child is so prosecuted in the sheriff court special provisions apply to keep the child away from adult criminals. In a case of murder the High Court will order a child or person under eighteen to be detained during Her Majesty's pleasure. In other cases a court may order a child to be detained, required to undergo residential training, put on probation, fined, admonished or discharged.

Most cases of delinquency are now dealt with by children's hearings. In each local authority area there has been established a Children's Panel made up of lay members appointed by the Secretary of State and removable by him. Groups of three members of the panel, including members of each sex, hold children's hearings in places dissociated from criminal courts and police stations. Each local authority has an officer called the Reporter, with deputies; they need not be legally qualified. The Reporter's function is to investigate cases of children likely to be in need of compulsory measures of care, not solely by reason of having committed offences,[90] and, if he thinks fit, to bring the child before a children's hearing. If he proposes to do so he must give the child and its parent a statement of the grounds of referral and call for a report on the child from the local authority social work department.

At the hearing [91] the child's parent has a right to be present at all stages and may be obliged to attend. Child and parent may be accompanied by a

---

[88] The law is now contained in the Children and Young Persons (Scotland) Act 1937 and the Social Work (Scotland) Act 1968.

[89] In summary cases the Lord Advocate's instructions are presumed given unless this is challenged. Even then general instructions will suffice: *M.* v. *Dean*, 1974 S.L.T. 229.

[90] For grounds for bringing before a hearing see 1968 Act s. 32. See also Children's Hearings (Scotland) Rules 1971.

[91] For procedure see A.S. (Social Work) (Sheriff Court Procedure Rules) 1971.

representative, who need not be legally qualified. Hearings are private and the public are excluded. The procedure is generally in the discretion of the chairman. The chairman must explain the grounds of referral alleged; if the child and his parent accept the grounds the hearing proceeds; if they do not the Reporter must apply to the sheriff for a finding as to whether the disputed grounds are established. Such an application is heard summarily, in chambers.[92] The sheriff must hold that none of the grounds for referral are established and dismiss the application and discharge the referral, or hold the grounds for referral established; he gives his decision orally. The case then goes back to the hearing.

In considering a case the hearing must discuss the case with the child, his parent and representative, and consider social inquiry and other available reports, and endeavour to obtain the views of the child and his parent on what arrangements would be in the best interests of the child. The chairman must inform the child, parent and representative of the decision and reasons for it. The disposal may be by discharging the referral and taking no further action, by making a supervision requirement which may require the child to reside in a named residential establishment.[93] A supervision requirement places the child in the care of the local authority and, unless discharged or varied, lasts till the child is eighteen. The hearing may not deal with the child by admonition or fine, nor impose any penalty on the parent.

An appeal lies from any decision of a children's hearing to the sheriff, on the ground of error in law or irregularity in procedure, or that the disposal ordered is not appropriate, and is heard summarily, in chambers.[94] The sheriff must allow the appeal if he is satisfied that the decision of the hearing is not justified in all the circumstances of the case; he may remit the case to a children's hearing for reconsideration, or may discharge the child. A further appeal lies to the Court of Session by way of stated case on a point of law or in respect of any irregularity in the conduct of the case at the instance of the child and/or his parent or the Reporter.[95] There may be appeals on both the sheriff's finding of fact on the grounds of referral and on the disposal of the case. No appeal lies against a decision to impose a supervision requirement solely on the ground that the treatment prescribed is inappropriate.

---

[92] Parents are competent and compellable witnesses: *McGregor* v. *T.*, 1975 S.L.T. 76.

A deputy Reporter not legally qualified has no right of audience: *Kennedy* v. *O.* 1975 S.L.T. 235.

[93] In deciding on a disposal a hearing may act only on grounds accepted by the parent or held established by the court: *K.* v. *Finlayson*, 1974 S.L.T.(Sh.Ct.) 51.

[94] Appeal against a decision of a children's hearing is competent only when the decision is a final disposal of the referral: *H.* v. *McGregor*, 1973 S.L.T. 110. When hearing an appeal any change in circumstances since the decision was reached must be considered: *Kennedy* v. *B.*, 1973 S.L.T. 38; *D.* v. *Sinclair*, 1973 S.L.T.(Sh.Ct.) 47. On procedure see *H.* v. *Mearns*, 1974 S.L.T. 184.

[95] See *e.g. D.* v. *Kennedy*, 1974 S.L.T. 168.

All supervision requirements imposed by children's hearings are subject to at least annual review and the child or his parent may require a review after three months, after six months after a review has continued a previous requirement or after three months after a review has varied a previous requirement. A local authority can require a review at any time. Review hearings are arranged by the Reporter and are conducted in the same way as an initial hearing. Supervision requirements cease to have effect when the child attains eighteen and within three months before that date the local authority must have the Reporter arrange a hearing so that it may advise whether the child still requires supervision and guidance. The Secretary of State may terminate a supervision requirement at any time.

PUNISHMENT AND TREATMENT OF CRIMINALS

Many changes have been made in the methods of punishment and treatment in recent years and experiment and change is constantly going on, the emphasis being now on training and reformation of criminals, not on mere punishment.[96]

The sentence of death can be imposed only by a judge of the High Court on a person convicted of treason.[97] The sentence will not be pronounced on a pregnant woman, nor on a person under eighteen, and capital cases are always reviewed by the Secretary of State for Scotland, who may recommend reprieve and commutation of sentence, or pardon.[98] Where a sentence is commuted to life imprisonment, the prisoner may be released on licence at any time. Persons convicted of murder are sentenced to life imprisonment, and the judge may recommend a minimum period which should elapse before the Secretary of State orders release on licence. The Secretary of State may not release a murderer on licence unless he has consulted the Lord Justice-General and the trial judge if available. Persons under eighteen convicted of murder are sentenced to be detained during Her Majesty's pleasure.

Transportation, penal servitude and imprisonment with hard labour have all been abolished. Imprisonment [99] may be imposed for such period

---

[96] In 1959 a new Scottish Advisory Council on the Treatment of Offenders was set up to advise and assist the Secretary of State for Scotland. There is also a Standing Advisory Council on Employment of Prisoners, appointed by the Home Secretary and the Secretary of State for Scotland. There is an Institute of Criminology at Cambridge University to study the causes and prevention of crime, while research is also pursued in various other universities and by the Home Office Research Unit.

[97] Homicide Act 1957; Murder (Abolition of Death Penalty) Act 1965 (expiring on July 31, 1970, but continued by affirmative resolutions of both Houses of Parliament).

[98] On the factors taken into account in murder cases, see *Report of the Royal Commission on Capital Punishment* (Cmd. 8932, 1953), paras. 36–49, 597 *et seq.* Milne, *The Scottish Office*, 153. See also Marshall, " The Prerogative of Mercy," 1948 *Current Legal Problems*, 104.

[99] Scottish prisons are at Aberdeen, Edinburgh (Saughton), Glasgow (Barlinnie), Greenock, Inverness, Low Moss, Perth and Peterhead, with an " open " prison at New-

as the court thinks fit or such period as may be authorised by any relevant statute. A sheriff acting under solemn procedure may not imprison for more than two years and, in summary procedure, unless statute authorises more, the maximum sentence is of three months' imprisonment, or six months' if there is a previous conviction of dishonesty or personal violence. There are restrictions on imprisonment of adult first offenders [1] and of young persons under twenty-one [2] and a prohibition on imprisonment of persons under seventeen. Corrective training and preventive detention are special forms of imprisonment for persistent offenders.[3] There is also provision for supervision of prisoners after release.

The Secretary of State for Scotland now has power [4] on the recommendation of the Parole Board for Scotland [5] to release on licence a person serving a sentence of imprisonment, other than imprisonment for life, after he has served one-third of his sentence or twelve months, whichever is greater. The licence may contain conditions and may be revoked. A person sentenced to life imprisonment may, on the Parole Board's recommendation, be released on licence only after consultation with the Lord Justice-General and the trial judge, if available.

Pecuniary fines are commonly imposed in addition to, or instead of, imprisonment. The amount of any fine is within the court's discretion save that, unless statute otherwise authorises, the sheriff court exercising summary jurisdiction, or a stipendiary magistrate, may not impose a fine of over £150 and district courts not over £100. In imposing a fine a court must have regard for the offender's ability to pay a fine of the amount imposed. The court may allow time for payment or order payment by instalments. If a fine or instalment thereof is not paid the offender is cited to a Means Enquiry Court, which may alter the mode of payment or impose imprisonment for non-payment.[6]

A probation order may be made, requiring the offender to be under supervision for a period of from one to three years, to be of good behaviour and to conform to the directions of the probation officer. He may be required to reside in a specified place, or to submit to mental treatment.

---

ton Stewart (Penninghame). The main women's prison is at Greenock (Gateside). There are detention centres for young persons at Glenochil and young offenders' institutions at Dumfries, Edinburgh, Glasgow and Perth (Friarton) and, for girls, Greenock Prison. Other custodial institutions are planned.

[1] Criminal Procedure (Scotland) Act, 1975, s. 417; *Winslow* v. *Farrell*, 1965 J.C. 49; *Auld* v. *Herron*, 1969 J.C. 4.

[2] *Ibid.*, ss. 208, 416; *Sillars* v. *Copeland*, 1966 J.C. 8.

[3] See Criminal Justice (Scotland) Act 1949, s. 21.

[4] Criminal Justice Act 1967, s. 60.

[5] Constituted under s. 59 of that Act. The Parole Board for Scotland has a chairman (Mr. D. A. P. Barry) and eight members, including two sheriffs.

[6] A Means Enquiry Court consists of a sheriff sitting alone. See *e.g. Fraser* v. *Herron*, 1968 J.C. 1. The period of imprisonment for non-payment of a fine is according to a statutory tariff. See also Smith and Gordon, "Collection of Fines in Scotland," 1972 S.L.T.(News) 181, 189.

Young persons aged sixteen to twenty may be discharged absolutely, admonished, put on probation for one to three years, fined or required to find caution for good behaviour. In more serious cases they may be detained in a remand home for observation and examination, or for reports,[7] or sent to a detention centre for three months,[8] or to a Borstal institution for an indefinite period (in practice about fifteen months)[9] or detained in a Young Offenders' Institution for the period for which they could, if adults, have been imprisoned. In cases of murder they must be detained during Her Majesty's pleasure.[10]

Minor penalties include forfeiture of instruments, being ordered to find caution for good behaviour, and admonition. A court may also defer sentence for a period, to give the accused an opportunity to repay money or establish his good conduct, or discharge an accused absolutely. In many circumstances the court must obtain and consider various reports before deciding on the appropriate penalty. In road traffic cases a licence may be endorsed or disqualification from driving be ordered.

FURTHER READING

Solemn Criminal Procedure
Renton and Brown: *Criminal Procedure According to the Law of Scotland* (4th ed.)

Summary Criminal Procedure
Renton and Brown: *Criminal Procedure According to the Law of Scotland* (4th ed.)
Trotter: *Summary Criminal Jurisdiction.*

Evidence
Walker and Walker: *Law of Evidence in Scotland.*

Punishment and Treatment
Fox: *The English Prison and Borstal System.*
Howard Jones: *Crime and the Penal System.*
Walker: *Crime and Punishment in Britain.*
HMSO: *Prisons and Borstals.*
    The Probation Service in Scotland.
King: *The Probation Service.*
Annual Reports: *Criminal Statistics, Scotland.*
    Prisons in Scotland.

---

[7] Remand institutions are at Polmont and Longriggend. Remand homes are provided by local authorities and " List D," formerly approved, schools by local authorities or other bodies, such as churches. The Secretary of State may regulate the constitution of the managers of an approved school, other than a local authority one.

[8] There is as yet no junior detention centre, for the 14–16 age-group, in Scotland.

[9] For the development of the system, see Fox, *The English Prison and Borstal Systems,* 327 *et seq.* The Scottish Borstals are at Polmont, Castle Huntly, Cornton Vale, Noranside, and in a separate section in Barlinnie Prison, Glasgow, and for girls at Greenock Prison.

[10] Criminal Procedure (Scotland) Act 1975, s. 206.

CHAPTER 15

THE MAKING OF NEW LAW

THE body of doctrines, principles and rules, and of exceptions and qualifications thereto, which constitutes the law is constantly being added to and modified. Consequently any statement in a textbook or judgment may be subsequently superseded or altered, and a perennial difficulty for the student or practitioner of law is to keep track of the constant changes and note how what he has hitherto understood to be the law on one point or another, or what is stated as the law in the latest available book, has been subsequently changed.

The Need for New Law

The need for new law and the alteration of old arises simply from the fact that society is not static. Views change on what the legal rule should be on particular topics, new situations develop calling for new controls, such as the growth of motor traffic, new forms of crime which become prevalent, changed views as to the proper disposal of convicted criminals, the grounds on which it should be permissible to terminate marriages, the persons who should be entitled to recover damages for the death of a breadwinner, the rights of illegitimate children, the need to limit hours of work in certain premises, and so on.

In brief the constant changes in our society and in the world in which we live, brought about by changing ideas, changing social habits and patterns, scientific and technological changes, and developments in medical science, in commercial practices, in international relations, all bring about constant need to modify the rules of law at some point or another if they are not to be out of touch with the general feeling of the community on the matter and the needs of the situation. Frequently some event, a particular crime, or disaster, or discovery, or court case, or other particular event, exposes a gap or defect in the existing law and generates a public feeling in favour of, or even demand for, a change. Increasingly in the twentieth century there have been movements for the deliberate consideration of topics of law and their reform to make them more consistent with current needs and views, rather than to rely on merely *ad hoc* stopping of gaps and correction of obvious defects.

Lawmaking by Judicial Decision

The superior court judges have no express power to alter the law or make new law [1] and judges at various times have disclaimed any law-

---

[1] Apart from powers to make or modify purely procedural rules, as by Act of Sederunt.

501

making power,[2] but it is undeniable that in the exercise of their duty to apply the law to cases coming before them, and, in so doing, to state what they understand the rules to be, they frequently in effect make new law or modify the existing law. Thus where a court overrules a prior decision, or limits or extends the application of a rule as compared with previous decisions on that point, the judges are really making new law or at least altering, albeit in detail, an existing rule, particularly when one has regard to the principle of *stare decisis*, which makes their reformulation of a rule binding for the future. The effect of a decision may be far wider than the mere decision of the issue between the parties. Thus when *Donoghue* v. *Stevenson*[3] was decided, the House of Lords not only decided the case before them, but in substance laid down a new general principle, namely, that in future every manufacturer of goods had to take reasonable care for the safety of the ultimate consumer of his goods, if there was no reasonable probability of the inspection of the goods between manufacture and consumption, and would be liable in damages if such a consumer were injured by reason of the original manufacturer's failure to take such care. This principle, laid down in the context of bottled drink, and in the first instance applicable only thereto, has been extended by other decisions to clothing, vehicles, food and other commodities. Its limits are not yet settled.

Again, when a court decides that a particular rule of law, common law or statute, is to a particular effect and not what it was hitherto thought to be, it is hard to say that there has not been a making of new law. So too where a court decides what has hitherto been undecided, even though the decision is not startling or surprising, there can be said to be a change in the law; what was formerly thought to be the law has now been authoritatively declared to be the law. Law is indeed created and declared and sometimes modified by the very acts of finding it, stating it and applying it in cases.

Limitations on Judicial Lawmaking

At the same time the severe limitations on judicial lawmaking are evident; the courts cannot lay down a rule for a set of facts by anticipation, but only if and when a case of such facts arises; they cannot deal with all such cases generally, but only with the one case which has arisen. And judges are very reluctant to state a rule more generally than the necessities of the case require them to do, so that it may be that the rule laid down is particular to that case, or class of case, and not a general rule at all. The power of the courts to alter any rule of law is dependent on the established conventions as to *stare decisis*, so that a court cannot alter the law on a point settled by a precedent binding on that court, though it may establish

---

[2] *e.g. Willis* v. *Baddeley* [1892] 2 Q.B. 324, 326; *Harnett* v. *Fisher* [1927] 1 K.B. 402, 424; *Baylis* v. *Bishop of London* [1913] 1 Ch. 127, 137.
[3] 1932 S.C.(H.L.) 31.

an exception or qualification if it can distinguish the precedent, and it may further define, or limit or extend the principle.[4] Still less can judicial lawmaking override any rule existing by virtue of legislation, however absurd or unjust the courts may consider the statutory rule. If it is applicable it cannot be ignored or altered by the court.

Not least, a decision of a point cannot be made solely on the basis of what the judge thinks is desirable or right; he cannot ignore the existing law and his decision must be consistent with the existing body of law on similar and related points, and based on some principle. Thus a judge cannot grant a divorce because husband and wife are incompatible in temperament, because the legally permitted grounds of divorce do not include that, but if the judge finds that the spouses were incompatible and as a consequence of incompatibility that the conduct of one was such as to be detrimental to the health of the other, he may find that that amounted to cruelty, which is a recognised ground of divorce. In *MacLennan* v. *MacLennan*,[5] a judge was faced, for the first time in Britain, with the problem whether the allegation that a wife had had herself artificially inseminated with the semen of a donor (an unknown male) and had had a child in consequence gave her husband grounds for divorce. It would have been blatant judicial legislation to hold that artificial insemination did so by itself. But could her conduct be held to amount to adultery? He might have held that impregnation by the unknown male's semen by medical intervention was equivalent to impregnation by the unknown male by normal physical intercourse, and therefore equally adultery. In fact he held that " adultery " involved extra-marital physical intercourse and that no conduct or insemination without physical intercourse, however morally wrongful, amounted to adultery. The decision therefore merely proceeded on the analysis and interpretation of the term " adultery," limiting it to what is generally understood by that term. The opposite view would have been such an extension of the term as to amount to judicial legislation, but might nevertheless have been right. Is the essence of " adultery " sexual fidelity or is it physical coitus?

Accordingly there are severe limitations on judicial lawmaking and only exceptionally can it go beyond redefinition, explanation, extension or qualification of existing principles, though even in these ways, particularly over a period of time, the courts can quite materially modify rules of law.

---

[4] Thus in the years before 1948 the courts could not get rid of " the rule of common employment," to the effect that an employer was not liable to one employee for an accident caused by the fault of a fellow-employee in common employment with the injured man. This rule, established for Scotland by the House of Lords in *Bartonshill Coal Co.* v. *Reid* (1858) 3 Macq. 266, could only be, and was, criticised and distinguished and its application limited. It was finally abolished by the Law Reform (Personal Injuries) Act 1948, s. 1.

[5] 1958 S.C. 105; the argument was on the law only and it was never determined whether the wife's plea was justified in fact or not; see footnotes on p. 115 of the report.

Lawmaking by Text writers

No jurist's statement of what the law should be, or, truly understood, is, on any unsettled point has any binding force against a decision of a competent court, still less against legislation, but the writings of jurists in textbooks and periodicals of high reputation have sometimes been influential on courts and been a factor in persuading a court to adopt a particular course of action or decision, and have thus indirectly played a part in shaping the law.[6] The text writer has greater freedom than a judge in suggesting what is wrong with the law and how it should be modified, but less effect in that unless his views are adopted by a court or a government department concerned they will be completely ineffective, however sensible or carefully thought out.

Lawmaking by Legislation

The main mode of lawmaking and law-changing today is undoubtedly parliamentary legislation. This mode has the theoretical advantages that it can deal with a problem in general and not merely with a particular case which has arisen, that it can make changes by anticipation, instead of having to wait on a problem arising, that it can completely abrogate pre-existing and contrary rules, however long-established or well-settled, get rid of anomalies, absurdities and injustices, and can formulate the new rule in a general statement and in a verbally authoritative form.

In practice this very rarely happens and much, far too much, legislation is piecemeal patching, dealing with particular problems rather than with the whole law on the subject, frequently merely adding to, or amending, or introducing an exception into, a substantial volume of existing legislation on the subject, so that the law on the topic consists, apart from cases, of many layers of legislation, each adding to or altering, but rarely completely restating or wholly superseding rules in an earlier layer. Frequently also legislation proceeds by applying a rule earlier enacted for one subject to a new and different, and possibly unsuitable, further set of circumstances, or by making exceptions and qualifications to previous enactments. Amendment is too frequently by the addition or deletion of words, rather than by the complete replacement of a section in an earlier Act by a rewritten section. In the result the state of the statute law on many topics is a patchwork of fragments of various statutes of different dates, a chaotic mess, wherein it is difficult, tedious and time-consuming to discover what words and fragments of sections appear to be still in force, let alone to determine whether they apply to, and what they mean in, particular circumstances.[7]

---

[6] *e.g. Bradford* v. *Symondson* (1881) 7 Q.B.D. 456, 462; *Haynes* v. *Harwood* [1935] 1 K.B. 146; *Shenton* v. *Tyler* [1939] 1 Ch. 620; *Re Egerton's Will Trusts* [1956] Ch. 593; *Boys* v. *Chaplin* [1971] A.C. 356; *Qureshi* v. *Qureshi* [1971] 1 All E.R. 325; *Richards* v. *H.M. Advocate*, 1971 J.C. 29.

[7] *Cf. Winslow* v. *Farrell*, 1965 J.C. 49, 52, *per* Lord Wheatley: " The ... Act ... has

Initiatives for Legislation

The initiative for legislation comes from many sources.[8] Most legislation is introduced by or on behalf of the Government of the day and must be taken to relate to something regarded by the Cabinet as of sufficient importance in the Government's programme to justify parliamentary time being found for its discussion.[9] Some of this is essential annual legislation, such as the Finance Bill, the Consolidated Fund Bill, the Appropriation Bill (the first of which always makes some, and frequently important, drastic and extensive changes in the law of taxation), and the Expiring Laws Continuance Bill, without which various statutes passed for only limited periods would lapse. Some is legislation necessitated by current world affairs, international relations, or relations with some part of the Commonwealth or a colony. Some is more or less emergency legislation to cope with some crisis or special circumstances.

In the sphere of public law and the management of the national economy the major initiating factor is the social, political and economic philosophy of the party in power at a given time. Thus the Acts which nationalised,[10] denationalised,[11] and renationalised the steel industry [12] were all passed because of the views of successive governments (of different political complexions) on whether the steel industry should be publicly or privately owned. Similarly, the transport industry has since 1945 been a shuttlecock thrown backwards and forwards by legislation founded on different political theories. The result is a chaotic mess of legislation.

Then there are Bills sponsored by departments of state in the furtherance of departmental policy on housing or agriculture or education or whatever else is that department's responsibility, because every department constantly sees the need for alteration and what it thinks is improvement of the law on some topic within its responsibility. Some of these raise little or no matter of political philosophy. Practically every year some alteration requires to be made to the rules of national insurance or industrial injuries or assistance to local authorities or the borrowing powers of nationalised industry or the like. Again, even when not seeking to make substantial changes, many government departments frequently have a number of small reforms which they would like enacted if parliamentary time can be found, and are consequently constantly in the queue for an opportunity to effect these changes.

---

been extensively amended by the . . . Act. In view of the devious and complicated ways by which this original four subsections Act was amended, one wonders why the statute was not simply re-enacted in its new form. It is perhaps not surprising that mistakes may be made by a person seeking the goal of enlightenment while wandering through the maze of amendment, cross-reference, substitution and deletion."

[8] Jennings, *Parliament*, Chap. 7.

[9] Morrison, *Government and Parliament*, Chap. 11.

[10] Iron and Steel Act 1949 (Labour Government).

[11] Iron and Steel Act 1953 (Conservative Government).

[12] Iron and Steel Act 1967 (Labour Government).

Pressure Groups

Numerous groups of persons, professional associations, federations, societies, trade unions, charitable and philanthropic bodies and similar organisations of many kinds are constantly pressing for legislation or legislative amendment of the law, on some matter affecting their and their members' interests, in the interest of the furtherance or preservation of the rights of their members or of some interest which they have at heart. They press their views on Ministers and their departments, on M.P.s, on Royal Commissions and Committees considering the state of the law, and on any person who may be able to influence parliamentary action in the way they want. Many such groups have one or more of their own leading members among M.P.s, or know a member who is sympathetic to their cause, and many of the members who ballot for the opportunity to introduce a Private Member's Bill are really doing so as the mouthpieces of some organisation or group or interest.

Particularly powerful among pressure groups are the T.U.C. and the major trade unions.[13] Thus the Trade Disputes Acts 1906, 1913 and 1965 and the Trade Unions and Labour Relations Act 1974, were all passed as a result of strong pressure from the trade unions, to overrule, or at least modify, the results of judicial decisions [14] or legislation [15] regarded by the trade unions as trenching on what they thought their privileged legal position was or should be. Bills affecting industry or trade, employment, pensions or related topics are also objects of pressure by trade unions and M.P.s supported by them and sympathetic to their views to secure that the law is changed in a manner beneficial, or at least minimally harmful, to the interests of trade unionists.

Other pressure groups include the Confederation of British Industry, the churches, the licensed trade, the motoring organisations, organisations of professional persons engaged in every kind of trade, profession, business, industrial or commercial undertaking, the farmers, the teachers, the doctors, those concerned for the protection of children, or animals, or birds, or the countryside, those representing disabled and handicapped persons, the old, the young, the widowed, the divorced, the homeless and every conceivable kind and group of individuals.[16] Some of these organisations may, of course, despite their names, actually represent and be supported by only a minority of the group for whose interests they campaign.

---

[13] On this, see Mackintosh, *The British Cabinet*, 470; see also Harrison, *Trade Unions and the Labour Party since 1945*.

[14] *Taff Vale Ry.* v. *Associated Society of Railway Servants* [1901] A.C. 426; *Amalgamated Society of Railway Servants* v. *Osborne* [1910] A.C. 87; *Rookes* v. *Barnard* [1964] A.C. 1129.

[15] Industrial Relations Act 1971.

[16] See further, Christoff, *Capital Punishment and British Politics*; Wootton, *The Politics of Influence*; Eckstein, *Pressure Group Politics: The Case of the British Medical Association*.

Private Members' Bills

Private Members' Bills [17] are accordingly sometimes expressions of the sponsoring members' own belief as to the desirability of some change in the law, which may be in some obscure detail, or may fundamentally affect some of the best-settled rules of law. Thus Private Members' Bills have several times altered the law of divorce [18] and other subjects affected in this way have been the death penalty for murder,[19] the medical termination of pregnancy,[20] and the provision of family planning advice by the National Health Service.[21] Frequently, however, a private member has taken up and is sponsoring a reform for which some pressure group or section of the community has been agitating, and he is as much, or more, the mouthpiece of that group as an independent legislator.[22] Numerous useful reforms, particularly in such fields as protection of animals, civic amenities, superannuation, and professional organisation of groups of persons, have sprung from measures originating in this way.

Technical Changes

In the more technical parts of the law, such as company law, conveyancing, bankruptcy, procedure, and the like, Parliament relies frequently on the reports and recommendations of Royal Commissions,[23] Departmental Committees,[24] the Law Commissions[25] or standing advisory committees.[26] At any given time there are usually, apart from permanent bodies, a dozen or more Commissions and Committees and similar bodies at work, gathering views, hearing evidence and suggestions, and formulating recommen-

---

[17] The monthly parts of *Current Law*, *s.v.* Parliament, list all Bills currently before Parliament, showing the stage of progress made to enactment, and marking those introduced by a private member as distinct from those sponsored by the Government.

[18] The outstanding instance is Mr. (later Sir) A. P. Herbert's championing of the Bill which became the (English) Matrimonial Causes Act 1937. See the story recounted by him in *The Ayes Have It*. The Divorce (Scotland) Act 1964 was also a private member's measure.

[19] Murder (Abolition of Death Penalty) Act 1965. Despite the title the Act only suspended the death penalty till 1970.

[20] Abortion Act 1967.

[21] National Health Service (Family Planning) Act 1967.

[22] Jennings, *Parliament*, Chap. 11.

[23] A Royal Commission is a body of persons appointed by the Crown under Royal Warrant, normally to inquire into and report on some specified matter. The report is addressed to Her Majesty and bears to be presented to Parliament by Command of Her Majesty; see *e.g.* The Royal Commission on Trade Unions and Employers' Organisations 1965–68 (Chairman: Lord Donovan; Report: Cmnd. 3623, 1968).

[24] A Departmental Committee is a body of persons appointed by a Minister of the Crown to inquire into and report on some specified matter. It is rather less important than a Royal Commission. The report is addressed to the Minister and bears to be presented to Parliament by him. See *e.g.* the Departmental Committee on the Sheriff Court in Scotland, 1963–67 (Chairman; Lord Justice-Clerk Grant; Report: Cmnd. 3248, 1967).

[25] On these bodies, see p. 516, *infra*.

[26] *e.g.* the Scottish Advisory Council on the Treatment of Offenders. See also P.E.P. *Advisory Committees in British Government*.

dations, which normally would require for their implementation some changes, sometimes far-reaching changes, in some branch or other of the law. The Cabinet or the Minister to whom the body reports has to decide whether and how far to accept the recommendations, and in the case of a Minister, he has then to fight for the opportunity to have the appropriate Bill drafted and launched on its parliamentary journey.

International Agreements

Some Bills again are introduced into Parliament to give the force of law in the United Kingdom to a treaty or convention to which Her Majesty's Government in the United Kingdom has become a party. In the United Kingdom, with a few exceptions, treaties and conventions cannot receive effect in municipal law unless adopted into the municipal law by statute.[27] Thus an international convention agreed at Warsaw in 1929, settling uniform rules as to the international carriage of goods by air, was adopted into British law by the Carriage by Air Act 1932, and when the convention was revised at The Hague in 1955, the revised version was enacted by the Carriage by Air Act 1961. So too certain rules relative to carriage by sea formulated by the International Convention on Maritime Law at Brussels in 1922 and 1923 were enacted by the Carriage of Goods by Sea Act 1924 and amendments contained in a protocol agreed internationally at Brussels in 1968 resulted in a revised Act in 1971. But an extensive unification of the law concerning carriage by rail accomplished by the Berne Convention of 1952, though ratified by the United Kingdom in 1954, has not yet been enacted into British law, and a convention signed at Geneva in 1956 has been given effect to by the Carriage of Goods by Road Act 1965, but the Act has not yet been brought into force. Similarly, the Diplomatic Privileges Act 1964 gave effect to a convention agreed at Vienna in 1961 on diplomatic immunities, and the Consular Relations Act 1968 gave effect to a Vienna Convention of 1963 on consular relations.

Lawmaking by Subordinate Legislation

In so far as legislative power has been delegated to Ministers and other authorities, any making or alteration of subordinate legislation by departments or other authorised bodies is legislative equally with direct legislation by Parliament.

Lawmaking by Other Means

In some spheres and to a limited extent the law can be changed simply by practice. In the criminal law of Scotland the centralised control of prosecutions by the Lord Advocate and the Crown Office permits a modest amount of, what is in effect, change in the law of the land by the practice

---

[27] McNair, *Law of Treaties*, 81 *et seq.*

of prosecuting or not prosecuting certain kinds of conduct. Thus adultery once was criminal in Scotland but for so many years now has not been prosecuted as such that, though not formally declared non-criminal, it cannot now be regarded as a crime.

Difficulties and Defects of Changes in the Law

This constant process of changes in the law is not without its difficulties and disadvantages. In the first place there is the constant and growing difficulty of finding and keeping up to date with changes, and of understanding how the changes made have affected the pre-existing rules. Frequently, this is not at all clear. In the second place new rules all too seldom completely supersede existing rules; more often they are superadded on the existing ones, replacing them in part, but to a large extent adding fresh conditions and a fresh layer of law onto a pile, already too thick, of Acts and decisions dealing with the topic. Again, changes not infrequently have unforeseen consequences or repercussions on other parts of the law, possibly creating a lacuna or a fresh complication elsewhere.

Lawyers are frequently accused of not being interested in law reform, or of being apathetic or unenthusiastic about it, or of having sought to block and obstruct changes. This is not really fair, because there are many factors which make the experienced lawyer frequently less than enthusiastic for law reform in general or for particular proposed reforms. In the first place an existing state of the law on any topic may be fairly well known, and its defects, difficulties and dangers have been uncovered. It is accordingly possible to predict with some confidence how the courts would apply the rules in question, and to advise an inquirer with some confidence. If the law is changed a new set of rules have to be assimilated, their interpretations and applications worked out, and for a very substantial time the lawyer has only his own guess as a basis for advice to a client on a matter involving this point of law. Reasonable certainty and predictability of application are valuable qualities of law; they are frequently lost when the law is changed and the lawyer is reluctant to see them lost. Furthermore, long and painful experience of legislation and parliamentary law changing has been that lacunae, mistakes, inconsistencies and other defects in the reforming legislation always occur and quite quickly become apparent in practice, so that a defective or out-of-date state of the law may have been exchanged for one defective in other respects. Thus *Adams* v. *Spencer* [28] revealed a lacuna in the Law Reform (Personal Injuries) Act 1948 which had to be corrected by the Law Reform (Personal Injuries) Amendment Act 1953. A reforming Act may create an absurdity. Thus the Law Reform (Miscellaneous Provisions) Act, 1971, s. 4, enacted that in assessing damages payable to a *widow* in respect of her husband's death

---

[28] 1951 S.C. 175

no account should be taken of her remarriage or prospect of remarriage. But the previous common law rule, that account should be taken of remarriage, applies to children [29] and to widowers. Lawyers sometimes complain, and with a great deal of justification, that Parliament always changes the law for the worse. Again, changes are frequently proposed and even carried through without any, or adequate, consideration of their repercussions on the law as a whole, and without regard to anomalies, difficulties and absurdities being created in other cases. Thus the Hire-Purchase Act 1964, ss. 27 to 29, introduced a rule about the passing to a purchaser of the right of property in a motor-vehicle sold to him but which was already the subject of a contract of hire purchase, which rule is different from the rule applicable to any other kind of property subject to such a contract, different from the rule applicable to the sale of goods which are subject to other kinds of transactions such as hire or loan, and itself subject to exceptions where the hire-purchaser is a company, or the value of the car is over a stated sum, or the buyer is a " trade or finance purchaser." Is this a rule of law of which any modern community can be proud? Was the creation of this anomaly justified, or ever really thought out? The Consumer Credit Act 1974 has created a maze of nightmarish complexity, introduced incomprehensible jargon, and raised a great mass of uncertainties.

Not least, a change in the law may be proposed in the guise of reform with which some, or many, lawyers quite conscientiously disagree. Thus some would regard the abolition of civil jury trial as a desirable reform, but others would regard it as the destruction of a valuable civil right, an essential element of justice.[30] Some see the abolition of the death penalty for murder as a great advance, others as an utterly wrong and stupid step. Not every change in the law is a reform, or change for the better, and a good deal of so-called reform is prompted by angling for votes or similar unworthy motives. Some legislation is motivated by jealousy, greed or plain stupidity.

The way in which legislation is framed has provoked and provokes much criticism. In fairness to the draftsmen, the Bill may have been drafted in haste and under pressure, it is always extremely difficult to formulate complex ideas in clear though formal language, and quite impossible to foresee, and provide for, every kind of instance and practical case which may arise under the legislation. Moreover the draftsman's work will be amended and tinkered with by many hands as well as by his own during the Bill's progress through Parliament, so that what finally emerges may have little resemblance to the draft as originally presented

---

[29] *Howitt* v. *Heads* [1972] 1 All E.R. 491; *Thompson* v. *Price* [1973] 2 All E.R. 846.
[30] See the Report of the Committee on Civil Jury Trial (Cmnd 851, 1959). The Committee was divided in opinion.

to the legislature.[31] Nevertheless judicial complaints and criticisms abound [32] and it would in many cases be surprising if Members of Parliament could themselves explain what they have enacted.

Frequently Acts seem to be badly planned. It is not easy to see why the Succession (Scotland) Act 1964 was so planned that a lawyer applying it must apply sections 1, 8, 9, 10 to 12, and 2 in that order! [33] Apart from defects in drafting and the expression of the enacted law, the state of the statute law in Britain is a disgrace and the courts, the legal profession and the public are very ill-served by Parliament. Too frequently different and even unconnected topics are dealt with in one Act. The law on one topic is sometimes altered by an Act dealing with quite a different topic. The statute law on any given topic is far too frequently scattered through many Acts, sometimes innovating substantially on the prior law, sometimes containing only verbal changes. Scotland and Scots law is particularly ill-served in that on matters where the law is roughly the same in Scotland as in England a fresh Act is normally drafted in terms applicable to England and English law with an " application to Scotland " section stating that certain parts of the Act are to apply to Scotland and that for certain words in the text certain other, Scottish, terms are to be substituted. That much of the law is a mess is Parliament's, and only Parliament's, fault. Particularly disgraceful is the chaotic muddle of injustices and incomprehensible verbiage which cumulatively amounts to our law of taxation.

Particularly objectionable, and the worst device of legislative technique of the twentieth century, is the Law Reform (Miscellaneous Provisions)

[31] Graham Harrison, " An Examination of the Main Criticisms of the Statute Book and of the Possibility of Improvement," 1935 J.S.P.T.L. 45; Ram, " Improvement of the Statute Book," 1951 J.S.P.T.L. 442.

[32] *e.g.* " It is not easy to penetrate the tangled confusion of these Acts of Parliament, and though we have entered the labyrinth together we have unfortunately found exit by different paths ": *G.W. Ry.* v. *Bater* [1922] 2 A.C. 1, 11; " ... to make some sort of path through the labyrinth and jungle of these sections and schedules ": *Parry* v. *Harding* [1925] 1 K.B. 111, 114; " It might be possible, but I doubt if it would be easy, to compress in the same number of lines more fertile opportunities for doubt and error ": *L.C.C.* v. *Lees* [1939] 1 All E.R. 191, 194: " I have not the least idea what sub-sec. 8 means ": *Bebb* v. *Frank* [1939] 1 K.B. 558, 568; " ... the almost insuperable difficulty of applying the obscure and complicated provisions of these Acts ": *Sharpe* v. *Nicholls* [1945] 1 K.B. 382, 384; " ... another almost insoluble problem arising from this welter of legislation ... "; *Vaughan* v. *Shaw* [1945] K.B. 400, 401; " ... this chaotic series of Acts ": *Cole* v. *Harris* [1945] K.B. 474, 478; " [The Rent Acts are] a byword for confused draftsmanship ... ": *Joint Properties* v. *Williamson*, 1945 S.C. 68, 74; " The obscurity of the Act has been frequently and severely criticised; indeed I think this Act has a strong claim to the distinction of being the worst drafted Act on the Statute book ": *Central Asbestos Co.* v. *Dodd* [1973] A.C. 518.

[33] A Committee on the Preparation of Legislation was appointed by Parliament in 1973 to review the form in which public bills are drafted, with a view to greater simplicity and clarity in statute law.

Act,[34] which is the name given periodically to a piece of legislation which embodies a number of small, usually unconnected, reforming provisions. It is a most unsatisfactory method of law reform, as the provisions are usually not very significant and are disconnected from each other so that the reforming Act is difficult to remember in any context. Reform in this way is the worst kind of tinkering with and patching of the law and the provisions of such an Act, and their effect on the existing law, are readily overlooked and forgotten.

Modes of Legislative Reform

There are four modes of legislative reform of the law. The first is by passing Acts which in some way alter the pre-existing common law, or statute law, or both, on a particular matter, and this is a mode which has been employed in Scotland and England for centuries. More sophisticated, more difficult, more valuable and more important are the other three, namely, statute law revision, consolidation of legislation, and codification of the law.

Acts altering existing law

Practically every Act in some way alters the existing common law or statute law or both. Its effect on common law can only be discerned by investigation of what the common law was; its effect on existing statute law is evident from the schedules of amendments and repeals appended to the Act, which are frequently lengthy.

Statute Law Revision

The process of statute law revision consists in repealing, and thereby expelling from the Statute Book, Acts which are spent or have served their purpose, or were enacted for a particular object which has been served, or have been superseded, or been virtually repealed by, or are inconsistent with, some later enactment, or are otherwise obsolete. The passing of Statute Law Revision Acts to cut away such dead wood commenced in 1856, and such Acts have been passed periodically since then.[35] A notable one was the Act of 1863, introduced by Lord Westbury in a speech explaining fully the principles on which such a Bill was founded.

In 1868 Lord Chancellor Cairns established the Statute Law Committee which supervised this work, and also the preparation and publica-

---

[34] Acts under this title were passed in 1940, 1949, 1966, 1968 and 1971. Distinct from these are the Law Reform (Contributory Negligence) Act 1945, the Law Reform (Personal Injuries) Acts 1948 and 1953, the Law Reform (Limitation of Actions, etc.) Act 1954 (extensively amended by the Limitation Act 1963), the Law Reform (Damages and Solatium) Act 1962, the Law Reform (Husband and Wife) Act 1962, the Law Reform (Jurisdiction in Delict) Act 1971, the Law Reform (Diligence) (Scotland) Act 1973, and certain other similar Acts applicable to England only.

[35] See *e.g.* Statute Law (Repeals) Acts 1971 and 1975.

tion of a *Revised Edition of the Statutes* in 18 volumes, brought down to the end of the year 1878. This edition was completed by 1885 and by the omission of repealed Acts substituted 18 volumes for 118. Twelve more Statute Law Revision Acts were passed between 1887 and 1898 and the second edition of the *Statutes Revised* was published in 16 volumes from 1888 to 1901, containing the statute law as revised down to 1886. Subsequent supplementary volumes brought the law down to 1920. A third edition of the *Statutes Revised* in 32 volumes was published in 1950, stating the statute law as amended down to the end of 1948 [36] and publication of a new loose-leaf edition, entitled *Statutes in Force*, commenced in 1972. [37] The classification of the statutes as Public General and Local and Private also dates from 1868. [38]

The Statute Law Committee dealt originally only with English Acts prior to 1707 and British Acts thereafter, including Irish Acts down to 1800. In 1897 the Committee was reinforced by three Scottish members and the revision of the pre-1707 Scots Acts was undertaken, resulting in the Statute Law Revision (Scotland) Act 1906 and the publication in 1908 of an edition of the Scots Acts still in force. A similar Act of 1964 was followed by the publication in 1965 of the *Acts of the Parliaments of Scotland, 1424–1707*, [39] setting out those Acts still in force as amended down to 1965.

The Statute Law Committee has also been responsible since 1870 for the publication annually of the *Chronological Table of the Statutes*, which sets out all the English and United Kingdom statutes in chronological order, showing which and which parts have been repealed or amended, and by what later Act, and the annual *Index to the Statutes in Force* which indexes the provisions of all the statutes in force under well-known legal heads and sub-heads.

In 1947 the committee was given the task of consolidating enactments and preparing editions of the *Statutes Revised* from which repealed and obsolete matter was omitted. It is now responsible for producing the *Statutes in Force*.

Consolidation of Legislation

Consolidation of statute law consists in bringing together and amalgamating into one Act all the then existing legislation on a particular topic, and repealing and superseding the individual statutes. It had been done occasionally in England in the time of Elizabeth I, and James I appointed a commission in 1609 for the purpose, while Bacon made similar proposals in 1616 and two committees were appointed for the purpose under the Commonwealth. [40]

---

[36] It does not contain pre-1707 Scots Acts.
[37] This does contain pre-1707 Scots Acts.
[38] Ilbert, *Legislative Methods and Forms*, 24–27, 65–67.
[39] H.M.S.O., 1965.
[40] Ilbert, 43–47.

In 1826 Sir Robert Peel began a series of Acts which consolidated
and amended parts of the English criminal law, while in 1833 a Royal
Commission was appointed to digest the common law and statute law
affecting crimes each into one statute. The commissioners made seven
useful reports before they were dissolved in 1845. A second commission
was appointed in 1845, made six reports, and survived until 1849.[41]
About the same time was appointed Macaulay's commission for digesting
and codifying the law of British India, the chief achievement of which
was the Indian Penal Code enacted in 1860, and in 1861 seven English
criminal law consolidation Acts were passed.

Particularly since about 1868 numerous consolidation Acts have
been passed, mostly initiated by the Statute Law Committee, among
the most notable being the massive Merchant Shipping Act of 1894.
The Consolidation of Enactments (Procedure) Act 1949 lays down the
current procedure for passing consolidating Acts, including corrections
and minor improvements in the existing law, but without change of
substance.

Consolidation is one of the most valuable forms of law reform, because
it enormously facilitates study, understanding and professional use of
the statutes to have all the statutory matter on a particular topic available
in one Act, and to be able to ignore the bits and pieces of legislation
replaced thereby. It also greatly reduces the volume of the statute law.
Thus the Police (Scotland) Act 1956 superseded and totally repealed
ten Acts, and amended or partially repealed ten others. Along with
the Police (Scotland) Act 1966 and certain lesser enactments it was
itself consolidated into the Police (Scotland) Act 1967. The Rent (Scotland)
Act 1971 superseded fourteen Acts and parts of fourteen more. Some
other consolidating Acts have embodied the substance of and replaced
considerably larger numbers of Acts.

Codification

Codification [42] is the reduction of the law, or the law on a topic, to
carefully formulated statutory form, comprising the substantial effect
of both the pre-existing common law, declared by cases and formulated
by jurists, and the pre-existing statute law, and intended to supersede
all the pre-existing statements of the law, and possibly including material
amendments and changes. In Europe large-scale codification has been
effected in many countries, and in most the major parts of the law are
embodied in Civil Codes, Commercial Codes, Criminal Codes, and so on.
Codes are never, however, all-embracing and some topics are found
in statutes outside the main codes. Also codification cannot stop the
development of the law, and codes need to be amended and even replaced

---

[41] Ilbert, 51–52; on the difficulties of consolidation, see Ilbert, 111–121.
[42] See generally Ilbert, 122 *et seq*.

in the same way as statutes in this country. With its civilian bias the codification of Scots law in the nineteenth century, had Scotland preserved her independence, would have been a natural development and would probably have presented no overwhelming difficulties, in view of the great work done by the jurists, particularly Erskine and Bell, in producing carefully formulated statements of the substance of the existing law. But the Anglo-American tradition has always been antagonistic to codification, though codification has been strongly urged in some parts of the United States.[43] But in Britain, only in particular and limited areas has small-scale codification by statute been attempted.

In 1853, following on the work of the Statute Law Commissioners, Lord Chancellor St. Leonards instructed the preparation of Bills for the codification of the criminal law, but none of the Bills prepared passed into law. In 1853 Lord Chancellor Cranworth, on succeeding St. Leonards, made ambitious proposals for a programme which he hoped might eventually result in a Code Victoria, and appointed a Board for the Revision of the Statute Law. This Board was later (1854) superseded by a Statute Law Commission consisting of judges and senior lawyers, including the then Lord Advocate and the then Solicitor-General for Scotland, and the first Statute Law Revision Act (1856) was based on their recommendations, while they stated that they had over ninety consolidating Bills prepared. In 1861 there were passed seven English Criminal Law Consolidation Acts based on the reports of the Commissioners of 1833 and 1849.[44] A Royal Commission was established in 1866 to consider the expediency of codification, but nothing resulted. Sir James Fitzjames Stephen, who had got passed for India a Criminal Procedure Code, an Evidence Act and a Contract Act,[45] drafted a Bill to codify the English law of evidence and a draft code of criminal law and procedure, and in 1878–83 several attempts were made to put through Parliament a Bill for codifying English criminal law and procedure but without success.

The Bills of Exchange Act 1882, the Partnership Act 1890, the Sale of Goods Act 1893 and the Marine Insurance Act 1906 are the only specimens of codification in British law, and each covers only a small part of the law. All are probably as lucid and plain as statute can be, in marked contrast to many more modern Acts, and have been generally successful, in that they have required little amendment and not provoked much litigation on their interpretation, but only on whether the particular case is or is not covered by a particular section of the Act.

In the United States the Civil Code of Louisiana, based on the French

---

[43] See Field, " Codification in the United States " (1889) 1 J.R. 18; Sweet, " The Recent Progress of Codification " (1891) 3 J.R. 97.

[44] Ilbert, 53–60.

[45] On codification in India, see Ilbert, 129–155; Sweet, " The Anglo-Indian Codes " (1895) 7 J.R. 330.

Code, was passed in 1808 and since 1850 several states have adopted codes as part of their law.

While a codified system of law is the ultimate state which should be attained by the legal system of a developed and civilised country, the enactment of a code does not, and should not, stop legal development and change.[46] Provisions of any code will become out of date, and will need to be replaced, revised or supplemented, while judicial and juristic interpretation, criticism and uncovering of errors and omissions will necessarily continue. Codification does not end the development of a legal system.

Planned Law Reform

In the twentieth century further conscious attempts have been made to achieve planned law reform.

In 1934 a Law Revision Committee was established in England. After the war it was reconstituted as the Law Reform Committee and a separate [English] Criminal Law Revision Committee was set up in 1959. There was also established in 1952 a Private International Law Committee. All these bodies consider and report on topics of law referred to them for consideration.[47] There is a standing Advisory Council on the Penal System, appointed in 1966, to make recommendations on the prevention of crime.

In Scotland the Law Reform Committee for Scotland was established in 1954 and did useful work in reporting on topics referred to it by the Lord Advocate, and some of its reports formed the basis for reforming legislation.[48] With the creation of the Scottish Law Commission the Law Reform Committee for Scotland was allowed to lapse into inactivity.

The Law Commissions

A fresh stage in the move for law reform was reached by the passing in 1965 of the Law Commissions Act 1965, which established the Law Commission and the Scottish Law Commission, each consisting of a Chairman and four other Commissioners appointed by the Lord Chancellor [49] for England and by the Secretary of State for Scotland and the Lord Advocate jointly for Scotland. By section 3 it is the duty of each Commission " to take and keep under review all the law with which they

---

[46] Experience in France has shown that though the Codes of 1803–1810 still stand, they have been amended and supplemented in many respects, and can be understood only in the light of interpretation. Since the Second World War a Commission for the reform of the Civil Code has been at work.

[47] See Winfield, " Law Reform " (1928) 44 L.Q.R. 289; Foster, " Law Revision " (1938) 2 M.L.R. 14; Wade, " The Machinery of Law Reform " (1961) 24 M.L.R. 1; Hutton, " The Mechanics of Law Reform " (1961) 24 M.L.R. 18.

[48] *e.g.* the Occupiers' Liability (Scotland) Act 1960.

[49] See Gardiner, " The Role of the Lord Chancellor in the Field of Law Reform " (1971) 87 L.Q.R. 326.

are respectively concerned with a view to its systematic development and reform, including in particular the codification of such law, the elimination of anomalies, the repeal of obsolete and unnecessary enactments, the reduction of the number of separate enactments and generally the simplification and modernisation of the law, and for that purpose—

(*a*) to receive and consider any proposals for the reform of the law which may be made or referred to them;

(*b*) to prepare and submit to the [Lord Chancellor or the Secretary of State and the Lord Advocate] from time to time programmes for the examination of different branches of the law with a view to reform, including recommendations as to the agency (whether the Commission or another body) by which any such examination should be carried out;

(*c*) to undertake, pursuant to any such recommendations approved by the [Lord Chancellor or the Secretary of State for Scotland and the Lord Advocate], the examination of particular branches of the law and the formulation, by means of draft Bills or otherwise, of proposals for reform therein;

(*d*) to prepare from time to time at the request of the [Lord Chancellor or the Secretary of State for Scotland and the Lord Advocate] comprehensive programmes of consolidation and statute law revision, and to undertake the preparation of draft Bills pursuant to any such programme approved by the [Lord Chancellor or the Secretary of State and the Lord Advocate];

(*e*) to provide advice and information to government departments and other authorities or bodies concerned at the instance of the Government with proposals for the reform or amendment of any branch of the law;

(*f*) to obtain such information as to the legal systems of other countries as appears to the Commissioners likely to facilitate the performance of any of their functions."

Programmes prepared by the Commissions and approved, any proposals for reform formulated by the Commissions pursuant to such programmes, and the annual reports of each Commission have to be laid before Parliament.

In pursuance of this Act there were appointed the [English] Law Commission under a High Court judge (Mr. Justice Scarman) and the Scottish Law Commission under a Court of Session judge (Lord Kilbrandon) [50] with, in each case, four other Commissioners.

---

[50] They returned to judicial duties and were replaced in 1972 by Mr. Justice Cooke and in 1971 by Lord Hunter respectively. The two Chairmen serve whole-time, being seconded from the Bench. The other English Commissioners serve whole-time, but of the Scottish Commissioners two serve whole-time, and two serve part-time.

The creation of these bodies offers some prospect of more continuous and constructive thought being given to legal reform, though the constant threat is that in the interest of uniformity the solution acceptable to England will always be adopted. The Commissions, separately and together, have produced numerous reports, memoranda and proposals, many of which have been enacted.[51]

The major obstacle is that any proposals for reform, even if generally agreed to be desirable, must find a place in the legislative queue to await their turn for consideration by a Parliament already grossly overburdened with proposed legislation. Moreover a reforming measure may well be talked out or emasculated or substantially destroyed in its passage through Parliament, or the most carefully prepared change rendered valueless by foolish amendments. Moreover law reform is not a popular or vote-catching plank in a party political programme. Votes may be won by promises to nationalise an industry, or give higher social security benefits, but few will be captured by proposals to amend the law of conveyancing or bankruptcy or procedure. The plain fact is that so long as Britain adheres to its present parliamentary system the chances of satisfactory large-scale law reform seem negligible. It may be significant that the two major successful codifications of modern times, the French Civil Code of 1804 and the German Civil Code of 1900, were passed through their respective legislatures by autocratic governing régimes. Parliament is ill-suited to the consideration and approval of really large-scale restatements of law.

International Unification of Rules of Law

Multilateral conventions have in several instances resulted in the adoption by several countries of common rules of internal law. Thus the Scandinavian countries have signed conventions unifying in their countries the rules relating to bankruptcy and the mutual recognition of judgments. The League of Nations entrusted to the International Institute for the Unification of Private Law, established by the Italian Government in Rome, the task of indicating on what lines ultimate unity of national legal systems might be sought, and proposals for the unification of the law of sale and related topics have been formulated.[52] This Institute is now linked with the United Nations and the Council of Europe. Conferences of Ministers of Justice of the countries which are members of the Council of Europe have also considered the possibilities of harmonising certain aspects of private law.

---

[51] *e.g.* Matrimonial Proceedings (Polygamous Marriages) Act 1972; Prescription and Limitation (Scotland) Act 1973.

[52] Gutteridge, " An International Code of the Law of Sale " (1933) 14 B.Y.I.L. 75. Conventions of 1964 were enacted into U.K. law by the Uniform Laws on International Sales Act 1967.

In the particular sphere of international private law, attempts have been made at Hague Conferences on Private International Law to minimise the number of topics on which the approaches of different countries diverge or conflict as to the choice of law.[53] In 1951 the Hague Conference was put on a permanent footing by the establishment by charter of a permanent bureau, which works under the general direction of the Standing Governmental Commission of the Netherlands, established in 1897 with the object of promoting the codification of international private law, and of which the main functions are to examine and prepare proposals for the unification of the rules of international private law and to maintain contact with the Council of Europe and with governmental and non-governmental organisations. The United Kingdom has sent representatives since 1951 but hitherto has accepted only a few of the major conventions concluded by the Hague Conference, such as on the formal validity of wills [54] and on the recognition of divorces and legal separations.[55] The Scandinavian and the Benelux countries have also concluded smaller multilateral conventions on certain limited topics.

Legal Change by International or Supranational Authority

International organisations, such as the United Nations Organisation, have no powers to change, or require change in, the internal law of member countries.

The Rome Treaty establishing the European Economic Community, however, imposes certain rights and duties direct on member states which may override domestic laws so far as they are inconsistent with the terms of the Treaty. Thus by Article 189 the Council and the Commission may adopt regulations which are binding in every respect and are directly applicable in each member state. Moreover there are common rules for the regulation of competition, co-ordination of economic policies and the approximation of domestic laws to the extent necessary for the functioning of the Community, and a member cannot legislate in contravention of these rules. Thus Article 100 provides that the Council may issue directives for the approximation of such legislative and administrative provisions in member states as have a direct incidence on the establishment or functioning of the Community. The Commission has also to consult with member states and promote collaboration particularly in respect of employment, labour law, social security, trade unions and collective bargaining. A considerable measure of harmonisation of the national legal systems of the member countries as to patents, trade

---

[53] Graveson, "The Hague Conference on Private International Law" (1953) 2 I.C.L.Q. 605; Van Hoogstraten, "The United Kingdom joins an Uncommon Market: The Hague Conference on Private International Law" (1963) 12 I.C.L.Q. 148; and see also 10 I.C.L.Q. 18; 14 I.C.L.Q. 528; 18 I.C.L.Q. 618.

[54] Implemented by the Wills Act 1963.

[55] Implemented by the Recognition of Divorces and Legal Separations Act 1971.

marks and designs will necessarily be sought and a common company law. It is obvious that the admission of the United Kingdom to membership seems likely to result in substantial changes in internal Scottish and English law to achieve the necessary harmonisation.[56]

FURTHER READING

Abel-Smith and Stevens: *Lawyers and the Courts.*
Cardozo: *The Growth of the Law.*
Farrar: *Law Reform and the Law Commission.*
Friedmann: *Law in a Changing Society.*
Finer: *Anonymous Empire.*
Gardiner and Martin (eds.): *Law Reform Now.*
Ilbert: *Legislative Methods and Forms.*
    The Mechanics of Law Making.
Jennings: *Parliament.*
Law Commission: *Annual Reports.*
Law Reform Committee for Scotland: *Reports.*
Morrison: *Government and Parliament.*
Potter: *Organised Groups in British National Politics.*
Scottish Law Commission: *Annual Reports.*
    Programmes, Memoranda and *Reports.*
Stewart: *British Pressure Groups.*
Statute Law Society: *Reports.*
Thring: *Practical Legislation.*

---

[56] See Bathurst and Others, *Legal Problems of an Enlarged European Community.*

INDEX

ABANDONMENT OF ACTION, 465
ABSENCE, decree in, 455
ABSOLVITOR, 461
ACCOUNTANT OF COURT, 285
ACCOUNTS, solicitors', 296
ACCURSIUS, 49, 168
ACT OF ADJOURNAL, 203
ACTIONS, 452
ACTS OF ASSEMBLY, 247
ACTS OF PARLIAMENT, 187
  codifying, 191
  consolidating, 191
  declaratory, 190
  general, 189
  local, 189
  personal, 189
  private, 189
  public, 189
ACTS OF SEDERUNT, 203, 501
ADJECTIVE LAW, 332
ADJOURNAL, Acts of, 203
ADJUDICATION, 477
ADJUSTMENT OF RECORD, 455
ADMINISTRATION, FEUDAL, 89
ADMINISTRATIVE COURTS. See COURTS
ADMINISTRATIVE LAW, 80, 304, 312
ADMINISTRATIVE REMEDIES, 453, 465
ADMIRALTY COURT, 62, 144
ADMIRALTY REMEDIES, 453
ADOPTION, 322
ADVERTISEMENT, prohibition of, 291
ADVISING, 468
ADVOCATE-DEPUTE, 276, 480
ADVOCATES,
  Faculty of, 146, 275
    Dean of, 147, 273, 276, 277
    Library of, 122, 134
  Society of, in Aberdeen, 282
ADVOCATES-GENERAL, 263
ADVOCATION, 493
AFFILIATION, 322
AGENCY, 336
AGRICULTURAL EXECUTIVE COMMITTEES, 222
AGRICULTURAL HOLDINGS, 338
AGRICULTURAL MARKETING, 230
AIDS TO CONSTRUCTION (of Statutes), 353
ALARIC, 46
ALIBI, 483
ALISON, Archibald, 181
ALLIANCE, AULD, 105
AMALFI, 62
AMBIGUITY, 347
AMENDMENT, MINUTE OF, 456

AMENDMENT of statutes, 197
ANALYSIS of legal problems, 440
ANALYTICAL METHOD of legal study, 27
ANGLO-SAXON INFLUENCE, 87
ANGLO-SAXON LAW, 56
ANSWERS to petition, 465
ANTHROPOLOGY, law and, 9
APPEAL,
  Court of, 255, 259
  Lords Justices of, 255, 259
  Lords of, 142, 219
APPEALS
  to Court of Session, 218, 221, 223, 243, 466, 469, 476, 478, 497
  to High Court of Justiciary, 215, 239, 241, 476, 486, 494
  to House of Lords, 126, 128, 140, 221, 223, 255, 472, 476
  to Parliament, 218
  to sheriff-principal, 216, 476
APPEARANCE, entry of, 455
APPLICATION of judgment, 473
APPLICATION of statutes, 196
APPREHENSION, 481
APPROVED SCHOOL, 500
ARBITERS, 335
ARBITRATION, 266, 335
ARBROATH, DECLARATION OF, 170
ARISTOTLE, 2
ARMS, law of, 221
ARREST, 481
ARRESTMENT, 477
ARTICLES, Committee of, 103, 107, 113
ASIA MINOR, 44
ASSEMBLY, GENERAL, 247
ASSENT, Royal, 192
ASSESSORS, nautical, 251
ASSIZES, 63
ASSOCIATIONS, voluntary, 323
ASSYRIA, law in, 43
ATHENS, law of, 44
ATTORNEY-GENERAL, 276
AUDITOR of Court, 294, 295, 297
AUDITORS, committee of, 104, 107
AULD ALLIANCE, 105
AUSTIN, John, 66, 181
AUTHORITIES, primary and secondary, 345
AUTHORITY OF RULES OF LAW, source of, 343
AUTHORITY OF STATUTES, 200
AVIATION licences, 231
AVIZANDUM, 458, 461, 468
AYALA, 71

521